DAVID M. KROENKE

BUSINESS COMPUTER SYSTEMS

AN INTRODUCTION

MITCHELL PUBLISHING, INC.
Santa Cruz, California

Composition Jonathan Peck, Typographer
Design Linda Marcetti
Illustrations Michael Abbey
Sketches Barbara Ravizza
Chapter Opener Photographs Steve Potter
Editor Alice Lescallet

Acknowledgments
We wish to acknowledge the following for permission to reproduce the listed materials:
Figure 1-1, C-3, C-4, C-12, D-14, Copyright 1979/1980 by CW Communications, Inc., Framingham, MA. 01701. Reprinted from *Computerworld;* 1-2, 2-3, 6-4, 7-5, A-8, Sperry Univac, a Division of the Sperry Rand Corp.; 1-8, NCR Corp.; 2-1, 2-2, A-12, p. 153, Honeywell Information Systems, Inc.; 2-7, 5-20, 6-8, 6-14, A-2, A-4, A-6, A-7, A-9, A-11, F-8, F-10, International Business Machines Corp.; 2-8, Inforex, Inc.; 2-16, Cabrillo College, Aptos, CA.; 3-6, Rocky Mountain Bank Note; 3-15, Recreational Equipment, Inc.; 3-18, Amana Refrigeration, Inc.; 5-9, Mohawk Data Sciences; 5-18, E-9, Qume Corp.; 6-5, BASE Corporation; 6-12, Verbatim Corp., Sunnyvale, CA., manufacturer of mini magnetic recording media; 7-3, 7-4, 8-17, pp. 59, 439, Data General Corp.; F-12, Diebold Corporation; 8-6, Northern Communications Corporation; 8-11*b*, CODEX Corporation; 8-18, Hewlett-Packard; 8-25, John M. McQuillan of Bolt, Beranek, and Newman, Inc.; A-1, A-3, pp. 3, 23, 93, 115, 193, 235, 277, 315, 379, 455, 511, 553, Steve Potter; A-10, Texas Instruments, Inc.; A-13, Digital Equipment Corp.; A-14, Intel Corp.; C-2, from Donn B. Parker, *Computer by Crime.* ©1976, Scribner & Sons (Compiled from "Sharpest Spurt Ever in Violence, Theft." *U.S. News and World Report,* November 24, 1975, p. 82; and from "Annals of Crime: Dead Souls in the Computer—I." *The New Yorker,* August 22, 1977, pp. 35–65.); D-2, The Boeing Company; D-8, Technicon Medical Information Systems Corp.; D-9, Robert J. Schulhof, Rocky Mountain Data Systems; D-11, FBI National Crime Information Center, FBI Headquarters, Washington, D.C.; D-12, Barbara Holt, Perkins, Cole, Stone, Olsen & Williams, Seattle; D-15, Congress of the United States, House of Representatives; D-16, p. 355, SRI International; E-1, Wang Laboratories, Inc.; E-10, Xerox Corp.; F-3, Radio Shack, a Division of Tandy Corp.

Library of Congress Catalog Card Number: 80-84140

ISBN 0-938188-00-3

Printed in the United States of America

10 9 8 7 6 5 4 3 2 1

To Vince and Joyce LoFranco, who have vision and foresight,
and the courage to act accordingly

Contents

Preface   xi

The importance
of computing in business

PART I
INTRODUCTION   1

Two cases:
A disaster and a success

CHAPTER 1
Why Study Business Computing?   3

Establishing the
five-component framework

CHAPTER 2
Introduction to Business Computer Systems   23

How are computer systems
used in business?

CHAPTER 3
Survey of Business Computer Systems Applications   59

How companies develop
computer systems

PART 2
FUNDAMENTAL BUSINESS
COMPUTER SYSTEMS   91

Introducing the systems
development steps

CHAPTER 4
Developing Business Computer Systems   93

The five components of
sequential processing

CHAPTER 5
Sequential File Processing Systems   115

The five components of
direct access processing

CHAPTER 6
Direct Access File Processing Systems   153

Decisions Alpine made,
how it all worked out

CHAPTER 7
Developing Business Computer Systems II   193

Systems with more capability
but also more complexity

PART 3
ADVANCED BUSINESS
COMPUTER SYSTEMS   233

Moving the user away
from the machine

CHAPTER 8
Business Teleprocessing Systems   235

Integrated processing creates
more information

CHAPTER 9
Business Database Systems   277

Processing applications on
the user's machines

CHAPTER 10
Distributed Business Computer Systems   315

A pot pourri of
computer knowledge

PART 4
SPECIAL COMPUTING TOPICS   353

Babbage made the classical
mistakes, 100 years ago!

MODULE A
History of Data Processing   355

Computers can't subtract,
and other mysteries revealed

MODULE B
Numbers Representation and Computer Arithmetic   379

Examples of crimes,
designing systems for prevention

MODULE C
Computer Crime, Security, and Control   395

Computer applications,
implications, privacy

MODULE D
Computers and Their Impact on Society   415

A counterpart to the industrial
revolution is underway

MODULE E
Word Processing Systems and the Automated Office   439

Exploding applications of
computers on chips

MODULE F
Microcomputers and Specialized
Input/Output Equipment   455

Developing your own programs

PART 5
STRUCTURED COMPUTER PROGRAMMING   469

What the computer does with
your source code, and why

MODULE G
Programs, Hardware, and Their Relationship   471

Secrets of professional
programmers: begin at the end

MODULE H
How to Design Simple Computer Programs   485

Basic BASIC for beginners

MODULE I
How to Write Simple BASIC Programs   511

Different languages for
different applications

MODULE J
Survey of Computer Programming Languages   553

Bibliography
Glossary and Index

Expanded Contents

Preface   xi

PART 1
INTRODUCTION   1

The importance of computer knowledge. Chuck Swanson, a computer user at TYCON, is asked to assist in a computer project. He doesn't know how. Meanwhile, ERD's Jan Forrest knows how to get the system she wants.

CHAPTER 1
Why Study Business Computing?   3

Case 1: TYCON Construction Products   6
Chuck's Mistakes   13
Case 2: ERD Pharmaceutical Company   14
The Difference between Jan and Chuck   19
A Word of Encouragement   21

Establishing the basic framework for understanding business computer systems: the Five-Component Model. Using this framework to describe an example: the Class Scheduling System.

CHAPTER 2
Introduction to Business Computer Systems   23

The Components of a Business Computer System   25
The Class Scheduling System   34
Data for Class Scheduling   35
Hardware for Class Scheduling   41
Programs for Class Scheduling   42
Procedures for Class Scheduling   48
Personnel for Class Scheduling   52

How do computer systems help business? A survey from a manager's viewpoint. Characteristics of systems in the major functional areas of business.

CHAPTER 3
Survey of Business Computer Systems Applications   59

Management Information Systems   60
Accounting   64
Finance   72
Sales and Marketing   75
Manufacturing   81

PART 2
FUNDAMENTAL BUSINESS COMPUTER SYSTEMS   91

Alpine Co-op needs help. Their growth made existing systems inadequate—too many errors in member records, and inventory expenses are too high. They think a computer can help. How should they proceed?

CHAPTER 4
Developing Business Computer Systems   93

Needs of Alpine Co-op   94
The Systems Development Cycle   99
The Alpine Feasibility Study   105
Alpine Co-op's Requirements   110

One of Alpine's alternatives: a sequential file system. Sequential hardware, data representation, record-matching algorithms, control totals, and more. Application to Alpine's Member Master File System.

CHAPTER 5
Sequential File Processing Systems   115

What Are Sequential File Systems?   117
Data and Hardware for Sequential File Processing   120
Hardware for Alpine's Member Master File System   125
Programs for Sequential File Processing   137
Procedures for Sequential File Processing   144
Personnel for Sequential File Processing   148
Sequential Processing for Alpine Co-op?   149

A second Alpine alternative: a direct access file system. Direct access hardware, data organization, direct access programs, special problems of backup and recovery, and more. Application to Alpine's Member Master File System.

CHAPTER 6
Direct Access File Processing Systems   153

The Nature of Direct Access Processing   155
Data and Hardware for Direct Access Processing   159
Direct Access Data Organization   169
Programs for Direct Access Processing   175
Procedures for Direct Access Processing   181
Personnel for Direct Access Processing   189

What should Alpine do? Documenting the alternatives and selecting one. How Alpine developed their system. Adding staff, system design, a few problems, development and testing, the Steering Committee approves implementation, and then . . .

CHAPTER 7
Developing Business Computer Systems II   193

Review of Systems Development Steps   194
Alternative Specification   196
Evaluation and Selection of an Alternative   209
Alpine Acquires Data Processing Personnel   213
System Design   214
Development and Testing   222
System Implementation   228

viii

PART 3
ADVANCED BUSINESS COMPUTER SYSTEMS   233

Wagner acquires a Florida subsidiary. How can the information services be quickly improved? Using the computer in Los Angeles. Characteristics of teleprocessing systems, the five components. Strange terms, and an interesting problem: selling the last item twice!

CHAPTER 8
Business Teleprocessing Systems   235

Wagner Pleasure Boats   236
What Are Teleprocessing Systems?   237
Teleprocessing Hardware   246
Teleprocessing for Wagner Pleasure Boats   259
Programs for Teleprocessing Systems   262
Teleprocessing Data and Data Protection   268
Procedures for Teleprocessing Systems   270
Teleprocessing Personnel   272

Why can't the bank get this address right? Problems of duplicated data. Expressing record relationships, but overhead, overhead. New ways of accessing data, and who can do what to which data? The need for a DBA.

CHAPTER 9
Business Database Systems   277

Problems of File Processing   278
What Is Database Processing?   281
Database Data   288
Database Hardware   298
Programs for Database Processing   298
Procedures for Database Processing   303
Database Personnel   307

Moving the computer to the user. Configurations of computers, and downline loading. Distribution of data, replication, and partitioning, and some very interesting problems (some unsolved). The issues of distributed people.

CHAPTER 10
Distributed Business Computer Systems   315

Three Examples of Distributed Processing Systems   317
Characteristics of Distributed Systems   326
Distributed Hardware   329
Programs for Distributed Processing   337
Distributed Data   340
Distributed Personnel   343
Procedures for Distributed Processing   346

PART 4
SPECIAL COMPUTING TOPICS   353

Charles Babbage made today's mistakes over 100 years ago. Early computers, early entrepreneurs, IBM takes the lead with a business-oriented

MODULE A
History of Data Processing   355

Charles Babbage and His Machines   356
Herman Hollerith   362

philosophy. Generations of
computers, and computers
today and tomorrow.

Early Computers   364
Computers in the 1960s and 1970s   367
Computers Today—The Fourth Generation   371

How computers represent
numbers. Subtraction by adding,
octal and hexadecimal
shorthand, conversions between
number systems, and more.

MODULE B
Numbers Representation and Computer Arithmetic   379

Decimal and Binary Numbers   380
Octal and Hexadecimal Number Systems   384
Conversions between Number Systems   387
Floating-Point Numbers   389
Decimal Numbers   391

Harold Johnson, an ambitious
and creative employee, is bored
and feels unappreciated. He finds
a niche as a modern Robin Hood,
he thinks. Other examples.
Computer crime, and what to do
about it. Establishing good system
controls. How Harold is caught.

MODULE C
Computer Crime, Security, and Control   395

Harold Johnson, Computer Criminal   396
What Is Computer Crime?   398
Preventing Computer Crime   403
Computer Auditing and Controls   404
MODREC—The Rest of the Story   411

Computers as boon and bane.
How computers impact business.
Application to nonbusiness
enterprises. Controlling computer
impact through legislation
and knowledge.

MODULE D
Computers and Their Impact on Society   415

The Positive Impacts of Computing   416
The Impact of the Computer on Business   417
Computer Systems in the Health Professions   422
Computer Systems in the Legal Professions   425
Computer Systems in Politics   427
Artificial Intelligence   428
The Negative Aspects of Computing   432
Controlling Computer Impact   435

An electronic typewriter? Yes,
and the start of a revolution.
Finally, after 400 years, offices are
helped by automation. A paperless
office? Perhaps in the office from
which you retire.

MODULE E
Word Processing Systems and the Automated Office   439

What Is Word Processing?   440
Word Processing Hardware   446
The Automated Office   451

Components of microcomputers,
RAMs, ROMs, PROMs, etc.
Myriads of new opportunities
for business products.
Entrepreneurs take note.
POS, OCR, MICR, and others.

MODULE F
Microcomputers and Specialized
Input/Output Equipment   455

Components of Microcomputers   456
Applications of Microcomputers in Business   458

PART 5
STRUCTURED COMPUTER PROGRAMMING   469

Tailoring general purpose machines to special functions. Source, object, and load module program forms. The role of the operating system: job, task, and data management.

MODULE G
Programs, Hardware, and Their Relationship   471

    Purpose of Computer Programs   472
    Machine Language and Program Translation   476
    The Operating System   479

The fundamental cycle of programming. Starting from outputs, then inputs, then processing steps. Tools for expressing logic: structured flowcharts and pseudocode.

MODULE H
How to Design Simple Computer Programs   485

    The Input/Process/Output Cycle   487
    General Strategy for Designing Simple Programs   487
    Adding More Logic—Initiation and Termination   494
    Using Pseudocode to Specify Program Logic   499

Writing programs in the BASIC language. Statements to express your logic. Nothing works until you've shown that it does, as you will see. BASIC and pseudocode.

MODULE I
How to Write Simple BASIC Programs   511

    Section 1—Getting Started   513
    Section 2—Additional BASIC Statements
      and Pseudocode Implementation   520
    Section 3—Program Loops: The FOR
      and NEXT Statements   533
    Section 4—Tables or Arrays   539

What language should DEMPCO use? A hot issue, with much in the balance. Characteristics of business, scientific, systems, and other applications. Languages used by each.

MODULE J
Survey of Computer Programming Languages   553

    Language Selection at DEMPCO Enterprises   554
    The State of Programming Languages Today   555
    Programming Applications and Languages   557
    Language Selection at DEMPCO Enterprises   571

Bibliography
Glossary and Index

Preface

The president of a $60 million-a-year company recently lost $200,000 on needless interest expense because a new computer billing system would not work. This president is an able and efficient executive. He lost this money because he did not know how business computer systems should be developed.

The Need for Business Computing Education

In another company, large payroll overpayments were made be-because a payroll clerk did not understand the need for following procedures. He submitted pay rate changes to Data Processing and *assumed* the changes were correct.

During an investigation, the clerk was asked, "How do you know the changes are made correctly if you don't examine the change reports?"

"If people are underpaid, they complain and then we change it," he responded.

"Yes," replied the interviewer, "but what if they're erroneously overpaid?"

"Well," he said, "that's only happened twice, and both times, the people were honest about it."

Needless to say, the clerk was very surprised when it was discovered that not everybody had been honest.

In May of 1980, the state of Colorado sent a memo to all licensed CPA's explaining that their annual permits would be delayed. The memo began, "An attempt to make a few minor program changes in order to process annual permits in a more expeditious manner back-fired with disastrous results." Although the error was caused by data processing personnel, the Director of the State Board of Accountancy became responsible. He did not know how to minimize his exposure prior to the problem.

In spite of these examples, many systems are successfully implemented every day. These systems indicate that disaster is avoidable, that people's needs can be satisfied by computer systems, and that computers can make people's work vastly easier.

Characteristics of Businesses That Use Computers Successfully

Why do these disasters occur? Why is some management seemingly impotent in controlling data processing activity? Why are some business people unable to communicate their needs to data processing personnel? Why do some users become bitter and antagonistic toward systems that are intended to help them?

In short, what distinguishes an organization that uses computers successfully from one that experiences disasters? In my opinion, the difference is *not* in the technical staff. Rather, the difference is in the minds of the organization's managers and computer users. *Where computer systems are successful, the managers and users have a clear understanding of the components of a business computer system. Further, they know the basic ways such systems should be developed and used.*

Is that surprising? Not really. Where components of computer systems are clearly understood, management and users know what to look for, and what to insist on. They know what the possibilities are, so they are able to find, select, develop, and manage the technical people to do the job correctly.

The Five-Component Model of a Business Computer System

What is a business computer system? In contrast to popular opinion, it is not a computer with a few programs. Rather, such a system is a collection of five interacting components: a *computer, programs, data, procedures,* and *trained personnel.* I believe the key to successful systems in business is that each one of these five components receives careful attention. Each is evaluated, designed, and implemented. Disasters occur where management and users do not understand these components, and where management lets Data Processing proceed in its own way.

The Role of Computer Education

How can computers be used more effectively in business? In the long run, the answer lies with education. In my opinion, it is the education of future managers and computer users that is crucial. These people need to learn the components of a business computer system, and they need to learn how computer systems should be developed (not to develop systems themselves, but rather to know what is supposed to occur, and to know when to take corrective action). They need to know what the possibilities are for effective systems development and use.

The education of data processing professionals is also vitally important. Industry seems to say the most successful professionals do not necessarily know the most about COBOL (or RPG, or database, or whatever). Rather, the most successful data processing professionals are those that have a solid grounding in business. These people know, as one business person put it, "where their bread is buttered." They know how to apply computer technology to business problems, and they do not attempt to force business problems into a given technology.

Thus the computer education needs of future business managers and computer users and the initial educational needs of data processing professionals are the same. All three groups need education that starts with business, and expands outward to show how computer technology can be applied to satisfy business needs. More specifically, all three groups need to know the five components of a business computer system, and how these components can be developed and used. Given this common grounding, each group can then proceed down their separate career paths. The communication among all of them, however, will be improved because of this common knowledge.

Discussions in this book originate with business needs, and proceed outward to computer technology. In every case, the five components of a business computer system are discussed. In addition to hardware and programs, data, procedures, and trained personnel are fully considered.

The Design of This Book

These last three components are crucial for future managers and computer users to understand. Few managers or users are likely to select hardware or develop programs, but many managers and users will have a role in designing and creating data, in developing and using procedures, and in selecting, training, and managing personnel.

I believe there are three reasons students should study computer programming. First, they should learn something about the programming process and experience the joys and sorrows of programming. In some cases, students will find that they like programming, and they will have found a new and perhaps unexpected career. Many professionals started just that way. Second, students should study programming because it may help them in their collegiate career. A knowledge of programming can be very useful in finance and production courses.

A Note on Programming

The third reason for studying programming is very important, but, because of a lack of facilities, it is seldom accomplished. Students need to learn the procedures they will follow as computer users. The payroll clerk who caused a disaster by not following procedures needed to learn how to use computer programs.

To support this education, Dr. Joby Renick has developed a software package to accompany the use of this book. This package is a professional-quality version of a simple class scheduling system. Students can use the system in the roles of administrators, clerks, professors, or students. The purpose of this activity is to learn what computer users should do. Chapter 2 introduces the class scheduling problem, and this system can be used to supplement that material.

Using the class scheduling system, however, is optional. Chapter 2 can be covered completely without it.

Introductory level students are not expected to program any part of the class scheduling system. Instead, they are expected to learn the roles of computer users, and they should learn the importance of systems procedures. (As an aside, advanced students can change the system, maintain it, or whatever.) Contact the publisher for more information about this package.

Philosophical Note

Computer hardware is becoming cheaper, and consequently, computers are being used increasingly in business. As long as systems are responsibly developed, this trend will be beneficial. However, computers are powerful, and like any powerful tool, they create hazards when improperly used. If irresponsibly developed, computer systems definitely pose a threat to personal privacy and freedom.

Professionals in data processing are concerned about this danger, and the computer profession is attempting to control itself. Still, the most effective controls will be those applied by managers and users—controls applied from the outside. Therefore, consumer knowledge about computer systems and how they should be developed and used is vital, not just for business efficiency and the profit and loss statement, but for the very quality of our lives.

Computer systems should be designed to serve people, and not the other way around. People should never be forced to conform to a computer system. Although people have been manipulated this way in the past, that era should be gone. The business leaders of tomorrow must ensure that it does not return. My sincere hope is that the knowledge you gain from this text will be applied to that end.

Acknowledgments

Many people contributed to the development of this book. Many helpful comments and criticisms were provided by the reviewers: Barbara Comfort of J. Sargeant Reynolds Community College, Caroline Curtis of Lorain Community College, Steve Deam of Milwaukee Area Technical College, Thomas Honnicutt of North Carolina State University, Ronald Lemos of California State University at Los Angeles, Gardner Mallonee of Essex Community College, Harold Stone of the University of Massachusetts, and Jim Williams of Davidson College. Additionally, Dee Stark, of North Seattle Community College, has made substantial contributions to this text. She also authored a creative study guide/casebook to accompany it.

Much encouragement for the general approach of this text came from those instructors who attended the National Computer Educators' Institutes during the summers of 1979 and 1980. Dr. Joe Kinzer of Central State University in Oklahoma, who has provided a stimulating environment at that Institute for many years, has been particularly supportive. Additionally, Marilyn Bohl of IBM has been a good friend and provided much encouragement, advice, and an occasional wrap on the knuckles when I strayed from my path. Thanks, too, to the students at Colorado State University who provided the impetus for this text and to those at North Seattle Community College who tested it in the classroom. Finally, I thank Louise, my wife, who has had a substantial, though indirect, impact on this book. Louise first showed me the human side of computing.

Ever since I finished writing *Database Processing,* I had a dream of writing this book. In 1978, I met with Steve Mitchell, who had a dream of starting a publishing company. We agreed to work together to transform those dreams into reality. Steve has the rare combination of skills needed to anticipate the needs of educators, to assemble a team of people to meet those needs, to manage the development of products, and to find economically feasible ways of disseminating those products. Without Steve's perseverance and boundless enthusiasm, this book would not have been written.

David M. Kroenke

CHAPTER 1

**WHY STUDY
BUSINESS
COMPUTING?**

CHAPTER 2

**INTRODUCTION
TO BUSINESS
COMPUTER
SYSTEMS**

CHAPTER 3

**SURVEY OF
BUSINESS
COMPUTER
SYSTEMS
APPLICATIONS**

PART 1

INTRODUCTION

INTRODUCTION

In the three chapters of Part 1 you will be introduced to business computer systems. Chapter 1 tells the story of two companies and their experiences in developing computer systems. One turned out very well, and the other one—well, you can read it.

Business computer systems are defined in Chapter 2. You will learn about the five components of a business computer system and study a familiar system—class scheduling. Chapter 2 is very important; we will refer to concepts in this chapter throughout the course. Finally, Chapter 3 surveys the applications of computers in business.

CHAPTER 1

Why Study Business Computing?

Requirements for TYCON's computer systems arise from business activity

CASE 1: TYCON CONSTRUCTION PRODUCTS

The Project Starts
Problems Develop
Mr. Miyamoto Acts

CHUCK'S MISTAKES

CASE 2: ERD PHARMACEUTICAL COMPANY

The Need for Computer Assistance

Analysis of the Problem
The Turnkey System
Resistance from Data Processing
A Proposal for Jan

THE DIFFERENCE BETWEEN JAN AND CHUCK

A WORD OF ENCOURAGEMENT

This book is about how computers are used to solve business problems. When you finish it, you will not be an expert, but you will know more about business computing than 90 percent of business people today. This knowledge will be of tremendous help to you whether you eventually work in accounting, finance, manufacturing, marketing, management, or some other aspect of business.

That's a bold statement but a true one. The first computer was built in 1946 and in the 35 years or so since then, business has been revolutionized. In the history of the world, no other factor has had a greater impact on business in such a short period of time.

Furthermore, many experts believe the true impact of the computer is yet to be felt. Computers get cheaper and yet more powerful every year. Thus each year a better product costs less money; even computer professionals are amazed to find they can buy Cadillacs at Pinto prices. (See figure 1-1.) As computers get cheaper, they become affordable to more and more businesses and it makes sense to use them for more and more applications. Also, as computers become cheaper, it makes sense to use more of their capability to make them friendly and easy to use. Consequently, computers will be applied for the first time in many more businesses and applications and the demand for computer-knowledgeable people will increase.

How will this knowledge of computing help your career? Suppose you and another person are both trainees in an accounting department. Suppose you both have about the same knowledge of accounting, but only you know something about computers. Whenever computers are talked about, installed, used, or create problems, you will have an advantage.

Figure 1-1 An Advertisement Appearing in *Computerworld*—A Computer Newspaper

To illustrate the need for knowledge about computing in business, we will consider two cases. These cases refer to business and computer terms that you may not understand. Do not be alarmed by this. You do not need to understand the details of these cases at this point. Try instead to get a feel for what can happen when computers are used in business.

<table>
<tr>
<td>

**Case 1:
TYCON
CONSTRUCTION
PRODUCTS**

</td>
<td>

"Oh, no, not a traffic jam, too!" thought Chuck Swanson as he pulled to a stop behind a long line of cars on the freeway. It was a gray, rainy, early fall day and Chuck had good reason to be upset. He was in the midst of problems at work and he needed to be there early.

Chuck was 32 years old and the staff assistant to the Director of Marketing for TYCON Construction Products. His problems had begun nearly two years previously. TYCON had been experiencing difficulties in processing orders. Because of a boom in construction, manufacturers' deliveries to TYCON had been irregular, late, and sometimes canceled. Thus, TYCON's inventory was erratic; customers and sales personnel couldn't depend on prompt deliveries. Also, some customers' bills were three, four, and five months overdue. Thus, Marketing wanted to check customer credit before authorizing orders. Unfortunately, since TYCON had over 8000 customers, authorizations were extremely time-consuming.

At this time, TYCON had a modest data processing (DP) department that was generally effective. The data processing manager, Tom Jackson, thought he could solve the order processing and credit authorization problems with a new, computerized order entry system.

A committee of Chuck, an accountant, a computer programmer, and Tom Jackson (as chairperson) was formed to study that idea. Chuck and the accountant told the computer people about the problem and their needs. The committee met five times over a period of three months and developed a data processing proposal for management.

This proposal recommended formation of an order entry department with 12 clerks. Each clerk would have a CRT (cathode ray tube — like a television set with a keyboard) connected to the computer. (See figure 1-2.) The clerks would receive orders over the phone, and use the CRT to obtain inventory and credit information from the computer. If the materials were in stock and the customer's credit was good, the order would be approved.

To implement this system, TYCON needed to buy or lease a computer and related equipment. Also, four programmers and five computer operators had to be hired. Tom Jackson said the system could be operational in 18 months.

The proposal was reviewed by Chuck's boss and eventually presented to Mr. Art Miyamoto, President. (TYCON's organization chart

</td>
</tr>
</table>

Figure 1-2 Order Entry Clerks Using a Cathode Ray Tube

is shown in figure 1-3.) Mr. Miyamoto liked the idea, but thought the costs were too high. Because of recent sales successes, however, the company was in a strong cash position and he approved the proposal providing the new system could be operational in a year. Jackson said he could compress the schedule if he could hire one more programmer on a temporary basis. Mr. Miyamoto agreed and the project was on.

Once approval was granted, the committee stopped meeting and Chuck Swanson didn't hear much from Data Processing. Ten months later Mr. Miyamoto called a meeting with the original committee, including

The Project Starts

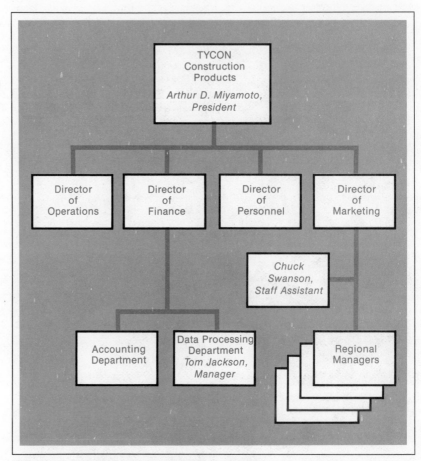

Figure 1-3 TYCON Organization Chart

Tom Jackson. (See figure 1-4.) He wanted to know the status of the project.

Tom Jackson stated that the new computer kept malfunctioning and that two programmers had quit and had to be replaced. Their programs had to be thrown out since nobody could understand them! Even worse, during testing they had discovered that two programs weren't compatible and one had to be rewritten. Also, Data Processing hadn't known about a new product line which would be required and which would take about a month or two to incorporate into the system. Further, order entry personnel needed to be hired and trained and procedures had to be developed. Altogether, Jackson reported it would be another six months before installation.

Mr. Miyamoto was furious. Why hadn't he been informed? Where did the $300,000 they had spent go? What were they going to do about the order processing problems for the next six months? Didn't Jackson

Figure 1-4 Tom Jackson Reporting Problems

know they were losing business and creating bad will? Did Jackson realize TYCON Construction Products existed to sell goods and make profit and not to support every itinerant programmer and computer peddler?

After the meeting, Mr. Miyamoto stopped Chuck in the hall and told him to drop what he was doing. "Chuck," he said, "I have half a mind to cancel this project, but I don't want to lose the money we've invested. Spend some time with the data processing people, and send me a memo about what you think we should do."

Chuck spent the next week with Tom Jackson and the data processing personnel. They seemed defensive, and they kept throwing terms at him he didn't understand. They claimed many of the delays were beyond their control. Also, programmers said the requirements kept changing, and they had to redo their work. Chuck tried to find a document describing the requirements so he could see what they meant, but no such document had been prepared.

On the positive side, it was clear to Chuck that the data processing personnel were highly motivated. They had spent long hours and were making an exhaustive effort to complete the system. Chuck decided to recommend continuing the project for six more months. His reasoning is given in the memo in figure 1-5.

Mr. Miyamoto decided to go along with Chuck's recommentation. He asked Chuck, however, to help the project every way he could.

The next six months were as hectic as any time Chuck could remember. He and Tom Jackson and most of the data processing staff regularly worked 10 to 12 hour days. Since Chuck was not qualified to help technically, he tried to remove the administrative burden from Tom.

Figure 1-5 Chuck Swanson's Memo

```
                    TYCON CONSTRUCTION PRODUCTS


                                  MEMO
                             July 17, 1979



        TO:      Mr. Arthur Miyamoto, President

        FROM:    Chuck Swanson

        SUBJECT:  Order Entry and Billing Systems

            I have reviewed progress on the order entry and billing
        systems as you requested. The following facts are pertinent:

            a. The project is definitely behind schedule. However, not
        all of the problems appear to have been Data Processing's fault.
        The computer vendor has caused several serious schedule slippages.

            b. Approximately $300,000 has already been spent or
        committed on this project. If we terminate it now, we will be
        able to recover only about $50,000 of this.

            c. Continuing this project for 6 more months will cost from
        $35,000 to $40,000.

            d. There is a significant chance that Data Processing will
        complete these systems within 6 months. The team members are
        highly motivated, and their enthusiasm is high.

            The cost of quitting now will be $250,000, plus we will
        still have order entry and inventory problems. The cost of
        continuing another 6 months will be $40,000, at most, and it is
        likely we will have a solution to our problems. In my opinion it
        is worth risking the $40,000 to continue the project.
```

After five months of the hectic schedule, Data Processing was ready to implement the new order entry system. Chuck and Tom checked with Mr. Miyamoto, and he told them to go ahead.

At first the new system operated fairly well and only a few small problems appeared. One time the computer displayed a minus amount of a siding product in inventory. Another time, several customers were accidentally dropped from the files. Basically, however, the system operated well — especially considering the hectic way it was developed.

Problems Develop

Disaster struck, however, at the end of the month. The existing computer billing system wouldn't work with the new order entry system! Something was wrong with the order data produced by the new system. The old billing system just wouldn't accept it. Figure 1-6 shows the relationship of the new order entry system and the old billing system.

Tom Jackson and the data processing staff worked through the weekend to determine what was wrong. They discovered a major design flaw in order entry. The person who had worked on it misunderstood how the billing system used order entry data. Much of the data needed by the billing system was in the wrong format, and some was simply unavailable.

Data Processing worked furiously to fix the problem. By the end of the next week, it was apparent that another month would be needed to make the billing system operate. Tom Jackson reported to Mr. Miyamoto that TYCON would not be able to prepare bills for four or five more weeks.

Clenching his teeth, Mr. Miyamoto provided Tom a lesson in business. "Tom," he said icily, "if we don't send our customers their bills, they don't pay them. If our customers don't pay their bills, we don't receive any money. If we don't receive any money, we can't pay

Figure 1-6 Relationship of Order Entry and Billing Systems

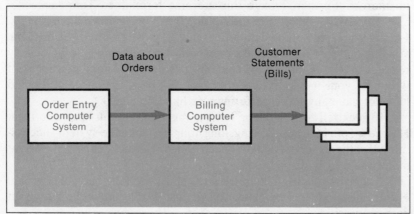

for our new computer and its staff, not to mention the other incidental expenses involved in running this company. This is called negative cash flow and we can't have two months of it. Go back to the old system!"

"Mr. Miyamoto, we can't," responded Tom. "It will take us three months to reconvert to the old system. All the data has been changed because of the new prices you wanted. We don't have the new prices in the old files."

Within a week it was clear to Mr. Miyamoto that Tom was right. They were going to fall six to eight weeks behind in their billing. Mr. Miyamoto had to borrow to cover the short term loss of revenue. Unfortunately, interest rates were at an all-time high, and TYCON spent over $75,000 on interest because of the problem.

At this point, Mr. Miyamoto had had it. He hired a computer consulting firm to investigate the situation. A team of three people spent several days at TYCON talking with Chuck, Tom, the data processing staff, users, and customers.

Mr. Miyamoto Acts

Such was the situation the dreary fall day when the traffic finally started moving as Chuck drove to work. Chuck was analyzing inventory reports when Mr. Miyamoto's secretary called to ask him to come to a meeting.

Mr. Miyamoto, Chuck's boss, and the three consultants were present as Chuck sat down at the conference table.

"Chuck," Mr. Miyamoto began, "our consultants have analyzed our order entry project from the beginning and they have given it some very black marks. They feel that fundamental principles of systems design were ignored and they question the professional competency of our data processing staff. Further, they believe we should have stopped the project as I wanted to five months ago.

"Consequently, I've decided to return to the old system even though we will lose about $350,000 of our investment plus $75,000 in interest. Further, I have this morning terminated Tom Jackson.

"Frankly, Chuck, I'm disappointed in your performance on this. I know you have limited data processing knowledge, but it seems to me you should have known that order entry and billing would be closely related. Also, couldn't you see this problem developing when you wrote me your memo five months ago? Go back to your staff job and let's not have any more performances like this one."

Chuck felt terrible as he left the meeting. He felt sorry for Tom. He knew Tom had worked long, long hours to make the system successful. Also, the experience hadn't been good for Chuck, either. Mr. Miyamoto was clearly displeased.

Later that night, Chuck tried to think where he had gone wrong. He decided that the problem was he just didn't know enough about data processing.

What should Chuck have known? If he had taken the course you are presently enrolled in, there is a very good chance the project would have turned out differently and TYCON would not have lost the $350,000. First, Chuck would have known how a business computer system should be developed. He would have known some of the pitfalls to avoid. He would have insisted on a documented definition of requirements. This by itself could have prevented the billing problem.

Chuck would have known of alternatives to Tom's plan and been certain that Tom at least considered them. He would have seen some of the mistakes that Tom made and had them corrected, or else recommended the project be canceled in his memo. Finally, Chuck would have known what users are supposed to do for themselves and what they can fairly expect from the data processing staff. He would have ensured that the users did their job and that Data Processing was providing appropriate support.

Don't worry if the above concepts are not clear to you. This is just a preview. You should realize, however, the importance of computing knowledge to every business professional.

CHUCK'S MISTAKES

QUESTIONS ABOUT TYCON CONSTRUCTION

1.1   Did Chuck have a chance? What could he have done differently before he wrote the memo to Mr. Miyamoto? What would you have done in his situation?

1.2   Do you think the memo in figure 1-5 makes sense? Do you agree with Chuck's reasoning?

1.3   What mistakes did Tom Jackson make? What could Chuck have done about them?

1.4   What mistakes did Mr. Miyamoto make? What could Chuck have done about them?

1.5   Do you suppose it is unusual for one data processing system to be dependent on another just as billing was dependent on order entry? What can companies do to eliminate problems like those TYCON had?

1.6   Do you think Chuck should have foreseen the billing problem? Would you?

1.7   What can Chuck do now? What do you suppose his attitude is toward data processing? Can Chuck be effective on other computer projects?

1.8   Did Mr. Miyamoto really want to cancel the project as he says in the last meeting? Do you suppose he remembers how he truly felt?

1.9   Suppose Chuck had taken a business data processing class before the disaster. Describe three aspects of data processing he could have learned that would have helped him prevent the disaster.

Case 2: ERD PHARMACEUTICAL COMPANY	Jan Forrest was the Manager of Marketing Analysis for ERD Pharmaceutical Company, a manufacturer of drugs and related medical supplies. She had a B.A. in education and had taught elementary school for several years. She decided that she really didn't want to teach, and so she returned to college and earned a degree in marketing.

In school, she had taken two courses in computing: an introductory one and a course in systems development. On graduation, Jan joined ERD's Marketing Analysis Group as a staff analyst.

Within a year she was one of the top analysts. She worked hard and had a good memory for sales facts. Her manner with people was friendly and easygoing. Jan was known among sales personnel as the person to call for client sales data.

Three years after Jan joined ERD, her boss was promoted to Regional Sales Manager. At that time, Jan was appointed to her present position as manager.

The Marketing Analysis Group was responsible for analyzing past drug sales and producing predictions, or *forecasts*, for future sales. They did this by developing mathematical equations that related future sales to past sales as well as to other economic and population factors.

The Need for Computer Assistance

One day as Jan walked past the offices of the seven analysts in the department (figure 1-7), she felt a familiar sense of unease. Her employees, who were trained to be business market analysts, were spending most of their time as clerks and calculators. It was a waste of their talents. She knew several were unhappy.

Why should so much of this work be done manually? ERD had a large computer that was used for other applications. Could it not be programmed to perform some of marketing's time-consuming calculations? If this were done, sales predictions could be developed for many more products. Her staff could then use their knowledge and experience to interpret and adjust predictions and stop being human calculators.

Jan discussed this situation with the Director of Data Processing, Peter Wandolowski. He promised to send a computer systems analyst over when he could spare one from other work.

Analysis of the Problem

Two months later the analyst finally appeared. His name was Fred Sanchez, and he was superb. He had 12 years of systems analysis experience, could communicate well, knew data processing inside and out, and had worked with Marketing in a previous job. Unfortunately, he was only available on a half-time basis.

Figure 1-7   Market Analysts Working as Human Calculators

Jan had learned in her computer courses how important it is for computer people to understand requirements. Therefore, she told Fred to present his understanding of their requirements to her staff when he was finished. Also, she wanted a document of requirements prepared.

Fred spent the next 10 days with Marketing Analysis. At the end of that time he presented his understanding of the marketing requirements to Jan and her staff. With a few minor adjustments, they believed Fred understood their problems very well.

As Fred handed Jan the requirements document he said, "Frankly, Jan, I've got some bad news. On the basis of these requirements, the job is too big for just me on a half-time basis. We need a full-time analyst and a programmer."

He went on to explain that he had put the matter before Peter Wandolowski and had been told no one was available. He would have to make do. He told Jan candidly that this seemed unfair to all the people involved.

After Fred left, Jan and her staff stared gloomily at one another. "Well, what will we do now?" Jan asked.

"Maybe we should try the yellow pages," said one of the analysts sarcastically.

"Hey, that reminds me," said Jan. "I got some material about a computer system in the mail the other day. Let's look at it."

The Turnkey System

Jan found the material. It contained information about a computer called a *turnkey system*. (See figure 1-8.) As Jan read on further, she gathered that meant it could be used by inexperienced personnel with no computing background. "Do you suppose we could run this thing ourselves?" she asked.

The next week was a busy one for the marketing analysis staff. In addition to their regular work, they investigated the possibility of leasing or buying their own computer. They called the computer vendor (the company that sells and services the equipment) and talked with the sales personnel as well as a specialist called a *systems engineer*.

Figure 1-8   User at a Turnkey Computer System

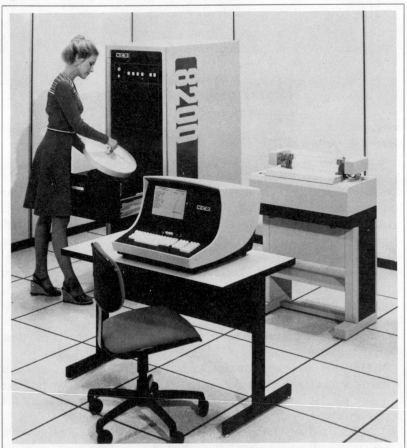

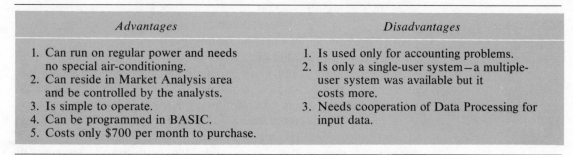

Advantages	Disadvantages
1. Can run on regular power and needs no special air-conditioning.	1. Is used only for accounting problems.
2. Can reside in Market Analysis area and be controlled by the analysts.	2. Is only a single-user system—a multiple-user system was available but it costs more.
3. Is simple to operate.	3. Needs cooperation of Data Processing for input data.
4. Can be programmed in BASIC.	
5. Costs only $700 per month to purchase.	

Figure 1-9   Advantages and Disadvantages of Turnkey System for Marketing Analysis

Also, Fred dropped by late one afternoon and they asked him questions until eight o'clock that night.

By the end of the week, Jan had a good picture of the alternative. The advantages were that the computer could run on regular power and it needed no special air-conditioning. This meant it could be located in their area and be controlled by them. Also, it was simple to operate, it could be programmed in a language called *BASIC*, which Jan knew from college was easy to use, and it cost only about $700 per month including charges for periodic maintenance. (See figure 1-9.)

Disadvantages of the system were that it was a turnkey system only for simple accounting problems; Jan and her staff would have to do their own programming to do market forecasting. Second, the $700 per month system was a single-user system. Only one person could use the system at a time.

Finally, to do market forecasts, Marketing Analysis needed to put the sales data into the computer. There was far too much of it for the analysis staff to type or key in. However, Data Processing already had the data in the big computer. The vendor told Jan the turnkey system could get this data from Data Processing's computer over a communication line (like a telephone line). Both he and Fred said this was feasible, but Fred doubted they would get much cooperation from Data Processing.

Jan thought seriously about this project over the weekend. On Monday and Tuesday she prepared a proposal for management. In it she discussed costs and benefits. She showed that considering only the most concrete benefits, the project would easily justify its costs. Also, she discussed Data Processing's busy schedule and explained how this project would relieve some of the burden on them.

She presented the proposal to her boss, the Vice-President of Marketing, and Peter Wandolowski on Wednesday. Pete was vehemently against Marketing's buying their own computer. He expressed a dozen or so objections in a 30 minute, emotion-filled meeting.

Resistance from Data Processing

To the Vice-President of Marketing, some of Pete's objections seemed rational. Pete believed that Jan had insufficient and unqualified staff to operate the system; he believed it would require much more support than the vendor said. Also, he was concerned about control of the data. How could Data Processing ensure that Jan's data was current? Or that her staff would maintain adequate security and control? Or that they would take appropriate backup and recovery actions?

In addition to these seemingly rational concerns, Wandolowski also felt threatened. He saw this project as an infringement on his territory. If Marketing did this, would Manufacturing or Shipping or Engineering be next? If programmers started popping up all over the company, would the Data Processing Department be out in the cold? What would happen to his staff? Pete was adamantly opposed.

"Well, all right, Pete," responded the vice-president, "since you're so opposed to this idea, let's put it before the Vice-Presidents Council. Maybe we can work out an official policy on these turnkey computer systems."

Later, Pete realized he couldn't let the matter go before the vice-presidents. It was simply too risky; suppose the policy approved users having their own computers? What then?

A Proposal for Jan

By now, Pete had a keen appreciation for Jan's business ability. He had to find a way to provide the service she wanted, or the long range damage to Data Processing would be great.

The next day, Pete made another appointment with Jan and he had his homework done. He explained to her the danger and agonies of running a computer. What would she do when it didn't work? What if the vendor blamed her programming for the malfunction? Who would be responsible for the communication line linking their computer with the main computer? What did she know about security, backup and recovery, or computer controls?

He asked if she knew how to manage a programming project. What is structured programming? What kind of documentation would her staff produce? What about testing? Could they design and implement a good test plan? How many people did she want to devote to program maintenance? These dangers are summarized in figure 1-10.

Once he covered the potential problems, Pete discussed her requirements. He had read Fred Sanchez's documentation and knew what needed to be done. He discussed reports that Data Processing could produce and indicated a willingness to implement whatever forecasting techniques Jan's staff would request. Finally, he presented a proposal: If Jan would withdraw her computer request, he would make Fred Sanchez available full time. Also (he had gone through his staff's profiles late the night before), he had a young programmer who had a degree in statistics. She was bright and had written major programs

Potential Problems
1. What to do when the computer doesn't work 2. How to deal with the computer vendor 3. Who will maintain the communication line 4. How to manage a programming project 5. What kind of documentation to produce 6. How to design and implement a test plan 7. What personnel to assign to maintain the system

Figure 1-10   Examples of Problems Identified by Peter Wandolowski

successfully. This programmer would be available full time to work with Fred.

Jan considered the proposal. She wasn't overly concerned with the dangers of running a computer. Sure, they might make a few mistakes but they would learn. On the other hand, did they want to learn? After all, their jobs were in marketing, not data processing. She decided if Pete would do as he promised, she'd rather have Data Processing develop the systems than her staff.

"I'll tell you what, Pete," she responded, "I won't cancel my request for a system, but I will postpone it. If Data Processing can provide the services we need, on a timely basis, I won't raise the issue again. If you don't deliver, though, I will; and I'll have a document a half an inch thick on how Data Processing failed."

"We'll deliver, Jan, I assure you," said Pete with a relieved sigh.

And they did. Whether from fear or respect for Jan or a sincere desire to provide better service, Peter Wandolowski ensured that Marketing Analysis was satisfied. Within three months, they had the basic capability operational. In six months they had an integrated system of several forecasting techniques and reports to select from. After 18 months, Marketing Analysis had (you guessed it) *their own computer.* This time, however, it was purchased, programmed, and maintained by Data Processing. It was in the Marketing Analysis area, however, and they used it whenever they wanted to.

Jan's situation turned out much differently than Chuck's. Why? They were about equal in intelligence. Both worked hard. They were both competent in their business specialties.

The difference was that Jan had some knowledge of computing. She knew how computer systems are supposed to be developed. She knew to request formal requirements from Fred. Furthermore, Jan was familiar with terminology and was not snowed like Chuck was when he

THE DIFFERENCE BETWEEN JAN AND CHUCK

wrote his memo. Consequently, she was able to communicate clearly with Peter. Also, she wasn't afraid to ask questions, challenge the DP experts, and do work on her own. She had confidence in her ability to relate to computing.

What would have happened if Jan and Chuck had had each other's jobs? We'll never know, but it seems likely that TYCON's problem would have been smaller. It also seems unlikely that ERD's Marketing Analysis Group would have had their own computer.

Think about these cases and consider that neither Chuck nor Jan wanted to work with data processing. However, in the course of their careers, both of them were required to. Either of these situations could occur in your business careers. In that event, the more you know about data processing, the more likely your own chances of success.

QUESTIONS ABOUT ERD PHARMACEUTICAL

1.10 In what ways did Jan Forrest differ from Chuck Swanson? How did this help her in the computer project?

1.11 Can you think of anything Jan did wrong?

1.12 What were some of the differences between Tom Jackson and Peter Wandolowski? How did these differences help Jan?

1.13 Do you think Jan should have agreed to postpone her computer request? What would have happened if she hadn't? What could have happened if she had withdrawn the request?

1.14 Explain how taking a data processing class helped Jan solve her computer problem.

A WORD OF ENCOURAGEMENT

If you are like many students, you are uneasy about taking this course. You may be fearful that business data processing is something you won't be able to understand. That is unlikely. Most students, like Jan, find there is no magic to computing, and contrary to popular belief, there is not a lot of math. If you'll invest the time, you'll probably find this course easier than you thought. The experience of hundreds of teachers has been that there are few college students who "just can't catch on." It will take time, however.

SUMMARY

There are important reasons for you to study business data processing even if you intend to work in some other business specialty. Computers have changed business practices drastically. Some experts believe the greatest change is yet to come. Computers are getting cheaper and so will find increased use in industry. In the future, many business people will be successful because of their ability to incorporate computer technology into their jobs.

A. Speculate on how you feel computers will affect your career. How will knowledge about computing help you?

B. Why are computers becoming so popular?

C. Neither Chuck nor Jan were data processing professionals, but their ability to perform their jobs depended on being able to work with data processing. Do you think this is rare? Is it becoming more frequent? Less? Staying about the same?

D. Think of any two business people in any field; real estate, banking, manufacturing, insurance, selling, and distribution are all possibilities. Suppose both people are well qualified but one has a knowledge of computers and what they can and cannot do. In what ways does the computer-literate person have an advantage over the other? How will their careers differ?

QUESTIONS TO CHALLENGE YOUR THINKING*

*To answer these questions, you will have to rely on your own intuition and experience. In later chapters, you may need to use additional references.

CHAPTER 2

Introduction to Business Computer Systems

Class scheduling using a computer system

**THE COMPONENTS
OF A BUSINESS COMPUTER
SYSTEM**

Hardware
Programs
Data
Procedures
Personnel

**THE CLASS SCHEDULING
SYSTEM**

The Problem

**DATA FOR CLASS
SCHEDULING**

Characters, Fields,
Records, and Files

**HARDWARE FOR CLASS
SCHEDULING**

**PROGRAMS FOR CLASS
SCHEDULING**

Developing Program
Algorithms

Pseudocode
Flowcharts

**PROCEDURES FOR CLASS
SCHEDULING**

The Need for Procedures

An Example of User
Procedures

**PERSONNEL FOR CLASS
SCHEDULING**

The term *business computer system* will be used throughout this book. In this chapter we will explain its meaning and describe system components. To do this, we will first introduce the concept and then examine a computer system familiar to most students, one that does class scheduling. This example will illustrate a business computer system and show how its components interact. We will use the definitions of these components many times in the pages that follow. Be sure you understand them.

A *system* is a collection of components that interact to achieve some purpose. A *computer system* is a collection of components, including a computer, that interact to achieve some purpose. Note the word *including*. A computer system is not just a computer; it includes a computer as one of its components. *A business computer system is a collection of components, including a computer, that interact to satisfy a business need.* For example, some business computer systems produce payroll; some compute taxes; some do accounting; and so forth.

Many business people are misinformed about the makeup of a business computer system. They think it is just a computer and that if they buy one their problems are over. Actually, the computer is only one of five components of a business computer system. Once the computer is obtained, many problems and considerable expense have just begun.

The five components of a business computer system are *hardware, programs, data, procedures,* and *personnel.* Each component is required to successfully satisfy a business need; take any of them away and the need cannot be satisfied. Let's consider each of them in turn.

THE COMPONENTS OF A BUSINESS COMPUTER SYSTEM

First there is computer equipment or hardware. Figure 2-1 shows a computer used by a bank. It is very large and actually is used to satisfy many different needs—not just one. Since there is a lot of computer

Hardware

Figure 2-1 A Computer

A (Card Reader)

D (Tape Drive)

B (CPU)

C (Printer)

Figure 2-2 The Central Processing Unit (CPU)

equipment, it may help you to divide it into categories. *Input equipment* is used to get data into the computer. In figure 2-1, arrow A points to a card reader; this is one example of input equipment. There are many other types.

Processing equipment actually does the computing once the data has been read in, or input. Arrow B of figure 2-1 points to the *central processing unit,* or *CPU.* You can think of this as the computer's brain.

Figure 2-2 shows a better picture of the CPU. Not very exciting, is it? Inside is a very complex electronic machine, but it is so small you can't see it. Visitors to computer centers are often disappointed with the appearance of the CPU; experienced guides usually spend most of the tour time on equipment such as tape drives. They are more exciting to watch but actually of much less importance.

Another category of computer hardware is *output equipment.* This hardware is used to transfer data from inside the computer to some more permanent form. Arrow C of figure 2-1 points to a computer printer; this equipment produces wide printouts with holes in the sides. In case you haven't seen them, an example is shown in figure 2-3.

A fourth and final category of computer hardware is equipment used to store data. An example of this *storage equipment* is the tape drive indicated by arrow D in figure 2-1. Unfortunately, the CPU (computer's brain) has a limited capacity to hold data. Consequently, storage equipment is needed to hold data that is not in use. This data is written onto tape so that it can be read back from tape when required.

To understand this, compare the CPU to your brain. You may have noticed you have a limited capacity to hold data (say, for example,

Figure 2-3 People Reading Computer-Printed Report

when you are taking a test). To help yourself, you put thoughts on a crib sheet. You read these thoughts into your mind when you need them. In this example, the paper serves as a storage device like the tape equipment in figure 2-1.

Figure 2-4 summarizes the five components of a business computer system and their subelements. We have just discussed hardware. The second component is *programs*. Most computers are general purpose machines. They can add, subtract, compare, but they are not designed to satisfy specific needs. A computer must have a program, or *sequence of instructions*, to satisfy a specific need. Thus, a computer with one

Programs

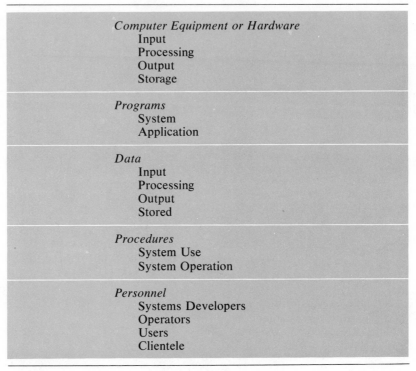

Computer Equipment or Hardware
    Input
    Processing
    Output
    Storage

Programs
    System
    Application

Data
    Input
    Processing
    Output
    Stored

Procedures
    System Use
    System Operation

Personnel
    Systems Developers
    Operators
    Users
    Clientele

Figure 2-4 Components of a Business Computer System

set of programs might be used to design airplanes. The same computer with different programs could be used to do general ledger accounting or to process insurance claims.

Figure 2-5 shows a simple program that reads two numbers, labeled A and B, adds them, and prints the result. Figure 2-6 shows a portion of a more complex program used to enroll students into classes.

Computer programs can be written in a variety of programming languages. Like human languages, these languages differ in vocabulary and structure. They all, however, have the same function: to instruct a general purpose computer to satisfy a specific need. The program in figure 2-5 is written in the BASIC language. The one in figure 2-6 is written in a language called *COBOL*. Although there are several hun-

Figure 2-5 A Computer Program Written in BASIC

```
10  INPUT A,B
20  LET C = A + B
30  PRINT C
40  END
```

```
IDENTIFICATION DIVISION.
    PROGRAM-ID.  CLASS01.
ENVIRONMENT DIVISION.
    INPUT-OUTPUT SECTION.
              .
              .
              .

DATA DIVISION.
    FILE SECTION.
FD  CLASS-MASTER
    LABEL RECORDS ARE STANDARD.
01  CLASS-MASTER-REC.
    05 CLASS-NUMBER                    PIC       9(4).
    05 CLASS-NAME                      PIC       X(10).
              .
              .
              .


PROCEDURE DIVISION.
    OPEN INPUT CLASS-MASTER.
    MOVE 0 TO EOF-FLAG.
              .
              .
              .
```

Figure 2-6   Portion of a Computer Program Written in COBOL

dred computer languages, only about six or eight of them are commonly used. For one reason or another, the rest have not been accepted. Programming and languages are discussed in detail in Part 5 of this book.

Since there is a wide variety of programs, they are often divided into categories according to their function. Two categories that are used in business are *system programs* and *application programs*. System programs control the computer. For example, they cause the computer to start and stop jobs, to copy data from one tape to another, and the like. Application programs are oriented toward a business need. They perform payroll, do accounting, etc. Usually the system programs come with the computer, but the application programs do not. Application programs must be developed or acquired separately.

Data

The third component of a business computer system is *data*. Before a need can be satisfied, all the pertinent facts must be gathered. This is a special problem for computer systems since all data must be put into some computer-sensible form before it can be read into the computer. Thus data is punched onto cards (see figure 2-7), is typed in directly by means of a keyboard of some type (figure 2-8), or put into computer-sensible form by some other means.

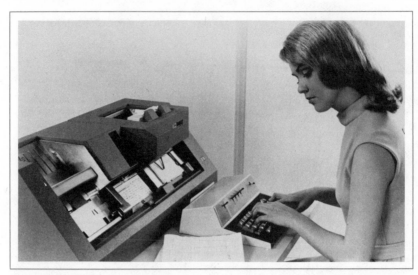

Figure 2-7   Keypunch in Operation

Complete and correct data is essential for the successful operation of a business computer system. Computers are fast but they have no intuition or judgment. They will work diligently with absolute gibberish and produce outputs that are equally gibberish. "Garbage in, garbage out" is an old (30 years is old in this industry!) but appropriate saying in the computer business.

Figure 2-8   Keyboard Data Entry Device

Computer data can be categorized in the same way that we categorized hardware. Thus there is *input data* that is read into the computer for processing. There is *processing data* inside the CPU. There is *output data*, or results, that are usually in human-readable form. Finally, there is *stored data*. This data is written onto some storage device and saved for later processing. (See figure 2-4.)

Data can be stored in a variety of ways. It can be recorded on magnetic tape (like on a tape recorder at home), it can be punched on cards, or stored in other ways. The term *storage medium* refers to the type of storage used. Magnetic tape is a storage medium, as are punched cards.

People in business computing distinguish between *data* and *information*. Data is defined as recorded facts or figures. Information is knowledge derived from data. Thus data and information are not the same. A list of sales made during the past month by 15 sales agents is an example of data. A summation of the sales of each, together with the names of the top three agents, is an example of information.

The last two components of a business computer system go hand in hand. They are procedures and trained personnel. *Procedures* are instructions for people on the use and operation of the system. Procedures describe how people are to prepare input data and how the results are to be used. Also, procedures explain what people are to do when errors are created and need to be corrected. Further, procedures explain how people are to operate the computer. They describe what programs to run, what data to use, and what to do with the outputs. Procedures must also describe what to do when the computer fails, or *crashes* as it is sometimes called.

Procedures

Trained people are the final component of a business computer system. People bring the other four components together and integrate the computer system into the business environment. The major categories of personnel are *systems development personnel*, *operations personnel*, *users*, and *systems clientele*.

Personnel

Systems development people design and produce business computer systems. There are two types of systems development personnel. *Systems analysts* investigate business needs, formalize requirements, and design all five components of a business computer system. Systems analysts work extensively with people and they need good communication skills. *Programmers* develop and test programs to meet requirements provided by systems analysts. Programmers work less with people and more with the computer. Sometimes an individual performs both jobs. He or she is then called a *programmer/analyst*.

Operations personnel run the computer and related equipment. *Computer operators* control the computer, start and stop jobs, mount tapes, load paper and special forms in the printer, and so forth. *Data entry personnel* key data into computer-sensible form using keypunches and similar equipment. *Data control personnel* are the liaison between operations and users. They accept data from the users, check for completeness, dispatch computer reports, and so forth. These people also serve as tape librarians if tapes are extensively used. (See figure 2-9.)

Users are individuals who interact directly with the computer system. They provide input data and utilize computer-generated information to accomplish their jobs. Examples are class scheduling clerks, order entry personnel, and airline reservation agents. Finally, the *clientele* of a computer system are people who receive the system's benefit. Examples are students in the class scheduling example, or customers who order food or services, or passengers on an airline.

Programmers or other systems development personnel do not have a role during system use. These people design and develop systems, and they make system changes (sometimes referred to as *system maintenance*). However, they have no part in the operation of a well-run system. In fact, as we will discuss in the Computer Control module of Part 4, there are important security reasons why programmers and systems analysts should not be involved in the operation of a system.

To be effective, both operations and user personnel must be trained in the system procedures. They should understand standard

Figure 2-9 Computer Personnel and Typical 1980 Salaries

Job Title	Typical 1980 Salary ($) (assuming 3 years experience at job)
Director of Data Processing	35,000 to 50,000
Systems Development Personnel	
Systems analyst	25,000 to 35,000
Application programmer	20,000 to 25,000
Systems programmer	25,000 to 30,000
Programmer/analyst	20,000 to 30,000
Operations Personnel	
Computer operator	15,000 to 25,000
Data entry operator	10,000 to 15,000
Data control clerk	15,000 to 20,000

procedures and know the location of procedure documentation for unusual conditions or errors.

Once again, the five components of a business computer system are hardware, programs, data, procedures, and trained personnel. Without all five components, the business computer system will not operate.

How does this relate to you? You already know more than Chuck Swanson did in the TYCON Construction case. If Tom Jackson presented his idea to you, you could ask, "Tom, where do you propose we get the data?" or "Tom, when are you going to define the procedures and train the users?" You could insist that these questions be answered adequately or you could protect yourself by withdrawing from the project.

This section introduced many terms. The following questions may help you to review them. Also, see the word list at the end of the chapter.

QUESTIONS

2.1 Define a business computer system.

2.2 What are the five components of a business computer system?

2.3 Describe one type of computer input equipment.

2.4 Describe one type of computer output equipment.

2.5 Describe one type of computer storage equipment.

2.6 What is the CPU?

2.7 What is the purpose of a computer program?

2.8 Name and describe two types of computer programs.

2.9 Name four types of computer data.

2.10 Why is storage data necessary? Give two examples of storage media.

2.11 Explain the difference between data and information.

2.12 What is the difference between procedures and programs?

2.13 Explain three types of procedures needed for a business computer system.

2.14 Name three types of systems development personnel. Explain what each does.

2.15 Name three types of operations personnel. Explain what each does.

2.16 What is the difference between systems users and systems clientele?

THE CLASS SCHEDULING SYSTEM

Now we will consider the components of a business computer system in greater detail by examining a typical system. The system we will discuss enrolls students into classes. The goal of this section is to help you remember the definitions already introduced and to show the interaction of the five components.

The Problem

The class scheduling problem is common to all colleges and universities. Departments of the college or university decide to offer one or more sections of a large number of classes. The offerings are published in a class schedule. Students, together with their advisors, select courses from the schedule. They then fill out class request forms and submit the request forms to the administration.

As every student knows, there are conflicts. Some classes are requested by more students than can be accommodated. Other classes are selected by too few students to be taught economically. Consequently, the department administrators close some classes, add more sections of others, and drop sections of still others.

This leads to a chaotic process known as *add/drop*. Here, students who were unable to enroll in the classes they requested are given an opportunity to wait in long lines to enroll in other classes. Eventually this process terminates. The students finally get acceptable schedules or become so worn out by the system that they decide to take whatever courses they can get.

The basic functions of the class scheduling system are listed in figure 2-10. Student IDs are compared to a list of valid students to ensure that the requester is officially enrolled and in good standing. Then the requests are examined to determine if any student tried to

Figure 2-10 Functions of the Class Scheduling System

1. Check student IDs against a list of valid students. Ensure that each student is enrolled in the university and in good standing.
2. Check class requests for time conflicts. Eliminate conflicting requests when necessary.
3. Enroll students in requested classes as space is available.
4. Count the number of students enrolled in each class. Close classes when the maximum number have enrolled. Count number of attempts to enroll in class once it is closed.
5. Store student class enrollment data for later use by add/drop, billing, grading, and other systems.
6. Print students' class schedules.
7. Print a summary report listing each class, the number of students enrolled, and the number of students attempting to enroll after the class is closed.

enroll in classes that meet at the same time. If so, all but one of the conflicting requests are dropped.

Next, students are enrolled in classes as space is available. No classes are to have more than the maximum number of students specified by the department. If a class is closed, the system counts the number of requests for the class after it is closed. Data showing which students are enrolled in which classes is saved for processing by other computer systems. Finally, student schedules and a summary report are printed.

To describe a business computer system that will solve this problem, we need to describe each of its five components. For this discussion, it will be convenient to consider the data first, and then the hardware, programs, procedures, and personnel.

Figure 2-11 summarizes the data involved in class scheduling. The output data shows what the system is to produce; there are three types of output. *Student/class enrollment data* shows which students are enrolled in which classes. This data will be stored on tape to be used by other business computer systems that do add/drop, billing, grading, and so forth. The other two types of output are both printed reports. *Student schedules* will be given to students. The *summary report* will be used by administrators when they decide whether to add or drop class sections.

DATA FOR CLASS SCHEDULING

There are also three types of input for the class scheduling system. Student class request data will provide the name, ID, and desired classes for each student. The *student status data* is stored data listing the ID, name, address, status (honors, probation, etc.) of all students enrolled at the university. Finally, the *class schedule data* describes the classes to be offered, their times, and locations.

Figure 2-12 presents a system flowchart. This diagram summarizes the interaction of the data and the class scheduling program. The strange shapes are not accidental; they are standard computing symbols. The ▰ represents a punched card; in figure 2-12 it indicates that the student request data is on punched cards. Since the arrow goes toward the program, the cards are being read. If the arrow were going away

Figure 2-11 Summary of Data Needed by the Class Scheduling System

Output Data	Input Data
Student/Class Enrollment Data	Student Class Requests
Student Schedules	Student Status Data
Summary Report	Class Schedule Data

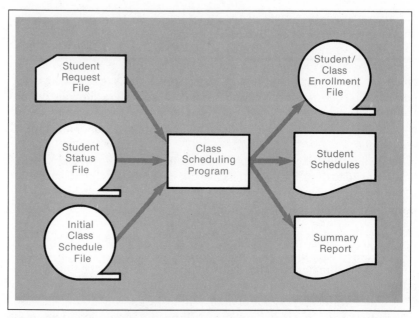

Figure 2-12   Class Scheduling System Flowchart

from the program, this would signify that the program is to punch the cards.

The ◖ represents stored data on magnetic tape. We can see from the figure that three tapes are required—two for input and one for output. Also, the ▬ represents a report or document. Figure 2-12 shows that two separate reports, the summary data and student schedules, will be printed. Finally, the ▪, which is called a *process symbol*, represents a program that will create the outputs from the inputs. In this case, the flowchart indicates that a program called *Class Scheduling* will do this function.

Characters, Fields, Records, and Files

Before we can describe this data further, we must define more data processing terminology. A *character* is a single letter or digit. For example, a character, say a Q or a 6, is appearing somewhere in computer data. A group of characters is called a *field*. Fields usually have logical meanings; they represent some piece of data. Thus the five characters in a postal zip code are the zip code field. The nine characters in a social security number are the social security number field.

A collection of fields is called a *record*. Thus a collection of fields about a student is called the *student record*. Figure 2-13 depicts a student status record. The numbers across the top of the record refer to character positions or columns. These numbers do not exist on the magnetic tape; they are shown here just for reference. If this record

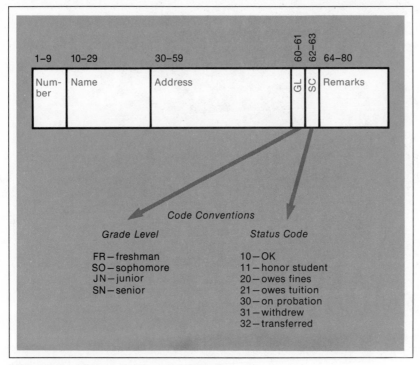

Figure 2-13 Fields in the Student Status Record

were printed, student number would appear in the first nine positions, name would appear in positions 10 through 29, and so forth.

Note the use of abbreviations and special codes. Rather than write out lengthy grade levels like SOPHOMORE, abbreviations are used. Also, the status code field contains numbers that are assigned meanings as shown in figure 2-13. These codes are set up as *conventions* when the system is designed. Thus an 11 in the code field is understood to mean the student is an honor student. When codes like these are used, they must be explained in procedures for users; otherwise, people will now know how to interpret results.

A collection of records is called a *file*. Thus all the student status records together are referred to as the *student status file*. The class schedule file contains all the class schedule records. Figure 2-14 summarizes this terminology: *Characters* are grouped into *fields;* fields are grouped into *records*; records are collected into a *file*.

Look again at figure 2-12. There are six files. Both the student status file and the class schedule file are on magnetic tape. For the time being, we will not be concerned with how the data got there. (This will be fully discussed in Chapter 5.) The format of the student status records was shown in figure 2-14.

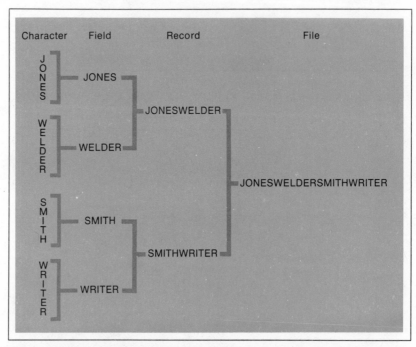

Figure 2-14 Relationship of Characters, Fields, Records, and Files

The format of the class schedule records appears in figure 2-15. All the field contents are self-explanatory except perhaps *Days Meeting*. This field will have letters representing the days of the week that the class meets. A Monday, Wednesday, Friday class will have MWF. A Tuesday, Thursday class will have TR. Also, the number of students enrolled and the number turned away will be zero initially.

The student request file is the remaining input file in figure 2-12. Students indicate their class requests by filling out forms like the one in figure 2-16. The forms are given to keypunch personnel who punch the data on cards as shown in figure 2-17. There is a set of cards for each

Figure 2-15 Class Schedule Record Format

Record Position	Field Contents
1–3	Class Number
4–30	Class Name
31	Section Number
32–35	Hours Meeting
36–40	Days Meeting (MTWRF)
41–43	Maximum Number of Students
44–46	Number of Students Enrolled
47–49	Number of Students Turned Away

Figure 2-16 Student Class Request Form

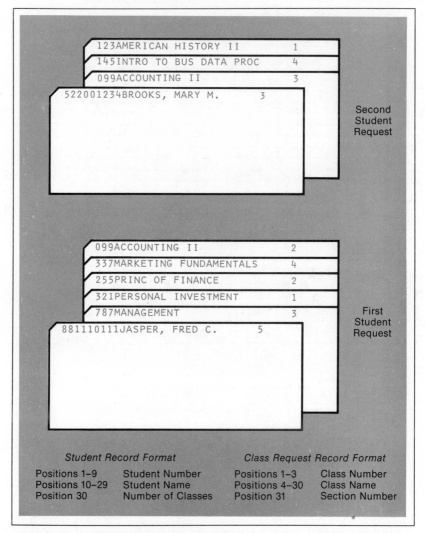

Figure 2-17 Format of Student Request File

student. The first card identifies the student; the remaining cards list the classes the student wants to take—one card for each class. When the class scheduling program is run, the cards for all the students will be combined into a single group called a *card deck*. This will be the student request file.

The remaining three files in figure 2-12 are output files. The student/class enrollment file lists classes and shows which students are in each class. We will not be concerned with its format here. The other two files are reports.

So far we have discussed one of the five components of the class scheduling system—data. We will now discuss a second component.

The hardware requirements for the class scheduling system can be determined from the system flowchart in figure 2-12. The system requires a card reader, a printer, and three tape drives. Only one printer is required because the reports can be produced in sequence. Also, with a little foresight and some manipulation, the same tape drive can be used for all three tape files. That, however, is beyond the scope of this chapter.

HARDWARE FOR CLASS SCHEDULING

Of course, the class scheduling system needs a CPU to process the program. The CPU will have two parts: a *main memory* that holds the program and the processing data, and an *arithmetic and logic unit* that actually executes the program's instructions. This brief description of hardware will suffice for this example. Chapter 5 contains much more detail.

2.17 What is a system flowchart?

QUESTIONS

2.18 Explain the meaning of ▭, ◯, ▱, and ▭ in a system flowchart.

2.19 Define character, field, record, and file. Explain how these terms are related.

2.20 Explain the conventions for status codes in the student status record.

Questions 2.21 through 2.23 pertain to the following flowchart:

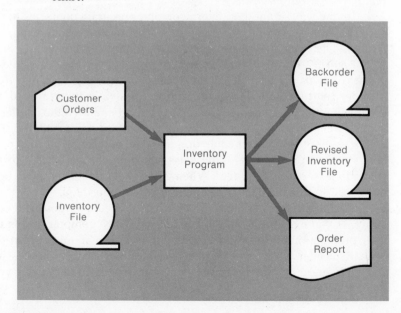

2.21   What computer hardware will be needed to run this pro-
       gram?

2.22   Is the order data input to the program or output from the
       program?

2.23   What data will be printed? What data will be stored?

**PROGRAMS FOR
CLASS SCHEDULING**
We will not discuss the details of programming and program languages
in this section—that is done in Part 5. However, you need to know
more about programs than we have described thus far. Consequently,
in this section we will discuss a logic pattern that occurs in many
programs and introduce two tools used by programmers.

Think for a moment about how you would solve the class scheduling problem manually. You would probably schedule the classes one
student at a time. You would gather the data you need for the first
student and the classes he or she requested. Then you would check for
conflicts, closed classes, and so forth, and produce a valid schedule.
Finally, you would write the student's schedule. You would then proceed with the next student. When all the student requests have been
processed, you would be finished.

Think about this process for a moment. Can you see that it has
basically three phases? There is a data gathering phase, a processing
phase, and a result writing phase. These three phases are common to
many business problems. In fact, this pattern occurs so frequently
that systems developers have given it a special name. It is called the
input/process/output cycle.

In one way or another, every computer program conforms to this
pattern. Data is read into the computer, it is processed, and results are
written. The cycle is repeated until all the data is processed.

Figure 2-18 shows how this pattern could be used to schedule
classes. For *input*, data about the student's request is read into main
memory (part of the CPU) along with the student's status record and
the relevant class schedule records. For *processing*, the student's
status is checked, and if it is acceptable, classes are scheduled. For
output, either the class schedule or a message describing the unaccept-
able status is printed. Also, the class schedule data is written to the
student/class enrollment file. When all student requests have been
processed in this manner, the summary report is printed.

This input/process/output cycle is an exceedingly powerful construct. If you ever find yourself floundering with a computer programming problem (in a test, as an assignment, or at work), think about this
cycle. Consider what activity is needed for input, what for processing,
and what for output. This pattern is very convenient for organizing your
thoughts. Try it!

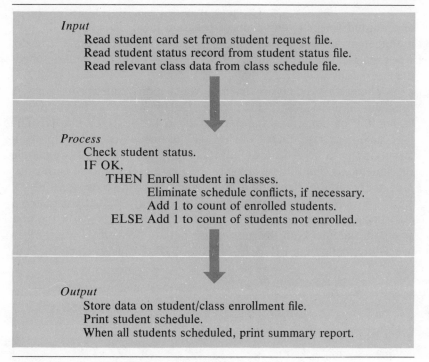

Input
  Read student card set from student request file.
  Read student status record from student status file.
  Read relevant class data from class schedule file.

Process
  Check student status.
  IF OK,
      THEN Enroll student in classes.
              Eliminate schedule conflicts, if necessary.
              Add 1 to count of enrolled students.
      ELSE Add 1 to count of students not enrolled.

Output
  Store data on student/class enrollment file.
  Print student schedule.
  When all students scheduled, print summary report.

Figure 2-18 Summary of Input/Process/Output Activity for the Class Scheduling Problem

In many ways, writing computer programs and writing English (or other languages) are similar. Programs vary in length and complexity just as written documents do. Some programs are simple, like a short memo. Some programs are longer, like term papers. Some programs are as long as books or even encyclopedias.

Developing Program Algorithms

It is difficult to write a long paper or a book without spending some time organizing thoughts. Often people make outlines, develop chapter descriptions, and so forth. Similarly, when writing all but the simplest computer programs, people need to organize their thoughts. This is sometimes called *developing the algorithm*. An algorithm is a set of specific actions to take in order to solve a problem in a finite number of steps. Computer professionals have developed a host of tools for this purpose.

The computer industry is new, and professionals disagree about many topics. Currently, one of the most heated debates concerns which are the best tools for developing and organizing program logic. In this section we will consider two of them that will be used throughout this book. They are *pseudocode* and *program flowcharts*.

Pseudocode   Pseudocode (*pseudo* means false, thus, false code) is an informal English equivalent of program logic. To write it, the programmer or analyst just explains in words what the program is to do. For example, consider figure 2-19, which shows part of the class scheduling program.

The pseudocode is divided into two sections, called *procedures*. A procedure is just a group of instructions that has a name and is performed as a unit. Program processing starts at the MAIN-PROCEDURE. The first statement says DOUNTIL. . . . This means that a group of instructions is to be repeated until a condition is met. In this example the statements that follow, down to the END-DO, are to be performed repeatedly until all the student requests have been processed.

A group of statements that are performed repeatedly is called a *loop* because the logic repeats, or loops back. In figure 2-19 the first group of statements in the loop cause data to be read. Next, another procedure, called the PROCESS-PROCEDURE, is to be performed.

Figure 2-19   Pseudocode for Part of the Class Scheduling Program

```
BEGIN MAIN-PROCEDURE
  DOUNTIL NO DATA REMAINS
      READ STUDENT REQUEST FROM STUDENT REQUEST FILE
      READ STUDENT STATUS FROM STUDENT STATUS FILE
      READ RELEVANT CLASS DATA FROM CLASS SCHEDULE FILE
      DO PROCESS-PROCEDURE
      STORE DATA ON STUDENT CLASS ENROLLMENT FILE
      PRINT ERROR MESSAGE OR STUDENT SCHEDULE AS APPROPRIATE
  END-DO
  PRINT SUMMARY REPORT
END MAIN-PROCEDURE

BEGIN PROCESS-PROCEDURE
  IF STUDENT STATUS CODE FROM STUDENT STATUS FILE IS ≥ 20
      THEN ADD 1 TO BAD-REQUEST-COUNT
      ELSE ADD 1 TO GOOD-REQUEST-COUNT
          /Now go through class schedule steps/
                    .
                    .
                    .
  END-IF
END PROCESS-PROCEDURE
```

PROCESS-PROCEDURE checks the student status and schedules classes if appropriate. The pseudocode to perform this function does not have to be in a separate procedure. It could be placed in the middle of the loop. However, doing so would make MAIN-PROCEDURE long and complex, and the author of this pseudocode elected to write it separately. Placement is purely a matter of personal creativity and taste.

Part of PROCESS-PROCEDURE is shown in figure 2-19. Note the IF statement. Checking conditions is very common in computer programs, and in fact, this capability gives programs much of their power. In figure 2-19 the IF statement is used to check student status in accordance with the convention shown in figure 2-13.

After PROCESS-PROCEDURE is performed, the program logic returns to MAIN-PROCEDURE. Here the output phase is performed. Either an error message or the student schedule is printed. (How would you like the schedule in figure 2-20?) After all requests have been processed, the summary report is written. Observe that MAIN-PROCEDURE has the input/process/output pattern.

Do not be misled by the simplicity of these statements. This is pseudocode. When the actual program is written in a programming language, many more details and more precise instructions must be specified. Pseudocode is a programmer's shorthand for organizing and developing program logic.

Flowcharts Flowcharts are a second way of organizing and presenting program logic. In figure 2-12 we have already seen one type of flowchart called a *system flowchart*. This flowchart showed how programs and files are related. Another type of flowchart is called a *program* or *detailed flowchart*. These flowcharts depict program logic. Figure 2-21 presents a program flowchart for part of the class scheduling program. This is the same logic shown in the pseudocode in figure 2-19.

Figure 2-20 Sample Student Class Schedule Report

```
    NAME:    SALLY J. PARKS

    STUDENT NUMBER:  500004128                    GRADE LEVEL:  SOPHOMORE


    CLASS                  HOUR         DAYS

    ACCOUNTING             8            MTWF
    COMPOSITION II         4            MWF
    HUMAN SEXUALITY        CLASS FULL
    STATISTICS             2-4          TR
    AMERICAN HISTORY II    UNABLE TO SCHEDULE DUE TO CONFLICTS
```

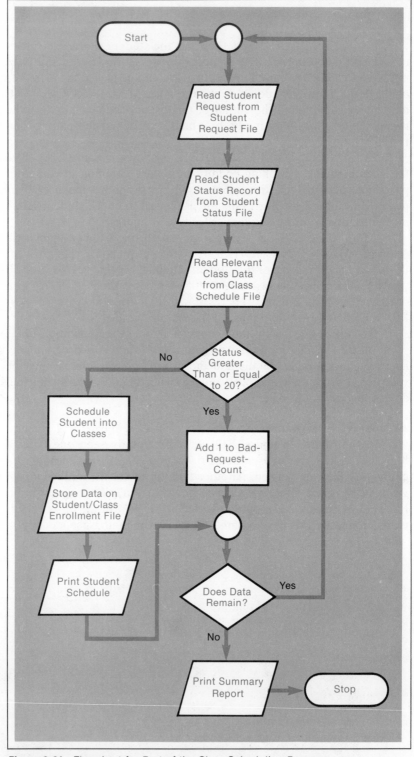

Figure 2-21 Flowchart for Part of the Class Scheduling Program

You probably recognize most of the symbols from figure 2-12. However, two new symbols are shown in figure 2-21. The parallelogram ▱ represents a read or write operation. The data to be read or written and the file name are put inside the symbol. The diamond ◇ represents a condition or decision. The condition is written inside the diamond, and the arrows out are labeled with answers to the questions. Thus, if the student status is greater than 20, the schedule will not be produced.

The computer industry is currently debating whether pseudocode or program flowcharts are better. Flowcharts are older and have an established position in the industry. Pseudocode is newer, but many experts think it is easier to produce and read than flowcharts. Others think that neither should be used and that one of the other techniques shown in Part 5 is the best. Both are used in industry, and you should be familiar with them.

We have described pseudocode and flowcharts as if their only use was for developing program logic. They have another important application. Both techniques can be used to document the logic of a program. Documentation is important when programs need to be changed, or when errors are discovered and programs must be fixed. Often the person who wrote the program is unavailable to make the change or *fix*. Even if that person is available, good documentation will make it easier for the modification to be made.

2.24   Explain the input/process/output cycle.   **QUESTIONS**

2.25   Describe input, process, and output activities for the preparation of paychecks.

2.26   Describe input, process, and output activities for balancing your checkbook.

2.27   Why are pseudocode and flowcharts necessary? Do professional programmers ever use them?

2.28   Explain the meaning of the following pseudocode:

```
BEGIN AVERAGE-PROCEDURE
    SET SUM TO 0
    SET COUNT TO 0
    DOUNTIL NO GRADES REMAIN
        READ NEXT SCORE
        ADD SCORE TO SUM
        ADD 1 TO COUNT
    END-DO
    SET AVG TO SUM DIVIDED BY COUNT
    PRINT AVG
END AVERAGE-PROCEDURE
```

2.29 Convert the pseudocode in problem 2.28 to a flowchart.

2.30 Explain the meaning of the following flowchart:

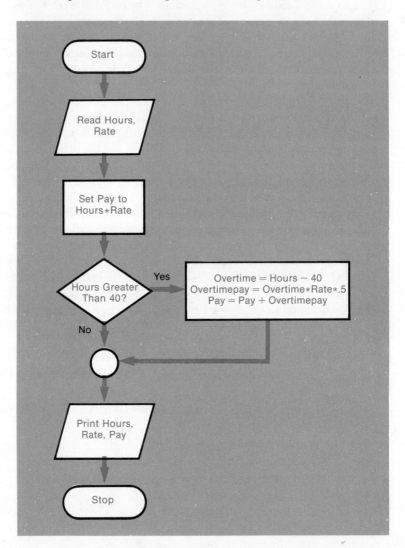

2.31 Convert the flowchart in problem 2.30 to pseudocode.

PROCEDURES FOR CLASS SCHEDULING Superficially, hardware, programs, and data are the major components of a computer system. In fact, many systems have been designed with this misconception. Unfortunately—as many businesses have painfully (and expensively) learned—two additional components are required. In this section we discuss one of them, *system procedures.*

Consider the case of George Shelton who tried to enroll in classes at a college using a class scheduling system similar to the one we have been discussing. When George examined his class schedule he found the college thought he owed money. George went to Scheduling to protest but they sent him to Finance. Finance agreed with George; he owed no money. They didn't know what to do, however, so they sent him to the computer center. The computer center sent him back to Scheduling. In desperation, George went to his adviser, who was sympathetic but didn't know what to do either. George went back to his room at the dorm, put his head in his hands, and wondered if college was for him, after all.

The Need for Procedures

What is the problem here? Obviously an error has been made, but why can't it be corrected? Is the hardware incapable? No. Can programs be written to correct the bad data? Certainly.

George has a problem because of the lack of procedures. No one knows what to do.

In the early days of data processing, procedures were an afterthought, something users and the data processing staff worked out during systems implementation. Today that is changed. Competent data processing personnel design procedures as part of the system.

Procedures are needed by users, operators, and systems developers. (See figure 2-22.) The users need to know how to input data, how to interpret results, and any special responsibilities they have. For example, in the class scheduling system, the users (scheduling clerks) have the responsibility of checking out all the bad schedule requests. Procedures need to be written to tell them how to do this. Additionally, users need to know how to correct errors that occur.

Figure 2-22   Examples of Procedures for Users, Operators, and Developers

Used by	*Procedure*
Users	How to prepare inputs How to interpret outputs Special user responsibilities How to correct errors
Operators	Who is authorized to provide inputs What format inputs should have When to run jobs What to do with outputs How to run jobs—tapes used, forms to mount, etc.
Developers	How to develop requirements Standards for systems design How to write and test programs How to implement new systems

Procedures for operators explain how to run the system. The operators need to know who is authorized to provide inputs, what inputs to expect, how often to run the jobs, where the outputs go, and so forth. Additionally, operators need to know the mechanics of running the job, such as which tapes will be read, what sort of paper to put into the computer printer, and how many tapes will be written.

Finally, systems developers need procedures that specify a standard way of building business computer systems. These procedures explain how to determine requirements, how to develop systems designs, how to write and test programs, and how to implement new systems. We will study these activities in greater detail in Part 2. The lack of systems development procedures was a major factor in the difficulties that TYCON Construction Products encountered in Chapter 1.

Procedures are ineffective if they are lost or forgotten, and consequently they must be *documented*. This means they must be written, evaluated by concerned personnel, and approved by management. Documentation is extremely important, not only as a way to preserve the procedures, but also as a way of ensuring that the procedures are complete and understood. Most computer systems have three volumes of documentation for each system. There is one volume for users, one for developers, and one for operators.

An Example of User Procedures

Figure 2-23 presents the table of contents for the users volume of procedure documentation for the class scheduling system. The first section summarizes the system. The next three sections are concerned with input, processing, and output. The input section describes required input data and presents data formats and input procedures. Note the section on how to verify data completeness and format.

The processing procedures for this system are minimal because the system is run entirely by computer operations. For some systems, however, the users have more responsibility and the procedures are documented here. Section IV, *Output Procedures*, summarizes the outputs generated by the system. It also defines the meaning of each output data item. This is essential when output data items have several possible interpretations.

Section V, *Error Correction Procedures*, is crucial. This section explains what users should do when errors are discovered in computer input or on reports. This documentation either was unused or did not exist at the college where George Shelton attempted to enroll. Finally, there is a section listing names and phone numbers of critical personnel to be called in emergencies. This list can be invaluable when a problem occurs at a critical time (like the middle of class registration).

Procedure documentation serves several important functions. First, personnel training can be more efficient and effective if new people read documentation before, during, and after training sessions. Second, written documentation helps to standardize processing and

CLASS SCHEDULING SYSTEM
Users Procedure Documentation

Table of Contents

  I. System Overview
     A. System Functions
     B. System Flowchart
     C. Summary of Users Procedures

 II. Input Procedures
     A. Summary of Input Data Needed
     B. Student Request Data
     C. Student Status Data
     D. Class Schedule Data
     E. Data Verification Procedures

III. Processing Procedures
     A. Summary of Operation
     B. User Responsibilities

 IV. Output Procedures
     A. Summary of Output
     B. Student Schedules
     C. Summary Report
     D. Student Class Enrollment File

  V. Error Correction Procedures
     A. Bad Input Data
     B. Incorrect Results
     C. Explanation of Error Messages

 VI. Critical Personnel
     (List of people and phone numbers for use in
     emergencies)

Figure 2-23 Example of Users Procedure Documentation

thus improve the quality of service. Without documentation, someone like George may happen to find a knowledgeable clerk and receive good service. Another person may find a substitute clerk and receive poor service, which can lead to ill will among the system clientele. Finally, documentation serves as a system memory. If the system is seldom used, people will forget the procedures. Also, if critical personnel quit or become otherwise unavailable, the documentation can be used to recover from the personnel loss.

PERSONNEL FOR CLASS SCHEDULING

The last of the five components of a business computer system is trained personnel. As mentioned previously, there are four types of people involved: systems development personnel (systems analysts, programmers, and programmer/analysts), operations personnel, system users, and system clientele.

Systems analysts are people who know both business and computing. When a system is being developed, systems analysts interview future users and determine what the requirements for the new system will be. They also design the computer systems to satisfy these requirements.

In the case of the class scheduling system, the systems analysts interviewed department heads, faculty members, scheduling personnel, college administrators, students, and computer center operators. From these interviews, they developed the requirements or the needs to be satisfied by the class scheduling system. Next, the system analysts developed a design by creating specifications for each of the five components. The program component was then given to a programmer to build and test. Finally, the systems analysts developed a plan to implement the system, and supervised this process.

Good systems analysts possess a rare combination of skills. They must be good at communicating with people, they must understand at least one business specialty, and they must know computing technology. Currently, systems analysts are in very short supply. If you would like to develop the needed skills, systems analysis would be an excellent career choice.

Programmers are computer specialists who write programs. In contrast to systems analysts, these people need not be as good in dealing with people nor do they need to know business as well. However, they must know more about computer technology. Specifically, they must know one programming language very well. Most programmers know two or three. Further, they understand the technical details of computing better than systems analysts do. Sometimes systems analysis and programming are combined into one job entitled *programmer/analyst*. This job requires all of the skills mentioned above. A good programmer/analyst is a rare and valuable commodity.

Once a system is designed, developed, and implemented, development personnel should cease involvement with it. Responsibility for using systems should lie only with users and operations. Most systems that last more than a few months, however, are required at some point to be changed. When this requirement occurs, the systems development personnel are called in to design and implement necessary changes to the system. This is sometimes called *system maintenance*. Note that these changes are not just changes to the programs; they can be changes to hardware, data, procedures, or personnel as well.

To do their job properly, systems development personnel need to know the latest in computer technology. Training is thus a recurring need. One month out of every year is not an unusual amount of training. (See figure 2-24.)

Operations personnel run the computer. They need to know how to start the computer, how to stop it, and how to run programs. They also need to know how to operate equipment like tape drives, card readers, and printers. When the computer fails, the operations personnel need to know what to do to minimize the damage, and they need to know how to restart the computer.

In a well-run data processing center, the majority of the processing is done according to a schedule. Also, everything the operators need to know about running a system is documented. Therefore, neither systems development personnel nor users need be in the computer room. To enforce this, access to the computer room is often controlled by locks. Only operations personnel are allowed in.

Operations personnel need to know how to run computer systems. They do not need in-depth knowledge of computing technology or even of how the computer works. Consequently, operations personnel usually have less technical knowledge than systems development per-

Figure 2-24 Examples of Training Needs of Systems Personnel

Personnel	*Training Requirements*
Systems Developers	Communication skills Business fundamentals and principles Programming languages Computer hardware Computer technology Project management
Operations Personnel	How to operate computer How to handle failures How to run business computer systems Requirements for preventive maintenance Operations staff supervision
Users	How to prepare inputs How to interpret outputs Special responsibilities Forthcoming changes to systems

sonnel. A typical operator has three to six months of formal training followed by about the same amount of on-the-job training.

The third category of personnel is *system users*. These people generally have no formal training in computing (that's why you will have an advantage). They do, however, have expertise in their business specialty. Users are typically trained by the development personnel on how to use a system. This training can be *initial training* in which the users are introduced to the system, shown its basic capabilities, and taught how to accomplish their jobs. *Recurring training* is given periodically to remind users of how they should (or can) be using the system and to inform them of any new features that have been developed. Also, if safety or public health is involved, users can be given proficiency examinations during the recurring training sessions.

The last group of systems development personnel is the *system clientele*. These are the people for whom the system is designed. You are a member of the clientele of a class scheduling system, of a grade posting system, and of many other systems as well.

The clientele of a system are usually not available nor even willing to be formally trained. Thus systems are designed so the requirements on the clientele are negligible. The input and output forms for the class scheduling system, for example, are simple and largely self-explanatory. The same is true for billing, grade posting, and other systems.

Where the system is complex, the clientele are often guided by the system users. A good example occurs when you make an airline reservation. The reservation clerk obtains needed data by a sequence of questions and then inputs the data. These questions, by the way, are often *prompted* by the computer.

The first three lines of figure 2-25 show an example of prompting. The computer typed ORIGIN: and the clerk filled in New York. Next the computer typed DESTINATION: and the clerk filled in Los Angeles. The third line was done similarly. Then the computer responded with possible flights.

The need for trained personnel is so obvious it is often overlooked. When users are not given formal training, system implementation is delayed until operators and users learn by experience. This is slow and costly. Also, when personnel are not properly trained, they often use the system ineffectively or inefficiently. They may take one or two hours to accomplish a task that would take a few minutes when done properly. Also, untrained users will not be able to service the clientele as well. Remember this situation occurred in George Shelton's case in the previous section.

Trained personnel are an important part of a business computer system. Users have a right to be trained by the development personnel. As a future business person, you should insist on proper training. Also, you should plan time and expense for training purposes.

ORIGIN: NEW YORK
DESTINATION: LOS ANGELES
APPROXIMATE TIME OF DEPARTURE: 9 AM

POSSIBLE FLIGHTS ARE:
UNITED 599 DEPARTING AT 8:45 NONSTOP
TWA   618 DEPARTING AT 9:20 1 STOP

Figure 2-25 Example of Computer Prompting

2.32 What are the three categories of systems procedures? **QUESTIONS**
Explain the need satisfied by each type.

2.33 What does the term *documentation* mean? Why is documentation important?

2.34 What is likely to happen when no procedures are defined?

2.35 Describe the job requirements of a systems analyst.

2.36 Describe what a programmer does.

2.37 Compare and contrast systems analysts' jobs with programmers' jobs.

2.38 Explain what training is required for:
a. Systems analysts   d. System users
b. Programmers   e. System clientele
c. Operators

SUMMARY

If you have learned the material in this chapter, you understand more about data processing than most business people. If you know that a computer system consists of hardware, programs, data, procedures, and trained personnel, then you will never be duped into thinking that if you buy a computer your problems will be over. You will know that many of your problems have just begun. Even if you obtain a small computer with programs that can be run like a simple office machine, you realize that you will still need to convert data, develop procedures, and train personnel.

Which of these components is the most important? We might as well ask which is the most important link in a chain. Without hardware there is no *computer* system. Without programs the computer won't solve a specific problem, for it is a general purpose machine. Without correct data the system cannot accurately or meaningfully solve the problem. Finally, without procedures or trained personnel the system cannot be used. Each of these five components is required. Without any one, there is no *system*. There are only four expensive components waiting to be integrated.

WORD LIST

Many terms are introduced in this chapter. Terms you should be certain to understand are listed here in the order they appear in the text.

System	*Input data*
Computer system	*Processing data*
Business computer system	*Output data*
Five components of a business computer system	*Stored data*
Computer hardware	*Storage medium*
Input, processing, output, and storage hardware	*Data vs information*
Central processing unit	*Procedures*
Computer program	*Crashes*
Computer programming language	*Systems development personnel*
BASIC	*Systems analyst*
COBOL	*Programmer*
Systems programs	*Programmer/analyst*
Application programs	*Operations personnel*
Garbage in, garbage out	*Computer operator*
	Data entry personnel

Data control personnel

System users

System clientele

Systems maintenance

System flowchart

Card flowchart symbol

Tape flowchart symbol

Document or report flowchart symbol

Processing flowchart symbol

Character

Field

Record

File

Coding convention

Main memory

Arithmetic and logic unit

Algorithm

Pseudocode

DO statement in pseudocode

IF statement in pseudocode

Program flowchart

Decision flowchart symbol

System procedures

Documentation

Initial training

Recurring training

Computer prompting

A. Suppose a computer salesperson tells you the total cost of a computer system is $65,000 for the computer plus $410 per month for maintenance. How do you respond? What other costs might there be?

B. Computer hardware is available in a tremendous variety of speeds and capacities. How, in general, can a business decide which computer to acquire?

C. Develop a system flowchart for an hourly payroll computer system. Assume hours worked are recorded on timesheets and there is an employee master file that has pay rates, year-to-date totals, etc., on it.

D. Suppose you manage the clerks in a payroll office.

   1. Develop an outline of documentation for hourly payroll computer system procedures.

   2. Describe how the payroll clerks should be trained.

E. Describe what you believe is the appropriate amount of education for systems analysts, programmers, and operators.

F. What do you think will happen if a system is designed with:

   1. The wrong hardware?

   2. Program errors?

   3. Improperly designed data?

   4. No procedures?

   5. Poor personnel training?

QUESTIONS TO CHALLENGE YOUR THINKING

CHAPTER 3

Survey of Business Computer Systems Applications

Financial analysts: typical business computer system users

MANAGEMENT INFORMATION SYSTEMS

Computer Applications Vary among Managers

ACCOUNTING

Characteristics of Accounting Computer Systems

Payroll

Payroll System Flowchart

Other Examples of Accounting Computer Systems

FINANCE

Characteristics of Financial Computer Systems

Examples of Financial Computer Systems

SALES AND MARKETING

Examples of Sales and Marketing Computer Systems

MANUFACTURING

Manufacturing Control

Examples of Manufacturing Computer Systems

This chapter surveys the application of computing systems in business. As you read, you should gain a general sense of how businesses use computers and how to relate computing to the areas of business you find interesting. You will also realize that computing is important in every business field.

MANAGEMENT INFORMATION SYSTEMS

Imagine yourself as president of a billion dollar-a-year business, say General Motors or IBM or some similar company. You sit in a plush office with 16 able assistants and secretaries outside your door. As a manager, your job is to *plan*, *organize*, and *control* business activity. To do this, you need *information*. You need information about the company's past performance, about competitors' performance, about new products, about costs, about inventories, about economic changes, about social changes, and on and on.

Why do you need this information? Your job is to make decisions and to start activity on projects you approve. To make good decisions and to start effective projects, you need current, reliable, accurate information.

As president, when you need information, you ask for it. You use your company's *management information system*, which is *a collection of business systems that provide information to managers*. Every company has a management information system (MIS) whether they know it or not. The secretary outside your door who has last year's profit and loss statement is part of the MIS, the contents of your file drawers are part, the annual report is part, as well as hundreds of other sources of information.

Look again at the definition of MIS. It is a collection of *business systems*. It does not necessarily include a computer. An MIS can be composed entirely of data, procedures, and personnel. Computer hardware and programs need not be involved. There have been management information systems for centuries—long before the computer was invented.

The focus of this book, however, is on business *computer* systems—a subset of the total MIS. As you proceed through this book, you will study many different kinds of business computer systems and much computer technology. Do not lose the forest because of the trees, however. Remember that you are studying a portion of an MIS, and the eventual goal of all the technology and complexity is to provide better information to managers.

The portion of the total MIS that is computer-based and the portion that is manual vary from company to company. Some companies do not have computers at all. Some companies buy computer service from other companies. Some have small computers that have just one purpose, like inventory accounting or billing. At the other extreme, some companies have joined their business computer systems with their typing, copying, and communications systems so that the entire MIS is computer-based. There are millions (yes, millions) of companies in between these extremes. (See figure 3-1.)

Business use of computers varies widely. One reason for this variance is that the needs of managers differ. You, as the president of a billion dollar company, have different needs than I, the tape librarian. You

Computer Applications Vary among Managers

Figure 3-1 Range of Computer Use in Management Information Systems

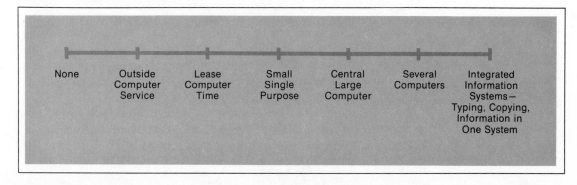

During my 30 years in business, I have seen many changes that I didn't recognize while they were occurring. Examples are the evolution of the near-standard multiple income family from the single family wage earner prototype; the conversion of a producer society to a consumer-oriented one; the dissolution of our inherent faith that Americans were always tops in production and technology. Above all else, I have observed the inexorable rise in the cost of human labor and the increased awareness of the value of time. This last change has led to our gradual and irreversible reliance on computer technology for economic survival.

The future in business, government, the military, and, in fact, all aspects of life is inextricably tied to computer technology. The high cost of labor and the value of time require decisions that can best be made by applying human judgment to information produced by computer systems.

In theory there is little difference between managing a production resource and managing a computer resource. However, perhaps because of the newness of computing, businesses tend to manage production better than computing. While computer systems are essential, they are also expensive. Without effective direction, the computer budget can grow like a cancer in an organization.

Having at least a basic understanding of computer technology is just as critical to one's future as a manager as fundamental skills in human relations and communications. This perspective of computer systems is best acquired early in your education.

COMPUTERS AND MANAGEMENT

Alan M. White

Alan M. White is President of Rocky Mountain Bank Note Company, a national producer of checks and other bank stationery. Mr. White is a native of Denver, and a graduate of Yale University. After service in the U.S. Army in the early 1950s, Mr. White joined Rocky Mountain Bank Note as a salesman. He was named Vice-President in 1964, and President in 1971. Mr. White is an enthusiastic mountain climber, skier, and bridge player.

manage the company, and I manage tapes. You don't care about the expiration date of tape number 07Q56T, and I don't care about the profitability of the Saskatoon plant. (Unless, of course, the profitability of the Saskatoon plant is on tape number 07Q56T!) Our requirements for a business computer system are therefore different.

In general, *the higher the level of management, the more summarized information tends to be*. At each level of management, consolidations, averages, and so forth are passed up to the next level. At the top, the information is consolidations of consolidations.

A second reason that computer use varies is that managers need different types of service. Sometimes business computer systems produce *status information*. The information may be *historical*, like accounting systems that produce year-end reports; it may be *current*, like inventory systems that maintain item counts; or it may be *future*, like market forecasting systems that predict the size of the market next year. (See figure 3-2.)

Not all managers use the computer to obtain status information. Some use computers for the *production of information-bearing documents*. A payroll system produces checks that inform banks to move money. Another such system creates insurance policies, and a third produces wills.

Finally, some managers delegate *control* to business computer systems. For example, an inventory system is designed to compare stock levels to projected sales and automatically generate orders when appropriate. Such control applications are actually combinations of status and production systems. The business computer system evaluates status (stock level) and produces official documents (orders). However, the judgment normally provided by the manager is programmed into the computer.

Suppose someone asks you, as the president of a billion dollar concern, to describe how your company uses computers. As you think, you realize there are probably thousands of ways. At every level of management and in every business specialty, there are computer-based information systems. One way you might organize such a description is by business area. That is what we will do in this chapter. We will examine business systems in accounting, finance, sales and marketing, and manufacturing.

Figure 3-2 Types of Service Provided by Business Computer Systems

Service Type	Example
Status Information	
Historical	Year-End Report
Current	Inventory Stock Levels
Future	Future Market Size Estimates
Information-Bearing Documents	Checks
	Insurance Policies
Automated Control	Automatic Ordering
	Operations Scheduling

ACCOUNTING

Accounting systems have been the most successful at satisfying business needs and have had the greatest acceptance in the business community. There are two major reasons for this success. First, the accounting profession has had many years' experience with computers. In fact, data processing grew out of the accounting machines prevalent in the 1940s and 50s. (See Module A in Part 4 for a history of computing.)

Second, computers are excellent recordkeepers. Given accurate data and correct programs, they can work many, many hours without error. Since computers never become bored and never complain, accountants have assigned them the most tedious, time-consuming aspects of accounting.

Basically, *the purpose of an accounting business computer system is to maintain data that accurately represents the financial state of the company*. To achieve this purpose, accurate data must be initially collected and it must be accurately modified whenever events of accounting significance occur.

Recall the five components of a business computer system from Chapter 2. To maintain accurate data, an accounting system needs (1) computer hardware of sufficient capacity, capability, and speed; (2) programs that correctly instruct the computer to modify data and to produce reports; (3) accurate data to start with and accurate data about transactions (events of accounting significance); (4) procedures for people to operate the system and correct the data; and (5) trained personnel.

Characteristics of Accounting Computer Systems

Several unique properties of accounting pose special requirements for the programs and procedures. First, accounting systems usually deal with transactions expressed in terms of money. Consequently, errors can have severe impact. Also, there is sometimes an incentive for computer crime: people can gain financially by making unauthorized changes to programs or data. This point is especially true for systems that produce negotiable outputs like checks.

Second, accounting systems usually have considerable input data. This data must be converted into some computer-sensible form like punched cards. Unfortunately, all types of data conversion are error-prone.

Consider these last two points together. Do you see the dilemma facing the designer of an accounting system? The system involves money and the impacts of errors can be severe. On the other hand, there is considerable data to be input by error-prone techniques. The consequence of this dilemma is that much of the processing in an accounting system is done to identify and correct errors. Also, considerable processing is done to provide checks and balances between the users and Data Processing, and thereby reduce the potential of unauthorized activity.

A final characteristic important to the design of accounting systems is the need to generate and save considerable data for annual audit. This data is also needed for income tax reporting.

During the audit, the auditors often want to trace a transaction (an order, for example) from its beginning to its final resting place. If the order is processed by a computer system, the auditors may want to examine computer records. Thus accounting systems must be designed to save data of potential interest to auditors.

Given these general comments, let's examine a familiar accounting system, hourly payroll. The requirements of this system are listed in figure 3-3.

Payroll

The first two requirements are self-explanatory. The third requirement refers to the *general ledger* or company accounts. The system needs to generate entries for accounting. These entries will reduce cash by the amount of the payroll, accrue taxes and FICA, and make other necessary bookkeeping adjustments.

Accounting for sick leave and vacation time requires the system to add time each pay period and deduct it as time is taken. Also, reports must be printed for the personnel department to use when authorizing vacations and sick leave payments.

The requirement to print W-2 tax forms at year end means the system must keep track of total pay-to-date, total taxes-to-date, total FICA, and the total of any other taxable income. This data must be kept even for employees who terminate.

The next two requirements refer to changes that will be made to the employee master file. (*Master file* will be defined in Chapter 5. For now, think of it as a file of permanent records.) As employees are hired, data for them must be added to the master file. Also, since pay rate is in the master file, changes must be made when employees re-

Figure 3-3   Requirements for Hourly Payroll

1. Compute pay, taxes, deductions
2. Print paychecks
3. Produce entries for general ledger
4. Account for sick leave and vacation time
5. Print W-2 tax forms at year end
6. Accommodate new employees and changes to employee data
7. Account for ex-employees until year end
8. Minimize risk of error or unauthorized activity

ceive pay increases. When an employee leaves the company, his or her record must be marked so that no further checks will be issued. The record cannot be deleted, however, until the W-2 form is printed at year end. Finally, all of these requirements are to be met in a way that minimizes the risk of error or unauthorized activity.

Payroll System Flowchart   Figure 3-4 shows a system flowchart for the payroll system. It is broken into three phases to provide checks and balances between the Payroll Department and Data Processing. During phase 1 the changes to the master file are keypunched and then *edited* by a computer program. Editing means the program will check the input to be sure it has the correct format, is plausible, and so forth. Note that no changes are actually made to the master file during phase 1. (The new symbol ▼ represents a manual operation.)

The report produced is called a *pre-edit* report. The users must check this report, and if they are satisfied with the changes, another run will be made to change the master file. At that time, a second report, called the *edit report*, will be produced that shows changes actually made.

The pre-edit report, shown in figure 3-5, is reviewed by the Payroll Department. If correct, Data Processing is instructed to proceed with phase 2. If not, then corrections are made and phase 1 is repeated. This sequence allows payroll personnel to ensure that only correct and authorized changes will be made.

In figure 3-5, the first two master file changes appear correct. However, the edit program detected an error in the third entry. This company had established a convention that all employee numbers start with 1. Since this number does not, it is flagged as an error. The new employee data for Joy Johnson must be verified by Payroll. The pay change for employee 17281 appears to have an error; probably the pay change should be 9.87 – not 98.70. Since the program has not detected an error, the responsibility lies with the Payroll Department to accept or reject this change.

These discrepancies point out the need for good procedures and trained personnel. Without them, an error may go undetected. Perhaps, too, you can see why *all* business people need some knowledge about computers.

During phase 2 the edited changes are actually applied to the employee master file. Another edit report is produced; the Payroll Department can check the pre-edit report against this edit report to ensure correctness. If the phase 2 edit report is correct, Payroll authorizes Data Processing to perform phase 3. Otherwise corrections are made and phases 1 and 2 are repeated.

In phase 3, employee timecards are input to the payroll program along with the updated employee master file. The timecards have gone through a pre-edit similar to that shown in phase 1. It is not shown

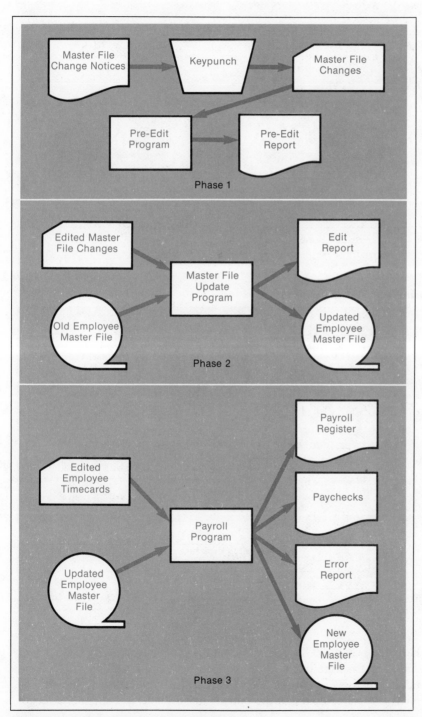

Figure 3-4 System Flowchart for Hourly Payroll

EMPLOYEE NUMBER	EMPLOYEE NAME	TYPE OF CHANGE
12481	FRED PARKS	PAY CHANGE TO 8.73
14618	SALLY BATTS	PAY CHANGE TO 7.50
✗✗✗ ERROR IN NEXT CHANGE		
02800	JOY JOHNSON	NEW EMPLOYEE
	ADDRESS	1418 S. TAMARACK
		ALEXANDRIA, VA 01042
	DATE OF BIRTH	DECEMBER 11, 1944
	TITLE	PRODUCTION ASSISTANT
	PAY RATE	7.52
	DEPENDENTS	3
	SOCIAL SECURITY NUMBER	522-00-1841
17281	ELMER NILSON	PAY CHANGE TO 98.70
16415	DOROTHY SUHM	PAY CHANGE TO 21.50

Figure 3-5 Payroll Master File Change Pre-Edit Report

Figure 3-6 Printed Payroll Checks

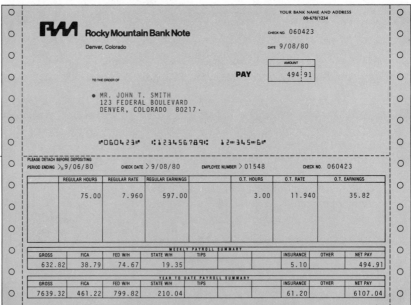

here for brevity. The program computes pay, taxes, and deductions; accounts for time off; and produces a new employee master file containing the new year-to-date totals. It also produces three reports. The *payroll register* contains the entries to be made to the general ledger and a list of every check written. Payroll uses this list to verify the amounts before signing the paychecks. The second report consists of the *paychecks*. (See figure 3-6.) The last report details any errors that have been detected—for example, a timecard for a nonexistent or terminated employee.

COMPUTERS AND ACCOUNTING

Donald E. Nilson, CPA

Knowledge of computing and computers is essential to the successful certified public accountant.

It is generally recognized that we are living in an age where computers impact almost everyone. Nowhere has this impact been any greater than in the field of accounting. In every aspect of accounting, whether it be the stewardship function, management decision-making, or financial reporting to owners, creditors, and governments, accountants deal with information. Until recently, even medium-sized organizations would process accounting information using manual methods; that is, pen and ink and ledgers and journals. Obtaining and putting accounting information into usable forms was time-consuming and expensive.

Within the last few years, the absolute cost and the price-per-formance ratio of computers have dropped drastically. Computers are no longer tools available only to large companies able to afford the expensive hardware and sophisticated staff necessary to run them. Computers are now available to everyone. Even the smallest businesses are able to and do justify the acquisition of a computer. In an overwhelming majority of these cases, the computer is acquired to handle accounting applications.

The public accountant is relied upon to assist in financial decision-making in working with financial institutions, government agencies, and owners, and to provide the kinds of financial knowledge which, in a large organization, is provided by the company's treasurer and controller. Because accountants deal with information, and because many businesses use computers to process this information, failure to gain a working knowledge of computing and computers may severely impair a certified public accountant's usefulness to his clients.

Donald E. Nilson was born and raised in Denver, Colorado. He graduated from the University of Colorado in 1967 and has been in public accounting since 1968, with firms ranging in size from one of the largest international accounting firms to his own practice. He was admitted as a partner in a large accounting firm in Denver at the age of 28. At 30, he was the second ranking partner in the accounting and auditing standards discipline of a national firm of certified public accountants. He is presently a partner in the firm of Scullion, Nilson, & Beekmann, Certified Public Accountants, in Denver. The firm's clients range from large manufacturing companies with overseas subsidiaries to small, closely held businesses.

This discussion demonstrates a typical accounting system. Can you see the need for user involvement to provide checks and balances over Data Processing? Also, note that the master files keep data about payments that can be used for audit and tax purposes. The payroll registers are another permanent record.

Other Examples of Accounting Computer Systems

Figure 3-7 lists common accounting systems. We will briefly summarize them here; several of these will be discussed further in subsequent chapters.

Billing systems generate bills or statements to customers. Figure 3-8 shows a typical billing statement. *Accounts receivable* systems keep track of debts owed to the company. Reports of this system are used for collection purposes, for checking credit on new orders, and for monitoring potential bad debts. Figure 3-9 shows a sample accounts receivable report.

Accounts payable systems produce checks to pay company bills. Since accounts payable systems generate checks, they usually have

Figure 3-7 Common Accounting Business Computer Systems

Payroll
Billing
Accounts Receivable
Accounts Payable
General Ledger
Inventory Accounting

Figure 3-8 Billing Statement

CONSOLIDATED INDUSTRIES

STATEMENT OF ACCOUNT WITH

TAYLOR CONSTRUCTION PRODUCTS   DECEMBER 1, 1981

INVOICE	SHIPMENT DATE	DESCRIPTION	COST
11046	10/20/81	ALUMINUM SIDING	$1148.12
11982	11/04/81	FASTENERS	37.15
12257	11/20/81	ROOFING MATERIALS	3894.84
TOTAL DUE			$5080.11

CONSOLIDATED INDUSTRIES

AGED ACCOUNTS RECEIVABLE   DECEMBER 1, 1981

CUSTOMER NUMBER	CUSTOMER NAME	CURRENT BALANCE	BALANCE OVER 30 DAYS LATE	BALANCE OVER 60 DAYS LATE	TOTAL BALANCE
37842	TAYLOR CONST.	$5080.11	$ 0.00	$ 0.00	$5080.11
39148	ABC SUPPLIES	0.00	438.10	300.14	738.24
40418	SHAKEWELL INC	127.13	541.27	1384.17	2052.57
41183	ZAVASKY INC	2312.47	0.00	0.00	2312.47
44817	ABLE ENTERPRISE	1497.12	348.97	0.00	1846.09

Figure 3-9 Accounts Receivable Report

the same controls and phased processing we observed in the payroll system. A common accounts payable problem concerns discounts. Suppliers often offer price reductions if payment is made within a certain time period. The company may or may not want to take the discount depending on cash available, the amounts of the debt and. discount, and other factors. Some accounts payable systems use these factors to determine the best time to pay debts.

General ledger systems maintain company accounts. They perform the bookkeeping function for the company. Balance sheets and income statements are usually produced, as well as other reports. (See figure 3-10.)

Figure 3-10 Computer-Generated Balance Statement

FRONTIER IRONWORKS

BALANCE STATEMENT   DECEMBER 31, 1981
(THOUSANDS OF DOLLARS)

ASSETS		LIABILITIES	
CASH	$ 127	ACCOUNTS PAYABLE	$ 197
ACCOUNTS RECEIVABLE	583	ACCRUED EXPENSES	
INVENTORY	317	EMPLOYEE BENEFITS	349
PREPAID EXPENSES	53	OTHER	23
MACHINERY	1,483	PREFERRED STOCK	987
FURNITURE AND FIXTURES	275	COMMON STOCK	2,384
LAND AND BUILDINGS	1,788	RETAINED EARNINGS	686
TOTAL ASSETS	$4,626	TOTAL LIABILITIES	$4,626

Inventory accounting systems maintain records of additions and depletions from stock of finished or unfinished goods. Computer systems are often advantageous for inventory accounting because some accounting techniques (last in, first out, or LIFO, for example) have sizable tax advantages but are complex. Without the computer, many companies cannot cope with the computational requirements of the more sophisticated techniques.

There are many accounting computer systems besides those described here. We have, however, discussed the major ones. Other systems are similar and have the same objective of maintaining data that accurately reflects the financial state of the company.

3.1 What are the functions of management?

3.2 What is an MIS? Which companies have an MIS? Does an MIS require a computer?

3.3 Characterize the difference in management information needs between the president and the production supervisor.

3.4 What are the three types of information service described in this section?

3.5 What is the purpose of an accounting business computer system?

3.6 Why is much of the processing in an accounting system oriented toward error detection and correction?

3.7 Explain the purpose of the pre-edit and the edit reports. Why are both types needed?

3.8 Briefly describe three accounting business computer systems other than payroll.

FINANCE

Finance is the specialty of managing money. People who work in the Finance Department assess the company's need for money, determine ways to raise capital when needed, and evaluate proposals to spend it when appropriate.

Finance personnel use the computer primarily for three reasons. First, the calculation of interest rates, rates of return, and other such financial measures is crucial to managing money. These calculations can become very complex for large expenditures or for expenditures on complicated projects. Computers can save employee time and they work very accurately when calculating these rates.

Second, much financial work is repetitive. Financial planning involves answering many "what if" questions. For example, a financial analyst may estimate earnings of $10,000 on a $100,000 investment for a new machine. He or she may then be asked, "What if sales go up 20 percent or down 5 percent?"

These kinds of questions can be answered easily by computer systems. The analyst may need to change only one or two input values and submit a request for another computer run to obtain the required answer. Hand-calculating a solution to the new problem might take nearly as long as determining the original solution.

A third reason for using computer systems in finance is that the alternatives to be evaluated often have complex interactions that can be processed better by computers than by humans. In the previous example, if sales go up by 20 percent, the machine will be used more. If the machine is used more, maintenance will increase, expenses will go up, and available time will decrease. If available time decreases, a backlog will develop, orders may be lost, and so forth. Many of these interactions can be processed by financial computer systems more easily and accurately than by manual calculations.

Financial systems have a character totally different from accounting systems. Figure 3-11 shows a typical financial system flowchart. Since most financial work involves planning only, there is much less incentive for unauthorized activity or crime. Also, the volume of input data is far less so the chances of input errors are lower. However, financial plans can have major impact on corporate strategy and long-run corporate health. Thus, for example, the cost of an error in a financial plan can be much greater than the cost of an error in a customer bill.

Characteristics of Financial Computer Systems

Reports from a financial system are usually fewer and less voluminous than from an accounting system. The clientele of a financial report are usually inside the firm, so the report format can be simpler and less elegant. Also, errors are less embarrassing and time-consuming to correct. Finally, financial data is often less precise than accounting data. Growth rates, interest rates, market shares, etc., are usually

Figure 3-11 System Flowchart of Financial Analysis System

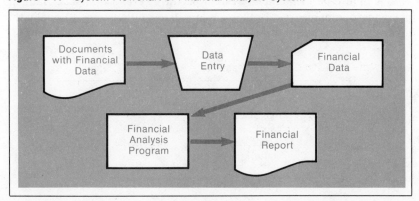

estimates. Consequently, several estimates may be used and the results compared.

A major difference exists between financial and accounting systems in the procedures and personnel required. Accounting systems have many reports, many users, and a large clientele. Formal, written procedures are needed to integrate these people and ensure good control. Financial systems have several reports, a few users, and a small clientele. Consequently, procedures are often simple and informal. Finally, financial system users are often highly skilled, highly educated people. They require less training than the clerks and data entry personnel who often use accounting-oriented systems. Also, there are usually fewer of them and less turnover, so the need for recurring training is less.

Examples of Financial Computer Systems

Figure 3-12 lists common financial systems. *Capital expenditure analysis* is done to determine if large and complex investments are worthwhile. Examples are an analysis of costs and benefits for building a new manufacturing plant, introducing a new line of products, or adding a new division to a corporation.

Financial planning is another type of financial computer system. The purpose of financial planning is to project revenues and expenses over several years of operation. *Cash planning* is another important financial system. Usually, in business, money must be spent on a project for some time before money is made. This practice can lead to a cash crisis or shortage where the long-run financial picture is good, but bills can't be paid in the short run. Cash planning systems identify these situations before they occur and allow management to find supplementary sources of cash to cover the short period.

Some financial systems do *merger analysis*. Here, data about two or more companies is input to a financial analysis program and a balance sheet and income statement are prepared assuming the companies have merged. This procedure allows management to learn the result of various merger strategies before the merger occurs.

A final type of financial system performs *credit analysis*. Banks, insurance companies, and other lenders use such systems to evaluate financial statements and determine the credit worthiness of potential

Figure 3-12 Financial Computer Systems

Capital Expenditure Analysis
Financial Planning
Cash Planning
Merger Analysis
Credit Analysis

borrowers. Similar systems are used by those companies that buy stock or otherwise invest in other companies.

Computers have an important role in finance. In fact, they have changed the nature of financial planning. Because of the computer, more alternatives can be evaluated than in the past. The analysis that is done is more complete and precise than that done previously. Because research is active in this field, it is likely that even more dynamic and effective financial planning systems will be developed in the future.

QUESTIONS

3.9   What are the responsibilities of people who specialize in finance?

3.10 What are the three reasons why financial personnel use business computer systems?

3.11 Compare and contrast a financial computer system with an accounting system.

3.12 Explain what each of the following financial systems does:
a. Capital expenditure analysis
b. Financial planning
c. Cash planning
d. Merger analysis
e. Credit analysis

SALES AND MARKETING

Sales and marketing are two closely related disciplines involved with the selling of goods and services. People who work in these departments have many widely varying responsibilities. They analyze potential sales markets, develop ideas for products, and develop plans for selling existing products. They present products to customers through advertising, telephone, and direct contact. They provide a point of contact for customers' questions and concerns. When sales are made, they handle paperwork like contracts and order entry documents. Sales personnel follow up to ensure delivery. When necessary, they investigate customer complaints and make corrections.

Sales personnel are often commissioned (their salaries are based on the amount they sell). An important sales management task is to devise proper incentive plans. Defining territories and product responsibilities and setting quotas are typical sales management tasks.

Sales and marketing systems fall into two broad categories. The first comprises systems used in direct support of business *operations* like order entry or the production of form letters. These systems are similar to accounting systems. They often have many files and reports, and they interface directly with customers. Since they deal with money

```
                              CUSTOMER  PROFILES

                              SOUTHWEST  REGION

                         PERIOD  ENDING  MARCH   1981

          CUSTOMER                      PRODUCT                    PURCHASES
   NAME                NUMBER    NAME                 NUMBER     UNITS     AMOUNT

   ACE  BILLIARD       10043     DISPLAY  CASE        P1040        4      $1287.50
                                 EXECUTIVE  DESK      Q3877        1      $1150.99

   AJ  ARCHITECT       70089     DRAWING  TABLES      J8897       12      $4588.85
                                 72  INCH  TABLES     J9789        4      $1768.04
                                 SECRETARY  DESK      Q0446        4      $1238.79
                                 EXECUTIVE  DESK      Q3877        3      $3452.97

   DR.  PAUL  A  AZURE  33879    EXECUTIVE  DESK      Q3877        1      $1150.99

                                         .
                                         .
                                         .
```

Figure 3-13 Customer Profile Report

and products, there can be a need for control over inputs, processing, and outputs.

Other systems do *analysis* of sales and marketing data. These systems are similar to financial systems in that they are used for determining strategies and plans, and they relate to business operations only indirectly. For example, *customer profiles* are reports of customer buying habits (figure 3-13). They can be used to plan marketing strategies, but they cannot be used to help produce or deliver goods directly.

Analysis-oriented systems are usually simpler than operational systems. Since their clientele are within the firm, they can be less elegant and errors are easier to correct. Also, analysis systems have less need for controls.

Examples of Sales and Marketing Computer Systems

Figure 3-14 lists common sales and marketing computer systems. The most common operational systems concern *order entry*. These systems receive order requests, check inventory levels, prepare invoices, and so forth. Another common operational sales system does *mail order processing*. Orders are received by mail, processed, and customer statements are prepared. Requests for backorders can also be printed. Forms used by a popular mountaineering and camping company are shown in figure 3-15.

Computer systems are also used to check *order status*. Some systems are designed to allow order entry clerks access to computer files

Operational Systems
    Order Entry
    Mail Order Processing
    Customer Credit Authorization
    Order Status
    Advertising Products

Analysis Systems
    Customer Profiles
    Product Penetration
    Sales Agent Effectiveness and Commission Calculation
    Market Analysis

Figure 3-14 Sales and Marketing Computer Systems

using CRTs. Thus an order can be monitored from order entry through production, packaging, and shipping. The customer can be informed of its progress. This capability is especially desirable for companies that manufacture goods to order that take a long time to produce.

A final type of operational sales and marketing system provides *advertising assistance.* Mailing labels, form letters, and customized advertisements are produced. Many companies have large files of customers' or potential buyers' names and addresses. Mailing labels can be produced easily from these files. Mailing lists on magnetic tape can also be purchased. Form letters and other types of personalized advertising are commonly produced.

Sales and marketing *analysis* systems are also listed in figure 3-14. Sales people use customer profile reports when making sales calls. Such reports are easily produced if order records are already stored on a computer-sensible medium. *Product penetration reports* show the sales of various products in different geographic markets. Using such a report, a marketing manager might decide to increase advertising or to assign additional personnel to underdeveloped markets.

A *sales agent effectiveness report* (figure 3-16) shows the sales of products by sales agent. These reports are helpful to sales people in analyzing their effectiveness with different products. Such reports also show commissions and bonuses earned. Sometimes these reports compare current sales effectiveness to prior years' performance.

Market analysis systems are used to estimate the total sizes of markets, a company's share of each of them, or the distribution of markets across geographic areas or age groups or demographic groups. For example, market analysis personnel may compare company sales over a period of time against the sales of its major competitors. This comparison may reveal that although company sales are increas-

Recreational
Equipment, Inc.
P.O. Box C-88125
Seattle, WA. 98188

FOR FAST TOLL FREE SERVICE PHONE:
Wash. Residents 1-800-562-4894
Alaska & Hawaii 800-426-4770
All other states 1-800-426-4840
Greater Seattle 575-4480
For Best Service Phone Between 7:00 am & 3:30 pm Seattle Time
TOLL FREE LINES NOT AVAILABLE FROM CANADA
Canadian Customers Please Call . . . . (206) 575-4480

MEMBER'S PERMANENT
MAILING ADDRESS   CO-OP NO. _____

SHIPPING ADDRESS, IF DIFFERENT
FROM PERMANENT MAILING ADDRESS

NAME _____

NAME _____

ADDRESS _____

ADDRESS _____

CITY _____ STATE_____ ZIP_____

CITY _____ STATE_____ ZIP_____

PHONE _____ AREA CODE_____

PHONE _____ AREA CODE_____

Is this an address change? ☐ Yes ☐ No

QTY ⑤	CATALOG NO.	CATALOG NO. 2nd Color Choice	SIZE	DESCRIPTION	PRICE	TOTAL

Shop R.E.I. by Mail or Telephone

Convenient. Order at your convenience. We are as near as your phone. No running from store to store.

Fast Service. Orders received by 3:00 pm are shipped the next work day.

Our Pledge of Quality. If any item you purchase from us proves to be unsatisfactory, please return it for a replacement or a full refund.

Send Your Friend a Catalog

Help your friend become a Co-op Member
We will send a current catalog

NAME _____

ADDRESS _____

CITY _____ STATE_____

FORM #186 REV. 10-78

SHIP MY ORDER:
⑨ ☐ SURFACE   ⑩ ☐ AIR

SHIPPING, HANDLING & INS. U.S. ONLY

Subtotal & Value	Surface	Air
0- 5.00	.35	.60
5.01- 10.00	.60	1.25
10.01- 25.00	1.00	1.75
25.01- 50.00	1.60	2.75
50.01-100.00	2.70	4.50
Over 100.00	3.20	5.50
Ski Sets @	4.00	10.00

Add $4.00 Per Package surface
or $10.00 Per Package air
for each ski package on
the reverse side.

Credit Card Number

Total—Ski Packages from other side		
Sub-total ㉘		
Current Sales Tax WA. & CA. only		
Shipping Charge		
Membership Fee ⑪		
Previous Due ⑫		
Total		

Method of Payment

☐ Check (U.S. Funds) ①
☐ Dividend ③
☐ COD ㉕
☐ Mastercharge ④
☐ Visa ④
☐ American Exp. ④
①

Expiration date _____

Customer Sig. _____

Thank you for your order!

a. Order Entry Form

Figure 3-15   Forms Used by REI Co-op

```
┌─────────────────────────────────┐   ┌─────────────────────────────────┐
│ REI CASCADE PARKA-MNS-BLUE      │   │ HEEL LOCATER                    │
│ LRG                      0150   │   │ PAIR                     9313   │
│                                 │   │                                 │
│ M222002404   D03   $164.95      │   │ M406600007   D08   >>$9.95      │
└─────────────────────────────────┘   └─────────────────────────────────┘

┌─────────────────────────────────┐   ┌─────────────────────────────────┐
│ KASTINGER HIGH TOUR DOUBLE      │   │ WONDER HEADLIGHT                │
│ BOOT   11                9319   │   │ 4.5 VOLT                 9345   │
│                                 │   │                                 │
│ M354402158   D08   $140.00      │   │ M236000006   D02   >>$8.95      │
└─────────────────────────────────┘   └─────────────────────────────────┘
```

b. Picking Slip

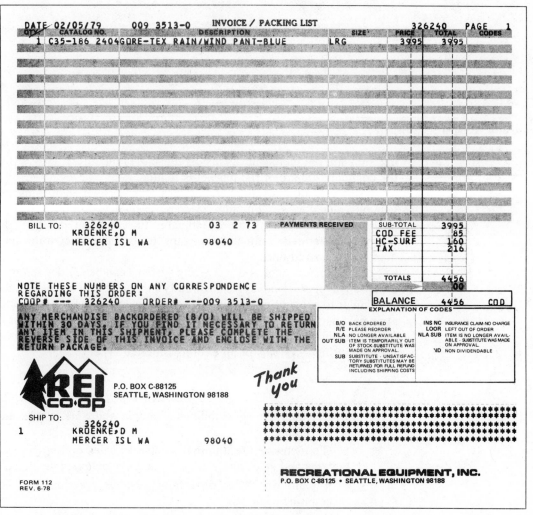

c. Customer Invoice

```
              SALES AGENT EFFECTIVENESS REPORT

                    FALL QUARTER, 1981


SALES AGENT              PRODUCT                         SALES
NAME             NAME              NUMBER      UNITS      AMOUNT

MARY PITTS       ZANSEN BOOTS      14327        319      $47,340
                 JET IV SKIS       36575        412       38,415
                 LAMBRETH POLES    55478        127        1,270

LENNY PORTZ      ZANSEN BOOTS      14327        450       66,780
                 NORDIC BOOTS      13788        139       27,845
                 JET IV SKIS       36575          7          653
                 K-3 SKIS          37782        539       73,422


                                     .
                                     .
                                     .
```

Figure 3-16 Sample Sales Report

ing, they are not increasing as fast as those of competitors. Obviously, the company's share of the market is falling.

This type of analysis often involves sophisticated algorithms and lengthy calculations. Computer systems ease the job of the market analyst and allow many more estimates to be prepared. Also, the computer-generated estimates are apt to be more accurate than manually prepared ones.

In summary, sales and marketing systems can be divided into two groups. The *operational* systems directly support company sales. They are similar to accounting systems. *Analysis* systems are used for evaluating past performance and making plans. These systems are similar to those used in finance. In the next section we will discuss computers in manufacturing—systems of an entirely different type.

QUESTIONS

3.13 Explain the responsibilities of people who work in sales and marketing.

3.14 Characterize the difference between sales operations systems and sales analysis systems. Give an example of each.

3.15 Explain why sales operations systems are similar to accounting systems.

3.16 Explain why sales analysis systems are similar to financial systems.

3.17   Describe the purpose of two sales operations systems.

3.18   Describe the purpose of two sales analysis systems.

A company's Manufacturing Department is responsible for integrating raw materials into finished products. This can be a complex task requiring four different activities. First, manufacturing personnel must order sufficient raw materials to produce the desired quantity of finished goods. This task may seem simple, but consider the great variety and vast number of components needed to produce a TV, an automobile, or an airplane! Often the lead time for ordering raw materials is six months or more. Manufacturing must determine its needs at least that far in advance so that the raw materials will be available when needed.

MANUFACTURING

Second, manufacturing personnel must schedule facilities so as to gain maximum use. For example, if a company has only two lathes, production should be scheduled to balance the use of these machines. Extra costs and time delays will occur if the machines are overloaded at one point in time and idle at another. The order of production needs to be arranged for uniform utilization of the equipment.

Another scheduling consideration is machine setup time. Suppose it takes 10 minutes to set up a saw to cut table legs and 15 minutes to set up the saw to cut tabletops. If five tables are to be produced, it makes sense to cut all the legs and then all the tops. Otherwise, if the legs for one table are cut, then the top, then the legs for the next table are cut, then the top, etc., much time will be wasted changing the saw setup. Many firms have increased production 20 to 30 percent simply by scheduling machines and people more effectively.

A third manufacturing activity is making components and assembling them into finished products. This task includes production labor, labor to make tools and machines, and labor for inspections and other quality assurance procedures.

The fourth activity is engineering. The design of new parts or new machines is an engineering responsibility, as is the incorporation of new materials or new technology into existing products.

Computer systems are used to support all four of these manufacturing activities. Some of these systems, particularly those supporting scheduling and engineering, are similar to the analysis systems discussed in the sections on finance and marketing. These systems have relatively few inputs but do considerable computing. Output reports are few, and the clientele are within the firm.

Some manufacturing systems, however, present a requirement that has not been emphasized before—control. Figure 3-17a shows the general control cycle, and figure 3-17b illustrates a typical manufacturing

Manufacturing Control

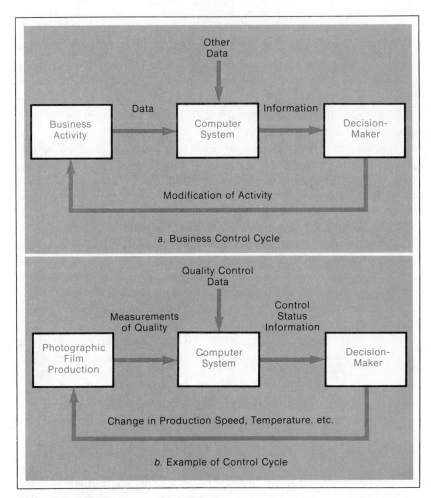

Figure 3-17 Manufacturing Control Cycle

control problem. Photographic film is produced and inspected for defects. This data is input into a computer system that combines it with quality assurance limits and produces information for a decision-maker. The decision-maker has the option of modifying the production activity. For example, if the number of defects is too high, the process can be modified by changing production speed, temperature, or some other production characteristic.

After the decision-maker modifies the business activity, the cycle starts again. Data is used to produce information. Information is used to develop modifications to the business activity. This is called the *control cycle* because adjustments are made to the activity to keep it "in control."

Figure 3-18 Microwave Oven with Control Loop to Maintain Constant Temperature

Computer systems can actually play two roles in figure 3-17. The computer can be used to produce information from the data as indicated. Additionally, however, it can be used as the decision-maker. The computer itself can electronically issue the instructions to modify the process. Manufacturing systems in which there is no human involvement are called *process control systems.*

In a process control system, the business activity is usually a machine of some type. It may be a lathe, a drill press, a blast furnace, blending equipment, machinery for an oil refinery, and so forth. Measurements (data) such as temperature, speed, or chemical properties are taken from the machine's product and analyzed by the computer system. If this analysis indicates some type of adjustment is necessary, a signal is sent to the machine and the adjustment is made without human intervention.

The microwave oven in figure 3-18 is an example of a simple process control machine. The microwave has been instructed to maintain the temperature of the turkey at 170 degrees. The temperature probe measures the heat of the food and when the temperature falls significantly below 170, say to 160 degrees, the microwave heat is turned on. The heat will stay on until the temperature again reaches 170 degrees.

Manufacturing is a material-intensive business. One of the biggest problems facing manufacturers is how to have just enough of the right material on hand, at the right time, without inflating inventories. A materials manager gave me an example recently. He wants to have $0.00 on hand in stockroom inventory. This means the material must arrive in stock at the exact moment it's needed for further production. The materials manager thus assumes a role something like an airline flight scheduler. If too many flights (raw materials) arrive at once, a traffic jam occurs and efficiency drops. On the other hand, if too few flights arrive, the airport (production) facilities may be under-utilized and there may not be enough empty planes (subassemblies) to send outbound flights (finished goods) on their way.

Good systems are required to accomplish this control. Yet, the development of computerized manufacturing systems is in its "youth" phase. Only recently have manufacturers learned to develop systems that reflect the way they actually accomplish materials control. An example is MRP (Manufacturing Resource Planning), which takes a master schedule and expands it to include needed quantities and dates for all subassemblies and raw materials. MRP recognizes that this month's demand for 6 inch bicycle spokes is directly tied to next month's production of children's bicycles.

Before MRP was developed and computerized, manufacturers often had to rely on simple, manual systems that didn't represent the way they really do business. An example of this type of system is an order-point material control system. An order-point system assumes that this month's demand for 6 inch bicycle spokes is somehow related to last month's demand for 6 inch bicycle spokes. It's like driving a car by using the rear view mirror and assuming you're okay if you're still between the white lines.

The success of systems such as MRP depends directly on their ability to mirror actual manufacturing techniques. Manufacturing professionals are quickly learning that in order to develop systems that reflect good business practices, it is better to teach manufacturing experts about computers than to teach computer experts about manufacturing.

Stacy Plemmons is employed by the General Systems Division of Hewlett-Packard Corp. He is in charge of support for a computerized manufacturing control package designed for small manufacturers. Prior to joining Hewlett-Packard, Stacy worked for Eastman Kodak as a business systems designer of material control systems.

He has a master's degree in information systems, and a bachelor's degree in marketing, both from Colorado State University. Married, and the father of two handsome sons, Stacy enjoys skiing, hiking, softball, racquetball, and woodworking.

WHY MANUFACTURERS NEED TO UNDERSTAND COMPUTERS

Stacy Plemmons

Figure 3-19 lists common computer systems used in manufacturing. Systems in the first category, *materials management*, support planning of raw materials purchasing and the control of raw materials and finished goods inventories. They also enable tracking of materials through the production process. Figure 3-20 shows a *bill of materials* for a simple backpack. If a company wanted to make 1000 of these, manufacturing personnel would need to compute the amount of raw materials needed. If, in addition, the company wanted to make tents, sleeping bags, and other products, they would need to compute the total materials required. *Materials requirements planning* (MRP) systems eliminate the manual effort required to make these computations.

> **Examples of Manufacturing Computer Systems**

Inventory control systems maintain the right quantity of parts in inventory. Inventory personnel must maintain a delicate balance. They do not want to run out of parts, but on the other hand, they do not want to have too many parts. Excess parts must be paid for and the cost of carrying inventory can be very high. Consequently, computer systems are used to keep track of the quantity of parts in inventory, the rate at which they are used, and the time it takes to receive a delivery once an order is made. These factors, together with the costs of the parts, are used to calculate the optimum reorder point and the quantity for each part.

Tracking of materials and *finished goods* is also accomplished using computer systems. Companies do not want to lose finished goods

Figure 3-19 Manufacturing Computer Systems

Materials Management
    Materials Requirements Planning
    Inventory Control
    Materials Tracking

Facility Scheduling
    Machine Balancing
    Production Scheduling
    Operations Research

Process Control
    Manufacturing Machines
    Environment Control
    Security Systems

Engineering
    Computer-Assisted Design
    Stress Analysis
    Spatial Conflict Detection
    Aerodynamics

```
                    BILL OF MATERIALS FOR

                    HIKER BACKPACK

                    PRODUCT NUMBER 14356


    MATERIAL              QUANTITY            DIMENSIONS (INCHES)

    CLOTH TOP                1                   20X12
    CLOTH SIDES              4                   8X22
    LEATHER BOTTOM           1                   8X14
    VELCRO HOOK TAPE         1                   6X1/2
    LEATHER TIEDOWN          3                   3X2
    WEB STRAPS               2                   2X35
    PADDED BELT              1                   3X40
    THREAD                   1                   400(FEET)
```

Figure 3-20 Bill of Materials Example

through accident or pilferage, nor do they want to lose material in the production line. Keeping track of materials can be a major task for a large manufacturer. Computer systems are used to process the large volume of data needed.

Facility scheduling systems are another category of computer applications in manufacturing. Systems are used to help balance machine utilization and to minimize the amount of time wasted because of machine setup or schedule conflicts. Since a typical manufacturer may have 50 machines and 500 products, production scheduling is not a trivial problem. A business specialty known as *operations research* uses mathematics to solve these problems. These techniques require extensive calculations. Computer systems are heavily used for this purpose.

As mentioned previously, the next category of applications, process control, uses computer technology to control and operate machines. In addition to controlling manufacturing machines, these computers control air-conditioning and heating, security systems, typewriters and copying equipment, and even timing equipment at sporting events.

The final category of manufacturing computer systems involves *engineering*. Systems are used to assist design in a variety of ways. Designs can be displayed on CRTs, and engineers can use the computer to make modifications. Once a design is approved, *computer-assisted design systems* translate design drawings into instructions for manufacturing machinery. In the coming years, robots will even be used.

Computer systems are also used to *analyze stress* in load-bearing structures and to check for *spatial conflicts* in drawings of large buildings. Other applications are to evaluate electronic circuits and to investigate *aerodynamic properties* of cars, boats, airplanes, and rockets.

QUESTIONS

3.19 Describe the four activities involved in manufacturing.

3.20 Explain the term *control cycle*. Make a sketch of it. How does the control cycle pertain to manufacturing?

3.21 Give an example, other than film manufacturing, of a control cycle that occurs in manufacturing.

3.22 Define *process control system*.

3.23 Give an example of a process control system.

3.24 Briefly explain how computers are used to support manufacturing.

SUMMARY

Are you, the president of the billion dollar company, satisfied with this application survey? Probably not. There are far too many applications to summarize them all in one chapter. We didn't discuss how computers are used for preparing budgets or for analyzing expenses. We didn't discuss how they are used for controlling the timing of people and deliveries on major projects like building construction. We didn't discuss computerized typewriters called *word processors* (but see Module E of Part 4). We could identify dozens of applications we didn't discuss.

However, did you gain an insight into the importance of computing in business? Can you see that knowledge of business computer systems is important to you, regardless of whether you want to be a manager, accountant, salesperson, or production supervisor? It's true. In fact, knowledge of computer systems will give you the competitive edge in any business position.

We began this chapter with a discussion of the collection of business systems called MIS. Some of these systems involve a computer, and they will be the focus of this book. We surveyed business computer systems in accounting and observed the need for control in accounting systems. Financial business computer systems tend to be analytical and involve fewer people than accounting systems. Sales and marketing systems fall into two categories: operational, like order entry, and analysis, like sales forecasts. Finally, manufacturing systems emphasize control over processes.

WORD LIST

(in order of
appearance in text)

Management information
system (MIS)

Status information

Information-bearing
documents

Control systems

Hourly payroll system

General ledger

Phased processing

Checks and balances

Editing

Pre-edit report

Edit report

Billing system

Accounts receivable system

Accounts payable system

General ledger system

Inventory accounting system

Finance

Capital expenditure analysis

Financial planning

Cash planning

Merger analysis

Credit analysis

Sales and marketing

Operational sales and
marketing systems

Analysis sales and marketing
systems

Order entry systems

Mail order processing systems

Advertising systems

Customer profile reports

Product penetration reports

Sales agent effectiveness
reports

Market analysis

Manufacturing

Machine setup time

Quality assurance

Control cycle

Process control system

Materials management

Bill of materials

Materials requirements
planning

Inventory control systems

Facility scheduling

Operations research

Engineering

Computer-assisted design

Stress analysis

**QUESTIONS TO
CHALLENGE
YOUR THINKING**

A. If you are interested in management:

1. What is PERT? How does it work, and are computers
   necessary for PERT applications? What is CPM? GERT?

2. Suppose you managed the production of a newspaper. How
   might you use the computer to reduce your costs of operation? To provide better reader services?

3. Interview one of your management professors. Find out other ways the computer is used to assist manufacturing personnel.

4. What role does a top level manager have in the development of business computer systems? What is the steering committee and how can it be used to control computer projects?

B. If you are interested in accounting:

1. What are the potential dangers of using computers for accounting purposes? What steps can be taken to reduce these dangers?

2. Interview one of your accounting professors and ask how computers have changed accounting. How do CPAs treat computer systems during an audit? Find out what SAS-3 is and why it is important to both data processing and accounting.

C. If you are interested in finance:

1. Find out if your computer has a package of financial programs. If so, determine the interest rate on a loan with a principal of $73,000 to be paid off in 72 payments of $1450 per month.

2. Ask one of your finance professors about financial planning. Determine how it has changed since the advent of the computer.

D. If you are interested in sales and marketing:

1. How are computers used to support marketing directly? Find out about a system that produces mailing labels. How can these systems detect whether or not they have a duplicate label on the list (a common and important problem of these systems)?

2. How are computers used to perform market forecasts? Has the ability of marketing people to make these forecasts changed since computers have started being used?

E. If you are interested in manufacturing:

1. What is MRP? Do MRP systems always use the computer? Why or why not? What do you suppose is the major computer problem in using an MRP system?

2. Bill of materials processors are very common manufacturing systems. What, specifically, do they do? Could this activity be done without the computer?

CHAPTER 4

**DEVELOPING
BUSINESS
COMPUTER
SYSTEMS**

CHAPTER 5

**SEQUENTIAL FILE
PROCESSING
SYSTEMS**

CHAPTER 6

**DIRECT ACCESS
FILE PROCESSING
SYSTEMS**

CHAPTER 7

**DEVELOPING
BUSINESS
COMPUTER
SYSTEMS II**

PART 2

FUNDAMENTAL BUSINESS COMPUTER SYSTEMS

FUNDAMENTAL BUSINESS
COMPUTER SYSTEMS

In this part we will discuss the fundamental types of business computer systems. For an example, the experiences of Alpine Co-op, a mail order company supplying camping and backpacking equipment, will be described. Initially, Alpine had no computing equipment or data processing staff. For several reasons, they decided to acquire a computer and do their own data processing. In the next four chapters we will discuss Alpine's experiences, the process they went through to acquire the equipment and develop the systems, the decisions they had to make, and the systems that were finally developed.

As you read this part, strive to attain three major objectives. First, learn the process or sequence of steps that are used to develop new computer systems. This process is known as the *systems development cycle*. It is a tried and true way of building new computer systems. To a large degree, Alpine followed this process, although they made some mistakes that we will note along the way. This cycle is important to you because system users have important responsibilities in it. Also, you need to know what data processing personnel are supposed to do so you can protect yourself if they are not doing it.

The other objectives you should attain while reading this part are to understand the two basic types of business computer systems: *sequential file systems* and *direct access file systems*. Alpine investigated each type during their analysis, and we will discuss those investigations.

In the first chapter of this part we will discuss the problems Alpine had that made them decide to acquire a computer and develop business computer systems. We will also describe their initial analysis effort. The next two chapters will describe the two basic types of business computer systems. In the last chapter, we will describe the decisions Alpine made and the results that followed.

CHAPTER 4

Developing Business Computer Systems

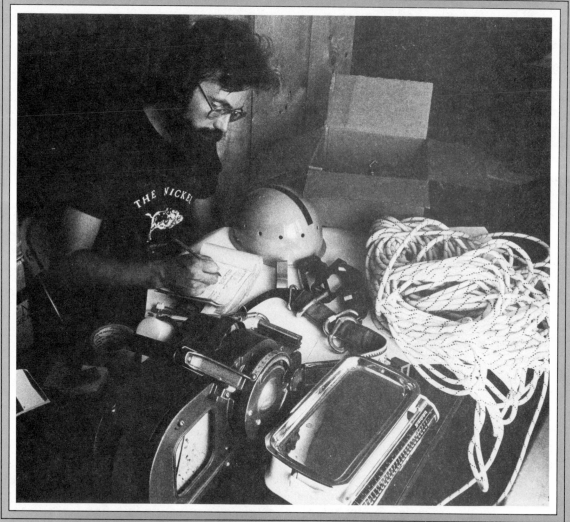

Alpine Co-op needs a computer system for inventory control

NEEDS OF ALPINE CO-OP

The Computer Committee

**THE SYSTEMS
DEVELOPMENT CYCLE**

The Feasibility Study

*Need for a Steering
Committee*

The Project Team

Requirements Definition

Alternative Specification

Evaluation and Selection
of an Alternative

System Design

Development and Testing

System Implementation

**THE ALPINE FEASIBILITY
STUDY**

Feasibility Results
Feasibility Summary

**ALPINE CO-OP'S
REQUIREMENTS**

NEEDS OF ALPINE CO-OP

Alpine Co-op is a cooperative that sells camping and backpacking equipment by mail order. The term *cooperative* means that the company is owned by its customers. At the end of the year, profits are distributed to customers in the form of refunds. Each refund, or dividend, is a percent of the total amount purchased by a member during the year. For example, assume profits are 10 percent of sales. If a customer orders $250 of merchandise during the year, his or her refund will be $25.00.

In 1976 Alpine experienced severe growing pains. Their membership of about 250,000 was growing at the rate of almost 30,000 per year. Sales were $3.5 million – up nearly 300 percent from $1.2 million in just three years. There were 6000 items in inventory. All orders were processed manually. The backlog of orders was growing. It sometimes took a month to add a new member to the membership files.

To place an order, a customer filled out an order form like the one in figure 4-1. The customer wrote his or her name, address, and member number. Then he or she listed the quantity and items ordered. All goods had to be prepaid, so the customer calculated the amount of the bill and sent in a check with the order.

When Alpine received the order, a clerk checked the item numbers and prices, and recalculated the total cost. He or she also checked the member number and captured a new address if appropriate. If the order was correct, or at least nearly correct, it went to the warehouse where the goods were picked from inventory. All the items in stock

ALPINE CO-OP ORDER FORM

P. O. Box A-8000 • Seattle, WA 98187 • Phone 1-800-562-4894

CITY ____________ STATE ______ ZIP ______

(Is this an address change? ☐ Yes ☐ No)

QTY.	CATALOG NO.	SIZE	DESCRIPTION	PRICE
			Sub-total	
			Tax	
			Shipping	
			Total	

Shop by Mail or Telephone

Convenient. Order at your convenience. We are as near as your phone. No running from store to store.

Fast Service. Orders received by 3:00 pm are shipped the next work day.

Our Pledge of Quality. If any item you purchase from us proves to be unsatisfactory, please return it for a replacement or a full refund.

☐ Check Enclosed ☐ COD ☐ Mastercharge ☐ Visa

Credit Card Number Expiration Date Customer Signature

FORM 101 REV. 10-80

Figure 4-1 Alpine Co-op Order Blank

were shipped to the customer. Items that were out of stock were backordered by Alpine, and the customer's order went into the backorder file. When the backordered goods arrived, Alpine shipped them to the customer. (See figure 4-2.)

As you might imagine, all sorts of errors and problems developed. First, customers often made mistakes when ordering. Sometimes the member number was in error. Sometimes the item numbers were wrong. Very often there were arithmetic errors in calculating prices. In the latter case, the amount of the check might be wrong. If it was too high,

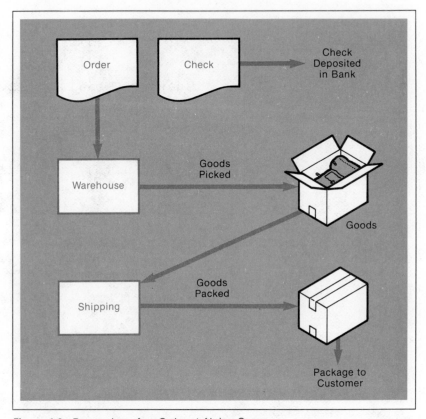

Figure 4-2 Processing of an Order at Alpine Co-op

the customer received a credit; if it was too low, the customer was billed for the difference.

Alpine's backorder file had grown to the point that buyers did not know how much of a product to order. They often ordered 100 units of an item, only to discover that 150 units were backordered and orders were still coming in. To prevent this development, some buyers ordered very large quantities. Then warehouse space became a problem. Also, the cost of carrying the large inventory reduced company profits. Members complained about smaller dividends.

To be fair, this manual system was designed when Alpine had fewer than 50,000 members and did about $500,000 in annual sales with 1000 products. It worked fine then, but it was no longer suitable. However, management had to spend so much time coping with the day-to-day problems that they had not found time to devise a new and better system.

In addition to these problems, Alpine was having trouble with their mailing list. They had hired a company that provides computer services (called a *computer service bureau*) to produce the mailing labels for the annual catalog and to compute and print the annual dividend checks. Once a week, Alpine sent data about new members and address changes for existing members to the computer service bureau. This data was supposed to be incorporated into the mailing list. Also, once a week Alpine sent a list of customer orders to the service bureau. The service bureau was supposed to use this data to keep the year-to-date sales total for each customer. At year end, this figure was used to compute and produce the dividend checks.

In 1976, Alpine had a 32 percent return on their annual catalog! Nearly one-third of the addresses were incorrect. Also, 17 percent of the dividend checks were either incorrect or sent to the wrong address. Alpine had repeatedly discussed this problem with the service bureau in previous years. The bureau was either unwilling or unable to improve the accuracy of the output.

In early 1977, Alpine's Board of Directors decided to investigate the possibility of acquiring their own computer. They hoped to be able to improve the accuracy of the mailing list. They also hoped that the computer could be used to find better ways of controlling inventory and processing orders. A committee consisting of an accountant, a buyer, and an inventory supervisor was formed.

The Computer Committee

The first meeting of the computer committee occurred in early April 1977. Within a few minutes the members realized that none of them knew anything about computers or knew anyone in Alpine who did. Consequently, the committee decided that the first order of business was to hire someone who did. They placed the ad shown in figure 4-3 in two local newspapers. One of the committee members said, "Let's place it under P for programmer." They did.

They had four applicants. The first two were unsuitable. One wanted part-time work. The other was inexperienced. The third had been a programmer for several years. He talked very impressively about the job he had done building an "online bill of materials processor" for a large manufacturing company. Unfortunately, none of the com-

Figure 4-3   Ad for a Programmer Placed by Alpine Co-op

WANTED

A programmer to select a computer and write programs for a mail order retail company. Salary negotiable depending on experience. Send resume to P.O. Box Z, care of this newspaper. An equal opportunity employer.

mittee members knew what that meant. (You will, before this course is over.) They weren't especially impressed because they didn't want to do any manufacturing, anyway. This programmer told them he had experienced great success with a Hewlett-Packard 3000 computer and suggested that's what they should acquire. With the HP 3000 he would be able to develop the programs they needed.

The fourth person, John Abrams, did not actually apply for the job. He was an independent, free-lance consultant. He wanted to sell them his services to develop the data processing department and systems. John had an impressive record of accomplishments in a variety of businesses, but the committee wasn't looking for a consultant. They nearly decided not to invite him for an interview. However, since they had had only three other respondents, they didn't have much to lose. He was invited.

The opening portion of the interview was as follows:

 Committee Chairperson: John, we're not actually looking for a consultant. As I said on the phone, we've talked with a good many applicants. We think we've found two or three possibilities. However, since you're so interested, we decided to spend an hour with you. What can you do for us?

(John didn't believe a word of this. He could tell from their ad that they didn't know much about business computer systems. He also knew that programmers were in short supply. He doubted that they had had six applicants, if that many. He judged these opening comments to be the insecure statements of someone who didn't know what he was doing.)

John: Look, let me come right to the point. It's obvious you have a good business. The outlook for your company is very bright. You committee members are probably very good at your business specialities. But it's equally obvious that you don't know very much about data processing.

You ran an ad for a programmer to select a computer and develop programs for a mail order business. First of all, programmers don't usually select computers. Someone called a data processing manager does that, with the assistance of people called systems analysts. So what you really want is a data processing manager and possibly other data processing personnel.

Second, you say you want to develop programs. What you really want to do is develop something called business computer systems. Programs are only one of five components of such a system. The other components are hardware, data, procedures, and trained people. Are you going to have a programmer develop those?

Finally, how do you know you want a computer? Have you done a feasibility study to see if a computer can solve your problems? Do you know how much a computer costs? Do you know how big a computer you want? Do you know how long it will take you to develop the business computer systems?

Chairperson: Well, John, it's true we aren't experts at data processing. You may have a valid point or two. We were thinking that a Hewlett-Packard 3000 computer might be what we need.

John: The HP 3000 is a good machine. However, there is a great deal of computer equipment to choose from. It's difficult to make a good choice until you know specifically what you want the computer to do. There might be better computers for you.

This conversation continued for an hour or so. Finally, John brought it to a close with this statement:

Let me summarize my position. I'll help you decide if a computer is for you. If so, I'll lead you through the process of acquiring the staff and equipment. I'll help you develop the business computer systems you need. It will likely take a year or more to get this done. My bill for this service will depend on the amount of time it takes me. The more you do, the less my services will cost. Based on my past experience, it will probably cost between $10,000 and $25,000.

If we come to an agreement, I want it structured so that you can terminate my services any time you aren't satisfied. Also, before we sign anything, why don't I give you a two-day course on how to develop business computer systems? I'll charge you $700, which is less than my usual fee, for the two days of instruction. You can listen to me and hear my philosophy before you make any bigger commitment.

After John left, the committee discussed his proposal for some time. They liked what he said. He seemed to know what he was doing, but $20,000, say, seemed a lot to pay for nothing more than advice. Finally, they decided to hire John to teach the two-day course and decide what to do after that.

"Well," said the accountant with a chuckle, "we could always run an ad under D for Data Processing Manager, or maybe under M for Manager, Data Processing."

The next week, John Abrams presented the two-day seminar at Alpine. In addition to the computer committee, all the vice-presidents and managers of Alpine departments were invited.

THE SYSTEMS DEVELOPMENT CYCLE

The course had two parts. The first part summarized the components of a business computer system. This discussion was very similar to the material presented in Chapter 2 of this book. The second part of the course considered the development of business computer systems.

John presented a sequence of activities which he called the *systems development cycle*. These activities are listed in figure 4-4. He explained that this sequence of steps had evolved over a period of time. It had been forged out of the mistakes and disasters of many systems development projects. Today, he said, most business computer professionals agree that these activities, in the order listed, are the best way to ensure that an effective system is developed.

Step	Development Action
1	Analyze feasibility
2	Determine user requirements
3	Specify alternatives
4	Evaluate and select an alternative
5	Design the system
6	Develop and test
7	Implement

Figure 4-4 The Seven Steps for Developing a Business Computer System

The Feasibility Study

The first step toward developing a business computer system is to determine whether or not one is needed and, in a general sense, whether it is practical. This is called the *feasibility study*, during which the problem is investigated and a precise definition written.

John defined a problem as a difference in the perception of what *is* and the perception of what *should be*. He was emphatic about producing a good problem definition. He told them about several companies that had wasted thousands of dollars trying to solve a problem that was vaguely stated. Eventually they discovered they had an elegant solution to the wrong problem.

Once the problem is defined, someone with computer expertise evaluates whether a computer can solve the problem. This step is called analyzing *technical feasibility*. Performing this analysis does not mean that the problem is solved. Rather it means that someone determines whether or not the problem has ever been solved by computer or whether it can likely be solved by computer.

In Alpine's case, if the problem is defined as producing mailing labels and dividend checks, then the technical feasibility is certain. Computers have been used for this sort of application for years. However, as we will see later, Alpine actually wants to solve several problems, not just one.

Once the technical feasibility is verified, then *cost feasibility* is examined by developing rough cost estimates. The approximate size and capacity of the computer required are determined. This information can be used to get a rough estimate of the cost of the computer. However, as John was quick to point out, other costs are also involved. Programs must be purchased or developed; data must be converted; procedures must be developed; and personnel must be trained. These are all initial costs. On top of these are the operational costs incurred as the system is used. Power, maintenance, and salaries of operations personnel are examples of these operational costs.

Again, rough cost estimates are used. The purpose of the cost feasibility step is to determine whether the cost of a computer system solution is in the right range. For example, if the cost of the system is $100,000 and the estimated worth of the solution is $10,000, then a computer solution to the problem is *cost infeasible*.

The final part of a feasibility analysis is to determine the *schedule feasibility*. If the computer system requires a year to develop, and if a solution must be found in six months, then the proposed system is infeasible. In Alpine's case, if a computer system requires 18 months, then the dividend checks will not be produced on time. Obviously, Alpine needs to find a faster solution. They might use the service bureau one more year, or find another service bureau.

Need for a Steering Committee   Once the problem has been defined and the technical, cost, and schedule feasibility has been determined, the results are documented. A report of findings is presented to management. If management believes the proposed computer system is feasible, then the project should be continued. Otherwise, another solution to the problem must be found.

Alpine personnel wanted to know which managers should be involved in these evaluations. John told them that any company using a computer should have a steering committee. The members of this committee should be senior people in the departments that will be the major users of the computer system.

If the steering committee exists, the results of the feasibility study should be presented to it. However, Alpine did not have such a committee, so the feasibility study results would have to be presented to others in management. If the decision is made to continue with the project, then the steering committee should be established.

John recommended that the results of any feasibility study be presented to a joint meeting of the board (since they requested the investigation) and the president and vice-presidents. If Alpine decided to go forward with the computer project, the steering committee membership could be decided then.

The Project Team   If the computer project is considered feasible, a second committee, called the *project team*, should be formed to develop the system. This team should include both users and computer personnel. The users are primarily responsible for developing requirements. The computer personnel build the components of the business computer system to satisfy those user requirements. Oftentimes, the best results occur if the project team is led by a user—not by someone from the data processing department.

For Alpine Co-op, John recommended that he and the computer committee become the project team to develop one or more computer systems. As data processing personnel were hired, they should be added to the project team.

**Requirements
Definition**

The second step of the systems development cycle is initiated only after the steering committee has approved the feasibility study and the project team has been formed. The purpose of this step is to determine the user requirements to be satisfied by the new business computer system.

As John pointed out, it is vital that future system users be involved in this process. Studies have shown that the number one cause of failure in a business computer system is a lack of user involvement in the requirements step. If users are not involved, the requirements are often not realistic. Also, if users are not involved, they have no psychological stake in the new system. In fact, they may be motivated to cause the system to fail. On the other hand, if users have had a part in the development of requirements, they feel a part of the process and are as anxious as anyone to see the system succeed.

The user requirements should be documented in a journal or written record. This journal must specifically state what the new system is to do. It becomes a storehouse of the team's knowledge about the problem. Further, writing the requirements forces the team members to clearly understand them. Finally, this documentation is useful during testing. Does the system accomplish what it is supposed to?

The first two steps of the systems development cycle are summarized in figure 4-5.

**Alternative
Specification**

After the requirements have been determined, alternatives for each component of the business computer system are developed. Each alternative specifies the hardware, programs, data, procedures, and personnel required to solve the business problem. Since Alpine had no computer equipment whatsoever, each alternative should specify the computer to be acquired as well as other components. John told the computer committee that he would help them to specify alternatives.

Figure 4-5 The First Two Steps of the Systems Development Cycle

Step	Remarks
1. Analyze feasibility	Define the problem. Determine feasibility: Technical Cost Schedule If feasible, form: Steering committee (if none exists) Project team
2. Determine user requirements	User involvement crucial. Document in requirements journal.

Once the alternatives have been determined, the next step is to evaluate them and select one for implementation. Basically, the alternatives should be evaluated by comparing the dollar values of benefits to costs. One way to do this is to form ratios of benefits to costs. The alternative with the highest ratio is selected. You will learn more about this process if you take a course in systems development or a course in business finance.

Evaluation and Selection of an Alternative

The next step after alternative selection is to develop the detailed design of the system. Each of the five components of a business computer system must be designed. Insofar as hardware is concerned, the term *design* is used loosely. Very rarely is computer equipment built; usually it is purchased or leased. Here, *design* means to determine the detailed specifications of the equipment needed and then to order it from a vendor.

System Design

Sometimes programs are purchased. Sometimes they are written by the project team. If purchased, the detailed specifications are developed and the programs are ordered at this step. If written as part of the systems development, the detailed design of the programs is produced. This is often the most time-consuming part of program development. If the design is done properly, the actual coding or programming may be done quite rapidly.

The other three components of the system must also be designed. Data formats are decided upon, including input forms, storage file structures, and layouts of outputs such as reports. Procedures that describe how users will employ the system and also how the operations personnel will run the system must be designed. Finally, both initial and recurring training programs are designed at this step.

According to figure 4-4, the next step is to develop and test the business computer system. Hardware and programs that have been ordered are installed and tested for correct operation. If programs are being developed as part of the system, they are coded and tested at this step. Test data files are built. The conversion of the actual data to computer format is begun. Procedures are documented and tested by operations personnel and by users. Training materials are prepared and initial training is completed. Finally, there is an integrated test of hardware, programs, data, procedures, and personnel. If all goes according to plan, the system is ready to be implemented.

Development and Testing

Proper implementation of a business computer system is vital. If done poorly, users will develop doubts and hostilities toward the system even if it is an excellent one.

System Implementation

There are four major types of implementation strategy. The first one is to *plunge*. The new system is started and any existing manual systems are stopped. This strategy is very dangerous. If the new system has some errors or other difficulties, there is no backup. This strategy should be used rarely, if ever.

A second strategy is to run the new system in *parallel* with the old manual system. If any problems develop, there is a backup. However, this approach is expensive because two systems must be supported for some period of time. Still, many companies view this expense as a form of insurance.

When following a *pilot* strategy, the new system is implemented on a small part of the clientele. For example, Alpine might implement a system on part of their membership, say on the members in the state of Minnesota. Once the system is working correctly it can be used for all members. The pilot strategy isolates the damages in case the new system works incorrectly.

Finally, implementing a system *piecemeal* means installing it in parts. Alpine could implement a catalog mail system and check it out before implementing the check mailing system. Problems identified in the catalog mailing could be fixed before mailing checks. Like the pilot method, piecemeal reduces the number of problems if the new system does not work.

The last five steps of the systems development cycle are summarized in figure 4-6.

John discussed all seven steps in considerable detail with the Alpine personnel. At the end of the two-day indoctrination, the com-

Figure 4-6 The Last Five Steps of the Systems Development Cycle

Step	*Remarks*
3. Specify alternatives	For: Hardware Programs Data formats Procedures People required
4. Evaluate and select an alternative	Evaluation is based on dollar values of benefits compared to costs (one example, benefit/cost ratio).
5. Design the system	Specify design for each of the five components.
6. Develop and test	All five components. Perform integrated test.
7. Implement	Parallel, pilot, piecemeal techniques are effective. Plunge technique invites disaster.

puter committee felt they had a much better idea of what developing computer systems involved. Because of their new knowledge, however, they also felt more vulnerable.

The committee considered their options. They were convinced they needed some outside expertise to help them. They didn't know whether to hire a data processing manager, hire John as a consultant, or hire another consultant. They wanted to hire a data processing manager, but they didn't know what kind of person to look for. If they hired the wrong person, it might take a long time to discover and then correct their error. Considerable money might be wasted.

They finally decided to hire John, but they hedged. They hired him just to help them with the first step, the feasibility analysis. After that, they would decide whether or not to hire him for more assistance. John agreed to these terms and the next week the feasibility study began.

QUESTIONS

4.1 Summarize the reasons why Alpine Co-op decided they needed a business computer system.

4.2 How should Alpine's ad have read to receive the help they actually needed?

4.3 List and describe activities for each of the seven steps of the systems development cycle.

4.4 What is the value of a steering committee? What do you suppose can happen without one?

4.5 What is the number one cause of failure in the development of business computer systems?

4.6 Define and explain the four types of implementation strategies.

THE ALPINE FEASIBILITY STUDY

For 10 days, John and the computer committee visited Alpine personnel in departments that seemed to be having the greatest problems. They wanted to gain an understanding of these problems and define them. Also, they wanted to gain a general sense of where computer systems might be useful. At the end of this period they wrote a report documenting their findings. It had seven major points, or problem definition results:

1. There was a need to keep an accurate file of member names, addresses, and year-to-date purchases. This file was needed for the catalog and other mailings as well as for dividend computation. This file needed to be updated accurately whenever a member moved or a

new member joined. The committee learned that the service bureau had not been able to keep an accurate file because their own staff made too many keypunch errors when inputting changes or posting sales to the file.

The member number was crucial. If the member misstated his or her number on an order, or if it was incorrectly keypunched, sales would be posted to the wrong member. A more accurate way to input member numbers had to be found.

2. All the problems regarding dividends related to inaccuracies in the customer file. If this file were accurate, producing dividend checks at year end would be simple.

3. Purchasing and inventory personnel needed a list of items in inventory. This list should show item name, item number, name of the buyer responsible for purchasing the item, name of the vendor who supplied it, and other data. Such a list was necessary because Alpine was adding about 100 items and deleting about 10 items a month. Several typewritten lists of items existed. Unfortunately, they often disagreed with one another. Consequently, orders were being taken for items no longer carried in stock, and Purchasing was buying items no longer listed in the catalog.

4. The most time-consuming part of processing an order was verifying prices and checking the computation of amount due. Orders could be processed much faster if a computer system computed the amount due. Order processing personnel wanted to give the computer the customer number, the item number, and the quantity for each item on the order, and then have the computer calculate the amount due.

5. The manual records of the items in inventory were a mess. At the last physical check of inventory, nearly 70 percent of the counts were in error. Shipments had arrived but had never been entered in the inventory records. Goods had been shipped and billed, but they were never taken out of the records. A computer system to keep track of inventory would be very helpful. John remarked, however, that a computer system would be useless unless the inventory management procedures in the warehouse were improved.

6. Orders were currently being filled in a chaotic manner. A picker took the customer's copy of the order and walked through the warehouse filling a basket with the items ordered. Whenever the picker couldn't find an item it was marked for backorder. Sometimes this was an error. The goods were actually in the inventory but the picker didn't know where to find them. In this case the item was backordered even though it was available.

Much of this chaos could be eliminated if a computer system processed the orders and generated picking slips. The system could keep an inventory file and determine whether or not each item was available. If an item was not available, it would be marked "backordered" on the picking slip. The picker would not waste time looking for it. Also, the computer could generate backorder recommendations for buyers and reduce the number of unnecessary backorders.

7. The computer could probably be used for other business functions such as payroll, accounts payable, and general ledger accounting.

However, there were currently no major problems in those areas. Such applications could easily be deferred until the immediate problems were solved.

After the problems were defined and documented, the computer committee and John considered the feasibility of developing business computer systems to solve any or all of these problems.

Feasibility Results

John stated that, from a technical standpoint, all of the problems could be solved by computer. He knew of several companies that were doing similar functions with computer systems. Consequently, the technical feasibility was considered certain.

From cost and schedule standpoints, however, feasibility was not so easy to determine. The costs and dates for developing systems depended on how many of the problems were to be solved. After considerable discussion, the committee decided to break the development into three phases as shown in figure 4-7.

During phase 1 the member master file and dividend systems would be developed. During phase 2 the inventory and pricing systems would be developed. The purposes of the inventory system would be to keep a master list of the items in inventory and to maintain a count of the items in stock, on backorder, and so forth. The pricing system, given the item numbers and quantities, would then calculate the total amount due for each order.

A pre-picking order processing system would be developed during phase 3. The system would be inputted the customer number, the item

Figure 4-7 Three Phases for Alpine's Systems Development

Phase	Systems to Be Developed
1	Member Master File System including: Master file maintenance Purchase updates Dividends Mailing labels
2	Inventory Master File System Inventory Accounting System Order Pricing System
3	Pre-Picking Order Processing System including: Picking slip generation Backorder management Order recommendations

Phase	Initial Expense	Annual Operating Expense
1	$100,000	$200,000
2	$275,000	$400,000
3	$600,000	$650,000

Assumptions:
1. Computer hardware is leased.
2. Growth in membership and sales is 10 percent per year.

Figure 4-8 Estimated Costs of Alpine Computer Systems

number, and the quantity of each item ordered. From these inputs, it would produce a picking slip, show items on backorder, and generate order recommendations for buyers.

Figure 4-8 shows cost estimates developed by the project team. The initial expense category includes the costs of hardware installation, program development, data conversion, procedure development, and training. It does not include the cost of hardware. Since the team assumed the hardware would be leased, its cost was included as an operating expense.

Operating expenses shown in the figure include the costs of the leased hardware; program and data maintenance; operating personnel salaries; training; and an allocation for overhead (a share of the expenses for lights, heating, buildings, taxes, and so forth). John explained that if Alpine decided to buy computer hardware, the initial expenses would increase but the operating expenses would decrease.

As the team examined the costs, it became apparent that phase 1 by itself would not be cost-justified. The cost was too great for the service. (Finding another service bureau would be a better solution.) However, it appeared that both phases 2 and 3 would be cost-justified if implemented in addition to phase 1.

Considering schedule, John said there was no realistic way that Alpine could hope to accomplish all three phases in the immediate future. Far too many tasks needed to be accomplished. Data processing personnel needed to be hired; the equipment needed to be selected and installed; and the other components of the systems needed to be developed. John predicted a disaster if all the problems were addressed at the onset.

After two days of thinking and discussion, the committee estimated that phase 1 would take about one year; phase 2 would take about 14 months; and phase 3 would take about two years. This estimate of phase 3 assumed that inventory personnel would make changes to their procedures on schedule. Thus, if Alpine started the project in

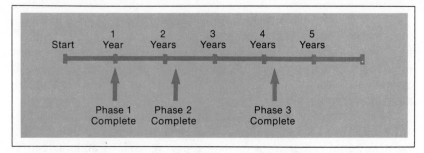

Figure 4-9   Timing of Alpine Systems Development Phases

May 1977, the earliest that all three phases could be finished would be July 1981. (See figure 4-9.)

To summarize, the computer committee found that all three phases were feasible from a *technical* standpoint. However, phase 1 by itself could not be *cost-justified*. Phase 1 followed by phase 2, or phase 1 followed by phases 2 and 3, could be cost-justified. Finally, the phases were *schedule* feasible if Alpine could wait one year for phase 1, slightly over two years for phase 2, and about four years for phase 3.

Feasibility Summary

The findings, phases, and results of the feasibility study were documented in a 15-page report. The report was sent to the board of directors, the president, and the vice-presidents. The board requested a meeting of top management, the computer committee, and John. Basically, the board was pleased with the quality of the analysis and work that had been done. They were disappointed that four years would be required to have complete capability.

Some board members tried to get the computer committee to reduce the estimates of time required. However, John had forewarned the committee of such an attempt and they adamantly refused to give in. As John had said, "Nine women can't make a baby in one month, no matter how badly someone wants them to."

In the feasibility study, the computer committee had recommended formation of a steering committee. The board of directors thought this was an excellent idea. They suggested that the president and all the vice-presidents be involved initially. Also, the board recommended that John Abrams be retained for the requirements phase of work and that he and the computer committee become the development project team. With this preliminary work accomplished, the president instructed the new project team to proceed with the requirements definition for phases 1 and 2. Phase 3 would be deferred until definite progress had been made on phases 1 and 2. The project team was instructed to report to the steering committee on a monthly basis.

**ALPINE CO-OP'S
REQUIREMENTS**

The project team worked steadily for the next four months to determine the requirements for the first two phases. The specific requirements are too detailed to present here nor do we need to know them for our current purposes. As an illustration, however, figure 4-10 summarizes some of the requirements—those for the member master file and dividend systems.

The first requirement specifies the data that is kept on the member master file. The second one states that new members are added daily. Note the requirement for a pre-edit report as well as an edit report. This requirement is similar to that of the payroll system discussed in Chapter 3. Updates to the member master file are made in two stages. During the first stage, the system edits changes to the master file without actually making them. A pre-edit report showing changes to be made goes to the users for inspection and approval. Corrections are made if there are errors.

After all the input data has been inspected and approved, stage two is run. Here the changes are made to the master file. An edit report showing the changes is printed; it will be useful if there are questions later. Membership cards showing name, number, address, and phone number are produced. Modifications to the membership file are handled in the same way.

Requirement four specifies that the year-to-date purchases total is kept current. This total will be used for computing dividends at year end. Note that the total is adjusted if returns are made, thus ensuring that members do not receive dividends for goods they did not keep.

The dividend checks are produced in two stages. During the first stage, the checks are not printed. The first stage is a pre-edit run.

Figure 4-10   Phase 1 and 2 Requirements for Member Master File and Dividend Systems

1. Maintain records of every member's name, number, address, phone, date of membership, date of last order, date of last file change, amount of last dividend check, and total purchases to date for the current calendar year.

2. Add new members to this file on a daily basis. Provide a pre-edit report prior to master file update. Provide an edit report of changes actually made. Print membership cards with name, phone number, and address. Print card mailers.

3. Modify member's name, address, or phone number as required. Provide both pre-edit and edit reports. Print new membership cards and mailers for cards.

4. Add amount of each order to year-to-date purchases. Correct this amount if returns are made.

5. Produce dividend checks on an annual basis. Provide both a pre-edit report and an edit report showing amount paid each member and total amount paid to all members.

6. Insert amount of dividend check into each member's master file record.

7. Develop a method for ensuring that all changes to the member file and all changes to amount purchased are made to the correct account.

Outputs are inspected by the users for correctness. Once correct, the run is made again to produce the checks and to insert the amounts of the dividends into the master file records. Finally, the last requirement specifies that some technique is developed to ensure better accuracy of processing.

The project team actually developed more specific requirements. They specified the format of the inputs to the system, the record formats, and the layouts of reports. Also, requirements for both user and operations procedures were specified.

After requirements for all the systems in phases 1 and 2 were documented, the project team reported back to the steering committee. The committee members read the requirements document and made a few minor changes. By and large, however, the requirements were considered sound. The team was instructed to specify alternative systems that would meet the requirements.

To initiate this process, John Abrams presented a tutorial on the two basic styles of file processing systems and described the equipment and components of each. We will consider these styles in the next two chapters. The Alpine case is concluded in Chapter 7.

QUESTIONS

4.7 Summarize the problem to be solved by Alpine's new business computer systems.

4.8 What are the three phases of development recommended by the project team?

4.9 What did the Alpine project team determine about the technical, cost, and schedule feasibility of business computer systems for their problems?

4.10 Summarize the requirements to be satisfied by Alpine's new business computer systems.

4.11 Why was it wise for the project development team to refuse to compress the schedule? Compare this to what Tom Jackson did in Chapter 1.

SUMMARY

This chapter has presented an introduction to the development of business computer systems. The experiences of Alpine Co-op have been used to illustrate the seven steps in the systems development cycle. In the first step, *feasibility study*, the problem is defined and the technical, cost, and schedule feasibility aspects are investigated. In *requirements definition*, the specific requirements for the system are defined and documented; then, in *alternative specification*, alternatives for each component of the business computer system are defined.

The fourth step is *alternative evaluation and selection*, in which the alternatives are compared to one another and the best one selected. During the fifth step, *design*, the components of the system are specified, and those components that are to be built as part of the project are designed. The components are *developed and tested* in step six, and finally *implemented* in step seven.

These seven steps are a tried and true method for developing a business computer system. They have been developed through the sometimes painful experiences of many companies. In this chapter, we discussed the first two of these steps for Alpine Co-op. We will discuss the last five steps in Chapter 7.

WORD LIST		
(in order of appearance in text)	*Computer service bureau*	*Program alternatives*
	Computer consultant	*Data alternatives*
	Systems development cycle	*Procedure alternatives*
	Feasibility study	*Personnel alternatives*
	Technical feasibility	*Alternative evaluation*
	Cost feasibility	*Cost/benefit ratio*
	Schedule feasibility	*Detailed design*
	Steering committee	*Develop and test*
	Project team	*Implementation*
	User requirements	*Plunge*
	Requirements journal	*Parallel*
	Alternative specification	*Pilot*
	Hardware alternatives	*Piecemeal*

QUESTIONS TO CHALLENGE YOUR THINKING

A. In general, how does a business decide whether or not it needs a computer? Describe a business that you know about that definitely does not need a computer.

B. Alpine was cagey in the way they hired John. They never committed themselves to hiring him for more than one step at a time. Why do you suppose they did this? Why do you suppose that John went along with their strategy?

C. How did John aid Alpine Co-op? Do you think they should have hired him? What is the worst that could have happened?

D. Suppose you wanted to hire a consultant but didn't know any. How would you proceed? For some reason, data processing seems to have more than its share of bad consultants — people who cost more than they are worth. How would you go about picking a good consultant?

E. What else could Alpine do besides hire a consultant?

F. Describe what can happen if the users are not involved in determining requirements.

G. Suppose you are a future user of a business computer system and the project team does not want your input. What do you do?

H. Computer sales personnel are notorious for pushing systems development into the alternative evaluation phase prematurely. Why do you suppose they do this? What should the management of a company like Alpine do to counteract this tendency?

I. Describe the dangers of implementing a business computer system with the plunge technique. Suppose you work for a company and the project team proposes to do this. What do you do?

CHAPTER 5

Sequential File Processing Systems

The sequential alternative: operator mounting a tape volume

WHAT ARE SEQUENTIAL FILE SYSTEMS?

Characteristics of Sequential File Systems

DATA AND HARDWARE FOR SEQUENTIAL FILE PROCESSING

Punched Card Data Representation

Magnetic Tape Data Representation

Data Representation in Main Memory

Numeric Data

HARDWARE FOR ALPINE'S MEMBER MASTER FILE SYSTEM

Punched Cards

Key-to-Tape Equipment

Tape Equipment for the Master Files

Record Blocking Magnetic Tape Speeds

Printers

Serial vs Line Printers

Impact vs Nonimpact Printers

Dot Matrix vs Full-Character Printers

Which System for Alpine Co-op?

PROGRAMS FOR SEQUENTIAL FILE PROCESSING

A Sequential File Record-Matching Algorithm

Pseudocode for Record Matching

Program Editing

PROCEDURES FOR SEQUENTIAL FILE PROCESSING

Batch Totals

Backup and Recovery Procedures

PERSONNEL FOR SEQUENTIAL FILE PROCESSING

SEQUENTIAL PROCESSING FOR ALPINE CO-OP?

In this chapter and the next we will examine two subjects that John Abrams presented to the Alpine project team. These subjects are the two basic styles of business computer systems. This chapter investigates sequential file processing; the next describes direct access file processing.

In this chapter we will first describe general characteristics of a sequential file system. Then we will examine the five components of a sequential-file-oriented business computer system. Concepts in this chapter will be illustrated by using the member master file and dividend systems introduced in Chapter 4.

Sequential file systems are business computer systems that have a special property: the records in files are processed in sequence. Think of your stereo tape player. You listen to songs in sequence. When you have a tape with a song in the middle that you like, you have to listen to the songs before it first. Sequential file systems are similar. To find a record in the middle of the file, all the records preceding it must be read first.

Figure 5-1 shows a system flowchart for the Alpine member master file system. This is a sequential file system. The punched cards hold data about membership changes, such as new members or address changes for existing members. The cards and the old member master file are read, and a new member master file is created. This poses a problem. Suppose there are 100 changes to be made to a file that has 100,000 members on it. How are the correct master file records to be found? If the first card says change the address of member number 10, how is member 10's master file record to be found?

Think about your tape player. Suppose you have a tape of nursery rhymes and you want to play "Lucy Locket." If you don't know where "Lucy Locket" is located on the tape, you will have to search the tape from the beginning until you find it. You might do this by using Fast Forward to advance the tape 10 feet, and then listening. If you do not hear "Lucy Locket," you would advance 10 feet again, listen again, and so forth. If there are 50 nursery rhymes on the tape, you can

WHAT ARE SEQUENTIAL FILE SYSTEMS?

Figure 5-1 Alpine Member Master File Maintenance System

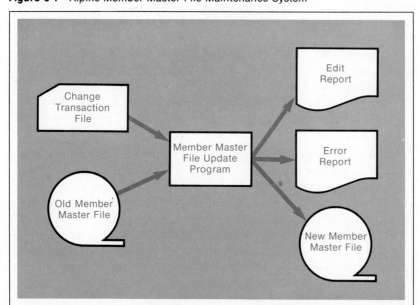

expect, on average, to search over 25 nursery rhymes to find the one you want.

Now suppose you want to listen to three nursery rhymes: "Ding, Dong, Bell," "Lucy Locket," and "Rub-a-dub-dub, Three Men in a Tub," in that order. If you don't know where these are located, you will have to search the tape three times. You may have to search over 75 (3 × 25) nursery rhymes before you find all three.

You can improve this process if you put the nursery rhymes on the tape in some order, say alphabetical order. Then, assuming you want to listen to the three rhymes in alphabetical order, you can search first for "Ding, Dong, Bell" and play it. Then, you can search for "Lucy Locket" and play it. Then you can find and play "Rub-a-dub-dub." At worst, you will only have to search through the tape once.

Also, you can catch mistakes more easily. Suppose you are searching for "Ding, Dong, Bell," but you find "Diddle, Diddle, Dumpling" followed by "Jack Sprat." What does this mean? It means "Ding, Dong, Bell" is not on the tape. If it were, it would be between "Diddle, Diddle, Dumpling" and "Jack Sprat." Thus, by having the rhymes in order, you eliminate having to search the whole tape only to find that "Ding, Dong, Bell" isn't there.

Now consider Alpine's member master file of 100,000 records. If the members' names are in no particular order on the file, then, on average, 50,000 will have to be searched to find the one we want. Therefore, to find master file records for 10 members, 10 times 50,000 or 500,000 records will have to be searched.

On the other hand, if the member master file is sorted by number, and if we also sort the required changes by number, then we can find all the records in one pass of the file. Also, invalid numbers can be identified quickly.

The essence of sequential file processing is that the records are sorted into some order. They are processed one after another in that order. *A sequential file system is a business computer system in which the files are sorted and processed in some predefined order.* This sorting saves considerable searching, and processing can be extremely fast.

Characteristics of Sequential File Systems

Sequential file systems have several identifying characteristics. First, there are two types of files. *Master files* keep data about continuing relationships. Examples are master files of employees, of customers, and of suppliers. Master files are usually relatively stable. In Alpine's case, a few members may join, and some members may terminate, but by and large the same members are processed year after year.

Transaction files contain records about events. When these records are processed, changes are made to master files or other outputs are produced. Transaction files are erratic. For example, changes to the member master file for one month will likely be completely different from changes for the next month. In figure 5-1 the member modifications are an example of a transaction file.

A second characteristic of a sequential file system is that a master file is completely rewritten whenever any records in the file are changed. This is because the records must be kept in some sequential order. If a new record is to be *inserted*, the file must be rewritten to make room for the record. (Similarly, to add a new nursery rhyme, the stereo tape needs to be rewritten.) If a record is to be *deleted*, the master file has to be rewritten to eliminate the unneeded record.

If a record is to be *modified*, the file has to be rewritten because the modified record may be larger or smaller than the existing one. Even if the record length does not change, the file is rewritten because of the difficulty of inserting the modified record in just the right place.

Have you ever tried to record a song in the middle of a group of songs? It is easy to wipe out the end of the prior song or the beginning of the next song. Also, it is easy to create a tape with a blank spot. These problems exist on magnetic tape, too. This is one reason that records on sequential files are not modified in place.

A third characteristic of a sequential file system is that transactions are usually processed in *batches*. The master file will be completely rewritten whether 1 percent or 100 percent of the records in the file are changed. Therefore, the more changes that can be made in one run, the better. Figure 5-2 shows a graph of the average time (time per updated record) plotted against size of the transaction file. The bigger

Figure 5-2 Average Time to Update a Sequential File

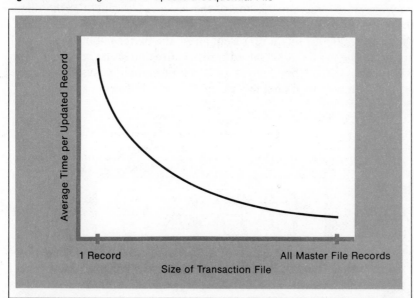

the batch, the shorter the average time to process a transaction. Since transactions are processed in batches, sequential file processing is sometimes called *batch processing*.

DATA AND HARDWARE FOR SEQUENTIAL FILE PROCESSING

In this section we will discuss computer hardware in more depth. To understand this discussion, you first need to know how computers represent data. The minimum essential facts are presented here; you can find more about computer data in Module B of Part 4.

The basic building block for representing computer data is called a *bit*, which is an abbreviation for *binary digit*. You know what a decimal digit is. It is one of the symbols 0, 1, 2, 3, 4, 5, 6, 7, 8, 9. A binary digit is similar, but there are only two symbols: 0 and 1.

Bits are used as the basic building blocks for computer data because they are easy to represent electronically. Bits can be represented by devices that are either on or off. For example, we can say that a light represents a 1 when it is *on* and a 0 when it is *off*. Figure 5-3 shows a panel of light switches. If we define *up* as 1 and *down* as 0, then this panel represents the *bit pattern* 1101. Computers are not composed of panels of light switches. They do have a variety of simple devices, however, that are either on or off.

Bits are represented in various ways in different parts of a computer system. In a punched card, for example, a bit is represented by the presence of a hole (1) or by the absence of a hole (0). We will see other examples as the discussion progresses.

Now, in the simplest terms, patterns of bits are used to represent *characters*. A character is one of the letters A through Z, the digits 0 through 9, or special symbols such as $, #, *, and %. For example, the pattern 000001 might represent an A; the pattern 000010, a B; and so forth. The word *might* is used here because there is no accepted code. The code varies depending on the type of computer system and the type of equipment. Examples are given in the following sections.

Figure 5-3   Panel of Light Switches Representing Bit Pattern 1101

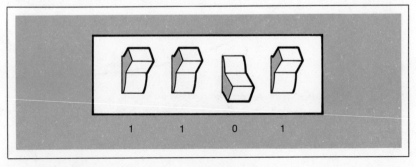

Figure 5-4 shows a punched card. This particular type of card is divided into 80 vertical columns and 12 horizontal rows. Each column is used to represent one character. By convention, the top row is called the 12 row; the next one is called the 11 row; and the next is called the 0 row. Then comes the 1 row, and so on, to the last row which is the 9 row.

Punched Card Data Representation

Each column represents a character. In figure 5-4 the character 0 (zero) is punched in column 36. By convention, this is done by punching a hole in the 0 row and by not punching any other holes in the column. A 1 is signified by punching a hole in the 1 row only, a 2 by a punch in the 2 row only, and so forth. Letters and special characters are represented by two (or more) punches in a column. Thus the letter A is represented by punching holes in both the 12 and 1 rows. Other characters are shown in figure 5-4. This scheme is commonly called *Hollerith code*, after Herman Hollerith, the inventor of punched card data processing. (See Module A in Part 4 for more about Hollerith.)

Now, if you think of a hole as a 1 and the absence of a hole as a 0, then each one of these columns can be visualized as a bit pattern. Starting from the top, the bit pattern for the character *zero* is 001000000000 because there is a 0 in the 12 row, a 0 in the 11 row, a 1 in the 0 row, and a 0 in all the other rows. The pattern for a character *one* is 000100000000, and that for an A is 100100000000.

Figure 5-4 80-Column Punched Card

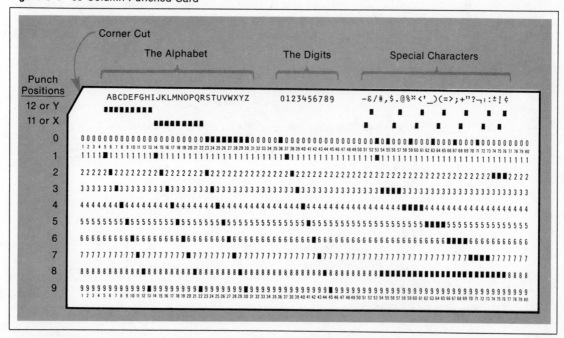

Hollerith code is just one example of a way to represent characters. Some punched cards have 96 characters and they use a different convention. Also, other conventions are used by tape and other devices.

**Magnetic Tape
Data Representation**

Figure 5-5 shows a section of magnetic tape. Bits are represented on magnetic tape by magnetized spots. If the spot is magnetized in one direction, it is considered to be a 0. If it is magnetized in another direction, it is considered to be a 1.

If you turn a section of tape on its side, its format is like a punched card. However, instead of having 80 characters as the card in figure 5-4 has, it can have as many characters as the tape is long. The section of tape shown in figure 5-5 has 9 characters. Also, instead of having 12 rows as the punched card did, the tape has 9. These are called *tracks*. Each character is represented by a column of the nine tracks.

Characters are represented by an 8 bit code. Figure 5-6 shows part of one popular code called *Extended Binary Coded Decimal Interchange Code* or *EBCDIC*. The character A is represented as 1100 0001, the character B as 1100 0010, the number 1 as 1111 0001, and the number 2 as 1111 0010. Other characters are shown in figure 5-6.

Characters are stored on tape by writing their codes in the bottom eight tracks. Thus, to store the character 1, a 1 is written in the bottom, or first, track, 0's are written in the next three tracks, and 1's are written in the top four tracks. (See figure 5-5.) To store the character A, a 1 is written in the bottom track, 0's are written in the next five tracks, and then 1's are written in the next two tracks.

If you're following this discussion, you have a burning question. What about the ninth track? Why have a nine-track tape to hold an 8 bit code?

The ninth track is called the *parity track*. (See figure 5-5.) It is used to help detect errors. Before the tape is written, a convention is estab-

Figure 5-5   Character Representation on Nine-Track Magnetic Tape

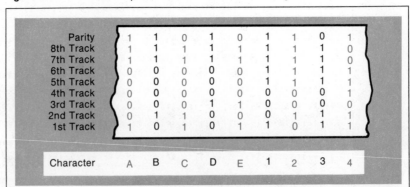

	A	B	C	D	E	1	2	3	4
Parity	1	1	0	1	0	1	1	0	1
8th Track	1	1	1	1	1	1	1	1	0
7th Track	1	1	1	1	1	1	1	1	0
6th Track	0	0	0	0	0	1	1	1	1
5th Track	0	0	0	0	0	1	1	1	1
4th Track	0	0	0	0	0	0	0	0	1
3rd Track	0	0	0	1	1	0	0	0	0
2nd Track	0	1	1	0	0	0	1	1	1
1st Track	1	0	1	0	1	1	0	1	1
Character	A	B	C	D	E	1	2	3	4

Character	Bit Representation
A	1100 0001
B	1100 0010
C	1100 0011
D	1100 0100
E	1100 0101
. . .	
1	1111 0001
2	1111 0010
3	1111 0011
4	1111 0100
5	1111 0101
. . .	

Figure 5-6 A Portion of a 9-Bit Character Code (Parity Bit Omitted)

lished that the tape will be written in either *even* or *odd parity*. If even, this means that each column of the tape is to have an even number of 1's. If odd, then each column is to have an odd number of 1's. The parity track is used to make each column obey the convention.

Suppose the convention is even parity. To represent the character 1 in EBCDIC, a 1 is written in the first track, then three 0's, and then four 1's. A total of five 1's are in the column. However, since each column is supposed to have an even number of 1's, a 1 will also be written in the parity track. After this is done, the column has six 1's, which is even, as it is supposed to be.

To represent the character 3, two 1's are written in the bottom two tracks, then two 0's, and then four 1's. A total of six 1's are in the column. Since this column has an even number of 1's, a 0 is written in the parity track. Examine figure 5-5 and you will see how the parity track is used to make every column have an even number of 1's.

How does this help with errors? Given an even-parity convention, if the tape unit misreads one of the tracks (reads a 0 as a 1 or a 1 as a 0), it will sense an odd number of 1's. Since the convention is even, the unit has made an error and will reread the character or stop. Also, if the tape has been damaged by mishandling, the tape unit will detect parity errors.

If you work around business computer systems, you will undoubtedly hear someone say, "That tape is full of parity errors." Now you know this means either the tape is damaged or the equipment is malfunctioning.

The code in figure 5-6 is not the only way data is represented by computers. There is another popular code that uses just 6 bits. Tape units that commonly process this code have only seven tracks.

**Data Representation
in Main Memory**

Character data is represented in main memory in several ways. The most common methods are similar to the seven- and nine-track tape representations. However, there is an inconsistency in terminology here. Main memory has one or more parity bits just as tape does, but they are seldom mentioned. When people talk about character representation in main memory, they usually talk of 6 bit or 8 bit codes; they ignore the parity bits.

A modern computer can hold literally millions of bits in its main memory. These bits are represented by circuitry. The size of voltage at a particular spot in a wire is one common means of bit representation. The particulars of these representations are complex and unimportant for your understanding of business computing. Therefore, they will not be discussed here. Just think of main memory as millions of bits that can represent either a 0 or a 1.

Sometimes you will hear the term *byte* used with regard to computer data. A byte is the group of bits required to represent one character. If 6 bits are used to represent characters, then a byte is 6 bits. If the computer uses 8 bits for each character, then a byte is 8 bits. Main memory is often described in terms of bytes. A small computer has about 100,000 bytes; a medium one has about a million; and a large computer may have as many as 30 million bytes or more.

Numeric Data   Numbers have several forms. They can have the character form just described. However, if the numbers are to be used for arithmetic, they are put into other forms. There is a *packed decimal form*, a *binary form*, and a *floating-point form*. These forms are used so that arithmetic can be performed efficiently and with the accuracy required by the application. When a number is to be used for arithmetic, it is read in from cards or other input medium in character form and converted to a numeric form.

While numbers reside in main memory, they stay in numeric form. However, numbers in one of these forms are hard for humans to understand. Therefore, they are usually converted back to character form when they are printed or displayed. When numbers are written to tape or other medium for storage purposes (humans won't be seeing them), they are sometimes left in numeric form. This practice saves conversion effort and reduces the amount of storage required.

Numeric format is described in detail in Module B in Part 4. We will not describe it further here.

QUESTIONS

5.1   Define sequential processing.

5.2   Why are records sorted on sequential files?

5.3   Explain the difference between master files and transaction files.

5.4   Why are transaction records usually batched in sequential file processing?

5.5   Why do master files need to be completely rewritten when they are changed?

5.6   What is a bit? Why are bits used to represent computer data?

5.7   Describe the way characters are represented on punched cards.

5.8   Describe the way characters are represented on magnetic tape.

5.9   What is EBCDIC?

5.10   Define parity and explain how it is used for error checking.

5.11   What is a byte? How many bits are there in a byte?

5.12   Why are numbers sometimes converted to binary form?

HARDWARE FOR ALPINE'S MEMBER MASTER FILE SYSTEM

Figure 5-1 shows the system flowchart for Alpine Co-op's member master file problem. The change transaction file is punched on cards, and the old and new member master files are stored on tape. A printer is used to output the reports. Consider each of these types of equipment.

Punched Cards

Punched cards have been used in business since the turn of the century. Figure 5-7 depicts how one type of card reader works. The cards pass between a light source and a light-sensitive receptor. When light passes through a punched hole, the card reader senses a 1. Otherwise, a 0 is sensed. Note that the cards are actually read twice; the results of the two readings are compared by the card reader. If they are different, the machine stops or takes other corrective action. Also, if the reader senses a combination of holes that has no meaning, a *read check* occurs and corrective action is taken.

Cards have two advantages: they are inexpensive and, unlike magnetic tape, it is easy to see what is stored on them. Unfortunately, they have important disadvantages. For one, they are bulky. A typical student's backpack will hold only about 4000 cards. Second, card readers are slow. Card readers can read about 600 cards per minute. If there were one change for every Alpine member (at year end, there could be a change for every member when dividend checks are recorded), it would take 333 minutes or about 5½ hours just to read the change transaction file. Because of these disadvantages, cards are being used less frequently in business computer systems.

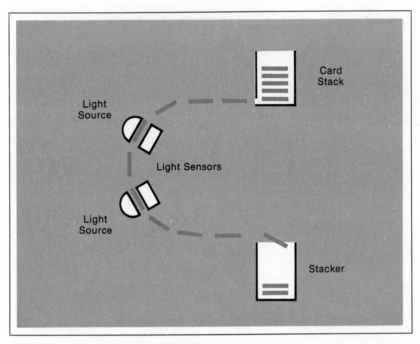

Figure 5-7 Schematic of Card Reader

Key-to-Tape Equipment

Figure 5-8 shows a system flowchart for an alternative to punched card data input. This flowchart is similar to the one in figure 5-1. Here the transaction file is keyed directly to tape instead of punched on cards. Since the transaction records are keyed in no particular order, they must be sorted into member number order. After sorting, the order of the transaction records will match the order of the master file records.

For the system depicted in figure 5-8, Alpine clerks initiate a change to the member master file by filling out a change request form. This form goes to data entry where it is keyed onto magnetic tape. A machine and an operator performing key-to-tape data entry are shown in figure 5-9. The tape that is generated can be a cassette tape like those used for home stereos, or it can be a reel of ½ inch tape commonly used for computers.

The record format for the change transaction file is shown in figure 5-10. The data entry personnel fill in this data on the CRT screens, and a tape is created that has one record for each change.

The record code field tells the update program what function to perform. A 1 in this field means add a new member; a 2 means delete a member; a 3 means change member data; and a 4 means print the member's record. This last action is taken to determine what data is on the member's master record.

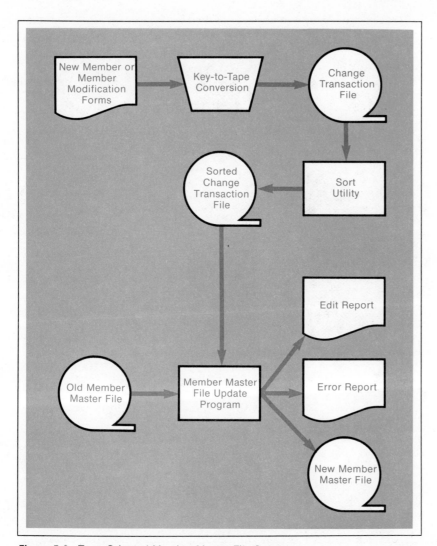

Figure 5-8 Tape-Oriented Member Master File System

The contents of the other fields in the change record vary, depending on the value in the record code field. For codes 3 and 4, only the member number need be specified. For code 1, all the data must be specified. For code 2, only the member number and the data to be changed must be specified. Figure 5-11 shows some examples of change records.

We will assume Alpine elected to input their transaction data using key-to-tape equipment. Now let's consider other components of the system in figure 5-9.

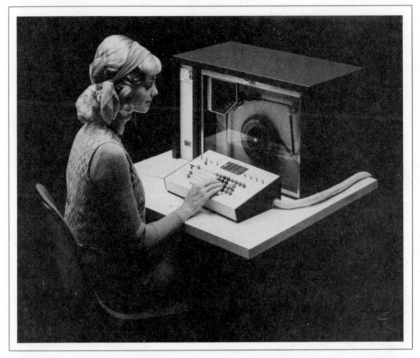

Figure 5-9 Operator Using Key-to-Tape Equipment

Column	Contents
1	Record Code
5–10	Member Number
11–30	Member Name
31–70	Member Address
71–80	Member Phone

Figure 5-10 Change Transaction File Record Format

```
1    201143FRED J.PARKS        316 E. TAMARACK, LOS ANGELES    CA 94123 2135551201
1    201144MARY ABERNATHY      934 S. LARCH, ALEXANDRIA        VA 02034 2033812347
2    101234
1    201145PETE WANDOLOWSKI     1123 17TH STREET, APT 6, MIAMI FL 11234 6053457769
3    001214
2    000109
4    000044
4    109877
3    154347REX BAKER
```

Figure 5-11 Change Transaction Data for Card-Oriented System

Both the old and new member master files are kept on tape. Figure 5-12 shows a typical magnetic tape format. The tape has a header section that contains the tape serial number, identity of the owner, and so forth. Then for each file on the tape, there is a file header that names the file and gives its date of creation and other identifying data. (There can be more than one file on a tape, although in Alpine's master file there would be just one.)

**Tape Equipment
for the Master Files**

The records in the file are stored after the file header. Following all the records, there is a file trailer that repeats the file header data. It indicates the end of the file. If there is another file, this grouping of file header–data–file trailer is repeated for as many files as are on the tape. Finally, the tape has a trailer that repeats the tape header data and signifies the end of recorded data on the tape. The headers and trailers are sometimes referred to as *labels*. A tape that has these labels is called a *labeled tape*.

This description generally applies to all labeled tapes. Slight variations exist among manufacturers, but the format is essentially the same. It is possible to force equipment to write tapes without the labels, but this is bad practice. Without labels, the computer cannot verify that the correct tape has been mounted. If the wrong tape is mounted, valuable data may be lost. When tapes are labeled, the computer hardware will ensure that the mounted tape is the one called for.

Figure 5-13 shows a reel of tape with a *write-protect ring* partially inserted. This ring must be in place before the tape can be written. Since the operator must insert the ring, this action is protection against inadvertently writing on a tape that was supposed to be read. The equipment simply won't write unless the ring is in place.

Figure 5-14 shows a simple schematic of a tape read/write unit. As the tape passes under the read/write heads, the magnetic spots are either sensed (read) or created (written). Typically, a tape unit will read or write one record and then stop; read or write another record and stop; etc. This means that the tape moves forward in jerks; a quick move followed by a stop, another quick move followed by a stop. To give the equipment time to stop, there is a gap between the records on

Figure 5-12   Magnetic Tape Structure

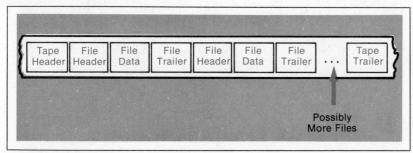

Possibly
More Files

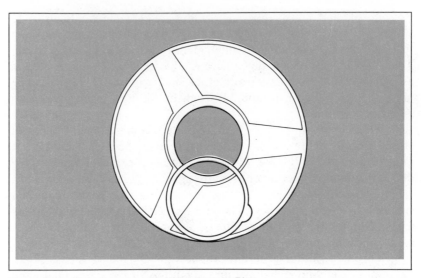

Figure 5-13   Tape Volume with Write-Protect Ring

Figure 5-14   Schematic of Tape Drive

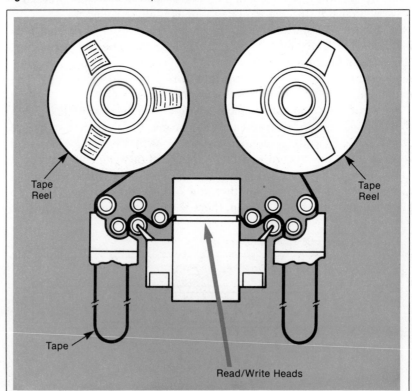

Position	Contents
1–6	Member Number
7–26	Member Name
27–66	Member Address
67–76	Member Phone
77–83	Year-to-Date Purchases (xxxx.xx)
84–89	Member Number
90–95	Date of Last Purchase (YYMMDD)
96–101	Date of Last Master File Update (YYMMDD)
102–107	Amount of Last Dividend Check
108–114	Amount of Last Year's Purchases (xxxx.xx)
115–120	Date Member Joined (YYMMDD)

Figure 5-15 Member Master File Record Format

the tape. This is called the *interblock gap*. This gap may be half an inch or more in size.

You may have seen pictures of magnetic tape drives in movies or on TV. Typically, the tape reels are shown whirling at great speed and not moving in jerks at all. That's because they are being rewound. Hollywood likes action and a tape drive actually reading or writing is apparently not dramatic enough.

Magnetic tape can be recorded in various *densities*. These are measured in *bytes per inch* (bpi). Typical values are 800 bpi, 1600 bpi, and 6250 bpi.

Consider Alpine's master file. According to figure 5-15, there are 120 characters per master record. If a tape is recorded at 1600 bpi, then it will take 0.075 inch to hold one member record. Do you see a problem? Most of the tape will be used for interblock gaps! If the gaps are 0.5 inch, there will be 0.075 inch of data followed by 0.5 inch of gap, then 0.075 inch of data, followed by 0.5 inch of gap, and so forth. (See figure 5-16.)

Figure 5-16 Alpine's Member Master File Record Format on Tape

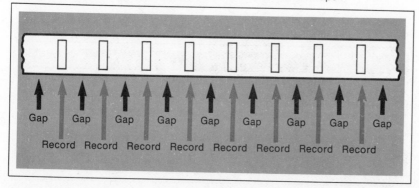

Record Blocking   To prevent this situation, records can be blocked. This means a group of records can be written or read together as a unit, or *block*. Figure 5-17 depicts a tape with a *blocking factor* of eight records per block. In this case, a block will take 0.6 inch (8×0.075) of tape and be followed by 0.5 inch of gap.

How much tape will be required to hold Alpine's member master file? There are 200,000 records. If they are blocked at eight records per block, then 25,000 blocks will be needed. Each block and its adjacent interblock gap take 1.1 inches. Consequently, 27,500 inches, or 2292 feet, of tape are required. Since reels of magnetic tape are available in lengths of 800, 1200, and 2400 feet, the master file will fit on one 2400 foot reel. There will be 108 feet left over for headers and trailers. (Isn't it amazing how textbook examples always work out!) Would the data fit if the blocking factor were 4? If it were 15?

You might be wondering why there are any gaps at all. Why not compress the data into one long record? The reason is that a block must be read into main memory in its entirety. A portion of main memory, called a *buffer*, must be set aside to receive the record as it comes in from the tape. If Alpine's master file were one long record, then $200,000 \times 120$ bytes, or 24 million bytes, of main storage would have to be set aside for the buffer. Only the very largest computers have that much memory and there are other uses for it. Consequently, records are usually blocked into more manageable-sized units, such as 1000 or 2000 bytes.

Magnetic Tape Speeds   How long will it take to read or write Alpine's member master file? The time to process a tape has two components: the time to actually move the data and the time to start and stop the tape between blocks. The time to move the data depends on the speed of the tape and the recording density. A typical speed (called the tape *transport speed*) is 200 inches per second. Thus at 1600 bpi, a total of 320,000 bytes can be transferred per second. The Alpine master file has 24 million characters, so 75 seconds (24 million divided by 320,000) will be needed to read or write the tape.

Figure 5-17   Schematic of Tape with Blocking Factor of 8

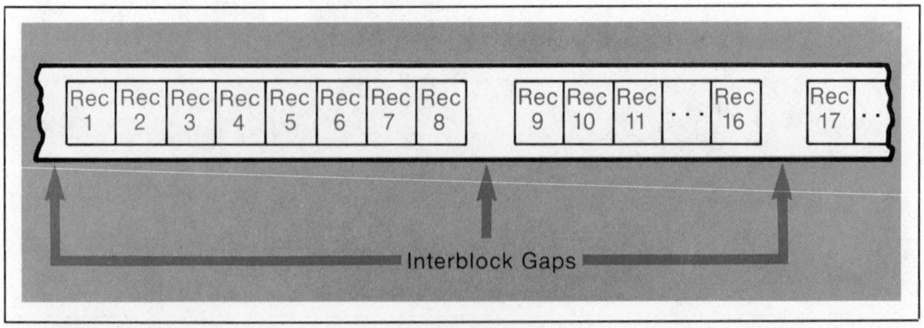

In addition, time is required to start and stop the tape between blocks. A typical time interval to stop and start a tape is 0.003 second. Assuming Alpine has 200,000 member records blocked eight per block, then 25,000 blocks will be needed. At 0.003 second for stop and start, a total of 75 seconds will be needed. Thus the total time to read or write the entire Alpine master file is 150 seconds.

This figure is somewhat misleading. The computer will not devote all of its time to reading or writing this tape. There will be interference from other activity. Still, five minutes is a very realistic estimate. This is a far cry from the 5 ½ hours needed to read 200,000 punched cards.

Both of the member master file systems in figures 5-1 and 5-8 required two reports to be written. In order to write these reports, Alpine will need some type of printer.

Printers

Serial vs Line Printers   Printers are characterized in three important ways. First, there are *serial* and *line printers*. Serial printers print one character at a time. They are similar to typewriters; in fact, the balls or "elements" that are used in IBM Selectric® typewriters are used in some serial printers. (See figure 5-18.) Serial printers operate at speeds of 15 to 60 characters per second. Some serial printers can print in both directions so that time is not wasted for carriage returns.

Line printers print a full line at a time. Figure 5-19 shows a sketch of a line printer that uses a print drum with 136 print positions. At each position is a band containing a complete set of characters. When a line is to be printed, the bands rotate to expose the correct character. The characters are then struck by hammers, thus causing the line to be printed. A printer like this operates at 300 to 2000 lines per minute.

Impact vs Nonimpact Printers   A second way that printers are characterized is *impact* or *nonimpact*. For impact printers, the characters strike the paper through a ribbon. Both the serial and line printers in figures 5-18 and 5-19 are impact printers. Some nonimpact printers write on specially coated or sensitized paper. Other types of nonimpact

Figure 5-18   Examples of Serial Printers

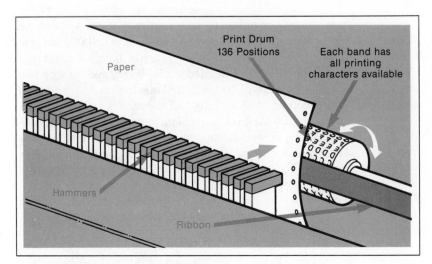

Figure 5-19 Print Drum of Line Printer

Figure 5-20 IBM 3800 Laser Printer

```
2.00    4.00   50.00    210.00    0      25
0.20    0.40   50.00     55.00    0     175
1.50    4.00   62.00    375.00    0     300
2.00    6.00   66.00    298.00    0      75
0.63    1.25   49.00     51.03    0      40
1.50    3.00   50.00    604.50    0     200
0.63    1.25   49.00     44.10    0      40
0.30    0.70   57.00    243.00    0     300
1.88    3.75   49.00    535.80    0      20
```

Figure 5-21 Dot Matrix Characters

printers spray the ink on the paper, or use the same technique as Xerox machines. Figure 5-20 shows a laser printer that uses a xerographic process.

Impact printers can make several copies at one time but they are noisy. Nonimpact printers are quiet, and some are much faster than impact printers. Speeds as high as 45,000 lines per minute are possible with ink jet printers. Nonimpact printers cannot make more than one copy at a time, but their faster speed can compensate for this. It is likely that nonimpact printers will be used more and more in the future.

Dot Matrix vs Full-Character Printers   A third categorization of printers is *full character* or *dot matrix*. Full-character printers print a whole character like a typewriter. Dot matrix printers (figure 5-21) print an array of dots. They do not produce as high print quality as do full-character printers; however, they are cheaper and faster. Figure 5-22 summarizes the categories of printers used in business computer systems.

Figure 5-22 Characterizations of Printers

Printer	*Characteristics*
Serial	Prints one character at a time.
Line	Prints a line at a time.
Impact	Can make multiple copies, but is noisy.
Nonimpact	Can make only a single copy, but is very fast and quiet.
Full Character	Prints characters like a typewriter, with possible high quality.
Dot Matrix	Prints characters using dots.

Which System for Alpine Co-op?

After discussing the data and hardware possibilities, the Alpine project team decided that either of the systems in figure 5-1 (the system with data entered on cards) or in figure 5-8 (the system with data entered on key-to-tape equipment) would be feasible. John Abrams suggested that they not attempt to choose between these two systems yet. Instead, he asked them to consider the next component of a business computer system: programs. A choice could better be made later.

John explained a common mistake is to evaluate alternatives only on the basis of hardware. Often, in terms of the total system cost, hardware is much cheaper than programs or people. Therefore, all five components of a business computer system should be considered in making systems decisions.

QUESTIONS

5.13 What are the advantages of punched cards? What are the disadvantages?

5.14 How do key-to-tape machines differ from card punches?

5.15 What is the purpose of the record code field in figure 5-10?

5.16 What is a labeled tape? Should most companies use labeled or unlabeled tapes?

5.17 Explain what file headers and trailers are.

5.18 Sketch the layout of a labeled tape that has three files.

5.19 What does bpi stand for? What are typical values of bpi for magnetic tapes?

5.20 What is the purpose of the write-protect ring?

5.21 What is the purpose of the interblock gap? What is its disadvantage?

5.22 What does it mean to block records? Why is this done?

5.23 How much tape would be required to hold the Alpine member master file if the blocking factor were 4? If it were 15?

5.24 How long would it take to read the Alpine member master file if the blocking factor were 4? If it were 15?

5.25 How long would it take to read 7500 200-byte records recorded at 1600 bpi?

5.26 How long would it take to write 7500 200-byte records recorded at 6250 bpi?

5.27 Distinguish between the following types of printers and give an advantage and a disadvantage of each:
a. Serial and line
b. Impact and nonimpact
c. Full-character and dot matrix

Figure 5-23 shows a system flowchart for Alpine's purchase update system. This system adds the total amount of a member's order to the year-to-date purchase total in the member's master record. This is a typical sequential file system.

The transaction records are sorted into the same order as the master file records. Then they are read by an update program. The update program matches a transaction record with the corresponding master file record, makes adjustments to the master data (by adding the order amount to the year-to-date total), and writes out the new master record.

PROGRAMS FOR SEQUENTIAL FILE PROCESSING

A Sequential File Record-Matching Algorithm

Figure 5-23 Alpine Purchase Update System

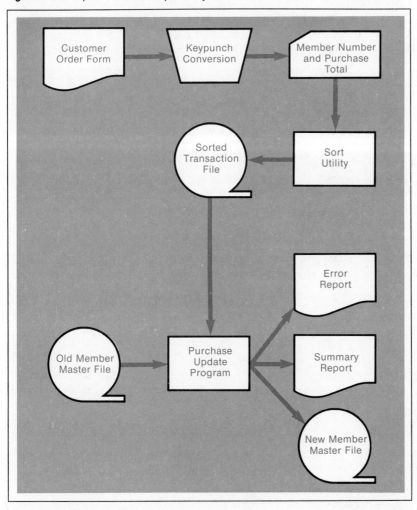

Records will be matched by member number. The master file will be kept in order of member number, and the transaction file will be sorted by member number. Fields that are used in the way member number is used in this example are called *control fields* or sometimes *keys*.

If the update program finds any transaction records that do not have a matching master record, then the unmatched records are written to an error file. Also, it is quite possible that there will be master records with no matching transactions; this means that some members made no purchases. In this case, the program will copy the master record from the old master file to the new one without making any changes.

Figure 5-24 lists data that could be input to a program like the purchase update program in figure 5-23. Each transaction record contains a member number and the amount of a recent sale. Each master record has a member number and other data that is not shown. If we examine this data, we see that member 100010 is on both the transaction file and the master file. The 7.95 will be added to his or her master record. Similarly, member 100020 is on both files; 124.85 will be added.

However, the next pair of member numbers in figure 5-24 do not match. Member 100040 on the transaction file does not match member 100030 on the master file. This means that member 100030 did not make any purchases; he or she had no transactions. In this case the program copies member 100030's data to the new file with no change.

After copying 100030's data, the program must read another master record to see if it matches transaction 100040. Note the program reads only the master file in this case. If it reads both the master and the transaction files, transaction record 100040 would be lost before it was processed.

The program now reads master record 100040. Sure enough, this record matches the current transaction record. Consequently, 382.17 is added to 100040's year-to-date total. The program now reads the

Figure 5-24 Data for Purchase Update Program

Transaction File		Master File	
Member Number	Amount of Sale	Member Number	Other Master Data
100010	007.95	100010	
100020	124.85	100020	
100040	382.17	100030	.
100045	081.29	100040	.
100050	176.76	100050	.
EOF		100060	
		100070	
		EOF	

next two records and finds a disagreement: 100045 from the transaction does not match 100050 from the master.

What does this mean? Both the transaction file and the master file are sorted by member number. The transaction number 100045 is *less than* the master number 100050. Consequently, we have detected a missing master record: 100045 is not on the master file. If it were, it would come before 100050 because the records are ordered. In this case, the program prints 100045 on the error file. Then it reads the next transaction record. It is 100050, which matches 100050 on the master file. The 176.76 is added to the master record and it is written on the new master file.

When the program tries to read the next records from the transaction and master files, it finds EOF on the transaction file. EOF stands for *end of file*. Here it simply means that there are no more file records to be read. All systems have ways of notifying a program that all the records in a file have been read. However, the way this is done depends on the type of computer and the language of the program. Your instructor can show you how your computer does this.

When the program encounters EOF on the transaction file, it copies all the remaining records from the old master to the new master file. If it did not do this, then all the remaining records on the master file would be lost. In this case, member records 100060 and 100070 are copied unchanged to the new master file.

It could happen that the master file runs out of data before the transaction file does. If so, then all remaining records on the transaction file are erroneous. They have no matching records on the master file. In this case, they are copied on the error report.

Figure 5-25 shows pseudocode for the purchase update program. This pseudocode has five procedures. The first one, MAIN-PROCEDURE, simply calls the other four procedures in the proper order. First, an initialization routine is called that sets two variables, EOF-MASTER and EOF-TRANSACTION. Then it reads the first master record and the first transaction record.

The two variables need explanation. EOF-MASTER is used to tell the program when EOF is detected on the master file. Initially, EOF-MASTER is set to 0, meaning EOF has not been reached. When the program detects the end of the master file, EOF-MASTER will be set to 1. The same is done for EOF-TRANS. Variables used in this way are sometimes called *flags*; if the flag is up (1), the end has been reached.

The second procedure is PROCESS-BOTH-FILES. This procedure is active as long as both files have data. It matches the records and does the processing. After one of the files runs out of data, the third procedure is called. This procedure, named FLUSH-NONEMPTY-FILE, does just that. If the nonempty file is the transaction file, then all the remaining transaction records are sent to the error report. If the

**Pseudocode for
Record Matching**

```
BEGIN MAIN-PROCEDURE
    DO INITIALIZE
    DO PROCESS-BOTH-FILES
    DO FLUSH-NONEMPTY-FILE
    DO WRAPUP
    STOP
END MAIN-PROCEDURE

BEGIN INITIALIZE
    SET EOF-MASTER TO 0
    SET EOF-TRANS TO 0
    READ OLD-MASTER-FILE IF END SET EOF-MASTER TO 1
    READ TRANS-FILE IF END SET EOF-TRANS TO 1
END INITIALIZE

BEGIN PROCESS-BOTH-FILES
    DOWHILE EOF-MASTER AND EOF-TRANS = 0
        IF MEMBER-NUMBER (MASTER-FILE) = MEMBER-NUMBER (TRANS-FILE)
            THEN /Add amount to year-to-date total in master record./
                WRITE MASTER-RECORD TO NEW-MASTER-FILE
                READ OLD-MASTER-FILE IF END SET EOF-MASTER TO 1
                READ TRANS-FILE IF END SET EOF-TRANS TO 1
            ELSE IF MEMBER-NUMBER (MASTER-FILE) < MEMBER-NUMBER (TRANS-FILE)
                    THEN /This means there is no activity on the member
                            record./
                        WRITE MASTER-RECORD TO NEW-MASTER-FILE
                        READ OLD-MASTER-FILE IF END SET EOF-MASTER TO 1
                    ELSE /This means there is a trans record with no
                            corresponding master./
                        WRITE TRANS-RECORD TO ERROR-FILE
                        READ TRANS-FILE IF END SET EOF-TRANS TO 1
                END-IF
        END-IF
    END-DO
END PROCESS-BOTH-FILES
```

Figure 5-25 Pseudocode for Purchase Update Program *(Part 1 of 2)*

```
BEGIN FLUSH-NONEMPTY-FILE
   IF EOF-MASTER = 1
      THEN /This means the master file is empty; send any remaining
             trans records to the error file./
             DOWHILE EOF-TRANS = 0
                WRITE TRANS-RECORD TO ERROR-FILE
                READ TRANS-FILE IF END SET EOF-TRANS TO 1
             END-DO
      ELSE /This means the transaction file is empty; copy any
             remaining master records to the new master file./
             DOWHILE EOF-MASTER = 0
                WRITE MASTER-RECORD TO NEW-MASTER-FILE
                READ MASTER-FILE IF END SET EOF-MASTER TO 1
             END-DO
   END-IF
END FLUSH-NONEMPTY FILE

BEGIN WRAPUP
   /Here program writes summary reports and takes other termination
      action./
END WRAPUP
```

Figure 5-25 Pseudocode for Purchase Update Program *(Part 2 of 2)*

nonempty file is the master file, then all the remaining master records are copied to the new master file.

After this process is complete, the last procedure, WRAPUP, is called. This procedure prints the summary report and performs any other needed termination work.

Examine procedure PROCESS-BOTH-FILES. The first statement is a DOWHILE statement. This statement means DO the following statements WHILE the condition is true. When the condition is not true, go to the next statement after the END-DO. If the condition is not true for the first time, do not perform the loop at all. For this example, the condition stated is that neither the master file nor the transaction file is out of data. If they are, control is returned to the MAIN-PROCEDURE.

The first statement inside the *loop* is an IF statement that checks to see if the member numbers match. If so, the amount is added to the member's year-to-date purchase total. Then, the new master record is written. The next records are read from both the master and the transaction files.

Note that if the READ statement detects end of file, the EOF flag will be set to 1. If this happens, the condition in the DO statement will not be true. Activity in PROCESS-BOTH-FILES will cease.

The pseudocode in figure 5-25 corresponds to the algorithm previously described. You should read through this to be sure you understand the algorithm and pseudocode statements.

This is a typical sequential file program. The need to match transaction and master records is universal to sequential processing. Consequently, this algorithm with a few modifications could be used for a large class of sequential processing programs.

For example, consider the master file maintenance problem summarized in figure 5-8. Additions, deletions, and modifications are to be made to the member master file. The algorithm shown in figure 5-25 could be used to solve this problem. The only difference is the action to be taken once two matching records are found.

So far in this book we have lightly skipped over sorting. This is not fair, since sorting is an important activity. The sort depicted in figure 5-23 would actually be done by a computer program. However, this program would most likely be a *system utility*, or program provided by the computer vendor to perform a common activity. Examples of other utilities are programs to copy data, to dump files (print their contents), merge files, and so forth.

The sort utility would have been written and tested by the vendor. Alpine personnel would simply run it. They would input the name of the file to be sorted, the fields to sort on, and the order (ascending or descending) in which to sort them. The utility would then sort the records and put them on an output file. If the data to be sorted is too large to fit into main memory at one time, tape or other storage equipment would be required.

Program Editing

Thus far we have assumed that programs always receive good data. Unfortunately, that is unrealistic. *Experienced programmers plan on bad data*. For example, we know that Alpine's service bureau had produced many errors because they could not input the member number correctly. Their keypunch operators made too many errors.

A good business computer program always *edits* or checks the input data. If the data is known to have been produced by keypunch or other error-prone methods, the checking should be extensive. If the input comes from a master file on, say, tape, then less checking need be done. However, this policy assumes that the data was heavily edited as it was added to the master file.

There are seemingly an infinite number of errors that could be made. Clearly, the program cannot check for all of them. However, certain types of checking are commonly done. A *reasonableness check* verifies that the input data items have reasonable values. For example, the update program in figure 5-8 might check member number to make sure it is all numeric, that it has six digits, and that it is positive.

Another type of check is a *range check*. Here the input data item is checked to be sure it falls in the correct range of values. Alpine may have a rule that no order can exceed $750.00. If so, then the purchase update program should edit the transaction record purchase amount to ensure that it is greater than 0 and less than or equal to 750.00. A program that reads ages might check to be sure they are greater than 0 but less than, say, 100 (depending on the system designer's optimism).

Value checks can be made if the number of values that a data item can have is small. For example, the value for sex should be M or F or perhaps blank. No other characters are acceptable. If a company has 10 plants numbered 1 through 10, the only values acceptable for plant number are the digits 1–10. The records in figure 5-10 had a code field in the first column. Its value was supposed to be 1, 2, 3, or 4. A value check could and should be made on this field.

Digit checks can be made on the individual digits of a field. A company may establish a convention that all part numbers are to start with 1, or that all company numbers are to end with 0. These digits can be checked.

An important extension to this concept is *check digits*. Here, a digit is added to a field to verify the correctness of the rest of the field. For example, consider Alpine's member numbers. They have six digits. Suppose we sum the digits individually. For the number 100040, the sum is 5. For the number 123456, the sum is 21. To create a check digit, we take the number in the ones column of the sum and append it to the member number. This forms a seven-digit number. Thus, 100040 becomes 1000405 and 123456 becomes 1234561.

Now suppose a data entry operator is to input member 100040, but miskeys the member number as 1000505. The program will sum the first six digits of the number and get 6. Since the 6 does not agree with the last digit (the check digit), an error will be detected. If 1234561 is miskeyed as 2234561, the check digit of 1 will not agree with the computed digit of 2 (the sum of 2, 2, 3, 4, 5, and 6 is 22). This is a type of *self-checking number*. Note that this scheme will not catch all errors. If 1234561 is miskeyed as 2134561, the check digit will not catch the error. The sum of the first six digits is still 21 even though the first two digits have been interchanged. Another type of check is required to detect this error.

What kind of a check can be used on the value of the purchase amount of the transaction file of the purchase update program? Range and reasonableness checks can be made, but these are not conclusive. If 555.00 were keyed for 055.00, neither of these checks would detect the error. Unfortunately, the program by itself cannot improve the checking of these amounts. Instead, this checking must be supplemented with manual checks by users and operations personnel. We will discuss this type of checking in the next section.

QUESTIONS	5.28 What is a control field? How is it used for sequential file processing?

	5.29 What does it mean when
	  a. there is a record on Alpine's member master file that does not match a record on the transaction file?
	  b. there is a record on Alpine's transaction file that does not match a record on the member master file?

	5.30 Why does the matching algorithm copy the last few member records to the new member master file?
	5.31 What is EOF? What role does EOF detection play in the matching algorithm?
	5.32 Explain what the DOWHILE statement means.
	5.33 What is a sort utility?

	5.34 Define the following edits and give one example of each:
	  a. Reasonableness
	  b. Range
	  c. Value
	  d. Digit
	  e. Check digit

	5.35 Why are edit checks not conclusive?
	5.36 Modify the pseudocode shown in this chapter to perform master file maintenance. Assume the records have the structure illustrated in figure 5-15.

PROCEDURES FOR SEQUENTIAL FILE PROCESSING

We described the general nature of systems procedures in Chapter 2. We will not repeat that discussion here. However, sequential file systems do impose some special requirements on systems procedures. Those special needs will be discussed in this section.

Correct data is important in all business computer processing, but it is given special emphasis in sequential systems. Because transactions are processed in batches, it is very easy for an erroneous update to slip through. It is very hard for humans to correctly check every item in a 1500-item list, for example. Also, once an erroneous update is made to a record in a sequential system master file, it is particularly hard to fix. The entire file must be rewritten just to change one record.

Two types of procedures are employed to reduce the likelihood of errors. First, updates to master files are often made in two phases. During the first phase, a dry run (dress rehearsal) is made; all of the processing is done but the master file is not updated. This type of processing was described previously in the Accounting section of Chapter 3.

Figure 5-26 shows a two-phased approach for the Alpine purchase update system. The edit program checks the transaction member master number and purchase amount fields. Both reasonableness and range checks can be made on these fields. Also, a form of value check can be made on the member number. To do this, the program checks the member number value by searching the master file for a matching number. If found, the number is assumed good.

If the master file is large, the dress rehearsal may be too expensive. In Alpine's case, reading the 200,000-record member master file may take more machine time than is judged practical. If so, then the transaction data will be edited, but the check on the member number will not be made until the actual update is done.

Unfortunately, even the check against the master file is inconclusive. If a valid member number is found on the master file, this is not a guarantee that *the* correct number was input. It is just a guarantee that *a* valid number was read. A check digit can be used as well, although as explained in the last section, this is also inconclusive. In truth, no check is conclusive. A variety of checks are made in the hope that at least one of them will catch any errors.

The edit report is sent to the users by Data Processing. Here it is checked. Any errors are sent to Data Entry for correction. Then the edit run is repeated. When all detected errors have been eliminated, the second phase is run. The master file is actually updated.

Another procedure often used with batch systems is to make manual calculations and to compare them to the computer program's results. For example, the number of transaction records can be counted by the users before they submit them to Data Processing. Later, when the edit report is available, the users compare the number of transactions that the program processed to the number that were submitted. In this way, users will detect that transactions have been duplicated or are missing. It is important for the users to check this number on both the edit and the final update reports.

An extension of these transaction counts is known as a *batch total.*   **Batch Totals**
Here, the users manually compute the total amount of all purchases in the batch. They then submit the orders to Data Entry. Later, when the edit report comes back, users compare the total determined by the program to the total computed manually. If the two disagree, then the difference can be traced to its cause. There may have been a manual addition error, a keypunch error, a missing record, or even an error

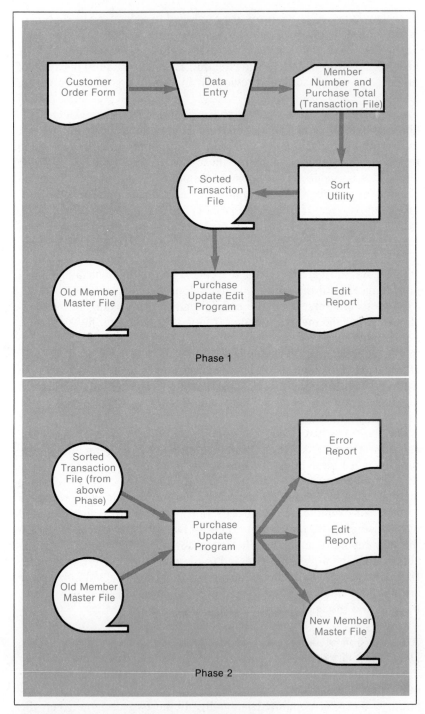

Figure 5-26 Two-Phased Purchase Update System

in the program. If the batch is very large, it may be divided into sub-batches to ease the burden of identifying errors. In this case, the program must be written to print the subbatch totals for comparison.

Thus, users and data processing personnel maintain checks and balances on one another. Simple counts or totals are produced by the two groups using different methods. If they agree, processing is continued. If not, the error is found and corrected. This system works only when both groups are aware of their responsibilities and perform their tasks correctly. Perhaps you can see why both the users and the data processing staff are considered parts of the system.

In addition to procedures on use, error detection, and error correction, a well-designed system also has procedures on *backup and recovery*. What happens if the computer malfunctions or crashes in the middle of a master file update run? What happens if the tape drive breaks and ruins the master file tape? What happens if an operator spills a Coke all over the transaction card file and the cards are so sticky that they won't go through the card reader?

Backup and Recovery Procedures

Here we see one of the great advantages of sequential file systems. Whenever a master file is changed, a complete new copy of the file is produced. If the old copy is kept, along with the transaction records, then the new copy can always be reproduced.

For example, the master file for the first week in January is used to produce the one for the second week. In turn, the second week's master file is used to produce the one for the third week, and so forth. If, for some reason, the master file for the third week is lost, it can be re-created from the second week's file. The transaction records for week three are just processed again.

A sequential system that is run weekly will generate 52 master files in one year. How many of these should be kept? Although the answer varies from application to application, a general rule is that three generations of master files and their associated transactions should be kept. Thus, when the master file for the fourth week of January is produced, the first week's file and transactions can be released. (See figure 5-27.) Because of the three generations, this procedure is sometimes called *child-parent-grandparent processing*.

Backup and recovery procedures are very important. There are countless horror stories of companies that have been dead-in-the-water because a critical system could not be recovered. Luckily, backup and recovery is easily done for sequential systems. For other types of systems, it becomes much more difficult and expensive. (We will see this situation in Chapter 6.) It becomes no less important, however.

To review, procedures for sequential file systems have three unique characteristics. First, a two-phased approach is often employed:

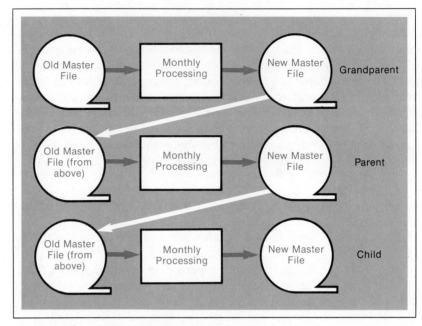

Figure 5-27 Child-Parent-Grandparent Processing

an edit run is made, then an actual update. Second, control mechanisms like transaction counts and batch totals are often used by users and data processing personnel as checks and balances. Finally, backup and recovery is accomplished by keeping at least three generations of master files and associated transactions.

PERSONNEL FOR SEQUENTIAL FILE PROCESSING

Users and operations personnel are the two groups involved with the utilization of a sequential file system. The users have two major responsibilities for which they need to be trained. First, they need to know what the control procedures are and what they are supposed to do. If transaction counts are to be made or batch totals produced, the users need to know what to do, how to do it, and what to do with the results. The design of effective control procedures is worthless if the procedures are not performed. Sometimes users take their control responsibilities lightly. They incorrectly assume that computer systems are infallible. Sometimes the users simply do not understand how the system works.

Second, the users need to know how to correct bad data. If an error is discovered during an edit run, it is easily corrected. If, however, an error gets through the edit and is applied to a master file, it may not be so easy to correct.

For example, suppose the price of an item in inventory is incorrectly stated in a master file. If orders for the item are processed with the incorrect price, it may be very difficult to correct the erroneous orders. Also, once the correction is made, strange results can occur. A customer can order the part under one price and return it under another. If the first price is less than the second one, the customer may make a profit! Consequently, error correction procedures need to be designed carefully and the users need to be trained in how to use them.

Operations personnel need to be trained in three major areas when executing sequential systems. First, they need to know about the two-phased activity; they must not initiate master file updates until the transaction data has been inspected and approved by users. Second, operations personnel need to know the backup and recovery procedures. They must be able to perform them without assistance from the users or the data processing staff. A 3 A.M. emergency call to find out what to do because the system crashed should be a rare event.

Finally, operations personnel must follow defined procedures for handling sequential files—especially master files. In addition to not updating master files without user approval, the operations personnel must release old versions of master files at the appropriate time. This requirement may sound simple, but when a tape library has thousands of tapes and many sequential systems are in use, it is easy to mount the wrong tape. File handling procedures must be carefully designed and well documented. Operations personnel must be trained to use them.

John Abrams presented the concepts in this chapter to the Alpine project team. After he was finished, the team members were ready to get started on designing a sequential file system.

"Hold on," said John. "We've only talked about one of the fundamental styles of file processing. Another style is direct access processing. This style has some big advantages over sequential file processing, as you'll see."

SEQUENTIAL PROCESSING FOR ALPINE CO-OP?

5.37 Why are errors easy to make with sequential file processing systems? Why are they hard to fix?

5.38 Explain the two-phased change process described for Alpine's purchase update system.

5.39 What is a batch total and how is it used?

5.40 Describe backup and recovery procedures for sequential file systems.

QUESTIONS

5.41   What is a child-parent-grandparent procedure?

5.42   Describe two user responsibilities for sequential systems.

5.43   Describe three operations personnel responsibilities for sequential systems.

SUMMARY

This chapter has surveyed the first of the two basic types of file processing systems: sequential file systems. We began by discussing the general nature of sequential systems. These systems usually have two types of files: master and transaction. Also, we found that when master files are changed, a new copy of the file is created. Changes are not made in the middle of a sequential master file. Sequential systems are designed to process transactions in batches. Although transactions could be processed one at a time or a few at a time, this would be expensive since all of the master file must be copied. A synonym for sequential processing is batch processing.

We discussed the data and hardware used for sequential processing. Data is represented by bit patterns. A common code of patterns is EBCDIC. Four categories of computer equipment were discussed: card readers, key-to-tape data entry equipment, tape units, and printers.

In addition to data and hardware, we discussed sequential-file-oriented programs. A common problem is matching transaction records with master file records. Pseudocode of a record-matching algorithm was illustrated. The importance of program editing was emphasized, and several types of edit checks described.

Finally, procedures and personnel requirements for sequential systems were discussed. The need for control procedures providing checks and balances between users and data processing was described. Also, backup and recovery procedures for sequential file systems were defined. Again, we stressed that the best designed procedures are worthless if they are not followed. Consequently, training for both users and operations personnel is crucial.

Sequential file systems are very common. They have advantages over other kinds of systems. They are relatively simple, they are fast, and they can be easily backed up and recovered. Unfortunately, they suffer one severe limitation: direct access to a record is impossible. To read record 1000, the first 999 records must be read or at least passed over. In the next chapter we will describe a type of file processing that does not have this disadvantage.

This is a big and important chapter. It you have understood the material presented, you know more than 99 percent of what all business professionals know about business computer systems. Do not lose your motivation and waver by the wayside. This knowledge will be invaluable to you throughout your business career.

		WORD LIST
Sequential file processing	*Buffer*	(in order of appearance in text)
Master file	*Transport speed*	
Transaction file	*Serial printer*	
Batch processing	*Line printer*	
Binary digit	*Impact printer*	
Bit	*Nonimpact printer*	
Bit pattern	*Dot matrix printer*	
Punched card	*Full-character printer*	
Hollerith code	*Control field*	
Magnetic tape	*Pseudocode*	
EBCDIC	*End-of-file (EOF)*	
Parity bit	*EOF flag*	
Parity track	*Loop*	
Even or odd parity	*Sorting*	
Byte	*System utility*	
Packed decimal form	*Reasonableness check*	
Binary form	*Range check*	
Floating-point form	*Value check*	
Read check	*Digit check*	
Key-to-tape equipment	*Check digits*	
Tape labels	*Self-checking number*	
Tape headers and trailers	*Transaction count*	
Write-protect ring	*Batch total*	
Interblock gap	*Backup and recovery*	
Bytes per inch (bpi)	*Child-parent-grandparent processing*	
Blocked records		
Blocking factor		

A. A county government maintains records about the ownership of parcels of land. They keep the legal description of the property, the name and address of the owner, and the date and price of purchase. They want to design a sequential file system to maintain this data.

QUESTIONS TO CHALLENGE YOUR THINKING

1. How should they sort this file?

2. If the length of the record is 150 bytes, how long would it take to read 45,000 of these records if they are stored on cards?

3. With the same assumptions as item 2, how long would it take to read or write a magnetic tape file?

4. Draw a system flowchart of a tape-oriented system to maintain this file.

5. Write pseudocode to insert, delete, and change the owner in these records.

B. A music production company keeps records about concerts they produce. They keep the name of the group, the date, the place, and the gross revenue of each concert. They want to keep this data on a computer file and periodically compute the average take of each group and the average take at each place. Assume they handle 50 groups and produce concerts in 200 places. The total number of concerts given so far is 3500 and they give 500 a year.

1. Design a system to keep needed records.

2. Draw a system flowchart of your recommendation.

3. Develop pseudocode for a program to add concerts to this file.

4. Develop pseudocode for a program to compute the averages.

C. Describe in detail a good application of a tape-oriented sequential file system.

D. Describe an ineffective application of sequential file processing.

CHAPTER 6

Direct Access File Processing Systems

The direct access alternative: disk packs appear like city of the future

THE NATURE OF DIRECT ACCESS PROCESSING

The Need for Direct Access Processing

Possible Direct Access Systems at Alpine

Order Pricing Application

Online Systems

DATA AND HARDWARE FOR DIRECT ACCESS PROCESSING

Data Layout on Disks

Data Transfer Time on Disks

Processing Times for Alpine's Member Master File

Other Direct Access Hardware

DIRECT ACCESS DATA ORGANIZATION

Random File Organization

Indexed Sequential File Organization

PROGRAMS FOR DIRECT ACCESS PROCESSING

Types of Programs

Alpine Member Master File Update

A Direct Access Program for Alpine's Member Master File

PROCEDURES FOR DIRECT ACCESS PROCESSING

Users Procedures for Normal Operation

The Need for Procedures

Error Correction Procedures

Control Procedures

Operators Procedures for Normal Operation

Backup Procedures

Users Procedures during Systems Failure/Recovery

Operators Procedures during Systems

Failure/Recovery

PERSONNEL FOR DIRECT ACCESS PROCESSING

User Training
Operator Training

When John Abrams summarized business computer system alternatives for the Alpine Co-op project team, he described two basic types of file processing systems. Sequential systems were presented in the previous chapter. Direct access systems are discussed in this chapter.

As John indicated, the initial business computer systems for most companies are one of these two types. There are other, more complex types of business computer systems, but these are usually not developed until a company has some experience with business data processing. Consequently, John did not recommend them to Alpine, and we will not consider them until Part 3 of this book.

The distinguishing characteristic of a direct access system is that records can be accessed (read or written) from a file in any order. In contrast to sequential processing, there is no need to read all preceding records to get to a particular record. Further, there is no need to rewrite all of the file when a record is changed, inserted, or deleted.

THE NATURE OF DIRECT ACCESS PROCESSING

We compared sequential systems to a stereo tape recorder. In a loose way, we can compare a direct access system to a stereo record player. You can play the third song without having to play the first or second. However, direct access computer systems can write records, whereas you cannot record music with your record player. Before considering how these systems operate, let's examine the need for such a capability.

Suppose you want to withdraw money from your bank account using a cash machine on a local street corner. You insert your card and then key in how much money you want to withdraw. If the bank keeps the balance of your account on a sequential file, you will have to wait while the file is searched to find your account. If there are a large number of depositors at your bank, this may take five minutes or more. Clearly you are going to become impatient. Perhaps you will find another bank to keep your money. The bank needs to be able to access your account balance directly—without sequentially searching through the depositors' records until yours is found.

The Need for Direct Access Processing

Suppose you decide to buy a new stereo. You want to pay for it using your Mastercharge or Visa or other similar bankcard. Since this is an expensive purchase, the salesperson must call for a credit authorization before he or she can sell you the stereo. If the bankcard processing center keeps all of its credit information on a sequential file, you and the salesperson will have to wait for the credit file to be searched. All of the records preceding yours in the file must be read. This search could take several minutes or more. To provide better service, the bankcard processing center needs direct access to accounts.

Suppose you call a parts distributor for an auto part or similar product. You want to know if they have the part in stock before you drive across town. If the distributor keeps the inventory records on a sequential file, and if there are many records in this file, you may have to wait some time for the inventory file to be sequentially searched. Again, the distributor needs direct access to the inventory file records.

In general, a direct access capability is called for when the batching and sorting of transaction records are infeasible. The bank cannot ask you to find 50 other people who want to withdraw money, and then require all of you to line up in ascending order according to your account numbers to obtain money (figure 6-1). The bank must be able to take the transactions (withdrawal requests) one at a time and in random order.

Figure 6-1. Here's What Could Happen without Direct Access Capability

Since a direct access system can process transactions in any order, it can always substitute for a sequential system. If transactions happen to arrive in batches in presorted order, it won't matter to the direct access system. The system will process them as if they were random. Since this is true, you may wonder why businesses use sequential systems at all. Why not use direct access systems for all applications? The answer is cost. Direct access systems cost more to design, to implement, and to operate than sequential systems do. Therefore, they are only used when the benefit is worth the cost.

Possible Direct Access Systems at Alpine

When John Abrams discussed direct access systems at Alpine, he described two possible applications. Figure 6-2 shows a flowchart for a direct access member master file system. Requests for changes to the member master file are submitted to the data entry clerks stationed at CRTs. These clerks input the changes to the member master file program via the CRTs. Each change is made immediately to the member master file. Note the symbol ▯. This symbol refers to direct access devices that we shall discuss in the next section. These devices

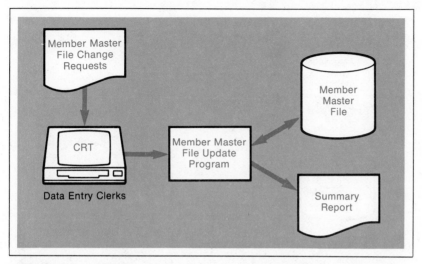

Figure 6-2 Direct Access Member Master File Maintenance

serve the same storage function as tape drives, but they have direct access capability.

The advantage of this system over a sequential system is that the clerks have immediate access to member records. If they need to know what the contents of a record are, they can bring the record up on the CRT screen and examine it. Also, changes can be made immediately. The clerks do not need to wait for keypunch operators to prepare punched cards and for a batch of the cards to be processed by the computer system.

Does Alpine need a direct access capability for this application? This is a good question. It will be hard for Alpine to answer. As John explained in his presentation, either a tape or a direct access system is feasible. The direct access system will allow immediate access to the member data, but it will also cost more to develop and operate. Alpine will have to decide whether the benefits are worth the costs. In the next chapter we will see what Alpine decided to do.

Order Pricing Application The second example John described concerned the pricing of orders. In this example, items are picked and packed, and then moved to a shipping area. Here, a clerk extracts a copy of the picking slip from each order and sends it to keypunch. The keypunch personnel prepare a sequence of cards like those used for the class scheduling system. There is a header card for each order, followed by cards giving the item number and quantity to be shipped for each item on the order.

These cards are read by the order pricing system shown in figure 6-3. For each order, the order pricing program obtains the price of each item, multiplies the price by the quantity of the item shipped (a

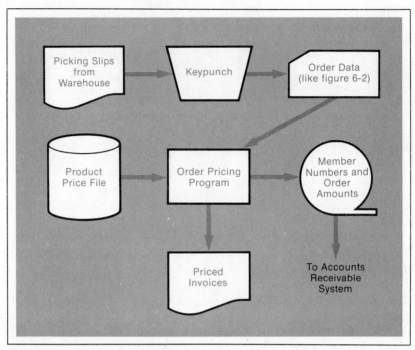

Figure 6-3 Order Pricing System

process called *price extension*), and computes the total cost of the order. The outputs are priced invoices that go with the orders and a magnetic tape file of member numbers and order amounts. This file is input to the accounts receivable business computer system (not shown).

To be able to price each order separately, the prices must be on a direct access file. If not, then the entire price file would have to be sequentially searched for each order. Extensive searching would be required just to find the prices of a few items on each order. This would be a very time-consuming process. Instead, the program shown in figure 6-3 reads the item number for each item on the order and uses this number to obtain the price of the item directly from the product price file. Then the price extension is done, and so forth.

Online Systems

Although the systems shown in figures 6-1 and 6-3 are both direct access systems, they have an important difference. In the system in figure 6-1, the clerks can communicate directly with the computer via CRTs. In the system in figure 6-3, there is no such direct communication. Inputs are made via punched cards.

A system in which the user is in direct communication with the computer is called an *online system*. This term means that the user is on line or has a communication link with the computer. The master file maintenance system in figure 6-1 is an online system. The user of the pricing system in figure 6-3 has no direct communication with the computer and so it is an *offline system*.

Online systems can be very complex and the technology involved is complicated. Consequently, we will defer discussing online processing until Chapter 8. For now, you should simply realize that direct access systems can be either online or offline systems. In fact, most direct access systems are online, but not all of them are. Do not make the mistake of assuming that direct access systems are *always* online systems.

Given this introduction, we will now consider each of the five components of a direct access business computer system. As in Chapter 5, first hardware and data will be considered; then programs, procedures, and personnel.

6.1 How does direct access processing differ from sequential file processing?

6.2 Is a credit card processing company for Mastercharge or Visa apt to keep credit information on a direct access file or a sequential file? Why?

6.3 Since a direct access system can always substitute for a sequential system, why have sequential systems at all?

6.4 Why is the Alpine member master file system shown in figure 6-1 called an *online system*?

6.5 Are all direct access systems online systems?

QUESTIONS

The most common type of direct access device is a *disk storage unit* (figure 6-4). It has two basic components. A *disk pack* is a collection of disks with recording surfaces. It looks much like a stack of phonograph records mounted on a spindle. (See figure 6-5.) The disk pack is mounted on the disk storage unit. It revolves at high speeds. (50 to 75 revolutions per *second* is typical.)

The surfaces of the disks are coated with an easily magnetized substance. Data is recorded on each disk in concentric circles as shown in figure 6-6. These circles are called *tracks*. Our comparison with a phonograph record is not perfect; the tracks on a disk surface are not continuous like the groove in a phonograph record is.

Figure 6-7 presents a schematic of a disk storage unit and its associated read/write heads. These heads are used to read data from or write data to the tracks. In most disk units, the heads are attached to access arms that move together to position the heads at any track on

DATA AND HARDWARE FOR DIRECT ACCESS PROCESSING

Figure 6-4 Disk Storage Unit

Figure 6-5 Disk Pack

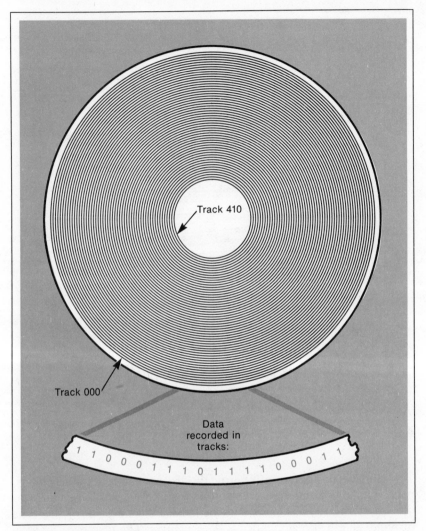

Figure 6-6 Disk Surface

the surfaces of the disks. Suppose a disk pack has 10 recording surfaces. When the access arms are fixed in a position, 10 tracks can be read—one on each surface. When the arms are moved to another position, another 10 tracks can be read. The collection of tracks that can be read when the access arms are stationed in a position is called a *cylinder.*

Not all disk storage units have movable read/write heads. Some units such as the IBM 2305 have fixed heads. Fixed-head units have one read/write head per cylinder. Consequently, they are more expensive than movable-head units. They may be faster, however, because no time is spent moving the read/write heads to the correct cylinder.

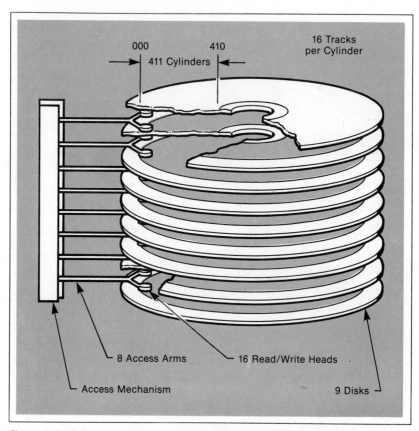

Figure 6-7   Schematic of Disk Storage Unit and Its Read/Write Heads

Some disk storage units permit the disk pack to be removed. Thus, packs containing different files can be mounted in the same unit. For other systems, the disk pack must be fixed. Figure 6-8 shows one type of removable disk pack called a *data module*. The disk pack and the access arm and heads are encased in a plastic housing and the entire package is removed. Data modules are more expensive than the disk packs shown in figure 6-4, but they have higher reliability and can store more data. Some data modules are so well protected that they require no preventive maintenance. Figure 6-9 summarizes the types of disk storage units.

You may be surprised to learn that the same amount of data is recorded on a small inner track as is recorded on a large outer track. The data is just recorded more densely on the inner track than on the outer one, thus keeping the data transfer rate constant. Since it takes the same amount of time for an inner track to make one revolution as it takes for an outer track, the same amount of data must be recorded.

Figure 6-8 Data Module

Otherwise, data would have to be transferred faster from the large tracks than from the small ones.

Figure 6-10 shows a general layout of data on a disk track. Each track has a starting point that is permanently marked on the track, then a track header, and then blocks of data. The track header bears the name of the track and other system data. As with tape, the application data is recorded in blocks that are collections of one or more logical records. (A block can include several Alpine member master file records, for example.) However, with disks, each block is preceded by a block header that identifies the block, gives its length, and may indicate the contents of the block. Each computer system has its own layout peculiarities, but the general structure is similar to that shown in figure 6-10.

Data Layout on Disks

Figure 6-9 Summary of Disk Characteristics

Types of Disk Storage Units	*Characteristics*
Fixed or Movable Heads	Fixed heads have one head per track. Variable heads have movable access arms.
Fixed or Removable Packs	Fixed packs stay in the unit. Removable packs can be interchanged. (Packs with disk and access arms removed are called *data modules*.)

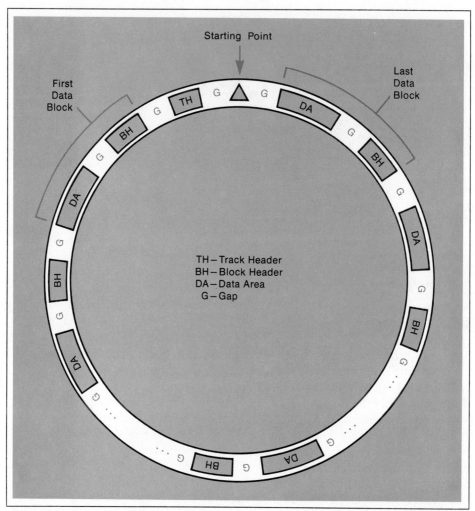

Figure 6-10 Layout of Data on a Disk Track

The capacity of a disk pack depends on the type of unit and its manufacturer. Capacities vary from several million characters to 350 million or more. As examples, the Hewlett-Packard 7920 disk storage unit has 815 cylinders per pack; each cylinder has 5 tracks; and each track can contain up to 12,000 characters or bytes. The total capacity is just over 50 million bytes. The IBM 3350 disk storage unit has 555 cylinders per pack; each cylinder has 30 tracks, and each track can contain up to 19,000 bytes. Total capacity for the IBM 3350 is 317.5 million bytes.

Not all of the stated capacity of a disk pack can be used for application data. Some of the space will be used for system data like addresses, block lengths, and so forth. Some will be used for interblock gaps. Depending on block sizes and other factors, somewhere between

75 and 95 percent of the available space can be used for application data.

Recall from Chapter 5 that the Alpine member master file has 200,000 records, each 120 bytes in length. This is a total of 24 million bytes. The file would easily fit on either of the two devices just discussed. It would fit on many other devices from other manufacturers as well.

The time required to transfer data to or from a disk has three major components. *Access motion time* is the time required to position the read/write heads over the correct cylinder. The amount of time depends on how far the access mechanism must move. On average, the HP 7920 and the IBM 3350 both take 25 milliseconds to move from one cylinder to another.

Data Transfer Time on Disks

The second component of time is *rotational delay*, or the time it takes for the required data to revolve under the read/write head. At best, this value is zero (when the head is over the required data); at worst, it is the time required for one complete revolution of the disk surface. The average of these time periods is often used for timing purposes. For the HP 7920, this time is 8.3 milliseconds, and for the IBM 3350, it is 8.4 milliseconds.

The final component of transfer time is the *data movement time*. This is the time taken to move data from the disk to main memory (for a read) or from main memory to the disk (for a write). The HP 7920 takes 0.00106 millisecond per byte; the IBM 3350 takes 0.00083 millisecond per byte. These specifications are summarized in figure 6-11.

From the above transfer time figures we can estimate how long it will take to read or write all of the Alpine member master file data. First, let's assume the data is read sequentially and then assume it is read in completely random order.

Processing Times for Alpine's Member Master File

Alpine has 200,000 120-byte records in the master file. Let's assume eight records are blocked together. Therefore, there are 25,000 blocks of data. Considering the HP 7920, we can assume that 12 of

Figure 6-11 Typical Time Requirements for Disk Units

Device Type	Average Access Motion Time	Rotational Delay Time	Data Transfer Time
HP 7290	25 msec	8.3 msec	0.00106 msec per byte
IBM 3350	25 msec	8.4 msec	0.00083 msec per byte

these blocks will fit on each track. Consequently, 25,000 divided by 12, or 2084 tracks will be required. Since there are 5 tracks per cylinder on the HP 7920, a total of 417 cylinders will be required to hold the data.

Now, consider each of the components of transfer time. For access motion time, it will take an average of 25 milliseconds to find each cylinder. Therefore, 417×0.025 or 10.42 seconds will be required for access motion. For rotational delay, it will take an average of 8.3 milliseconds to find each block, so $25,000 \times 0.0083$ or 207.5 seconds will be required. Finally, a total of 24 million bytes of data must be transferred. Thus, 24 million $\times 0.00106$ milliseconds or 25.44 seconds will be required to transfer the data. Consequently, the total time to read or write the Alpine member master file is 243.4 seconds, or about four minutes.

The time required to read or write the data for the IBM 3350 is not vastly different and will be left as an exercise.

How long will it take to read this data completely randomly? Assuming the worst, the unit will read one block of data for each master record. Further, the block will, in the worst case, be located on a different cylinder than the previous block was. Therefore, the access mechanism will have to be moved to read each record. On average, this will take 25 milliseconds for the HP 7920. Also, the unit will have to wait for the correct block to come under the read/write head for each record read. This will take 8.3 milliseconds. Thus, 33.3 milliseconds will be required just to find each record.

Once found, the entire block (not just the record wanted) must be read. This is because the unit is designed to read only whole blocks (not parts of them). There are 960 bytes per block, so, at 0.00106 millisecond per byte, a total of 1.02 milliseconds will be required to read the entire block. In total, then, 34.32 milliseconds will be required to read each record. Since there are 200,000 records in the file, a total of about 6864 seconds, or about two hours, will be required to read the file in random order.

Comparing this to the answer we obtained for sequentially reading the file, we see one of the reasons why direct access processing is more expensive than sequential processing. To read a record randomly, 34.32 milliseconds are needed. To read the same record in sequential order, only about 1.2 milliseconds are required.

Why is there such a big difference in the times required to read the file? There are two reasons. First, for direct access processing the access arms must move back and forth across the disk pack, which takes about 5000 extra seconds. Second, for sequential processing, when a block is read, all eight records in the block are processed. For direct access processing, when a block is read, only one of the contained records is needed; therefore each block is read eight times instead of just once. This fact accounts for the balance of the extra time.

In addition to disk storage units, three other types of direct access media are in common use. One is called a *floppy disk*, or sometimes just *floppy*. This media is similar to a conventional or *hard* disk storage unit, but there is always only one disk (like a phonograph record) instead of a stack of disks. Further, this disk is flexible, hence the term *floppy*.

Other Direct Access Hardware

The arrangement of data on a floppy is very similar to that on the disks previously described. One difference is that floppies, because of their design, contain less data. A typical floppy has two surfaces with 70 tracks per surface and 7680 bytes per track. The total capacity is just over one million bytes. Also, the times for access motion, rotational delay, and data transfer are considerably longer for floppies. Figure 6-12 shows a floppy disk.

Another type of common direct access media is called a *drum*. A drum is a cylinder that can have data recorded on its outer surface. The tracks on a drum are circles around this surface, as shown in figure 6-13. Each track has its own read/write head, so there is no access motion and hence no delay for moving the access arms. Drums were more prevalent in the past than they are today. Newer, faster, greater capacity disks have replaced many of them.

A final type of direct access device is actually a hybrid, or a combination of tape and disk technology. Figure 6-14 shows a *mass storage device*. Data is stored on small rolls of magnetic tape and then moved

Figure 6-12 Floppy Disk

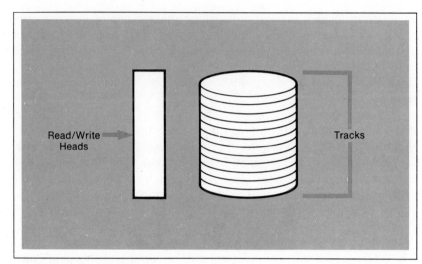

Figure 6-13 Drum Schematic

Figure 6-14 IBM 3850 Mass Storage Subsystem

or staged to direct access devices when needed. After the data is processed, it is moved from disk back to the small rolls of tape. The capacity of this unit and similar units manufactured by other companies is typically in the range of 400 billion bytes. Thus, they provide very large capacity, direct access capability.

The cost per byte of stored data is less for a mass storage unit than for the several pure direct access devices required to yield the same capacity. The disadvantage is that the data must be staged from tape to disk and back. This staging, however, is automatic; it requires no human intervention. These units, by the way, are amazing to watch. If you have the opportunity to see one, don't pass it up.

		QUESTIONS

6.6   Define the terms *disk storage unit, disk pack, disk, track,* and *cylinder.*

6.7   The XYZ 2000 disk pack has 10 surfaces, 200 tracks per surface, and 10,000 bytes per track. What is the total capacity of the XYZ disk pack?

6.8   What is the difference between a record and a block?

6.9   What is access motion time? Rotational delay? Data movement time?

6.10   Average access motion time for the XYZ 2000 is 50 milliseconds to move from one cylinder to the next. What is the access time to read a file of five cylinders sequentially?

6.11   Rotational delay for the XYZ 2000 is 10 milliseconds. What will be the total rotational delay to read 500 records?

6.12   The XYZ 2000 transfers data at the rate of 0.001 millisecond per byte. How long will it take to read 500 records if they are 200 bytes long?

6.13   What is the total time for the XYZ 2000 to sequentially read a file of 500 records, 200 bytes long, that occupies five cylinders? The records are not blocked.

6.14   Why does it take so much longer to process a file randomly than it does to process it sequentially?

6.15   What is a floppy?

DIRECT ACCESS DATA ORGANIZATION

To do direct access processing, each record in the file must have an identifier or *key*. The key is usually one of the fields of the record. For example, the member number could be the key for Alpine's member master file. A part number could be the key for a file of parts in inventory. Usually, keys are required to be unique; only one record in the file is allowed to have a given key value. Consequently, names are seldom chosen as keys.

Now, the fundamental problem for direct access processing is to relate a particular key value to the location of the record on a direct access device. There are two primary techniques or file organizations to do this. One is called *random*, or *direct*, *file organization* and the other is called *indexed sequential file organization*.

Unfortunately, the terminology as used in industry is confusing in this area. To review, there are two types of file processing: sequential and direct access. Under the category of direct access file processing, there are two file organizations: random or direct and indexed sequential. Thus, the term *direct* is used in two ways, as the name of a type of file processing and as the name of a type of direct access file organization. To make matters worse, the term *random* is used in the same two ways.

In this book, we will use the term *direct* only to refer to a type of file *processing* (in contrast to sequential file processing) and the term *random* only to refer to a type of file *organization* (in contrast to indexed sequential file organization). This is awkward, but it can't be helped. Industry uses the terms this way and you should be aware of its terminology.

Random File Organization

There are a variety of ways to allocate records to a random file organization. We will describe one common technique sometimes called a *hashing algorithm*. Basically, the value of the key is arithmetically manipulated to determine the record's location on the file.

For example, suppose Alpine has an inventory file of less than 1000 items. One way of determining record locations would be to take the last three digits of the part number as the address of the record. Thus, part number 12345 would be assigned record location 345 on the file. Part number 14592 would be at location 592.

As you can see, there is a problem if two different parts have the same three last digits. Both part 12345 and part 32345 are assigned location 345. One way to solve this problem is to put one of these records in location 345 and to put the other in the next available location. Thus, the calculated address is the place to start looking for the record. Other ways are used but are not important for your understanding of business computer systems (at least in this course). This addressing scheme is summarized in figure 6-15.

When this file is first created, the direct access device is formatted with 1000 empty records. These records can be thought of as empty buckets or place holders. Then the file is loaded with the inventory data by assigning the records to file locations according to their last three digits.

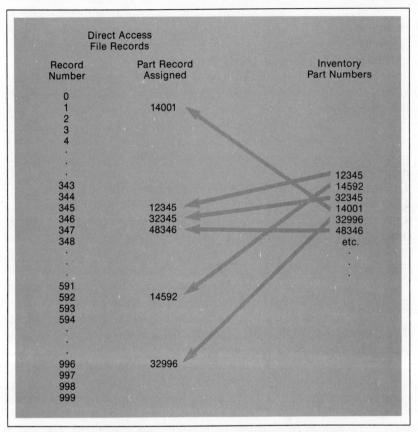

Figure 6-15 Allocating Records to Random File Using Last Three Digits

Can you see the problem that could occur if the file were completely full? Suppose that when the 1000th record is loaded, the only remaining empty record is record 999. Further, suppose the part number of the last item is 12000. Its assigned location is zero, but the next available location is 999! For this reason, randomly organized files should be only 60 to 70 percent full. Even at that, similar problems can occur.

Now, how does the system find a record? Given part number 12345, it will first find the record at location 345. If record 12345 is in location 345, the system will stop because the desired record has been found. If not, it will read the next record and so on until record 12345 is found. To modify a record, the system will first read it into main memory as just described, then modify the record contents, and then write it back out to the location in which it was found. To delete a record, the system will first find it, and then replace it with an empty record, or indicate that the record is deleted by putting a special mark on it (a question mark in the first position, for example).

This discussion has assumed that the records are unblocked. If there are several inventory records per physical block, then the algorithm for computing addresses must be a little more sophisticated. Otherwise, the process is nearly the same.

Random file organization is the fastest direct access file organization. Unfortunately, it suffers from several disadvantages. First, the records are allocated to the file in a haphazard fashion. If the records are read in the order in which they are stored on the direct access device, they are not in any logical sequence. Second, it is hard to expand a randomly organized file. If Alpine wants to have 2000 items in inventory, the file and some of the programs must be altered. Finally, as mentioned, randomly organized files should never be full. Consequently, 20 or 30 percent of the file space is wasted. However, in spite of this, if the application calls for very fast retrieval, random organization can be effective.

Indexed Sequential File Organization

The second type of direct access file organization is called *indexed sequential*. This organization allows both sequential and direct access processing by storing the records in sequential order of the key. Indexes (similar to the index of a book) are constructed for direct processing. Thus, to do sequential processing, the records are processed in physical order of the file. To do direct processing, the indexes are used to locate a desired record and it is then read from the file.

Since records are to be kept in sequential order of the key, inserts pose a problem. Rather than rewrite the entire file as is done with sequential processing, indexed sequential organization puts the new records in their correct places on a track, and moves the last record on the track to a special place called an *overflow area*. Thus, in figure 6-16, when record 12 was inserted, record 20 was moved to the overflow area; when record 14 was inserted, record 15 was also moved into the overflow area.

When the file in figure 6-16b is processed sequentially, the system will read records 5, 10, 12, and 14 from track 1. It will then find records 15 and 20 in the overflow area. Then it will process the records on track 2. Thus, all of the records will be retrieved in the correct sequential order.

Indexed sequential organization is an excellent compromise between straight sequential and pure random file organizations. It is most useful in applications that call for both sequential and direct processing. A good example is credit card authorizations. At the end of the month, the credit file is processed sequentially to produce the customer bills. However, throughout the month, it is processed directly when doing credit authorizations.

Unfortunately, like all compromises, indexed sequential organization has disadvantages. Sequential processing is faster for a sequen-

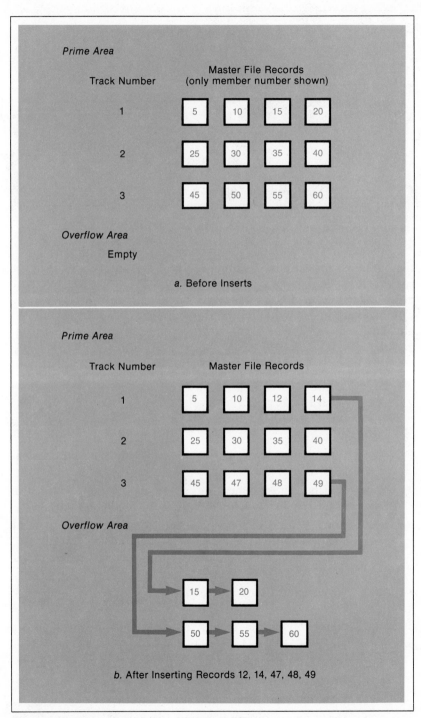

Figure 6-16 Inserts in an Indexed Sequential File

File Organization	Advantages/Disadvantages
Sequential	Is simple to use. Is fast and efficient for large batches. Cannot update in middle of file.
Indexed Sequential	Can update in middle of file. Both sequential and direct processing are possible. Processing may be slow.
Random	Can update in middle of file. Processing is very fast. Has wasted file space.

Figure 6-17 Comparison of File Organizations

tial file than for an indexed sequential file. Direct processing is faster for a random file than for an indexed sequential file. Also, the overflow areas take up extra file space. Finally, after many inserts, record retrieval becomes slow. Figure 6-17 summarizes advantages and disadvantages of sequential, random, and indexed sequential file organizations.

QUESTIONS

6.16 What is a key?

6.17 What are the two possible meanings for the term *direct processing*?

6.18 What are the two possible meanings for the term *random processing*?

6.19 Which of the two meanings of direct processing will we use in this book? Which will we use for random processing?

6.20 For the random file organization in figure 6-15, to what location will part number 45897 be assigned? Where will part number 22345 be assigned? Where will part number 22345 actually be stored?

6.21 Why should a randomly organized file never be completely full?

6.22 Name three disadvantages of random file organization.

6.23 Does an indexed sequential file allow direct access or sequential processing?

6.24 How are inserts made to an indexed sequential file?

6.25 Describe a good application for random file organization.

6.26 Describe a good application for indexed sequential file organization.

Before you can get a clear picture of how direct access programs operate, we need to define three programming terms. So far in this book we have discussed programs as one homogeneous category. There are actually three categories of computer programs.

Application programs direct the computer to solve specific business problems. The Alpine master file update program is one example of an application program. Application programs do not usually come with the computer; the using organization has to develop them or buy them from some program vendor.

    System support programs are the second type. The sort utility described in Chapter 5 is one example of a system support program. Other examples are the language translators or compilers. If you have written programs, you have used the COBOL, BASIC, or some other language compiler. System support programs usually come with the computer. They are written and tested by the computer manufacturer. Data processing personnel simply have to learn how to use them.

    The third category of programs is referred to as the *operating system*. These programs manage the computer's resources. They start and stop application programs; allocate tape, disk, and other types of equipment; and manage the computer's memories. Also (and this is the reason for introducing the topic here), the operating system programs provide *data management services*. In most instances, operating systems are provided by the computer manufacturer.

    When an application programmer wants to read or write a record, he or she simply codes a command like READ MEMBER-FILE or WRITE INVENTORY-RECORD. The application programmer does not need to be concerned with blocking or deblocking the record or with filling and emptying buffers, and so forth. Instead, all these activities are performed by the data management portion of the operating system.

    When the command READ MEMBER-FILE is translated by the compiler, computer instructions are inserted into the application program. These instructions ask the operating system to control the input/output (I/O). It does this by executing a very complex set of instructions that cause the data to be read or written.

    Because of this operating system service, the job of the application programmer is greatly simplified. He or she need not be concerned with the details of how to do input and output. The programmer can spend more time solving application problems instead of computer system problems.

    Figure 6-18 illustrates the read process. The application program issues requests to read data, one record at a time. Each request goes to an operating system program where it is executed. A block of data is brought in from the file, deblocked, and sent to the application program.

PROGRAMS FOR DIRECT ACCESS PROCESSING

Types of Programs

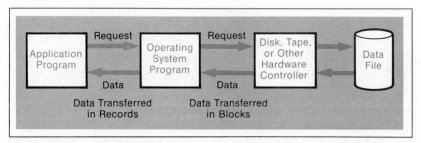

Figure 6-18   Application and Operating System Program Roles in File Read Records

**Alpine Member
Master File Update**

To illustrate a direct access application program, consider the Alpine member master file update program shown in figure 6-1. Again, a clerk at a CRT inputs requests to the update program. The program then accesses the direct access member master file. For this example, we assume that this file has indexed sequential organization and that the key is the member number.

Four basic actions can be taken in maintaining a master file. Records can be inserted, deleted, modified, and read. Corresponding to each of these actions is a command that the application programmer may use. Thus, when he or she codes the INSERT command, the operating system will cause a new record to be added to the file. Now, since this is a direct access application, the operating system needs to know what to call the new record, or put another way, what the key of the new record will be. Usually this is done by a command like INSERT 123456 INTO MEMBER MASTER FILE. This means insert a new record whose key is 123456 into the member master file. The data for the new record will also be supplied by the application program, but the way that this is done depends on the language used. (Ask your instructor to explain how it is done in the language you use.)

Examples of other indexed sequential commands are DELETE 123456 FROM MEMBER MASTER FILE, REPLACE 123456 IN MASTER FILE, and READ 123456 FROM MEMBER MASTER FILE.

Recall that the commands for processing a sequential file included only an operation (like READ) and the name of a file. The identity or key of the record was not needed. The next record in sequential order was assumed to be the one to be processed.

**A Direct Access
Program for Alpine's
Member Master File**

Figure 6-19 shows the pseudocode for the member master file update program. This pseudocode references three files. MEMBER MASTER FILE is the indexed sequential file having the member data. SUMMARY REPORT is a printed report of the actions taken by the clerk at the CRT. This report documents changes that have been made for later reference if errors are discovered. The third file is called TERMI-NAL and corresponds to the CRT employed by the user.

At first, it may seem surprising to consider a user at a terminal as a file. However, since the user supplies data to the program, and since the program outputs data to the user, the CRT is like a storage file. Therefore, terminals are often processed as files in application programs.

The member master file update program has six procedures as shown in figure 6-19. This program obtains a request code from the user that indicates the activity to be performed. A 0 means stop, a 1 means insert, a 2 means delete, a 3 means modify, and a 4 means read a record. To start the process, MAIN-PROCEDURE opens the files. (This means the system will take whatever action is necessary to prepare to use the files.) Then it asks the user for the first request code. Next PROCESS-PROCEDURE is called. PROCESS-PROCEDURE will stay in control until the user types a request code of 0, at which time MAIN-PROCEDURE will regain control. It will close the files and stop.

Activity in PROCESS-PROCEDURE is controlled by a DO-WHILE statement. As long as the value of REQUEST-CODE is nonzero, PROCESS-PROCEDURE will be executed. The first statement in the DO loop is a new pseudocode statement: the *case statement*. It sends control to a location, depending on the value of RE-QUEST-CODE. (See the comment in figure 6-19.) If the value of REQUEST-CODE is 1, 2, 3, or 4, then one of the four processing modules will be called. However, if the value is greater than 4, an error message will be written.

What happens if the user accidentally types in a negative number? There is no telling. As this pseudocode stands, an error of some unknown form will occur. This is a defect that you will be asked to fix in question 6.31.

The four procedures called by PROCESS-PROCEDURE are similar. We will discuss only one of them. The first statement in the INSERT-PROCEDURE obtains the member number and data for the new member record. Then, it checks the validity of this number by attempting to read a record using it as a key. If the member number is a valid new number, this read should be unsuccessful. If the read is successful, the member number provided by the clerk is erroneous because it is already in use.

If the member number is valid, the program inserts the new master record. It writes messages to SUMMARY REPORT and to the user at the CRT terminal. Then, control is returned to PROCESS-PROCEDURE where the user is asked for the next REQUEST-CODE. If nonzero, another transaction is processed against the master file. Otherwise, the program terminates.

```
BEGIN MAIN-PROCEDURE
    OPEN MEMBER MASTER FILE, SUMMARY REPORT FILE, TERMINAL FILE
    INPUT REQUEST-CODE FROM TERMINAL
    DO PROCESS-PROCEDURE
    CLOSE MEMBER MASTER FILE, SUMMARY REPORT FILE, TERMINAL FILE
    STOP
END MAIN-PROCEDURE

BEGIN PROCESS-PROCEDURE
    DOWHILE REQUEST-CODE ≠ 0
        GO TO
            INSERT-SECTION
            DELETE-SECTION
            MODIFY-SECTION
            READ-SECTION
            ERROR-SECTION
                DEPENDING ON REQUEST-CODE
        INSERT-SECTION
            DO INSERT-PROCEDURE
            GO TO EXIT
        DELETE-SECTION
            DO DELETE-PROCEDURE
            GO TO EXIT
        MODIFY-SECTION
            DO MODIFY-PROCEDURE
            GO TO EXIT
        READ-SECTION
            DO READ-PROCEDURE
            GO TO EXIT
        ERROR-SECTION
            PRINT "ERROR. INVALID REQUEST CODE. TRY AGAIN." ON TERMINAL
            GO TO EXIT
        EXIT
            INPUT REQUEST-CODE FROM TERMINAL
    END-DO
END PROCESS-PROCEDURE
```

(This is called a *case statement*. If the value of REQUEST-CODE is 1, control will go to INSERT-SECTION. If 2, control will go to DELETE-SECTION. IF 3, to MODIFY-SECTION, etc. If 5 or greater, control will go to ERROR-SECTION.)

Figure 6-19   Pseudocode for Member Master File Update Program *(Part 1 of 3)*

```
BEGIN INSERT-PROCEDURE
    INPUT MEMBER-NUMBER AND OTHER DATA FROM TERMINAL
    READ RECORD MEMBER-NUMBER FROM MEMBER MASTER FILE
    /Check to see if this member number is already in use./
    IF RECORD ALREADY ON MEMBER MASTER FILE
        THEN PRINT MEMBER-NUMBER AND MESSAGE "THIS IS AN INVALID
                MEMBER-NUMBER. MEMBER ALREADY ON MASTER FILE." ON TERMINAL
        ELSE INSERT NEW RECORD ON MEMBER MASTER FILE
            PRINT "NEW MEMBER ADDED. MEMBER-NUMBER IS". MEMBER-NUMBER
                ON SUMMARY REPORT
            PRINT "INSERTION SUCCESSFUL." ON TERMINAL
    END-IF
END INSERT-PROCEDURE


BEGIN DELETE-PROCEDURE
    INPUT MEMBER-NUMBER TO BE DELETED FROM TERMINAL
    DELETE RECORD MEMBER-NUMBER FROM MEMBER MASTER FILE
    IF DELETION SUCCESSFUL
        THEN PRINT "MEMBER DELETED. MEMBER-NUMBER IS", MEMBER-NUMBER ON
                SUMMARY REPORT
            PRINT "DELETION SUCCESSFUL." ON TERMINAL
        ELSE PRINT MEMBER-NUMBER AND MESSAGE "THIS IS AN INVALID
                MEMBER-NUMBER. MEMBER NOT DELETED." ON TERMINAL
    END-IF
END DELETE-PROCEDURE
```

Figure 6-19   Pseudocode for Member Master File Update Program *(Part 2 of 3)*

If you compare this pseudocode to the pseudocode for making updates to the sequential file in figure 5-25, you will find the direct access pseudocode is simpler. It is simpler because there is no need to match records against one another as there is in sequential processing. In actuality, direct access processing is a good deal more complex than sequential processing. Most of the extra work, however, is taken care of by the operating system so the application programmer does not see it.

Since the member master file is an indexed sequential file, it could also be processed sequentially. This means that the pseudocode in figure 5-25 could be used to update the member master file with sales data. In fact, John Abrams recommended that the Alpine project team

```
BEGIN MODIFY-PROCEDURE
   INPUT MEMBER-NUMBER TO BE MODIFIED AND MODIFYING DATA FROM TERMINAL
   READ RECORD MEMBER-NUMBER FROM MEMBER MASTER FILE
   IF READ SUCCESSFUL
      THEN MAKE CHANGES TO RECORD JUST READ
           REPLACE RECORD MEMBER-NUMBER ON MEMBER MASTER FILE
           PRINT "RECORD MODIFIED. MEMBER-NUMBER IS", MEMBER-NUMBER ON
              SUMMARY REPORT
           PRINT "MODIFICATION SUCCESSFUL." ON TERMINAL
      ELSE PRINT MEMBER-NUMBER AND MESSAGE "THIS IS AN INVALID
              MEMBER-NUMBER. MEMBER NOT MODIFIED." ON TERMINAL
   END-IF
END MODIFY-PROCEDURE


BEGIN READ-PROCEDURE
   INPUT MEMBER-NUMBER TO BE READ FROM TERMINAL
   READ RECORD MEMBER-NUMBER FROM MEMBER MASTER FILE
   IF READ SUCCESSFUL
      THEN PRINT "READ SUCCESSFUL. MEMBER DATA FOLLOWS.", MEMBER
              MASTER FILE DATA ON TERMINAL
      ELSE PRINT MEMBER-NUMBER AND MESSAGE "THIS IS AN INVALID
              MEMBER-NUMBER. MEMBER NOT FOUND." ON TERMINAL
   END-IF
END READ-PROCEDURE
```

Figure 6-19 Pseudocode for Member Master File Update Program *(Part 3 of 3)*

consider this as an alternative. He said Alpine could construct the member master file as an indexed sequential file, and use sequential processing to update the member records with sales data. They could use direct access processing to maintain current member data and add new members. Also, John said that at the end of the year, they could use sequential processing to generate the members' dividend checks. We will observe what Alpine decided in Chapter 7.

Random organization of direct access files places more burden on the application programmer than indexed sequential does. To explain it well, we would need to consider more detail than is probably necessary for your business career. Consequently, we will not present pseudocode for a randomly organized file. References 38 and 48 contain complete discussions if you are interested.* For now, it will be sufficient to remember that random organization exists, and that it is one of two major types of direct access file organization.

Direct access file organizations are not standardized across makes and models of computers. The syntax of commands as well as the details of the file organizations vary from one computer to another. The commands described in this section are generalized. They do not correspond to any particular manufacturer's language. Also, some operating systems provide a larger variety of direct access organizations. These organizations are variations and extensions of the two basic types described here. If you understand these two organizations and their capabilities and limitations, you should be able to understand other variations that you encounter.

QUESTIONS

6.27   What are the three categories of computer programs?

6.28   Which one of the three categories of programs requests I/O operations? Which actually processes the I/O requests?

6.29   When performing direct access I/O, the application program must specify an extra parameter. What is it?

6.30   Why consider a user at a terminal as a file?

6.31   How can the member master file pseudocode be changed to trap any negative REQUEST-CODE and print an error message?

6.32   Explain what the case statement means.

PROCEDURES FOR DIRECT ACCESS PROCESSING

 "Let's suppose," said John Abrams, "that Alpine had the member master file on an indexed sequential file, and that clerks made changes to this file directly using a member update program. Could a clerk accidentally delete the wrong member? Would this be hard to do? Also, could a clerk change his or her sales amounts and thereby get an extra large dividend at year end?"

These questions started a loud and active conversation during which the project team discovered an important fact: *Although direct access systems have great advantages and are easy to use, they are also very hard to control.* Errors are easily made and the data is vulnerable to unauthorized activity. As the discussion progressed, John explained how system procedures can be used to provide control over direct access systems. He described two categories of procedures: those

*All references are listed in the bibliography at the end of this book.

used for normal operations and those used when there is a system failure. We will consider the procedures for normal operation first.

Users Procedures for Normal Operation

Procedures need to be defined for each operation on the file. For example, there should be an insert procedure that describes the steps a clerk takes to add a new member. There should also be procedures for deletion, for modification, and even for read.

The insert procedure is summarized in figure 6-20. When the clerk receives a membership request document, he or she first verifies that the name, address, and phone number are on the request form. If not, the request is sent back to the requester for more data. If the needed data is present, the clerk then obtains a new member number from a prepared list of new numbers. When the number is taken, it must be checked off the list so that other clerks do not attempt to use the same number. (In many systems, the new number would be assigned by the computer program. Alpine elected not to do this because they wanted manual control over member numbers.)

Next, the order entry clerk uses the CRT to access the member update program to add the new member. If the program rejects the member number (see INSERT-PROCEDURE in figure 6-19), then the clerk records this problem in an error log and obtains another new number from the prepared list. Later, a supervisor will examine the error log to determine the cause of the error. If the program accepts the member number, then the member's record is added to the file. A membership card is prepared and sent to the new member.

Figure 6-20   Users Procedure for Inserting New Member on Master File

```
CHECK INPUT DATA FOR COMPLETENESS
IF NOT COMPLETE
    THEN RETURN DOCUMENT TO APPLICANT FOR MORE DATA
    ELSE OBTAIN NEW MEMBER-NUMBER FROM MASTER LIST
         CROSS OUT NUMBER ON LIST
         ACCESS MEMBER UPDATE PROGRAM USING CRT
         ATTEMPT TO ENTER NEW MEMBER
         IF SUCCESSFUL
             THEN PREPARE AND SEND MEMBERSHIP CARD TO NEW MEMBER
             ELSE POST PROBLEM ON ERROR LOG
                  TRY AGAIN WITH ANOTHER MEMBER-NUMBER
         END-IF
END-IF
```

Why is this procedure necessary? Without it, as John explained, clerks will input new members with incomplete data, or they won't know what to do if some data is missing. Each clerk will take a different action and the results will be unpredictable. Worst of all, some requests with insufficient data will not be inserted, nor will they be returned to the requester either. This leads to the situation in which someone submits a membership request but then never hears from Alpine again. Also, without the procedure, clerks won't know how to obtain new membership numbers, and chances are that some clerks will try to use numbers already used by another clerk. Finally, there will be no means for reporting errors and for correcting them when they occur.

The Need for Procedures   Think for a moment about the "computer errors" publicized in the news. Frequently, these are not errors of the computer at all, but errors in procedures or errors in following procedures. Suppose that Alpine implemented this system with poorly defined procedures and as a result two members were given the same member number. If that happened, one person could receive another person's order, and someone else could receive a bill for goods that he or she never received. These errors might incorrectly be blamed on the computer.

The problems that can be caused by incorrect modifications and deletions are even worse. If a clerk modifies the wrong member record, say by changing the address, then two errors are generated: the desired address change is not made, and another member's address becomes incorrect. Also, if the wrong record is deleted, a member will inexplicably disappear from the file, while a member that was to have been deleted stays on.

Because of these potential difficulties, modification and deletion procedures usually call for some type of verification before the action is taken. For example, the clerk may first read a member record and verify that the name on the file is the name that is on the change request form. If this is not so, the change is not made.

The verification step can be coded in the program. Thus, when the clerk requests the program to delete a member, the program will display a message like "THIS IS THE RECORD OF JOHN PARKS IN OMAHA, NEB. IS THIS THE RECORD YOU WISH TO DELETE?" If the clerk then types YES, the deletion is made. Otherwise, the deletion is not made, and the clerk must find the correct number or return the deletion request to get the correct data.

Error Correction Procedures   If the procedures are well designed, if they are documented, and if the clerks are trained in their use, many errors will be detected before the member master file is incorrectly modified. In spite of this, however, some erroneous changes will be made. When this occurs, procedures are needed to correct the errors.

For example, suppose a member writes Alpine complaining that his address has not been changed even though he requested a change several weeks previously. To determine the source of the error, a supervisor or other employee could check past records. He or she could examine past change request forms to find out whether Alpine had received the request. If so, the supervisor could find out whether it had been processed, and if so, when and by whom it was processed. Then the supervisor could examine the summary report for that date to determine what happened. If a change was made to the wrong record, the supervisor could initiate action to correct both of the records involved.

Observe that the supervisor cannot just correct the record for the member who complained. The other member's record would remain in error. Also, note the need for data about past processing. Both the old change request forms and the summary report were required in order to find the error. Error correction procedures need to be carefully designed ahead of time so that necessary data and training can be developed.

Control Procedures   A third type of procedure concerns controls. The data entry clerks can willfully make erroneous changes for their own gain or for the gain of their associates. The only certain control is to maintain accurate records of the transactions processed and to compare these with the source documents.

For example, periodically a supervisor should compare the activities recorded on the summary report with the member change request forms. Every change made to the master file should correspond to an authorized change request form. If there are changes made to the master file that do not have matching change request forms, the supervisor should investigate them to be certain they are authorized. This can be a long and exhausting process if there are many changes. In some cases, it suffices to check summary data. Thus, the summary report may print the total number of insertions, the total number of deletion documents, etc. If the counts do not agree, then a more detailed investigation can be conducted.

In summary, the normal-use procedures for the users of a direct access system have three primary purposes. First, they must specify how the users are to employ the system to obtain correct results. This procedure includes actions to be performed when special conditions occur. Second, the procedures must detail what actions are to be taken to correct errors when they are discovered. The procedures include steps for ensuring that all the data needed to correct an error are saved for a reasonable period of time. Finally, procedures are designed to provide checks and balances against unauthorized and possibly criminal

> *Users need procedures that explain:*
>
> 1. How to use the system to accomplish their job.
> 2. How to minimize errors.
> 3. How to correct errors.
> 4. How to ensure that only authorized activity occurs.

Figure 6-21   Users Procedures for Normal System Operation

activity. Procedures are especially important for direct access systems because the users have a much greater impact and work more independently than with other types of systems. (See figure 6-21.)

The computer system operators also need to follow system procedures. The operations staff needs to know how to start programs, what files to mount in the direct access equipment, and how to stop programs. Additionally, security procedures need to be defined so that computer operators know who has authorized access to the programs and data, and when.

Operators Procedures for Normal Operation

Unlike tape files, direct access files are not always dismounted. If the data resides on a disk pack that is not removable, or if a removable pack is left resident for some reason, then the data can be readily accessed. Whereas an operator is required to mount a tape volume, no action is required at all to access an available direct access file.

This practice is both an advantage and a disadvantage. It is less work for the operations staff; but on the other hand, it results in less control. The operators do not necessarily know what users and programs are accessing the data.

Several controls can be developed to counteract this disadvantage. First, users can be assigned *account numbers* and *passwords*. These are special numbers or codewords. If the user cannot provide the correct number or codeword, then the computer will not allow access to certain programs. Users in the shipping department will be restricted from the programs in the membership department if they do not know the membership account numbers and passwords. Further, files themselves can have passwords. A user may have to specify both a password to use a program and a password to access a critical file. Additionally, passwords can be restricted as to function. One password may permit read only access. Another may allow both reading and inserting. A third may allow reading, inserting, deleting, and modifying.

The operations staff may be involved in setting up passwords. If so, they need procedures. Further, they need to know the importance of passwords and not circumvent them for the users' convenience.

Another procedural responsibility of operations is to run computer jobs only in accordance with established schedules. These schedules are set up to ensure that all the computer workload can be accomplished in a timely manner, and also as a control measure. Since the user of a direct access system can have nearly unlimited ability to modify the contents of a file, such systems are often restricted for use only during normal business hours. The hope is that the activity will be adequately supervised during this time.

Thus, procedures need to be defined that describe what programs are to be run at what times. Also, the operations staff needs to have a procedure for making exceptions to the schedule. This procedure may merely be the name of someone to call to authorize the changes in schedule.

A final procedure for the operation of a direct access system is to periodically obtain *backup copies* of the direct access files. This need can be met by copying or dumping the direct access data to a tape file. Unlike sequential systems, new generations of master files are not created as a by-product of processing. Updates are made in place. When this is done, the old data is lost. If the file is damaged in some way, the data can only be restored from a backup copy.

Backup Procedures   Procedures need to be defined that tell the operations personnel when and how to back up the direct access files. Also, procedures should be defined for the operations supervisors to periodically check on backup activity to ensure that it is properly performed. This step is crucial. Many companies have learned through great agony and expense how important appropriate backup is for direct access systems.

The procedures for normal use for operations personnel are summarized in figure 6-22. We will now discuss procedures used when there is a failure in some part of the system.

Figure 6-22 Operators Procedures for Normal System Operation

Operators need procedures that explain:
1. How to start and stop programs.
2. Which files to mount on devices.
3. How to assign account numbers and passwords.
4. How to maintain integrity of the security program.
5. How to run jobs in accordance with the established schedule.
6. How to handle exceptions.
7. How to back up direct access files.

When there is a failure in a direct access system, both the users and the computer operators need procedures describing the action they should take. The users need to know what to do while the computer is out of operation. Later, they need to know what to do when the computer first becomes operational. If the system is on line and the users rely on it for the performance of their jobs, they need to know what to do while the system is down. For example, if bank tellers use an online direct access system to post deposits and withdrawals to banking accounts, the tellers need to know what to do when the system fails. Do they continue to accept deposits? If so, what data do they gather for entry to the system when it is again running? Can the tellers allow withdrawals? If so, how do they verify account balances? And so forth.

Users Procedures during Systems Failure/Recovery

The problem for Alpine is not as severe as it might be for a bank. If the member master file update program won't work, the data entry clerks can simply wait until the system is operational: they have no customers waiting in line. If Alpine uses direct access processing to price orders, failure might be more disruptive. The shipping area may fill up with orders that have been filled but not priced. The picking of new orders may have to be deferred until the shipping area is cleared. In this case, procedures have to be developed describing what to do until the system is again functioning.

Once the system is repaired, users need procedures describing their recovery activity. Usually, some work must be redone. The amount of rework depends on the severity of the error, the adequacy of the backup and recovery techniques, and luck. Users need procedures for determining how much work must be redone. For example, the users of the Alpine member update program could check to see if the last five changes they made to the file were recovered. If not, then the users might go back through 25 changes to see if they were recovered. Continuing in this way, the users could discover how much work needed to be redone. Sometimes the operations personnel can help; they may know that the files were recovered accurately as of 8:00 in the morning and that all subsequent changes must be redone.

Considering computer operations, recovery of a direct access system is a three-step process. First, the operators must have a procedure for determining the general source of the problem. It might be a direct access device malfunction, a CPU or memory failure, a program error, or whatever. Operations needs to know which of these sources of error are at fault so that they can notify the appropriate personnel.

Operators Procedures during Systems Failure/Recovery

This notification is the second step of recovery. Since operations personnel generally are not trained or experienced in fixing problems, they call in appropriate experts to make repairs. Consequently, they need a list of names and phone numbers for repair purposes, as well as special instructions for the large variety of errors that can occur.

Once the repairs are in progress, operations can begin preparing for the final step of recovery: recovering files and restarting programs. Whenever there is an unscheduled stop of a direct access computer system, there is always a chance that some data is lost. If the computer fails in the middle of an update, for example, part of the record can be changed and part not changed.

To recover from this failure, it is necessary to restore the file to its condition before the failure and to restart the programs where they were when interrupted. This is easy to say but difficult to do. The file can be restored from its most recent backup copy, but then all of the changes since the backup was made must be reapplied. The computer can take this action if all of the changes have been recorded. Otherwise, the users will have to repeat all of the activity since the backup copy was made.

Since these backup and recovery activities are so complex, operations personnel need detailed procedures to follow. Procedures for recovery from system failure are summarized in figure 6-23.

To review, direct access systems can be much easier to use than sequential systems. However, this ease of use means that errors can be more easily made and that unauthorized activity is harder to control or prevent. Further, direct access systems are considerably more difficult to back up and recover than are sequential systems. This difference is because updates are made in place and no backup files are generated as a by-product of processing, as they are with sequential systems.

These disadvantages can only be counteracted by people following well-designed and well-documented procedures. It is impossible to counteract these disadvantages with more hardware, a faster CPU, or other types of equipment. Thus, the careful design of procedures for both users and operations personnel is crucial to the successful implementation and use of direct access systems.

Figure 6-23 Procedures for Recovery from System Failure

Personnel	Procedures
Users	What to do while the computer system is inoperative
	What to do when the computer system first becomes operational
Operators	How to detect the general cause of the failure
	Whom to contact to have the problem fixed
	How to restore files and restart programs

The final component of a direct access business computer system is trained personnel. Again, there are two groups to be trained: users and operations personnel. Both groups need training in the use of equipment and in following established procedures.

PERSONNEL FOR DIRECT ACCESS PROCESSING

Users need to be trained in how to prepare inputs and how to use outputs. If the direct access system is off line, then this training is similar to that for sequential systems. If the system is on line, then users need to be trained in the use of CRTs or other devices.

User Training

Generally, users will be more comfortable if they are given some minimal introduction to computer processing during this training. Also, they need to be assured that they cannot ruin millions of dollars of computing equipment from their CRT. (They may, however, be able to ruin data files, so they should be trained in how *not* to do this.) After these preliminaries, users should be shown how to use the CRT.

When they have learned how to use the equipment, users need to be trained in the use of procedures. They should be given the documentation they will have on the job and then shown how to accomplish their job using the computer system and the documentation. Even the best procedures are worthless if users do not understand or believe in them. Therefore, users should be given procedure rationale. Some activities may seem silly or inconsequential when considered just from the user's viewpoint. Often, when this is the case, the users will stop following the established procedures. To prevent this situation, users should be given insight into the need for all procedures.

Training for operations personnel is similar. The operators need to be taught how to use the direct access equipment and how to perform any special maintenance or testing activity. They should be shown how to handle removable disk packs and the like so as to minimize the chance of damage. Finally, operations personnel need training in the established procedures. As indicated previously, backup and recovery is especially important for direct access processing, and operators should be trained and rehearsed in the backup and recovery procedures. Periodic inspections should be made to ensure that the procedures are known, remembered, and followed.

Operator Training

6.33 What are the two categories of procedures needed for direct access systems?

6.34 Describe three types of procedures for users of a direct access system.

6.35 What procedures do operators of an online system need?

QUESTIONS

6.36   What user procedures are needed when a direct access system fails?

6.37   What operations procedures are needed when a direct access system fails?

6.38   Describe training needed by users of direct access systems.

6.39   Describe training needed by operators of direct access systems.

SUMMARY

This chapter has presented an introduction to direct access file processing systems. We began with a discussion of the need for direct access processing. In those situations in which sorting and batching are infeasible, direct access capability is required. We then described the characteristics of each of the five components of a direct access business computer system. Direct access hardware includes disks, floppy disks, drums, and mass storage equipment. Direct access data can be organized in either of two basic forms. Indexed sequential file organization permits both direct access and sequential processing. Random file organization can be very fast, but it permits only direct access processing.

We described the pseudocode for a direct access program to maintain the Alpine member master file. The program itself is actually simpler than a sequential program because many functions are taken care of by the operating system. After this, we described procedures for direct access processing. The importance of these procedures cannot be overemphasized. Direct access systems are easy to use; this means errors can easily be made. The only effective controls over these errors are well-designed and well-implemented procedures. Finally, we briefly summarized the training requirements for direct access system users and operations personnel.

This chapter concludes the discussion of the fundamental types of business computer systems. In the next chapter we will return to the Alpine Co-op case to see what decisions they made and why.

WORD LIST

(in order of appearance in text)

Direct access

Flowchart symbol for direct access devices

Price extension

Online system

Offline system

Disk storage unit

Disk pack

Disk surface

Track

Cylinder

Movable read/write head disk storage device

Fixed-head disk storage device

Data module

Access motion time

Rotational delay

Data movement time

Floppy disk

Drum

Mass storage device

Key

Sequential file processing

Direct access file processing

Random file organization

Indexed sequential file organization

Hashing algorithm

Overflow area

Application programs

System support programs

Operating system programs

Data management services

Case statement

Users procedures for normal operations

Operators procedures for normal operations

Account numbers

Passwords

File backup copies

Users procedures for failure/recovery

Operators procedures for failure/recovery

A. Estimate the amount of time required for an IBM 3350 to read the Alpine member master file both sequentially and randomly. Use the same file data as used for the HP 7290 estimates. The IBM 3350 performance characteristics are summarized in figure 6-11.

B. Although random and indexed sequential file organizations are standard, many computer systems have special varieties of these. Find out what variations your computer has and compare them to random and indexed sequential as described in this chapter.

C. Find out if your college or university has business computer systems using direct access technology. If so, investigate the five components of the direct access system. In particular, determine whether or not you believe that the procedures in use are sufficient. Are they well documented?

QUESTIONS TO CHALLENGE YOUR THINKING

CHAPTER 7

Developing Business Computer Systems II

Alpine's master file system keeps records of purchases

REVIEW OF SYSTEMS DEVELOPMENT STEPS

ALTERNATIVE SPECIFICATION

Hardware

Microcomputers
Minicomputers
Mainframes

Alpine Looks for a Mini

Using a Request for Proposal

Programs

Sources of Programs

Data and Procedures

Personnel

Alpine's Organizational Alternatives

The Complete Alternatives

EVALUATION AND SELECTION OF AN ALTERNATIVE

Analysis of Costs

Analysis of Benefits

Alpine's Alternative Analysis

Alpine's Decision

ALPINE ACQUIRES DATA PROCESSING PERSONNEL

Alpine Project Planning

SYSTEM DESIGN

Design of the Alpine Member Master File System

System Controls

Detailed Design

Design Walkthrough

DEVELOPMENT AND TESTING

Documentation

Data Preparation

Training and Testing

Procedures

SYSTEM IMPLEMENTATION

REVIEW OF SYSTEMS DEVELOPMENT STEPS

In Chapter 4 we summarized seven steps in the systems development cycle. The first two of these, feasibility study and requirements definition, were illustrated by discussing the case of Alpine Co-op. When we came to the third step, identifying alternatives, we needed to define new concepts and vocabulary, so we departed from the Alpine case to discuss sequential file processing in Chapter 5 and direct access file processing in Chapter 6. In this present chapter, we will discuss the last five steps of the systems development cycle and resume the case of Alpine Co-op.

To refresh your memory, these seven steps are listed in figure 7-1. These activities should be completed for each business computer system that a company develops. For the first system, these steps are more involved because the hardware must be selected and installed.

Step	Development Action
1	Analyze feasibility
2	Determine user requirements
3	Specify alternatives
4	Evaluate and select an alternative
5	Design the system
6	Develop and test
7	Implement

Figure 7-1   The Seven Steps for Developing a Business Computer System

Once a company has a computer, then only additions to hardware need be considered in the systems development.

Figure 7-2 summarizes the systems that Alpine Co-op's users wanted to be developed. Phase 1 was to be implemented first to provide improved accuracy in member names and addresses so that catalogs and dividend checks could be mailed successfully. In phase 2, systems were to be developed that would keep a file of items in inventory, provide inventory accounting, and price orders after they had been picked. Finally, in phase 3, systems were to be developed that would process the orders before they were picked. This included generating picking slips, handling backorders, and providing order recommendations for the buyers.

Figure 7-2   Three Phases for Alpine's Systems Development

Phase	Systems to Be Developed
1	Member Master File System including: Master file maintenance Purchase updates Dividends Mailing labels
2	Inventory Master File System Inventory Accounting System Order Pricing System
3	Pre-Picking Order Processing System including: Picking slip generation Backorder management Order recommendations

As stated, Alpine should complete the seven steps of the systems development cycle for each of the systems to be produced. However, since Alpine had so much work to do, the project team decided to combine systems activities where possible. The steering committee had approved starting work on phases 1 and 2, but had deferred work on phase 3. Consequently, the team decided to consider alternatives for the systems in phases 1 and 2.

This is typical of a company that is just starting out in data processing. However, if you work for a company that has had computers for some time, you will probably not see systems developed in groups. Rather, they will be developed on an individual basis. We will now consider the remaining five steps of the systems development cycle.

ALTERNATIVE SPECIFICATION	The objective of this step is to find three or four feasible alternatives that will accomplish the user's requirements. To do this, each of the five components of a business computer system is considered in the light of the requirements produced in step 2. Then, an alternative is created by specifying the hardware, programs, data, procedures, and personnel required to meet the requirements.

Sometimes, one of the business system components is the same for all alternatives. For example, if a company already has a computer, then the hardware may be the same for each alternative. Also, the data needed may be the same or the procedures to be used may be equivalent. When this correspondence occurs, the component that stays the same does not form part of the alternative.

You might wonder when the data or procedures would ever be different. If one of the alternatives was a batch system and another a direct access system, then the data format might be different and the procedures certainly would be different. In this case, data and procedures should be specified in the alternatives so that management can be made aware of the different impacts on people of the two styles of processing.

Developing an alternative is an iterative process. The five components are interdependent. A decision on one may change the others. This process may necessitate going back and reassessing other components. For example, one type of computer hardware seemed feasible to the Alpine project team until the personnel component was discussed. At that stage the team realized that a systems engineering specialist would be required to put the computer together and keep it running. The team deleted that alternative.

Further, the choice of one component can impact choices on other components. For example, if Alpine decided to build computer programs, a systems development staff would be required. Otherwise, a development staff would not be needed.

We will discuss the major considerations when identifying alternatives in the context of Alpine Co-op. As we left them, John Abrams, the Alpine consultant, had presented a course describing sequential and direct access systems. The Alpine project team (John, an accountant, a buyer, and an inventory supervisor) had done a feasibility study and a detailed study of requirements. They were about to begin specifying alternatives. They discussed each of the five components as follows.

The project team discovered there are three basic types of computer systems. These are called *microcomputers, minicomputers,* and *mainframes.*

Hardware

Microcomputers Microcomputers (figure 7-3) are the cheapest and smallest computers. They are available from personal and hobby computer stores. Computers of this type are generally slower and smaller than the other types. A typical microcomputer has 32,000 to 250,000 bytes of main memory and executes instructions at the rate of 250,000 per second. The maximum amount of direct access storage is approximately 5 to 10 million bytes. Microcomputers typically cost in the range of $2,000 to $10,000.

Figure 7-3 Microcomputer

The reliability, or *mean time between failures* (sometimes abbreviated *MTBF*), is not as high for microcomputers as it is for computers of the other two types. Also, since microcomputers cost much less than other types, the micro vendors cannot afford to provide as much support in the way of documentation, training, and programs like operating systems and utilities. Furthermore, maintenance for a microcomputer is often harder and slower to obtain than for other types of computer systems.

Microcomputers are not hard to build. A large number of under-financed micro vendors have come and gone. The purchaser of a micro needs to carefully check the background of the manufacturer to be sure it will remain in business and will back up its products.

Minicomputers　*Minicomputers* (figure 7-4) are the next group of computers in terms of size, speed, and expense. Minicomputers were first developed in the 1960s as small, special purpose computers. However, as time went on, minicomputers became more and more powerful. In the late 1960s, general purpose business minicomputers became available. Today, minicomputers have grown in capability to the point where they overlap the mainframe category of computers.

Figure 7-4　Minicomputer

A typical minicomputer has 500,000 to 1 million bytes of main memory and executes instructions at the rate of about 1 million per second. The maximum direct access storage supported is around 1 billion bytes. The typical minicomputer costs between $50,000 to $150,000 for the CPU and an average amount of peripheral equipment.

Minicomputers usually have more vendor support than do micros. The operating systems are usually more sophisticated, and there is a wider range of utilities available. Further, more documentation is typically available. Training is often provided by the vendor.

Mainframes The largest, fastest, and most expensive computers are called *mainframes* (figure 7-5). These computers typically have several million bytes of main memory. They execute instructions at the rate of 4 to 8 million per second. Online storage can be as great as 10 to 20 billion characters. Mainframes start at about $200,000 and go up to $5 million or more.

At this price, considerable vendor support is provided. Usually, there is a choice of several different operating systems. A complete package of utilities is provided. Systems documentation is extensive. Comprehensive, 24 hour, quick-response maintenance is available. The mainframe vendors offer literally dozens of training courses in the application and operation of their equipment.

Figure 7-5 Mainframe Computer

All microcomputers and many minis operate in a standard office environment. No special power or air-conditioning is needed. However, the larger minicomputers and nearly all mainframes require air-conditioning and special power. Further, these computers require raised floors for the cables that connect components.

One way to distinguish micros, minis, and mainframes is by their physical size. A micro can be picked up by two fingers, a mini by two arms, and a mainframe by two elephants! Other characteristics of these three computer types are summarized in figure 7-6.

Alpine Looks for a Mini   The Alpine project team discussed these categories of equipment in relation to Alpine's needs. John felt that although microcomputers are excellent for home use and for use by very small or specialized businesses, Alpine would be better off to pick a computer with greater vendor support. Mainframe computers would certainly be able to handle Alpine's workload, but they might cost considerably more than Alpine could afford to pay. Consequently, the team decided to concentrate first on business minicomputers. If no feasible mini could be found, then they would investigate mainframes. John doubted they would need to.

One morning John came to work with two large volumes under his arm. "These," he explained, "are summaries of business minicom-

Figure 7-6   Characteristics of Typical Computer Systems by Category

Parameter	Computer Characteristics		
	Micro	Mini	Mainframe
Main Memory Size (bytes)	32,000 to 250,000	500,000 to 1 million	5 to 10 million
Instruction Speed (instructions per second)	250,000	1 million	4 to 8 million
Maximum Direct Access Storage (bytes)	5 to 10 million	1 billion	10 to 20 billion
Typical System Cost	$2,000 to $10,000	$25,000 to $200,000	$200,000 to $5 million +
Operating System and Utilities	Minimal	Required capabilities provided	Extensive—choice of several systems
Maintenance	Often hard and slow to obtain	Usually adequate	Comprehensive; several plans available

puters that are available today. These summaries are produced by companies that keep abreast of all the recent developments." (See references 19 and 33.)

The team examined the reference books. It quickly became apparent that there were literally hundreds of possible choices for minicomputers. Since Alpine was new to the data processing business, they decided to pick large vendors that could provide support in terms of training, documentation, and maintenance. John explained that computers from such vendors may cost more, but the cost is worth it to a company like Alpine. Companies with experienced staff members, however, might do well to obtain cheaper, less well-supported equipment.

Large vendors usually have several computers grouped into a family. Thus, one vendor offers the System X, with Models I, II, and III. John explained that usually it is not hard to convert from one computer to another in the same family. Since Alpine planned to expand its data processing activity during phase 3 and beyond, John recommended they pick a computer that meets their current needs and is in the low end of a family. Alpine could obtain the Model I, for example. Then, as their needs expanded, they could switch to the Model II or III. If they picked the top model of a less powerful family, they would have to switch to another family or even to another vendor's computer as their needs expanded. This approach would likely be time-consuming and expensive.

The team had decided that Alpine needed both sequential and direct access file processing capability. In phase 1, sequential processing was needed to produce mailing labels and dividend checks, and to add new purchase amounts to the member master file records. Further, they had decided to use direct access processing to update the member master file with new members, member changes, and deletions. Also, direct access was required to allow the clerks to quickly access member data when answering telephone queries from members.

In phase 2, sequential file processing was needed to produce the inventory item list and to produce reports for inventory accounting. However, direct access capability was also needed to price the orders.

The team also had estimates of the amount of direct access file space that would be needed for member master and inventory processing. Given the need for sequential and direct access processing, and the estimates of file sizes, they searched for large vendors having families of minicomputers such that the models on the low end of the family would satisfy the immediate Alpine need. Within a day they had a list of three possible minicomputers and candidate vendors.

In this example, Alpine picked specific vendors and systems to consider. This is not the only way to select equipment alternatives. Another approach uses a *request for proposal* or *RFP*. The RFP is a

Using a Request for Proposal

document that describes the requirements of a new or proposed system. It is sent to many computer vendors, who are invited to propose the system they believe best meets the described needs. This way, vendor personnel, who know the most about their own equipment, decide which of their systems to propose for the new system. The disadvantage is that Alpine would need to spend considerable time preparing a complete RFP and evaluating many responses. Also, the vendors have a financial incentive to sell, and the responses are not always confined to reality.

John did not use the RFP approach because he believed he knew the appropriate systems and he wanted to shorten the acquisition time. Such expertise is one advantage of hiring a consultant. (That, however, doesn't mean John was right. Did he really know all of the systems that could have been used? If so, Alpine will not be damaged by this decision. Otherwise, using an RFP probably would have been more appropriate.)

QUESTIONS

7.1   What are the five components of a business computer system alternative?

7.2   Is it possible for one of these components to be the same for all alternatives? If so, what should be done?

7.3   What is a microcomputer? Describe its characteristics.

7.4   What is a minicomputer? Describe its characteristics.

7.5   What is a mainframe? Describe its characteristics.

7.6   Why was it important for Alpine to pick a computer in the low end of a computer family?

7.7   What is an RFP? What are the advantages and disadvantages of using an RFP to identify hardware alternatives?

Programs

The second component of a business computer system is programs. At this stage, the Alpine project team had two sets of programs to consider: one group for the member master file system and another for the inventory and pricing system. John described five basic ways to obtain programs.

Sources of Programs   First, Alpine could develop its own programs by designing, coding, and testing them in-house. To do this, it would need to acquire a systems development staff. John approximated the staff needed for both systems to be two systems analysts and two programmers for a 20 to 24 month period. These were the minimum requirements; he felt that they might increase once the detailed system design was done.

Not all these people would have to be full-time, permanent employees. Alpine could hire programmers and maybe even analysts through a temporary employment service. Also, they could find temporary or part-time employees directly.

The second way of acquiring programs is to contract with a *software house* (a company that writes programs to specification) to develop the programs they needed. This way would be more expensive in the short run, but would save the long-run expense of building and maintaining a systems development staff. Unfortunately, if Alpine used a software house, they would also have less control over the quality of the programs. They would run the risk that the programs might be developed incorrectly.

A third way to acquire programs is to buy them. If programs that meet the needs already exist in another company, the best and cheapest way to acquire them is to purchase them. This method works well in industries where operations are standardized. Accounting firms are a good example.

John knew that programs had been developed for mail order businesses. Some of them might be applicable to Alpine's situation. The team made a list of several possible sources of programs for both member master file and inventory accounting and billing systems. They decided to investigate whether any of them could be used at Alpine.

As John pointed out, buying programs is risky. Even if they appear to do the job required, they may be difficult to install or use or they might even have errors or bugs in them. Once a program has been purchased, it is difficult to get money back or to get compensation for problems caused by defects. Also, the project team needs to be certain that the programs will run on the type of hardware that Alpine plans to acquire. If not, the team might need to add another computer to its list of candidates.

A fourth way to obtain programs is a combination of the second and third. Programs are purchased and then modified to fit a company's needs. This can be a good way to obtain tailored programs. The cost can be much less than starting development from scratch. To be successful, however, the programs need to have been written so that they can easily be changed. Also, good programmers documentation must be available, and the amount of change required must be minimal. John felt that if more than 20 or 30 percent of any program had to be rewritten, then it would be better to start from scratch.

The personnel required to make changes to the programs could either be full-time Alpine employees, or Alpine could contract with a software house to make the changes. Also, temporary programmers or analysts could be hired.

The fifth way to acquire computer programs is to buy what is termed a *turnkey system*. These systems are combinations of computer hardware and programs that solve specific problems. For example, turnkey systems are available to handle doctor billing and accounting, or to keep track of inventory for parts distributors.

The term *turnkey* refers to products like cars or boats. When the consumer buys one of these, he or she simply turns the key. No development is required. In data processing, the organization that buys a turnkey system just starts the computer, responds to a few basic questions on the CRT, and the computer and programs are ready to go.

Unfortunately, such a plan seldom works out so simply. Usually there are variances in the ways that businesses operate that necessitate adjusting and tuning. Also, such systems are only feasible in industries that have standard ways of operating. In Alpine's case, John knew of no suitable turnkey system that would handle their member master file and inventory and pricing requirements. Also, he believed that Alpine's future requirements would grow beyond the capability of the turnkey systems in the mail order business. As he pointed out, most large businesses eventually acquire their own systems development staff.

The project team discussed these alternatives for some time. They concluded that no programs or turnkey systems could be found to meet all of Alpine's needs. Thus, even if they found programs that were close to meeting the need, some systems development would be required. They decided to try to find programs that were well written and documented, and to plan on changing them. If no such programs could be found, then Alpine would have to write its own.

The team could not decide whether Alpine should plan on acquiring a systems development staff or to use outside services. Eventually, it occurred to them that this decision had long-run consequences and should be made by their management. Consequently, they decided to present both possibilities as alternatives to the steering committee.

The five sources of computer programs are summarized in figure 7-7. Note these sources apply to any new system—not just the Alpine problem. Also, these sources can be used even if a company already has a computer.

Figure 7-7 Five Sources of Computer Programs

Ways to Obtain Programs
1. Develop programs by in-house Alpine staff.
2. Develop programs by software house (vendor).
3. Purchase programs.
4. Purchase programs and rewrite to fit Alpine's needs.
5. Obtain turnkey system.

As the project team discussed the data and procedures for the new systems, they discovered that data and procedures were nearly the same for all of the hardware and program alternatives. Data requirements did not change from one computer to another. Consequently, they decided not to include data and procedures as part of the alternatives to be presented to the steering committee. Those would be designed and developed later.

While discussing data, however, the team discovered they had forgotten to include input hardware for the pricing system. How were the filled orders to be priced as they went to shipping? Somehow the order data had to be input to the pricing programs. After some discussion, the team decided that clerks sitting at CRTs could do this best. The team updated their list of hardware needs to include CRTs for these people.

Also, while discussing procedures, the team realized that Alpine needed some type of password protection for data files. Otherwise, procedures could not be developed to ensure that only authorized changes could be made to the files. They added the need for an operating system that would provide passwords to control both file accessing and updating.

Data and Procedures

The last of the five components of a business computer system is trained people. Here the project team could find several alternatives. First, there was the issue of how systems development was to be accomplished. Either the staff could be hired permanently, or Alpine could obtain temporary help or contract for development with a software house.

Second, data entry personnel needed to be hired and trained. The team thought four clerks would be necessary initially for the member file system. Eight more would be needed later for the inventory and pricing system. For whom should these people work? One possibility was to form a data processing department and have the clerks work for the DP Director. Another was to have the member clerks work for the membership department, and the other clerks work for the order processing department.

Finally, operators would be required to run the new computer. John believed that initially Alpine would need 10 hours per day of operation. He recommended that two operators be hired. A third backup operator could be obtained by training one of the data entry clerks so that he or she could run the computer when one of the regular operators was absent.

Personnel

Alpine's Organizational Alternatives   After considerable discussion, the team proposed three alternative organizations as shown in figure 7-8. For the organization in figure 7-8*a*, the Director of Data Processing manages three groups: systems development, computer operations,

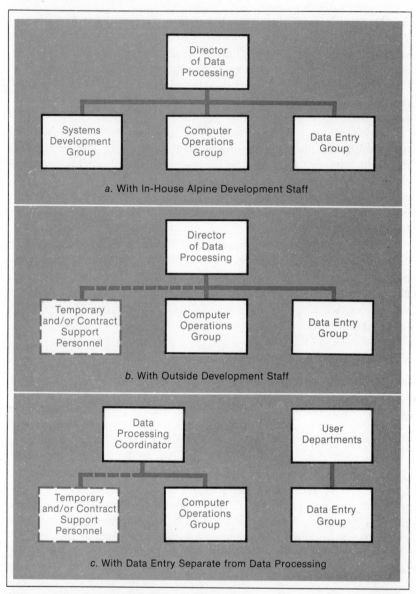

Figure 7-8 Proposed Organizational Alternatives

and data entry. For the second alternative (figure 7-8*b*), the director manages just operations and data entry. This organization assumes only temporary or contract systems development personnel are used.

The third alternative (figure 7-8*c*) shows a data processing co-ordinator who manages just the operations group, but also supervises the temporary and contract development efforts. The data entry personnel report to the user departments.

At this point, the project team reviewed their work and conclusions. By now they had decided that only two computers would provide what they wanted. One of the original three had proven to be infeasible. They labeled the two remaining computers A and B.

Their attempts to find programs that might be adapted to Alpine's problems had uncovered two products. One was MAIL-CUST, a package of programs that a bulk mail company had developed. It could be run on computer B. With some rewriting, the team felt it could be used for the Alpine member master file system.

Another package was a group of programs developed by a general merchandise mail order company. It was called INV/PRICE/80 and had been sold to several mail order companies. It could be run on computer A or B.

Considering these facts together with the organization charts shown in figure 7-8, the project team developed five basic alternatives as listed in figure 7-9.

Alternative 1 assumes that both packages would be purchased, and that the work required to make the programs suitable for Alpine would be done by temporary or contract development personnel. Only computer B could be used for this alternative because MAIL-CUST would not run on computer A.

Alternatives 2 and 3 assume that only the INV/PRICE/80 package would be purchased. The programs for the member master file and changes to the package would be developed by Alpine or through outside help. For these two alternatives, any of the organizations in figure 7-8 could be used. Alternative 2 assumes computer A would be used, and alternative 3 assumes computer B would be used.

Alternatives 4 and 5 assume that no programming packages would be purchased at all. Programs for both the member and the inventory and pricing systems would be developed by Alpine. For these alternatives the project team believed that only the organization in figure 7-8a would be workable. This group could be supplemented by

Figure 7-9 Five Alternatives Developed by the Alpine Project Team

Alternative	Computer	Programs Needed		Organization (from figure 7-8)
		Member Master File	Inventory/ Pricing	
1	B	MAIL-CUST	INV/PRICE/80	7-8b or c
2	A	Develop	INV/PRICE/80	7-8a, b, or c
3	B	Develop	INV/PRICE/80	7-8a, b, or c
4	A	Develop	Develop	7-8a
5	B	Develop	Develop	7-8a

outside help, if necessary. Alternative 4 assumes computer A would be used, and alternative 5 assumes computer B would be used.

After the team had developed these alternatives, they documented them and presented them to the steering committee. That group was pleased with the work and believed the alternatives represented a feasible range of possibilities. The steering committee directed the project team to evaluate the alternatives and to recommend one of them for implementation.

In the above discussion we briefly surveyed the actions that Alpine took to develop alternatives for the new business computer systems. Figure 7-10 shows other aspects that the Alpine team considered that we did not discuss. These issues were addressed in their report to the steering committee.

The steering committee was particularly concerned about user procedures. They wanted to be sure only simple, easy-to-learn tasks would be required. Otherwise, the committee members thought users would make too many errors.

Figure 7-10 Considerations When Developing Systems Alternatives

System Component	Issues Considered
Hardware	Type of CPU Amount of main memory Type and amount of tape, direct access, and other storage equipment Type and number of terminals Type and number of data entry devices
Programs	Number needed Build vs buy Language choice
Data	Number of files and rough format Style of processing Type of data input

Procedures	Users
	    Input activity
	    Use of outputs
	    Data editing and control responsibilities
	Operations
	    How to use equipment
	    How to operate systems
	    Backup and recovery
	    Control responsibilities

7.8   Name the five ways of acquiring computer programs.

7.9   Which of these five ways do you think is most appropriate for Alpine to use?

7.10 What is a software house?

7.11 Explain the term *turnkey system*.

7.12 Why did Alpine decide not to include data and procedure components in the specification of their alternatives?

7.13 Speculate on the advantages of organization 7-8*b* as compared to 7-8*c*. What do you suppose are the disadvantages?

EVALUATION AND SELECTION OF AN ALTERNATIVE

The purpose of this step of the systems development cycle is to compare the alternatives to one another and select the best. To perform this step in a systematic way, the alternatives are compared in terms of their costs and benefits. Basically, estimates are made of all the costs of each alternative, and of the dollar values of all the benefits. The best alternative is the one for which the benefits exceed the costs by the greatest amount. If none of the alternatives have benefits exceeding costs, then the project should be discontinued.

Analysis of Costs

In practice, this step never works out as simply as stated above. For one thing, costs are hard to estimate. In Alpine's case, determining the costs of developing programs for alternatives 2 through 4 is very difficult. There are too many unknowns. Further, costs of modifying the packages in alternatives 1 through 3 are hard to estimate. Sometimes programs are easier to change than anticipated. Sometimes they are much harder to change. One change to a program can cause many errors that are hard to track down.

Each of the five components of a business computer system costs something. In addition to the programming costs just mentioned, there is the cost of acquiring and operating the computer hardware. Also, there is the cost of gathering the data and putting it into computer-readable format. Input and output forms and documents must be purchased.

There are costs associated with developing procedures, documenting them, and ensuring that they are followed. Finally, there is the cost of the personnel to operate, use, and support the system. This item includes salaries as well as training costs.

Analysis of Benefits

Unfortunately, benefits can be even harder to quantify than costs. In cases where the new system will reduce labor hours, then benefits are not too hard to estimate. The benefits will be the cost savings of the labor reduction. However, if the benefits are more vague—like providing more or better information, or enabling the company to provide better customer service—then they are hard to quantify.

Sometimes the benefits are separated into *tangible* and *intangible* ones. Examples of tangible benefits are cost savings or increases in revenues. Tangible benefits relate directly to dollars. Examples of intangible benefits are better service or increased customer goodwill. Intangible benefits relate indirectly to dollars.

For each alternative, the dollar value of the tangible benefits is computed and compared to its costs. The alternatives are compared. If the tangible benefits for the best alternative will cover its costs sufficiently, the project is continued. Otherwise, management must decide whether the intangible benefits make the project worthwhile. This will be a subjective decision, not a quantified one.

Alpine's Alternative Analysis

The Alpine project team evaluated the five alternatives shown in figure 7-9 by computing the costs and the dollar values of the tangible benefits. Two facts became obvious. First, alternatives 4 and 5 (developing all programs from scratch) were much more costly than the first three alternatives. Consequently, the project team eliminated those two alternatives.

Second, they found that the MAIL-CUST package of programs was not as complete or as close to the Alpine needs as they had hoped. To adapt the package would cost considerably more than the team thought was worthwhile. Thus, the team eliminated alternative 1.

This left alternatives 2 and 3, which were the same except for the choice of computer. Before making a decision on which computer to use, the team wanted to be sure that the benefits were worth the cost of either alternative.

They identified the tangible and intangible benefits of both the member master and the inventory/pricing systems. Considering the member system, the tangible benefits were a reduction in mailing and processing expenses. If the master file could be made more accurate, fewer catalogs would be returned and more checks would be sent correctly. These savings were not significant, however, compared to the cost of the systems. An intangible benefit was better customer service. Members would get catalogs on a more timely basis. Also, new customers could be added sooner. Even more important, as a cooperative, Alpine had a responsibility to disburse dividend checks. Surprisingly, some 12 percent of the checks had not been delivered the previous year. Alpine hoped to reduce that percentage with the new system. (See figure 7-11.)

The inventory/pricing system offered substantial tangible benefits. If the inventory could be better controlled, the number of items of

System	Tangible Benefits	Intangible Benefits
Member Master	Reduced mailing costs Reduced processing costs	More timely delivery of catalogs Customers added sooner Timely delivery of checks
Inventory/Pricing	Reduced inventory size Reduced inventory costs Less inventory processing	Fewer backorders Quicker order response Less chaos

Figure 7-11   Benefits of Member Master and Inventory/Pricing Systems

each type in inventory could be reduced. This reduction would mean substantial savings in the cost of maintaining the inventory. Intangible benefits concerned better customer service. Since fewer items would be back-ordered, customers would receive goods more quickly.

The team determined that the tangible benefits of the member and inventory systems together would more than justify the cost of the new systems. Therefore, they decided to proceed and choose between computers A and B.

The two computers were essentially priced the same. System A was about $7,000 more expensive than B; but in terms of the total system cost, this difference was deemed insignificant. Therefore, the project team held extensive discussions with the hardware vendors to learn as much as possible about the relative merits of both computers. They also called on companies that were using these types of computers. The project team found that users of computer A were very satisfied by the service they received, but that the users of B were not. They learned that vendor B did not have a local sales or service and support office. These personnel traveled from a city 200 miles away when they were needed. Once the team learned this, they decided to recommend computer A and alternative 2 to the steering committee.

If alternative 2 was to be developed, Alpine needed to acquire the personnel to build programs for the member master file system and to modify and install INV/PRICE/80 on their new computer. These personnel could be either full-time Alpine employees or temporary or contract personnel. The team could not decide which way would be best for Alpine. They could not decide which of the organizations in figure 7-8 to propose. Therefore, they agreed to propose two versions of alternative 2 to the steering committee and let them make the decision.

Alternative 2A assumed that Alpine would acquire a systems development staff to write the programs and implement the systems.

There would be a data processing department as shown in figure 7-8*a*. Alternative 2B assumed that systems development would be done by outside services and temporary employees. The development effort would be managed by John Abrams. The organization would be as shown in figure 7-8*b*.

Costs and tangible benefits were summarized for these two alternatives. A list was made of the intangible benefits. These were put into a report and presented to the steering committee.

Alpine's Decision

Strangely, it did not take the committee long to decide what to do. They listened to the two versions of alternative 2 and decided they wanted neither. Rather, they wanted a combination. They wanted Alpine to begin to develop a systems staff, but not to the extent described in alternative 2A.

The committee's thinking was as follows: They did not believe development would stop with phases 1 and 2. Phase 3 and systems beyond that needed to be implemented. Further, they expected that Alpine would continue to grow, perhaps at a faster rate. Therefore, Alpine needed to begin building a systems development staff. The committee viewed work done by outside personnel as only putting off the problem. Eventually the outside development work would become so expensive that Alpine would have to build their own systems staff.

On the other hand, the committee did not want to rely exclusively on a new team to develop the member master and inventory/pricing systems. Consequently, they wanted to form a nucleus of employees for the data processing department and to supplement this with part-time, temporary, or contract personnel as necessary. They also wanted John to stay involved until the staff was effectively operating.

After some discussion, John indicated that three people in addition to the operators could be hired to form such a nucleus. They would need a director of data processing, one experienced systems programmer/analyst, and one programmer/analyst trainee. In this case, John felt that the best organization would be the one shown in figure 7-8*a*. The committee agreed. On the matter of hiring data entry personnel, the committee wanted to use existing employees instead. An accounting office had been reorganized. Four clerks would become available for training in the next two or three months.

The committee thanked the project team for their efforts and instructed them to proceed as agreed.

The result reached in this case is unique to Alpine. You should not assume that every company needs a systems development staff. If Alpine's business had been stable and if little future development had been anticipated, they probably would have reached a different conclusion.

7.14 The dollar values of _____ and _____ are compared to select the best system alternative. (Fill in the blanks.)

7.15 Name one cost for each of the five components of a business computer system.

7.16 What two types of benefits are considered in the evaluation of system alternatives?

7.17 Do you think the team should have eliminated alternatives 4 and 5 as quickly as they did? Discuss.

7.18 Why did the project team eliminate computer B? Do you agree?

ALPINE ACQUIRES DATA PROCESSING PERSONNEL

After the steering committee meeting, the project team met to decide the next course of action. They agreed that before more progress could be made, they needed to hire the new personnel. John Abrams worked with the Alpine personnel department to locate several candidates for the job of director of data processing. He did this by calling on his professional acquaintances, talking with vendors, and discussing Alpine's needs with friends. He wanted to find someone for that position who was personally recommended. Consequently, Alpine never did run an ad under M for data processing manager.

After several candidates had been interviewed by the project team and the members of the steering committee, Barbara Carlson was selected. She was 34 and had been in data processing for 10 years. She began as a supervisor of keypunch, then went back to school to earn a B.S. in information systems. She had worked two years as a programmer, three years as a systems analyst, and two years as a project manager. In addition to this experience, she had worked extensively with computer A and, in fact, was recommended by that vendor.

Even before Barbara officially started work, she and John met several times to locate someone for the programmer/analyst position. Within a month, Jim Gianola was hired. Jim had a B.S. in accounting and five years of experience as a systems programmer/analyst. He knew the mail order business very well, and had even worked for a period of time for the service bureau that Alpine had been using! He had been involved in the development of both member processing systems and inventory systems while employed by other companies.

Finally, Barbara and John located a recent graduate of an information systems program for the trainee position. Her name was Carol Denton. In addition to programming and other information systems coursework, Carol had a good background in business.

Barbara and Jim joined the project team as soon as they reported to work. At this point, the representatives from Accounting, Purchasing, and Inventory became less active on the team. They were called upon when the user's viewpoint was needed, but they were not involved in the more technical work.

Alpine Project Planning As soon as the three data processing employees had been hired, the project team met to lay out priorities and a work schedule. The member master file was clearly the most pressing project. Alpine wanted to terminate the service bureau as soon as possible. It was late January. The team hoped to be able to convert to the new system in time to produce the dividend checks for the year.

After some discussion, Barbara laid out the following work assignments. Jim and Carol were to begin immediately reviewing the requirements for the member master file system. They were to produce the design as soon as possible. John was to line up any temporary or part-time help they might need. Also, John would review the design with Barbara when it was complete. Meanwhile, Barbara would begin negotiating an agreement to buy INV/PRICE/80. She would try to have the package in-house within six months so that Jim and Carol could start on it whenever they finished the member master file system. Also, Barbara would begin to set up the data processing operation by writing procedures of operation and standards for documentation. She would develop procedures for users to formally request data processing services. With this plan established, the design phase was begun.

SYSTEM DESIGN

During the design phase, the structure of each of the five components of a business computer system is created. To proceed, the requirements are analyzed in relation to the alternative that has been selected.

Most designs are produced in top-down fashion; that is, the design progresses from the general to the specific. First, the major parts of the system are designed. Then, subparts of these parts are designed. Next, sub-subparts are designed, and so forth. Work progresses in this downward manner until the smallest components have been specified.

You can use a similar process when producing topic outlines for composition courses. First, you identify major topics, then subtopics, then sub-subtopics, and so forth. Proceeding in this way, you build the outline from the top down.

In the Alpine case, the top-down strategy was used to develop the design of the member master file system. First, the overall systems flowchart was developed. Then, for each of the components, the major structure was created. For hardware, the configuration of CPU, disk units, terminals, and other equipment were designed. For programs, the names and major functions of each of the programs in the system were specified. For data, file names, contents, and basic formats were determined. The high level structure for procedures and for personnel requirements and training was also produced.

After this, each of these components was broken up into major parts and they were designed. Major portions of the programs were identified and functions allocated to them. More precise formats for data were specified, and the relationship of programs and data was made precise. Documentation showing which programs access or modify which data items was developed. Similar activities were performed for procedures and personnel components.

For hardware or for programs that are being purchased, the term *designed* is a misnomer. A better term is *develop specifications*. However, since the term design is appropriate for the other components, we will use it for hardware or purchased programs as well. Remember, however, that hardware is very seldom designed and built from scratch. It is nearly always purchased or leased.

Another problem must be solved for hardware and other purchased components. Negotiations with vendors must be conducted and completed. Further, contracts must be written, approved by all parties' legal counsel, and signed. Once this stage is completed, the company must prepare sites or do whatever else is necessary to receive the products.

We will discuss these activities only for the Alpine member master file system. A discussion of the inventory/pricing system would be repetitive and probably not that informative for you.

Figure 7-12 shows subsystems of the Alpine member master file system that Jim and Carol identified. The member maintenance subsystem is used to obtain data from the master file for customer queries and to update the master file with new members or member changes. The purchase update subsystem adds purchase amounts to the member records. The total of these amounts is needed to compute the dividend

Design of the Alpine Member Master File System

Figure 7-12 Functions of the Alpine Member Master Subsystems

Subsystem	Functions
Member Maintenance	Retrieve data from member master file Update member data Add/delete members
Purchase Update	Edit purchase transaction records Update member master file with purchase amounts
Label and Check	Produce mailing labels Calculate dividends and print dividend checks

at the end of the year. Finally, the label and check subsystem produces mailing labels and checks at year end.

Figure 7-13 presents the system flowcharts for each of these subsystems. The member maintenance subsystem has three programs. Two are accessed by CRT. The member data retrieval program obtains data from the master file. The member master file update program is used to change the file. These functions were separated into two programs to control changing of the master file. Only users authorized to make changes will be allowed to access (through passwords) the member master file update program.

Whenever a change is made to the member master file, a record is written to the change file. Periodically, say once a day, this file is read by the change report program. A formatted report showing changes to the members' records in member number order is produced. The reports are kept on file for at least a year.

The purchase update subsystem is shown in figure 7-13*b*. Order data is keyed to floppy disks. These are then consolidated, edited, and stored on the edited purchase transactions tape file. Actually, some editing (like checking for only digits in numeric fields) is done by the key-to-disk equipment. Other editing (like checking for a valid member

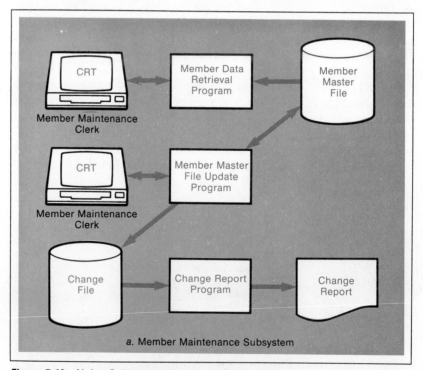

Figure 7-13 Alpine Subsystem Flowcharts *(Part 1 of 3)*

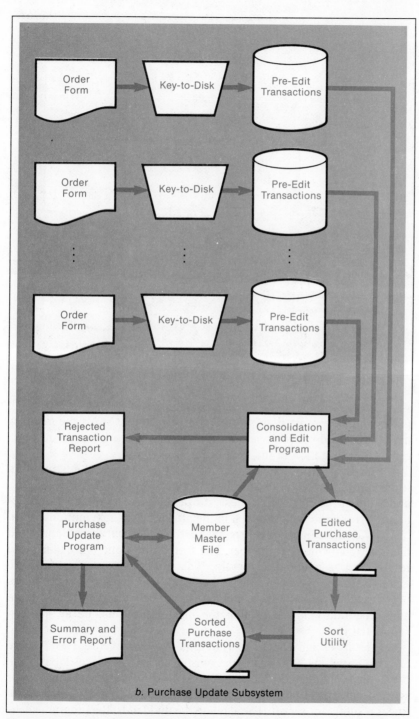

b. Purchase Update Subsystem

Figure 7-13 Alpine Subsystem Flowcharts *(Part 2 of 3)*

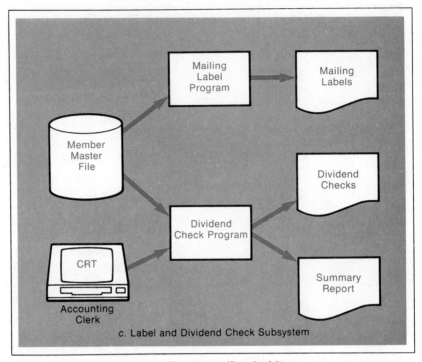

c. Label and Dividend Check Subsystem

Figure 7-13 Alpine Subsystem Flowcharts *(Part 3 of 3)*

number) can only be done by the edit program. It reads the member master file to do this. Rejected transactions are printed on an error report for correction in the next cycle.

Jim and Carol's plan called for the consolidation and edit program to be run twice a day: once around noon, to edit the morning orders; and again at the close of business, for the afternoon orders. A transaction in error could be corrected in the afternoon or next morning's run.

After the edit run has been made, the edited purchase transaction file is sorted by member number. The sorted transactions are then input to the purchase update program. This program adds the purchase amounts to the member's master record. The member master file is processed sequentially here, whereas it had been read randomly in the edit program. This means that the master file must be an indexed sequential file.

The label and check subsystem is shown in figure 7-13c. There are two programs. One reads the master file and produces labels. The other reads the file to produce checks. Both of these outputs will be written on special forms on the printer. The check program also produces a summary report. To calculate the dividends, the program needs a dividend percent. This amount is to be input via the CRT.

Because of its financial nature, the design team planned special controls for this system. The blank check forms will be locked up and
accounted for by serial number. Also, the computer program itself will
be taken off the system library immediately after it is used. The files
containing the source and object code will be locked in a vault not
accessible to data processing personnel. Finally, the procedures stipulate that the program will be run by only two people: one user and one
operator. The systems development staff will not be involved in the
operation of this system.

System Controls

Once this basic system structure had been developed and agreed on
by the project team (including the members from Accounting, Purchasing, and Inventory), Jim and Carol began to design the next-level
components.

Detailed Design

    Since Alpine did not have a computer, they needed to specify
exactly what equipment would be needed. Figure 7-14 shows the hardware required by the member master subsystem. The inventory/pricing
system needed eight more terminals. Once the hardware requirements
were known, Barbara Carlson and the Alpine legal staff conducted the
negotiations with the hardware vendor and the contract was signed.

    The program structures were designed next. For this design,
pseudocode for the general logic of the programs was created. Figure
7-15 shows the logic for the dividend check program. The logic for the
member master file update program was shown in figure 6-19. The logic
of the purchase update program was shown in figure 5-25.

    While the program logic was developed, Jim and Carol determined
the formats of the member master and purchase transaction files. The
format of the member master was shown in figure 5-15. Also, the formats of the checks and mailing labels were developed jointly with the
users. The formats of the change, edit, and summary reports were
developed and approved by the users. Finally, the *screen formats* (the

Figure 7-14 Hardware Components Required to Support Alpine Member Master
File System

Quantity	Hardware Component
1	CPU with 512,000 bytes of main storage
7	CRT terminals (4 for data entry, 3 for development staff)
3	Disk drives (75 million bytes of storage)
1	Printer (1200 lines per minute)
1	Tape unit (1600 bpi, 9 track)
1	2 million byte floppy disk
4	Key-to-disk stations

```
BEGIN MAIN-PROCEDURE
    DO INITIALIZE-PROCEDURE
    IF AUTH-CODE = 'OK'
        THEN DO DIVIDEND-AND-CHECK-PROCEDURE
            DO WRAPUP-PROCEDURE
    END-IF
END MAIN-PROCEDURE

BEGIN INITIALIZE PROCEDURE
    OPEN TERMINAL FILE
    INPUT USER'S ACCOUNT NUMBER, PASSWORD
    IF ACCOUNT NUMBER, PASSWORD ACCEPTABLE
        THEN OPEN MASTER, SUMMARY-REPORT, AND CHECK FILES
            SET EOF-FLAG TO 0
            INPUT DIVIDEND-PERCENT
            EDIT DIVIDEND-PERCENT
            IF DIVIDEND-PERCENT TOO LARGE OR TOO SMALL
                THEN PRINT DIAGNOSTIC MESSAGE
                    SET AUTH-CODE TO 'BAD'
                ELSE SET AUTH-CODE TO 'OK'
                    READ FIRST MASTER RECORD; IF EOF SET EOF-FLAG TO 1
            END-IF
        ELSE SET AUTH-CODE TO 'BAD'
    END-IF
    CLOSE TERMINAL FILE
END INITIALIZE-PROCEDURE
```

Figure 7-15 High Level Logic for Dividend Check Program *(Part 1 of 2)*

way the data appears on the CRT screens) for the member maintenance subsystem programs were designed and approved. (See figure 7-16.)

While Jim and Carol were developing these designs, John was working with the users to develop procedures and training courses for the users and operators. Procedures were designed for each of the three subsystems. The outlines for the training manuals and courses for these two groups were also produced.

By April, the detailed design was complete. The computer had been installed. Jim and Carol were ready to begin programming. They had planned work for a temporary programmer for two months. Consequently, John arranged for someone to come in during May and June.

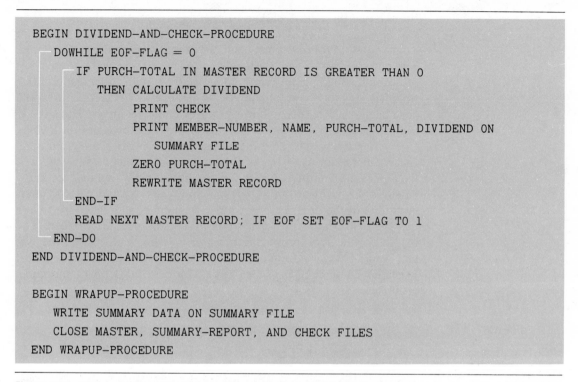

```
BEGIN DIVIDEND-AND-CHECK-PROCEDURE
    DOWHILE EOF-FLAG = 0
        IF PURCH-TOTAL IN MASTER RECORD IS GREATER THAN 0
            THEN CALCULATE DIVIDEND
                    PRINT CHECK
                    PRINT MEMBER-NUMBER, NAME, PURCH-TOTAL, DIVIDEND ON
                        SUMMARY FILE
                    ZERO PURCH-TOTAL
                    REWRITE MASTER RECORD
        END-IF
        READ NEXT MASTER RECORD; IF EOF SET EOF-FLAG TO 1
    END-DO
END DIVIDEND-AND-CHECK-PROCEDURE

BEGIN WRAPUP-PROCEDURE
    WRITE SUMMARY DATA ON SUMMARY FILE
    CLOSE MASTER, SUMMARY-REPORT, AND CHECK FILES
END WRAPUP-PROCEDURE
```

Figure 7-15 High Level Logic for Dividend Check Program *(Part 2 of 2)*

Carol was very anxious to start programming. She had wanted to start in February, but Jim and Barbara had been holding her back until the design was complete. Carol believed that they would not have enough time to develop and test the program before the new year. The more experienced personnel assured her that if the design was well done, programming would be quicker than she thought. On the other hand, if the design was poor, much rework would be needed. The programs would be full of errors and hard to test.

Figure 7-16 Formats Designed by Alpine Personnel

Formats
Master File
Purchase Transaction File
Checks
Mailing Labels
Change, Edit, Summary, and Rejection Reports
Screen

Design Walkthrough For the first three days of April, Jim and Carol presented what is called a *walkthrough*. They described their design and development plans to a committee of John, Barbara, and one of the users on the project team. The purpose of the walkthrough was to see if there were any defects or misunderstandings of requirements in the design. As a result of this walkthrough, the logic of the edit program was corrected. It would have been much harder to correct this logic if development had already begun. Detecting this one error made the walkthrough worthwhile.

After the walkthrough had been completed, Barbara, John, and Jim presented an overview of the member maintenance subsystem to the steering committee. Since the committee members did not know much about hardware or programs, they concentrated most of their questions in the areas of procedures, personnel, and data. They were satisfied with the answers the data processing people provided. The only real concern expressed during this meeting was whether the system would be ready soon enough. Barbara expressed her hope that it would be, but did not agree to compress the schedule from their original estimates.

QUESTIONS

7.19 What does the term *top-down design* mean?

7.20 Why is the term *design* a misnomer for the hardware component?

7.21 What is the function of the consolidation and edit program shown in figure 7-13?

7.22 What is the function of the purchase update program shown in figure 7-13?

7.23 What special controls were designed because of the system's financial nature?

7.24 What is a screen format?

7.25 Why did the experienced staff not want Carol to start programming right away?

7.26 What is a walkthrough? What purpose does it serve?

7.27 Why do you think Barbara did not agree to compress the development schedule?

DEVELOPMENT AND TESTING During this phase of the systems development cycle, the five components of a business computer system are built and tested. Initially, each component is tested by itself. Gradually all five components are integrated into a single system.

Considering the hardware component, there is usually not much to be built. During this step, the equipment is installed and tested to see that it operates according to the manufacturer's specifications. Sometimes, computer equipment is obtained with a 90 or 120 day warranty. If this is the case, the company needs to be certain to thoroughly check out the hardware in this period, before the warranty expires. If this is impossible, an extension to the time period should be negotiated.

During this systems development step, the programs are written and tested. As discussed in detail in Part 5, programs should be written and tested in top-down fashion, in relatively small pieces. First, the high level modules are written and tested, then the next level modules, and so forth.

Written documentation should be produced at this stage that describes the input, processing, and outputs from each section of code or *module*. In the past, programmers have deferred writing documentation until the programming is over. This practice is ineffective because some details are quickly forgotten, and because the documentation often does not get done.

Documentation

Program documentation will be needed when the programs have to be changed or when errors are detected. As long as the person who wrote a program is available, and as long as that person can remember the program, the need for documentation is not evident. However, most programs need to be changed sometime—often long after the original authors have departed or else forgotten the code. At that point, documentation is critical. Unfortunately, that's the very time in which it cannot be easily produced. Consequently, professional programmers and analysts develop documentation as the system is being built.

Additionally, procedures for orderly operation of the system and for error correction and backup and recovery must be finalized and documented. Procedures for both operations personnel and users should be developed.

By this step, the data files and report formats have already been designed. The major task remaining is to build the files by copying the raw data into the format needed by the system. This activity cannot begin until the hardware and programs to edit and store the data are available. Until then, the team can assemble the raw data, hire temporary personnel that may be needed to create the master files, and train them.

Data Preparation

Once the hardware and programs are ready, test data can be produced. Then, the files containing real data are created. This data must be edited carefully. After the files are created, they should be thoroughly checked manually to be sure that the edit process worked correctly. If the data is bad, the system cannot operate successfully. If the system does not operate successfully at first, the users will form a low opinion of it and Data Processing will face an uphill battle gaining user acceptance and support.

Training and Testing

Finally, the operators and users are trained. They are shown how to use the equipment and how to follow the procedures. If the philosophy of the system is explained, they will better understand why procedures are designed as they are. Even better results occur if the operators and users have had a hand in designing the procedures. The development and test tasks just described are summarized in figure 7-17.

In Alpine's case, this stage went very smoothly. Barbara thought this smooth operation was due to the complete design job on which John and Jim had insisted. The vendor had to make two calls to fix the connections between the CPU and one of the disk units, but the hardware was installed with no major problems. The programmers were hard at work within three days of the hardware acceptance inspection.

Jim had decided to write the member maintenance subsystem programs first, so that the data entry clerks could begin inputting the master file data. He and Carol and a temporary programmer worked diligently for five weeks to write and test the member master file system programs. Then, they turned the system over to the data entry personnel for training. The member maintenance subsystem had a few minor bugs, but largely it worked successfully from the start.

They were not as fortunate on the purchase update subsystem. There was a miscommunication between Jim and Carol about the editing of transactions generated on the key-to-disk equipment. Some

Figure 7-17   Tasks for the Development and Test Phase

Component	Task
Hardware	Install and test Check before warranty expires
Programs	Write from pseudocode designs Follow top-down, modular approach Test small modules before integration Document
Data	Build test files and check for errors Assemble data from sources Train data conversion personnel Build files Examine data for errors
Procedures	Complete and document users procedures Complete and document operators procedures
Personnel	Train operators Train users
	Perform integrated test

editing was done by the programs in the key-to-disk system, and some was done by the edit program. Carol misunderstood what was to be done on each component. Consequently, some programs had to be rewritten, causing some long nights and several weekends of work. Eventually, the programs were corrected successfully, however.

As soon as the member maintenance subsystem was fully tested, the data entry personnel began building the member master file. First, a tape of the member records was obtained from the service bureau that had been doing Alpine's processing. This tape was input to the member maintenance subsystem. The clerks went through a printout of this file and eliminated all erroneous entries. The Alpine staff was amazed at the number of duplicate records and the number of incomplete records in the service bureau's file.

Next, the data entry personnel began adding new members and making modifications. Alpine had changed their order form to request new addresses as orders came in. These address changes were made by the clerks as necessary.

The data entry clerks did not like the arrangement of fields on the CRT screen. They asked Jim to change it. Barbara intervened; she did not want Jim diverted from the purchase update program. However, she told Jim to make one small change and the other changes were put on data processing request forms for action at a later time. (The clerks had seen and approved the screen formats before they were implemented. However, after working with them for a period of time, they had a better idea of what they wanted. Jim thought that was frustrating but typical of systems work.)

While the programs were being written and the data converted to the new format, John was busy completing and documenting the procedures shown in figures 7-18 and 7-19. He had the part-time assistance of one data entry user and one operator.

Procedures

One procedure was written for each type of user activity, as well as more general procedures for what to do in case of system failure. Also, there were procedures for operations personnel to use when running the member master file programs. One other procedure explained how the operators were to dump the member master file for backup, and another explained how to use these backup files to recover.

These procedures were written in pseudocode similar to that used by Jim and Carol for designing the programs. John felt that pseudocode was easily understood. The users and operators were initially put off by the pseudocode format, but once they had used the procedures for awhile, they began to like it. As one of them said, "Once you understand this form, it is easy to use and very complete and concise." Figure 7-20 shows part of the procedure for processing rejected transactions.

Subsystem	Type of Procedure
1. General	a. System overview b. User responsibilities c. Backup and recovery procedures
2. Member Maintenance	a. Subsystem overview b. Retrieving data from the member master file c. Updating data in the member master file d. Reviewing the change report
3. Purchase Update	a. Subsystem overview b. Key-to-disk operations c. Preparing order entry information d. Reviewing the rejected transaction report e. Correcting rejected transactions f. Reviewing the summary and error report
4. Label and Dividend Check	a. Subsystem overview b. How to create mailing labels c. How to produce dividend checks

Figure 7-18 Users Procedures for Member Master File System

Figure 7-19 Operators Procedures for Member Master File System

Subsystem	Type of Procedure
1. General	a. System overview b. Operators responsibilities c. Backup and recovery procedures

2. Member Maintenance	a. Subsystem overview
	b. Program run instructions for:
	   (1) Member data retrieval program
	   (2) Member master file update program
	   (3) Change report program
	c. Backup activity
	d. Recovering the member master file

3. Purchase Update	a. Subsystem overview
	b. Key-to-disk operations responsibilities
	c. Run instructions for:
	   (1) Consolidation and edit program
	   (2) Purchase transactions sorting and merging
	   (3) Purchase update program
	d. Backup and recovery procedures

4. Label and Dividend Check	a. Subsystem overview
	b. Run instructions for:
	   (1) Mailing label program
	   (2) Dividend check program
	c. Backup and recovery procedures

```
General.
    The rejected transaction report has one line of data for each
rejected transaction. The first item on a line is the reason for
rejection; the second is the transaction number. The rest of the line
presents the data that was entered.
    You should review each line of this report and take action depending
on the reason printed as follows:

BEGIN-Procedure
DO for each rejected transaction
    IF reason is Invalid Number, No Such Number, or Purchase Amount Out of
      Bounds,
      THEN check the transaction printout against the original order
           IF a data entry error was made
              THEN submit a correction to data entry department
              ELSE send original order and error message to data quality
                     control for correction
           END-IF
      ELSE IF reason is Bad Master Record
           THEN send transaction data to operations for data
                     correction
           ELSE error is unknown. Send recycled transaction to your
                     supervisor.
           END-IF
    END-IF
END-DO
END-Procedure
```

Figure 7-20 Users Procedure for Correcting Rejected Purchase Order Transactions

Training occurred during all of this step. The operators, who had already been trained to use the equipment, were trained again on the member master file procedures. Also, the users were taught how to operate the CRTs and how to use the programs to accomplish their jobs. Data entry personnel were trained in the use of the key-to-disk equipment.

By the end of August, the member maintenance subsystem had been thoroughly checked. The member master file appeared to be in better shape than the one the service bureau was using for their processing. Testing was complete on the purchase update subsystem.

Work had not been completed on the label and check subsystem, but it appeared the work would be done and tested by the end of November. Barbara decided to ask the steering committee for approval to implement the system. The committee agreed.

SYSTEM IMPLEMENTATION

As stated in Chapter 4, there are four basic styles of implementation: *parallel*, *piecemeal*, *pilot*, and *plunge*. Alpine had the ideal situation in which to use parallel. They continued the service bureau processing for six weeks after they had begun to use the member maintenance subsystem. After one month, they compared the results from the service bureau to those produced by their own system. They found that several transactions that were to have been corrected were lost. A data entry clerk had accidentally thrown them away. Better controls were developed to ensure that all the transactions that were rejected were actually corrected.

Also, Alpine found that several changes were incorrectly made by the service bureau. Occasionally, the wrong member address was changed. It appeared that the service bureau occasionally mismatched transaction and master records. Alpine pointed that out to them with a sense of pride at the quality of their new system. After this review was complete, Barbara petitioned the steering committee to discontinue the service bureau contract. This action was taken. The member maintenance subsystem was up and running!

The Alpine implementation was considerably simpler than most. It is unusual for a system to be as clean and as well tested as the member maintenance subsystem was. Also, the system itself was simple and straightforward. Systems that are more complex, or that are to be used by companies that are more decentralized than Alpine, are harder to implement.

In theory, however, implementation should be easy. If the system is well-designed and tested, and if all the critical personnel are trained and have a positive attitude toward the system, it should go well. After all, it is not hard to drive a new car. However, easy implementation can only occur in situations where appropriate attention has been given to all five components of the business computer system—not just, say, programs and hardware.

QUESTIONS

7.28 What actions are taken with regard to hardware during the development and test phase?

7.29 When should program documentation be produced during development? Why?

7.30 Which of the five components of a business computer system should be tested?

7.31 What happens if bad data is allowed in the original data files?

7.32 Whose fault was it that Jim had to redo portions of the CRT screens?

7.33 Alpine had an unusually easy time of implementation. Why do you think this was true?

7.34 Could Alpine have used the piecemeal or plunge techniques of implementation?

SUMMARY

We began this part with a general discussion of the seven steps in the systems development cycle. Then, the first two were illustrated using Alpine Co-op as an example. In Chapters 5 and 6, we made a diversion from systems development to discuss the two fundamental styles of data processing: sequential and direct access. After that, we again resumed systems development to discuss the final five steps.

Hopefully, these chapters have given you an appreciation of the tasks that a systems development team must accomplish. In your business career, you will probably interface with one of these teams at some point, and the chances are good you will even be a team member. In that case, you should ensure that the team operates along the lines described here. If it doesn't, you should force some change. Disaster will surely result from a poorly organized systems development effort. You do not want to be put in the position of Chuck Swanson, who wrote the unfortunate memo at TYCON Construction Products.

Figure 7-21 (shown on the following page) summarizes the actions to be taken during the systems development process. Study this figure carefully. You should be able to list the seven steps shown in rows and the five components shown in columns. Further, for the alternatives, design, and development steps, you should know the actions specific to each business system component.

In particular, think about the roles of users and business managers. What should users do during feasibility analysis? What is management's role?

How can users ensure that the systems development staff understands requirements? How can management tell if the requirements phase has been successfully completed?

Ask the same question for the remaining stages of systems development. What roles do users and managers play? The answers to these questions will prove very useful in your business career.

Seven Development Steps	*Five Components of a Business Computer System*				
	Hardware	*Programs*	*Data*	*Procedures*	*Personnel*
Feasibility Study	Determine cost/technical/schedule feasibility. Form project team and steering committee (if necessary).				
Requirements Definition	Determine user requirements. These requirements then determine requirements for the five components.				
Alternative Specifications	Determine vendors of needed equipment.	Build vs buy (five sources of programs)	Processing styles (sequential, direct access, etc.)	Ways to meet users needs— depends on other components.	Organizational structure (users, operations, systems development)
Evaluation and Selection of an Alternative	Determine costs and dollar value of tangible benefits. Identify intangible benefits. Compare costs and benefits; select best alternative if cost-justified.				
System Design	Determine specifications. Initiate procurement.	Top-down design Pseudocode (Procure if choice is buy.)	File contents Data formats Relationship to programs	Design users and operators procedures.	Develop or procure training programs.
Development and Testing	Install and test.	Write programs, document, and test.	Create and test production files.	Document and test.	Conduct training. Test with rehearsals.
System Implementation	Choose parallel, piecemeal, or pilot integrated test. Do not take plunge.				

Figure 7-21 Summary of Actions on Components for Systems Development

WORD LIST		
(in order of appearance in text)	*Systems development cycle*	*Implement*
	Feasibility analysis	*Microcomputers*
	Determine requirements	*Minicomputers*
	Specify alternatives	*Mainframe computers*
	Evaluate and select alternatives	*MTBF*
	Design	*Computer family*
	Develop and test	*Request for proposal (RFP)*

Software house

Tailored programs

Turnkey systems

Password protection

System cost

System benefit

Cost/benefit analysis

Tangible benefits

Intangible benefits

Top-down design

Negotiation

Rejected transactions

Walkthrough

Module

Written program documentation

Requirement change

Parallel

Piecemeal

Pilot

Plunge

A. Which of the seven steps in the systems development process do you think is the most important? Which is the most difficult?

B. Do you think John should have used an RFP? Speculate on how the case could have developed differently if he had.

C. Describe an ideal business application for a microprocessor. Describe one for a minicomputer. Describe one for a mainframe.

D. What will happen if a company chooses a microcomputer when they really need a minicomputer?

E. What will happen if a company chooses a mainframe when they actually need a minicomputer?

F. Compare and contrast the risks of in-house written programs with turnkey systems.

G. In what situations is the cost/benefit analysis technique most likely to be successful? When is it likely to be unsuccessful?

H. Why is top-down design and programming likely to be more successful than bottom-up design and programming?

I. Why is a design walkthrough important?

J. Rank the four styles of implementation in the order of desirability. Explain your ranking.

QUESTIONS TO CHALLENGE YOUR THINKING

CHAPTER 8

**BUSINESS
TELEPROCESSING
SYSTEMS**

CHAPTER 9

**BUSINESS
DATABASE
SYSTEMS**

CHAPTER 10

**DISTRIBUTED
BUSINESS
COMPUTER
SYSTEMS**

PART 3

ADVANCED BUSINESS COMPUTER SYSTEMS

ADVANCED BUSINESS COMPUTER SYSTEMS

The fundamental business computer systems discussed in Part 2 are adequate for many business environments and problems. However, they have drawbacks and limitations that make them unsuitable for some businesses. In this part we will consider three types of advanced computer systems that provide more capability. Unfortunately, these systems are also more complex, more expensive to develop and operate, and more difficult to manage and use effectively.

Chapter 8 examines business teleprocessing systems. The prefix *tele* means distance. In these systems, the processing is done some distance from the user, or the originator of the request for processing. Chapter 9 is devoted to a discussion of database systems. These systems store data in an integrated manner. They allow data items to be processed by their relationship to one another. This type of processing results in easier access for the user, better data accuracy, and more information. Finally, Chapter 10 discusses distributed computer systems. These systems are similar to teleprocessing systems, except that the processing is not centralized in one location. Instead, data storage, update, and control are distributed among several geographically distributed computers.

These three chapters have a common format. First, we will discuss the essential character of the advanced computer systems. Then, we will examine the five components of the systems, and show how they differ from the components of the more fundamental systems presented in Part 2.

If you want only a summary of these topics, you can read the first five or six pages of each chapter. To obtain a greater understanding, you should read the descriptions of the advanced system components as well.

The systems development process will not be considered as heavily in Part 3. Although this process is just as important for advanced systems as it is for fundamental systems, there is too much material to include both advanced concepts and systems development. You can get greater exposure to systems development by taking the course following this one.

CHAPTER 8

Business Teleprocessing Systems

Wagner Pleasure Boats requires teleprocessing

WAGNER PLEASURE BOATS

WHAT ARE TELEPROCESSING SYSTEMS?

Three Examples of Teleprocessing Systems

Alpine Co-op

Medium-Sized Bank

Worldwide Shipping Company

Rationale for Teleprocessing Systems

Teleprocessing Applications

TELEPROCESSING HARDWARE

Transmission Media

Line Speed
Line Mode
Line Type

Sources of Communication Lines

Line Management

Communication Terminals

Multiplexers and Concentrators

Teleprocessing at the Central Computer

Communications Front-Ends

TELEPROCESSING FOR WAGNER PLEASURE BOATS

PROGRAMS FOR TELEPROCESSING SYSTEMS

Teleprocessing Application Programs

Protocols

Synchronizing Processing

TELEPROCESSING DATA AND DATA PROTECTION

PROCEDURES FOR TELEPROCESSING SYSTEMS

Concurrent Update Procedures

Backup and Recovery Procedures

TELEPROCESSING PERSONNEL

WAGNER PLEASURE BOATS

 Wagner Pleasure Boats manufactures motor and sailing boats for recreational use. Their smallest boat is a 14 foot runabout. The largest is a 35 foot sailboat. Wagner is located in Los Angeles, California.

Seven months ago, Wagner bought another company called Sabre Marine Hardware, located in Tampa, Florida. The cost of parts for boat construction had skyrocketed. They hoped to be able to reduce these costs by producing parts themselves.

Within a few months, it became apparent that Sabre was an unhealthy company. Their inventory was mismanaged; the costs of manufacturing were far too high; and employee morale was low. Consequently, Wagner Pleasure Boats decided to send their chief hotshot problem solver to

Florida to clean house. The problem solver was to fire inept managers and replace them with well-qualified personnel. Also, inventory costs were to be reduced and the manufacturing process made more efficient.

Suppose you are Wagner's chief hotshot problem solver. After you arrive at Sabre, one of your first observations is that there is little, if any, reliable information available on the company's operation. The accounting system is in shambles. The few computer reports that are produced are nearly worthless. The inventory system is so full of errors that no one pays attention to it. And so on.

This situation is particularly shocking to you because you are accustomed to the high quality data processing service you have received at Wagner. There, reports are accurate and delivered on time. The manufacturing business computer system is the backbone of the company's operation. You decide to eliminate Sabre's ineffective computer systems and to convert to the systems used at Wagner.

The question is, how? Sabre's current computer is too old and too limited to handle the Wagner programs and data. One possibility is to acquire another computer at Sabre and to install the programs from Wagner's data processing department. However, since you took business data processing in college, you realize that a business computer system is more than just hardware and programs. In addition, you will need data, procedures, and trained personnel.

It's this last component that concerns you. Sabre has been so mismanaged for so long that you doubt you can find enough high quality personnel to make the Wagner system operate. You could start a training program and build a data processing staff. You have enough other problems, however, and don't want to take the time to do this.

Another possibility occurs to you. Is there a way that you can access the Wagner computer in Los Angeles from the Sabre facility in Tampa? Could you somehow send the input data to Los Angeles for processing and have the results returned to Tampa? Even better, is there a way that people in Tampa can use CRTs that are connected to the computer in Los Angeles?

When you finish this chapter, you will know the answers to these questions.

Until the mid-1960s, most data processing was done on centralized, batch-oriented computers. However, for many business applications (like Wagner's), it was undesirable or infeasible for the data to be brought to the computer center for processing. The movement and delivery of the data on punched cards, magnetic tape, printed reports, etc., took too long and was too expensive.

Business people began to wonder whether telephones or other communications facilities could be used to transfer data. Today, a wide range of capabilities for such data transfer has been developed.

WHAT ARE TELEPROCESSING SYSTEMS?

Simply stated, *teleprocessing* is data processing at a distance. The term is derived from a combination of the terms *telecommunications* and *data processing*. Hopefully you know by now what data processing is, so only telecommunications need be defined.

Telecommunications is communicating at a distance, usually using some form of electromagnetic signal similar to that used for radios and TVs. The subject of telecommunications is a broad one that includes the transmission of voice, messages such as telegrams, facsimile (pictures), and data. The latter, called *data telecommunications* or *data communications*, is concerned with moving data from point to point, from terminal to computer, and even from computer to computer.

Now we can be more specific. A business teleprocessing system is a business computer system in which one or more of the five components are physically (geographically) distributed and the components are connected into a system using telecommunications facilities. All forms of telecommunications can be used. Data communication is used to transfer data from one site to another, voice communication is used to integrate distributed personnel, and message communication is used to implement distributed procedures.

Three Examples of Teleprocessing Systems

Alpine Co-op Alpine Co-op represents the simplest form of teleprocessing systems. Data entry clerks use CRTs to process the direct access files for the member master file and inventory/pricing systems. (See figure 8-1.) This is considered a teleprocessing system because the clerks and the CRTs are physically removed from the computer.

Figure 8-1 Teleprocessing System Used by Alpine Co-op

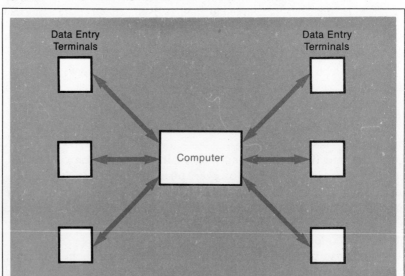

This is a simple system. Most clerks are in the same building as the computer and the others are not more than 100 meters (about 300 feet) away from it. As is frequently the case, all of the hardware is supplied and maintained by the same vendor, which eliminates compatibility problems. Both the CPU and the operating system are designed to support just this type of teleprocessing. Only a modest amount of work is required to install the hardware. (The other four components may require extensive work, however.) Consequently, Alpine does not need a staff specialist for communications processing.

Medium-Sized Bank Figure 8-2 shows the teleprocessing configuration for a bank that has three branches and operates a credit card authorization center. In addition to the CRTs and CRT-like terminals, there are cash machines and a remote job entry (RJE) station. The RJE station has a card reader, a printer, and a CRT for the operator to use.

Figure 8-2 Teleprocessing Equipment Configuration for Medium-Sized Bank

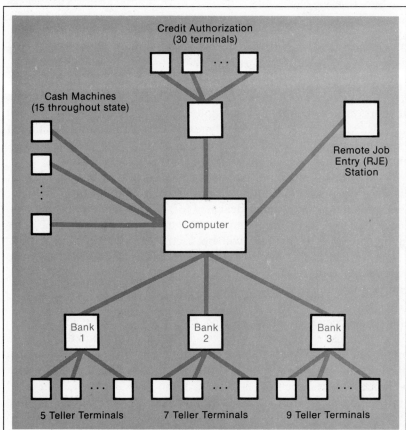

This equipment is used to submit batch jobs from the remote card processing center.

The bank's teleprocessing system is considerably more complicated than Alpine's. The communication lines are much longer and involve the telephone company and other organizations. The hardware is supplied by several vendors. Getting it to work together is not easy. Maintenance and problem fixing are sticky when one vendor blames the problem on another. Further, the operating system was designed to be general purpose. Someone must tailor it to the bank's environment. The bank needs one or more communications and operating system specialists on staff to install and maintain the hardware and programs.

The bank has less control over the terminal environment than does Alpine. The equipment may be misused, abused, or even fraudulently used. Since the applications are financial in nature, efforts must be taken to provide security. Finally, *response time* (the time it takes the computer to respond to a request or statement) is important to the bank. If response is too slow, customers will be kept waiting in line. Customer service will suffer. This case differs from the Alpine case where clerks, not customers, must wait.

Worldwide Shipping Company   A third teleprocessing configuration is depicted in figure 8-3. Clearly, this is the most complex of the three. Here, computer users in Alaska, Hawaii, and Europe communicate with the company's headquarters in New York. Not only are multiple vendors involved, but also multiple communication media. Phone, microwave, satellite, and other types of communications equipment are used. All of it must work together in spite of different speeds, conventions, and vendors.

Additional problems occur because of the international link. Europe, Canada, and the United States have different laws and customs. Also, the equipment is designed to operate to different standards. Since this is a large and complex configuration, multiple CPUs are involved. Some computers will be used to handle communications resources and traffic, but not to process data. The company may use several hundred CRTs. To build this system and maintain all the equipment requires a large staff of communications specialists.

Rationale for Teleprocessing Systems

Businesses develop teleprocessing systems for two major reasons. First, because the business is geographically distributed; the data originates, is processed, and is used at different places. In the example of the bank, customers transact business at a local bank, but the data is processed at a central facility. Outputs like the bank's financial statements then go to the bank's headquarters at still another location.

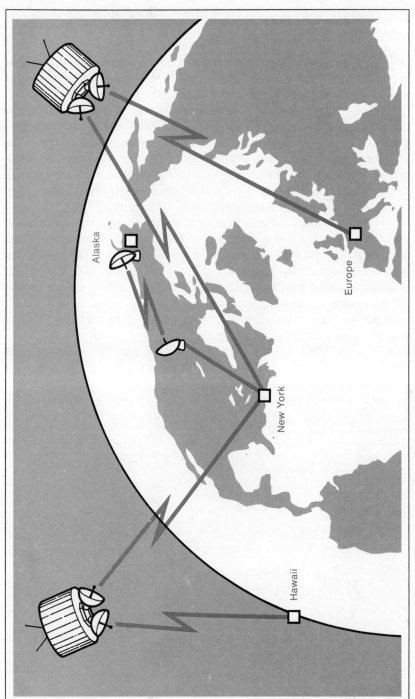

Figure 8-3 Teleprocessing Configuration for Worldwide Shipping Company

Second, teleprocessing systems are developed for economic reasons. Rather than separate data processing facilities for every bank, a central facility is established. The banks are connected to it via telecommunication links. This system allows the business to gain *economies of scale,* or cost reductions, by having one large computer instead of several smaller ones.

Unfortunately, these economies of scale do not extend indefinitely; as more systems are added to the central computer with teleprocessing, the facility becomes hard to manage and expensive to operate. Figure 8-4 shows the average cost of data processing as it relates to the size of the computing facility. At first, the average cost decreases as the size increases; but at some point, the computer becomes hard to manage and the average costs go up.

When a single, central computer becomes too large to manage effectively, another will be acquired and some applications transferred to it. At this point, the company will have two (or more) teleprocessing systems. (See figure 8-5.) Usually, these systems need to communicate in order to share data or facilities. Consequently, they are connected via telecommunications. The result is one large teleprocessing network with applications processing occurring at two separate sites. This is called *distributed processing*, because the processing of application data is distributed on two or more computers in the teleprocessing network.

To review, there are three major configurations of data processing systems. In the first, called *centralized processing*, processing is

Figure 8-4 Average Cost of Data Processing vs Size

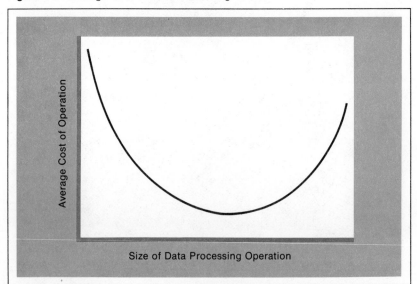

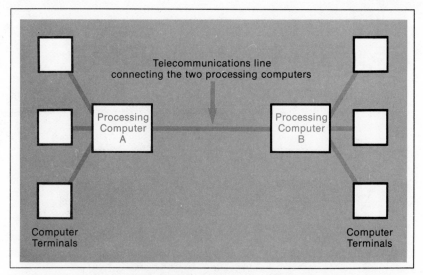

Figure 8-5 Example of Distributed Processing Using Two Computers

centralized on a single computer. Applications are batch-oriented; inputs arrive at and outputs depart from the computer center on physical media like cards or printed reports.

In the second major configuration, the components of the business computer system are geographically separated. They are united into a system, however, by telecommunications equipment. Processing of the data is still done on a single computer, however. Systems of this type are called *teleprocessing systems.*

Finally, in the third configuration, the system components are geographically separated and applications processing is done on more than one computer. Systems of this type are referred to as *distributed systems.*

In the past, data processing services have evolved from centralized to teleprocessing to distributed configurations. Recently, however, some businesses have started with minicomputer systems that support teleprocessing and thereby skipped the centralized stage. Alpine Co-op is a case in point.

We will consider teleprocessing systems in this chapter. Centralized systems were considered in Part 2. Distributed systems will be discussed in Chapter 10.

Teleprocessing Applications

Teleprocessing applications can be divided into two broad categories: offline and online. For offline applications, the data is transmitted from a remote location to the processing computer and stored. When a batch of data is complete, the computer processes it and then returns the output to the remote location as a batch.

Figure 8-6 Remote Job Entry (RJE) Station

Remote job entry (RJE) is a good example of offline teleprocessing. A computer run is input via RJE equipment like that in figure 8-6. The run is transmitted to the processing computer and stored on its files. After some period of time, the run is processed and the results stored on files at the central computer. Later still, the outputs are sent to the RJE station for printing.

Batched data transmission is another example of offline processing. Here, groups of data are sent to the central computer in batches. For example, a day's worth of sales data may be sent. The batch of data is then processed by one or more application programs at the central computer. The results are returned to the remote terminal and printed as a batch.

For online teleprocessing applications, the remote terminal is directly connected to the processing computer. Data is not sent in batches. Rather, a single record or message is sent, acted on by the processing computer, and the results returned. Then, another message is sent, and so forth.

Query and response systems are online applications. Here, the user sends a request for information like, "How many seats are available on Flight 102?" The processing computer determines the answer and returns it to the terminal. Such questions are acted on one at a time, not in batches.

Application	Teleprocessing System
Offline	Remote Job Entry
	Data Transmission
Online	Query and Response
	Transaction Processing
	Online Program Development

Figure 8-7 Types of Teleprocessing Systems

Transaction processing is another online application. The user sends a transaction like, "Add $1000 to Account Number 123123," and the processing computer takes the indicated action. A message is then returned indicating whether the operation was successfully executed or not.

Online program development is a third example. Users write programs at terminals by sending one line of code at a time to the processing computer. The computer then either translates the code and stores it if correct, or stores the code for later translation. Either way, the user sends one line at a time. Unlike RJE, the program is not sent as a batch. Figure 8-7 summarizes these classifications of teleprocessing applications.

This discussion completes a general introduction to teleprocessing systems. We will now consider each of the five components of a teleprocessing system and show how they differ from components of a centralized business computer system.

QUESTIONS

8.1 Why did Wagner's problem solver want to access the Los Angeles computer from Tampa?

8.2 What two terms is the word *teleprocessing* derived from?

8.3 What is telecommunications?

8.4 Define a business teleprocessing system.

8.5 Why is a medium-sized bank's teleprocessing system more complicated than Alpine's?

8.6 What are the two major reasons for developing a teleprocessing system?

8.7 How does centralized processing differ from teleprocessing?

8.8 How does teleprocessing differ from distributed processing?

8.9 Describe an offline teleprocessing application.

8.10 Describe an online teleprocessing application.

TELEPROCESSING HARDWARE

If you examine the teleprocessing systems in figures 8-1, 8-2, and 8-3, you will see that three basic types of hardware are involved in each: terminals, transmission media (lines), and central computers. Consider the transmission media first.

Transmission Media

A wide variety of media can be used to transmit signals. The simplest and easiest is a pair of wires that connect the terminal to the computer. The most sophisticated is communication via satellite. In between these extremes are telephone lines, radio, cable TV lines, etc. These media are classified according to their *speed*, *mode*, and *type*.

Line Speed The speed of a communication line is measured in bits per second (bps). Transmission media fall into three groups of speed. The slowest is called *narrowband* and permits communication at the rate of 45 to 150 bps. A simple pair of wires will allow narrowband communication. The second group is called *voice grade* and permits maximum transmission rates of 1800 to 9600 bps. These lines are called voice grade because their speeds are typical of those that can be obtained over a voice-oriented telephone line.

Regular telephone lines like those in your apartment or home can be used for data transmission. However, such lines only allow a maximum of 1800 bps processing. To obtain higher speeds, a line must be leased from the telephone company and given special *conditioning*. Only then is the 9600 bps maximum speed possible.

The third category of communication lines is called *wideband*; these lines permit very high speed communication at the rate of 500,000 bps or more. Communication via satellite is a good example of wideband service. Figure 8-8 summarizes these three categories.

Communication line speeds are sometimes given in another unit called *baud*. This term refers to the number of times per second that a line signal can change its status. This is not the same as bps; the speed in terms of baud is less than the speed in terms of bps. For data processing purposes, the term *bits per second* is always more informative than baud, and you should use it.

Line Mode In addition to speed, communication lines are classified according to mode. Two modes are possible: *analog* and *digital*. Analog lines carry signals that are continuous waves. The sounds of a siren or of a smooth melody can be thought of as analog signals. Voice telephone lines are analog lines. (See figure 8-9a.)

Digital lines carry signals that have sharp peaks and valleys. The sounds of a barking dog and of a dripping faucet are similar to digital signals. The graph in figure 8-9b illustrates a digital signal.

When a terminal sends a message to the central computer, it will do so by sending a series of bits. Thus, it might send the sequence 1, 1,

Line Speed	Transmission Rate
Narrowband (telegraph)	45 to 150 bps
Voice grade (telephone)	1800 to 9600 bps
Wideband (microwave or satellite)	500,000 bps or more

Figure 8-8   Speed of Communication Lines

0, 1, 0, 1. As you might guess, such a message is more easily carried by a digital line than by an analog one. The peaks of the digital line can be used to represent 1's and the valleys can represent 0's. (See figure 8-9*b*.)

Sending a series of bits on an analog line is not as simple. Somehow the continuous signal must be transformed to carry the bits. This transformation is called *modulation* and *demodulation*.

Figure 8-10 shows a common type of modulation called *frequency modulation*. This type works by causing the signal to oscillate faster to represent a 1 and to oscillate slower for a 0. *Amplitude modulation* works by making the signal larger (louder) for a 1 and smaller for a 0.

Figure 8-9   Modes of Communication Lines

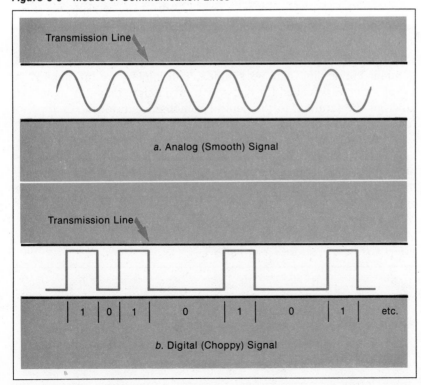

Transmission Line

a. Analog (Smooth) Signal

Transmission Line

| 1 | 0 | 1 | 0 | 1 | 0 | 1 | etc. |

b. Digital (Choppy) Signal

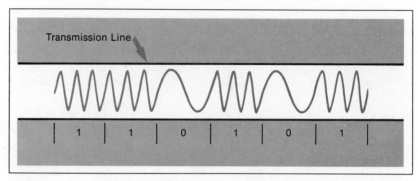

Figure 8-10 Analog Signal Representing 1, 1, 0, 1, 0, 1 Using Frequency Modulation

To transmit digital signals over an analog line requires a special device called a *modem*, or *mo*dulator/*dem*odulator. As shown in figure 8-11*a*, when the terminal sends a message to the central computer, it sends its digital message to the modem. The modem encodes the message into an analog signal and sends it over the analog communication line. At the other end, another modem receives the analog signal and converts it back to digital (binary) form.

Although modems, or *data sets* as they are sometimes called, are innocuous looking (figure 8-11*b*), they are expensive. Five to ten thousand dollars is a reasonable estimate of their cost.

Line Type   The third classification of a communication line is type. A communication line can be simplex, half-duplex, or full-duplex. A *simplex line* is designed for one-way transmission; that is, a signal can go from the terminal to the central computer, but not back. Simplex lines are cheap, but not very useful for business teleprocessing.

Half-duplex lines can carry a signal in either direction, but only one way at a time. Thus, the terminal can send a message to the computer, but the computer must wait until the terminal is finished before it sends a message. Half-duplex lines are like a road that is only wide enough for one car.

Figure 8-11 Use of Modems *(Part 1 of 2)*

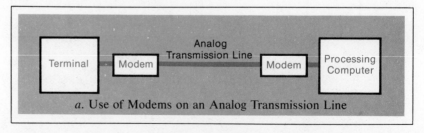

a. Use of Modems on an Analog Transmission Line

b. Modem

Figure 8-11   Use of Modems *(Part 2 of 2)*

    Full-duplex lines can carry messages in both directions simultaneously. Thus, while the terminal is sending a message to the computer, the computer can be sending a message to the terminal. A good application for a full-duplex line is an RJE station. While the terminal is sending the computer a job, the computer can be sending the terminal the results from a previous job for printing.

    The characteristics of communication lines are summarized in figure 8-12.

Figure 8-12   Summary of Characteristics of Transmission Lines

Line Classification	Characteristics
Speed	Narrowband (45 to 150 bps maximum)
	Voice grade (1800 to 9600 bps maximum)
	Wideband (500,000 plus bps maximum)
Mode	Analog (modems required)
	Digital
Type	Simplex (one way transmission)
	Half-duplex (one way at a time)
	Full-duplex (both ways simultaneously)

**Sources of
Communication Lines**

When a company decides to implement a teleprocessing system, it must determine not only the characteristics described above, but also the sources from which the communication lines will be obtained. One obvious choice is for the company to *build its own communications system*. For several reasons, however, this option is seldom chosen. First, the distances involved must be small enough so wires or coaxial cable can be used. Second, considerable expertise is required and such experts may be unavailable or too expensive. Third, communications technology is rapidly changing; most companies do not want to become locked into a system using present technology. This circumstance would happen if the company built an expensive communications capability.

A second source for communication lines are *common carriers*. In the United States, many common carriers belong to the Bell System owned by American Telephone and Telegraph. Common carriers provide two types of lines: switched and private. *Switched lines* are like those in your apartment or home; they are called switched because you can dial any other phone and the connection will be made by switching various phone circuits together.

If the communication line is to cover a long distance, companies have choices of programs. Using *direct distance dialing*, the company pays for each minute of the call just as you do when you dial long distance. This practice is expensive if there is much traffic to be sent.

Another option for switched lines is to obtain WATS (Wide Area Telephone Service) capability. Here, the company pays a fixed amount for a large number of long distance calls. The fixed amount is considerable (in the range of $1500 per month), but will be cheaper than direct distance dialing if there is heavy use. Other choices are becoming available as communications processing becomes more prevalent.

Private lines (or sometimes, *leased lines*) are a second type of service that can be obtained. Private lines are leased from the common carrier and provide a fixed path from one point to another, or from one point to several others. Since the path is fixed, special improvements or *conditioning* can be made so that the maximum transmission rate can be as high as 9600 bps. Figure 8-13 compares the advantages and disadvantages of switched and private lines.

In the United States, analog lines can currently be obtained on either a switched or private basis. However, digital lines are only available on a private basis. In Canada and other countries, digital capability can be obtained on both switched and private lines.

A third source for communication lines are the *satellite carriers* such as RCA AMERICOM. These companies either have their own satellites or pay to use those of other organizations. They provide both wideband and voice grade lines. The satellites are used as reflectors; they receive signals and transmit them back to an earth station. (See figure 8-14.) In this way, large amounts of data can be transmitted very

Type of Line	Advantages	Disadvantages
Switched	Destination points not fixed Costs based on use	Slower speed May possibly get busy signal Noise problems
Private (Leased)	Line never busy Fast speed Fixed cost Line conditioning possible	Fixed destination High cost for low volume

Figure 8-13 Advantages and Disadvantages of Switched and Private Lines

long distances. Unfortunately, there is a lengthy delay in the transmission.

A final source of communication lines are the *value-added carriers* such as ARPANET. These companies lease communication lines from the common and satellite carriers, add additional services, and sell the improved capability to other companies. In this way, they act as dis-

Figure 8-14 Example of Satellite Communications

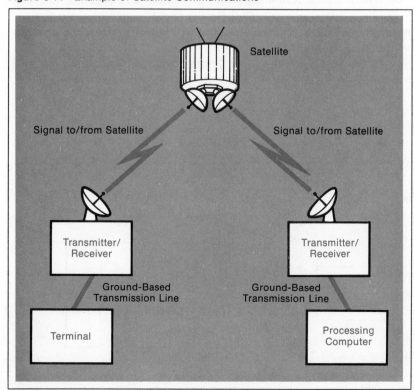

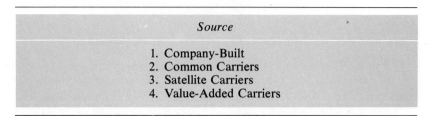

Source
1. Company-Built
2. Common Carriers
3. Satellite Carriers
4. Value-Added Carriers

Figure 8-15   Summary of Communication Line Sources

tributors of communication lines. The term *value added* is used because these companies add better error detection and recovery and faster response. Value-added carriers also have more flexible lease plans. Companies can pay for just the service they use. Lease periods are shorter. Figure 8-15 summarizes the sources of communication lines.

Line Management

A common problem in telecommunications processing is that the terminals are not active enough to keep the lines busy. To avoid this situation, several terminals can be connected to the same line as shown in figure 8-16. This is called a *multidrop* configuration because the terminals are "dropped off" the line.

When several terminals share the same line, a potential problem is created. If two or more of them use the line simultaneously, their messages will become garbled. To prevent this effect, two line management methods are used.

In the *polling* method, the central computer asks each terminal if it has a message to send. If so, the terminal is directed to send it.

The central computer then asks the next terminal, and so forth, in round-robin fashion. In figure 8-16, the terminals are polled in the order 5, 4, 3, 6, 2, 1, 5, 4, 3, 6, 2, 1, and so forth.

Polling works well but can waste CPU time. If none of the terminals has a message to send, the CPU is asking a lot of questions for

Figure 8-16   Multidrop Transmission Line

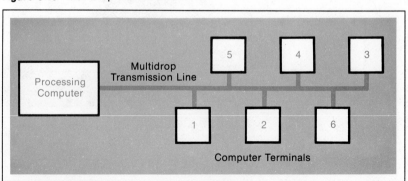

nothing. A second technique, called *contention*, overcomes this disadvantage.

When a line is managed by contention, each terminal listens to the line before sending a message. If the line is busy, it waits a period of time and listens again. Eventually, when the line is not busy, the terminal sends its message. When two terminals start to send messages at the same time, they notice the contention and stop. They then wait different lengths of time and try to send their messages again.

Contention is similar to a human discussion without a leader. It works well as long as no one monopolizes the conversation, and as long as no one speaks very long at a time. Using this comparison, if a terminal sends messages too frequently, or sends a single message that is too long, then other terminals will incur long delays in sending messages. Also, to work well, the line must have considerable excess capacity. Otherwise, terminals will get too many busy signals.

Like so many data processing alternatives, neither polling nor contention is better for all situations. Polling allows the line to be busier but takes CPU time; contention requires idle time on the line but does not involve the CPU. It becomes a question of which is cheaper — CPU time or line capacity.

Communication lines provide the vital link to integrate terminals with the processing computer in a teleprocessing system. However, to be effective, additional hardware is required at both the terminal and the computer ends of this link. We will consider terminal-oriented communications hardware next.

QUESTIONS

8.11   What are the three types of teleprocessing hardware?

8.12   All communications media can be classified according to speed, _____, and _____.

8.13   Narrowband communication lines transmit at the rate of _____ to _____ bps.

8.14   What are two other speeds of communication line (besides narrowband)?

8.15   What are the two communication line modes?

8.16   Which mode is closer to the format of computer data?

8.17   What is the function of a modem?

8.18   Name the three communication line types.

8.19   Why do most companies not build their own communications system?

8.20   What is a common carrier?

8.21   Explain the difference between switched and private lines.

8.22   What is a value-added carrier?

8.23   Explain the difference between polling and contention.

Communication Terminals

Primarily three kinds of terminal equipment are used in teleprocessing systems. The first type are the CRT devices. *Teleprinters* are the second type. This equipment has a keyboard with a printer enclosed or attached. Figure 8-17 pictures a typical teleprinter. The third type of equipment is used for remote job entry. Typically, RJE stations have a card reader, a printer, and a CRT or teleprinter. Some RJE stations also have disk storage to accumulate input before sending it, or to receive output before printing.

In the past few years, terminals have changed drastically. At first, terminals were slow, difficult to use, and functioned as slaves of centralized computers. They were essentially human-oriented input/output devices. Recently, however, inexpensive microprocessors have been integrated into the terminal equipment. The result is termed an *intelligent* (sometimes *smart*) *terminal*.

Since these terminals have microprocessors, they can be programmed to perform any number of tasks. They can have sophisticated

Figure 8-17   Teleprinter

Figure 8-18 Example of Sophisticated Screen Format

screen formats like the one in figure 8-18. They can have special key-strokes that allow data to be *scrolled* up or down when there is more data than can fit on the CRT screen at one time. Other special functions include inserting or deleting text; moving data items, lines, or other groups of characters on the screen; and so forth.

Additionally, intelligent terminals can be programmed to perform data editing. Input data can be checked for type limits (character vs numeric) and completeness, and check digits can even be calculated and checked during input.

Finally, if a terminal has storage equipment like a floppy, it can be used to store data for batch transmission. As the operator keys in data, it is edited and stored. After some period of time, say an hour, the data is then transferred from the floppy to the central computer in a batch. Processing in this mode can reduce communication costs. Instead of using the communication line for an hour, it is used only for the time required to send a batch. The line is not active while the operator pauses, corrects errors, and so forth.

Some terminals can be extended with intelligence and storage to the point that they are computers themselves. They can do batch processing or even handle queries and transactions. However, this makes the system a distributed one, so we will not consider this possibility until Chapter 10.

**Multiplexers
and Concentrators**

Typically, a communication link operates at much faster speeds than a terminal. A medium-speed line transmits data at the rate of 9600 bps, whereas a human reads at about 50 bps and types at about 15 bps. Further, there are human delays for thinking time. To reduce this imbalance, two types of communications equipment are used: multiplexers and concentrators.

A *multiplexer* receives several slow-speed transmission lines and combines them into one high-speed line. One method, shown in figure 8-19, is called *time-division multiplexing*. Here, five 300 bps lines are combined into one 1500 bps line. Each slow line is allocated one out of every five character positions on the fast line. If it has nothing to send, a blank character (shown as b in the illustration) is sent in its position.

Note that on the receiving end, the signal must be demultiplexed into its components; in this case there would be five outputs. Demultiplexing is similar to a line at the post office. People (messages) enter in one line and are distributed to windows (terminals). Unlike the post office, however, a message must go to a specific terminal.

A *concentrator* is an intelligent multiplexer. It combines slow-speed lines into a single fast line, but it does it more efficiently and performs other services as well. Concentrators allocate time on the fast line in accordance with need. For example, instead of allocating every fifth character to a terminal, it allocates many characters to busy terminals, and no characters at all to idle ones. Blanks are not sent.

Additionally, concentrators can compress data by removing repeated characters and by other more sophisticated techniques. The compressed data is sent over the transmission line and then decompressed into its original format. Concentrators provide error detection and correction capabilities not found in multiplexers.

Also, some terminal equipment operates on a different character code than others. (Remember character codes in Chapter 5?) One terminal may represent characters with a 7 bit code, while another uses 9 bits. A concentrator can convert all of these codes to a single convention.

Finally, concentrators can help the central computer to manage communications equipment. For example, a multidrop line might be connected to a concentrator. If so, the concentrator can poll the terminals and send their messages down the fast line to the central computer. This capability relieves the CPU of the responsibility of polling and also reduces traffic on the fast line. Figure 8-20 shows such an application.

Do not confuse polling and contention with multiplexing and concentration. The objective of polling and contention is to allow multiple terminals to share the same line but with no change in line speed. The message is received at the central computer at the same

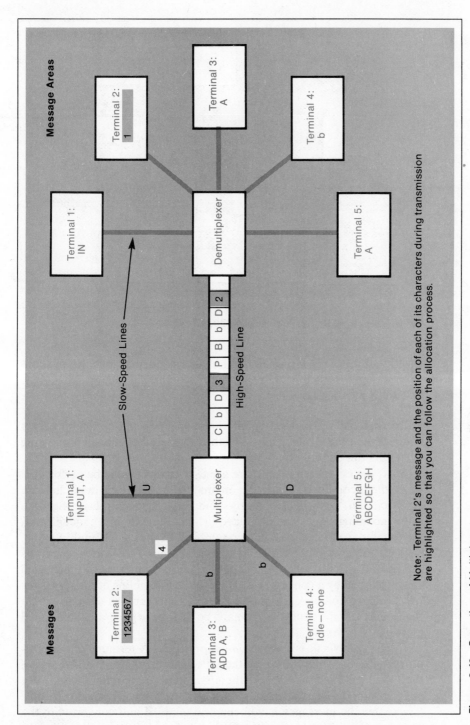

Figure 8-19 Operation of Multiplexer

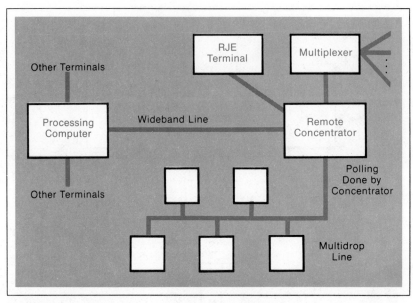

Figure 8-20 Example of Remote Concentrator Application

speed that it left the terminal. On the other hand, multiplexing and concentration allow the line to be shared by combining several slow-speed lines into one fast line.

Teleprocessing at the Central Computer

So far, we have discussed communication lines and communications equipment at the terminal end. The third component of a teleprocessing system is the central computer.

At the computer's end there are four basic tasks to be performed. First, the incoming transmission on analog lines must be demodulated. As discussed, this will be done by a modem at the central site. Second, if the incoming signal was produced by a multiplexer or a concentrator, the original messages must be reassembled. In the case of multiplexing, each character must be added to the correct message. For our previous example, every fifth character is part of the same message. If the signal was produced by a concentrator, then the reassembling of the messages will be more complex. In simple terms, whatever was done to create the signal from the concentrator must be undone to generate the original messages.

The third task is called *code conversion*. A terminal may represent characters differently than the CPU and other terminals do. If so, the CPU will have to convert the characters to a common code. If a concentrator is in use, some of this work will have been done by it.

After the messages have been reassembled and converted to the correct code, the final task of the CPU is to pass them to the application

Tasks

1. Demodulate analog signals
2. Demultiplex multiplexed signals (includes undo concentrator's work, if applicable)
3. Convert character codes
4. Pass data to correct application program or other destination (file, for example)

Note: Repeat action in reverse order to send output to terminals

Figure 8-21   Teleprocessing Tasks at the Central Computer

program. This is done by the operating system when the application program executes an instruction like "INPUT A, B."

Once the messages have been processed by the application programs, outputs may have to be returned to the terminals. In this event, all the steps just described are completed in reverse order. Also, if some terminals expect to be polled, the CPU must do this unless a remote concentrator has the responsibility. Figure 8-21 summarizes these tasks.

Now, this is a lot of work for the CPU. When you consider that the CPU is also supposed to execute the application programs, as well as run the rest of the operating system to manage file input/output and other tasks, you may wonder if it will have enough time to accomplish all of its tasks. In fact, for some systems this effort is a problem. The CPU has too many things to do and can't keep up with the workload.

Communications Front-Ends   In these situations, two solutions can be taken. One is to acquire a larger, more powerful CPU. Unfortunately, this can be expensive. A second solution is to acquire another, smaller CPU to handle just the communication tasks. Such computers are called *front-end processors*, or *communications controllers*.

A front-end computer acts in many ways like a concentrator, but it physically resides close to the central computer. It accepts inputs from terminals, multiplexers, and remote concentrators, and merges them together for the CPU. It performs code conversion, does error checking and correction, and polls the terminals if necessary.

 As you may have guessed, Wagner's chief hotshot problem solver wasn't really you. Instead it was Joan Adams. She did investigate the possibility of remotely processing from Tampa to Los Angeles, and within two months, Sabre Marine Hardware had a remote job entry terminal that was connected to the computer in Los Angeles. Two sharp data process-

**TELEPROCESSING
FOR WAGNER
PLEASURE BOATS**

ing individuals were sent to Tampa for six months to convert the most important applications over to the Wagner systems.

As it turned out, those two people stayed in Tampa. As fast as they could convert a system, Joan and some of her new managers were requesting that other systems be converted. Soon, the Tampa operation outgrew the single RJE terminal; users in Manufacturing, Engineering, and Purchasing were processing from CRTs that were connected to the computer in Los Angeles.

Figure 8-22 shows the communications hardware configuration two years after Sabre had been acquired by Wagner Pleasure Boats. The CRTs and the RJE station in Tampa were connected to a concentrator. It sent all of the traffic to Los Angeles over a wideband digital leased line. Some of the terminals in Tampa were connected to the concentrator over a multidrop line. The terminals in Manufacturing were polled by the concentrator. The terminals in Purchasing were managed by contention. The Engineering terminals were not active more than two weeks out of four. When they *were* active, however, they required very high transmission rates. They were displaying engineering drawings on the CRT screens that had a lot of detail to be transmitted. Since these terminals needed high speeds, they were connected directly to the concentrator.

As you might imagine, all this activity had quite an impact on data processing operations in Los Angeles. Wagner upgraded their CPU to a faster and larger model. After a year, even this measure wasn't enough. Consequently, they acquired a small computer to act as a communications front-end. This computer received input from Tampa and dispersed outputs. Additionally, it managed local CRTs on multidrop lines as shown. Figure 8-22 shows messages coming to the front-end labeled IN-WATS. These messages are sent by salespeople in the field who carry small teleprinters with them. The salespeople call the IN-WATS number (an 800 number) and are connected to the computer. They then key in orders and receive information from their hotel rooms, phone booths, etc.

The terminals in figure 8-22 generate a chaotic situation. All of them can be sending or receiving messages simultaneously. The concentrator and the front-end work together to bring order out of this chaos. The result of their efforts is an organized stream of input from the front-end to the processing CPU. To understand what happens next, we need to discuss the second component of a business teleprocessing system: programs.

QUESTIONS

8.24   What is an intelligent terminal?

8.25   Explain the difference between a multiplexer and a concentrator.

8.26   How is polling different from multiplexing?

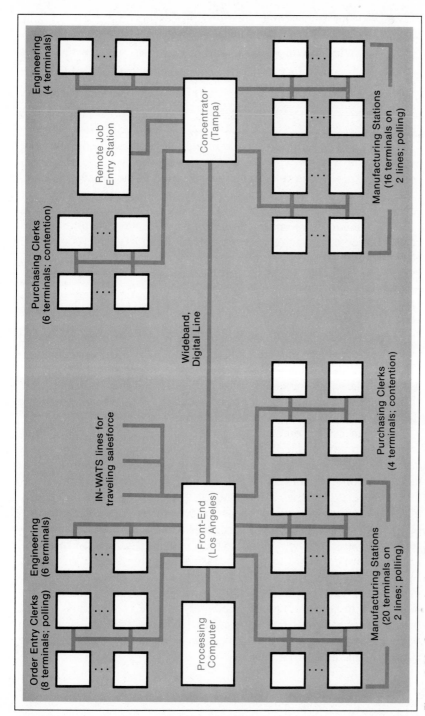

Figure 8-22 Communications Equipment Used by Wagner

8.27   Describe communications processing that must be done by a CPU or front-end.

8.28   Why do companies use front-ends?

8.29   Examine figure 8-22. Explain the function of each piece of equipment illustrated.

PROGRAMS FOR TELEPROCESSING SYSTEMS

Three types of programs are used in the teleprocessing environment: the *operating system*, *communications control programs*, and *application programs*. The operating system controls the processing computer's resources (not including communications equipment), and the application programs process the user's data to produce information.

Communications control programs control the flow of messages across the communications equipment. In figure 8-22, there are three places where programs are used to control the flow of messages. Both the concentrator and the front-end have programs to perform polling, multiplexing, code conversion, etc. In addition, the processing computer has a program to control the flow of messages inside its own memory.

Programs for the concentrator and the front-end can be purchased from the vendors of this equipment and tailored to the specific environment, or they can be developed by the using organization. The details of these programs are beyond the scope of this book and probably beyond your need as a business person. You should be aware that they exist, however, and that they must be acquired.

(As an aside, some of the earlier concentrators and front-ends were not programmable. They were easier to install, but not nearly as flexible as later ones. With the advent of inexpensive microprocessors, nearly all concentrators and front-ends are programmable.)

Figure 8-23 shows a schematic of the contents of main memory of the processing computer. The *operating system* is shown at the top of memory; this is the set of programs that control the computer's resources, allocate and deallocate files, execute I/O, and so forth. As messages are delivered to the processing computer, they are received by the operating system and delivered to another program, the communications control program. This program determines whether the message is to be acted upon immediately (online applications) or is to be stored on a file for later processing (offline). If the message is an online type, the communications control program routes it to the correct application program.

Teleprocessing Application Programs

Two *application programs* are shown in figure 8-23. One performs inventory processing. The other is used to process customer orders. In reality, there could be many more application programs. Messages are delivered to these programs and processed. When results are

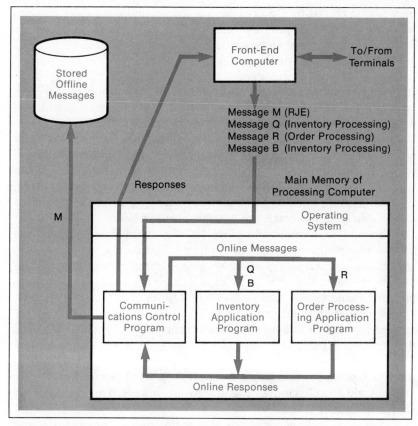

Figure 8-23   Programs Involved in Communications Processing

available, they are sent back to the communications control program and routed to the terminal that is waiting for a reply.

In figure 8-23, four messages are being transferred to the processing computer by the front-end. The first will be sent to the inventory application program; the next will be sent to the order processing program; the third to inventory processing; and the fourth will be stored on the file for later processing.

You should recognize an important detail. Although there may be many order entry clerks, there will only be one order processing program. As transactions arrive for order processing, they will have to wait in line just as humans do at the grocery store. When the order processing program is finished with an order, it will take the next one in line, and so forth. If orders arrive faster than the order processing program can handle them, a wait will develop.

Teleprocessing systems are amazing when you think of the work involved. In the Wagner Pleasure Boats case, a message originates on a terminal in Tampa, is sent 3000 miles to a front-end in Los Angeles, then is transferred to a processing computer, and eventually finds its way into the correct program residing in a main memory of perhaps 5 million bytes! It is then processed, and a return message retraces all of these steps. This entire operation may be done in five seconds or less!

Protocols

In order to route the message through this maze of processors, it must be packaged. When you want to send a package through the mail, you wrap it and put To and From addresses on the outside. A similar technique is used to package messages. As shown in figure 8-24a, header and trailer data is added to a message for routing and error control purposes. The header shows where the message is to be delivered and where it is from. The trailer contains parity bits for error checking. In fact, in some systems the trailer has enough data so that the error can be detected and corrected without retransmission.

There is a difference between the way that post office packages and teleprocessing messages are wrapped, however. In teleprocessing applications, a message may be wrapped several times. The process can be compared to putting a package inside a bigger box, then rewrapping and readdressing, and so on several times.

Consider an order entry transaction that originates in Tampa. It is wrapped as shown in figure 8-24a and sent to the concentrator. Now, the message is marked for delivery to the order processing program. The concentrator does not know just where that is. So, the concentrator wraps the message again, specifying the front-end as the To address and the concentrator as the From address. This procedure is shown in figure 8-24b.

When the message is received at the front-end, the outer layer of packaging is removed. Another one may be added. This time, the To

Figure 8-24 Message Packaging Techniques

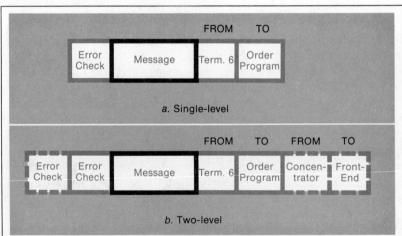

address becomes the processing computer and the From address becomes the front-end.

The number of layers of packaging depends on the complexity of the communications facilities. In one important international standard, up to seven levels of packaging have been defined.

The term *protocol* is used in the communications business to refer to the way that a message is packaged and handled between two communicating programs. Since the equipment on a communications system is likely supplied by different vendors, it is important that national and international standards on protocol be used. If two computers, say a concentrator and a front-end, conform to the same standard, they can interface successfully with one another. However, if they operate on different protocols, they cannot be used together. Consequently, one of the important considerations when designing a communications facility is to ensure that all components operate on the same protocol.

A question you may be asking is what happens if a computer sends a message and it is never received on the other end? For example, suppose the concentrator sends a message to the front-end, but a lightning bolt strikes the phone line and the message is never received. Without some type of control, the concentrator will wait and wait for a response, but none will ever come because the front-end never knew it was supposed to do something.

Synchronizing Processing

To prohibit this situation, the programs in the concentrator and the front-end are structured so that whenever one of them receives a message, it sends an acknowledgment to the other. Consequently, if a processor sends a message, but does not receive an acknowledgment in an agreed-upon time, it will retransmit the message. Also, these programs are written to ensure that the messages are received in the correct order and that no errors occur in transmission.

Figure 8-25 shows two algorithms used to control message transmission in this way. One of these is for the processor sending the message, and the other is for the receiver. These algorithms are simpler than those actually used, but they illustrate the programming that must be done.

The essential idea in these algorithms is that the sender receive an acknowledgment for every message it transmits. Furthermore, the sender will not transmit the next message until acknowledgment is received for the current one.

In figure 8-25a, the sender builds the message, transmits it, and waits for acknowledgment. If no acknowledgment is received in a given period of time, the message is retransmitted. Additionally, if a bad acknowledgment is received, or if the acknowledgment is for the wrong message, the sender will still wait and retransmit if necessary.

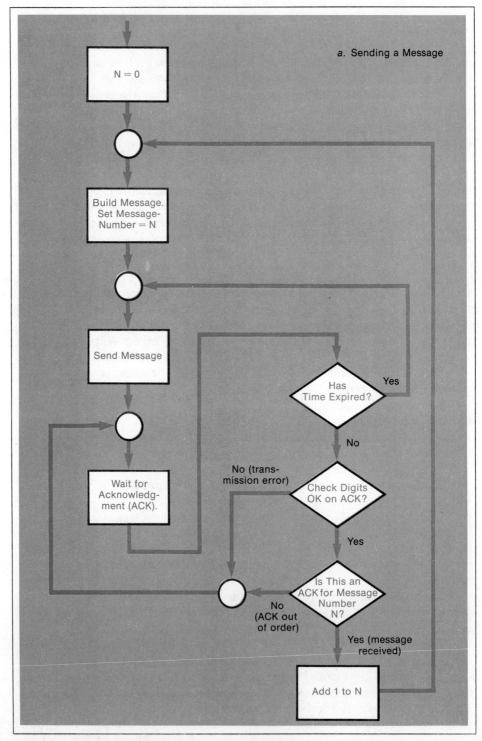

Figure 8-25 Simple Algorithms for Controlling Transmission *(Part 1 of 2)*

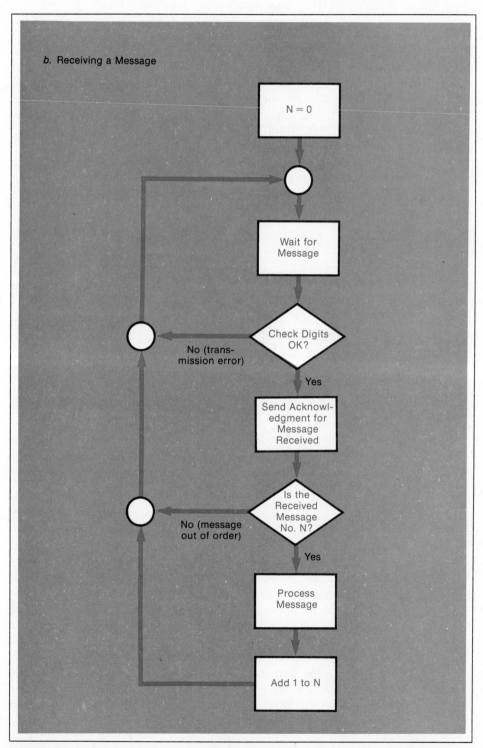

Figure 8-25 Simple Algorithms for Controlling Transmission (*Part 2 of 2*)

There are two reasons why an acknowledgment may not be received. First, the receiver may not have received the message (lightning bolt, for example). In this case, it is appropriate for the sender to retransmit. Second, the receiver may have received the message, but the acknowledgment may have been destroyed on its way back to the sender. In this case, the sender will retransmit even though the receiver got the message. Therefore, when the duplicate message is received, the receiver must send another acknowledgment; otherwise, the message will be sent again and again and again.

The easiest way to understand how these algorithms work is to try them. Ask your roommate to play the part of the receiver, and send a few messages to him or her. See what happens if either the message or the acknowledgment is lost.

QUESTIONS

8.30   What types of programs are used in the teleprocessing environment?

8.31   What are the functions of the communications control programs?

8.32   If there are 10 order entry clerks, all performing the same function, must there be 10 order entry programs?

8.33   What is a protocol?

8.34   Illustrate the packaging of a message with a three-level protocol.

8.35   What happens if a message is lost between a terminal and a computer? What keeps the terminal from waiting indefinitely for a response to a message the computer never received?

TELEPROCESSING DATA AND DATA PROTECTION

The third component of a business computer system is data. In the teleprocessing environment, data is subject to three special considerations. First, it must reside on direct access files; sequential processing takes far too long. Imagine your reaction if, when you wanted to withdraw money from your bank, you had to wait while the bank's entire depositor file was sequentially processed. It might take 20 minutes or more.

In the case of Wagner Pleasure Boats, the purchasing, order entry, and manufacturing personnel want their data to be available immediately. So, the data must reside on direct access files. Further, the files must be mounted on the devices. Thus, if the files are stored on removable volumes, the operators must be sure that the volumes are mounted.

The second special consideration for teleprocessing data concerns its vulnerability. Efforts must be made to preserve the accuracy (sometimes referred to as the *integrity*) of the data. Because the data is on line, and because there can be multiple users of the same data, it is easy for the files to be changed incorrectly. Furthermore, because the files are shared, when problems develop it is difficult to determine who or what is responsible.

Consider the case of Wagner Pleasure Boats. Suppose an order entry clerk confuses two part numbers. He uses the part number for bolts whenever he orders diesel engines, and he uses the part number for diesel engines whenever he orders bolts. Chances are that after two or three days, the order entry files will be a mess. There will be a great backlog on diesel engines. Furthermore, other order entry clerks will be misinformed. If one of them tries to input an order for a diesel engine, he or she will be told there is a great backlog. The company may lose an important order.

As another example, suppose Wagner has two order files — one for customer orders and one for in-plant orders for items used in production. If the order entry clerk accesses the wrong file (this is possible since both files are on line) havoc will result on the production line. This havoc, by the way, will all be blamed on the computer, even though the order entry clerk is at fault.

Since data is on line and since data integrity can be a problem, adequate security must be provided for the files. As a minimum, all online files should be protected by account numbers and with passwords. Only users with certain account numbers should be able to access the file. Additionally, these users must be assigned passwords that restrict the actions they can take. For example, read-only passwords might be used.

The account number restriction will prohibit users in Purchasing, say, from accessing order entry files. The passwords will keep order entry clerks from making unauthorized changes to order entry files. These features are needed not just to keep computer criminals out. They are needed to bring control and order to everyday business activity.

In addition to these precautions, some businesses use encryption to protect their data. *Encryption* is the coding of data so that it is unintelligible. Substituting one character for another is a simple encryption scheme. More sophisticated techniques are needed for real applications. Data can be encrypted when it is sent over communication lines and when it is stored on the files. Encryption is *not* effective unless the programs that do the encrypting and that use the data are protected from would-be infiltrators as well.

IN-WATS capability like that shown in figure 8-22 is particularly susceptible to unauthorized access. Some companies have automatic answering. A caller is connected to the computer with no human intervention. This facility is convenient but not secure. A much better approach is to have the caller identify him or herself to an operator who then transfers the call to the computer. Some computer terminals initiate conversations by broadcasting their identities. The front-end or processing computer can be programmed to check this identifier against a list of authorized terminals before proceeding.

To review, there are three special considerations for data in the teleprocessing environment. The data must be on line, and consequently, data integrity must be carefully managed. Finally, since online data is vulnerable, security is vitally important.

PROCEDURES FOR TELEPROCESSING SYSTEMS

The procedures needed to successfully operate a teleprocessing system are an extension to the procedures we have discussed previously. Concerning users, there must be procedures describing how to use the system under normal conditions. These include how to start and stop the system, as well as how to use it. Additionally, there must be procedures describing user activity during abnormal operation. These include how to tell if the system is operating incorrectly, what to do if it is, and so forth. Also, there must be procedures for users to follow when the computer system has failed. These describe what data must be gathered for restoration and what activities the users can allow before the system is operational. For example, bank tellers may allow deposits to accounts, but not withdrawals.

For operations, there need to be similar procedures both for normal operation and for operation during failure. The operations staff needs specific instructions about how to identify failures, what to do or whom to call, and how to recover files and restart programs.

In addition to these standard system procedures, teleprocessing systems require two other types of procedure. To illustrate the first, consider what happened at Wagner.

 About six weeks after a new teleprocessing order entry system had been implemented, Wagner's customer service department got a few complaints from customers who had been promised goods that had never arrived. Customer service personnel checked the order entry procedures. They seemed all right. The order entry clerks had checked to ensure that the items were in inventory, they were, and an order had been generated.

Furthermore, Shipping reported that they had received orders for goods that were not in inventory. At this point, data processing personnel were brought in to examine the situation.

Eventually, the source of the error was discovered; it had to do with the interaction of two clerks attempting to order the same part simultaneously. Figure 8-26 summarizes the action.

Clerk A's Activity	Clerk B's Activity
Read inventory record for item X.	Read inventory record for item X.
Take last item X from inventory.	Take last item X from inventory.
Set item count to 0.	(Clerk B's copy of the record does not show that clerk A just took the last one.)
	Set item count to 0.
Replace item X inventory record.	Replace item X inventory record.

Figure 8-26   Example of Concurrent Update Problem

Concurrent Update Procedures

The processing computer has only one CPU. Consequently, it cannot actually process two orders simultaneously. Instead, it will do some processing on one, then some processing on another, and so forth, until both are completed. However, the computer works so fast that it appears to the users that their orders are processed simultaneously. In computer terminology, the orders are processed *concurrently*.

What happened in the example in figure 8-26 is that the computer read an inventory record for clerk A, and then read the same record for clerk B. Next, clerk A took the last item from inventory and updated the inventory record. Subsequently, clerk B took what he thought was the last item from inventory and updated the record. At this point, the inventory showed 0 items for that part, but the last part had been issued twice!

This is called the *concurrent update problem*. It can occur in any system in which more than one user is allowed to update the same file. To get around the problem, programs have to be written to *lock* records before updates are made. The record is locked by giving exclusive control of it to one user. Other users cannot obtain the record until the first person is through with it.

In Wagner's case, this portion of the order processing program had been written by a new programmer who did not understand the need for locking and unlocking. Once the problem was fixed, Wagner's data processing department developed new procedures for the coding of programs to ensure that this situation would not recur.

Additionally, Wagner developed new procedures for users to prevent concurrent update problems. Basically, the users were given two new commands. One was a read command for information purposes only. The other was a read command for update purposes. Thus, if a clerk only wanted to know the number of items in inventory, he or she would use the first read. However, if the clerk wanted to determine if there were a sufficient number of items in inventory, and if so, to order them, then he or she would use the second read command. Programs were written so that if the user tried to update after using the first command, an error message was generated.

To summarize, teleprocessing systems are multiple-user systems. As such, they are susceptible to the concurrent update problem. Obviously, procedures must be developed for both programmers and users to ensure that such problems do not occur.

Backup and Recovery Procedures

Teleprocessing backup and recovery also require extensions to the standard procedures. Examine figure 8-23. Imagine what happens if the computer fails after all four messages have been input to the processing computer's main memory. Parts of order transactions and parts of inventory transactions may have been completed. Then again, they may not have been. When a computer fails, there is no sure way to tell what has occurred.

Since the status of the machine is unknown, the status of the files is also unknown. Suppose, during recovery, the first inventory message is processed again. It may have been processed successfully before the failure as well. In this case, it will be processed twice. On the other hand, there is the danger that it was not processed before the failure. In this case, it will be skipped if it is not processed during recovery.

One solution to this problem is to restart from a backup file and reapply all the transactions processed since the backup was made. However, this procedure can be very time-consuming. The users will be impatient if they are waiting for the system to return so that they can resume their jobs.

Another problem when reprocessing is that it is difficult to repeat the exact sequence. If two transactions are recovered in a different order than they were processed originally, strange results can occur. For example, if during the original run, customer A got the last part 123, but during recovery, customer B gets the last part 123, then the order documents produced during the original run will disagree with the recovered files. This situation can create great havoc in a company.

Another interesting possibility is to consider what may happen if the front-end in figure 8-22 fails. Assume it just quits. Then none of the terminals can talk to the processing computer, and the processing computer cannot talk to the terminals. This standoff is material for the nightmares of the systems staff.

Backup and recovery for teleprocessing systems is a difficult subject. We cannot solve Wagner's problem here. You should be aware of the need for backup and recovery, however, and know that procedures must be written to cover all possibilities.

TELEPROCESSING PERSONNEL

The personnel required to operate a teleprocessing system are also an extension to those required for batch systems. As with any business computer system, both the users and the operations staff must be trained in procedures. Further, the systems development staff must know how to build and maintain programs for online processing. Programming in this mode is different from batch programming. Some additional training may be required.

In addition to these standard personnel requirements, several specialists may be needed. *Hardware communications specialists* know how to maintain and repair communications-oriented hardware. They also are important members of a communications design team. These people maintain an inventory of diagnostic equipment. They are called upon whenever there is a communications hardware failure.

These personnel are expensive and hard to find. Therefore, only companies having large communications systems have such specialists on staff. Other companies contract with vendors or with independent communications consulting companies to supply these personnel when needed. For simple telecommunications systems like that described for Alpine Co-op, the vendor provides communications support under the maintenance contract for the computer. Independent expertise is needed when several vendors are involved.

Software communications specialists know how to build and maintain the programs on communications processors like concentrators and front-ends. They also specialize in products like the communications control program shown in figure 8-23. The level of expertise needed to maintain these programs is much the same as the level of expertise needed to maintain the operating system. Some companies have one or more people who maintain all of these programs. This group is sometimes referred to as the *systems shop* because they maintain the systems programs.

In addition to these experts, there is a person who is woefully neglected in most companies. He or she is vital to the success of a large teleprocessing system. That person is the *buyer* or *purchaser* of this equipment. Buying or negotiating leases for communications equipment is tricky business. The equipment is complex; there are many pitfalls; and there are more than a few fly-by-night companies. Companies that intend to build large communications systems are well advised to use trained buyers when contracts are to be negotiated and signed.

A final person who is especially important in teleprocessing systems is called the *data administrator*. This person is the custodian of the shared data in the teleprocessing system. He or she is responsible for resolving conflicts between users, for ensuring that procedures are followed, and, in general, for protecting the data. This job is especially important in the database environment. We will discuss it in detail in the next chapter. For now, you should realize the need for someone to have responsibility for protecting shared data.

QUESTIONS

8.36   The three special conditions for data in teleprocessing systems are _____ data, careful management of data _____, and a vital need for data _____ .

8.37   Why are passwords needed for online teleprocessing files?

8.38   What is encryption?

8.39   Describe the concurrent update problem. How can it be prevented?

8.40   Why are teleprocessing systems difficult to back up and recover?

8.41   What two types of specialized personnel are needed to support a teleprocessing system?

SUMMARY

This chapter has introduced the major concepts of business teleprocessing systems. We defined the terms *teleprocessing* and *telecommunications* and described three examples. Businesses develop teleprocessing systems because the business enterprise is geographically distributed and for economic reasons. Because of economies of scale, it can be cheaper to have one central computer with communications capability than to have many disconnected, distributed computers.

We identified three stages in the growth of computer capability: *centralized*, in which all computing is done in batch mode on a single computer; *teleprocessing*, in which all computing is done on a single computer, but the users are connected via telecommunications equipment; and *distributed*, in which computing is done on distributed computers.

In the remainder of the chapter we discussed the five components of a business teleprocessing system. Considering hardware, communication lines were discussed in some depth. Lines can be classified according to speed (narrowband, voice grade, and wideband), according to mode (analog and digital), and according to type (simplex, half-duplex, and full-duplex). Also, we discussed sources of communication lines.

Other hardware components discussed included teleprinters, remote job entry terminals, and CRTs. Finally, multiplexers, concentrators, and front-end computers were described.

Two types of programs are needed in the teleprocessing environment. Message control programs are written to transmit messages from a terminal to the relevant application program and then back again. Such programs are used on concentrators, on front-ends, and as the communications control programs inside the processing computer's main memory. The second type are application programs that perform tasks like inventory, order entry, and other user-related functions. Application programs in teleprocessing systems and batch systems are nearly the same.

In the teleprocessing environment, data is used by more than one person. The integrity of the data can easily be lost. Therefore, the data must be subjected to rigorous security controls. Also, since problems can occur as a result of concurrent updates, special procedures for users and programmers must be devised. Further, special backup and recovery procedures are needed because of the complexity of teleprocessing systems.

Finally, we discussed personnel needed for teleprocessing systems. In addition to the usual people, communications specialists for both hardware and software are needed. Also, a specially trained buyer is important. Finally, because the data is shared among many users, there is a need for a data administrator.

WORD LIST

(in order of appearance in text)

Teleprocessing

Telecommunications

Data communications

Remote job entry (RJE) station

Response time

Economies of scale

Distributed processing

Centralized processing

Offline processing

Online processing

Batched data transmission

Query and response systems

Transaction processing

Online program development

Communication line speed

Communication line mode

Communication line type

Narrowband

Voice grade

Wideband

Bits per second (bps)

Baud

Analog lines

Digital lines

Modem

Data set

Frequency modulation

Amplitude modulation

Simplex lines

Half-duplex lines

Full-duplex lines

Common carrier

Switched lines

Private (leased) lines

Direct distance dialing

Wide Area Telephone Service (WATS)

Line conditioning

Satellite carrier

Value-added carrier

Multidrop line

Polling

Contention

Teleprinter

Intelligent terminal

Multiplexer

Time-division multiplexing

Concentrator

Front-end

Operating system

Communications control program

Application program

Protocol

Message acknowledgment

Online data

Data integrity

Data security

Passwords

Encryption

Concurrent update problem

Locking mechanism

Backup and recovery procedures

Hardware communications specialists

Software communications specialists

Systems shop

Data administrator

QUESTIONS TO CHALLENGE YOUR THINKING

A. Suppose again that you are Wagner's problem solver. How would you decide whether to expand your own local data processing facility or to communicate with the facility in Los Angeles? What costs would you consider? What benefits would you measure? How would you proceed?

B. Suppose Wagner did not acquire a concentrator in Florida. How would the system configuration in figure 8-22 change? How many lines would be needed between Tampa and Los Angeles? What additional equipment might be needed?

C. Suppose the users of the teleprocessing system shown in figure 8-22 complained that response time was too slow. What could be done to improve it?

D. Find an organization that has a teleprocessing system. Interview the Director of Data Processing or other responsible individual to find out how they do backup and recovery. What backup files are kept? How often are they obtained? How are transactions saved? How is the recovery performed? What procedures are there for users and for operations personnel? Are there any special programming restrictions?

E. In the past few years, several notorious computer crimes have been accomplished using teleprocessing systems. Pick any one of them and find what you believe was the cause or causes of the crime. Was the problem in hardware, programs, data, procedures, or personnel? What can be done to prevent the recurrence of the crime in the future?

CHAPTER 9

Business Database Systems

Cash machine accesses centralized database for transaction processing

PROBLEMS OF FILE PROCESSING

Batch-Oriented File Systems

Disadvantages of File Processing Systems

WHAT IS DATABASE PROCESSING?

Advantages of Database Processing

Disadvantages of Database Processing

DATABASE DATA

Integrated Files

Hierarchical Record Relationships

Network Record Relationships

Three Views of Database Data

Database Overhead Data

Inverted Files
Linked List Structure

DATABASE HARDWARE

PROGRAMS FOR DATABASE PROCESSING

Using the DBMS

Database-Oriented Application Programs

DBMS Commands and Precompilation

Locking Commands

PROCEDURES FOR DATABASE PROCESSING

Procedures for Sharing the Database

Processing Rights and Responsibilities

DATABASE PERSONNEL

Data Activity Management

Managing Database Structure

Evaluating the DBMS Performance

DBA Organizational Placement

PROBLEMS OF FILE PROCESSING

 "This darn bank," thought Jeremy Williams. "They still don't have my address right. I've told them to change it twice already, but they still have it wrong!"

"Look at this, John," said Tricia Lucero. "We get three separate mailings from the bank. One is for our checking account; another is for our savings; and the third is for the car loan. It's confusing. Every week we get another piece of paper from them. Why don't they put it on one statement? It would sure save on their mailing costs and be less confusing for me."

"Fred, FRED, FRED! Where is that data I wanted on the Parks loan application? I asked for it a week ago. We need to take some action on this request. Get it for me!"

"I'm sorry, Ms. Baker, I can't find it in all these computer printouts. I asked Data Processing to give me the data last week. They said it would take a month to write the programs. I told them you had to have it right away. The next morning these three boxes of computer printouts were on my desk. I guess the data's here somewhere."

These people are all expressing frustration at the information system used to process customer accounts. These systems are all batch-oriented file processing systems. They are shown in figure 9-1.

Figure 9-1a depicts the system used to process checking accounts. Every evening, deposit slips and canceled checks are input to the check processing program, along with the check master file. The deposits are made to the accounts. Checks are canceled as long as the balance is large enough. The program produces a new check master file and a file of bank transfers as output. Further, a summary of account balances is printed for use by the tellers the next day. At the end of the month, the master file is used to print customer statements.

Batch-Oriented File Systems

The customer savings system is shown in figure 9-1b. This system is similar to the check processing system except that no file of bank transfers is produced. Finally, figure 9-1c shows the system used to account for customer loans. Payments are posted to the accounts as they arrive. Once every two weeks a report is printed showing the status of the various loan accounts.

These three systems are typical batch-oriented file processing systems. They are effective in that they account for financial transactions accurately, and they allow the bank to conduct business in an orderly manner. However, as we have seen, they have disadvantages.

First, file processing systems like these have *duplicated data*. The customer's name, address, and other data may be recorded several times. If a customer has both checking and savings accounts, his or her personal data will be recorded twice: once in the check master file and once in the savings master file. People who have checking, savings, and loans will have their data recorded three times. If a customer has multiple checking or savings accounts, his or her data will be recorded even more times.

Disadvantages of File Processing Systems

Why is this a problem? Consider what happens when a customer moves, changes names, or changes other personal data. All files containing the data must be updated. The new address, for example, must be inserted in the checking, savings, and loan master files if the customer has all three types of accounts. This task isn't hard as long as the bank realizes the customer has all three account types, and as long as the bank can readily find all three account numbers.

In practice, most such modifications are made successfully and customers are satisfied. On occasion, however, someone slips up and

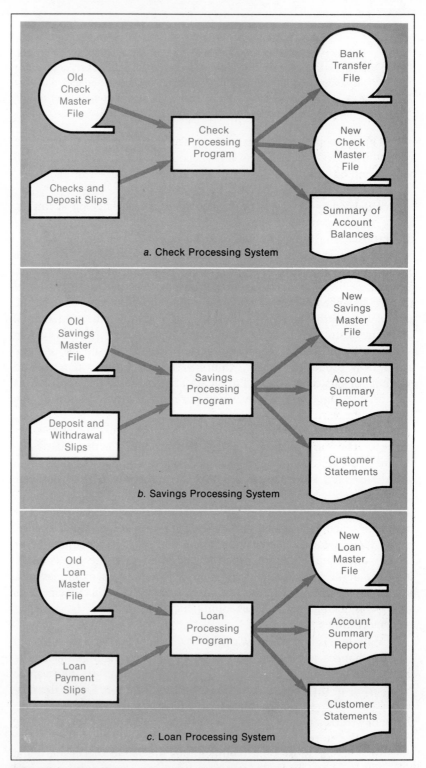

Figure 9-1 Batch-Oriented File Processing Systems

some of the necessary changes are not made. This happened in Jeremy Williams' case. He had three separate checking accounts; one for personal use, one for a part-time business; and one because he was treasurer for a local chess club. When he moved, the bank just changed the address in one account. He kept complaining and eventually the addresses in all three accounts were changed.

Another disadvantage of duplicated data is wasted file space. This can be a problem when files are large. Typically, however, adequate file space is available and not very expensive. Therefore, the problem of data integrity is a more important disadvantage.

A second disadvantage of file processing systems like those in figure 9-1 is that data is not integrated. For example, it is difficult to obtain all the data for one customer. People like Tricia Lucero like to have a single, integrated statement. This is a reasonable request. And she's right; the bank's mailing expense would decrease substantially if they produced a single statement for each customer.

However, as the files are structured, this is a difficult task. A program would have to be written to obtain customer data from each of the master files and print it on a single form. Since the account numbers are different for the three types of accounts, the bank would need a file that showed all account numbers for every customer. Even then, producing integrated statements from the files would not be easy. (If you wonder why, try to write pseudocode to produce the report.)

A third disadvantage of systems structured like those in figure 9-1 is that new requests and one-of-a-kind requests are difficult to implement. Ms. Baker knew that Mr. Parks had had trouble paying his loans in the past and that he had written several bad checks. She wanted her assistant, Fred, to determine how many such checks had been written and what his loan repayment situation was. Fred was frustrated because Data Processing couldn't seem to give him that data. In fact, Data Processing itself was frustrated because it couldn't provide the data Fred wanted.

In this chapter, we will discuss a style of data processing that overcomes these disadvantages. Called *database processing*, it represents data in an integrated manner.

WHAT IS DATABASE PROCESSING?

Database processing is a technique for organizing and manipulating data files in an integrated manner. Relationships among the records are represented, and these relationships are used to process the data. For example, suppose a company keeps records about company departments and about employees. In a database application, these two types of records are integrated into a single database. Furthermore, the relationship between department and employee records is represented.

ADVANCED BUSINESS COMPUTER SYSTEMS

Thus, it is possible to retrieve all the employees who work in department 123 or to determine the name of the department in which employee Jones works.

Figure 9-2 shows how programs relate to the database. Contrast it with figure 9-1. In figure 9-1, the programs perform I/O on the files directly. In figure 9-2, the programs call upon an intermediary, called a *database management system* (DBMS), to do the I/O. Programs in a database application do not have READs and WRITEs for data. Instead, they call the DBMS and ask it to retrieve or enter needed data.

In a sense, the DBMS operates like a data librarian. Programs pass data to it for storage. Later, they recall it, and perhaps change the

Figure 9-2 Bank Processing Using Database Technology

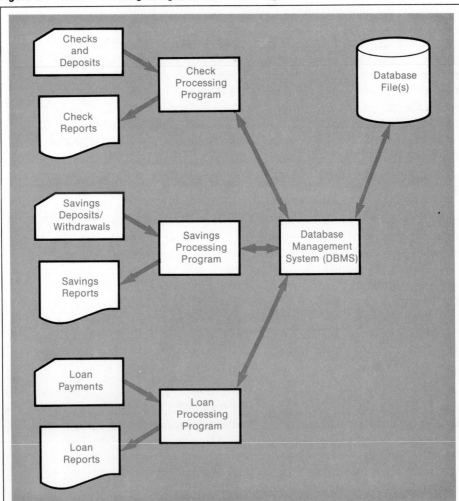

data and store it again. Also, the programs might ask the DBMS to delete the data. To do this, the program needs to identify the data by key. The DBMS uses the key value to find the data in the database. Also, users or application programs share the data just as books are shared in a library.

To show the advantages of database processing, consider the processing needs of the bank discussed previously. Figure 9-3 shows four types of records. The first record contains data about a customer, such as name, address, and other data. The second record is a checking account record. It has account number, account type, balance, and so forth. The remaining two record types have data about savings accounts and loans.

Advantages of Database Processing

Figure 9-4 shows some examples or instances of these record types. The lines represent *relationships*. Thus, customer Jones has checking account number 1000 and savings account number 5050.

Figure 9-3 Four Record Types in Bank Database

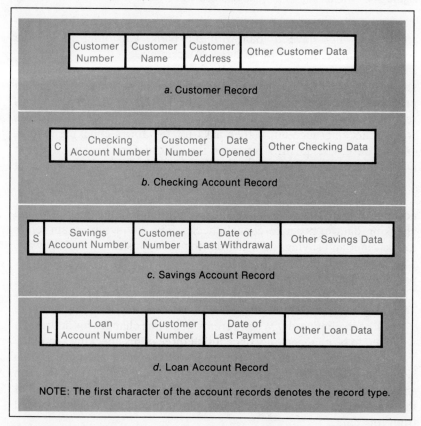

a. Customer Record

b. Checking Account Record

c. Savings Account Record

d. Loan Account Record

NOTE: The first character of the account records denotes the record type.

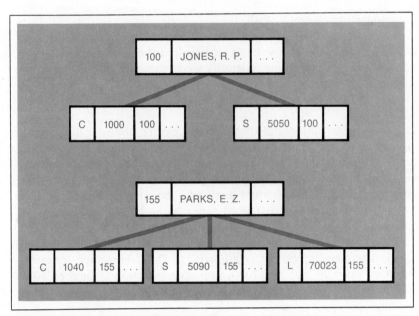

Figure 9-4 Two Examples of Bank Records

Jones does not have a loan with the bank. Customer Parks, the second example, has all three types of accounts.

In a database application, all of this data, including the relationships, is sent to the DBMS for storage. Later, when an application program asks for data about Jones, the DBMS retrieves the Jones record shown in figure 9-4. If the application program wants to process Jones' checking account, it then asks for the Jones checking record. In this case, the DBMS retrieves the record for checking account number 1000 and sends it to the application program. The retrieval was done by *relationship* — not by key value or sequential position.

Using database technology, the bank has three programs to do its account processing. The checking program refers to customer and checking data in order to cancel checks. The savings program refers to customer and savings data in order to post deposits and withdrawals. The loan program refers to customer and loan data in order to post payments against loans.

All three programs refer to the same copy of the customer data. Thus, the duplicated data that we noticed for file processing in figure 9-1 has been eliminated. When Jeremy Williams changes his address, it will need to be changed only once for all three of his checking accounts.

Additionally, integrated processing of customer accounts is possible. To produce a consolidated statement, an application program simply retrieves a customer record from the database along with all of that customer's accounts. The consolidated statement can be produced from this data.

Finally, database applications provide more general ways of accessing data. As just illustrated, records can be accessed by *relationship*. Additionally, records can be accessed by any of several keys. In Chapter 6, we defined *key* as a field that is used for identification purposes. Database systems generalize on this concept. Several fields can be used as keys. Thus, customer records can be accessed by customer bank number, or by customer social security number, or by some other key. Additionally, database systems support *nonunique keys*. Such keys identify groups of records. A key on ZIP code, for example, identifies all the customers living in a particular area.

Thus, a DBMS is a general purpose program that provides multiple ways of accessing data. This means that new requests and one-of-a-kind requests are more easily satisfied by database applications.

In addition to these multiple access paths, most DBMS vendors supply a special utility called a *query/update program* to complement the DBMS. Such a utility provides an English-like capability to access or update data in the database. Using multiple keys and the query/update utility, someone like Fred can obtain data such as that required by Ms. Baker.

In addition, database processing can provide one more advantage as compared to file processing systems. Some database systems create *program/data independence*. That is, the programs are independent of the format of the data on the files. To understand this concept, examine figure 9-2. The application programs do not process the files directly; rather, they ask the DBMS for the data. Therefore, when a file format is changed, only the DBMS is impacted. Although DBMS processing must be changed, the application programs can be left alone.

The database processing environment differs drastically from the file processing environment. For file processing, when a file is changed, all of the programs that process the file must be changed. In a large system, this could be 50 programs or more. In fact, in a file processing environment, sometimes desired changes to the files are not made because of the amount of work necessary to modify the affected application programs.

The advantages of database processing that we have discussed are summarized in figure 9-5.

Figure 9-5 Database Processing Advantages and Disadvantages

Advantages	*Disadvantages*
Elimination or reduction of duplicated data	Expensive
	Difficult initial development
Integrated processing	Vulnerability to crash
Generalized access to data	High equipment requirements
Program/data independence	

**Disadvantages of
Database Processing**

Unfortunately, in the data processing environment, nothing is all good, and so it is with database systems. Database processing has several major disadvantages. First, it can be expensive. The DBMS shown in figure 9-2 is a large, complex computer program. For mainframe computers, the DBMS program alone can cost $100,000 or more. For minicomputers, the cost is more reasonable — say around $5,000 — but it is still a factor.

Since databases can be complex, the systems development personnel must be well trained. This training can be time-consuming and expensive. One company spent over $100,000 in two years just on training.

Another disadvantage is that database applications are difficult to develop initially. The DBMS must be informed about the structure of the database. To do this, computer specialists define a *schema*, or definition of the database structure. The schema describes data items, record contents, and record relationships. Figure 9-6 shows a simple schema for the bank database.

After the schema is defined, the data must be loaded into the database. Special utilities are used for this purpose. Furthermore, application programmers must learn to use special commands to process the database. This learning process takes time. Finally, since a database will be shared among many users, procedures that describe who can do what to which data must be negotiated and documented. All these activities mean that substantial initial work is required.

A third disadvantage of database processing is *vulnerability*. If the check master file in figure 9-1*a* is damaged, checks cannot be processed, but savings and loan applications continue to run. In the database environment, however, when something happens to the database files, none of the applications can operate. The bank is incapacitated until the database file is fixed.

A final disadvantage of database processing is high equipment requirements. All database files must reside on direct access devices, and the storage requirements can be large. In fact, an integrated database usually requires more storage space than the sum of the files it contains. For example, if file A takes 10 cylinders and file B takes 20 cylinders, a database containing files A and B might take 40 or 50 cylinders. The additional space is used to keep data representing the relationships between records, as well as data to enable processing by multiple keys.

Also, the DBMS is an additional program. The CPU must execute application programs, the DBMS, the operating system, and, in a teleprocessing system, a communications control program. This is a lot of processing. A large, powerful CPU is often required for database processing.

These disadvantages are also summarized in figure 9-5.

```
RECORD DEFINITION: NAME IS CUST-RECORD,
   FIELD IS CUSTOMER-NUMBER, INTEGER (10),
   FIELD IS CUSTOMER-NAME, ALPHA (20),
   FIELD IS CUSTOMER-ADDRESS, ALPHA (30),
   . . . other customer fields here
RECORD DEFINITION: NAME IS CHECKING-RECORD,
   FIELD IS TYPE, ALPHA (1) VALUE IS 'C',
   FIELD IS CHECK-NUMBER, INTEGER (8),
   . . . other customer fields here
RECORD DEFINITION: NAME IS SAVINGS-RECORD,
   FIELD IS TYPE, ALPHA (1), VALUE IS 'S',
   . . . other savings fields here
RECORD DEFINITION: NAME IS LOAN-RECORD,
   FIELD IS TYPE, ALPHA (1), VALUE IS 'L',
   . . . other loan fields here
RELATIONSHIP DEFINITION: NAME IS CUST-CHECK,
   PARENT IS CUST-RECORD,
   CHILD IS CHECKING-RECORD.
RELATIONSHIP DEFINITION: NAME IS CUST-SAVINGS,
   PARENT IS CUST-RECORD,
   CHILD IS SAVINGS-RECORD.
RELATIONSHIP DEFINITION: NAME IS CUST-LOAN,
   PARENT IS CUST-RECORD,
   CHILD IS LOAN-RECORD.
```

Figure 9-6 Example of Schema for Bank Database

Database processing trades machine resources for human resources. It uses the computer less efficiently, but it enables people to work more efficiently. They can get the data they need in less time. Since people have become increasingly expensive, and computers have become drastically cheaper, tradeoffs of this kind are often smart business decisions. For this reason, database processing is likely to be used more and more. In fact, some people believe that eventually all computer processing will be database processing.

The first part of this chapter has presented a brief introduction to database processing. Now, we will discuss each of the five components of a database-oriented business computer system. Since data is the component most drastically impacted by the database approach, we will discuss it first.

QUESTIONS

9.1 Why didn't the bank correctly change Jeremy Williams' address?

9.2 Why did the bank send three separate mailings to Tricia Lucero?

9.3 Why didn't Data Processing give Ms. Baker the data she wanted?

9.4 What is database processing?

9.5 What is the function of a DBMS?

9.6 How does a DBMS eliminate data duplication?

9.7 How does a DBMS allow integrated processing?

9.8 How does a DBMS generalize on the concept of a key?

9.9 What is program/data independence?

9.10 Name four advantages of database processing.

9.11 Name four disadvantages of database processing.

9.12 Why do some people think database processing will be used more and more frequently in the future?

DATABASE DATA

To understand the data component of a business database system, you need to understand three concepts. First, a database contains a collection of *integrated files*. Second, in a database system, there will be a variety of *forms*, or *views*, of the same data. Third, to represent record relationships and enable processing by more than one key, database systems create systems data, sometimes called *overhead data*. We will consider each of these in turn.

Integrated Files

In Chapter 5, we said a field is a collection of characters, a record is a collection of fields, and a file is a collection of records. We extend this now to say a database is a collection of *integrated files*. Another way of saying this is that a database is a collection of *files and record relationships*.

The words "and record relationships" are important. If a database were only a group of files, they would not be integrated. The employee records in the employee file, for example, would have no correspondence with the department records. In a database, a facility must be provided to relate records to one another.

What are these record relationships? Database experts have determined that there are three basic ways in which records can be related.

Hierarchical Record Relationships   The first kind of record relationship is called *hierarchical*, or *tree*. A tree is a collection of records such that all the relationships between record types are one-to-many. Figure 9-7a

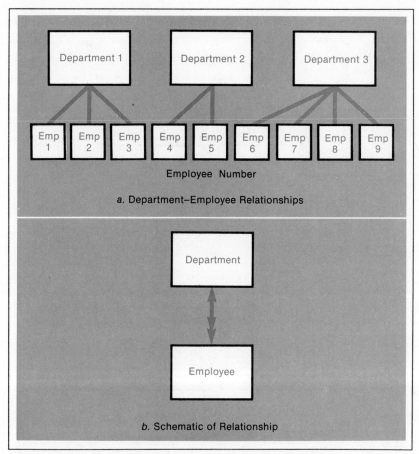

Figure 9-7 Example Tree Relating Departments to Employees

shows an example of a tree relating department records to employee records. For each department, there are many (more than one) employees. However, each employee works in only one department. This one-to-many relationship is symbolized by the single, double-arrowhead notation in figure 9-7*b*.

Figure 9-8 shows a tree of records for the banking application. Four record types are involved. The first is the customer record; the second is a checking record; the third is savings; and the fourth is loans. Again, notice the one-to-many relationships. Each customer can have many checking accounts, but an account corresponds to only one customer (joint accounts are considered one customer with two names). Each customer can have many savings accounts or loans, but these belong to only one customer.

These record structures are similar to family trees. In fact, the terminology *parent* and *child* is sometimes used. In figure 9-7, the department records are parents and the account records are children.

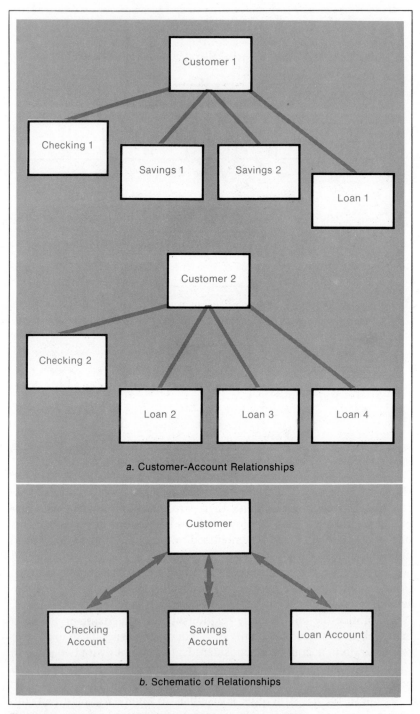

Figure 9-8 Example Tree Relating Customers and Accounts

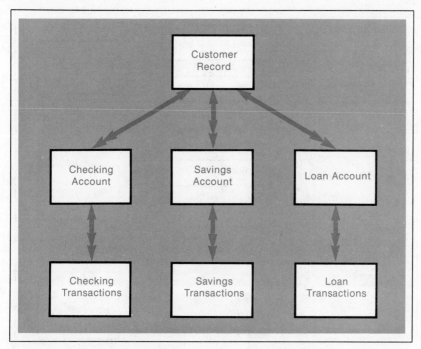

Figure 9-9   Schematic of Bank Relationships

In figure 9-8, customer records are parents and transaction records are children. Account records are both children (to customer) and parents (to transactions). In a tree structure, each child has at most one parent.

Trees can involve many record types and have several levels. Figure 9-9 shows a tree used for processing at the bank introduced at the start of this chapter. There are seven record types, six one-to-many relationships, and three levels. Trees are common relationships in database applications.

Network Record Relationships   The other two kinds of record relationships are called *networks*. Networks allow a record to have more than one parent. Figure 9-10 shows a *simple network*. Here, an order record has two parents: a customer record and a salesperson record. The network is called simple because the parents of the order record are of different types.

The third record relationship is called a *complex network*. In this type of structure, a record can have multiple parents, and the parents can be of the same type. Figure 9-11 shows a complex network between student and class records. One student is enrolled in many classes, and a class is composed of many students.

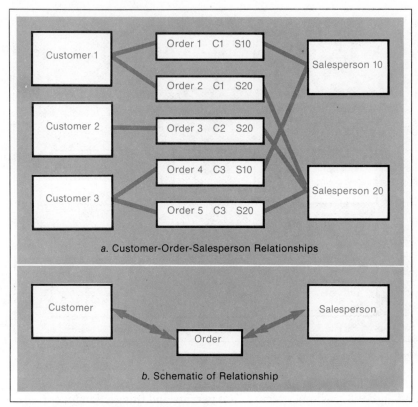

a. Customer-Order-Salesperson Relationships

b. Schematic of Relationship

Figure 9-10 Illustration of Simple Network

Database management systems vary in the ease with which they represent these structures. For example, IMS (Information Management System), a DBMS supplied by IBM, represents hierarchies well, but it does not easily represent complex networks. IDMS (Integrated Data Management System), a DBMS sold by Cullinane Corporation, represents hierarchies and simple networks readily, but complex networks require redefinition. Similar statements can be made of all other commercial DBMS products.

You may be wondering why these relationship types are important to you. When the database is created, all the record relationships have to be defined. To define them, the data processing personnel will make a sketch similar to those in figures 9-7b through 9-11b. You may be asked to specify what kind of a relationship exists between records in your area of business. Knowledge of the three types of relationship will be helpful to you if this occurs. In any case, this knowledge will enable you to communicate better with data processing personnel.

To review, a database is a collection of files and relationships. Three types of record relationship can exist: tree or hierarchy, simple

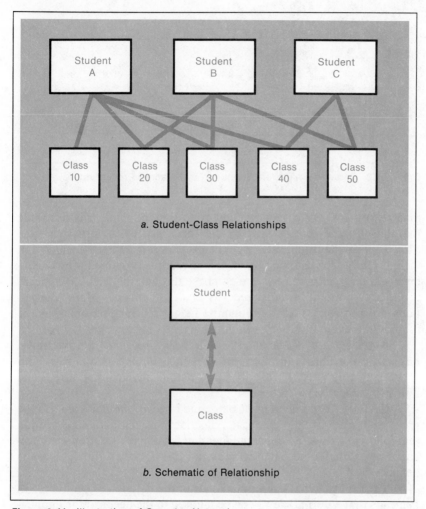

a. Student-Class Relationships

b. Schematic of Relationship

Figure 9-11 Illustration of Complex Network

network, and complex network. These relationships are defined in the database. Now, we will turn to the subject of database views.

In a database system, a variety of forms, or views, of the data are defined. One such view is called the *schema*, or *conceptual view*. It is the complete logical view of the data. The term *logical* means the data as it appears to a human. In fact, the data may be stored on the files in a form completely different from what humans see.

A second view of the data is called the *subschema*, or *external view*. This view is a subset or, in some cases, a transformation of the conceptual view. For example, consider the schema in figure 9-6. The check processing program (in figure 9-2) does not use the savings or

Three Views of Database Data

Type of View	Description
Schema (Conceptual)	Complete logical view of the data
Subschema (External)	Subset or transformation of schema
Physical (Internal)	Appearance of data to computer

Figure 9-12 Three Views of Data Supported by Database Processing

loan records. From a security and control standpoint, it is desirable that these records not be seen by the check processing program.

To provide such security, a subschema or external view that includes only the customer and checking records is defined. The checking program then processes the database through this view. It appears to the program that no other records exist. Other types of transformations are possible, such as renaming fields, rearranging fields in the record, and even modifying relationships.

A third view of the data is called the *internal*, or sometimes, *physical view*. This is the form of the data as it appears to a particular processing computer. It describes how data is physically arranged and how it is allocated to files.

Each of these views must be defined before the database can be processed. Usually, the database administrator (see personnel section that follows) writes the conceptual and external views. Often the internal view is created automatically by the DBMS when the database is defined.

The ability to have multiple views of the data is very convenient. It means that external views can be tailored to the needs of the application. Even though the data is centralized and shared, it can appear to each user in a format that is familiar and useful to him or her.

Figure 9-12 summarizes the three views of data. Again, the essential concept for you to understand is that in database processing there are a variety of views of the same data.

Database Overhead Data

The third concept essential to an understanding of data in database systems is that systems data, sometimes called *overhead data*, is created to enable processing by more than one key and to represent record relationships. Because of this overhead data, the size of a database may be 200 or 300 percent greater than that of the original data. The exact amount depends on how many keys and record relationships are represented, as well as on the particular DBMS in use.

There is a hot debate among database experts regarding the best way to structure and process overhead data. Rather than get involved in that debate, we will show two examples that are typical of the structures used.

Consider first the problem of having more than one key. Suppose we have a group of customer records on a direct access file. Also, suppose the primary key for these records is customer number. A hashing algorithm is used to allocate a customer record to a relative record number in the file. (In case you've forgotten what this means, the customer number will be input to a formula that will produce an address on the file for this record. See Chapter 6, figure 6-15, for more detail.) The data might appear as in figure 9-13.

Now, suppose that in addition to accessing the records by account number, the users want to access them by zip code. One way to do this is to read the entire file, looking for all the records with the desired zip code. However, this is a time-consuming, wasteful process if there are many records in the file and if few of them have the desired zip code.

Inverted Files To make this process more efficient, some database systems build a file of overhead data called an *inverted file*. This file

Figure 9-13 Customer Records on Direct Access File

Record Number	Customer Number	Zip Code	Other Data
1	1000	22042	
2	1010	22042	
3	2030	98040	
4	4030	22042	
5	1050	01418	
6	2055	98040	
7	4070	01418	
8	3070	01418	
9	3090	53520	
10	4090	53520	
11	1095	22042	

Zip Code Value	Customer Records Having Corresponding Value
01418	5, 7, 8
22042	1, 2, 4, 11
53520	9, 10
98040	3, 6

Figure 9-14 Example of Inverted File for Figure 9-13

is similar to an index for a book. It shows which records have which values of zip code. Figure 9-14 pictures such an inverted file.

If a user or application program wants to know all of the customers with zip code 22042, the DBMS will search for 22042 in the inverted file. It will find 22042 in the second entry. Then, the DBMS will use the indicated record numbers to find customer records desired. Thus, record locations 1, 2, 4, and 11 contain customer records with zip code 22042.

Whenever customer records are added, changed, or deleted, the DBMS will modify the inverted file. If there are several inverted files (there will be one for each key in use), their modifications will become burdensome. That is the price you pay for having the additional access capability.

Linked List Structure   Record relationships can be represented by inverted files also; but for variety, we will study another approach. Suppose we want to represent the one-to-many relationship between departments and employees. Assume both types of records are loaded on a direct access file as illustrated in figure 9-15. Locations 1, 3, and 5 hold department records. The other locations hold employee records.

To represent the relationships, we will add a *link field* to each record. This field has a record location, or address, of another record. In a department record, this link field points to the first employee record for that department. In an employee record, the link field points to the next employee in the same department. The last employee record in a department has a zero in the link field.

Examining figure 9-15, we see that Department 100's record points to location 2, or Employee 20's data. This means that Employee 20 is in Department 100. Employee 20's link field points to record position 7 which contains Employee 80. Finally, Employee 80's link field points to position 10 which contains Employee 15's data. The link field for Employee 15 is zero, indicating that there are no more employees in the department. Thus, Employees 20, 80, and 15 work in Department 100.

Record Number	Link	Record Type	Contents
1	2	D	Department 100 data
2	7	E	Employee 20 data
3	4	D	Department 200 data
4	8	E	Employee 25 data
5	9	D	Department 300 data
6	0	E	Employee 40 data
7	10	E	Employee 80 data
8	0	E	Employee 70 data
9	6	E	Employee 30 data
10	0	E	Employee 15 data

Figure 9-15 Linked Lists Used to Represent Record Relationships

If you follow the links in the other records you will discover that employees 25 and 70 work in Department 200 and that Employees 30 and 40 work in Department 300.

Data structures like this are called *linked lists* because link fields are used to maintain relationships as lists of data items. Linked lists are also used to represent multiple keys.

This section has presented three essential concepts about data in the database processing environment. First, a database is a collection of files and relationships. Second, databases allow multiple views of the same data. Finally, to enable multiple-key processing and to represent record relationships, databases contain overhead data. We will now consider the other four components of a database-oriented business computer system.

QUESTIONS

9.13 What is another way of saying a database is a collection of integrated files?

9.14 Describe a hierarchical or tree record relationship other than those shown in this book.

9.15 For question 9.14, which records are parents and which are children?

9.16   What is a simple network relationship? Give an example.

9.17   What is a complex network relationship? Give an example.

9.18   Name and describe the three views of a database.

9.19   Why is the external view or subschema necessary?

9.20   Why is the internal view necessary?

9.21   Suppose a company has a database that includes a file of sales data. One of the fields of a record in this file is month of sale. If there is an inverted file on this field, how many entries will it have?

9.22   Sketch an example for the situation in question 9.21. Use the format shown in figures 9-13 and 9-14.

9.23   Consider the example in figure 9-15. Suppose a department that has employees 72, 82, and 92 is added. Also, suppose Employee 20 is moved to the new department. Sketch the appearance of the file after these changes are made. Use the format in figure 9-15.

DATABASE HARDWARE

Database systems do not require special hardware. However, they may require more hardware. Since database files must be direct access files, a company may need to increase the amount of direct access space. Also, database processing places a greater burden on the CPU because of the processing required. A larger, more powerful CPU may thus be needed.

Aren't you relieved? After studying about all the extra hardware used in teleprocessing systems in the last chapter, you deserve a break.

PROGRAMS FOR DATABASE PROCESSING

There are two considerations regarding programs in database applications. First, the database management system (DBMS), a large and complex program, must be acquired and integrated into the company's processing environment. Figure 9-16 shows the relationships of the operating system, a communications control program, the application programs, and the DBMS.

The jobs performed by the DBMS can be organized into three types: creation, processing, and utility. When the database is created, the DBMS must structure the database files according to the definitions given in the schema. To do this, the DBMS builds *skeleton files* for both user and overhead data. Then, the initial data is loaded into the skeleton database files.

Processing tasks done by the DBMS include reading, modifying, inserting, and deleting records. These tasks are complicated because

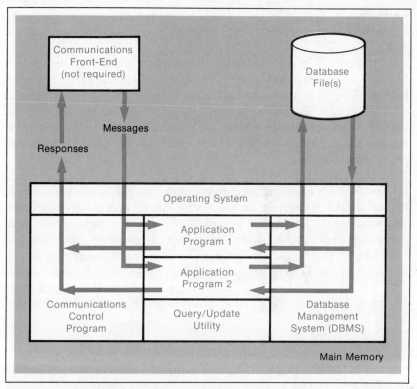

Figure 9-16 Program Relationships in the Database Environment

application programs access records by their relationships to one another and by more than one key. Remember, too, whenever data is added, changed, or deleted, the DBMS has to modify any affected overhead structures. Utility tasks include backing up the database, restoring it, reformatting it, and so forth.

Users can interface with the DBMS in one of two ways. First, they can use application programs that call the DBMS for record processing. In terms of figure 9-16, the user sends a message or transaction to the pertinent application program. In the course of processing the transaction, the application program calls the DBMS. Also during transaction processing, the application program sends messages back to the user.

Using the DBMS

The second mode of access to a database is through a query/update facility. This is a utility or a portion of the DBMS that provides generalized access to the database. Query/update programs are not application programs in that they do not solve problems like order entry or inventory. Instead, they are used to access records and perhaps to modify them. The user names a file and gives the key or keys for records desired. The query/update program responds with qualifying records. Commands are available to insert and delete records as well.

In figure 9-16 a query/update command is entered to the system like any other command. The communications control program routes it to the query/update utility instead of to an application program.

Other utilities besides query/update change the structure of the database and reload the data; clean up files by consolidating unused space; improve the efficiency of the overhead data; and back up and recover the database.

The cleanup programs require explanation. As the database is processed, both user and overhead data is changed. Sometimes data is moved around. After thousands of such changes, processing sometimes slows down. Data that was consolidated initially is now spread over many cylinders or even many disk packs. To improve efficiency, the data can be rearranged on the files. Utility programs are sometimes provided by the DBMS vendor for this purpose.

Processing tasks of the DBMS are summarized in figure 9-17. Figure 9-18 lists several popular DBMSs and the companies that sell or lease them.

Database-Oriented Application Programs

Application programs are different in a database processing environment. The ability to process records by many keys and by record relationships is a characteristic unique to database processing. Common

Figure 9-17   DBMS Processing Tasks

Type of DBMS Job	Processing Tasks Performed
Creation	Compile schema and subschema and store results Build database skeleton Load initial data
Processing	Read records Modify records Insert records Delete records Access records by multiple keys Access records by record relationships Manage overhead structures
Utility	Use query/update facility to access or modify records Change database structure and reload data Clean up database Perform backup and recovery function

Database Management System	Supplier
ADABAS	Software AG of North America
IDMS	Cullinane Corp.
IDS	Honeywell Corp.
IMS	IBM Corp.
IMAGE	Hewlett-Packard Corp.
TOTAL	CINCOM Corp.
SYSTEM 2000	MRI Corp.
MODEL 204	Computer Corp. of America

Figure 9-18   Examples of Database Management Systems (DBMS)

programming languages do not have commands or statements for this capability. For example, the BASIC language has INPUT and PRINT statements, and the COBOL language has READ and WRITE statements, but these are inadequate to initiate the powerful actions that a DBMS can perform.

DBMS Commands and Precompilation   In response to this problem, some DBMS vendors have defined *special commands* for the application programmer to use. These commands augment the standard language statements. Since these statements are not part of the standard language, the language translators (or compilers) cannot process them. Therefore, the application program with special database commands is first translated by a program supplied by the DBMS vendor. This program is called a *precompiler*. The precompiler translates the special database commands into standard language commands. Thus, a FIND command that is not part of COBOL will be translated into a legitimate COBOL command.

   This procedure is illustrated in figure 9-19. The application program INVOKES a named subschema and thereby declares what database it will process. The INVOKE is not a standard command. Therefore, the precompiler must translate it. The precompiler finds the named subschema in the schema library. It uses this data to substitute the correct code in the COBOL program's data division. The particulars of this translation are not important to you at this stage. Rather, you should strive to understand the precompilation process.

   The dictionary shown in figure 9-19 is a special file or database maintained by the DBMS for its own use. It contains names of programs, fields, records, files, procedures, and the relationships of all of these. In figure 9-19, the precompiler is inserting data about the program it is compiling, such as program name, subschema used, processing type (read vs modify), and so forth.

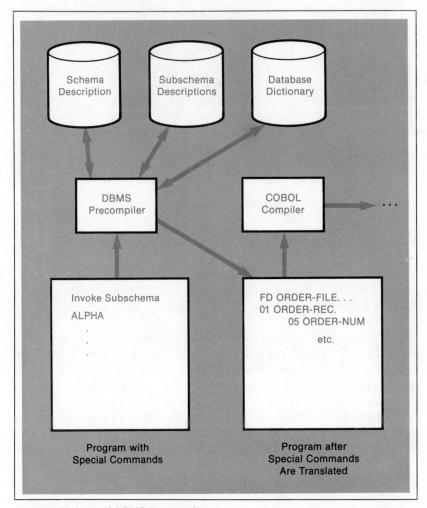

Figure 9-19 Use of DBMS Precompiler

Of course, it would be possible to have a DBMS without a precompiler. In that case, the application programmer has to insert the necessary data statements and calls to appropriate DBMS routines. In fact, some primitive database management systems require this action as they have no precompiler. This extra effort is a disadvantage, however, since it is much easier for the application programmer to use the special commands. Using special commands also results in programs that are easier to read and cheaper to maintain.

Locking Commands A database is a shared resource. Many different application programs and many different users can access it concurrently. Consequently, databases are susceptible to concurrent update problems like those we discussed in Chapter 8. If two users try to modify the same record concurrently, errors can be generated.

To prevent these problems, DBMS systems have *special commands to lock records* that might be modified or deleted. When the application program issues one of these commands, the DBMS will not allow other users to access the record until the first user is finished.

To summarize, the DBMS is a program that processes the database. It creates the database structure, processes the user's or application program's requests, and provides utility services. Additionally, in the database environment, application programs are different. They have special commands to request the advanced services that a DBMS can provide. Some DBMS vendors provide a program precompiler to translate these commands.

Summary

QUESTIONS

9.24 Do database systems require any special hardware? Do they require any more hardware?

9.25 What three types of tasks are performed by the DBMS?

9.26 What is a query/update utility?

9.27 Why do application programs contain special commands to process a database?

9.28 What is the function of a DBMS precompiler?

9.29 What are the contents of the data dictionary? How is it used?

PROCEDURES FOR DATABASE PROCESSING

The procedures necessary for database-oriented business computer systems are extensions to those required for more basic types of processing. Like other systems, database systems must have user procedures explaining how to use the system under normal and abnormal operating conditions. Also, procedures must be developed to ensure that only authorized personnel can perform authorized activity using the system.

Since database systems are often online teleprocessing systems, procedures are needed to prevent *concurrent update problems* and to ensure that the database can be *recovered* in case of failure. For the former, programmers need to be taught how to use the DBMS lock commands. Controls need to be developed to ensure that programmers follow these procedures. Additionally, if users have a role in preventing concurrent update errors, procedures need to be written for them.

We saw an example of this in figure 8-26, where Wagner users were told to use one command for read-only and another command for read followed by delete or modify.

Regarding backup and recovery, users must have procedures describing what they should do when the system is unavailable because of failure. They should know how best to carry on their responsibilities, what data to keep, and what to do first when the system becomes operational.

In addition to these procedures for users, procedures must be developed and documented for operations personnel. These procedures should explain how to run the system, how to perform backup and recovery operations, and how to control the system to ensure that only authorized activity occurs.

Procedures for Sharing the Database

In addition to these, special procedures must be developed because the database is a shared, integrated resource. Without careful management, users can interfere with one another. For example, consider the database depicted in figure 9-9; this schema could be used by the bank discussed at the beginning of this chapter.

Suppose a customer who has a checking account and a bank loan decides to move to another city. In the process of moving, the customer closes his checking account. If the clerk in the checking department deletes both the customer's checking account and the customer's record, then information about the customer's loan may be lost. The reason for this loss is that when the customer record is deleted, the loan record will not have a parent. Depending on the DBMS in use, records without parents may be deleted automatically.

A simple solution to this problem is to have the checking department clerk examine the database to determine whether the customer has accounts in other departments. However, the clerk may be processing a subschema that does not include the loan or savings records. If so, he or she will be unable to determine whether the customer has other accounts.

This example illustrates the problems that can occur when processing a database. These problems occur not only because the data is shared, but also because the data is integrated—there is only one customer record for all checking, savings, and loan processing.

Processing Rights and Responsibilities

To prevent users from interfering with one another, the company must determine the *processing rights and responsibilities* for all users. For each record (or even each field), the company must decide which users can read, insert, modify, or delete data. Furthermore, each of these users must have a procedure to follow when performing the activity.

Command	Customer Records	Checking and Transaction Records	Savings and Transaction Records	Loan and Transaction Records
Read	New Accounts Checking Savings Loan	Checking Savings	Savings Checking	Loan
Insert	New Accounts	Checking	Savings	Loan
Modify	New Accounts	Checking	Savings	Loan
Delete	New Accounts	Checking	Savings	Loan

Figure 9-20 Department Processing Rights for the Bank Database

Figure 9-20 shows the processing rights negotiated at the bank. All departments can access customer records, but only New Accounts is allowed to add, modify, or delete such records. Further, when deleting records, New Accounts must follow the procedure in figure 9-21.

Authorities for the other record types are shown in the remainder of figure 9-20. Note that the checking and savings departments are allowed to read each other's records. This option allows them to check

Figure 9-21 Bank Procedure for Deleting Customer Records

```
SEND REQUEST FOR CUSTOMER DELETION TO CHECKING, SAVINGS, AND
    LOAN DEPARTMENTS
IF ALL THREE DEPARTMENTS APPROVE DELETION REQUEST
    THEN IF CUSTOMER HAD NO SAVINGS OR LOAN ACCOUNTS
            THEN DELETE CUSTOMER RECORD
            ELSE CHANGE CUSTOMER STATUS TO INACTIVE
                CHANGE ADDRESS IF APPROPRIATE
        END-IF
    ELSE DEFER OR DESTROY DELETION REQUEST IN ACCORDANCE WITH
            DEPARTMENT INSTRUCTIONS
END-IF

AT YEAR END, SEND TAX FORMS FOR SAVINGS AND LOAN ACCOUNTS
    DELETE ALL INACTIVE CUSTOMERS
```

that transfers from savings to checking (or checking to savings) are successfully made.

Figure 9-21 shows the procedure that New Accounts must follow when a customer record is to be deleted. First, the checking, savings, and loan departments must all certify that the customer's accounts are successfully closed. If all three concur, and if the customer has no savings or loan accounts, the record is deleted.

If the customer does have savings or loan accounts, the record is then marked as inactive. It will not be deleted until the close of the calendar year. This delay is because year-end statements need to be sent to the savings and loan customers for tax purposes. If the customer's record were deleted, the bank would then have no address to send the statements to.

This discussion has illustrated the decisions the bank must make about processing rights in order to ensure that users' activities do not interfere with one another. A similar community-oriented view must be taken when considering changes to the database schema.

For example, suppose the checking department wants to add a code letter to the customer number in the customer record. Making such a change will impact the savings and loan departments. Most likely they will have to change their application programs as well as their forms and documents. Clearly, the code letter change cannot be made without agreement from these departments.

Suppose they are opposed to it. Then negotiations will have to be conducted to determine the best solution for all concerned. If the code letter change is so important that it justifies the additional expense and effort to the savings and loan departments, then it will be done. Otherwise, another way must be found to satisfy the needs of the checking department.

The point of this example is that changes to the database can only be made after the needs of all users have been considered. Thus, procedures for change must be developed. The procedures describe how changes can be suggested, how the input of all using departments is received, and how the change decisions will be made. Such procedures bring order to the change process, and ensure that all proposals receive fair and adequate consideration. They also ensure that all departments have a chance to express opinions.

To summarize, special procedures are needed in the database processing environment to ensure that one group of users do not take actions that are harmful to another group. The processing of the database must be carefully coordinated. Changes to the database must be thoroughly discussed and well planned before they are implemented. In addition to these special procedures, the standard systems procedures are also needed.

Database environments have users, operations personnel, and systems development people just like all other business computer systems. In addition, however, one or more individuals are concerned with managing and protecting the database resource. This individual (or group) is called the *database administrator* (or *office of database administration*). Both the individual and the office are abbreviated *DBA*.

    Databases are shared; and since the beginning of the human race, whenever people have had to share something, conflict develops. In a broad sense, the job of the DBA is to anticipate conflict, provide an environment for the peaceful resolution of conflict, and protect the database so that it can be used effectively. The DBA does this by accomplishing three separate functions as summarized in figure 9-22.

First, the DBA manages data activity. Note the wording here. The DBA does not perform data activity (inserting accounts, canceling checks, etc.); users do that. The DBA manages this activity.

    As discussed in the last section, it is necessary for the processing rights of all users to be carefully determined. The DBA is the focal point for negotiating these rights. The DBA meets with the users to determine who is authorized to do what to which data. The DBA is

DATABASE PERSONNEL

Data Activity Management

Figure 9-22 Job Responsibilities of the Database Administrator (DBA)

DBA Tasks and Subtasks

1. Manage data activity
   a. Processing rights
      (1) Provide focal point for negotiating
      (2) Document
      (3) Enforce
   b. Concurrent update and backup and recovery problems
      (1) Define problems
      (2) Develop solutions and standards
      (3) Ensure that adequate training is done
      (4) Evaluate problems

2. Develop database structure
   a. Manage schema and subschema designs
   b. Determine data standards
   c. Document database structure
   d. Manage changes to structure

3. Evaluate DBMS
   a. Resolve performance problems
   b. Determine need for new features

an unbiased (hopefully) arbitrator for resolving any conflicts. As time goes by, the business will change and user needs will change. The DBA serves as a focal point for changing the user processing rights as necessary.

Once the processing rights have been determined, they need to be documented. The DBA is responsible for developing this documentation. Also, the DBA is responsible for enforcing the processing rights. If a department or individual violates the agreed-on policy, complaints are given to the DBA. The offender is informed of the need to follow the policy. More stringent measures are taken if necessary.

Since the DBA is charged with the responsibility for protecting the database, the problems of concurrent update and backup and recovery are important to him or her. First, the DBA must determine what the potential problems are and how serious they can be. These problems vary from one DBMS to another, as well as from one application to another. Once the problems are known, the DBA meets with users, operations personnel, and the systems development staff to develop solutions.

As mentioned previously, part of the concurrent update solution may be to develop standard ways of processing the database. Application programs may need to lock records before they are updated, for example. In addition, standard procedures must be developed for backing up the database. Procedures for recovery are also important.

The DBA is responsible for ensuring that adequate means are found to solve concurrent update and backup and recovery problems. Further, these means must be documented. All involved personnel from the user and operations departments must be trained. Although the DBA may not do all of this documenting and training, he or she must ensure that it gets done.

Finally, the DBA is charged with the responsibility for investigating problems that occur and for finding solutions to prevent recurrence. This task may mean meeting with involved personnel and changing standards, procedures, processing rights, or other activity.

Managing Database Structure

In addition to managing data activity, the DBA must manage the database structure. If the DBA has been appointed at design time, he or she leads the tasks of defining the schema and subschemas. These tasks include identifying the fields, records, and relationships that will exist in the database. Also, subschemas must be defined that allow users or application programs to accomplish their assigned tasks and support the negotiated processing rights. Subschemas should not contain unnecessary data.

Defining the schema is the same as developing data standards for the company. Users must agree on how many characters will be in the customer account number, for example, or which fields will be in the customer record. Further, the relationships that can exist between records must be standardized. Again, whenever more than one person develops a standard, conflict will develop. The DBA has the responsibility for resolving this conflict.

Once the schema and subschemas and related standards have been determined, the DBA ensures that the decisions are documented. Also, the DBA must ensure that the database is developed in accordance with these decisions.

Business is a dynamic activity. No schema, however well developed, will last without change. Users will want to add new capability or to change existing procedures. The operations staff will want to add new equipment, or to change computers. The systems development staff will find a better way to do things.

The DBA is charged with the responsibility of managing change to the database structure. As discussed in the procedures section, such changes must be made carefully. If not, a change made for the benefit of one user will cause problems for others.

To manage change, the DBA must receive requests for changes and periodically present these requests to a group representing all using organizations, computer operations, and systems development staff. Potential changes should be discussed with the representatives. In a subsequent meeting, the changes should be discussed again and potential problems identified. If there are no conflicts, or if ways of eliminating the conflicts can be found, the changes can be made. This change process is managed by the DBA.

A third area of DBA responsibility concerns DBMS performance. Since the DBA is the focal point for conflict resolution, when users complain that the system performs too slowly or that it costs too much to run certain jobs, the DBA will be involved. He or she will serve as an interface between the users and the operations and systems development staffs.

Evaluating the DBMS Performance

Sometimes the performance problem can be resolved by *tuning*, or changing DBMS parameters set at installation time. The amount of main memory allocated to the DBMS is an example of such a parameter. Other performance problems can be fixed by cleaning up the database using utility programs supplied by the vendor. In some cases, a high-performance feature of the database can be acquired. At worst, a more powerful CPU can be obtained.

Periodically, vendors of DBMS announce new features for their products at extra cost. When such announcements are made, the DBA must determine whether the new features are needed. Each feature is considered in light of user requirements. Again, the DBA will meet with users, operations, and systems development personnel to make this determination.

DBA Organizational Placement

Figure 9-23 shows two acceptable alternatives for organizational placement of the DBA in the company. Both of these organizations have worked well. Experience has shown that a lower placement gives the DBA too little power and exposure to be effective. A higher placement removes the DBA from the day-to-day problems.

A close look at either of these organizations reveals a problem for the DBA. The DBA has responsibility for all aspects of database processing, but he or she has direct line control over few of the personnel involved. In fact, the DBA works closest with users, yet the

Figure 9-23 Two Acceptable Alternatives for DBA Placement

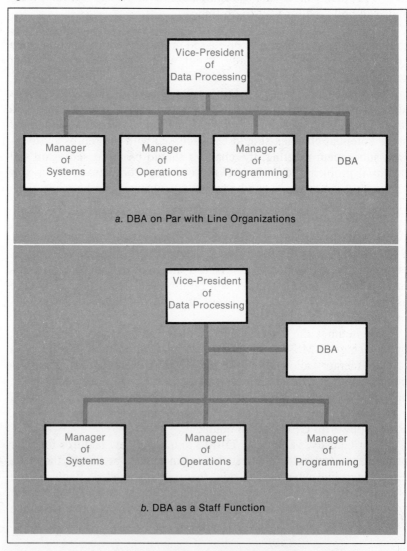

a. DBA on Par with Line Organizations

b. DBA as a Staff Function

DBA and the users are not even shown on the same organization chart!

Consequently, the DBA must be a diplomat. He or she must be able to convince people to conform to the database standards primarily on the basis of rational argument. This requirement calls for good communication skills and a thorough knowledge of organizational politics. The DBA must have good rapport with senior managers in the using departments as well as those in Data Processing.

If worst comes to worst, the DBA is not without weapons. He or she can control the priority of user jobs and thus determine how much service a user gets. People who do not cooperate will find it harder and harder to use the computer. Also, frequent violators of established procedures may find the computer won't process their jobs at all.

Who should be the DBA? Generally, database experts agree it should be a nontechnical person who has been in the company for some time. Although the DBA has responsibility for some technical matters, the expertise to perform these duties can be borrowed when needed. It is more important to have a diplomat than to have a technical giant. The DBA needs to know personnel well, which generally means that the person should have worked in the company for some time.

9.30	What procedures do users need for operation of a database system? What do they need for backup and recovery?	QUESTIONS
9.31	What procedures do operators need for operation of a database system? What do they need for backup and recovery?	
9.32	Explain why the activities of one user must be coordinated with the activities of another.	
9.33	What does the phrase *processing rights and responsibilities* mean?	
9.34	What procedures are needed to ensure orderly change to the database structure?	
9.35	What does DBA mean?	
9.36	In a broad sense, what is the job of the DBA?	
9.37	What three major functions are performed by the DBA?	
9.38	Does the DBA perform data activity? If not, who does?	
9.39	What role does the DBA have in defining processing rights and responsibilities?	
9.40	What is the DBA's responsibility with regard to concurrent update and backup and recovery problems?	
9.41	What does the DBA do with regard to developing the database structure?	

9.42 What is the major management problem of the DBA?

9.43 What characteristics should the DBA have?

SUMMARY

Database processing is a technique for organizing and manipulating data files in an integrated manner. Relationships are represented, and these relationships are used to process the data. To provide this capability, a large, complex computer program is required. This program is called a *database management system*, or DBMS. The DBMS is an intermediary between the application programs and the database.

The advantages of database processing are an elimination or reduction of duplicated data, integrated processing, easier implementation of new requests and one-of-a-kind requests, and the creation of program data independence.

The disadvantages of database processing are expense, difficult initial development, vulnerability of data problems, and the need for much hardware.

Three concepts are crucial to understanding database data. First, a database contains a collection of integrated files. Second, in a database there exists a variety of forms, or views, of the same data. Third, to represent record relationships and enable processing by more than one key, database systems create overhead data.

There are two modes of accessing database data. One is through an application program, and the other is using a query/update facility. If the database is processed in a teleprocessing environment, access to the DBMS may be controlled by the communications control program.

Since a database is a shared resource, procedures must be developed to control conflicts that arise. Users must process the database in ways that will not adversely impact other users. Further, the rights and responsibilities of all users must be well known and documented. Backup and recovery is important and even more difficult for database systems than for teleprocessing systems.

Finally, the database administrator or office of database administration is required for successful operation of a database system. The job of the DBA is to anticipate conflict, provide an environment for the peaceful resolution of conflict, and protect the database so that it can be used effectively.

WORD LIST (in order of appearance in text)		
Duplicated data	*Record relationship*	
Integrated data	*Key*	
Database processing	*Multiple keys*	
Database management system (DBMS)	*Nonunique key*	

Query/update program

Program data independence

Database structure

Database schema

Vulnerability

Database form or view

Overhead data

Hierarchical or tree relationship

One-to-many relationship

Parent

Child

Simple network

Complex network

Schema or conceptual view

Subschema or external view

Internal view

Inverted file

Link field

Linked list

Skeleton files

Special DBMS commands

DBMS precompiler

Database dictionary

Lock commands

Concurrent update problem

Processing rights and responsibilities

Database administrator

Database administration

Data activity management

Database structure development

DBMS evaluation

Tuning

QUESTIONS TO CHALLENGE YOUR THINKING

A. Suppose you work for Alpine Co-op. The Director of Data Processing asks you whether Alpine needs a database capability. How do you respond? What would be the advantages to Alpine? The disadvantages? How should Alpine determine whether or not a database is appropriate?

B. Sketch a schema for an academic database. Follow the form in figure 9-9. Your schema should include data about students, classes, faculty, departments, colleges, advisers, and grades. Show all the appropriate record relationships and label them with their type (hierarchical vs simple network, for example). Define a subschema or external view that would be used by a grade processing program. Define another subschema that would be used by a class scheduling program.

C. Show how inverted files could be used to represent all three types of record relationships.

D. Show how linked lists could be used to represent nonunique keys.

E. Extend the structure in figure 9-15 to represent simple networks. Extend it to represent complex networks.

F. Locate a nearby organization that is using a DBMS. Interview a responsible person to find out the name of the DBMS, its cost, and how satisfied the organization is with it. How long did the conversion to the database take? Were there any special problems that other organizations should avoid? How has the support from the vendor been?

G. For the organization in question F, determine if any special procedures have been instituted since the database was installed. How does the organization handle concurrent update problems? Have processing rights and responsibilities been negotiated and documented? Have there been conflicts among users? Has the company appointed a DBA? If so, what are the DBA's responsibilities? What organizational or management problems have developed since the database was implemented?

CHAPTER 10

Distributed Business Computer Systems

Distributed microcomputers in Super-Burger cash registers

THREE EXAMPLES OF DISTRIBUTED PROCESSING SYSTEMS

ERD Pharmaceutical

FRAMCO Distributing

Computer Communication

Super-Burger Restaurant Franchises

Distributed Programs
Distributed Personnel

CHARACTERISTICS OF DISTRIBUTED SYSTEMS

Evolution of Distributed Systems

Advantages of Distributed Systems

Disadvantages of Distributed Systems

DISTRIBUTED HARDWARE

Distributed Hardware Configurations

Star Configuration
Ring Configuration
Hybrid Configuration

Comparison of Star and Ring Configurations

Cost

Performance
Reliability

PROGRAMS FOR DISTRIBUTED PROCESSING

Types of Distributed Programs

Application Programs

Problems When Distributing Programs

DISTRIBUTED DATA

Local and Global Data

Centralized or Partitioned Data

Data for Super-Burger Restaurants

Data Directory

Updating Distributed Data

DISTRIBUTED PERSONNEL

Alternatives to Distributed Personnel

Systems Development Personnel

PROCEDURES FOR DISTRIBUTED PROCESSING

Remember Jan Forrest? Remember ERD Pharmaceutical Company? They were introduced in the second case in Chapter 1. Because of your hard work in this course, we are now in a position to discuss the technical aspects of what Jan wanted to do.

Jan Forrest was the Manager of Marketing Analysis who wanted her own minicomputer. She wanted to do marketing analysis. The existing centralized computer system did not or could not meet the needs of her staff. Eventually, Jan got a minicomputer that supplemented the company's centralized computer. The two computers were connected by a communication line.

The system that resulted when ERD acquired the second computer is called a *distributed data processing system*. The term *distributed* is used because applications are processed on computers that are distributed throughout the company. Distributed processing systems, then, are data processing systems in which multiple computers are used to run *application* programs.

Distributed data processing is not the same as teleprocessing. Figure 10-1 shows a teleprocessing system. Users and terminals are distributed. Also, there are multiple computers: the concentrator, the front-end, and the application processing computer. However, only one of the computers is used to process application programs. Applications processing is not distributed.

THREE EXAMPLES OF DISTRIBUTED PROCESSING SYSTEMS

Figure 10-2 shows the distributed processing network used by ERD Pharmaceutical. This system is an extension to a teleprocessing system. Users and terminals are distributed. However, two computers are doing applications processing. The minicomputer does marketing analysis and the other computer processes all other application programs.

ERD Pharmaceutical

Therefore, the unique characteristic of a distributed system is not that users or terminals are distributed. It is not that there is more than one computer in use. The unique characteristic of distributed processing is that more than one computer processes application programs.

Distributed processing allows the applications processing to be done in the best place for the application — not in the place where a large, centralized computer happens to be. This arrangement leads to two advantages. First, it can be cheaper. When applications processing is moved toward the user, there is less traffic on the communication lines. Data need not be sent to a centralized location for processing and then have the results returned. Thus, communication costs go down.

Second, distributed processing gives the users greater control over the data and its processing. Often, the users operate distributed computers. They can determine the data to be processed, the order of processing, and the quality of service. Also, users in one department are not inconvenienced by users in another department if each group of users has its own computer.

If you view data processing as a method of producing information from raw data, then data processing is a type of manufacturing. In these terms, distributed data processing is similar to distributed manufac-

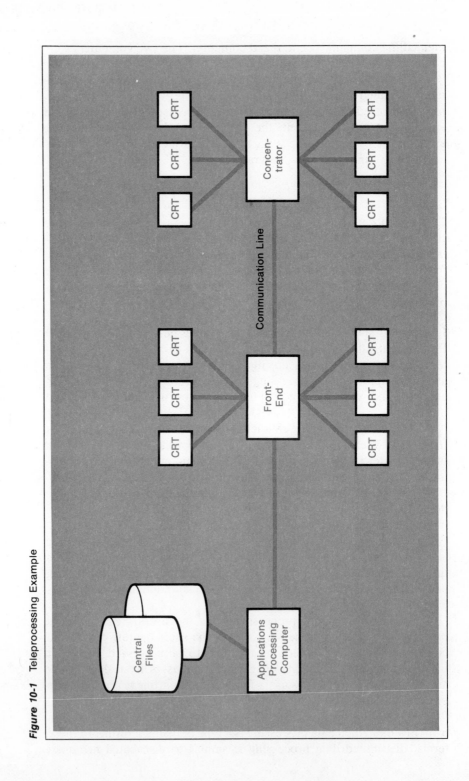

Figure 10-1 Teleprocessing Example

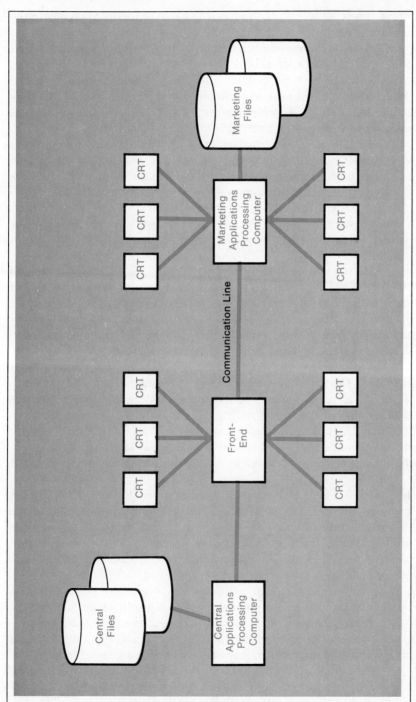

Figure 10-2 ERD Distributed Processing System

turing. The computer (plant) is moved close to the location where the product is needed.

An *application node* is a computer in a distributed network that does applications processing. Each application node has a computer, programs, data files, procedures, and users. Thus, each node has all the components of a business computer system. However, within this definition, there is a wide variety of capability because different amounts of each of these components can be distributed.

Examine ERD Pharmaceutical's distributed network in figure 10-2 again. Once a day, all of the sales data is sent from the mainframe computer to the minicomputer over the communication line. This data is saved on a local minicomputer file. The marketing analysis department later scans this data and copies parts of it to several other files. These files are then used by analysis programs to produce marketing reports. Also, the marketing analysts examine the data in these files using a query utility.

This is a simple distributed system. There is only one distributed computer, and it processes only marketing-related data. The flow of data is one way; the marketing department does not send any data back to the mainframe. This means that marketing analysis does not change any files used by any other department. If they make a mistake, only the marketing department will suffer the consequences.

In this system, the mainframe is a *master* and the minicomputer is a *slave*. The mainframe decides when to send the data, and it decides what data to send. There is no interaction between the two computers to determine what to do. Also, the mainframe never receives data from the minicomputer. No interactions are initiated by it. Finally, since the mainframe keeps a copy of everything it sends to the minicomputer, the mainframe is not dependent on the minicomputer for any data.

FRAMCO Distributing   Figure 10-3 shows a distributed data processing system that is more complex than ERD's. FRAMCO Distributing has seven locations throughout the United States and Canada that operate as autonomous profit centers. Each location is considered to be an independent company. Each location manager shares in the profits made by his or her company.

Each location has its own computer and does its own data processing. However, for compatibility and maintenance reasons, the programs are the same and the files have a common format. The programs are used for order processing, inventory, and accounting. There are files of customer, price, inventory, order, and general ledger data.

Additionally, FRAMCO headquarters has a computer of its own. It receives data from the other seven computers and produces consolidated financial statements. It also extracts marketing and other data

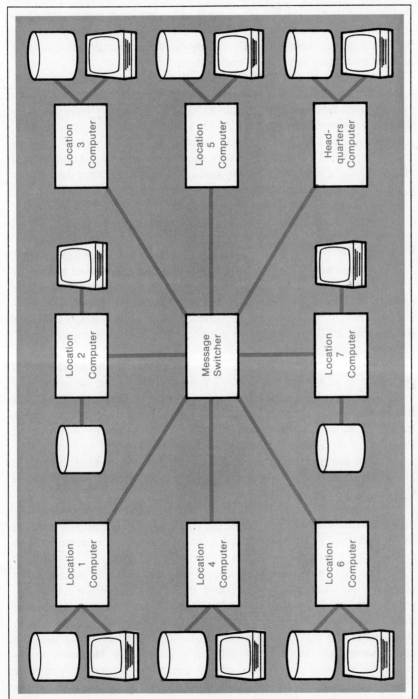

Figure 10-3 Computer Network for FRAMCO Distributing

that is used by centralized purchasing and planning departments. Consequently, each location computer must be able to communicate with the headquarters computer. Furthermore, the application nodes must be able to communicate with each other.

According to FRAMCO policy, if one location is out of a part, it must try to locate the part at another location. Before the distributed system was developed, order clerks did this manually over the telephone. This method was too slow to be effective. Consequently, FRAMCO built the distributed system so that all seven location computers could communicate with one another. Now, when the local inventory does not have a part in stock, the local computer determines if another FRAMCO location has it. If so, the part is ordered from the other location. This processing is done by the computers. The order entry clerks need not call or take other direct, human action.

Computer Communication   Figure 10-3 shows a processor labeled *message switcher*. This is a computer much like a front-end processor that receives messages and sends them to the correct location. It is used to reduce the number of communication lines necessary to connect all the computers to one another. To illustrate, we will calculate the number of lines needed to connect all the computers without a message switcher.

First, seven lines will be needed to connect the headquarters computer to all seven locations. (See figure 10-4.) Then six more lines will be needed to connect location 1 to locations 2 through 7 (location 1 is already connected to the headquarters computer). Next, five more lines will be needed to connect location 2 to locations 3 through 7 (location 2 is already connected to headquarters and to location 1). Four lines are needed to connect location 3 to locations 4 through 7, and so on. In total, $7 + 6 + 5 + 4 + 3 + 2 + 1$, or 28, lines will be needed if there is no message switcher.

Examine figure 10-3. Observe that with the message switcher, only eight lines are needed. Thus, the message switcher greatly reduces the number of lines needed and hence reduces the communication costs.

The distributed network shown in figure 10-3 is considerably more complex than the one in figure 10-2. First, there are eight computers instead of just two. FRAMCO must operate all of these, ensure they are properly maintained, and have them repaired when necessary. Also, programs must be maintained for each computer. Since they are all the same, this task is not as difficult as it could be. However, maintaining seven uniform copies of a program is not easy. Whenever changes are made to one program, great care must be exercised to ensure that the same changes are made to all copies of it. If not, over a period of time the programs will diverge. Processing will not be identical at each location.

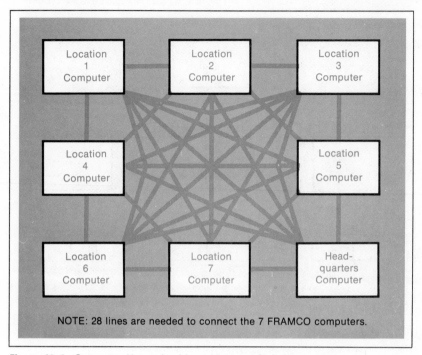

Figure 10-4   Computer Network without Message Switcher

   Another complexity of the FRAMCO system is that there is no clear master/slave relationship. The eight computers operate as colleagues. As with humans, equality requires more frequent and more sophisticated communication. The computers can request services from one another, but they must be prepared for rejection. Another computer may be too busy, or may be inoperative. Furthermore, while a computer is requesting a service from one computer, it may be receiving a request from a different computer. All these actions must be coordinated and the processing must be done systematically without error.

   Finally, unlike the ERD system, FRAMCO's computers are very *dependent on one another for data.* No computer in the network possesses all the FRAMCO data. Backup and recovery must be carefully performed at each node so that no data is lost. This system demands close coordination of activity and careful data management.

A third example of a distributed processing network is shown in figure 10-5. Super-Burger Restaurant Franchises has 20 restaurants in each of four regions throughout the United States. Each restaurant has a microcomputer that controls the operations of the cash registers (which also have micros). The restaurant computer keeps track of raw goods received, goods produced, foods sold, cash receipts, and so forth.

Super-Burger Restaurant Franchises

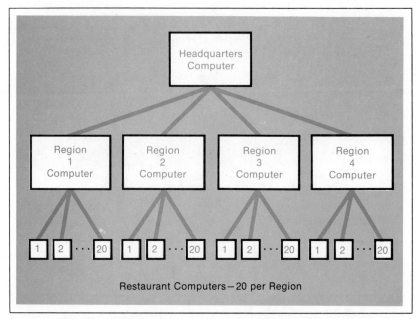

Figure 10-5 Computer Network for Super-Burger Restaurant

The restaurant microcomputers are connected to regional mini-computers via communication lines. The regional computers obtain data from the restaurant computers twice a day. This data is used to maintain a raw goods inventory for each restaurant, and to order and schedule deliveries of raw goods three times per week. The regional computers also produce bimonthly financial statements for each restaurant and for the region as a whole.

Finally, the four regional computers are connected to a head-quarters computer. They send financial statements as well as other marketing and inventory data to headquarters. This computer, also a mini, produces consolidated financial statements, ranks the profita-bility of the 80 franchises, develops marketing forecasts, and sched-ules procurement of major supplies. Furthermore, this computer is used to assess the market potential of future franchises and to estimate the best location to place new restaurants.

Super-Burger considered obtaining a mainframe computer for their headquarters. When they evaluated alternatives, however, they found that a minicomputer would do the job. This option was possible because so much processing was done in the regions. From this exam-ple you can see that mainframes are not always needed to manage minicomputers.

The computer network shown in figure 10-5 is an extension of the simple network used by ERD. Super-Burger has a two-level hierarchy of computers connected in multiple master/slave relationships. The headquarters computer is a master over the regional computers. The regional computers are masters over the restaurant computers. Thus, the regional computers operate as both masters and slaves.

Distributed Programs   In order for the headquarters computer to produce useful summaries, the data that it receives from the regional computers must be consistent. To ensure this consistency, all of the programs used at the regional and restaurant computers must be the same. This uniformity is difficult to manage since whenever a restaurant computer program is changed, programs at all 80 restaurants must be updated.

There are two ways to accomplish this task. First, Super-Burger could send computer professionals to each of the restaurants with a new copy of the program and have them install it. This approach would be expensive. It would involve many people and a lot of travel. It would also be wasteful because the task to be performed is very simple.

A better approach, and the one that Super-Burger uses, is to have the regional computers *downline load the new programs*. In other words, the regional computers will install the new versions of the programs remotely over the communication lines. This approach not only saves money, but enables the entire process to be completed in a few hours. Consequently, changes to the restaurant programs can be made more frequently.

The data in the Super-Burger Restaurant system is duplicated just as ERD's data is. The restaurant computers send copies of their data to the regional computers. The regional computers in turn send copies of their data to the headquarters computer The restaurants computers keep one week's worth of data for their own processing and for backup of the regional computer's data. The regional computers keep data on an annual basis. The headquarters computer keeps financial data indefinitely.

Distributed Personnel   There are no data processing personnel at the restaurants. The microcomputers receive input from the cash registers and requests from the regional computers. There is no need for computer operators. Many of the restaurant employees do not even know the computer is there. A restaurant manager can get some data by using special keys on one of the cash registers. He or she also gets reports from the regional computer. (See figure 10-6.)

At a regional facility, there are no systems development personnel, but there are three computer operators. These operators run programs and disperse outputs. The users at the regional locations are purchasing agents and managers.

The headquarters has a full complement of data processing personnel. There are systems development personnel (application programmers, systems analysts, communications specialists, and systems

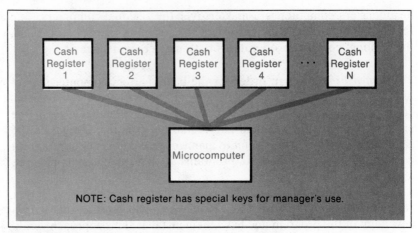

Figure 10-6 Super-Burger Restaurant Microcomputers

programming experts). The headquarters computer is supported by a staff of three operators. There are also marketing, purchasing, and management users.

Because of the large number of computer locations without onsite systems development personnel, there is a great need for well-documented, standardized procedures. Each restaurant manager has clear instructions on how to start and stop the computer and what to do in the event of a failure or an emergency. The names and phone numbers of critical personnel are also available. The data processing department is proud of the fact that these names have been seldom used. The microcomputers have been very reliable.

CHARACTERISTICS OF DISTRIBUTED SYSTEMS

As with teleprocessing systems, the components of a business computer system in a distributed environment can be physically distributed. In the Super-Burger example, the consolidated financial statements are produced by hardware and programs at headquarters. Also, the personnel, including users, of this system are at headquarters. However, the data and the procedures for obtaining the data are distributed throughout the company.

In contrast to a teleprocessing system, however, a distributed system has at least one complete business computer system resident at each application node. For at least one system, the node has processing hardware, programs, data, procedures, and users. This fact is one way to discriminate between teleprocessing and distributed systems.

Evolution of Distributed Systems

As you can imagine, distributed systems are complex to develop. In fact, almost no company starts out to build a distributed computer system. Instead, a company usually moves to a distributed system in one of two ways. First, a company that has a very large central computer may decide to *offload* some of their processing to a distributed computer. This usually happens when the central computer processing load is so big that it is hard to manage. There may be so many systems to run that the operations staff has trouble scheduling them. The quality of service may be poor because it becomes impersonal. Also, cost considerations may indicate that expanding the existing computer is more expensive than acquiring an additional, smaller one. (Refer back to figure 8-4.)

Another common reason for offloading a central computer is that the systems development staff is far behind in development effort. In some companies, it takes 18 months or more before work starts on a new project. In these companies, the users sometimes become so frustrated that they acquire turnkey systems to install and run themselves. (Recall Jan Forrest at ERD Pharmaceutical.) The systems development staff may be happy to be relieved of another request. This situation can lead to problems, however, if the turnkey system is not properly integrated into the rest of the company's data processing function.

A second way a company can move to a distributed system is to *build up to it*. Here, the company may have one minicomputer or a small mainframe that is easily and perhaps inexpensively upgraded in capability. However, they decide not to upgrade it but to buy more small computers instead.

Usually, a company takes this second course of action if local control of the data processing resources is important. In FRAMCO's case, for example, each location is considered to be an independent company. FRAMCO therefore decided to let each location have its own data processing center under its own operational control. It would have been feasible for FRAMCO to develop a centralized teleprocessing system, but they decided not to do this for organizational and political reasons.

Capt. Grace Hopper, USN, one of the pioneers of the data processing profession, has an interesting analogy about distributed systems. She says we should think about the pioneers as they struggled across the Great Plains. When they wanted to move a rock, they would hitch an ox to the rock. If the rock was so big the ox couldn't move it, they didn't attempt to grow a bigger ox. Instead, they used two oxen for the job.

A company with a distributed system uses the same technique. Instead of trying to build a bigger computer, it uses two or more computers to accomplish its work.

There are several advantages of distributed processing systems. First, they can be less expensive. It is often cheaper to use minicomputers and microcomputers to perform a task instead of a larger mainframe. If the data processing organization operates on the right-hand portion of

Advantages of Distributed Systems

the graph in figure 8-4, it will be cheaper to obtain additional, smaller computers. Also, distributed systems can reduce data communication costs because data is processed close to the source instead of being sent away for processing.

Second, distributed systems give the users greater control over the processing of their data. Often, users operate the computer themselves. They can determine the quality and the scheduling of the services they receive. Additionally, distributed systems can be useful in companies in which the systems development staff is behind development schecules. Turnkey systems may be available that will successfully accomplish the users' jobs.

Finally, distributed systems can be tailored to the company's organizational structure. For example. FRAMCO has seven autonomous locations that are connected on a more or less equal basis. This decentralized configuration matches the company's decentralized philosophy. On the other hand, Super-Burger has a computer configuration that matches a traditional organizational hierarchy. The regional computers are supervisors of the restaurant computers. The headquarters computer supervises the regional ones. Each of these systems meets the needs of the organizational structure of the company that owns it.

The advantages of distributed processing systems are summarized in figure 10-7.

Disadvantages of Distributed Systems

There are also several disadvantages of distributed processing systems. First, they are complex to set up. Communications facilities must be obtained. The computers must be connected to one another. Furthermore, the programs must be made to interact with one another. Close coordination is required throughout the distributed system to ensure that all data is compatible. Confusion will result if one division of the company reports sales data from the previous month, while another reports sales data from the current month.

Additionally, distributed systems are often run without the guidance of data processing professionals. This practice is risky unless the personnel are well trained and have complete, well-written documen-

Figure 10-7 Summary of Distributed Processing Systems

Advantages	Disadvantages
Can be less expensive	More complex to build
Greater control to users	Close coordination required for
Quicker development if turnkey systems	data compatibility
can be used	Greater need for standards and documentation
Tailored to organizational structure	Problems of multivendors

tation of all necessary procedures. Finally, distributed systems are often a mixture of equipment. The computers may be supplied by a variety of vendors; the communication lines, by other vendors; and the programs, by still other vendors. In this environment, compatibility can be a problem. It may be difficult to make the equipment operate together. Also, recovery may be difficult if one vendor inaccurately claims that a problem is due to another vendor's equipment. Figure 10-7 summarizes the disadvantages of distributed processing.

Given this overview of distributed processing, we will now describe the five components of a distributed system in greater detail.

		QUESTIONS

10.1 What is the difference between teleprocessing and distributed processing?

10.2 Why may distributed processing be cheaper than teleprocessing? Refer to figure 8-4 for your answer.

10.3 How does distributed processing give the users greater control?

10.4 What is an application node?

10.5 Describe two reasons why ERD's distributed system is simpler than FRAMCO's system.

10.6 What is a message switcher? Why is it useful?

10.7 If FRAMCO had 10 computers instead of 8, and if there were no message switcher, how many communication lines would be needed?

10.8 What does the phrase *downline loading* mean?

10.9 Why does Super-Burger need well-documented, standardized procedures?

10.10 Why may a company decide to offload its centralized or teleprocessing computer system?

10.11 Why may a company decide to install new computers even though its existing computer could be expanded to meet its needs?

10.12 Explain the statement, "A distributed system can be tailored to a company's organizational structure."

DISTRIBUTED HARDWARE

The basic hardware components of a distributed computing system are computers and high-speed communication lines. The computers at each application node of the network can be micros, minis, or mainframes—all types are used. These computers are employed for both applications processing and communications control. In some, a single computer is used for both functions. In others, one computer is dedicated to applications processing and another is dedicated to communications control. Front-ends and concentrators are examples of this last type of application.

Distributed Hardware Configurations

There are three basic configurations of computers in networks: *star, ring,* and *hybrid.*

Star Configuration Figure 10-8 shows a star configuration. A central computer is connected to other computers on the periphery of the star via communication lines. Usually in a star configuration, the central computer is a master. It controls the operation of the computers at the points of the star. Furthermore, the master can serve as a message switcher to enable communication from one peripheral computer to another. Note, however, the master computer has control. It can shut off such communication if it so chooses.

An extension to the star configuration is called a *hierarchical star.* Here, the central computer is connected in star fashion to computers that are themselves the centers of other stars. Figure 10-9 shows an example. If you examine this figure carefully, you will see that it is the arrangement of computers used by Super-Burger Restaurant Franchises in figure 10-5.

Figure 10-8 Star Network Configuration

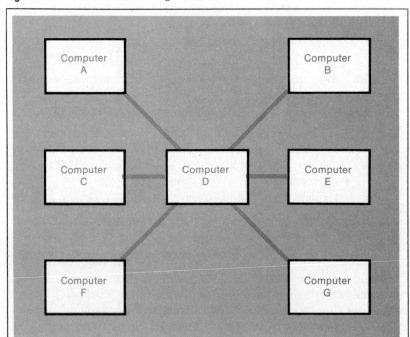

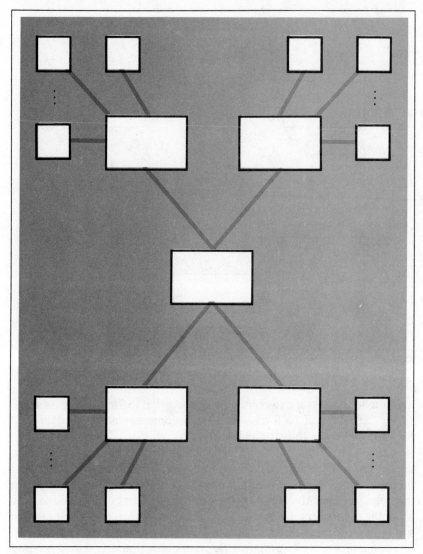

Figure 10-9 Hierarchical Star Network Configuration

Ring Configuration Figure 10-10 illustrates computers connected in a *ring*. Each computer is connected to some or all of its neighbors on basically an equal relationship. Usually in a ring configuration, no computer has central control over all the others. Each computer operates autonomously. The computers function as cooperating partners or *colleagues*.

In figure 10-10, not all computers are connected directly to all the other computers. This is acceptable. More than likely, computer A seldom needs to communicate with computer C. When it does need to,

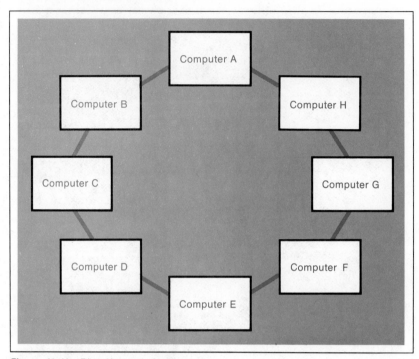

Figure 10-10 Ring Network Configuration

it can send its message to computer B, and ask B to forward the message to C, C to D, and so forth. Thus each computer needs programs to forward messages to its neighbors.

FRAMCO Distributing elected to connect its computers in basically a star configuration as shown in figure 10-5. However, the central node of the star is not really a master computer. Rather, it is just a message switcher that reduces the communication costs of connecting all of the computers. FRAMCO could have connected its computers in a ring like the one shown in figure 10-10. In this case, for computer A to communicate with computer D, computers B and C would have to forward the message.

Hybrid Configuration   The third type of distributed hardware configuration is called a *hybrid*. This is a combination of a ring and a star structure. As shown in figure 10-11, the hybrid consists of a ring of computers, each of which is the center of a star. The hybrid configuration is used for very large networks of computers.

For one important application of the hybrid configuration, the nodes of the ring form what is called a *communication subnetwork*. The nodes are sophisticated message switchers that do no applications pro-

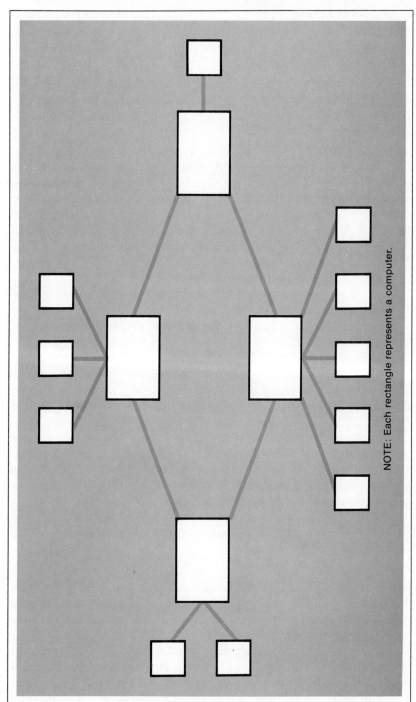

NOTE: Each rectangle represents a computer.

Figure 10-11 Hybrid Network Configuration

cessing. Instead, they communicate with one another on the ring and with the computers on their star. Their sole purpose is to route messages.

Comparison of Star and Ring Configurations

Suppose you work for FRAMCO and you are trying to decide whether the star configuration in figure 10-5 or the ring structure in figure 10-10 is more appropriate for your company. To do this, you might decide to examine the *cost, performance*, and *reliability* of these configurations.

Cost   Considering costs, which of these two configurations is cheaper? The costs of the communication lines are proportional to distance, so you might favor the alternative that has the minimum distance. To simplify the discussion, assume the computers are arranged in a circle.

For a star configuration, there is one communication line for each computer on the periphery of the circle. If the length of the radius of the circle is r, then the total length of the communication lines will be $N \times r$, where N is the number of computers on the periphery.

For the ring configuration, the length of the communication lines is the same as the circumference of the circle. From high school geometry you may remember that this is $2\pi r$, where again r is the radius of the circle. Since π is about 3.14, the length of the star communication lines is about $6.28 \times r$.

Therefore, the length of lines for the star is $N \times r$, and the length of lines for the ring is $6.28 \times r$. This means that if N is less than or equal to 6, the star has shorter lines. However, if N is 7 or greater, the ring has shorter lines. In FRAMCO's case, N is 8, so the ring has shorter communication lines.

However, there are other costs. The computers on the ring must be programmed to pass messages. This program may be expensive. Also, the computers on the ring may have to be large to handle the message switching workload. On the other hand, the ring does not need a message switcher like the star does.

If you worked for FRAMCO, you could compute these costs. Most likely, you would find the ring configuration to be cheaper. What about performance and reliability, however?

Performance   The performance of the network depends on how performance is defined, and on the workload to be processed. Suppose FRAMCO considers the time to process transactions as the only important performance consideration.

If the computers seldom need to communicate with computers other than immediate neighbors, then the ring configuration may give better performance. Messages do not need to be sent to the switcher before arriving at their destinations. On the other hand, if some computers frequently communicate with nonneighbors, the star structure may give better performance. Another factor to be considered is the speed of the message switcher vs the speed of the computers. If the message switcher is fast, it will speed communications in the star. If the computers pass messages quickly, the ring will be faster. Assume you do an analysis for FRAMCO and determine the star is faster.

Reliability   So far you have found the ring is cheaper and the star is faster. Now, consider the reliability of the two configurations. What happens if one of the communication lines between two computers fails in the ring structure? Suppose the link between nodes A and B fails. Then, if B wants to send a message to A, B will have to send it in a roundabout fashion. The message will be sent backwards—across all computers. B will send the message to C, then C will send it to D, and so on until H sends it to A. This sequence will be very time-consuming, but the message will get through. Now, suppose that another link fails, say the link between E and F. At this point, the ring is broken into two *noncommunicating sections*: B-C-D-E and F-G-H-A. Messages cannot get between nodes on these two sections. (See figure 10-12.)

Consider the same case for the star structure. Assume two links fail: one between node A and the message switcher, and another between node E and the message switcher. In this case, neither A nor E will receive any messages at all, but the rest of the network will be unimpaired. (See figure 10-13.)

Figure 10-12   Broken Ring Caused by Two Line Failures

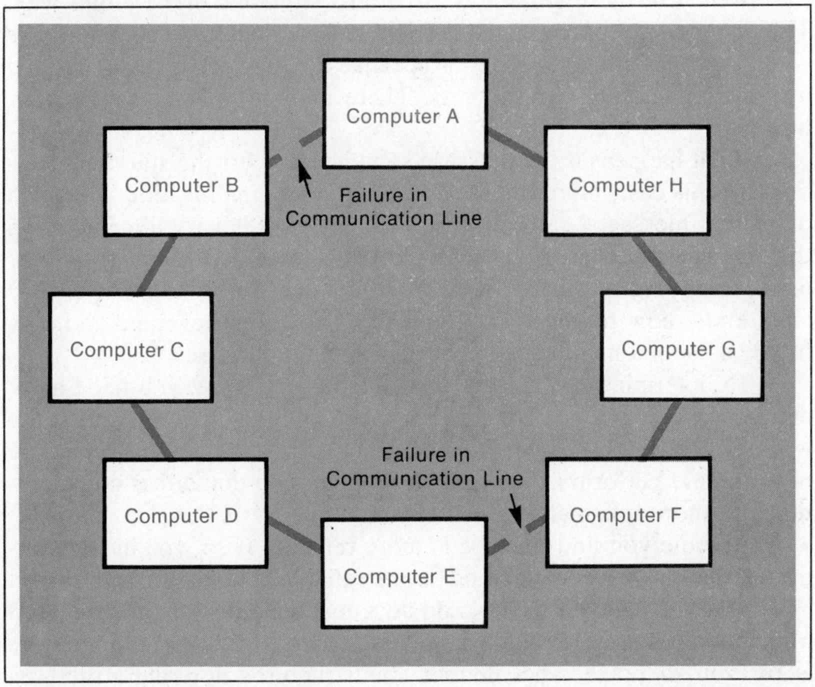

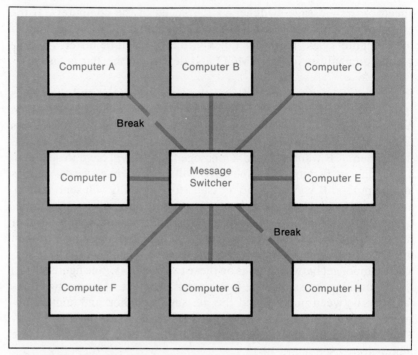

Figure 10-13 Star Network with Two Line Failures

Which of these situations is better? We could argue either way. The ring is better because at least some of the nodes can communicate with A and E. The star is better because the network is never divided into noncommunicating sections. There is another important factor, however.

What happens if the message switcher fails for the star configuration? In this case, all of the nodes are out of communication with each other. No messages can be sent at all. The star is very dependent on the message switcher. For this reason the message switcher should be high-quality, very reliable hardware. When it does fail, FRAMCO must know how to get it fixed quickly. They might even go so far as to buy a second message switcher for backup purposes.

To determine the answer to the reliability issue, you need more data about the reliability of the computers and the lines, and about the workload to be processed. You could build a statistical model of the network and perform an analysis. You might find that either configuration was more reliable.

Assume you find the ring is more reliable. If so, you have determined the ring is cheaper and more reliable, but the star is faster. Which do you choose? You would do a cost benefit study as discussed in Part 2 to determine the best system for FRAMCO. The point here is for you to realize that neither star structures nor ring structures are the best for all circumstances. Both can work well. Both can lead to disaster. The appropriate choice depends on the application.

We have discussed the characteristics of communication lines in detail in Chapter 8, so we will not repeat that discussion here. However, you should realize that computers operate at very high speeds, millions of times faster than a person at a terminal. Consequently, the communication lines must be very high speed. Wideband satellite communications are often used in large computer networks.

QUESTIONS

10.13 What are the three basic computer configurations in distributed networks?

10.14 Under what conditions does a star configuration have shorter communication lines than a ring? Under what conditions does a ring have shorter communication lines than a star?

10.15 Which costs less, a ring or a star configuration?

10.16 Which has better performance, a ring or a star configuration? What factors must be considered to answer this question?

10.17 Which has greater reliability, a ring or a star configuration?

10.18 What happens to a ring structure if one of the communication lines fails? What happens if two communication lines fail?

10.19 What happens to a star structure if one of the communication lines fails? What happens if two communication lines fail?

10.20 What happens to a star configuration if the message switcher fails?

10.21 Should the communication lines in a distributed network be narrowband, voice grade, or wideband? Why?

PROGRAMS FOR DISTRIBUTED PROCESSING

The programs used at application nodes of a distributed network are the same types as those used by teleprocessing computers as discussed in Chapter 8 (at least at the level of detail we are concerned with in this book). However, additional functions must be added to these programs. Each node must have an operating system that controls the system's resources, a communications control program (CCP) that controls the message transfers, and application programs. The node may also have a database management system (DBMS) if databases are being processed.

Types of Distributed Programs

The operating system (excluding the CCP) will be different in the distributed environment. The differences are primarily in the data management or I/O processing. The operating system must be written to recognize that application programs may attempt to access files that reside on a computer at a different location. When this occurs, the operating system must generate a message to the other computer to obtain the data. Also, a computer may receive a transaction that must be processed on a different computer. In this case, the operating system must route the transaction to the correct computer.

Similar considerations apply to the DBMS. Local application programs may try to extract data from a database that resides on another computer. Again, when this occurs, the DBMS must recognize it and obtain the data from the correct source by generating the appropriate message request.

The CCP also has additional duties in the distributed environment. It must be able to receive messages from any of the computers connected to its node, translate them if necessary, send them to the appropriate application program or to the DBMS, or take other action. The translation may be required because the computer that generated the message may be an entirely different type from the local computer. The character code, number of bits per word, etc., may be different.

Also, the CCP will be required to receive messages from local application programs or the DBMS, format them, and transmit them to the correct nodes for processing. Such messages may be responses to requests from these other nodes, or they may be requests for other nodes to perform some actions.

In addition, the node may have its own terminals with which to communicate. The CCP, therefore, must not only talk with other computers, but also control the terminals as is done in a teleprocessing environment. Clearly, the CCP will be a large, complex program.

Application Programs

Since it is impractical to rewrite application programs every time they are moved from one node to another, these programs must be written so as to minimize their dependence on local computer systems. Therefore, systems developers go to great pains to make distributed system applications independent of their environment. Thus, an application program is designed to access a file without knowing where that file is. Similarly, an application program may converse with a user at a terminal, without knowing whether that user is connected to the local computer or to another computer in the distributed network.

This independence actually makes the job of the applications programmer easier. He or she need not learn the details of every computer system in the network. Instead, the programmer learns a generalized way of performing I/O or accessing terminals. The burden is on the operating system and the CCP to execute these generalized commands.

System/Program	Function
Operating System or DBMS	Locate input/output files on another computer Generate messages for remote I/O Access and update directory of data
Communications Control Program	Receive messages from other nodes Send messages to other nodes Translate computer codes
Application Programs	Issue location-independent requests for I/O

Figure 10-14 Special Tasks for Distributed Programs

Developing and maintaining the types of programs just discussed is difficult in distributed systems. First, the computers on a distributed network are often smaller and more limited than centralized mainframes. Main memory is smaller. The programs will not have as much storage space in which to operate as they have on a mainframe. Constraints on main memory, CPU processing speed, and online file space can cause systems developers to limit the capability of the programs more than they would like to.

    Another complicating factor is that the nodes of a distributed network are often operated by the users without the assistance of experienced data processing personnel. Thus, the application programs have to be *self-instructional*, or written so that minimum formal training is needed. Also, the computer itself must be easy to run. Users cannot be expected to perform all of the functions that a well-trained operator can perform. This fact places constraints on the operating system as well as on the CCP, the DBMS, and the application programs.

    As discussed in the Super-Burger example, programs must sometimes be *downline loaded*. That is, a program can be changed or installed remotely using another computer. In some systems, all types of software must be downline loaded—not just application programs. The need for this capability is especially great when there are many nodes in the network, or when the nodes are separated by great geographical distances, or when they are located in hazardous working areas. Figure 10-14 summarizes considerations for distributed programs.

Problems When Distributing Programs

10.22 Are application programs different on a distributed system than on other types of systems? Why or why not?

10.23 Is the operating system on a distributed system different from that on other types of systems? If so, how?

QUESTIONS

10.24 Is the DBMS (if used) on a distributed system different from that on other types of systems? If so, how?

10.25 Is the communications control program on a distributed system different from that on other types of systems? If so, how?

10.26 Name two reasons why programming can be difficult on distributed computers.

DISTRIBUTED DATA

The characteristics of data in the distributed environment can best be examined by considering two questions that the designer of a distributed computer system must answer. First, where is the data to be located? Second, how will it be updated? We will consider each question in turn.

Local and Global Data

In a distributed system, data can be broken into two broad categories: local and global. *Local data* is only needed at the local node. Local data is processed solely by the application programs that run on the local computer. Nodes never request data that is local on a different node. For example, consider FRAMCO Distributing. At a given location, the number and amount of a given sales invoice is local data. Only the local order processing or accounts receivable programs need the data. The data is of no use to any other computer in the FRAMCO system.

Global data is needed by a program or programs that run on at least two computers in the distributed system. For example, the total sales at a given FRAMCO location are needed by the local general ledger programs and also by the headquarters general ledger programs.

The percentage of local vs global data varies from company to company, and from application to application. One rule of thumb in data processing is that 80 percent of the data at a node tends to be local and 20 percent tends to be global. These percentages are not based on any scientific study, but they are a rough guideline.

Turning now to the question of where to locate the data, one basic principle is that *local data stays local*. It almost never makes sense to move local data from the node on which it is used. The communication costs are too high.

Centralized or Partitioned Data

Unfortunately, it is not so easy to decide where to put global data. The first consideration is whether it should be *centralized* or *partitioned*. If centralized, one of the computers in the distributed network stores all of the global data. Then, whenever a node needs some global data, it sends a message for it to the global data computer. In the FRAMCO example in figure 10-3, one of the computers, perhaps the headquarters computer, could store all of the global data.

If the global data is partitioned, then it is spread on several computers throughout the network. Whenever a node needs some global data, it must first determine where the global data it needs is located. Then it can access the data on that computer.

One advantage of centralized data is simplicity. Every node knows where the data is located. The concurrent update problem can be handled by one processor. A disadvantage of centralized global data is that the global data computer can be a performance bottleneck. All computers are dependent on the global data computer for data. If it is slow, processing on all other computers will also be slow.

A second disadvantage concerns reliability. If the global data computer fails, then all the nodes in the network will be unable to continue any processing requiring global data.

Partitioning global data eliminates the performance bottleneck and the reliability problems. Unfortunately, updates of partitioned data are much harder to control.

The systems development personnel must decide not only whether to centralize or partition global data, but also whether or not the data is to be *replicated*. If replicated, several copies of the data are stored around the network. Either centralized or partitioned data can be replicated as illustrated in figure 10-15.

To replicate centralized global data, the entire collection of global data is stored at several locations in the network. When this is done, the nodes need only keep lists of the computers having the replicated data. They do not need directories that show the locations of particular kinds of data; all of the data is located at each of the nodes. Also, replicating global data eliminates the bottleneck and reliability problems discussed above, but introduces the problem of concurrent update control.

Figure 10-15 Allocation of Global Data in Distributed Networks

Category	Number of Copies	
	Nonreplicated	*Replicated*
Centralized	All global data is located on a single node.	Complete copies of all the global data exist on several nodes.
Partitioned	Global data is broken into pieces. Only one copy of each piece exists, but the pieces reside on different nodes.	Global data is broken into pieces. Several copies of some pieces exist or copies of all pieces exist.

Data for Super-Burger Restaurants

Super-Burger Restaurant Franchises might decide to have replicated, centralized global data. If so, they might store all of the global data on each of the regional computers. (See figure 10-5.) Then, when any of the restaurant computers needs global data, it simply accesses its regional computer.

Super-Burger would decide to take this course only if the restaurant and regional computers frequently needed all of the global data. If these computers needed only part of the global data, Super-Burger might decide to have replicated, partitioned global data. In this case, multiple copies of the partitioned global data would be stored.

Suppose, for example, that each restaurant needs access to the summarized sales data for the region in which it resides. Further, suppose the regional computers need summarized sales data for all four regions. In this case, Super-Burger would divide the global data into five parts: the summarized data for region 1, the summarized data for region 2, the summarized data for region 3, the summarized data for region 4, and the summarized data for all four regions.

Now, the summarized data for region 1 would be replicated at each of the 20 restaurant computers in region 1, that for region 2 would be replicated at the 20 restaurants in region 2, and so forth. Further, the summarized data for all four regions would be replicated at each of the four regional computers. This scheme is illustrated in figure 10-16.

Data Directory

When data is partitioned or replicated, each node must have access to a *dictionary* or *directory* that gives the location or locations of each type of data. This dictionary is used by the operating system or the DBMS whenever a user or application program attempts to access global data.

Since the dictionary is global data, an interesting question is, Should it be partitioned or replicated? If so, then a dictionary of dictionaries is necessary. This situation becomes complex and is beyond the scope of this text, but you might enjoy puzzling over this question.

Replicated, partitioned data allows for the greatest flexibility in storing data across the distributed network. Unfortunately, it is also the most complex and the hardest to control.

Figure 10-16 Example of Replicated, Partitioned Data for Super-Burger Restaurant

Global Data Partitioned into Five Parts	Global Data Replicated on Nodes
Summarized sales data for region 1	All restaurant computers in region 1
Summarized sales data for region 2	All restaurant computers in region 2
Summarized sales data for region 3	All restaurant computers in region 3
Summarized sales data for region 4	All restaurant computers in region 4
Summarized sales data for entire company	All four regional computers

At the start of this section, two questions were mentioned. One was, Where is the data to be located? As shown in figure 10-15, there are four philosophies for allocating data in the network. The second question was, How is the data to be updated? This second question poses some very difficult problems for the designers of distributed systems.

What happens when two users or application programs want to update the same record concurrently? As we saw in Chapter 8, it is possible for one of the updates to be lost. This predicament occurs when user A reads a record, user B reads the same record, user A updates the record, and then user B updates the record. In this case, user A's update is lost.

Updating Distributed Data

To prevent this situation, users or application programs are supposed to lock records before they update them. This solution is reasonably straightforward for centralized, nonreplicated data. The lock only involves the computer that has the global data. However, what happens if the data is replicated? Then, the lock must be in place on two computers. This doesn't sound too difficult until you consider what happens if the locks are applied simultaneously (as they could be). Then, one user has the record locked on one computer, and another user has the record locked on a different computer. Both locks are in place, but neither user has absolute control over the record. One of the locks will have to be released, and control of the record given to the other user. This is difficult to coordinate and is very time-consuming.

Even nonreplicated, partitioned data is susceptible to these problems. An application program may need to update several records with the same transaction. For example, to record a sale, an application program may need to insert a new order record, modify the contents of a customer record, and modify a salesperson record. These last two records should be locked throughout the update process. However, if they are located on different computers, then we again have the problem of invoking locks on separate machines, and the potential for two users locking each other out.

So, of the four styles of allocating data to a distributed network, three of them pose significant problems regarding the concurrent update problem. It is beyond the scope of this book to solve these problems; in fact, some of them have not yet been solved. You should be aware of them, however.

It is easier to distribute hardware, programs, and data than to distribute personnel. First, hardware, programs, and data are cheaper than personnel. With the advent of microprocessors and other cost-saving electronic technology, hardware is becoming cheaper and cheaper.

DISTRIBUTED PERSONNEL

Meanwhile, because of inflation and other factors, personnel are becoming more and more expensive.

(Since people write computer programs, and since the cost of people is rising, you might think the cost of distributed programs is also increasing. However, once a program is written and tested, the cost of producing a second copy is negligible. Therefore, if a program that already exists can be installed and used on a distributed node, its cost is minimal.)

People are hard to distribute not only because they are expensive, but also because they are harder to obtain and train. More computers can be manufactured, and additional copies of a program can be inexpensively made by a computer. But, training a systems analyst or programmer takes a long time. Therefore, there is currently a critical shortage of data processing personnel. Companies cannot easily locate another 20 programmers or operators to staff a distributed network.

In addition to these problems, people are hard to distribute because they need support organizations. An operator needs a boss. He or she needs someone to report to, someone to learn from, someone to provide positive feedback or correction when required. A single operator is apt to feel out of place and isolated from the mainstream of the company's data processing activity.

Alternatives to Distributed Personnel

Because of these problems, data processing personnel are often not distributed with the hardware, programs, and data. Instead, distributed systems are designed to be operated by the users who are already present in the distributed locations. These people are already hired; they are already trained in their jobs; and they already have a support organization.

Clearly, a user cannot be expected to perform the same tasks as a well-trained operator or programmer. This fact is considered in the design of distributed systems. The programs are written to be easily used. Operations procedures must be simple, well-documented, and as self-explanatory as possible.

For example, to start the computer, the user should only have to turn it on. Messages that prompt the user's next action should be displayed on the CRT screen. These messages must be easy to understand. The required action must be such that a person with only a week or two of training can accomplish it. Additionally, it is absolutely essential that standardized procedures be well documented and that users be trained in following them.

To reduce the burden of training, some organizations have chosen to have two or three users at each site designated as *key personnel*. These key people are given special training. They are called upon when the equipment fails, when a user has difficulty accomplishing a task, or when special actions such as file backup must be performed. In this way, these people become para-operators at the distributed location.

There are some tasks that are too difficult for even key user personnel to perform. Examples may be installing new programs, or initially operating new equipment. These tasks can be performed by data processing personnel who travel on a temporary basis to the distributed location, or they can be performed *downline* from a remote computer as discussed previously.

Operations personnel are sometimes distributed when the workload is too heavy or complex for users to perform. Also, in some cases, tasks arise that are too difficult for users and that cannot be done by data processing personnel on a temporary basis. An example is running a daily system having a complex sequence of jobs, each requiring tape and disk files. In such cases, some operations personnel have to be distributed. This distribution usually occurs only in the larger, more sophisticated computer installations.

How operators are distributed depends on the configuration of equipment and the data processing needs. For example, consider Super-Burger Restaurant Franchises. Super-Burger has no computer operators at any of its 80 restaurant locations. However, even though it would like not to have operators at the regional centers, the users cannot perform all the tasks required. Consequently, Super-Burger has three operators at each regional location. These distributed personnel are in addition to a full staff of operators at the headquarters computer center.

Systems Development Personnel

In addition to users and operators, systems development personnel are required to develop and support distributed computer systems. Programmers, systems analysts, and specialists are needed. The specialists include communications experts, hardware experts, and probably personnel for maintaining the operating systems, communications control programs, and database management systems. If there are several types of computer hardware in the network, a company may need experts for each type.

In most instances, the systems development personnel will be consolidated in one location. Super-Burger, for example, has its entire systems development staff at the headquarters facility. There is really no need for the development staff at distributed sites. In fact, Super-Burger wants to maintain tight *control* over developmental projects and refuses to authorize the development of any systems in the field. They believe this is the only way they can ensure strict *standardization* of their programs.

Figure 10-17 summarizes the considerations for distributed personnel. Generally, as few data processing personnel as possible should be distributed. People cost too much, are hard to find, and require support organizations. Consequently, users take on as much of the operations functions as they can.

Why Data Processing Personnel Not Distributed	Ways to Avoid Distribution
Too expensive Hard to obtain and train Difficult to support and control	Training users to run systems Designing systems for ease of use Training key personnel Loading downline Providing temporary data processing personnel Centralizing development

Figure 10-17   Distributing Considerations for Data Processing Personnel

Systems development personnel are required for distributed systems, and considerable expertise may be needed to maintain the distributed network. These personnel are generally not distributed, for control as well as economic reasons.

PROCEDURES FOR DISTRIBUTED PROCESSING

The procedures needed to successfully operate a distributed system are generally the same as those for other data processing systems. However, because the computers may be operated by inexperienced personnel, the procedures must be better documented and easier to understand than other systems procedures. Also, the procedures must be complete and unambiguous. The computers will be operated by personnel who are miles apart and who in fact may never meet. If the processing is to be uniform from one computer to the next, the procedures must be clear and complete.

Since the distributed computers are intended to communicate with one another, there must be procedures explaining how to make such a connection, and what to do if the connection does not work. Also, users (or operators) must know what their responsibilities to other computers are when their computer fails. They must also know what to do when another computer in the network fails.

This knowledge is particularly important for networks having partitioned data. If a computer that has critical global data fails, the personnel involved with other computers must know what to do. Procedures are required to explain how to get needed data, or how to get along without it until the failed computer has been repaired.

Users of a distributed system need the usual procedures on how to interact with the business computer systems they use. However, with a distributed system, they may also need procedures on how to run the computer, including backup, recovery, and other special tasks.

Procedures and standards for program development are particularly important in distributed systems. Programmers must know how to lock data before updating it, what conventions must be followed to obtain data, special techniques to be used (or avoided) in order to communicate with other programs, and so forth. Programs used in the distributed environment should be well tested and be able to handle erroneous conditions without failing themselves. This requirement is necessary because these programs will be run by inexperienced personnel in locations remote from the systems development staff.

10.27	What are two broad categories of data?	QUESTIONS
10.28	Where should local data be stored in a distributed environment?	
10.29	Global data can be either centralized or _____.	
10.30	Into how many pieces is centralized global data broken?	
10.31	What is the maximum number of pieces that partitioned data can be broken into?	
10.32	What is an advantage of centralized data?	
10.33	What is an advantage of partitioned data?	
10.34	Explain the difference between replicated, centralized data and nonreplicated, centralized data.	
10.35	Explain the difference between replicated, partitioned data and nonreplicated, partitioned data.	
10.36	What is the purpose of a distributed system dictionary or directory?	
10.37	Explain why problems occur when locks must be invoked on two separate computers.	
10.38	Of the four methods of allocating data to distributed computers, which one does not pose significant problems regarding concurrent update? Why is it not used in all cases?	
10.39	Why is it easier to distribute hardware, programs, and data than to distribute personnel?	
10.40	What is meant by the statement that people need support organizations?	
10.41	Since data processing personnel are hard to distribute, how do companies staff their distributed computers?	
10.42	What is the function of distributed key personnel?	
10.43	Under what conditions are computer operators distributed?	
10.44	Are systems development personnel likely to be centralized or distributed? Why?	

10.45   What are the differences between procedures used in distributed systems and procedures used in other types of systems?

10.46   What special procedures are needed for systems that have partitioned data?

10.47   What procedures are needed for program development in a distributed system?

SUMMARY

In a distributed data processing system, application programs are run on more than one computer. These computers are connected to one another via communication lines. Distributed systems are like teleprocessing systems in that the terminals and users are distributed, and there can be more than one computer. However, distributed systems differ from teleprocessing systems in that application programs are run on more than one computer. For a teleprocessing system, the application programs are run on a centralized computer.

There is a wide variety of distributed data processing configurations. Computers can be connected in master/slave relationships, and they can be connected as partners or colleagues. The nodes of the distributed networks can be simple microprocessors or large mainframes. Distributed computers can be totally interconnected or there can be few connections. Distributed computers can be autonomous and independent, or they can be interconnected and very dependent.

Distributed processing has several advantages. It may be cheaper than teleprocessing because communication costs are less. Also, distributed systems allow more control to users because the computer is located close to the need for the data processing services. Further, a distributed system can result in shorter development if turnkey systems can be found that meet user requirements and that can be integrated into the distributed system. Finally, distributed networks, because of their flexibility, can be tailored to the organizational structure of the company.

Distributed processing also has several important disadvantages. First, such systems are difficult to build, and close coordination is required to keep data compatibility. Also, there is a greater need for standards and documentation. Finally, distributed systems usually involve multiple vendors, and this fact can lead to maintenance problems.

There are three basic configurations of distributed hardware: star, ring, and hybrid. In a star configuration, a central computer is surrounded by distributed computers. In a ring, the computers are connected in a circular manner without a central controller or computer. A hybrid configuration is a combination of these two.

None of these three configurations is superior to the other two for all circumstances. A choice depends on the requirements, the budget, and the equipment that is already in place.

Application programs in the distributed environment are not much different from application programs in the teleprocessing environment. The major difference is that application programs or users may request data that does not reside on the local node. In this case the operating system or the DBMS, whichever controls the data, must determine where the data resides and obtain it.

The communications control program is different in the distributed environment. It must be able to communicate with other nodes; that is, it must accept messages from them and respond as well. This interaction may be difficult if the computers in the system are made by several manufacturers.

Distributed data can be local or global. Local data nearly always stays on the local node. Global data can be centralized or partitioned. Also, global data can be replicated or nonreplicated. There are significant problems regarding concurrent update for partitioned or replicated data.

It is difficult to distribute data processing personnel. Consequently, systems are designed to be as independent of operators and systems development personnel as possible. Users thereby have a greater responsibility for running computer systems, but they also gain greater control.

Finally, distributed systems must be well documented and procedures must be very clear. Users will not be computer experts, and they must be able to remember and understand necessary procedures. Also, users must coordinate with one another over some distance. Thus, procedures must be standardized and uniformly documented.

Distributed data processing system

Application node

Master/slave relationship

Message switcher

Colleague relationship

Data dependency

Hierarchy of computers

Downline loading

Offload processing

Star configuration

Ring configuration

Hybrid configuration

Hierarchical star configuration

Self-instructional programs

Local data

Global data

Centralized data

WORD LIST

(in order of appearance in text)

Partitioned data   *Distributed data directory*

Replicated data   *Simultaneous locks*

Nonreplicated data   *Key user personnel*

Data directory

A. Suppose you work for Alpine Co-op. Do you think distributed processing is appropriate for their environment? How would you determine whether or not it is?

B. Suppose Alpine Co-op decided to open retail stores and to add several warehouse shipping points. Would distributed data processing be appropriate? If so, should data processing costs or other considerations play a role in determining the location of the new installations?

Assume Alpine opened stores in Los Angeles, Anchorage, Denver, Atlanta, and Boston. Also, assume warehouse/shipping points were located in Los Angeles, St. Louis, and Richmond. Describe one feasible distributed processing configuration. Show where application nodes, and equipment like concentrators, message switchers, RJE stations, and terminals could be located. Describe communication lines connecting the hardware.

C. Suppose FRAMCO Distributing has five locations instead of eight. Further, suppose the locations are Seattle, Los Angeles, Atlanta, Montreal, and Chicago. The headquarters is in Atlanta. All the other facts introduced about FRAMCO are the same. What sort of a distributed configuration do you think is appropriate? If you need more data, stipulate the data you need and then assume values for it that support your recommendation.

D. Do you think distributed processing is appropriate for your college or university? What organizations might have their own processing computers? Describe the kinds of hardware and programs you think would be appropriate for these user organizations. Is there any global data? If so, should it be centralized or partitioned? Should it be replicated or nonreplicated? What personnel and procedures will be required to operate this distributed system?

E. For some organizations, teleprocessing is more appropriate than distributed computing. For other organizations, just the opposite is true. Characterize the organizations for which teleprocessing is more appropriate and those for which distributed computing is more appropriate. How are they structured? What management philosophies are prevalent? How is senior management rewarded? What services do their customers expect? What products do they buy and which do they sell? Describe other characteristics you think are important.

F. To answer this question, first read Module C, *Computer Crime, Security, and Control.*

Discuss special considerations when designing controls for distributed systems. Are distributed systems more vulnerable to computer crime? How can organizations be structured to improve control in distributed systems? Is is desirable for distributed personnel to know how to program? What should distributed personnel know?

MODULE A

**HISTORY OF DATA
PROCESSING**

MODULE B

**NUMBERS
REPRESENTATION
AND COMPUTER
ARITHMETIC**

MODULE C

**COMPUTER CRIME,
SECURITY, AND
CONTROL**

MODULE D

**COMPUTERS AND
THEIR IMPACT ON
SOCIETY**

MODULE E

**WORD PROCESSING
SYSTEMS AND THE
AUTOMATED OFFICE**

MODULE F

**MICROCOMPUTERS
AND SPECIALIZED
INPUT/OUTPUT
EQUIPMENT**

PART 4

SPECIAL
COMPUTING TOPICS

SPECIAL
COMPUTING TOPICS

This part contains six independent sections, or modules, on a variety of computer topics. They provide information that may not be of interest to all students. You can read none, one, or all of these sections, in any order. The discussions assume you have read Chapters 1 and 2. The following topics are discussed:

Module A   History of Data Processing
Module B   Numbers Representation and Computer Arithmetic
Module C   Computer Crime, Security, and Control
Module D   Computers and Their Impact on Society
Module E   Word Processing Systems and the Automated Office
Module F   Microcomputers and Specialized Input/Output Equipment

MODULE A

History of Data Processing

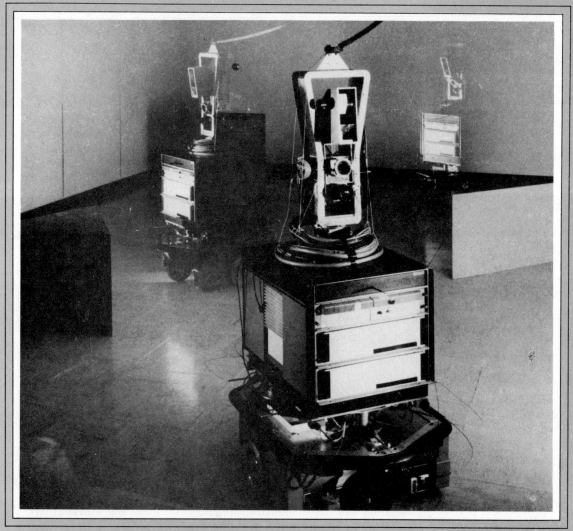

Computer history or computer future? History—Shakey the Robot is now retired

CHARLES BABBAGE AND HIS MACHINES
  Babbage's Life
  Lessons We Can Learn
  from Babbage
HERMAN HOLLERITH
EARLY COMPUTERS
COMPUTERS IN THE 1960s AND 1970s
COMPUTERS TODAY — THE FOURTH GENERATION

The history of computing began centuries ago when people first started to count on their fingers. In fact, fingers and toes were probably (no one knows for sure) the earliest computational devices. As business and commerce developed, however, a need arose for a calculator with capacity greater than 20.

The abacus shown in figure A-1 is an early form of such a calculator. Versions of it were used for centuries by people of many nations and areas of the world. The abacus was used even before numbers had a written representation. Other computational devices were constructed throughout the centuries. The numerical wheel calculator (figure A-2) was the predecessor of the adding machines and manual calculators that were commonly used before the rise of the electronic calculator. The slide rule (figure A-3) was another type of computational device.

CHARLES BABBAGE AND HIS MACHINES

As far as we know, Charles Babbage is the father of computing. This amazing man was far ahead of his time. He developed the essential ideas of a computer over 100 years before the first computer was constructed. He was so far ahead of his time that nearly none of his contemporaries appreciated him. In addition to computing, Babbage made contributions to the fields of mathematics, optics, underwater navigation, railroads, industrial engineering, mechanics, and others.

Many of the mistakes that Babbage made continue to be made today, and so it is worth considering his life's activities in some detail.

Figure A-1   Abacus

Babbage was born in England in 1792 (George Washington was still alive). His father was a wealthy banker who left him a sizable fortune. Babbage says he suffered from high fevers and so he was sent to a private tutor "with instructions to attend to my health; but, not to press too much knowledge upon me: a mission which he faithfully accomplished." [62, p. 11] Babbage says, "My invariable question on receiving any new toy was, 'Mamma, what is inside of it?'" Apparently, if she couldn't answer, he tore it apart.

    Some time prior to 1822, Babbage and his friend John Herschel were checking data calculated for the Astronomical Society. In frus-

Babbage's Life

Figure A-2   Numerical Wheel Calculator

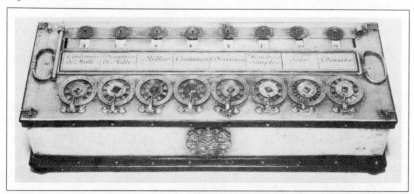

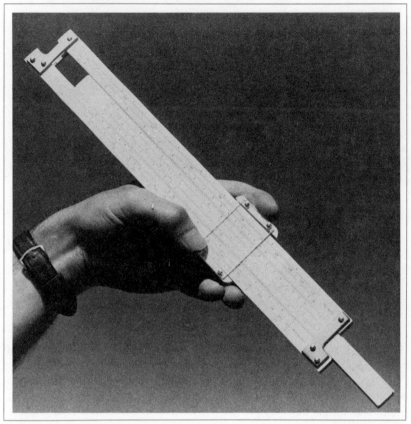

Figure A-3   Slide Rule

tration, Babbage remarked to Herschel, "I wish to God these calculations had been executed by steam." (Steam engines were common.) In 1822, Babbage proposed the design of a difference engine composed of gears and wheels. (See figure A-4.) This engine would automatically compute functions of the form:

$$y = a + ax + ax^2 + \cdots + ax^6$$

In 1823 the British Government granted Babbage money to build the engine. The first government-sponsored computer project was on! Like most of those to follow, the project fell behind. By 1833 the government had invested £17,000 and only part of the difference engine was completed. Meanwhile, Babbage's active mind had been extending the possibilities of automated computing. By 1834 he had developed the idea of an analytical engine. The analytical engine would compute *any* mathematical function. It had most of the concepts embodied in early computers.

Figure A-4 Babbage's Difference Engine

Babbage asked the government in 1834 whether it wanted him to finish the difference engine or start on the analytical engine. After eight years of frustrating correspondence, Prime Minister Robert Peel told Babbage the government was going to abandon the project. This case established a record of governmental delay that is yet unbroken!

The analytical engine had a main memory which Babbage called *the store*. It was to have room for 1000 variables of 50 digits each. It had an arithmetic and logic unit which he called *the mill*. Programs for the mill were written on punched cards. The engine would drive a typesetter. It had logical capability and could ring a bell or take other action when a variable passed zero or exceeded the capacity of one of the words. All these operations were to have been implemented mechanically.

People had a hard time understanding the concept. Mathematicians asked him how it would use logarithms. He told them it wouldn't need logarithms since it could compute any function. Some people didn't believe this, so he showed them how it could be programmed to ask an attendant to supply a logarithm from a library of cards. Furthermore, it would check for the correct logarithm. The procedure he described in 1864 is exactly the procedure used today to check tape labels. (See Chapter 5.)

Ironically, Babbage got more attention outside of England than from within. He had two automated devices in his home, a clockwork lady who would dance and a portion of the difference engine. He reported that his English friends would gather about the dancing lady, whereas an American and a Hollander studied the difference engine. In fact, a Swedish printer, George Scheutz, made the only complete version of the difference engine (except for the one IBM recently made). Babbage was delighted and helped Scheutz explain it.

We know about the analytical engine largely because of a paper written by an Italian, L. F. Menabrea. This paper was written in French, and translated into English by Ada Augusta, the Countess of Lovelace. There is interesting social commentary here.

Ada Augusta was the only legitimate daughter of the poet, Lord Byron. She was an excellent mathematician, and understood Babbage's concepts perhaps better than anyone. In 1842, when she translated Menabrea's paper of 20 pages, she added 50 pages of "notes." Babbage wanted to know why she didn't write a paper of her own. "I never thought of it," she replied. In fact, she didn't sign her translation or her notes, but used the initials A.A.L. instead. Ladies didn't do such things (which probably explains why "Anonymous" was a woman!).

However, ladies could go to the racetrack. The Countess loved racing, and it may have been inevitable that she would use the difference engine to determine horse bets. Apparently, it didn't work too well. She lost the family jewels at the track. Her mother, Lady Byron, had to buy them back.

The Countess died of cancer at the age of 36, just 10 years after reading Menabrea's description. This was a big loss to Babbage and perhaps to the world. The new programming language, ADA, is named after Ada Augusta Lovelace. (See Module J.)

Babbage was a fascinating person. He was very social; he worked and played hard. Charles Darwin reported lively dinner parties at Babbage's home. Another person complained of barely being able to escape from him at 2:00 in the morning. Babbage once said he would be glad to give up the rest of his life if he could live for three days 500 years in the future.

Babbage once spent several months riding railroad cars around the United States. He was doing research on railway and train design. It is sad that he could not know the very tracks he was riding on would someday carry trains controlled by computers having the design he envisioned. Also, he would have been interested to know that those same computers would someday be used to steal over 400 railway cars. (See Module C.)

Babbage died in 1871. He never saw the analytical engine developed. And he never knew how right he was. At the time of his death, he was bitter about the lack of government support. However, his autobiography does not seem bitter, and he probably was not the frustrated and unhappy man some people report. If you're interested in Babbage, read the excellent book, *Charles Babbage and His Calculating Engines*, edited by Philip and Emily Morrison. [62]

Many of the errors Babbage made have been repeated again and again in the computer industry. For one, Babbage began with vague requirements. "Let's compute numbers by steam" sounds all too much like, "Let's use a computer to do billing." Much more precise statements of requirements are necessary.

Lessons We Can Learn from Babbage

Second, it appears Babbage started implementing before design was complete. Much work had to be redone. His engineers and draftsmen often complained that they would finish a project only to be told the work was wrong or not needed because the design had been changed. The very same complaint has been made by countless programmers since then. Another mistake Babbage made was to add more and more capability to his engines before any of them were complete. As his work progressed, he saw new possibilities, and he tried to implement them into his existing projects. Many data processing systems have failed to be completed for the very same reason.

Work on the difference engine was set back considerably when Babbage and his chief engineer, Joseph Clement, had a crisis over Clement's salary. Clement quit, and Babbage had little documentation to recover that loss. Further, Clement had the rights to all the tools. Who knows how many systems projects have failed because indispensable programmers quit in the middle? As stated in Chapter 4, working documentation is crucial for successful system implementation.

Even Lady Lovelace's losses at the track have a lesson. Systems ought not to be used for purposes for which they weren't designed. The computer industry has suffered much inefficiency because systems are applied to problems for which they weren't designed.

There was no electronics industry to support Babbage's ideas. All of the concepts had to be implemented in mechanical components, and the tolerances were so fine they could not be manufactured within 19th century technology. Also, Babbage's plans were grandiose. Building a computer with a thousand 50 decimal digit numbers was a large task. He might have been more successful at completing a smaller computer and building credibility with his government and solidifying his funding before starting on a large one. Many government-sponsored

---

Babbage's Mistakes
Vague problem definition and requirements
Implementation started before design was complete
Requirements added during implementation
Working documentation not complete
Dependency on one person
System used for unintended purposes
Grandiose plans that exceeded existing technology

Figure A-5   Mistakes Babbage Made That Are Still Made Today

projects fail today because of a lack in technology to support grandiose plans. These lessons are summarized in figure A-5.

We do not know what impact, if any, Babbage's work had on future development. One pioneer, Howard Aiken (see p. 364), reported he worked three years before discovering Babbage's contributions. We do not know about the others.

HERMAN HOLLERITH

In the late 19th century, the U.S. Census Bureau had a problem. The Bureau was supposed to produce a census of the U.S. population every 10 years. However, the 1880 census took seven and a half years to finish. By the time the census data was processed, much of its usefulness was gone. Furthermore, at the rate of growth of the U.S. population, the Census Bureau was afraid the 1890 census would not be finished before the 1900 census was due to begin.

In 1879, the Bureau hired Herman Hollerith to help them. He worked for the Census Bureau for five years, and then started his own company. Hollerith designed and managed the construction of several punched card processing machines. (See figure A-6.)

In 1889 the Bureau held a contest among Hollerith's and two other competitors' systems to determine which system was the fastest. Hollerith's system required only one-tenth of the time needed by his nearest competitor. Using this equipment, the first count of the 1890 census took only six weeks! However, the final, official count was not announced until December of 1890.

Hollerith's equipment was an extension to the work of the Frenchman, Joseph Marie Jacquard. Jacquard designed looms in which punched cards controlled the pattern on woven material. In Jacquard's looms, needles fell through holes in the cards. The needles lifted threads in a way to cause a pattern to be produced. This technique had been used in the weaving industry since 1804.

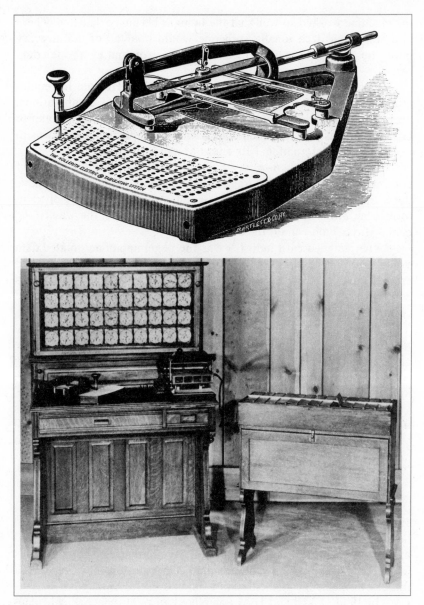

Figure A-6 Hollerith's Punched Card Machines

Hollerith extended this concept by using the cards to control electric circuits. Data was punched on three by five inch cards and fed into a machine that moved the cards over a group of pins. If there was a hole in a card, the pin would fall through the hole and touch a pan of mercury. This closed a circuit and registered on a meter. Apparently, the machine worked so well that the humans became exhausted. There is a story that occasionally someone would pour all of the mercury into a nearby spittoon. The machine would stop and everyone could rest!

Hollerith decided he had a marketable idea. He sold his equipment to railroads and other large companies that had computational problems. This was the start of the punched card industry. Hollerith built up his business and then sold it to the company that later was to become IBM (International Business Machines).

Hollerith didn't know it, but he was setting the pace for many entrepreneurs to come. Literally hundreds of computer people have done the same thing. They have taken a good idea, developed it, formed an attractive company, sold it, and laughed all the way to the bank. Maybe you can do the same thing.

The punched card industry was the beginning of automated data processing. The earliest business computer systems were developed around punched card technology. Companies found that to use this new technology successfully, they needed to build systems composed of hardware, programs, data, procedures, and trained personnel.

Programs? Well, sort of. As the punched card equipment became more sophisticated, it became possible to change the wiring of the equipment to make it do different things. People who changed the wiring were doing an elementary form of programming. Programming as we know it today did not occur until stored-program computers were developed in the middle of the 20th century. However, the concepts used in business computer systems started evolving with the 1890 census. That is when the idea of developing systematic procedures to direct machines to turn data into information was born.

EARLY COMPUTERS In 1937, Howard G. Aiken proposed the use of electromechanical devices to perform calculations. He was a graduate student at Harvard at the time, and the IBM Corporation gave him a grant to pursue his ideas. IBM was active in the punched card industry. They may have felt electromechanical calculators would be useful to them.

In 1944, Aiken and IBM completed an electromechanical calculator called the Mark I. This computer had mechanical counters that were manipulated by electrical devices. The Mark I could perform basic arithmetic, and it could be changed to solve different problems. (See figure A-7.)

At about the same time, the U.S. Government signed a contract with the University of Pennsylvania to develop a computer to aid the military effort during World War II. As a result of this contract, John W. Mauchly and J. Presper Eckert developed the first all-electronic

Figure A-7 Mark I Computer

computer called the Electronic Numerical Integrator and Calculator, or ENIAC. Unlike Mark I, there were no mechanical counters; everything was electronic.

Although Mauchly and Eckert are often given credit for developing the first electronic computer, this is apparently not true. Their work was based in part on work that had been done by John V. Atanasoff. Atanasoff was a professor at Iowa State and in 1939 had developed many ideas for an all-electronic computer. In 1942, he and a graduate student, Clifford Berry, completed an electronic computer that could solve systems of linear equations.

ENIAC (the Mauchly/Eckert machine) was used to perform many different calculations. It had 19,000 vacuum tubes, 70,000 resistors, and 500,000 soldered joints. The ENIAC could perform 5000 additions per second. It used 150,000 watt-hours of power a day—so much that when it was turned on, the lights in one section of Philadelphia dimmed. Unfortunately, it was inflexible. Changing its program required rewiring and thus considerable time and resources. Since it could be changed, it was programmable. However, it was not programmable in the sense we know it today.

In the mid-1940s the mathematician, John von Neumann, joined the Mauchly/Eckert team. Von Neumann proposed the design of a computer that stored programs in its memory. He also proposed other concepts that were to become the foundation for computer design for 30 years. Two computers evolved from this work: the EDVAC (Electrical Discrete Variable Automatic Computer) and the EDSAC (Electronic Delay Storage Automatic Calculator). Both machines stored programs. EDSAC was completed in England in 1949, and EDVAC in the United States in 1950.

At the time, the potential of these machines was not understood. Atanasoff couldn't get support from Iowa State. The administration thought there would be a need for only three or four of these devices throughout the United States. Furthermore, another computer pioneer, Hermann Goldstine, reports that in the late 1940s none of the ENIAC-EDVAC staff was promoted to full professor at the Moore School of Engineering. People didn't seem to feel the work was going to be very important.

Another social commentary: the first programmers for the Mark I and the ENIAC were women. Capt. Grace Hopper, USN, programmed the Mark I and Ms. Adele Goldstine programmed the ENIAC. Both of these women were talented mathematicians. Their presence undoubtedly helped to establish women's strong position in the computer industry.

John Mauchly and Presper Eckert decided to follow Hollerith's entrepreneurial footsteps, and in 1946, they formed the Eckert-Mauchly Corporation. This ripe young company was purchased by the Remington-Rand Corporation. Their first product was UNIVAC I (Universal Automatic Computer). This was the first computer built to sell. The Census Bureau took delivery on the first one in 1951, and it was used continuously until 1963. It now resides in the Smithsonian Institution. (See figure A-8.) Sperry Rand still manufactures a line of computers under the name UNIVAC. These computers are a far cry from the UNIVAC I.

Figure A-8   UNIVAC I

Meanwhile, other companies were not idle. IBM continued development on the Mark I computer and eventually developed the Mark II through Mark IV as well as other early computers. Burroughs, General Electric, Honeywell, and RCA were also busy with computer developments.

IBM took an early lead in the application of this new computer technology to business problems. They developed a series of business-oriented computers and sold them to their punched card customers. Since IBM had a near monopoly on punched cards (they had been sued by the U.S. Trust Department in the 1930s for this), they were in a strong position to capitalize on the new technology.

Furthermore, IBM had an extremely effective marketing philosophy. They emphasized solving business problems. They developed products that were useful to businesses, and they showed business people how to use those products. IBM provided excellent customer service and good maintenance.

This philosophy paid off. Some other companies had better computers, but their computers weren't packaged to provide total solutions to business problems. IBM was the first company to understand that intelligent business people don't buy the best computers; they buy the best solution to their problem. Today, many vendors have adopted this philosophy. They sell solutions to business problems (not just computers). However, the fact that IBM understood this principle first has much to do with their strength in the computer market today.

The computers manufactured in the 1950s are often called *first-generation computers*. They had vacuum tubes as their major components. Most of them used magnetic drums as their primary storage devices. Main memory as discussed in this book did not exist at that time.

Because of the number and size of the vacuum tubes, these computers were huge. Also, they generated tremendous amounts of heat, were expensive to run, and failed often. A large first-generation computer occupied a room the size of a football field. It contained rows upon rows of racks of tubes. A staff of a half dozen people was required just to change the tubes that burned out.

COMPUTERS IN THE 1960s AND 1970s

In the late 1950s and early 1960s, vacuum tubes were replaced by transistors. This led to *second-generation computers*. These computers were much smaller than vacuum tube computers, and they were more powerful. A new type of main storage was developed. It was called *core memory* because it used magnetized doughnut-shaped cores. The term *core* is still around today. Some people use core synonymously with main memory. This usage is incorrect. Most main memories today do not contain magnetic core.

The first high-level programming languages were developed during this stage. First-generation computers were programmed in machine code, but second-generation computers were programmed in assembly language and English-like languages such as FORTRAN and ALGOL. (See Module J.) Also, primitive operating systems were installed on second-generation machines. Operating system programs controlled the use of the computer's resources.

Most second-generation computers could run only one program at a time. Therefore, to speed things up, certain input and output operations were done *off line*. For example, punched cards were read and their contents copied onto tape without the computer's involvement. Then, the data on the tape was read into the computer, processed, and the generated output was written to tape. The tape was then dismounted and printed on a separate machine. This process was done because tape units could read and write much faster than card readers or printers could operate. Figure A-9 shows the IBM 7094, a typical second-generation computer.

Most of the business computer systems at this stage were accounting in nature. The computer was used to produce checks for payroll and accounts payable, and to keep track of inventories. General ledger was also computerized. However, processing was done in batches. Inputs were gathered into groups, processed, and outputs produced. Applications that required interaction, like order entry, could not be done.

Figure A-9   A Second-Generation Computer — The IBM 7094

In the 1960s the *third generation of computers* became available. In these, *integrated circuits* were used instead of transistors. An integrated circuit is a complete electrical circuit on a small chip of silicon. (See figure A-10.) Because of these chips, third-generation computers are smaller and more powerful than second-generation computers. Figure A-11 compares the sizes of vacuum tubes, transistors, and integrated chips.

Also, vast improvements were made in programming during the third generation. Sophisticated operating systems were developed. These systems allowed many programs to be executed concurrently. Slow input and output operations like card reading or printing could be performed "in the background." One job would be in processing

Figure A-10   Integrated Circuit on a Silicon Chip

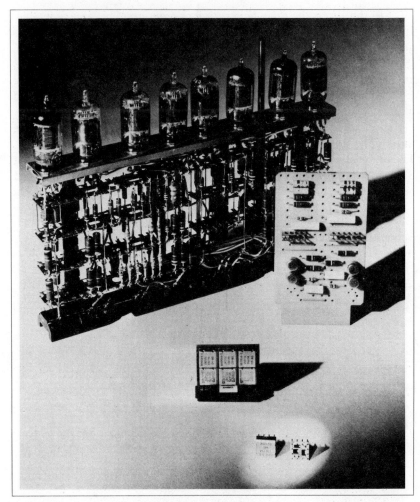

Figure A-11   Three Generations of Hardware Components

while another was being read and the outputs of a third were being printed. The computers ran programs and every now and then took a little time to handle slow I/O. This procedure eliminated the need for offline processing typical of second-generation computers. Figure A-12 shows a typical third-generation computer.

Also, third-generation computers supported online, interactive processing. Users could interact with the computer to perform functions like online order entry or online airline reservations. Although some online processing had been done by earlier, military systems, these were very specialized and not economical. The third generation of computers made it possible for online processing to be a standard product.

Figure A-12   A Third-Generation Computer—The Honeywell 6000

Minicomputers were announced in the mid-1960s. Initially, these were small, special purpose machines designed for military and space applications. Gradually, however, the capability of these machines was increased until the more powerful minicomputers and the less powerful mainframes (the big computers) overlapped. Figure A-13 shows a Digital Equipment VAX minicomputer, which is a very powerful machine that exceeds the capability of many so-called mainframes. Thus, it is hard to distinguish between the two categories of computers. See Chapter 7 for more discussion of this topic.

Today, computers are entering the *fourth generation*. The distinguishing characteristic of this generation is the tremendous decrease in the price/performance ratio of new computers. Simply put, computers are becoming incredibly cheaper and yet more powerful. Thus, while the first three generations were characterized by changes in hardware (tubes to transistors to integrated circuits), the fourth is characterized by economics.

COMPUTERS TODAY— THE FOURTH GENERATION

The lower prices are possible because of the continued development of integrated circuits. Today, because of large-scale integrated circuits, it is possible to put an entire computer on a small chip of

Figure A-13   The DEC VAX Minicomputer

silicon. The computer that may have occupied an entire room in 1952 resides today on a silicon chip half the size of a penny.

Large-scale integrated circuits can be mass produced. This means they can be manufactured and sold in quantities of thousands. Because so many are sold, the costs of research, development, and tooling are spread over many items. Thus, large-scale integrated circuits are extremely cheap. A circuit that may have cost $50,000 10 years ago can be purchased in quantity now for $100 or less.

A computer on a chip is called a *microprocessor*. When the chip is installed with electronics to perform input and output and other functions, it is called a *microcomputer*. Microprocessors were not designed with forethought. They just happened. The companies that manufacture silicon chips found ways to put more and more circuitry on the chip. They were doing this to support other products. For example, the Intel 8008, a microprocessor, was originally intended to be the controller for a CRT terminal. For a variety of reasons, the chip was not used for this purpose.

Since Intel had developed the product, however, they put it in their catalog. Apparently, to their surprise, it sold very well. The company saw the demand, put a design team together, and a year later introduced the Intel 8080 microprocessor shown in figure A-14. This has become one of the most popular microprocessors. Other manu-

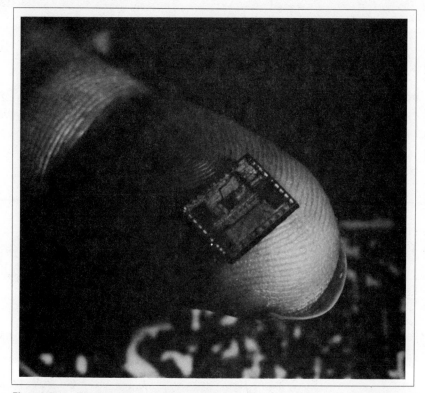

Figure A-14 The Intel 8080 Microprocessor

facturers quickly followed suit. Today there are dozens of microprocessor products to choose from.

All this development means that computers have become cheaper
and cheaper. Some experts believe the cost of computer CPUs will
soon be essentially zero. At least the cost will be negligible compared
to that of other components of a business computer system.

These inexpensive microprocessors may well lead to entirely new
computer architectures. Since microprocessors are so cheap, it becomes feasible to develop and market *supercomputers*, or computers
that are banks of many microprocessors. For example, a supercom-
puter could be a 100 by 100 array of microprocessors. It boggles the
mind to consider the power of such a machine.

In addition to price reductions, the fourth generation is characterized by increased use of data communications. Computers are
linked to one another via very high speed data lines. Satellites are used
to communicate around the world. Figure A-15 shows part of the
configuration of a network of large computers called the ARPA
(Advanced Research Project Agency) network. Chapter 8 has more
details on communications processing.

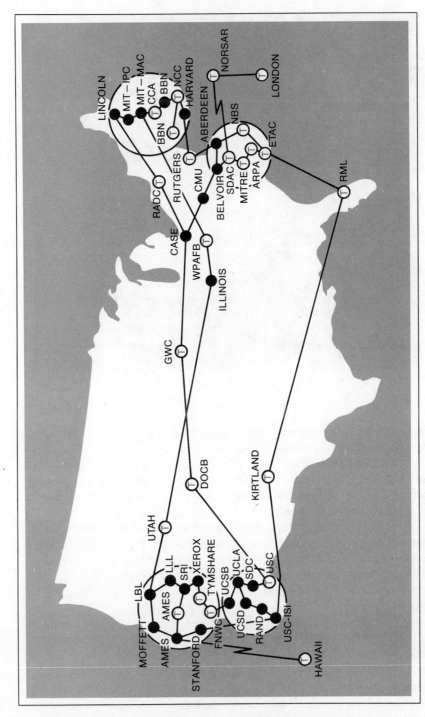

Figure A-15 A Portion of the ARPA Network of Computers

Many people believe there will soon be a data utility. Such a utility will supply computer processing and data banks to subscribers much like other utilities supply electricity. Initially, the subscribers will be businesses, but eventually individuals could be members. With this capability, people could obtain news, magazines, business statistics, even books or other literature at home. This communication could take place over cable TV lines. Individuals could use the data utility to order goods and services as well as to receive information.

In addition to hardware developments, other significant capabilities have emerged since 1970. One is *database technology*. (See Chapter 9.) Database processing allows data to be integrated and thus allows more information to be gleaned from the data.

To do database processing, a company must obtain a database management system. The system is a complex set of computer programs that acts as an intermediary between application programs and user data. Such programs have only become available since 1970. In the future, database management systems may be integrated with microprocessors to form database machines.

Another significant development since 1970 has been the rise of *distributed data processing*. This aspect of data processing is discussed in detail in Chapter 10. As explained in that chapter, the availability of cheap computers has allowed applications to be distributed away from a centralized data processing center. This development has given business users much greater control over their data.

Although the cost of hardware has dramatically decreased in the fourth generation, the cost of programs has increased. Thus, developing business computer systems is not necessarily cheaper. Cost decreases in hardware are often overcome by cost increases in program development. Additionally, program complexity is increasing, and developing programs is becoming more and more risky.

For these reasons, the biggest computing problem in the 1980s is likely to concern programs. Where possible, businesses will buy programs from outside vendors. The programs they buy will need to be general purpose, and flexible enough to meet varying business needs. Probably the most successful programs will sacrifice machine efficiency to gain ease of use and generality. Gradually, the needs for computer specialists will change. There will be less need for programmers and greater need for systems analysts.

Although the history of computation began thousands of years ago, the development of computers is a recent phenomenon. In the early 1800s, Charles Babbage developed many of the design concepts used in

SUMMARY

today's computers. However, these concepts were not implemented at that time. Many of the mistakes that Babbage made are still being made today.

In the late 1800s, the U.S. Census Bureau had a problem. They hired Herman Hollerith to develop automated ways of computing census data. This effort led to the development of punched card equipment and started the punched card industry.

Computers were not actually developed until the mid-1940s. Early computers were produced through the cooperation of universities, government, and industry. There have been four generations of computers so far. First-generation computers had vacuum tubes, and main storage was magnetic drum. These computers were huge and very hard to maintain. Programs were written in machine code.

Computers in the second generation were made of transistors and had main memory made of magnetic core. They were smaller, and still very expensive. High-level languages were developed for programming, and rudimentary operating systems were invented.

The third-generation computers are composed of integrated circuits on silicon chips. The chips are used both for the arithmetic and logic unit and for main memory. Third-generation computers are much smaller and cheaper than first- or second-generation computers.

Today we are in the fourth generation. Computers have become significantly cheaper and more powerful. In the near future, the cost of a CPU will be essentially zero. We may see the development of supercomputers that are banks of microprocessors.

Computer programs are being continually improved. Today we have database processing, which allows for integration of data. Also, distributed data processing is becoming prevalent. However, the cost of programming is increasing. Consequently, in-house programming is likely to decrease in the future. More emphasis will be placed on purchased programs.

QUESTIONS

A.1 Explain what people can learn today from the experiences of Charles Babbage.

A.2 What role did the U.S. Census Bureau play in the development of computers?

A.3 Explain the contribution to the development of computers made by each of the following individuals:

Charles Babbage	J. Presper Eckert
Herman Hollerith	John V. Atanasoff
Howard Aiken	John von Neumann
John Mauchly	Capt. Grace Hopper

A.4 How did Herman Hollerith set the pace for computer entrepreneurs?

A.5 What was the IBM marketing philosophy in the early days of computing? How did this help them?

A.6 Characterize the machines and programs of each of the four generations of computers.

A.7 Explain why computers are becoming inexpensive.

WORD LIST

(in order of appearance in text)

Abacus

Charles Babbage

Difference engine

Analytical engine

Ada Augusta Lovelace

Herman Hollerith

Howard G. Aiken

Mark I

John W. Mauchly

J. Presper Eckert

ENIAC

John V. Atanasoff

John von Neumann

EDVAC

EDSAC

Capt. Grace Hopper

Ms. Adele Goldstine

UNIVAC I

First-generation computers

Second-generation computers

Machine code

Transistors

Core memory

High-level languages

Offline input/output

Third-generation computers

Integrated circuits

Online processing

Minicomputers

Fourth-generation computers

Large-scale integrated circuits

Microprocessors

Microcomputers

Supercomputers

Data communications

Database processing

Distributed data processing

Purchased programs

QUESTIONS TO CHALLENGE YOUR THINKING

A. The rate of computer technology development has been astronomical in the last 30 years. What impact do you think this has had on industry? How do you think a company can best cope with this type of growth if it continues in the future?

B. What impact do you think the rapid change in technology has had on education? Do you think it has been hard for educators to keep pace? How would you stay current if you were a computer educator?

C. Judging from the past, what do you think is going to happen in computing? What impact will computers of the future have on business? What do you think business data processing will be like in the year 2000?

MODULE B

Numbers Representation and Computer Arithmetic

What's missing in this picture of binary arithmetic?

DECIMAL AND BINARY
NUMBERS
  Binary Arithmetic
OCTAL AND HEXADECIMAL
NUMBER SYSTEMS
CONVERSIONS BETWEEN
NUMBER SYSTEMS
FLOATING-POINT NUMBERS
  Fractions and
  Roundoff Error
DECIMAL NUMBERS

This module discusses how computers represent numbers and do arithmetic. This information supplements material in Chapter 5. It will be helpful if you read Chapter 5 before continuing with this section.

Computers represent two basic types of data: *numeric* and *alphanumeric*. Numeric data is numbers that can be processed arithmetically. Alphanumeric data is numbers, letters, and special symbols like #, $, %. Alphanumeric data is not processed arithmetically. Even if alphanumeric data is all numbers, the computer represents it in such a way that it is impossible to perform arithmetic on it.

Alphanumeric data is represented by character codes like EBCDIC. This was discussed in Chapter 5, and we will not repeat that discussion here. Instead, we will discuss the format and processing of numeric data.

DECIMAL AND BINARY NUMBERS

To understand how numbers are represented in the computer, it will be helpful for you to remember your second grade math. Recall Mrs. Gazernenplatz (your second grade teacher)? When she wrote a number on the board like 5437, she said the 7 is in the ones place, the 3 is in the tens place, the 4 is in the hundreds place, and the 5 is in the thousands place. The meaning of the symbols is 5 times 1000, plus 4 times 100, plus 3 times 10, plus 7 times 1.

Later, in algebra, you learned that another way to write 1000 is $10^3 (10 \times 10 \times 10)$, another way to write 100 is 10^2, to write 10 is 10^1,

5437 Decimal Is:		
5×1000		5×10^3 (thousands place)
$+ 4 \times \ \ 100$	or	$+ 4 \times 10^2$ (hundreds place)
$+ 3 \times \ \ \ 10$		$+ 3 \times 10^1$ (tens place)
$+ 7 \times \ \ \ \ 1$		$+ 7 \times 10^0$ (ones place)

Figure B-1 Decimal Place Notation

and to write 1 is 10^0. Thus, each place is a power of 10. The power starts with 0 and increases by 1 for each place to the left of the decimal point. (See figure B-1.)

In the computer, numeric data is often represented in binary form. The binary number system has only two digits (or symbols), 0 and 1. Each binary place has a *bit*, or binary digit. Examples of binary numbers are 110110, 01110, 11111, and 00000. The number 0121 is not a binary number. The symbol 2 is not defined in binary. As explained in Chapter 5, binary is used because the symbols 0 and 1 are easy to represent electronically.

Binary numbers are constructed the same way as decimal numbers, but instead of using powers of 10 in the places, powers of 2 are used. Thus, there is the ones place (2^0), the twos place (2^1), the fours place (2^2), the eights place (2^3), and so forth as shown in figure B-2. The binary number 1010 is interpreted as 1 times 8 plus 0 times 4 plus 1 times 2 plus 0 times 1 or 10 in decimal. Figure B-3 shows the first 16 binary numbers.

Humans like to work with decimal numbers, but computers are more efficient when working with binary numbers. Therefore, when many calculations are to be performed, the computer converts decimal inputs to binary form. Calculations are made in binary. Results are then reconverted to decimal before they are printed. We will discuss how to perform these conversions after we discuss binary arithmetic.

Figure B-2 Binary Place Notation

1010 Binary Is:		
1×8		1×2^3 (eights place)
$+ 0 \times 4$	or	$+ 0 \times 2^2$ (fours place)
$+ 1 \times 2$		$+ 1 \times 2^1$ (twos place)
$+ 0 \times 1$		$+ 0 \times 2^0$ (ones place)
Note: This equals 10 in decimal form.		

Binary	Decimal	Binary	Decimal
0000	0	1000	8
0001	1	1001	9
0010	2	1010	10
0011	3	1011	11
0100	4	1100	.12
0101	5	1101	13
0110	6	1110	14
0111	7	1111	15

Figure B-3 The First 16 Numbers in Binary and Decimal

Binary Arithmetic

Binary numbers can be added much like decimal numbers. You add each column at a time and carry when necessary. In binary,

$$0 + 0 = 0$$
$$0 + 1 = 1$$
$$1 + 0 = 1$$
$$1 + 1 = 10$$

Thus when two 1's are added, a 1 is carried into the next place. The following are examples of binary addition:

```
Carries              1          1111
          0010      1010        1111
        +0101      +0010       +0001
         0111       1100       10000
```

Although subtraction can be done in binary the same as it is done in decimal, computers usually do not do this. In fact (here's an amazing thing), *most computers cannot subtract*! Instead, they find the result of a subtraction by adding in a special way. This technique is called *complement addition*.

Suppose you want to compute 8 minus 3 in decimal. To do this using complements, you add the tens complement of 3 to 8, and throw away the carry. The tens complement of a number is the value you add to the number to get 10. Thus, the tens complement of 3 is 7 because $3 + 7 = 10$. The tens complement of 6 is 4 ($6 + 4 = 10$) and the tens complement of 2 is 8 ($2 + 8 = 10$).

Now, to find 8 minus 3, you add the tens complement of 3 to 8 and throw away the carry. Thus, 8 plus 7 (the tens complement of 3) is 15. Throwing away the carry, we get 5. This equals $8 - 3$ as shown in figure B-4. Like magic, isn't it? Try it! Compute 9 minus 2. The tens

To compute 8 − 3,

   a. Find the tens complement of 3, which is 7.

   b. Add 8 to the complement of 3 to obtain 15.

   c. Throw away the carry to obtain 5, the difference of 8 and 3.

To compute 9 − 5,

   a. Find the tens complement of 5, which is 5.

   b. Add 9 to the complement of 5 to obtain 14.

   c. Throw away the carry to obtain 4, the answer.

Figure B-4 Subtraction Using Complement Addition

complement of 2 is 8. Add $9 + 8$ to get 17. Throw away the 1, and you have 7, which is 9 minus 2!

Try it again. Compute $9 − 5$. The tens complement of 5 is 5 ($5 + 5 = 10$). Adding 9 plus 5, you get 14. Throw away the carry to get 4, which is 9 minus 5.

What happens if you get a negative number? Suppose you compute 3 minus 6. The answer should be −3. If we do this using complements, we add the tens complement of 6 to 3. Thus, we add 3 plus 4 and get 7. This is not −3.

What happened? There is an additional rule. If there is no carry to throw away, the answer is negative. In this case, take the tens complement of the answer and add a minus sign.

Thus, $3 − 6$ is computed by adding 3 to 4 (the tens complement of 6) to get 7. However, there is no carry, so the answer is negative. We take the tens complement of 7 and add a minus sign. The answer is −3, which it should be. (See figure B-5.)

Figure B-5 Subtraction Using Complement Addition − Negative Answers

To compute 3 − 6,

   a. Find the tens complement of 6, which is 4.

   b. Add 3 to the complement of 6 to obtain 7.

   c. There is no carry, therefore the answer is negative. Take the tens complement of 7, which is 3, and add a minus sign. The answer is −3.

To compute 7 − 9,

   a. Find the tens complement of 9, which is 1.

   b. Add 7 to the complement of 9 to obtain 8.

   c. There is no carry, therefore the answer is negative. Take the tens complement of 8, which is 2, and add a minus sign. The answer is −2.

Try $7 - 9$. The answer should be -2. Take the tens complement of 9, which is 1. Add 7 and 1 to get 8. There is no carry, therefore the answer is negative. Take the tens complement of 8 and add a minus sign. The answer is -2. It works! You probably think it's done with mirrors.

Computers do the same thing in binary. To form the twos complement of a binary number, the computer just turns all the 1's to 0's and all the 0's to 1's. Then it adds 1. Thus, the twos complement of 0110 is $1001 + 1$ or 1010.

Suppose we want to compute 1111 minus 0110. The answer should be 1001. To compute this, we add 1111 and the twos complement of 0110. Using the complement from above, we add 1111 to 1010.

```
Carries              111

                    1111
                  +1010
                   11001
```

Now, we throw away the carry and the answer is 1001 as it should be. If there is no carry, the number is negative. Complement the answer by switching 1's and 0's and adding 1.

Thus, computers do not know how to subtract. Instead they add complements. They can do this very fast. Forming twos complements is quick and easy. Adding is also easy.

Computers multiply by successive additions. Thus, to multiply 7 times 8, the computer adds eight 7's together. To multiply 1234 times 438, it adds 438 1234's together. Division is done by successive "subtractions."

OCTAL AND HEXADECIMAL NUMBER SYSTEMS

Working with binary numbers is easy and convenient for computers, but it is a hassle for people. Adding the binary number 11010101110100 to the binary number 110100100001111101100110101 is a chore. It is also very easy to drop a symbol and get the wrong answer. To make errors less likely, people have found a way to shorten binary numbers.

One way is to group the binary symbols into threesomes, and to represent the threesomes by a number. The table in figure B-6 shows how this is done. The first column has all the possible three-place binary numbers, and the second column has the symbol used to represent them.

Now, let's use this table to shorten some binary numbers. Group the following binary symbols into threes and substitute the number above:

Binary Number	Octal Equivalent	Binary Number	Octal Equivalent
000	0	100	4
001	1	101	5
010	2	110	6
011	3	111	7

Figure B-6   Binary Numbers and Their Abbreviations (Octal Equivalents)

111011 becomes 111 011 or 73

011010 becomes 011 010 or 32

111000 becomes 111 000 or 70

111111 becomes 111 111 or 77

Notice that the symbols 8 and 9 are not used in this abbreviation scheme; 7 is the biggest symbol. We have created a number system that has only eight symbols: 0, 1, 2, 3, 4, 5, 6, and 7. This number system is called *octal* because it has eight symbols.

Figure B-7 shows the decimal equivalents of an octal number. In the decimal system, we have the ones, tens, hundreds, and so forth places. In binary we have the ones, twos, fours, eights, and so forth places. In octal, we have the ones, eights, sixty-fours, and other powers of 8 places. The octal number 3456 is equal to 3 times 512 ($8 \times 8 \times 8$) plus 4 times 64 plus 5 times 8 plus 6 times 1, or 1838 in decimal.

As mentioned, octal is used primarily as a shorthand for binary. It is very easy to convert from octal to binary. We just replace each octal symbol with the three binary symbols that it represents. Thus, 234 octal equals 010 011 100 in binary.

Several manufacturers produce computers that abbreviate binary with octal. Control Data Corporation makes computers that have 60 bits per word. When the binary value of a word is printed by their

Figure B-7   Octal Numbers and Their Decimal Equivalents

Octal Number	Decimal Form		
47	$4 \times 8 + 7 \times 1$	or	39
312	$3 \times 64 + 1 \times 8 + 2 \times 1$	or	202
4057	$3 \times 512 + 0 \times 64 + 5 \times 8 + 7 \times 1$	or	1583

machines, it is usually shown in octal. Thus, instead of printing 60 binary symbols like

1111111111111111111111111111111111111111111111111111111111111

they print the octal number 7777777777. This form is much easier for humans to understand and manipulate.

Sometimes computers print a *dump* at the end of a run that terminated abnormally. This dump shows the values in certain critical areas of main memory. The values in these critical areas will be in binary, but the computer will print them in octal so that they will be easier for humans to understand.

Some computers such as IBM machines have 32 bits per word. In this case, the octal number system cannot be used readily to abbreviate the stored values. Thirty-two bits cannot be broken into groups of three. Instead, the word is divided into eight groups of 4 bits. This presents a problem, however.

Four bits can represent the decimal values 0 through 15. To abbreviate 4 bits by one character we need 16 symbols. We can use the symbols 0 through 9 to represent the first 10 numbers, but we need other symbols to represent the last six. Figure B-8 shows how this is done.

The binary values 0 through 1001 are represented by the decimal characters 0 through 9. The binary value 1010 equals decimal 10. However, we need a single symbol to represent 1010. Hence we use the letter A. Letter B represents 1011, C represents 1100, and so forth.

This scheme creates a number system with 16 symbols: 0 through 9 and A through F. It is called the *hexadecimal* number system. The places in this system are powers of 16. There is the ones place, the sixteens place, the 256's place, the 4096's place, and so forth by powers of 16. As shown in figure B-9, the hexadecimal number

Figure B-8 Binary Numbers and Their Hexadecimal Equivalents

Binary Number	Hexadecimal Equivalent	Binary Number	Hexadecimal Equivalent
0000	0	1000	8
0001	1	1001	9
0010	2	1010	A
0011	3	1011	B
0100	4	1100	C
0101	5	1101	D
0110	6	1110	E
0111	7	1111	F

Hexadecimal Number	Decimal Form		
79	$7 \times 16 + 9 \times 1$	or	121
E4	$14 \times 16 + 4 \times 1$	or	228
A1C	$10 \times 256 + 1 \times 16 + 12 \times 1$	or	2588
A14E	$10 \times 4096 + 1 \times 256 + 4 \times 16 + 14 \times 1$	or	41,294
1F7C8	$1 \times 65,536 + 15 \times 4096 + 7 \times 256 + 12 \times 16 + 8 \times 1$	or	128,968

Figure B-9 Hexadecimal Numbers and Their Decimal Equivalents

A14E represents 10 times 4096 plus 1 times 256 plus 4 times 16 plus 14 or 41,294 in decimal.

On IBM and other computers that have 32 bit words, the dumps and other binary printouts are produced in hexadecimal. To convert from hexadecimal to binary, just substitute the bit pattern for each character from figure B-8. Thus, A14E in hexadecimal represents 1010000101001110 in binary.

So far we have discussed four number systems. Decimal numbers are traditionally used by people. Binary numbers are used by computers, mostly because the binary symbols 0 and 1 are easy to represent electronically. However, it is hard for people to work with binary numbers. Therefore, binary numbers are sometimes abbreviated using either octal or hexadecimal numbers.

CONVERSIONS BETWEEN NUMBER SYSTEMS

Sometimes people and computers need to convert a number from one system to another. For example, we may need to know what the hexadecimal number A1A equals in decimal. Also, we may need to know what the decimal number 789 equals in octal, and so forth.

It is easy to convert from binary, octal, or hexadecimal to decimal. In fact, we have already shown how. Just multiply each symbol by its place value. In binary the place values are powers of 2, in octal they are powers of 8, and in hexadecimal they are powers of 16.

Also, it is easy to convert from binary to octal or binary to hexadecimal. Just use the table in figure B-6 or B-8. To convert from decimal to binary or to octal or to hexadecimal is not so easy, however.

Such conversions can be done by the *division/remainder* method. This method uses successive divisions by the base number. For example, to convert decimal to binary, the decimal number is successively divided by 2. To convert from decimal to octal, the decimal number is successively divided by 8. As the divisions are done, the remainders are saved; they become the transformed number.

Examine figure B-10. Three conversions are shown. In the first, the decimal number 37 is converted to binary. 37 is repeatedly divided by 2 until the quotient is 0. As the division is done, the remainders are written on the righthand side. The equivalent binary number is read

Figure B-10   Decimal to Binary, Octal, and Hexadecimal Conversions

Division   Remainder

2 | 37
                 1
2 | 18
                 0
2 | 9
                 1
2 | 4
                 0
2 | 2
                 0
2 | 1
                 1

Answer: 100101 binary

a. Decimal 37 Converted to Binary

Division   Remainder

8 | 92
                 4
8 | 11
                 3
8 | 1
                 1

Answer: 134 octal

b. Decimal 92 Converted to Octal

Division   Remainder

16 | 489
                 9
16 | 30
                 E
16 | 1
                 1

Answer: 1E9 hexadecimal

c. Decimal 489 Converted to Hexadecimal

from these remainders, from the bottom up. Thus, 37 decimal equals 100101.

In the second example, the decimal number 92 is converted to octal. 92 is repeatedly divided by 8 until no whole division is possible. Then the number is read from the remainders. 92 decimal equals 134 octal. Finally, 489 is converted to hexadecimal. Again, 489 is repeatedly divided by 16 until no whole division is possible. The remainders are kept on the righthand side. Note the remainder of 14 is represented by the hexadecimal symbol E and not by 14. 489 in decimal equals 1E9 in hexadecimal. In practice, such conversions are done by special hand calculators.

FLOATING-POINT NUMBERS

The binary format just described is only one of the ways that computers represent arithmetic numbers. Another format is called *floating point*. This term is used because the decimal point of the number is allowed to move, or float. The same form can represent 0.45 and 4500. The advantage of this form is its flexibility. It can represent very large and very small numbers, as well as fractions.

Floating-point numbers are represented in *exponential* or *scientific form*. The decimal number 1257 is represented in exponential form as 0.1257×10^4. This notation means that $1257 = 0.1257 \times 10 \times 10 \times 10 \times 10 = 0.1257 \times 10,000$. Numbers from other number systems can be represented similarly. Thus, the binary number $1011 = 0.1011 \times 2^4$ or $0.1011 \times 2 \times 2 \times 2 \times 2$. Also, the octal number $765 = 0.765 \times 8 \times 8 \times 8$.

In each of these cases, the fractional number is called the *mantissa* and the power of the base is called the *exponent*. The mantissa of 0.1257×10^4 is 0.1257 and the exponent is 4.

Scientific notation represents fractions as well as whole numbers. The decimal number 0.0123 is 0.123×10^{-1}. The number 0.000345 is 0.345×10^{-3}. In this latter case, the mantissa is 0.345 and the exponent is -3.

Floating-point numbers use exponential notation. Each computer word has two sections. One section holds the exponent, and the other holds the mantissa. On IBM computers, for example, the first 8 bits of a word hold the exponent (a power of 16), and the remaining 24 bits hold the mantissa. (See figure B-11.)

On Control Data computers, the first 12 bits hold the exponent (a power of 8) and the remaining 48 bits hold the mantissa. Since more bits are used to represent the mantissa on CDC computers than on IBM computers, greater precision is possible. The mantissa can have a larger number of characters.

Both the mantissa and the exponent have a sign. The sign of the mantissa indicates whether the number is positive or negative. The

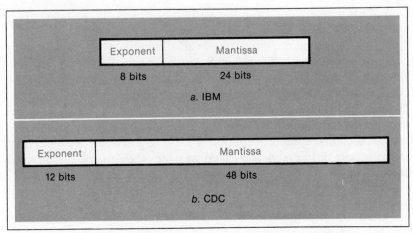

Figure B-11   Floating-Point Word Formats

sign of the exponent indicates whether the number is greater or less than 1.

The particular method of representing floating-point numbers is beyond the scope of this book. You should know that they exist, and that they are represented in a special way in the computer. Also, because of the special format, extra instructions (and time) are required to process floating-point numbers.

Some small computers have only one type of numbers. Some microcomputers have only integer numbers and integer instructions. Others have only floating-point numbers and instructions. If you purchase one of these computers, you should ensure that it has floating-point capability if you need it. Otherwise, you will have to program your own floating-point capability, and this is a chore.

Fractions and Roundoff Error

Fractions can be represented in two ways. First, floating-point format can be used as just described. A second way is to use *fixed-point binary format*. For this format, numbers are represented in binary, but a binary point is assumed to exist. For example, a binary point could be defined to be to the left of the third bit in a word. Then, the binary number 110111 would be interpreted as 110.111. See figure B-12 for other examples. When using this format, the program defines where it wants the point to be, and all operations are based on that definition. Note in this case that the binary point cannot float; every number has the same number of places to the right of the point.

There is a curious fact about fractions. A fraction that can be represented exactly in one number system may not be representable exactly in another. For example, the decimal fraction 0.1 cannot be evenly represented in hexadecimal (or binary). It is slightly more than hexadecimal 0.199.

Fixed-Point Format	Binary Number	Is Interpreted As
XXX.XX	11101	111.01
	10011	100.11
	10001	100.01
X.XXXX	11101	1.1101
	10011	1.0011
	10001	1.0001
.XXXXX	11101	.11101
	10011	.10011
	10001	.10001

Figure B-12   Examples of Fixed-Point Binary Numbers

The fact that 0.1 cannot be evenly represented in binary is very important in business. The dollar value $12.10 does not have an even representation. More importantly, the value $1.1 trillion does not have an even representation either!

Assume you ask the computer to sum the value $0.01 one hundred times. If 0.01 is represented in binary, you may not get $1.00. Instead you may get $0.99999999999999. This can be inconvenient and embarassing to computer personnel. Sometimes it looks like the computer can't add.

DECIMAL NUMBERS

Because of this problem, some computers have the ability to perform arithmetic in decimal. In this case, the inputs are never converted to binary, and the roundoff error does not occur. Unfortunately, decimal arithmetic is slower than binary arithmetic. Therefore, decimal arithmetic is only done when calculations are minimal.

In business, this is often the case. Many business systems need only perform simple additions or multiplications. Therefore, the decimal form of data is often used in business.

Figure B-13 shows decimal digits represented in the EBCDIC code. Two "hex" characters are used to represent each decimal. F1 represents 1, F2 represents 2, and so forth. Note how inefficient this scheme is. Two hex characters or 8 bits are needed for each decimal character. In binary form, these 8 bits can represent all of the numbers from 0 to 255. In decimal form, they can only represent the numbers from 0 to 9.

Using the code shown in figure B-13, the decimal number 287 is represented as F2F8F7. Other examples are shown in figure B-14. This format is sometimes called *unpacked* (or *zoned*) *decimal form*.

Decimal Number	EBCDIC Code (Hexadecimal)	Decimal Number	EBCDIC Code (Hexadecimal)
0	F0	5	F5
1	F1	6	F6
2	F2	7	F7
3	F3	8	F8
4	F4	9	F9

Figure B-13 EBCDIC Code Representation for Decimal Numbers

In figure B-13, the first hex character for each of the digits is F. To reduce the storage taken by decimal numbers, all but one of the F's can be removed. This is called *packed decimal form*. Thus, in figure B-14, the decimal number 287, which has unpacked decimal notation F2F8F7, has the packed decimal notation 287F. All but one of the F's has been removed. The remaining F is put at the end of the number.

In many applications, numbers must have signs. They can be positive or negative. In packed decimal notation, the last hex position is used to denote a sign. This format is called *signed decimal form*. If there is a hex C in the last character, the number is positive. If the last character is a D, the number is negative. Thus, 287C represents +287. 287D represents −287. The notation 287F is still valid. It just means that the number 287 is unsigned. Figure B-14 has other examples.

Figure B-14 Unpacked, Packed, and Signed Decimal Data Formats

Decimal Number	Decimal Form		
	Unpacked	Packed	Signed
287	F2F8F7	287F	287C (+287) 287D (−287)
1492	F1F4F9F2	1492F	1492C (+1492) 1492D (−1492)
77	F7F7	77F	77C (+77) 77D (−77)

QUESTIONS

B.1 Which of the following are valid binary numbers?
a. 1101
b. 1200
c. 9812
d. 0000

B.2   Decimal places have values of ones, tens, hundreds, and so forth.
    a. What are the values of binary places?
    b. What are the values of octal places?
    c. What are the values of hexadecimal places?

B.3   Add the following binary numbers:
    a. $110 + 001$
    b. $110001 + 001110$
    c. $111111 + 0000001$
    d. $11101 + 00011$

B.4   How do most computers perform subtraction?

B.5   Do the following subtractions using complements:
    a. $9 - 4$ (decimal numbers)
    b. $1101 - 0001$ (binary numbers)
    c. $1111 - 0101$ (binary)
    d. $4 - 9$ (decimal)
    e. $0011 - 0100$ (binary)

B.6   What are octal numbers used for?

B.7   Convert the following numbers to decimal:
    a. 1101 binary
    b. 1110101 binary
    c. 453 octal
    d. 7671 octal
    e. A21 hexadecimal
    f. ABC hexadecimal

B.8   What are hexadecimal numbers used for?

B.9   Convert the following numbers to binary:
    a. 789 decimal
    b. 1234 decimal
    c. 643 octal
    d. 77777 octal
    e. CE4 hexadecimal
    f. FEBCAD hexadecimal

B.10   What causes roundoff error? Why is it important in business?

B.11   How can roundoff error be eliminated?

B.12   Show the unpacked and packed decimal forms of the following numbers:
    a. 12345   c. 23
    b. 484930   d. 1

B.13   Show the signed decimal form of the following numbers:
    a. -19 c. -78965
    b. 7345   d. 0

SUMMARY

Computers represent two types of data: numeric and alphanumeric. This section has described the representation and processing of numeric data. The binary number system is most often used to represent numeric data. In binary there are only two symbols, 0 and 1. In decimal the place values of a number are ones, tens, hundreds, thousands, etc. In binary they are ones, twos, fours, eights, sixteens, and so forth.

Binary numbers are added like decimal ones. However, instead of carrying when the sum of two numbers exceeds 9, we carry when the sum exceeds 1. Subtraction is usually done by computers in complement form. The complement of the number to be subtracted is added to determine the result.

Two other number systems are used to abbreviate binary numbers. The octal number system has eight symbols; each octal symbol represents three bits. The hexadecimal number system has 16 symbols; each hex symbol represents 4 bits. Octal is used when the computer's word size is a multiple of 3 bits. Hexadecimal is used when the word size is a multiple of 4 bits.

Floating-point numbers allow the decimal point to shift. They represent both very large and very small numbers. They can also represent fractions. In addition to floating-point form, fractions can be represented by fixed-point binary. Here, a fixed location of the binary point is assumed.

Decimal fractions are not necessarily represented evenly in binary. For example, 0.1 does not have an even representation in binary. This difference means computers can make roundoff errors. To eliminate this, some computers can perform decimal arithmetic. In this case, numbers are not converted to binary. Arithmetic is done in decimal form. Data is carried in packed decimal format.

WORD LIST

(in order of
appearance in text)

Numeric data	*Floating-point number*
Alphanumeric data	*Exponential form*
Bit	*Scientific form*
Complement addition	*Mantissa*
Tens complement	*Exponent*
Twos complement	*Fixed-point number*
Octal number system	*Roundoff error*
Dump	*Unpacked decimal format*
Hexadecimal number system	*Packed decimal format*
Division/remainder method	*Signed decimal format*

MODULE C

Computer Crime, Security, and Control

Evidence of the need for computer control and security

**HAROLD JOHNSON,
COMPUTER CRIMINAL**

WHAT IS COMPUTER CRIME?

  Pacific Telephone

  Penn Central Railroad

  Equity Funding
  Corporation

  Types of Computer Crime

**PREVENTING COMPUTER
CRIME**

**COMPUTER AUDITING AND
CONTROLS**

  Management Controls

  Organizational Controls

  Data Center Resource Controls

  Input, Processing,
  and Output Controls

  Other EDP Controls

**MODREC—THE REST OF
THE STORY**

HAROLD JOHNSON, COMPUTER CRIMINAL

 Harold Johnson applied for a systems analysis/programming job at Modern Record Distributing Company (MODREC). Harold was young, only 25, but he had an impressive background. He had major responsibility in the development of three different computer systems at his prior employment. His reason for leaving was that he believed the major challenges were over and he wanted something new.

In fact, Harold was very bright and eager for new opportunities to apply his problem-solving skills. He was highly motivated and willing to spend long hours solving difficult problems. Furthermore, he was courageous and would stand up to anybody when his ideas were disputed. He was also creative and adventuresome, and enjoyed challenges posed by people. In short, he had all the skills and traits to be a superior systems developer.

MODREC was a spinoff company. At one time it was a division of a large, traditional record manufacturer. The separate company was created when MODREC's sales exceeded $5 million, and the directors of the parent company thought it made sense to form a subsidiary. MODREC specialized in distributing rock music of interest to people under 30.

MODREC's first president was the son of one of the parent company's directors. He was promoted into his position through influence and not ability. Consequently, MODREC sales began to slip, personnel morale fell, and MODREC lost many sales opportunities.

MODREC's small data processing department was managed by the chief accountant. The accountant meant well, but he was very uneducated about data processing. When Harold Johnson applied for the job, the chief accountant was delighted. He made Harold an excellent offer and Harold came to work.

In his first year, Harold made many contributions to data processing. The level of service vastly improved. Sales people were given better information about their customers. The time to deliver an order was cut in half. Sales went up. Further, the accounting systems were improved, and the chief accountant had better information than ever.

Unfortunately, Harold began to feel discontented. Nobody paid attention to him. He felt no one recognized the contributions he made. He probably would have gone to another company, but after a year, MOD-REC gave him a substantial pay increase. He thought he would have trouble earning as much money elsewhere.

As Harold worked with the accounting systems, he began to notice MODREC's large profits. These were possible in spite of ineffective management because MODREC had very large markup. Harold concluded MODREC was ripping off their customers.

One day, Harold mentioned this to Joan Everest, the manager of a record store that ordered from MODREC (figure C-1).

"Harold," said Joan, almost in jest, "why don't you reprogram one of those computers to offer special discounts to my store? Perhaps I could share the savings with you."

Figure C-1   Harold and Joan Plotting a Computer Crime

Harold was never quite the same. He was bored at work, and the technical challenge of such special discounts excited him. Also, he was angry with the way MODREC had treated him. He believed it was unfair for them to make so much profit. Joan needed the financial help, and MODREC could easily afford to lose $40,000 to $50,000 per year. In some ways he felt he was playing a game of Robin Hood—stealing from the rich and giving to the poor.

Once Harold decided to cooperate, the technical aspects were easy. In fact, Harold was disappointed at the lack of challenge. He changed the pricing program to look for Joan's customer number and to reduce her prices by 85 percent. Only he saw the special copy of the program. The unchanged version was kept in the program documentation library for appearances.

Harold Johnson is a typical computer criminal. He was also caught. We will explain how as this module progresses.

WHAT IS COMPUTER CRIME?

No one knows for sure how many computer crimes have occurred. In an excellent book entitled *Crime by Computer,* Donn Parker estimates that $300 million is lost per year through computer crime. Experts at the National Bureau of Standards estimated that the U.S. lost $200 million in 1974. In 1976, the average loss per crime was estimated at $430,000. (See figure C-2.)

There are many stories of computer crimes. Some seem downright ludicrous. It's hard to tell what is fact and what is fable. The following three cases, however, have been well documented.

Figure C-2 Average Amount Stolen in Various Types of Crime

Type of Crime	Average Amount Stolen ($)
Larceny-Theft	150
Burglary	320
All Robberies	400
Branch Bank Robbery	2,000
Full-Service Bank Robbery	10,000
Conventional Bank Embezzlement	19,000
Computer-Related Embezzlement	430,000

Jerry Schneider was a child prodigy who developed his own telecommunication system at the age of 10. By the time he was in high school, he had started his own electronics company. While he was a part-time college student, he found a way to steal electronic equipment from Pacific Telephone. He used a terminal in his home to order parts and not be charged for them. He learned the correct account numbers, passwords, and procedures by taking old computer printouts and other documentation from a Pacific Telephone trash container.

Pacific Telephone

He had expensive telephone components delivered to his home and other locations. He got bored with the project, and to add more excitement, had the company deliver a $25,000 switchboard to a manhole cover at the intersection of two streets. The company delivered and he picked up the switchboard in the Pacific Telephone truck he bought at a company surplus auction.

Much of the equipment that he stole in this way he resold to Pacific Telephone. In fact, he used their own information system to determine what they were low on so he would then know what to steal.

Schneider was caught when one of his own employees informed on him. The employee wanted a pay raise, and Jerry refused. When he was apprehended, Pacific Telephone refused to believe he had stolen as much inventory as he claimed. He said he had stolen $800,000 to $900,000; they said $70,000.

Another famous computer crime concerned the Penn Central Railroad. In the early 1970s, someone modified a freight-flow system to send boxcars to a small railroad company outside Chicago. There, the boxcars disappeared! They were apparently repainted and sold to or used by other railroads. Estimates vary, but approximately 400 boxcars disappeared. Somehow the computer system was modified so as not to notice the missing railroad cars.

Penn Central Railroad

The Penn Central case is mysterious. Although a Philadelphia Grand Jury was convened to investigate the case, and although some stolen boxcars were found, Penn Central refused to acknowledge the affair. For some reason, it was in Penn Central's interest to minimize attention on the crime. No prosecution occurred. There were rumors that organized crime was involved.

A third famous case occurred in 1973. This large fraud involved the Equity Funding Corporation. Over 20 people were convicted on federal charges. Estimates of loss are as high as *$2 billion.*

Equity Funding Corporation

Equity Funding was a conglomerate of companies that specialized in investments and insurance. Top-level management distorted the company's financial situation to lure investors. Also, they created artificial insurance policies.

Former Students Indicted for Altering Grades

By Marguerite Zientara
CW Staff

JAMAICA, N.Y. — Two former Queens College students — one who had been employed at the school's DP center — were indicted last month on charges of falsifying a total of 154 grades in the computerized records of 19 different students. The alterations allegedly took place from 1974 to 1977, with some students reportedly paying hundreds of dollars for the revised grades [CW, March 20].

James Chin, 35, and Tom Tang, 26, voluntarily surrendered to New York police on the day the indictments were announced. At their arraignment later that day, both Chin and Tang plead not guilty.

Both were freed without bail since neither had any prior arrests and since they had voluntarily surrendered. The hearing was adjourned to Jan. 15, when a trial date may be set, according to a spokeswoman for the district attorney's office.

Queens District Attorney J. Santucci said the indictments of Chin and Tang resulted from an investigation begun last spring by his office's Rackets Bureau and his detective squad, with the assistance of the city Department of Investigation, the Board of Higher Education's Office of General Counsel and the administration of Queens College.

Chin, formerly Queens College's senior computer operator, is employed by Printronics Corp. of America in New York. He was indicted on one count of falsifying business records, first degree; one count of bribe receiving, second degree; two counts of receiving a reward for official misconduct, second degree; and one count of violating a state education law section dealing with unlawful acts in respect to examinations.

Tang, a salesman for Burroughs Corp. in Warrendale Heights, Ohio, was not employed at the college during the period of his alleged crime, but was a student. He has been indicted on one count of falsifying business records, first degree.

The Chin indictment charges him with 131 grade falsifications on the computer records of 15 students, including himself, and with receiving approximately $300 from one student for whom he falsified 22 grades and $100 from another for whom he falsified 11 grades.

The Tang indictment charges him with arranging for the falsification of 23 grades on the computer records of four students, including himself. Tang did not accept money for his part in the falsifications, according to the spokesman for the district attorney's office, and the 23 grade changes he is charged with arranging are separate from the 131 grade changes allegedly made by Chin. If convicted, Chin could receive a sentence of up to seven years in jail and Tang could get a four-year sentence.

Figure C-3 Computer Crime Committed by Students

Crime Expert Foresees DP-Aided Murder

By Jeffry Beeler
CW West Coast Bureau

SAN JOSE, Calif.—Computers have already been involved in a wide assortment of crimes including fraud, theft and espionage. Someday they might even be used to commit murder, according to computer security expert Donn B. Parker.

In fact, the first known computer-aided murder attempt may have already taken place, Parker said last week at the Hewlett-Packard Co. (HP) General Systems Users Group meeting here.

The suspected murder attempt occurred only about a month ago when the air traffic control system at New York's Kennedy International Airport suspiciously malfunctioned and nearly caused a mid-air collision involving an airliner carrying Soviet Ambassador Anatoly Dobrynin [CW, Feb. 11]. No one was harmed during the incident, but Parker plans to investigate the equipment failure anyway to find out whether it resulted from human tampering, as some observers have speculated.

Appearing at the HP users group meeting as keynote speaker, Parker voiced fears that the traditional traffickers in computer crime will soon be joined by much more dangerous practitioners, especially organized groups like hostile foreign powers, the Mafia and international terrorist bands. Computers are rapidly replacing bank vaults as the preferred method of "storing" money, and as the world traffic in electronic "cash" steadily grows, so does the threat that it will one day become the target of large, unscrupulous organizations with a vast capacity to cause harm.

Figure C-4 Possible New Wave of Crimes

Although the media described this crime as a modern computer fraud, there is some debate about whether it can be blamed on the computer. Most of the criminal activity did not involve the computer. All of the phony accounting was done manually.

The Equity Funding case is very complex. Over 50 major lawsuits were filed. Basically, the fraud was accomplished by inflating the company's reported income. This was done in two ways. One, the company's officers declared income and assets that didn't exist. They did this simply by writing them into financial statements. The firm's auditors have been severely criticized for not detecting this activity.

The second way income was inflated did involve the computer. Massive numbers of phony documents were generated by a computer system. These documents were supposed to be valid insurance policies. In fact, they were computer fabrications. The phony policies were sold to other insurance companies for cash.

In retrospect, it is amazing that these documents were accepted at face value. The system was audited, but it was designed to print only valid policies at those times. Further, insurance industry personnel believed in computer-generated documents. It didn't occur to them that the computer could produce phony data.

Types of Computer Crime

These three short stories represent only a few of the ingenious ways people have found to commit crimes with computer help. Most computer crimes fall into one of the five categories shown in figure C-5. Sometimes, the *input to the computer is manipulated*. This was done in the Pacific Telephone case. Other crimes are perpetrated by changing computer programs. This was Harold Johnson's approach.

A third type of computer crime is to *steal data*. Such data might be the names and addresses of a company's customers. It might be proprietary designs or plans. Fourth, *computer time can be stolen*. The criminal either uses the time or sells it to others who may not be aware the time is stolen. For example, a computer communications system may be used to transmit unauthorized data. In one case, a company's message-switching system was used daily to broadcast racing results.

Finally, *computer programs can be stolen*. Computer programs are very expensive and time-consuming to produce. They can give a company a competitive edge in its marketplace. Therefore, stealing programs is a criminal act.

The theft of computer data and computer programs is very hard to detect. Such theft can be done simply by copying the computer files having the data or programs. Since the original copy is not missing, companies have difficulty knowing that a crime was even committed.

Many computer crime experts think the cases we know about are only the tip of the iceberg. Some companies have been victims of crimes and have not acknowledged it. They wanted to avoid adverse publicity. A bank that lost money by computer crime will not want its customers to know it. Further, businesses do not want to advertise their vulnerability. They may not know how to prevent similar crimes in the future, and they certainly do not want the crime advertised in the newspapers. Therefore, they do not prosecute.

Figure C-5 Types of Computer Crime

Type of Crime
Manipulating computer input
Changing computer programs
Stealing data
Stealing computer time
Stealing computer programs

1. The computer seems to run the company; management just reacts.
2. Management expects computers to solve major existing problems.
3. Management does not (cannot) communicate with the EDP staff.
4. Users are told how their systems will be designed.
5. There are no documented standards for the development of new applications or the maintenance of existing ones.
6. Technical management is actively involved in programming and troubleshooting.
7. Programmers are uncontrolled; they can do what they want with the computer.
8. EDP staff has easy access to data and to program libraries.
9. Errors occur so frequently that adequate investigation is not possible.
10. Auditors treat the computer like a mysterious black box.
11. Management fails to implement audit recommendations.
12. No EDP audits are performed.

Figure C-6   Signals Indicating Potential for Computer Crime

For this reason, computer criminals are often not penalized. Further, when they are, they typically receive light sentences. Jerry Schneider spent only 40 days in jail, and lost just $8,500 in a court battle.

Figure C-6 shows 12 warning signals of computer crime. These are characteristics of companies in which crimes have occurred. Hopefully in the course of your business career, you will not work for a company that has many of these signs. However, if you do, you should be aware of the possibility of computer crime.

Most of the characteristics in figure C-6 indicate poor data processing management. Except for the items concerning audits, every one of these characteristics is a violation of a principle discussed in this course. Thus, good data processing management is needed to build and use systems that are less susceptible to computer crime.

PREVENTING COMPUTER CRIME

Unfortunately, there is no such thing as a completely secure data processing installation. First, computer manufacturers do not provide completely secure computers. An ingenious programmer can find a way to modify the operating system. Once this is done, computer security features like passwords and account numbers are ineffective.

Second, many, if not most, data processing departments are so busy just keeping up with the business and the change in computer technology that they do not find the time to adequately consider computer security. Inputs to the computer are not as well controlled as they should be. Outputs are not checked for accuracy and completeness. Also, security issues are not considered when systems are designed or when programs are written. Most companies take the attitude that computer crime won't happen here.

Finally, effective security can be costly. It takes time and resources to build a secure system. Also, the system may be more expensive to operate because of security features. If a user must spend half of each working day to verify outputs, then in a year, half of the person's salary is spent for security. Also, good security on the computer will mean that programs operate more slowly. More instructions must be processed for security functions. Thus, more computer power will be required.

Most companies must strike a balance between no security at all, and as near to perfect security as possible. How much security is needed depends on the potential loss and the amount of threat. An accounts payable system probably needs more security than a system that produces company telephone lists.

In *Crime by Computer*, Parker reports a surprising and distressing fact. Most computer crimes are caught by accident. In some cases, the computer failed and irregularities were discovered while someone was fixing it. In other cases, people consistently spent more money than they were earning, and the source of the additional money was traced back to a computer system. The Internal Revenue Service has caught some of these people for not paying taxes on their criminal earnings. In other cases, the FBI caught them in illegal gambling activities.

The distressing part of this discussion is that few crimes are caught as a result of controls in the business computer system. Apparently few systems provide protection against computer crime. However, this need not be the case; systems can be designed to thwart unauthorized activity. We will see how in the next section.

COMPUTER AUDITING AND CONTROLS

The American Institute of Certified Public Accountants has recognized the possibility of computer crime or other unauthorized activity. This organization has issued an official statement (called *SAS-3*) directing CPAs to pay special attention to business computer systems. As a result of this statement, auditors are paying more and more attention to data processing departments and personnel.

Further, groups of auditors and data processing personnel have worked together to develop recommended procedures or *controls* over data processing operations. In the remainder of this module, we will discuss these controls. To show their usefulness, we will relate each control to the MODREC case introduced at the start of this module.

The term *EDP controls* originated with the accountants and auditors. EDP is an accounting term that means electronic data processing. EDP controls are features of any of the five components of a

> Management
> Organizational
> Data center resource
> Input/processing/output
> Data administration
> Systems development

Figure C-7   Categories of EDP Controls

business computer system that reduce the likelihood of unauthorized activity. Figure C-7 summarizes the basic categories of EDP controls.

 Harold Johnson was dissatisfied with his management. He felt under-appreciated. Since his boss was only the chief accountant, Harold was buried in the finance department. Consequently, neither he nor any one else in data processing had access to top management.

  Top management did not have access to Harold or data processing, either. They knew little of what he was doing, and had only a limited idea of how data processing operated. They spent considerable money on data processing operations, but they did not know how the money was spent. In short, there was a large gulf between top level management and data processing.

Management Controls

  Over the years, professionals have learned that such a situation is an invitation to trouble. Senior management of a company should take an active part in the management of the data processing function. This does not mean that they should be down on the machine floor mounting tapes. However, it does mean that they should recognize the importance of data processing to the company, and they should set the direction and be actively involved in data processing plans.

  It may seem surprising that this even needs to be said. However, in the past, too many managers have washed their hands of data processing. They have stayed as far away from the computer as possible. Perhaps they didn't understand computing; perhaps they were afraid of it; or perhaps the data processing personnel spoke in strange ways. In any event, data processing went its own way. In some cases (like Harold's), data processing personnel felt disassociated with the company. They felt rejected and unappreciated, and computer crime was the result.

  Senior management can manage data processing in several ways. First, they can demonstrate an appreciation for and interest in the data processing function. Occasional visits to the computer staff, recognition in the company newsletter, and references to data processing in the year-end report are examples of showing their interest.

  Senior management can recognize data processing in another large and important way as well. They can place the data processing function high in the organizational structure. Instead of burying data processing somewhere in accounting or finance where none of the senior managers ever see or hear of it, they can place it as a department on par with other business departments. Figure C-8 shows two ways

Figure C-8 Two Organizational Structures Recognizing the Information Systems Department

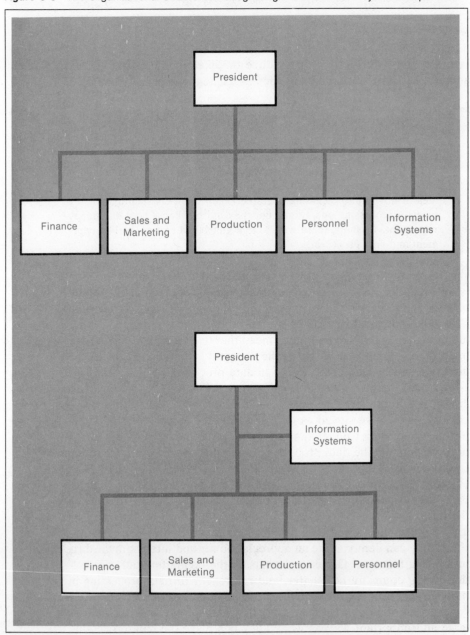

1. Data processing is placed at high organizational level.
2. Senior management demonstrates knowledge and good attitude toward data processing.
3. Data processing steering committee takes active role in DP
4. Management requests and reviews periodic reports.

Figure C-9 Management Controls

that data processing can be raised from the company bilges to gain the attention it deserves.

Next, management can understand the company's vulnerability to computer crime. Once they do, they can communicate the importance of controls to the entire organization. As we shall see, controls on the data processing function involve more than just data processing. To encourage other departments to cooperate, management needs to be very positive about the need for controls.

Another responsibility for management is to form a steering committee. As stated in Chapter 4, this committee controls data processing development efforts. They receive reports about project status and provide go/no go decisions as appropriate. Refer to Chapter 4 for more information about the steering committee.

Finally, management can take a role in data processing by requesting and paying attention to periodic operations reports. Management should know how well the computing resources are being used, how happy or unhappy the users are with the data processing function, and what the major data processing problems are. These reports increase the amount of communication between data processing and senior management. Management control responsibilities are summarized in figure C-9.

 Harold Johnson had free access to the computer and all of its resources. When Harold needed a tape file to determine Joan's account number, he walked into the tape library and got it. When he wanted to obtain the pricing program, he instructed the computer to print a copy of it. After he made the changes, Harold put the changed program into the standard program library. No one checked Harold's authority to do these things.

Organizational Controls

Organizational controls concern the organizational structure of the company. We have already mentioned that data processing should be organizationally on par with other functions of the company. In addition, the company should be structured so there is separation of authorities and duties.

The MODREC case is a good example of what can happen when there is no separation. Data processing employees had unlimited access to the computer. MODREC should have at least two categories of data processing personnel: operations and development. These groups should provide checks and balances on each other. The operations group should control the equipment and the production program library. The development group should develop new programs in accordance with requirements. They should not have access to the tape library or to the production programs.

If this were the case, the authorities would be separated. Only the programmers could develop program changes, and only the operations department could change the production library. Further, making changes to the program library would require a supervisor's authorization.

Separating authorities and duties provides checks and balances in the system. In general, the more people and the more levels of management that are involved in authorizing and performing duties, the less susceptible the system is to unauthorized activity.

Data Center Resource Controls

 After Harold Johnson changed the pricing program to give Joan the special discounts, he wanted to test it. After all, he didn't want to make a mistake and give the discounts to the wrong customer. However, to test the change, he needed to mount the customer and price files on the tape drives. To avoid suspicion, Harold stayed at work after hours the next week. Since none of the managers paid any attention to data processing, they didn't ask what Harold was doing. In fact, nobody asked Harold what he was up to. Harold took his time, and after three short nights, he had fully tested his program. Not only was he sure it would work, he was also sure no one could trace the changes to him.

Data center resources should be controlled. Use of computer equipment should be restricted to authorized personnel. Processing should be controlled by schedules, and records of use should be reviewed. To do this, access to the computer must be controlled. Only authorized personnel should be allowed in the computer room. This restriction not only protects the equipment from damage, but also helps to ensure that outputs are delivered only to the right people. Furthermore, limiting access to the machine room reduces the level of chaos and helps eliminate operator errors.

Computer operations should be controlled as well. Procedures and job schedules should be documented and followed. A supervisor should examine operations to ensure that the procedures are followed, and records should be kept of all computer activity. These records should be reviewed. It should be very difficult for operators to deviate from the established schedule and procedures.

In addition to protecting computing resources during normal operations, plans and procedures should exist to recover from problems. All files and libraries should be backed up by copies stored in secure off-premise locations. Further, recovery procedures should be well documented and the staff trained in the execution of them.

> Controlled access to computer center
> Documented operating procedures
> Secure program libraries
> Backup and recovery procedures
> Protection from natural hazards
> Documented emergency procedures

Figure C-10   Data Center Resource Controls

There should be a disaster recovery plan that explains what to do in case of fire, flood, earthquake, or other disaster. The company should consider having backup hardware and programs available in other locations. The procedures and data necessary to use the hardware should be available in the backup location. Resource controls are summarized in figure C-10.

 Harold Johnson did not have to modify program inputs. He found a way to provide special discounts by changing the processing. This process changed the outputs. If anyone had ever examined the invoices generated by the pricing program, they would have seen that something was amiss. Luckily for Harold, MODREC had no policy to examine outputs.

Input, Processing, and Output Controls

In general, there should be controls over inputs, processing, and outputs. First, the authorized form of input data should be documented. The operations personnel should be trained not to accept improper input data. Second, data processing personnel should be trained not to make changes to input data. Such changes should be made by the system users.

Where appropriate, control totals should be used. For example, when the users send the weekly payroll to data processing, they should calculate (independently) the sum of the hours worked or a similar total. The payroll program should be written to calculate the total number of hours worked, and to print this total on a summary report. The report should be examined by the payroll department after the payroll run to ensure that the manually prepared total and the computer-generated total match.

Similar totals can be kept on changes to master files, number of accounts payable checks to be issued, etc. Users must be trained to compute these totals and to treat them seriously. Oftentimes they are the most important control in the business computer system.

Inputs to teleprocessing applications are harder to control. A program can be coded to accept only certain inputs from certain users or certain locations. However, it is possible to fool such a program. Therefore, the use of terminals must be limited to certain individuals

Category	Type of Control
Input	Documentation of authorized input format
	Separation of duties and authorities
	Verification of control totals
	Online system input controls
Processing	Documented operating procedures
	Reviews of processing logs
	Adequate program testing
Output	Documented output procedures
	Control over disposition of output
	Users trained to examine output

Figure C-11 Input/Processing/Output Controls

at specified times. Further, the supervisors of these individuals need to be trained to review their subordinates' terminal activities.

There must also be controls over the processing of data. As stated earlier, all operations procedures should be documented and followed. The performance of the operators should be monitored periodically. The operations department should keep records of all errors and system failures. The corrections for each of these should be documented. These records should be reviewed periodically by data processing supervisory personnel to determine whether or not the failures are related to (or are covers for) unauthorized activity. Also, the records can be used to determine whether or not there is a need for additional training and to assess employee performance.

Finally, the outputs of all data processing activities should be controlled. Procedures for disseminating outputs should be documented and followed. Outputs should be given only to authorized users, and these users should examine the outputs for completeness and accuracy. Control totals produced by programs should be reconciled against input control totals.

Outputs from online systems are hard to control. Where data is changed on line, it can be very difficult to trace the sequence of activities. For example, a price might be changed several times and no written record generated. The absence of records can make the job of the auditor impossible. Consequently, online programs are often programmed to log transactions on computer tape. These logs are saved and used to correct errors or for audits. Figure C-11 summarizes input, processing, and output controls.

Other EDP Controls

Some EDP controls are not oriented toward preventing criminal activity. Instead, their purpose is to encourage effective use of EDP systems. Data administration controls are one example. Controls over

DP Training Seen Leading Inmates to Computer Crime

By Brad Schultz
CW Staff

NEW YORK—Federal agencies sometimes launch convicted felons on careers in computer crime by offering prison inmates DP training as well as access to income tax and other sensitive federal data banks, according to Sen. Abraham Ribicoff (D-Conn.).

The Senate investigation of federal computer security Ribicoff directed last year found the Bureau of Prisons training and then paying prison inmates to write computer programs for the U.S. Department of Agriculture.

In the process, some convicts learned to crack Internal Revenue Service (IRS) computer codes. They filed bogus tax returns and then received large tax refunds while serving penitentiary sentences, Ribicoff said last week in his Computer Expo '79 keynote address here.

One convict received a $25,000 IRS refund while doing a stretch at Leavenworth federal peniten-

tiary. He was caught and convicted of tax fraud, Ribicoff said. The IRS knows of many similar cases and is "deeply concerned" about the extent of tax fraud behind prison walls, he added.

Training in Wrong Area

Many of the inmate DPers are serving sentences for white-collar crimes such as counterfeiting and securities violations, the senator said. One convict-programmer has been arrested 25 times and convicted of 14 felonies; he is still in his early 30s.

"It was not my committee's intention to question the very valid principle of rehabilitation for prisoners. But a man with 25 arrests and 14 felony convictions might be better taught to be an auto mechanic or [learn about] some other worthwhile trade that would not require him to be involved in sensitive financial transactions for the federal government," Ribicoff said.

Figure C-12   Possible Inappropriate DP Training

systems development are another. We will not discuss these controls in this module. They are important to systems designers and auditors; and if you make either of these professions your career, you should learn more about them.

Harold Johnson and Joan Everest were able to continue their crime for 18 months. During that period, they obtained $150,000 worth of records for $22,500. The crime would have gone on longer, except for a change of MODREC management.

A new president was hired, and he expected better performance from the entire company. As part of his improvement program, the sales-

MODREC—THE REST OF THE STORY

force was required to increase sales. When one of the new sales managers reviewed the performance of the region having Joan's store, he detected something suspicious. It seemed that the volume of sales should have netted larger income. He examined the sales invoices over the last year and saw what had been going on. He contacted the new president, and the game was up.

Harold was actually relieved. The strain of perpetrating the crime had begun to wear on him. Also, he was frustrated. He liked to brag about his creations, and he wanted to tell his friends about the crime. He thought it was clever and he wanted credit for it.

MODREC threatened to sue for damages, but a settlement was made out of court. Harold and Joan paid MODREC $50,000, and Joan turned over a sizable part of her record inventory. Surprisingly, Harold had all but a few hundred dollars of the money that Joan had paid him. He really didn't participate for the money.

Criminal action was taken. Since both Harold and Joan were first-time criminals, they received light sentences. They each spent 60 days in jail and were fined $5,000.

QUESTIONS

C.1 According to Parker, how much is lost due to computer crimes?

C.2 Describe five types of computer crime.

C.3 What are 12 indications that an organization is vulnerable to computer crime?

C.4 How have most computer crimes been discovered?

C.5 What are EDP controls?

C.6 List the categories of EDP controls described in this module.

C.7 Describe management controls.

C.8 Describe organizational controls.

C.9 Describe data center resource controls.

C.10 Describe input/processing/output controls.

SUMMARY

Computer crime is an important issue. Millions of dollars are lost each year. There are five types of computer crime: manipulating input, changing programs, stealing data, stealing computer time, and stealing programs.

The characteristics of companies that are vulnerable to computer crime are known. Most of these characteristics reflect bad data processing management and violate the principles of effective data processing discussed in this book.

In order to prevent crime, companies need to develop better controls within their business computer systems. These controls fall into several areas: management, organizational, data center resources, input/processing/output, data administration, and systems development. EDP controls will not guarantee that crime is eliminated, but they will reduce the likelihood of crime.

Computer crime	*Data center resource controls*	**WORD LIST**
EDP	*Input/processing/output controls*	(in order of appearance in text)
EDP controls		
Management controls	*Data administration*	
Organizational controls	*Data administration controls*	

QUESTIONS TO CHALLENGE YOUR THINKING

A. What organizations or industries do you believe are particularly vulnerable to computer crime? If you worked for one of these companies, what would you do to reduce the likelihood of computer crime?

B. What would you do if you believed computer crime was happening at a company for which you worked? Would you report it? If so, to whom? Suppose you didn't report it but later someone found out you knew about it all along? What might happen?

C. How can computer crime be detected? What role do you think accountants and auditors have in the detection of computer crime?

D. Find out more about SAS-3. (Ask an accounting professor.) What does this mean to public auditors? What does this mean to data processing professionals? How do you think you should react to an EDP auditor?

E. Are existing laws sufficient for prosecuting computer criminals? Are special laws needed? What is the Ribicoff Computer Crime Bill? What actions do you think need to be taken?

MODULE D

Computers and Their Impact on Society

U.S. Congress uses computerized voting system

THE POSITIVE IMPACTS
OF COMPUTING

THE IMPACT OF THE
COMPUTER ON BUSINESS

   Electronic Funds
   Transfer

COMPUTER SYSTEMS IN
THE HEALTH PROFESSIONS

COMPUTER SYSTEMS IN
THE LEGAL PROFESSIONS

COMPUTER SYSTEMS IN
POLITICS

ARTIFICIAL INTELLIGENCE

THE NEGATIVE ASPECTS
OF COMPUTING

CONTROLLING COMPUTER
IMPACT

In the 1950s some people said we were entering the atomic age. It didn't turn out that way. It became the computer age instead. Computers have invaded every corner of our society, changed it, and altered the lives of the people who live in it. People over 50 have a hard time visualizing machines that can think. People under 30 expect machines to think. People in between are the pioneers of the computer age.

Computer technology has been both beneficial and harmful. In this module, we survey its benefits and discuss its costs. We try to determine what people can do to increase the good and minimize the bad. In today's society, the relevant question is, "How can we best use computer technology?" For good or ill, computers are here to stay.

THE POSITIVE IMPACTS OF COMPUTING

Since we in North America have ready access to computing resources, we tend to take them for granted. Some people say the major reason the Russians never put a person on the moon was a lack of computer technology. In the 1960s the Russians wanted desperately to send someone to the moon for publicity purposes. They had the rocket power and technology, but they could not develop sophisticated enough control systems. Their space flights had to be controlled from the ground. The United States put computer control capability into the spaceships. (See figure D-1.) Few people know the importance that computing had on the space program. Even fewer know the importance the space program had on computing. (It led to the development of microprocessor technology.)

Figure D-1   Computer Technology Made the Moon Landings Possible

To show the positive impact of computing, we will survey the application of computer technology in our society. We will discuss computers in business, health, law, and politics. Also, we will describe some exciting developments in a field called *artificial intelligence.*

THE IMPACT OF THE COMPUTER ON BUSINESS

Computers are one of the few bright spots on the business horizon. In a time of rising prices, computers are the only resource that is getting both cheaper and better. We have discussed specific business computer systems throughout this book. Therefore, we will not discuss more of them here. Instead, we will discuss the impact that computing has made on the character of business.

The biggest change that computers have made to business concerns the control of organizations and the allocation of resources. Their impact in this area is so subtle it is hard to notice, but computers have gradually changed the character of business. Giant corporations like IBM, American Telephone and Telegraph, or The Boeing Co.

could not exist without computers. Without computers they could not account for their operations, control their personnel, or manage projects. The design of the Boeing 747 took 16 million engineering hours. This work could not have been coordinated without computing. (See figure D-2.)

Largeness may seem bad to you, but consider that if these companies were smaller, there would be fewer computers, fewer telephones,

Figure D-2   Boeing 747 Could Not Be Produced without Computers

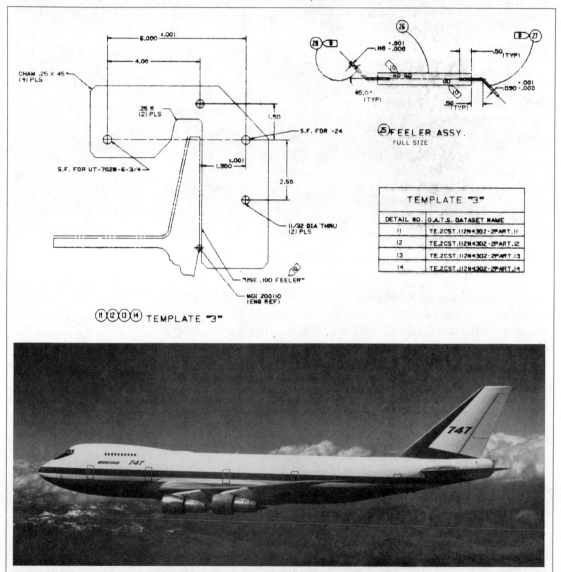

and fewer airplanes. Think about it the next time you fly nonstop from Chicago to Hawaii! (From Chicago to Milwaukee?) Also, many people are employed by these companies. Without them, these people would have to be doing something else, or perhaps would be doing nothing.

Computers have changed more than just the size of business. They have improved the control of resources. Consider the chair you are sitting in. The production, distribution, and sale of that chair and others like it were most likely controlled by computer systems. (Unless you made it yourself, in which case, think about the tools you used.)

Why did the manufacturer decide to make the chair? Most likely, a market study was done by a computer system. Where did the raw materials come from? The manufacturer probably used a computer system to decide what to order and to control its raw material inventory. How was the chair routed through the manufacturing process? A computer system may well have been used to determine the production schedule and routing. Computer systems were used to put the chair in inventory, to accept the order for the chair, to take the chair out of inventory, to ship the chair to the distributor, and to route the train or truck that carried the chair. Computer systems were used to put the chair into the distributor's inventory, to accept the retailer's order, to take the chair out of inventory, to transport it to the retailer, to put it into the retailer's inventory, to price it, and to record the fact that someone bought it. The chair has been handled by so many computer systems, it should have bit marks on it! (See figure D-3.)

Furthermore, the process isn't over. If the chair belongs to a company or organization, computer systems are used to keep it in the

Figure D-3 Chair Processed by Too Many Computer Systems—Bit Marks Visible

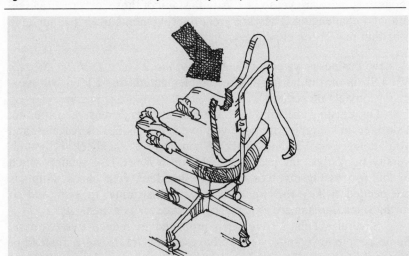

equipment inventory, to depreciate it, to consider it for balance and income statements, to consider its impact on taxes, and eventually, to scrap it. However, the process continues. If the chair is made of metal, it may be sent to a scrap dealer who will use computer systems to control the shipment of the scrap and the production of new metals. The new metals will be sold, distributed, and stored in inventories using computer systems until the day (you guessed it) it finds its way into the production of a new chair! The cycle will repeat itself. There is no escaping computer systems; they are everywhere.

Now, why is this good? It is good because products can be manufactured cheaper when they are well controlled. There may be six different ways of producing, delivering, and selling a chair. Of the six, we want to use the least expensive way. Why spend more than we have to? By improving control, computers help management to produce goods for less.

Given the inflation rates today, it may seem that goods are terribly overpriced. However, if goods were not made in large quantities (allowing economies of scale to be realized), they would be much more expensive than they are. Prices are high, but no society in history has had as many products to choose from. Some people say we live as well as kings lived in previous times.

Additionally, computers have improved the quality of work. They have eliminated many tedious chores. Accountants, for example, can spend more time on creative work like designing accounting systems or providing better auditability and control and less time on ticking and tacking (adding columns of numbers).

Furthermore, computer technology has created a whole new industry. Thousands of jobs have been created by computers, and thousands more are yet to be created. Many of these jobs are creative, fun, and challenging. They are great improvements over the mundane jobs that have been eliminated.

Electronic Funds Transfer

A new business system, called *Electronic Funds Transfer System* (EFTS), is on the horizon. When implemented, this EFTS will have major impacts on society.

Our existing checking and banking system is expensive to operate. Consider an example. Suppose you live and bank in Los Angeles, and you attend school in New York. When you write a check to the university bookstore, the processing shown in figure D-4 occurs. Much of this processing involves physically handling your check. Humans are needed to key the input, to sort, to distribute, to mail, and so forth. Since humans are expensive, the process is expensive.

Several schemes have been proposed to reduce this expense. Some people have suggested we have a *checkless society*. Instead of physical checks, all purchases would be made by electronic transactions. Individuals and businesses would have national account

Step	Processing Action
1	You deposit money in your Los Angeles checking account for school expenses.
2	You write a check to purchase books at your university bookstore in New York.
3	The bookstore deposits your check with its New York bank.
4	The New York bank deposits the check for credit in the Federal Reserve Bank of New York.
5	The Federal Reserve Bank in New York sends the check to the Federal Reserve Bank in Los Angeles for collection.
6	The Federal Reserve Bank in Los Angeles forwards the check to your Los Angeles bank. The amount is deducted from your checking balance.
7	Your Los Angeles bank tells the Federal Reserve Bank in Los Angeles to deduct the amount of the check from its deposit account.
8	The Los Angeles Federal Reserve Bank pays the New York Federal Reserve Bank for the amount of the check.
9	The New York Federal Reserve Bank pays the bookstore's bank in New York.
10	The bookstore's bank credits the bookstore's account.
11	Your Los Angeles bank photographs the check and sends you the canceled check at the end of the month.

Figure D-4 Existing System for Processing Checks

numbers. When someone makes a purchase, the merchant would input both numbers and the amount of the purchase. This amount would be deducted from the customer's account and added to the merchant's account (less a processing fee). This is an extension to the VISA and Master Charge systems.

Individual deposits would be handled the same way. When people are paid, their employers make electronic deposits to employee accounts. At the same time, the employer's account is reduced.

If this system were operational, there would be no obvious need for money. This could lead to the *cashless society.* Here, both checks and money are eliminated. All purchasing and payments are handled electronically.

Other forms of EFTS have been proposed. *One-way checks* are physically moved only to the bank of first deposit. In figure D-4 that is the bookstore's bank. Thus, the physical check does not go beyond step 3. The bookstore's bank creates an electronic transaction that represents the check in steps 4 through 11. Canceled checks would not be returned. Instead, people would receive a monthly printout of the transactions recorded. This is sometimes called *truncated check flow.*

The one-way check system is a compromise between existing systems and the checkless society. It would save physical processing and yet be similar to the existing system. This similarity is important

1. Invasion of privacy
2. Secret monitoring of individuals' activities
3. Control over individuals' lives
4. Reduced bank competition
5. Large-scale theft
6. Disaster due to system outages or sabotage

Figure D-5 Potential Problems of Electronic Funds Transfer

to bank customers. Research and experience have shown that people will not regularly use credit cards in place of checks. In January of 1980, Seattle First National Bank had to offer 5 percent discounts to encourage use of its checkless system. The response was hardly overwhelming. People like checks.

In spite of this preference, some form of EFTS is probably inevitable. Unfortunately, EFTS creates the potential for serious social problems. These are listed in figure D-5. First, the *invasion of individual privacy* can occur. Currently, checks are not stored in computer-sensible form. Therefore, the systematic investigation of one account is impossible. EFTS would make such investigations possible. Second, governmental agencies could *secretly monitor* the activities of individuals. Furthermore, they could *control people's lives* by restricting the types of purchases that could be made.

A fourth disadvantage is *reduced competition* among banks. Possibly a few large superbanks or financial utilities would be created. In this case, bank service would suffer and expenses would probably increase. EFTS opens the door to *large-scale thefts*. Billions of dollars would be vulnerable to computer criminals. Very large thefts could go undetected for years.

Increased vulnerability is another problem. The financial industry would become susceptible to credit blackouts when computers or communications failed. Furthermore, EFTS introduces the possibility of financial sabotage by terrorist groups or foreign governments.

Clearly, there are substantial problems to be overcome before EFTS becomes a reality. Congressional hearings have been held on the subject, and hopefully, problems will be thoroughly solved before EFTS is implemented. In the meantime, keep your checkbook handy.

COMPUTER SYSTEMS IN THE HEALTH PROFESSIONS

Both hospitals and doctors have used computers to improve service and reduce costs. First, they use computers for typical business functions—general ledger, billing, accounts receivable, inventory, and so forth. Additionally, they use computing for problems unique to health as summarized in figure D-6.

1. Administrative business functions
2. Patient records
3. Pharmacy records
4. Nursing stations
5. Radiological analysis
6. Monitoring of patient health
7. Diagnosing illnesses

Figure D-6 Computer Applications in Medicine

Computer systems are used to keep *patient records*. Because of the large number of diagnoses and the technical terms used, these systems are difficult to build. The system shown in figure D-7 has been successfully implemented, however. Technical terms are often given unique codes. Once the records are input to the computer, it is easy to search on these codes. Thus, the computer can be used to determine the effectiveness of different treatments.

Pharmacy systems are used to record the drugs used by patients. Such systems can even assist the doctor in planning the treatment course. Furthermore, these systems can notify the pharmacist if harmful combinations of drugs have been prescribed. (One doctor may prescribe a drug that conflicts with a drug prescribed by another doctor. The doctors won't know about each other's treatment if the patient doesn't tell them.)

Some pharmacists use computers to provide income tax records for their customers. The system records the cost of each prescription and a receipt for the total is printed at year end. This process saves customers' recordkeeping. Pharmacists like it because the customers have an incentive to use only one pharmacy.

Computer systems are used to help nurses. The *nursing station* shown in figure D-8 prints patient drug histories and treatment plans. The nurses record patients' vital signs (pulse, blood pressure, etc.) via this station.

Computers are used in radiology to *analyze X-rays*. Patterns are identified and reported. In figure D-9, a computer is used to help

Figure D-7 Steps Required to Input Patient Data

1. Doctor dictates patient data into tape recorder.
2. Nurse screens tape for time-critical actions.
3. Tape transcriptionist inputs data using CRT.
   Codes are used for technical terms.

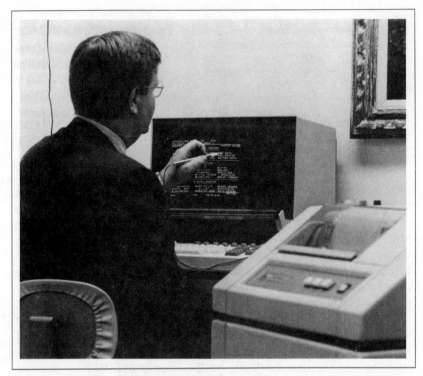

Figure D-8 Doctor Using Computer Nursing Station

orthodontists plan treatments. The dentists send patient X-rays to the computer service company. These X-rays are input to the computer. The effect of different treatments is them simulated by computer. From this record the orthodontist can plan the best treatment.

Computers are used to *monitor patient health.* Seriously ill patients such as those having cardiovascular problems (heart attacks, for example) can be connected to computer monitoring systems. Sensors are taped to the patient and the computer watches for abnormal activity. If it is detected, messages are displayed on terminals at a central location. There are even plans to remotely monitor patients after they leave the hospital.

Further, computers are used to help doctors *diagnose illnesses.* Patient symptoms and other data are input to a computer program. A list of possible illnesses and suggested treatments is produced. To date, these systems have not been overwhelmingly successful. The computer may respond with two or three thousand illnesses. Human judgment is hard to duplicate. Still, these systems have had some success — especially in treating rare diseases.

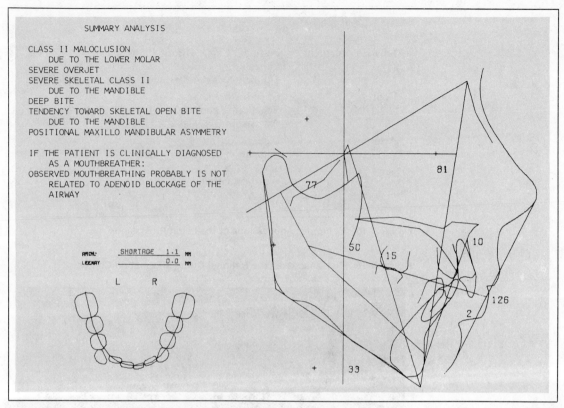

SUMMARY ANALYSIS

CLASS II MALOCLUSION
    DUE TO THE LOWER MOLAR
SEVERE OVERJET
SEVERE SKELETAL CLASS II
    DUE TO THE MANDIBLE
DEEP BITE
TENDENCY TOWARD SKELETAL OPEN BITE
    DUE TO THE MANDIBLE
POSITIONAL MAXILLO MANDIBULAR ASYMMETRY

IF THE PATIENT IS CLINICALLY DIAGNOSED
    AS A MOUTHBREATHER:
OBSERVED MOUTHBREATHING PROBABLY IS NOT
    RELATED TO ADENOID BLOCKAGE OF THE
    AIRWAY

Figure D-9   Computer Used to Analyze and Plan Orthodontic Treatment

Computers are used in all of the legal professions. (See figure D-10.) In *law enforcement*, computers are used to keep criminal data. The FBI maintains the National Crime Information Center (figure D-11). Records of criminals, stolen property, and crimes are kept on files in this system. State law enforcement agencies can query this system when they need information. They can also add data to the system. Other computer files are also maintained by the FBI and the CIA.

Many states also use computers in law enforcement. The State of Washington keeps driver license information in computer files. When a car is pulled over by the State Patrol, the driver's license can be checked immediately. The officer sends the license number to a central location by radio, and a terminal operator accesses the license files. Within minutes, the officer can obtain a complete driving history.

Courts use computer systems for a variety of purposes. Case histories are kept by computer systems. Courtrooms, personnel, and

COMPUTER SYSTEMS IN THE LEGAL PROFESSIONS

Legal Element	Application
Law Enforcement	National Crime Information Center Other crime centers Online access to drivers' licenses and other data
Courts	Case histories Scheduling courtrooms, personnel, and cases Administrative tasks
Attorneys	General business applications Allocation of attorney time Trial support Word processing Legal research

Figure D-10   Computer Applications in the Legal Professions

Figure D-11   Clerk Accesses the National Crime Information Center

Figure D-12   Legal Librarian Using Computer for Legal Research

cases are scheduled by computer. Administrative tasks such as keeping track of costs are also handled by computer systems. Computers are used to help select juries.

Attorneys are major users of computer systems. Law firms use computers for standard business applications like general ledger, billing, and accounts receivable. Computer systems are used to record expenses and to allocate attorneys' time to clients. Trial support systems keep case histories, maintain inventories of evidence and lists of witnesses, and keep schedules of activities for the trial attorneys. Word processing systems (see Module E) are frequently used in the legal profession.

One of the most promising legal applications of computing concerns research. Computers are used to query files of legal history (figure D-12). Relevant past cases and legal precedents are found much faster by computer systems than by humans.

COMPUTER SYSTEMS IN POLITICS

Computer systems are frequently used by politicians. (See figure D-13.) *Computer voting systems* are popular. Using these systems, citizens vote by punching holes in cards or otherwise creating a computer-sensible document. These documents are read by computers and votes are tabulated to determine election outcomes.

Computers are used to predict election outcomes. For national elections, all of the major TV networks use computers to predict results. As the early returns on the East Coast become available, they are used to predict the national outcome. This presents a problem. If

1. Election support—vote tabulation
2. Predicting election outcomes
3. Campaign letterwriting
4. Legislative administration

Figure D-13 Computer Applications in Politics

the predictions are made before the polls close on the West Coast, some people may not vote. They may think it is not worthwhile to vote for someone who is obviously losing. Thus, the predictions may influence the election. In fact, it would be possible for someone to sway an election by manipulating these predictions.

Politicians use computers to *raise money*. Records of potential campaign contributors are kept on computer files. At intervals, these records are used to produce "customized" letters asking for money or making political statements. According to the article in figure D-14, Ronald Reagan's organization sent out 250,000 letters per month prior to the 1980 election.

Computers are also used by legislatures. The United States Congress uses computers to tally votes. Congressional personnel use the computer system to determine the status of votes, the names of members present or absent, and so forth. (See figure D-15.)

ARTIFICIAL INTELLIGENCE

Probably the most fascinating projects in all computing are the efforts to build machines that think. The capability of these machines goes beyond the logical and arithmetic activity normally associated with computers. In some ways, these machines appear humanlike.

"The brain," said Marvin Minsky of MIT, "happens to be a meat machine." Many scientists agree with this philosophy. And they take it one step further. If the brain is a machine, then it may be possible to build another machine that has the same capability, or even greater capability. Research to build parts of such machines is called *artificial intelligence*.

Although work began in this field in the mid-1950s, results were slow to come. There were early programs that could successfully play easy games like tic-tac-toe. There were also programs that could play reasonable games of checkers. Promises were made that there would soon be chess-playing programs, but this was overly optimistic. Respectable chess-playing programs have only become available in the last five years.

Language translation was also harder than expected. In the 1950s people said it would only be a short time until computers could trans-

In Less Than Four Months
Reagan Nets $2 Million From Mail

By Marguerite Zientara
CW Staff

WASHINGTON, D.C.—"Ronald Reagan is a tremendously well-known commodity and therefore a very well-received and successful letter-signer," according to the head of the Reagan for President Committee's direct mail fundraising campaign, which has netted almost $2 million, since Nov. 13.

Roger Stone, who has been involved with direct-mail fundraising for seven years—"a very long time when you're 27 years old"—now heads both the fundraising and political persuasion mailing efforts as the committee's director of finance communications and deputy political director.

In direct-mail efforts, vast lists of names, addresses, political and interest group affiliations and previous donations can be stored on computer tape for eventual feeding to laser printers or word processors.

By culling from such lists the names of individuals with specific interests or donors who have given at particular monetary levels, direct mailers can aim "personalized" letters at those most likely to respond favorably.

"Our people are used to a tremendous amount of personalization," Stone noted, "and that does have a very definite effect" on the success of our appeals.

Stone has sent out an average of 250,000 letters monthly for a total of about 1.5 million letters since November. Divulging one of the secrets of the campaign's success, he said, "You should never, in my view, mail out any letter without asking for money.

"The fund-raising letter has a much stronger pitch for funds" compared with a political persuasion letter, in which the request for funds is "almost incidental," but always there.

Another criterion for success is timeliness, Stone explained. "Our mailings are based on what the current political happening is, whether it's Iowa or New Hampshire, whatever the goal is."

Figure D-14   Using the Computer to Raise Funds

late. However, they discovered that human language is very complex. Early programs simply substituted a word in one language for an equivalent word in another. With this procedure, the phrase "The spirit is willing but the flesh is weak" was translated to "The booze is good, but the meat is rotten." One scientist said programs had to be taught that when Mary had a little lamb, she didn't have it for lunch!

Attempting to translate human language led to a greater understanding of language. The theory of transformational grammar resulted from this work. Today there are programs that can do limited forms of translation. Considerable work still needs to be done.

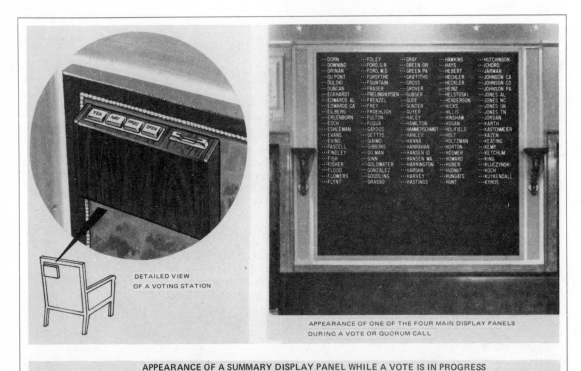

DETAILED VIEW
OF A VOTING STATION

APPEARANCE OF ONE OF THE FOUR MAIN DISPLAY PANELS
DURING A VOTE OR QUORUM CALL

APPEARANCE OF A SUMMARY DISPLAY PANEL WHILE A VOTE IS IN PROGRESS

Figure D-15 Computer System Used by the United States Congress

One subset of artificial intelligence is oriented toward simulating human dialog. In 1963 at MIT, Dr. Joseph Weizenbaum decided to build a machine that would simulate the conversation between a psychoanalyst and his or her patient. Weizenbaum's program was called ELIZA. This program was enhanced by Dr. Kenneth Colby and renamed DOCTOR. In *Machines Who Think*, Pamela McCorduck reports the following conversation between DOCTOR and a distinguished foreign visitor [59, p. 254]:

Doctor: Good afternoon. Please type in your name.
(This visitor typed his name.)
Doctor: What brought you here to see me today?
Visitor: Oh, nothing much. I'm feeling a bit tired, that's all.
Doctor: Why do you think you're feeling a bit tired?
Visitor: Well, I've been traveling a lot, and away from home.
Doctor: Tell me about your family.

According to Ms. McCorduck, the conversation continued in an intimate manner. Even though the visitor knew he was talking with a machine, he continued to reveal his personal fears and concerns.

Scientists debate whether this program has any therapeutic value. Weizenbaum says it does not. He wrote it only to simulate a conversation. Others think it may provide some therapy.

One of the most impressive developments in artificial intelligence is robotics — the production of robots. The Stanford Research Institute developed a famous robot named Shakey. Shakey could propel itself and avoid objects in its path. It could also be programmed to perform simple tasks such as picking up toy blocks or boxes. One of the most complex tasks it performed was to assemble an automobile water pump from parts scattered on a table. (See figure D-16.)

Robotics is becoming important in industry. Plans call for using robots to perform boring and repetitive jobs. They can also be used in hostile environments where humans cannot work. Nuclear powerplants are one example; space is another.

The work in artificial intelligence continues. Many of the problems have been more difficult than anticipated, and a keen appreciation for the human mind has resulted. Still, many scientists think it is only a matter of time until intelligent machines exist. Hermann Kahn, an analyst at the Hudson Institute, thinks machines will ultimately surpass human beings. He says,

I find it a very unpleasant prospect. . . . The computer may write better poetry than human beings, better drama, make more perceptive judgments . . . before the end of the century. It may turn out that the only way to do this is that the computer itself will have to learn by experience. [58, p. 56]

Figure D-16 Shakey—Stanford Research Institute's Robot (It is no longer "living")

THE NEGATIVE ASPECTS OF COMPUTING

Unfortunately, the impact of computers has not been entirely positive. There have been social costs in the application of computer technology as well. These are summarized in figure D-17.

Some aspects of computing have served to decrease the quality of life. For one, computers have eliminated jobs. While it is true they have created other jobs, these jobs have not always been available to the people whose jobs were eliminated by the computer.

For example, suppose a new order entry system is installed at a company. When this is done, several order entry jobs may be eliminated, and several data processing jobs may be created. But the people who were data entry clerks yesterday probably are not qualified to be systems designers or programmers today. Thus, computers can put some people out of work. (This, by the way, is all the more reason for you to learn all you can about computers.) Unfortunately, the people out of work tend to be the least skilled; it may be hard for them to find other work.

In addition to eliminating jobs, computers have changed the environment of some business activities. Business has become more impersonal. People have been treated as numbers instead of as human beings.

Actually, this treatment should not be blamed on computers; it should be blamed on people. Computers themselves don't make business more impersonal. Laying the blame for impersonalization on the

1. Elimination of jobs
2. Impersonalization of business
3. Human abuse caused by
     Improper data handling
     Poor systems design

Figure D-17   Societal Costs of Computing

computer is like laying the blame for murder on the weapon used. Suppose a person is found standing over a gunshot victim with a smoking gun. The person explains to the investigating officer that he is not responsible because the gun shot the man. How far would that line of reasoning go?

Surprisingly, this reasoning goes far in business computing. How often have you heard, "The computer won't let me do that."? Did you ever want to ask, "Who controls the computer? Who programmed the computer? Does the computer make decisions for itself?" Obviously, it doesn't. Since the computer cannot speak up to defend itself, people hide behind it to avoid responsibility for their own mistakes.

Now, back to the coldness in business. In some cases, when computer systems were installed, businesses became inhumane. This occurred partly because people were discovering how to use computer technology; they made mistakes. It occurred partly because the people who designed and developed the computer systems tended to be machine-oriented. They had little regard for the machine's impact on people. As people learn how to integrate computer technology into businesses, impersonalization will be less likely to occur. However, there is little doubt that computer processing is standardized processing. It will always be hard for computer systems to deal with exceptions as well as humans can.

In addition to these disadvantages, there has been a certain amount of computer abuse. The abuse stems from two sources: *improper data handling* and *bad systems design*.

Data is relatively easy to collect and store. Once data is in magnetic form, billions of characters can readily be sent from one computer to another—even across the nation or across the world. Further, the data doesn't wear out; it doesn't fade with time as people's memories do. Under these conditions, it is hard for people to have privacy. If someone defaults on a home mortgage, a record of the default may be distributed across the nation. It may be available to credit bureaus for years.

Lenders may consider this capability an advantage, but many people do not. People change and grow. Doesn't everyone have something in their past they would prefer to forget about? With computer technology, forgetting about the past may be a thing of the past.

The potential for totalitarian government is tremendous. It is technically possible to gather enough data to know the earning and spending habits of every person in the nation. With EFTS it is possible to prohibit certain people from making certain purchases, or from living in certain areas, or from working at certain jobs. Again, this capability may be an advantage in some ways, but it is clearly a disadvantage in others.

Thus, computer technology presents the opportunity for serious infringements on individual rights and privacy. Today, these infringements are mostly possibilities, but the potential is certainly real.

Perhaps the greatest abuse occurs when computer systems produce inaccurate information. There are many stories about people who have been refused employment or credit because their records were in error, or because they were confused with someone having the same name. The individuals who learned about such errors were the lucky ones. The unlucky ones didn't receive jobs, or credit, or whatever, and never knew why.

Just thinking about this possibility fills us with anger and disgust. Yet, should we blame computer technology for these errors? Although computer technology created the possibility of these errors, they were not made until some person created a system and another person misused the system to create a problem. Ultimately, the responsibility for the errors lies with people.

The second category of computer abuse occurs when systems are designed poorly. For example, the class scheduling system in Chapter 2 would not enroll George Shelton in classes because it thought George owed money to the university. In fact, George did not. George's frustration occurred because the finance people recognized that George was in good standing, but the computer did not. Further, George found no one who knew how to correct the error.

In this example, the class scheduling system was poorly designed. It was too difficult to rectify an error. There have been many similar cases. One person was sent threatening letters because she refused to pay a bill for $0.00. Finally, she sent a check for $0.00. The letters stopped coming, but then her bank refused to process the check for $0.00. She had to explain the situation several times to rectify the error.

Sometimes, people are abused by computer technology because they are unable to obtain services they need and deserve. There are cases of utility companies terminating service to homes because computer systems determined incorrectly that bills were several months overdue.

Perhaps the worst situations develop when the computer is used to intimidate people. Computer-generated letters that look and sound official sometimes cause people to do things they are not obligated to do. People who do not know their rights or how to deal with computer errors are likely victims.

All such cases of systems abuse are preventable. When they occur, they reflect poor systems design or personnel errors. The computer is nearly never at fault. The problem lies with incomplete or inaccurate procedures or with poorly trained personnel.

Computers have the capacity to be a boon to mankind and to help us solve our greatest difficulties. However, they also have the capacity to be destructive, to limit personal freedom, and to eliminate personal privacy. How can we best obtain the benefits of computer technology while minimizing the dangers?

CONTROLLING COMPUTER IMPACT

First, the greatest strength we have is knowledge. As people take courses like this one, as they learn what business computer systems should be, and as they learn what the dangers of computing technology are, they will demand better treatment.

Hopefully, you will not believe anyone who says, "The computer won't let me." If you hear that statement, speak to as many of the involved supervisors as you can. Let the supervisors know you are aware that people often hide behind the computer to avoid responsibility. Encourage them to take control over their organization. Computers are not supposed to be dictators; they are supposed to be servants. Go to the president of the organization if you need to. He or she deserves to know who the apparent company leader is—the computer!

As more and more people learn how to deal with computers, they will exercise more power as consumers. They will learn to observe the quality of computer service and will choose to do business with companies that have good systems. As time passes, competition in the marketplace will eliminate companies that operate substandard computer systems.

In addition to consumer knowledge, legislation will help to eliminate computer abuse. Several laws have already been passed. Others are pending. The Fair Credit Reporting Act of 1970 established laws that give individuals the right to see credit data that is maintained about them. Also, this act stipulates that people can challenge the credit data and that it must be changed if it is erroneous. The Freedom of Information Act of 1970 also gave individuals access to data collected by government agencies.

Another law gives citizens rights with respect to data gathered by the government. The Privacy Act of 1974 stipulates that individuals must be able to learn what information the government collects about them. Also, the government must state what the data will be used for. Data gathered for one purpose cannot be used for a different purpose without permission of the individual. Further, individuals have the right to have erroneous data changed. Finally, this act clearly lays the responsibility for maintaining correct data on the organization that keeps it. The responsibility for ensuring that data is not misused lies with the government.

Unfortunately, this act applies only to governmental agencies. Legislation that applies to private organizations and companies is yet to be adopted. Some states have passed such legislation, and others are considering it. Such legislation is not popular with businesses because the costs of compliance will be high.

Knowledge and legislation are the tools we have to control the impact of the computer on society. As citizens, we have the responsibility to make our voices heard. We can do this through consumer power, by knowing our rights and insisting on fair and legal treatment from businesses, and by expressing the need for responsible computer systems and operation to our governmental representatives. If you become involved with the design or operation of computer systems in business, you will have an opportunity to ensure that the systems are responsibly designed and used.

QUESTIONS		
	D.1	How has computer technology improved the quality of life in our society?
	D.2	Explain how computer technology has changed the character of business.
	D.3	Explain five ways that computers are used in medicine.
	D.4	Explain five ways that computers are used in the legal professions.
	D.5	Explain four ways that computers are used in politics.
	D.6	How has computer technology improved the quality of work?
	D.7	How has computer technology decreased the quality of life in our society?
	D.8	React to the statement, "Computers create more jobs than they eliminate."
	D.9	Explain how the philosophy, "But officer, this gun shot this man," applies to computer abuse.
	D.10	Explain how you can use your knowledge of computers to control the impact of computer technology on our society.

D.11   Explain the benefits of the following laws:
  a. Fair Credit Act of 1970
  b. Freedom of Information Act of 1970
  c. Privacy Act of 1974

SUMMARY

In the future, we can expect society's problems to increase. Energy will be more scarce; natural resources will be more scarce; increasing population will place a greater burden on the environment; and competition for scarce resources will cause considerable social unrest. Improving the allocation and control of resources is essential to the solution of these problems. As we have seen, allocation and control are strengths of business computer systems. Further, computers are getting cheaper. From these facts, it seems apparent that computers can and should play a major and increasing role.

The computer has brought both benefits and harm to our society. Without the computer, many of our present activities would be impossible. In business, the computer has greatly improved the control and allocation of resources. Activities on a large scale are possible only because of computing. In medicine, new techniques and treatments have become possible because of computers. Computers are used in important ways in the legal professions and in politics. Finally, the computer industry has provided many challenging jobs.

On the other hand, computers have been harmful. Jobs have been eliminated. Standardization has resulted in people being treated as numbers. Business has become more cold in some cases. Data has been in error and people have been unfairly denied credit or jobs. Also, it is difficult for people to have privacy in the computer age. Finally, some systems have been poorly designed and have caused people to be mistreated.

In the future, we must hope to maximize the benefits of computer technology while minimizing their harmfulness. In this effort we have two main strengths: our knowledge about how computers can be used, and legislation. Computers are not in themselves bad. They only become bad when people misuse them. We must use our strengths to avoid this misuse.

WORD LIST

(in order of appearance in text)

Electronic Funds Transfer System (EFTS)

Checkless society

Cashless society

One-way checks

Truncated check flow

Artificial intelligence

Robotics

QUESTIONS TO CHALLENGE YOUR THINKING

A. Imagine that for some reason all the computers in existence stopped operating. For some reason, they just quit. What would be the impact on our society?

B. Suppose you could wind time backwards 40 years. Like Superman in the movie, you could fly around the earth and undo time. If you could, would you eliminate computers? Do you think the world would have evolved in a better way without computers?

C. Do you think a machine can think? Do you think computers can be built that will duplicate or surpass the human mind?

D. Do you think machines should think? Do you think it is morally right for people to build intelligent machines? Is it possible to build machines that will someday be smarter than we are? Could they enslave us?

MODULE E

Word Processing Systems and the Automated Office

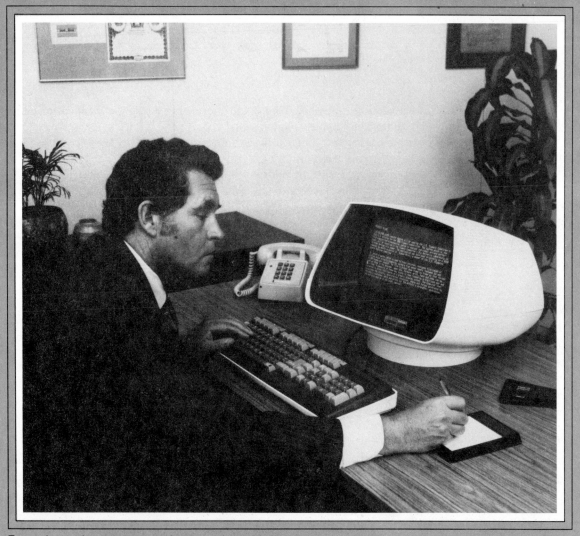

Executive reviews contents of electronic mailbox

WHAT IS WORD PROCESSING?

Word Processing Example

Advantages of
Word Processing

WORD PROCESSING HARDWARE

CONNECTING WORD PROCESSORS TO OTHER EQUIPMENT

THE AUTOMATED OFFICE

This section describes a new and increasingly popular application of computers in business called *word processing*. These systems are like computer-driven typewriters, although as we will see, they have much greater capability than any ordinary typewriter.

First, we will introduce word processing by describing its features, capabilities, advantages, and costs. Then, typical word processing hardware will be illustrated. Next, the possible interfaces of word processing with data processing and other office machines will be discussed. Finally, we will describe the potential of a completely automated office.

WHAT IS WORD PROCESSING?

Word processing systems use computer technology to facilitate the preparation of documents. A person uses a keyboard to compose or type a document that appears on the CRT screen. When the person makes a typographical error, he or she simply backspaces and types the correct character over the error. Additionally, a powerful set of tools is available to move words around, to insert and delete words, and to perform other editing functions.

Once a document has been prepared, it can be saved on magnetic disk. It can be printed using a high-speed, computerlike typewriter. Once a document has been stored on disk, it can be retrieved, edited, and printed again. Thus, word processing is particularly useful in environments where documents go through several drafts before they are finished.

Word Processing Example

This book, its accompanying workbook, and other supporting materials were written on a word processor. (See figure E-1.) To illustrate

Figure E-1 Use of Word Processing Equipment

the power of such systems, we will show how the paragraph immediately above could be changed using special word processing commands.

Figure E-2 shows how that paragraph appeared on the word
processor CRT screen. Now, suppose you decide to change the first
sentence, beginning with the words,

> *Once a document has been prepared, it can be . . .*

to read,

> *A document can be saved . . .*

On a word processor, there is a replace key or command. To
make the above change, you simply hit the replace key, and then show
the system which words you want to replace. Word processors have a
cursor, which is an underline character that moves to different places
on the CRT screen. There are buttons to push to move the cursor
around. To replace the words, "Once a document has been prepared,
it . . . ," you move the cursor to the letter O and hit a particular key.
Then you move the cursor to the letter t in "it," as shown in figure E-3.
Then you hit a key labeled *Execute.* At this point, the word processor
will remove these words and ask you what you want to replace them

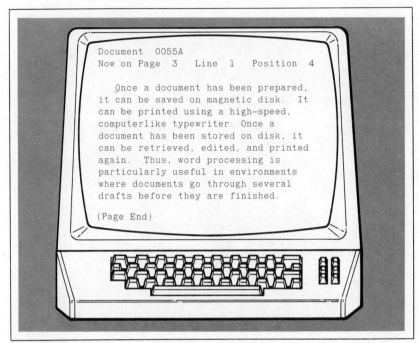

Figure E-2   Paragraph of This Book on a Word Processor

Figure E-3   Replacing a Phrase on the Word Processor

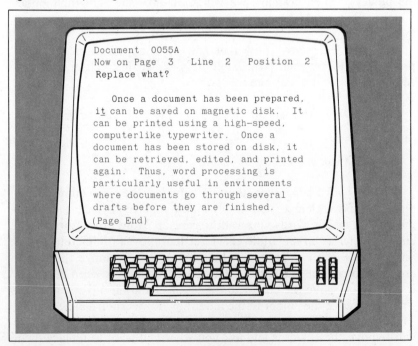

```
Document  0055A
Now on Page  3   Line  1   Position  4
Replace with?




can be saved on magnetic dis*
```

Figure E-4   Word Processor Is Ready to Accept New Phrase

with. (See figure E-4.) You then type the words, "A document," into the hole that the system has created and hit the key again. The paragraph now reads as shown in figure E-5.

You shortened the sentence by making this change. Therefore, the system automatically moved words to the left and adjusted the paragraph to fill the hole. The format of the whole paragraph has been automatically changed.

In addition to replace, word processing systems can delete and insert. When a deletion is done, words and lines are adjusted to fill any gaps created. When an insert is made, words are moved to allow space for the new characters.

Many other features are provided. Special keys are available to allow indentions, to cause one or more lines to be centered on a page, and to move or copy characters. For example, the paragraph used to illustrate figures E-2, E-3, and E-5 was typed only once. The word processor made copies for the examples.

Another feature of word processors is variable margins. Suppose you want to type the same paragraph but with narrower margins. To do this you set the new margins and hit a special key. The word processor then moves words from line to line to conform to the new margins. Thus, that same paragraph appears as shown in figure E-6.

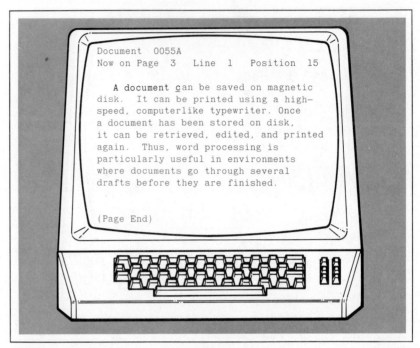

Figure E-5 Paragraph of This Book After Replacement

Figure E-6 The Same Paragraph After Margin Changes

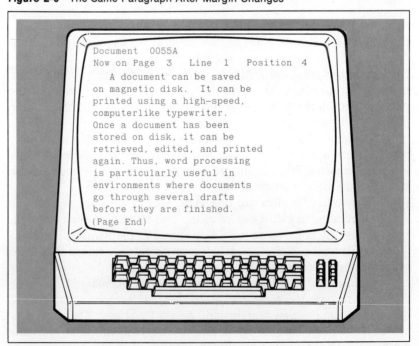

All of this is done simply by hitting a few keys. As you can see, a word processor makes it easy to add or delete words, sentences, or paragraphs. In fact, whole pages can be added to a document, which will be adjusted to accommodate the changes.

There are many other useful features of word processing systems. Documents can be merged, form letters can be prepared, many "original" copies can be made, columns of numbers can be added, numbers can be aligned on decimal points, and so on.

Advantages of Word Processing

Word processing systems have simplified secretarial activity. Before word processing systems were developed, secretaries and typists had to completely retype pages or even entire documents when changes were made. They had to be careful not to make mistakes because fixing errors took considerable time. With word processing, changes are simple to make and typographical errors are easily corrected.

Because of these advantages, secretaries with word processing systems can be much more efficient. In fact, it has been estimated that word processors reduce typing time by 50 percent. Thus, if a secretary spends half of his or her time typing (say 4 hours per day), a word processor will save half of this time (2 hours per day). That is 25 percent of the total time available!

While these savings are significant, word processors can be used to obtain even greater savings. Some companies have found they do not need to employ typists to prepare documents. Since mistakes are easy to correct and since editing is easy to do, many professionals have found they can compose directly on a word processing screen. In this case, typists are not needed. For example, some lawyers can produce more work by typing on a word processing system than by writing on paper or dictating. They do this not so much to eliminate the cost of a typist, but rather to speed up their own work.

People in other professions have learned this shortcut, too. For years, programmers and systems analysts have used computer text editors to do documentation. These text editors were the predecessor of word processing systems. Some auditors and consultants have begun to use word processors for composition as well.

Great cost savings are possible when professional people compose on word processors. People who can produce work in one-half to one-third as much time are then free to do other work. Also, people who do their own editing have greater control over the quality of their work.

The cost of a basic word processing system is between $5,000 and $20,000. This may seem expensive, but the annual salary of a typist is in that range. If the word processor can save the work of one typist, it pays for itself in a year. This savings does not consider the income tax advantages of this equipment, either.

WORD PROCESSING HARDWARE

The configuration of a typical word processing system is shown in figure E-7. It has four components: *workstations* (the CRTs used to input documents), a *CPU*, a *disk system*, and a *printer*.

The CPU of a word processing system need not be very powerful, at least not by data processing standards. Only a little intelligence is required to move text around and to keep track of it. Because typists and printers operate at slow speeds, the CPU need not be fast. Often, microprocessors are used as CPUs in word processing systems.

Two types of disks are used in word processors. The most common are floppy disk systems. (See Chapter 6 for a discussion of floppies.) Usually, there are master and backup drives. The master drive maintains the system programs and the copies of documents that are currently being produced, edited, or printed. The floppy disk on the master drive is semipermanently mounted. The master floppy typically holds about 100 pages of documents.

The backup drive is used to copy documents for storage. Floppies are readily mounted and dismounted on this drive. When a document is to be stored, a floppy is mounted on the backup drive and the document is copied to it. The floppy can then be filed in a cabinet or on a bookshelf. Later, when the document is needed, the floppy is mounted

Figure E-7 Components of a Word Processing System

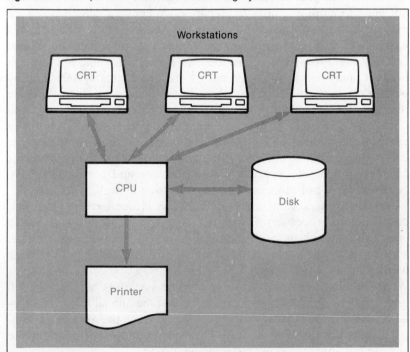

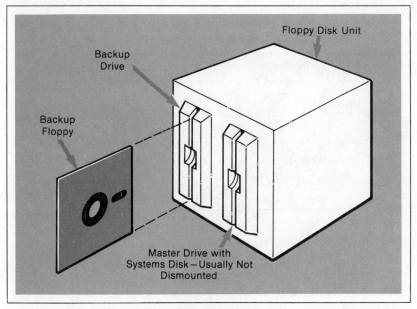

Figure E-8 Using a Floppy Disk System for Backup

on the backup drive and the document copied onto the master disk. Once there, it can be edited or printed. A backup floppy typically holds more data than the master; 120 pages is typical. (See figure E-8.)

The second type of disk is a hard disk similar to that used for direct access file processing. (See Chapter 6.) These disks are much more expensive than floppies, but they have far greater capacity. Five hundred or a thousand pages of documents can be held on them. When hard disks are available, the system programs and current documents are kept on them. Floppies are still used for backup.

The fourth component of a word processing system is a printer. It is important to have good quality print for word processing applications, so the printers are generally expensive. Daisy wheel printers are often used. These have removable print wheels as shown in figure E-9. A variety of print styles are available.

Word processing printers typically operate at 40 to 50 characters per second. Although this is much slower than regular computer printers (4000 characters per second is typical for them), it is much faster than manual typing. Also, the quality of the print is better than that of a typical computer printer. Both uppercase and lowercase letters are available.

Word processing printers are bidirectional. Instead of returning the carriage to the left margin on every line, they print in both directions. Thus, every other line is printed backwards. This is surprising to see, but is actually simple for the CPU to control.

Figure E-9   Daisy Wheel Point Mechanism

Word processing systems can become very large. It is possible to have 20 or 30 workstations and five or six printers on a single system. Systems that are this large are very expensive, however. A cost of $100,000 to $200,000 is typical.

CONNECTING WORD PROCESSORS TO OTHER EQUIPMENT

Often, much can be gained by connecting word processors to other office equipment. One common connection is to tie a word processor to an *intelligent copier* like the one in figure E-10. These copiers are like Xerox machines, but they can accept both printed source documents and electronic input.

When word processors and intelligent copiers are used together, the word processor sends instructions and text to the copier. For example, a secretary at a word processing workstation might issue a command to make 100 copies of a certain document. The word processor would retrieve the text of the document from storage and send it to the copier with a command to make 100 copies. Since the copier operates at much higher speeds than the word processing printer, this method will be more efficient than printing 100 originals.

Another possibility is to connect several word processing CPUs together. This is effective for companies that have offices in several geographic locations. By connecting word processors together, documents that are prepared in one location can be printed in others. This is called *electronic mail*. Instead of sending a printed document to

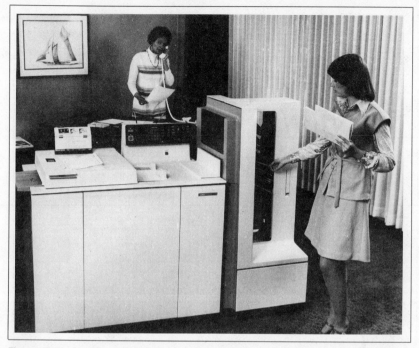

Figure E-10 Intelligent Copier

another location by regular mail, the electronic form is sent over communication lines.

A system of distributed word processors and intelligent copiers is shown in figure E-11. This system is used by a law firm with offices in Los Angeles, Washington, D.C., and Anchorage, Alaska. Since all three cities have word processing systems, documents prepared in any of the locations can be transmitted electronically to any of the other locations for printing. Also, since both Los Angeles and Washington have intelligent copiers, the text of source documents can be sent from either of these cities to the other.

Although the possibilities for distributed word processing are great, the possibilities for combining word processing and data processing are even greater. When combined, the word processing CPU is connected to the data processing CPU by communication lines or by shared files. In the latter case, a hard disk is connected to both computers. The computers leave messages for each other on the disk.

Accounts receivable is one application that can benefit from this combination. The data processing system can maintain the accounts receivable file and process order invoices and payments as they occur. Periodically, the data processing computer can send messages to the word processing computer to generate form letters to customers. For

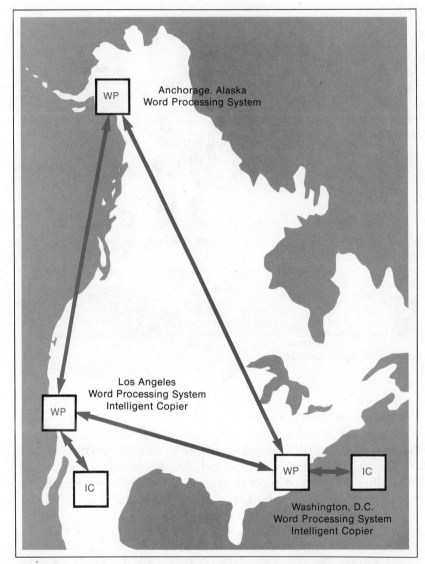

Figure E-11 Network of Word Processors and Intelligent Copiers for a Law Office

example, if a customer's bill is overdue, the data processing computer can direct the word processing computer to prepare a letter asking for payment. This action can be recorded in the data processing computer's files. Subsequent letters can be made more threatening if needed. (But, the system should consider the social issues of computing.)

One law firm has developed an even more ingenious and profitable application for a data/word processing combination system. This firm has several hundred standard paragraphs for wills. When a lawyer prepares a will, he or she selects the standard paragraphs that are appropriate. If slight modifications are needed, they are made and recorded on the word processing system. The word processor passes a file of paragraph numbers and modifications to the data processing computer where this data is stored, along with the name of the client.

Whenever a law change impacts one of these paragraphs, a data processing program searches all of the wills to determine which ones contain that paragraph. A file of names of people with affected wills is then sent to the word processor computer. The computer prepares form letters to these people telling them that the law has changed and asking if they want their wills updated.

Meanwhile, a firm lawyer rewrites the standard paragraph to conform to the new law. The new standard paragraph is then added to the files of the word processor.

When responses are received from people who want their wills updated, this fact is input to the data processing system. The system sends the list of paragraph numbers to the word processing system which then generates the new wills. The data processing computer also conveniently prepares a bill for each client. It is typed by the word processor and sent to the client a few days later.

Using this system, a will can be updated for about $2.50, including postage and handling. The standard charge for updating a will is about $50.00. Therefore, the firm makes considerable profit on each will that it updates. Furthermore, the clients of this firm receive high quality, up-to-date service.

Many other intriguing possibilities exist when data and word processing computers are connected. Undoubtedly, creative people will find many ways to use this technology to save money and increase profit. Good luck!

THE AUTOMATED OFFICE

Word processing, intelligent copiers, online data processing systems —computers are bringing automation to the office. Just as the industrial revolution brought automation to the factory, the computer revolution is bringing automation to the office.

Given the current trend of cheaper computers and more expensive people, we can expect this automation to increase. Some experts think the paperless office is not far off. At that time, business communication will mostly be done electronically.

The *paperless office* is technically feasible today. Documents can be maintained in word processing files and recalled when necessary. Reports generated by computers can be stored on online files. When someone needs a document or report, he or she can simply use the CRT in his or her office to access the word or data processing computer.

Furthermore, intracompany communication can be done electronically. Each employee is assigned a CRT location and a personal file or *electronic mailbox*. When someone generates a memo, he or she composes it on a word processor and prepares a list of the people to receive it. The word or data processing system then routes the memo to those people's CRT terminals. Communication like this is much quicker than preparing documents, copying them, and routing them through company mail.

As communication systems are standardized, intercompany communication can also be done electronically. In the not-too-distant future, letters as we know them today can be eliminated. They will be prepared on word processing systems, shipped electronically from one company to another, and then stored in an individual's electronic mailbox. After reading such mail, the recipient can destroy it or store it on a word processing file. A letter sent this way may never be printed.

The automated office may sound futuristic, but it is probably not as far away as you think. It is probably not yet economically justifiable. But, as people become more expensive, and as computers and their equipment become cheaper, this picture will change. The office you retire from will likely be automated. You will be a pioneer in the development of automated offices.

QUESTIONS

E.1   What is a word processing system? What does it do?

E.2   Describe three word processing edit facilities.

E.3   How has word processing simplified the typist's job? According to the text, about how much time do word processors save?

E.4   How can professional people take advantage of word processing systems?

E.5   How much does a small word processing system cost? How much does a large one with 20 terminals and several printers cost?

E.6   Name the four components of a word processing system.

E.7   What is an intelligent copier? What are the advantages of coupling word processors and intelligent copiers together?

E.8   What are the advantages of coupling two or more word processing computers together?

E.9   What are the advantages of coupling word processing and data processing computers?

E.10 Describe the automated office. How does it differ from offices today? Is it technically feasible?

SUMMARY

Word processing systems apply computer technology to the preparation of documents. People use CRTs to input source documents and edit them using powerful word processing commands. Documents can be stored on disk, and they can be printed.

Word processors greatly simplify the job of the typist. However, the greatest savings occur when professionals compose documents directly on word processors. This practice not only eliminates the need for a typist; it also enables the professional to work more productively.

Word processors can be connected to other office equipment. When tied to intelligent copiers, they can produce many copies of documents. When interfaced with other word processors, they allow electronic mail. When word processors are connected to data processing computers, great savings and improvements in service become possible.

Computers are bringing automation to the office. The paperless office is technically feasible today. Physical forms of memos and letters can be eliminated. The automated office is probably not yet cost justifiable except in special cases. However, as people become more expensive and computers less expensive, this situation will likely change.

WORD LIST

(in order of appearance in text)

Word processing

CRT

Replace command

Cursor

Insert command

Delete command

Variable margins

Word processing workstation

CPU

Floppy disk

Hard disk

Daisy wheel printer

Intelligent copier

Electronic mail

Automated office

Paperless office

Electronic mailbox

QUESTIONS TO CHALLENGE YOUR THINKING

A. What are the dangers of an automated office? Do you think the potential for computer crime is enhanced in an automated office?

B. Can the automated office have an undesirable impact on working environments? What do you think can be done to reduce the chance of abusing people in an automated office environment?

MODULE F

Microcomputers and Specialized Input/Output Equipment

Student uses microcomputer

COMPONENTS OF MICROCOMPUTERS

APPLICATIONS OF MICROCOMPUTERS IN BUSINESS

Microcomputers as Components of Business Computer Systems

Microcomputers as Components of Products

Microcomputers and Specialized Input/Output Equipment

This module discusses microcomputers and their applications in business. The components of microcomputers are defined, and typical business uses are described. Finally, examples of specialized microcomputer-based input/output equipment are presented.

COMPONENTS OF MICROCOMPUTERS

A microprocessor, shown in figure F-1, is a CPU mounted on a small chip of silicon. In spite of its small size (about like this ▮), the microprocessor contains over 2000 transistors and other electronic equipment. In simple terms, the functions of a microprocessor are to receive binary data, to perform arithmetic or logical operations on the data, and to output results.

Microprocessors are very cheap. They range in price from ten to a few hundred dollars. In spite of their small size and low cost, microprocessors can be powerful. Even the first ones, like the Intel 8008, had more power than huge, expensive, early computers like ENIAC. (See Module A for information about ENIAC and also about the development of microprocessors.)

Several components need to be added to a microprocessor to construct a *microcomputer*. First, some type of main memory is needed. Also, an input/output interface is needed to connect the processor with

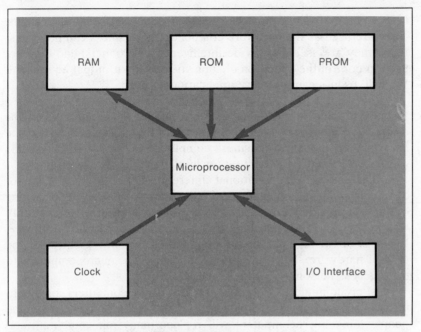

Figure F-1 Components of a Microcomputer

devices like CRTs, printers, disks, and so forth. Finally, a clock is needed to synchronize activity among these components.

Several types of main memory are used in microcomputers. *Random access memory* (RAM) is high speed memory used for storing intermediate results. Data from input devices is read into RAM. The microprocessor obtains the data from RAM and operates on it. Results of the operations are returned to RAM. Finally, data is written from RAM to storage or output devices.

Read only memory (ROM) is also high speed. However, the contents of ROM cannot be changed. Programs like the operating system and compilers are stored into ROM by the computer's manufacturer. These programs are accessed by the microprocessor, but the contents of ROM are never changed.

Programmable read only memory (PROM) is a compromise between RAM and ROM. It is like ROM because the microprocessor cannot change its values. However, it can be changed by other means. The contents of a PROM can be erased by exposing it to ultraviolet light. Then the PROM can be reprogrammed.

Microprocessors are classified by the number of bits (see Module B) that they can process in a single operation. The earliest microprocessors processed 4 bits. Later, *8 bit microprocessors* became available. Today, *16 bit microprocessors* are common.

APPLICATIONS OF MICROCOMPUTERS IN BUSINESS

Microcomputers are commonly used in business for three reasons. They are used as the hardware component of business computer systems; they are used to provide intelligence in products; and they are used to control the operation of sophisticated input/output equipment. We will discuss each of these applications in turn.

Microcomputers as Components of Business Computer Systems

Because of their low cost and high performance (sometimes called *low cost/performance ratio*), microcomputers are increasingly used as the hardware component of business computer systems. When used this way, microcomputers substitute for minicomputers or mainframes.

There is no real functional difference between using a microcomputer and using other types of computers. The concepts regarding business computer systems that you are learning in this class apply whether you use a microcomputer, a minicomputer, or a mainframe. Business computer systems are designed the same, regardless of the type of hardware. Thus, the prime importance of microcomputers to the business person is that they cost less.

Microcomputers have not replaced minicomputers or mainframes. They are not yet as powerful as these others. However, some people think microcomputers will replace many minicomputers and mainframes. Today, though, microcomputers are used only for small applications.

Microcomputers as Components of Products

Microcomputers are having a much greater impact on the design of business products. Here, because of the low cost, microcomputers are being used for new and highly creative applications.

Figure F-2 presents a schematic of a microcomputer application to a gasoline filling station. Sensors in the gas pumps and the gas tanks are connected to the microcomputer. The microcomputer monitors the level of fuel in the tanks and relates it to the amount of gas sold. It can detect tank leakages and theft. Additionally, the station office has a small terminal. Employees use it to input the amount of each purchase. They also input whether the purchase was for cash or credit. The station owners can detect missing cash from the records kept by the microcomputers.

The microcomputer can be connected via a telephone line to a mainframe at the gasoline supplier. It communicates the amount of gas sold. From this, the supplier can determine when to send a truck to replenish the fuel supply. This process is all done automatically.

Home and *personal computers* are another application of microcomputers. Figure F-3 shows a typical home computer system. Computers like this can be used to keep household records, to balance the checkbook, to compute interest payments, and to perform other domestic recordkeeping activities. They have recreational applications

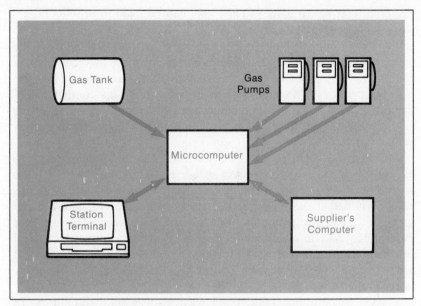

Figure F-2   Microcomputer Application for a Gasoline Station

Figure F-3   People Using a Microcomputer as a Home Computer

like computer-based games. They also can be used to provide home-work drill for school children.

The automotive industry is using microcomputers to improve the operating efficiency of automobile engines. For these applications, the gas pedal is disconnected from the gas line. Instead, as shown in figure F-4, the pedal is connected to a microcomputer. This computer continually senses the engine temperature, the fuel-to-air ratio of air entering the engine, the level of pollutants in exhaust, and other operating characteristics.

When the operator steps on the pedal, the microcomputer computes the best strategy to increase speed. The result may be to increase air pressure, change spark timing, and recycle more exhaust. Perhaps no gas is added at all. The computer monitors the increase in power and speed and makes adjustments as necessary. Microcomputers used for this application can maximize fuel economy while meeting the federal auto pollution constraints. Unfortunately, this application makes it hard for the average person to tune his or her car on a Saturday afternoon.

Even restaurants have found ways to use microcomputers. In figure F-5, a microcomputer is connected to terminals at the head-waiter's station, at three different waiter service stations, at the cashier's station, in the kitchen, and in the bar. Reservations are input at the

Figure F-4 Schematic of Microcomputer Application in an Automobile

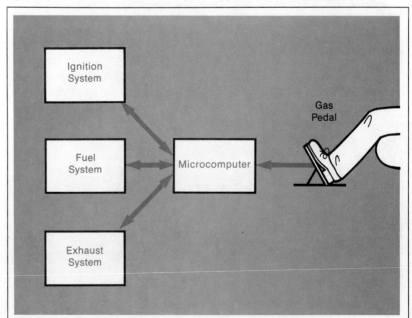

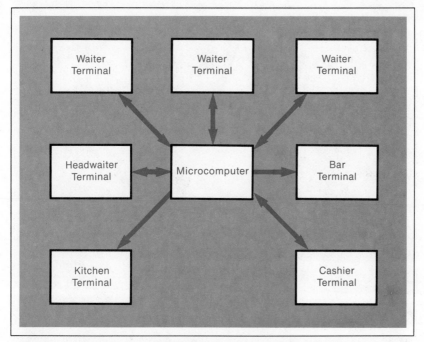

Figure F-5   Schematic of Microcomputer System for a Restaurant

headwaiter's station, and the status of tables is displayed there. When guests are seated, table status is changed from empty to occupied.

The waiters input orders on the service terminals. Orders are displayed in the kitchen for preparation. Also, orders for beverages are displayed in the bar. As the meal progresses, the waiters use the terminals to request preparation of the next course. The display in the kitchen tells the chefs what to prepare. Finally, when the meal is over, the computer calculates the check. The cashier uses a terminal to record the amount and method of payment.

This system improves control over restaurant operations. The status of all tables and meals is known. Better service can be provided by the kitchen. Also, operating records are kept. The managers use this data to purchase food and supplies. They can also determine the fastest and most efficient waiters. Since the checks are prepared by computer, there are no arithmetic errors. Finally, the system results in better control of cash and receipts.

The technology for these applications has been available for 10 years or more. However, until microcomputers were developed, these applications were not cost-justifiable. The amounts saved were not worth the cost of a minicomputer or mainframe. The lower cost of microcomputers makes computer application possible.

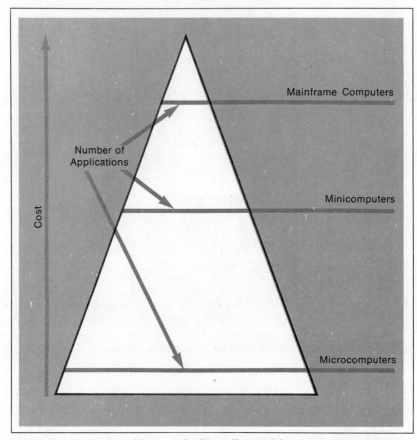

Figure F-6 Expansion of Demand for Three Types of Computer Equipment

Figure F-6 relates the number of business applications to the cost of technology. Using high-cost mainframes, only a small percent of business applications can be computer-based. The number of applications increases dramatically for lower cost minicomputers. For microcomputers the number of applications drastically increases.

Entrepreneurs take note: Since microcomputers are relatively new, only a few of the possible applications have been developed. Many, many opportunities are available. There may not be a market for the intelligent toothbrush, but any of the areas listed in figure F-7 are ripe with microcomputer-based product possibilities.

Microcomputers and Specialized Input/Output Equipment

The availability of cheap microcomputers has enabled hardware manufacturers to build many types of sophisticated input/output equipment. Figure F-8 illustrates a *point-of-sale* (POS) terminal. The cash register has a microcomputer inside it. When the salesperson moves the wand over the sales tag, the microcomputer reads the item

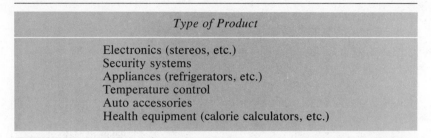

Type of Product
Electronics (stereos, etc.)
Security systems
Appliances (refrigerators, etc.)
Temperature control
Auto accessories
Health equipment (calorie calculators, etc.)

Figure F-7   Home Products with Possibilities for Microcomputer Applications

number. From this it computes the price, taxes, and so forth. Additionally, the microcomputer may remove the item from inventory. Most likely, it does this by communicating with the store's minicomputer or mainframe.

Figure F-8   Microcomputer-Based Point-of-Sale (POS) Terminal

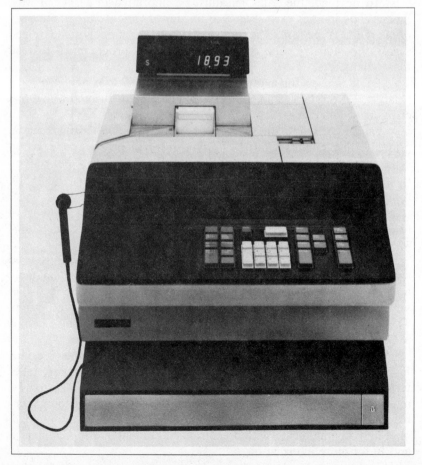

a. Optical Character Recognition (OCR) Type Font

b. Universal Product Code (UPC) Bar Code Example

Figure F-9 Examples of OCR and UPC Equipment

To be read, the sales tag must be imprinted in a special way. Several possibilities exist. Figure F-9*a* shows *optical character recognition* (OCR) type font. The format of these characters is standardized across the industry. The POS terminal can be programmed to read these characters.

OCR is used for many other applications. For example, Master Charge, VISA, and gasoline credit card invoices are printed with OCR characters.

Instead of OCR, the sales tags read by the POS terminal can be printed with bar codes (figure F-9*b*). The universal product code (UPC) is a standardized bar code format. It is used in the grocery and general retailing businesses. Products you have at home are undoubtedly printed with UPC bar codes. (See figure F-10.)

A third type of print that can be read by the POS terminal is magnetic ink. Here, the ink used to print the sales tag is magnetized so that it can be sensed by the POS terminal.

Actually, magnetic ink character recognition (MICR) is used most frequently in the banking industry. Check numbers and amounts are encoded with MICR characters. Perhaps you have noticed that your canceled checks have the check amount typed on the bottom. These characters are magnetized so that they can be read by a bank's MICR equipment. (See figure F-11.)

There are many types of microcomputer-based equipment besides POS terminals and UPC readers. Figure F-12 shows a bank teller terminal. This machine has a microcomputer inside it. When customers make deposits or withdrawals, the microcomputer checks account numbers and passwords, and records transactions. It may be self-contained, or it may communicate with a centralized computer. See Chapters 8 and 10 for more information.

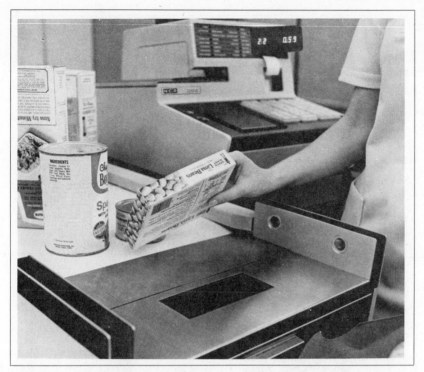

Figure F-10 UPC Sensing Cash Register

Figure F-11 MICR Characters and Their Use

234 89

a. MICR Character Codes

DAVID M. KROENKE   284

MERCER ISLAND, WASHINGTON 98040   1/15 19 80   19-2/1250

Pay to the
order of _Postmaster_ $ 15.00

Fifteen and 00/100 _____ Dollars

FIRSTLINE
SEATTLE-FIRST NATIONAL BANK
MERCER ISLAND BRANCH/MERCER ISLAND 98040   _David M Kroenke_

For _____

⑆125000024⑆ 93178 000⑈ 0 284   ⑈0000001500⑈

Rocky Mountain Bank Note B

⌐ MICR Characters ¬

b. Cancelled Check with MICR Printing

Figure F-12 Customer Using Bank Teller Terminal

QUESTIONS

F.1 What is the difference between a microprocessor and a microcomputer?

F.2 Are business computer systems designed differently when microcomputers are used as hardware?

F.3 Why haven't microcomputers replaced minicomputers and mainframes?

F.4 Discuss three microcomputer applications in business.

F.5 Explain why microcomputers can be used for a larger number of applications than minicomputers.

F.6 What is a POS terminal? Describe how sales tags can be read by POS terminals.

F.7 What is the UPC? What is it used for?

SUMMARY

Microprocessors are CPUs on a silicon chip. A microcomputer is a microprocessor with memory, a clock, and an input/output interface. Microcomputers can substitute for minicomputers and mainframes in business computer systems. They have not yet replaced minicomputers or mainframes for all applications because they are not yet as powerful.

Because of the availability of cheap microcomputers, many new business products and applications are being developed. Additionally, many opportunities exist for entrepreneurs to create new intelligent products.

Microcomputers are also used in specialized input/output equipment. POS terminals and UPC readers are examples. To use this equipment, special type fonts and codes have been developed. Microcomputers are used to add intelligence to computer terminals like CRTs. More microprocessor-based input/output equipment will undoubtedly be announced in the future.

WORD LIST

(in order of appearance in text)

Microprocessor	*POS terminal*
Microcomputer	*OCR*
RAM	*UPC*
ROM	*MICR*
PROM	*Intelligent terminals*
Personal or home computer	

MODULE G

PROGRAMS, HARDWARE, AND THEIR RELATIONSHIP

MODULE H

HOW TO DESIGN SIMPLE COMPUTER PROGRAMS

MODULE I

HOW TO WRITE SIMPLE BASIC PROGRAMS

MODULE J

SURVEY OF COMPUTER PROGRAMMING LANGUAGES

STRUCTURED
COMPUTER PROGRAMMING

STRUCTURED COMPUTER PROGRAMMING

In this part we will consider the purpose and construction of computer programs. In Module G we will discuss what computer programs are and how they relate to hardware. We will include a brief discussion of how programs are translated and controlled by the computer.

Modules H and I are a pair. They should be read in order. Module H discusses techniques for designing simple computer programs. These techniques will help you develop program logic for programs you will write. In Module I, we introduce one common programming language: BASIC. This language is relatively easy to learn; you will be encouraged to write programs with it. For those of you who have a greater interest in programming, a separately bound, alternate version of Module I is available. It introduces the programming language COBOL. Although COBOL is harder to learn than BASIC, it is a more powerful language, and finds much wider use in business. Module J surveys computer programming languages. First, a general orientation to computer programming languages is presented. Then, several popular programming languages are discussed.

As you read this section, try to learn what a program is, how programs are used by computer hardware, what some of the advantages and disadvantages of the different programming languages are, and how programs are constructed. If you accomplish these objectives, you will be in an excellent position to assist and direct computer personnel in the course of your business career.

MODULE G

Programs, Hardware, and Their Relationship

What does computer hardware do with these people's programs?

PURPOSE OF
COMPUTER PROGRAMS

MACHINE LANGUAGE
AND PROGRAM
TRANSLATION

THE OPERATING SYSTEM

In this module we will discuss what computer programs are, and how they relate to computer hardware. We will see how programs reside in the computer's main memory, and how they are translated. Also, we will discuss the functions of the computer's operating system (which is itself a set of computer programs), and show how the operating system manages and assists application programs.

PURPOSE OF COMPUTER PROGRAMS

Suppose you own a car rental agency. You charge your customers $25.00 for each day they rent a car, and 20¢ for each mile they drive. You decide that your clerks are making too many errors, and that the manual computation of customer bills takes too long. You decide to get a computer to compute bills automatically.

You approach a group of computer specialists and ask them to build a system to compute your bills. Suppose there is no such thing as a computer program. In this case, the computer people will build a *special purpose electronic machine* to compute your bills. You will input the number of days of rental and the number of miles driven, and the machine will output the customer charge. This operation is shown in figure G-1.

Now, before they build this machine, the computer people will ask you for the maximum number of miles and days. Suppose you say 500 miles and 10 days. Given this information, they will then build the electronic equivalent of the table shown in figure G-2. The table will have 5000 entries, one for each combination of miles and days. The machine will have transistors and resistors and other electronic gadgetry that cause it to find the right entry for each combination of days and miles.

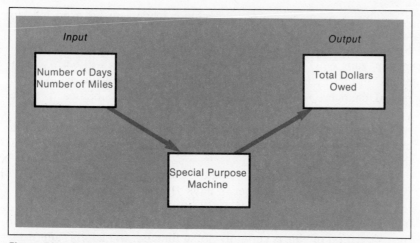

Figure G-1   Computing Rental Charges Using Special Purpose Machine

Figure G-2   Table Showing Charges for Combinations of Days and Miles

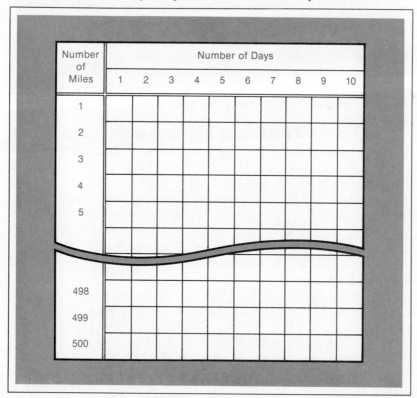

This is a special purpose machine; when you have no bills to compute, the machine will be idle. This is a waste of the resource. Further, you may not want to have a single-function machine cluttering up your workspace. So, although this machine will satisfy your needs (in fact many such machines exist—in microwave ovens, cars, record changers, etc.), there are other, better possibilities to solve your problem.

Suppose that instead of acquiring a special purpose machine you buy a calculator that adds and multiplies. You then give your employees the formula:

Total due = \$25 × Number of days + \$.20 × Number of miles

You show them how to use the calculator. This approach works, but the calculation of bills is certainly not automatic. In fact, this approach is probably not an improvement over the manual process.

Suppose you buy a calculator that has a *memory* that can hold the sequence of steps necessary to compute a bill. Suppose also that this calculator performs these steps whenever you request it to. In this case, you have an automatic machine like the one in figure G-1, but it is not a special purpose machine. You can load different sequences of steps into the machine depending on what you want to do.

A sequence of steps, or instructions, is called a *program*. Calculators that can execute instructions held in their memories are called *computers*. (Actually, computers are more than this, but for our purposes, think of them as the same.) To see how this computer is different from the special purpose machine, examine the memory shown in figure G-3.

First, note that this memory is divided into boxes or cells. Each box has a numerical address. The boxes can hold instructions or data. In figure G-3, the boxes in the top of memory hold instructions; those at the bottom hold data; and those in the middle are unused.

The contents of these boxes are groups of binary digits or *bits*. On most computers, the boxes are called *bytes*. Instructions and data can occupy one or more bytes. In figure G-3, the first two instructions each take 3 bytes, and the other instructions each take 2 bytes. The first instruction starts in byte 1, the next in byte 4, the next in byte 6, and so forth.

Bytes 83 through 96 hold data. In this example, each data item takes 2 bytes. This statement is not always true; some data items take more and some take less. Working backwards (for convenience), bytes 95,96 hold the constant 25. Bytes 93,94 hold the constant .20. Bytes 91,92 will hold the number of days rented, and bytes 89,90 will hold the number of miles driven. Bytes 87,88 and 85,86 will hold two temporary values. Finally, bytes 83,84 will hold the amount that is computed.

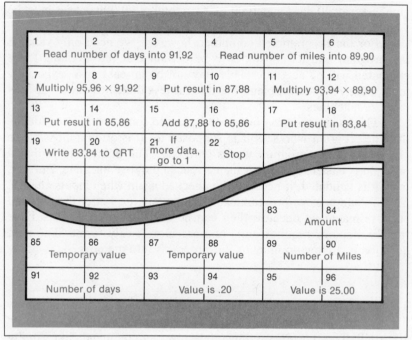

Figure G-3 Example of Memory with Instructions and Data

Now, to compute a customer bill the computer will begin executing the instructions starting at byte 1. It will execute the instructions in sequence. Note that the next to last instruction is conditional. If there is more data, the computer will go to byte 1; otherwise it will stop.

Now you may ask, why is this an improvement over the special purpose machine in figure G-1? There are three reasons. First, the contents of the computer's memory can be changed. Another program can be read into the computer's memory and the computer will then solve a different problem. Thus, the computer can be used for many different purposes.

Second, the memory requirement for the general purpose computer, program, and data is much smaller than that for the special purpose machine. The table in figure G-2 has 5000 entries. Even so, it only allows for cars driven no more than 10 days or 500 miles. The program and data in figure G-3 occupy much less space, and they are far more general. The program is not limited to cars driven no more than 10 days or 500 miles.

The third reason the program and general purpose computer are preferred over the special purpose machine concerns testing. To verify the accuracy of the special purpose computer, 5000 different entries must be validated. If the machine is built to allow more realistic numbers, say 90 days and 1000 miles, a total of 90,000 entries must be validated!

For the programmed computer, however, we need only validate the program and its constants to be certain that the amounts to be computed will be accurate. This may not be an easy task, especially for a more realistic problem, but it is far less difficult than for special purpose machines.

The term *validation* means to ensure to some level of confidence that the program works as it is supposed to. It is often impossible to *guarantee* that a program works correctly. The point here is that a program is easier to validate than a special purpose machine. Further, once it is validated, it need not be checked again when inputs change.

To summarize, programmable computers are better than special purpose machines because they can be used for several tasks, have smaller memory requirements, and are more easily tested. The next question is, "How do humans put programs into memory?"

MACHINE LANGUAGE AND PROGRAM TRANSLATION

The boxes in figure G-3 represent bytes that hold groups of binary digits. Thus, the content of a box is a sequence of 0's and 1's, say, 10010110. This presents a difficulty. How can commands like "multiply the contents of location 95,96 by the contents of location 91,92" be represented by 0's and 1's?

The answer is that instructions are represented by codes. Figure G-4 shows a few *binary instruction codes* for the IBM System 370 family of computers. Multiply is represented by the code 10011100, divide is represented by the code 10011101, and so on. The addresses of the locations containing the numbers to be multiplied or divided are also represented in binary format. We need not consider that here.

In the early days of computing, programmers had to memorize binary instruction codes. Thus, someone might spend an hour or two to produce the following program:

```
11001000100011111010101010101110101011101000111110100101010001 0101
01010010101011110010101010101010000000101111011110001110111011111 0111
01010101110010010010001011111010011100101010100010101010101111110 101
01000101010100101111110001010101100001110010100111100100011100100 010
01010111001010101010100100101010101111101011010001011101101001111 101
```

Writing such gibberish might be fun for a few hours, but clearly it is no way to spend a lifetime. Also, programs produced by this method often had errors, and the errors were very hard to find and fix. Consequently, people looked for a better way to produce programs.

Since these people were computer professionals, it was natural that they look to the computer for a solution to the problem. Even-

Instruction	Binary Code
Add	10011010
Divide	10011101
Multiply	10011100
Subtract	10011011
Move	10010010

Figure G-4 Examples of Binary Instruction Codes for IBM Computers

tually they developed what is known today as a *high-level language*. This is an English-like language in which programmers can express commands. This language is then translated into machine language (binary form) by the computer.

For example, a programmer might write a program like:

    Input A, B
    Let C = A + B
    Print C

These English-like statements are translated into a sequence of 0's and 1's that cause the computer to read two numbers, add them together, and print the result.

Figure G-5 illustrates the translation process. The English-like statements that are produced by humans are called *source code*. These statements are input to a translation program called a *compiler*. A binary (0's and 1's) version of the program is produced. This binary version is called *object code*.

There are many programming languages and dialects of programming languages. Each language or dialect has its own compiler. Programs written in BASIC use one compiler. Programs written in COBOL use another.

The compiler is a program. It is *not* a piece of hardware or a special machine. It is a program that resides in main memory and it accepts other programs as its data. As a program, it was written by someone. Unless it was written in binary, it, too, had to be *compiled* or *translated*.

In figure G-5 the object code generated by the compiler is stored on a file (a disk is shown here). Even though it has been translated, it may not be ready for execution. The program may contain references to other programs. For example, a programmer may write an application program that requires the current time of day to be printed on a report. Although the programmer can write his or her own routine to determine the time, there is probably a routine that determines the time on a *system library*. When the programmer needs the time routine,

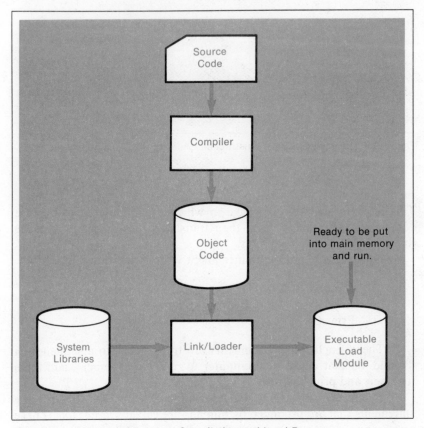

Figure G-5 Example of Program Compilation and Load Process

he or she will consult the library documentation to determine the name of such a routine. Suppose the name of this routine is TIME and it is used as follows:

$$X = TIME$$

This statement sets the variable X to the current time of day.

Now, when the application program is translated, the compiler will recognize TIME as the name of an external routine. Since the compiler does not have the source code of the TIME routine, it cannot translate it. Instead, the compiler inserts a note into the object code indicating that TIME is an external reference. This instruction means that the TIME routine should be taken from a library.

Now, before the application program object code can be executed, the object code of TIME must be appended to it. This action is done by a program variously called a *link/loader, linkage editor,* or some other name. The link/loader searches the libraries for the TIME routine as well as for any other external programs. These programs are then appended to the object code. The output of this process is an *executable load module*. This module is ready to be read into main memory and executed.

If the program is to be used over and over again, the executable load module is saved. This way, the program need not be compiled and link/loaded every time it is run. For example, a weekly payroll program is not compiled each week. Instead, its load module is saved from week to week. It is only compiled when changes are made to the program.

Thus, every program has three versions or formats. It is written by a human in *source form*, it is compiled (translated) into *object form*, and it is merged with other routines to form an *executable load module*.

Unfortunately, our story is not yet complete. Once the program is placed in main memory and begins execution, it may need special services like reading data from disks or tapes. Also, computers that are used for business data processing are not as simple as the computer shown in figure G-3. Usually, more than one program is running at a time, which requires that the activities of several programs must be coordinated. These functions are managed by a set of programs called the *operating system*.

The operating system is a program that controls the computer's resources. It normally is provided by the computer's manufacturer. The operating system allocates main memory and CPU time to other computer programs. It also coordinates activity between the CPU and peripheral devices such as tape and disk units.

Since the operating system is a set of programs, it is written in a source language by humans and then translated into machine code. Most operating systems are large and complex; they contain thousands or even millions of instructions.

The operating system has three main functions: job, task, and data management. The goal of *job management* is to control the flow of work through the computer. As jobs are submitted at batch terminals, or as requests for action are received from interactive terminals, they are saved on a file known as the *input queue*. (See figure G-6.) As space becomes available in main memory, jobs or transactions are selected from the queue and processed.

The operating system uses a *scheduling algorithm* to select the next job. This algorithm considers factors such as how much space is available in main memory, what devices are available, how much space each waiting job will need, what files each will need, how long each has been waiting, and so forth. The job management portion of the operating system selects the next job, brings it into main memory, and turns it over to task management.

THE OPERATING SYSTEM

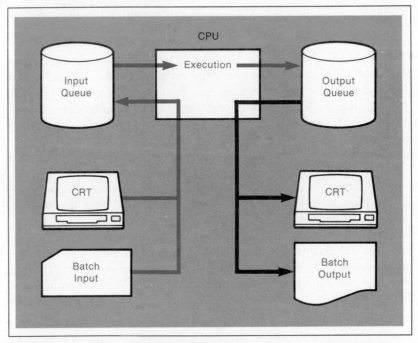

Figure G-6   Program Input/Execution/Output

As shown in figure G-6, once the job is completed, its output is placed on another queue. Job management controls this queue, schedules outputs to the printers, and otherwise dispatches the job outputs.

While the job is executing, it is controlled by the other two portions of the operating system. *Task management* allocates the CPU by assigning main memory and scheduling the execution of programs. This is a complex process because more than one job can be in execution at a time.

For example, figure G-7 shows main memory when four application programs are in execution. Each of the application programs and the operating system occupy main memory space. As the application programs run, the amount of space they need may change. If this occurs, task management may adjust the space boundaries between jobs. When a job terminates, the space it occupied becomes unused, and the next job selected by job management is brought into the available space.

Most computers can only execute one program at a time. Therefore, when four programs are in main memory, the part of the CPU that executes instructions (called the arithmetic and logic unit, or ALU) must shift its attention from one program to another.

This process is called *time slicing*. The ALU devotes a segment of time (say 50 milliseconds or 0.050 second) to application program

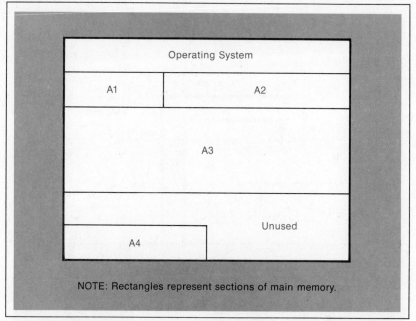

Figure G-7 Main Memory with Operating System and Four Application Programs

1; then a segment of time to application 2; then to application 3; and then to 4. It repeats this sequence until the applications are finished.

Because this process occurs so fast, it appears to humans that the applications are being processed simultaneously. Actually, they are not. True simultaneous processing requires two ALUs. Instead, applications processed by time slicing are said to be running *concurrently*.

The third responsibility of the operating system is called *data management*. When an application programmer wants to input or output data, he or she does not actually code all of the instructions necessary to transfer the data to or from a file. Instead, he or she codes a READ, WRITE, or other I/O command. This command is translated by the compiler into a request to the data management portion of the operating system.

A typical read from a disk is shown in figure G-8. Data management receives the read request, and sends a signal to a device known as a *channel* to obtain the data. The channel is actually a small, separate computer that transfers data between devices and main memory. When the channel receives the command, it accesses the disk unit and causes the data to be read. The channel then places the data in main memory and signals the operating system that the I/O is complete. Data management routines then place the data requested by the user into the application program memory space.

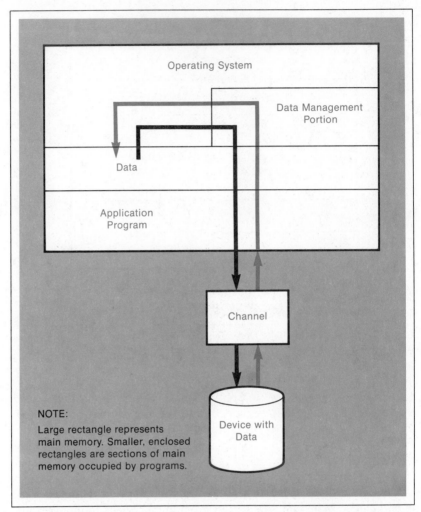

NOTE:

Large rectangle represents main memory. Smaller, enclosed rectangles are sections of main memory occupied by programs.

Figure G-8 Role of Channel and Data Management Portion of Operating System

In general, then, the data management portion of the operating system provides data access services to application programs. These services include sequential processing like that in Chapter 5 and direct access processing as described in Chapter 6. Data management also maintains indexes or catalogs to data libraries. It provides security by controlling data access. It allows such access only to authorized programs and users.

The operating system is, in a sense, the supervisor of the application programs. It starts and stops them; it allocates resources to them; and it provides data to them on demand. In fact, sometimes the term *supervisor* or *executive system* is used instead of operating system.

In this module we have introduced the concept of a computer program. **SUMMARY**
We have seen that programs are sequences of instructions that can be
stored in the main memory of the computer and executed by the computer's ALU. Programs are used to tailor general purpose computers
to solve specific problems. Without programs, there would have to be
a separate machine for each problem. Also, these machines would be
harder to test than general purpose computers with programs.

Main memory is divided into boxes with addresses called bytes.
Bytes can contain instructions and data. Instructions and data can
vary in length; each instruction or data item can occupy from one to
many bytes.

Programs are written in source code, translated into object code
by a compiler, and then formed into executable load modules by the
link/loader. A compiler is a program that translates other programs.
It is not a piece of hardware or a special machine. There is a separate
compiler or compilers for each computer language.

The operating system is a set of programs that controls use of the
computer. These large and complex programs control the computer's
resources and manage computer jobs. It has three major parts: job
management, task management, and data management. Job management starts and stops jobs and allocates complete resources. Task
management supervises jobs in execution and allocates the CPU. Data
management provides data access services to application programs.
Synonyms for the operating system are supervisor and executive
system.

G.1 Explain the purpose of a computer program. Describe three   **QUESTIONS**
     advantages of programmable computers over special pur-
     pose computers.

G.2 Explain the term *byte*. Can an instruction occupy more than
     one byte? Can data occupy more than one byte?

G.3 What is the purpose of a compiler? Is the compiler a
     machine? A person? What is it?

G.4 Explain the purpose of a link/loader. How does it integrate
     programs from a system library with a compiled program?

G.5 Name and explain the three functions of an operating
     system.

G.6 What is a scheduling algorithm?

G.7 What role does a channel have in the input and output of
     data?

WORD LIST

(in order of appearance in text)

Special purpose machine

Memory

Program

Bit

Byte

Program validation

Binary instruction code

High-level language

Source code

Object code

System library

Link/loader

Linkage editor

Executable load module

Operating system

Job management

Task management

Arithmetic and logic unit (ALU)

Time slicing

Concurrent execution

Data management

Channel

Supervisor

QUESTIONS TO CHALLENGE YOUR THINKING

A. If the compiler is a program, what compiles the compiler?

B. Since microcomputers are becoming so inexpensive, the architecture of computers may change. In this module, the ALU is assumed to be one unit. It could be possible to have multiple microprocessors acting as ALUs. For such a machine, how might the processing in figure G-7 change? How would time slicing change?

MODULE H

How to Design Simple Computer Programs

Student using flowcharts and pseudocode to design a simple program

THE INPUT/PROCESS/OUTPUT CYCLE

GENERAL STRATEGY FOR DESIGNING SIMPLE PROGRAMS

ADDING MORE LOGIC— INITIATION AND TERMINATION

USING PSEUDOCODE TO SPECIFY PROGRAM LOGIC

If you are like many students, you do not have a clear idea of how to design and write a computer program. You have a vague notion of what a program is, but when you sit down to write one, you don't know where to start. Hopefully, you will know how to proceed after you read this module.

There are two phases to writing a simple program (for real-world problems there are more than two—see Part 2). The phases are (1) design and (2) programming and test. During design, you figure out a logical sequence of steps to solve the problem. You determine the *algorithm*. During programming, you write statements conforming to this design. Then you test the program.

Many beginners try to omit the design phase. They pick up a pencil or sit down at a programming terminal with no idea how to solve the problem. *This is a big mistake*. Sure, they can solve simple problems this way, but they will have difficulty with larger problems. Also, experience has shown that the total time to develop a fully tested program is less if a thorough design is made. Therefore, you are strongly encouraged to design before you try to program.

This module teaches you how to design simple programs. First, we will discuss a logical pattern common to most computer programs. Then, a general strategy will be given for designing programs. Next, three examples to illustrate the technique will be shown. Finally, a few hints on how to write good flowcharts and pseudocode are presented. In the next module (I) you will learn how to transform these designs into BASIC language programs.

First of all, what is a computer program? It is a sequence of steps, or instructions, for the computer to execute in order to solve a particular problem. Most computers are general purpose machines. They can add, subtract, and do other arithmetic. They can also make simple decisions. However, they do not know how to solve specific problems like order entry or payroll. To solve a specific problem, they must be given detailed instructions. These instructions are the program.

Most computer programs follow a pattern. Once you understand this pattern, it will be easy to see how to develop the logic for programs. To understand the pattern, think about how you would solve a business problem like payroll. How would you produce the payroll for 10 people?

First, you would gather the data, say hours worked and pay rate, for one of the employees. Then, you would compute the amount to pay, and finally, you would write the check. You would perform these steps for each employee until the paychecks for all 10 had been written.

Notice the pattern in your work. You first gather data (input), then you compute the pay (process), and then you write the check (output). After you have done this for one employee, you cycle back and repeat the process for another employee. You repeat these steps until all the input has been processed.

This pattern occurs so frequently in business computing, it has been given a special name: the *input/process/output cycle*. Nearly all business computer programs conform to this pattern. First, they input data, then they process it, and then they produce output. After this, they repeat the process. If, for example, there are 150,000 employees on the payroll, the payroll program will repeat these three steps 150,000 times.

Think about this cycle. Input, process, output, repeat; input, process, output, repeat. Whenever you start to design a computer program, look for this pattern. If you start to get confused or lost, think about this cycle. You want to input, process, output, and repeat as long as there is input data.

**THE INPUT/
PROCESS/
OUTPUT CYCLE**

Over the years, many programmers have learned a trick. They initially approach a program design problem backwards. They start with the output! The first thing an experienced programmer does is to determine what a program is supposed to produce. For example, suppose we are given the following programming problem:

Design a program to compare the performance of pairs of salespeople. The program should read the names of two salespeople and the amount each has sold in the last month. Then it should print the name of the

**GENERAL STRATEGY
FOR DESIGNING
SIMPLE PROGRAMS**

person selling the larger amount. If they have sold the same amount, print the words "TIE BETWEEN" and both of their names. Repeat the process for the next pair of sales people until all data has been processed.

Now, what is the output of this program supposed to be? It should be one of two messages:

THE PERSON WHO SOLD MORE IS_____

TIE BETWEEN_____AND_____

We now know exactly what the program is to produce. The next step that professional programmers take is to identify the input. What data is available? It's like cooking. Having decided to make an apple pie, what ingredients do we need to make it?

What are the inputs in our example? There are two names and two amounts. For discussion purposes, let's call the first salesperson N1, and the second salesperson N2. Also, let's call the amount for the first salesperson A1, and the amount for the second, A2.

These abbreviations, N1, N2, A1, and A2 are *program variables*. They are called *variables* because their values vary. At one point, the variable N1 can have the value MARY JONES. At another point, it can have the value FRED SMITH. In our program, the variables will have different values each time we go through the input/process/output cycle.

So far, we have identified two steps that are followed by professional programmers. First, they identify the outputs of the program, and then they determine the inputs. The third and final step is to determine the program logic, or how the inputs can be used to produce the outputs.

Think again about cooking. The program logic is equivalent to the directions in a recipe. We know the outputs (pie) and the inputs (ingredients). We now must determine a method of producing the outputs.

There are two common ways of expressing program logic. One is called *flowcharting*, and the other is called *pseudocode*. Both techniques can be effectively used. Programming professionals do not agree which is the better technique. We will look at both.

Figure H-1 shows a flowchart for the program logic in our example. Four symbols are shown. The ⬭ is used for initiation and termination only. The parallelogram ▱ is used to represent either input or output processing. A rectangle ▮ is used to represent operations. Finally, a diamond ◇ is used to represent decisions or questions.

Examine figure H-1. As promised, it has the input/process/output structure. First, we input the data about the two salespeople. The

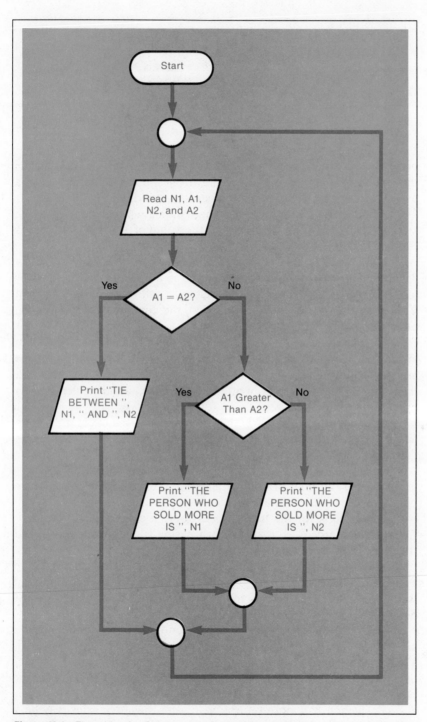

Figure H-1 Flowchart for Salesperson Comparison Problem

MARY JONES	10348	FRED SMITH	9345
JACK STALLONE	8745	BILL NICHOLS	11234
TIM BROWN	23891	GWEN APPLE	24671
SALLY DUNCAN	12678	BARRY GREEN	12678

Figure H-2 Sample Data for Sales Comparison Problem

program tells the computer to read N1, A1, N2, and A2. This means the computer is to obtain these values from a punched card or from a user at a terminal, or from some other input medium.

Assume the computer reads the data shown in figure H-2. The value of N1 is MARY JONES and the value of A1 is 10,348. N2 is FRED SMITH and A2 is 9,345.

Now, what is to be done with this data? The next operation is a decision instruction. Inside the diamond is a question. If the answer to this question is yes, the computer is to follow the arrow labeled Yes. If the answer to the question is no, the computer is to follow the other arrow labeled No.

Decisions are always represented in this way. There is a question inside the diamond, and the yes and no answers are written on the arrows leading out of the diamond. In figure H-1, if A1 equals A2, then the TIE message is written. Otherwise, another decision is executed.

This next question is whether A1 is greater than A2. If so, then name N1 is written to the report. Otherwise, name N2 is written as the person with greater sales.

Note all the arrows ultimately point to the bottom of the flowchart. Here, the flow of control goes back to the read operation to obtain the next set of data.

Again, look for the input/process/output cycle in this flowchart. Data is read, processed (here the processing is decision-making), and then messages are output. The cycle is then repeated.

Have you noticed something strange about the flowchart in figure H-1? It has no end. The process never terminates. Clearly, we do not want to continue feeding data to this program until doomsday. We must determine a way to cause the computer to stop.

We want the computer to stop executing this program when we are out of data, that is, after the last two salespeople are processed. There are several ways to do this. For one, we can input a special data item at the end of the input to signal end of data. Thus, we might put a negative amount sold in A1 to represent the end of data. However, if a salesperson has more returns than sales, negative sales may be a valid data item. Therefore, this may not be the best approach.

Another possibility is to put a special label in the N1 name position. Thus, when we read a record with name equal to END-OF-DATA, we can cause the program to terminate. This possibility is shown in figure H-3.

A different approach is to allow the computer to determine when we are out of data. Using this approach, after each read, we ask the computer's operating system if we are out of data. If not, we process. When the computer signals end of data, we stop. This approach is often used. The only difficulty is that each computer signals end of data in a different way, and we may have to change our program to make it run on another computer.

Now, let's review the general strategy. There are three steps. First, determine what the outputs of the program will be. A good technique is to write (by hand) sample lines of output. This approach will help you to be sure you understand what the program is to do. Second, determine what the inputs to the program will be. What data items will be available to produce the desired outputs? Third, specify the program logic. So far, we have shown how to perform this step using flowcharts. Before going any further, you should try out this sequence. Consider the following problem:

> Design a program to read a customer name and total purchases for one month. If the total purchases is equal to zero, print the customer name and a message stating the customer had no orders. Otherwise, print the customer name and the amount of the orders. Repeat the process for the next customer. Stop when END-OF-DATA is read.

Perform the three problem-solving steps for this problem before you go on.

Are you cheating? Did you perform the three steps? Your brain will turn to jelly if you go on without performing the three steps.

How did you do? What are the outputs? There should be either of two messages appearing something like the following:

```
CUSTOMER_____HAD NO ORDERS.

CUSTOMER_____ORDERED_____THIS MONTH.
```

What are the inputs? Two variables. One is customer name, which we will call C, and the other is amount ordered, which we will call A.

What is the program logic? Figure H-4 shows one potential solution to this problem. Note that it has the input/process/output cycle structure.

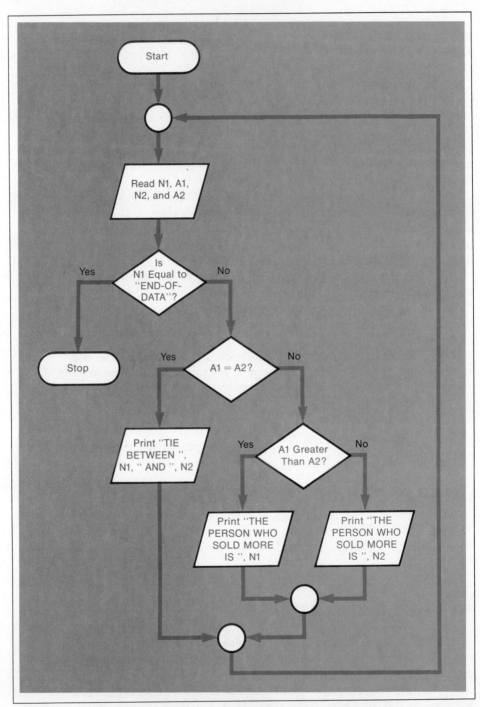

Figure H-3 Terminating Flowchart for Salesperson Comparison Problem

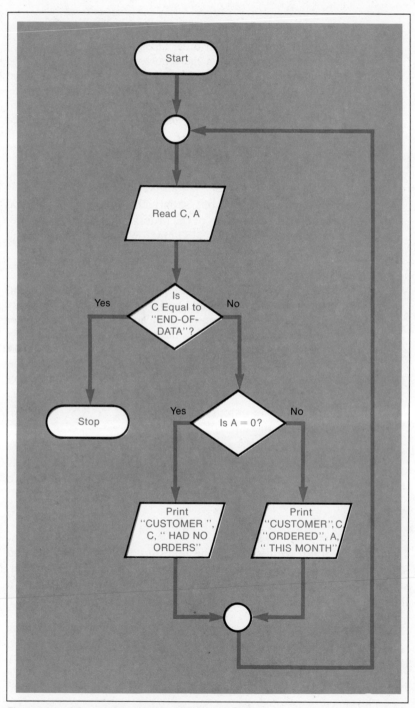

Figure H-4 Flowchart for Customer Order Problem

EXERCISES

H.1 Consider the following problem:

A program sums customer order amounts. The program reads a record having customer name followed by three amounts. The amounts are added together. Then the name of the customer and the sum of the orders are printed. After a customer record is processed, the program repeats for the next customer's record. End of data is signaled by a −9999 in the first amount ordered field.

a. What is the output from this program?

b. What is the input?

c. Develop a flowchart of the program logic.

H.2 Repeat exercise H.1 but satisfy the following additional requirement: If the sum of the orders is greater than 10,000, print the words "BIG CUSTOMER" after the sum of the orders. Specify the outputs, inputs, and flowchart.

H.3 Consider this problem:

A program computes employee pay. It reads a record having employee name, pay rate, and hours worked. It calculates gross pay (rate times hours). Employees are not paid extra for overtime. The program prints the name of the employee and his or her gross pay. If the number of hours worked is zero, the message "DID NOT WORK" is printed. The program repeats to process the next employee record. End of file is signaled by a −99 in the pay rate field.

a. What are the outputs?

b. What are the inputs?

c. Develop the program flowchart.

H.4 Repeat exercise H.3 but assume that the employee gets time and a half pay for all hours in excess of 40. What are the inputs, outputs, and the flowchart?

ADDING MORE LOGIC – INITIATION AND TERMINATION

In the last section, we discussed the input/process/output cycle, and showed how it is fundamental to most business programs. However, some business problems require an extension to this pattern. To illustrate this extension, consider the following problem:

A company maintains a computer file of employee records having employee number, employee name, age, pay rate, and total pay-to-date. They want to print the total pay-to-date for each employee. Also, they want a report that shows the total number of employees, their average age, their average pay rate, and the sum of the pay-to-date for all employees.

If you were to write a program to produce such a report, how would you proceed? That's right. You would identify the outputs, then the inputs, and then specify the program logic. Proceeding in this way, we have:

Outputs

The following message should be written for each employee:

EMPLOYEE_____HAS BEEN PAID $XXXXXX.XX.

Also, at the end of the report, the following messages should be output:

THERE ARE XXXX EMPLOYEES IN THIS COMPANY.

THE AVERAGE AGE OF THE EMPLOYEES IS XX.X YEARS.

THE AVERAGE PAY RATE IS $XX.XX PER HOUR.

THE TOTAL PAYROLL SO FAR THIS YEAR IS $XXXXXXX.XX.

Inputs

The program will need to read values for the following variables from the data records:

> NAME, the name of an employee
> AGE, the age of an employee
> PAY-RATE, the pay rate of an employee
> EMP-PAY, the total pay-to-date for an employee

Now to specify the program logic, we need to make a flowchart or pseudocode (we will discuss pseudocode soon). However, before we do that, do we know how to get averages? To get the average of 10 numbers, we sum them and divide by 10. To get the average pay rate, we need to sum the pay rates and divide by the number of employees. This operation presents some questions: How do we know the number of employees? How do we sum the pay rates?

Suppose we create two more program variables. One we will call NEMP for the number of employees. The other we will call TPR for total pay rates. Now, every time we read an employee record, we will execute the following statements:

> ADD 1 TO NEMP.
> ADD PAY-RATE TO TPR.

Since we are adding to the variables every time we read an employee record, when we are finished, NEMP will have the total number of employees and TPR will have the total pay rates. To get the average pay rate, we will divide TPR by NEMP.

Now, we have created a problem. What was the beginning value of NEMP? Before we read the first employee record, what was NEMP equal to? If you are like most students, you have assumed NEMP was zero. After all, when you count something, you always start your count value at zero.

Unfortunately, the computer is not that smart. NEMP is equal to whatever happens to be in the main memory location assigned to NEMP. It might be zero, but it might be −345673822 or 1819.786540 or even the characters YES. Therefore, before we use the variables NEMP or TPR, we must *initialize* them to zero.

This operation is easy enough to do—we just insert statements like,

> SET NEMP TO 0.
> SET TPR TO 0.

There is a problem, however. Where do we put these statements in our program design? So far, we have said every program has the pattern: input, process, output, repeat. Now, if we put these initializing statements in the *process* part of this pattern, the variables will be reset to zero every time we repeat. We have to change our pattern.

The more complete pattern for business computer programs looks like this:

> INITIALIZE ACTIVITY.
> INPUT, PROCESS, OUTPUT, REPEAT.
> TERMINATE ACTIVITY.

Note we have inserted a step before we begin the input/process/output cycle, and we have inserted a step after this cycle. In the initialize step, we will give starting values to all the variables that need them. In the termination step, we will perform any activity that needs to be done after all the inputs have been processed.

What termination activity do we have in this problem? We are supposed to print the number of employees, their average age, their average pay rate, and the total pay-to-date. We cannot print these items in the input/process/output cycle because we must wait until all employees have been processed. Therefore, we will do it in the termination step.

Figure H-5 shows a flowchart for this program logic. The initiation, input/process/output, and termination sections of this flowchart are boxed in the figure. The arrow on the righthand side of the flowchart represents the repeat portion of the input/process/output cycle.

Figure H-5 illustrates how the initiation and termination portions fit in the program. The initiation portion is performed once in the beginning. The termination is performed once at the end. In between, data is input, processed, and output. This cycle is repeated over and

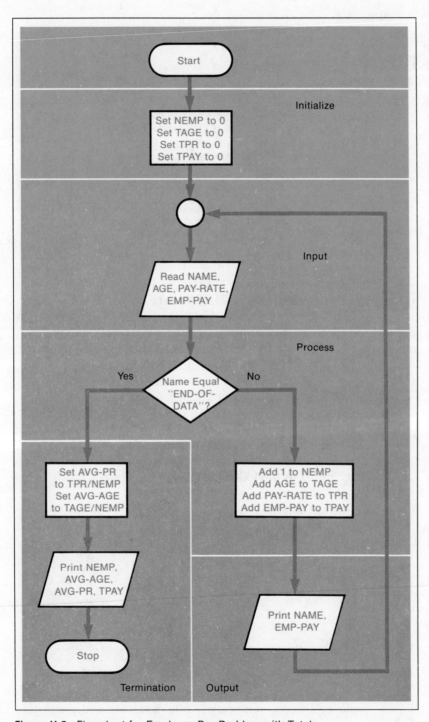

Figure H-5 Flowchart for Employee Pay Problem with Totals

Step	Action
1	Identify the outputs.
2	Identify the inputs.
3	Specify the program logic:
	a. Determine whatever equations, variables, etc., are required to transform the inputs into the outputs.
	b. Develop a flowchart of the input/process/output cycle.
	c. Add necessary initialization activities prior to beginning the input/process/output cycle.
	d. Add termination activities necessary to perform after all the data is processed.

Figure H-6 Summary of Steps to Develop Program Logic

over until the data is exhausted. This fact is detected in figure H-5 by reading the characters END-OF-DATA in the name field of a record.

This discussion is summarized in the sequence of steps shown in figure H-6. Hopefully, this sequence will help you to develop program logic. You might want to try that sequence on the following problems.

EXERCISES

H.5 Suppose a company keeps records of employee names, numbers, hourly pay rates, and numbers of hours worked. Develop the logic of a program that will compute gross pay, assuming no special payment for overtime. Compute taxes according to the following table:

If Pay Is Greater Than or Equal to:	But Less Than:	Then Taxes Are:
$ 0.00	$ 5,000.00	15%
5,000.00	10,000.00	$750 + 20% of the amount exceeding $5,000.00
10,000.00 or greater		$1,750 + 30% of the amount exceeding $10,000.00.

For each employee, the program should print the employee's name, number, pay rate, hours worked, gross pay, and taxes. Also, the company wants to know the total number of hours worked, the total gross pay, and the total taxes for all employees. The report should also show the average tax per employee.

Follow the steps in figure H-6 and show all your work.

H.6 Assume a company keeps computer records of sales. On each record are the customer number, customer name, salesperson number, salesperson name, and dollar amount of the sale. The records are ordered by customer number; all the records for a given customer are contiguous (next to each other).

The company wants a report that lists the name of each customer and the amount of each purchase. Also, the company wants to know the total number of sales, the number of customers, the total of all the sales, and the average sales amount.

Follow the steps in figure H-6 and show all your work.

In Chapter 2 and elsewhere in this book, we have used pseudocode to specify logic. In this section we will show how you can use it to portray program designs.

The term *pseudocode* means false code. This name is appropriate because pseudocode looks like a programming language, but it isn't. Pseudocode statements are simpler. They are free-form English. They do not conform to the strict punctuation rules of a programming language.

As illustrated in Chapter 2, to use pseudocode you break up the program into parts called *procedures* or *modules*. Each procedure or module will be a major step in the program logic. Every procedure is given a name. Within a procedure there are three types of instructions. Imperative statements tell the computer to do something like ADD 1 TO NEMP. These instructions are executed in sequence.

A second type is the IF-THEN-ELSE instruction. It is used to portray a decision. The form is:

USING PSEUDOCODE TO SPECIFY PROGRAM LOGIC

```
IF condition
    THEN group-1 of statements
    ELSE group-2 of statements
END-IF
```

If the condition is true, then the group-1 statements are executed. Otherwise, the group-2 statements are executed. For example, in the statement:

```
IF A IS LESS THAN B
    THEN ADD 1 TO B
            SUBTRACT 2 FROM C
    ELSE ADD 1 TO A
END-IF
```

If A is less than B, then 1 is added to B and 2 is subtracted from C. If A is equal to or greater than B, then 1 is added to A.

Sometimes there is nothing to do if the condition is not met. In this case, the IF structure appears as follows:

```
IF condition
    THEN group of statements
END-IF
```

There is no ELSE and there are no statements to execute if the condition is not true. This is sometimes called a *null ELSE*.

The final type of pseudocode statement is the DO statement, which is used for iteration. There are two forms. The first is the DOWHILE statement.

```
DOWHILE A IS LESS THAN B
    ADD 1 TO A
    SUBTRACT 1 FROM B
    ADD 1 TO COUNT
END-DO
```

Figure H-7 shows a flowchart of the logic of this DOWHILE. In this example, the three statements in the DO loop are executed as long as A is less than B. When A becomes equal to or greater than B, the next instruction after the DO loop will be executed. If A is less than B the first time, these statements will be skipped and never executed.

The DOUNTIL structure is similar to DOWHILE except that the group of statements in the loop is always executed at least once. Consider the statements:

```
DOUNTIL A IS EQUAL TO OR GREATER THAN B
    ADD 1 TO A
    SUBTRACT 1 FROM B
    ADD 1 TO COUNT
END-DO
```

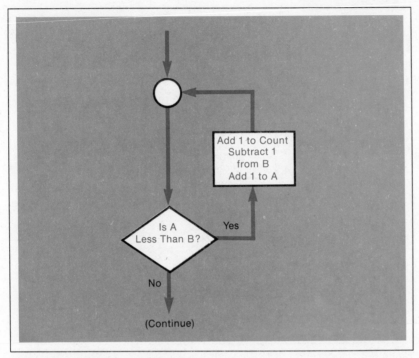

Figure H-7 Flowchart of DOWHILE Logic

As shown in figure H-8, these statements operate the same as the DOWHILE with one exception. The three statements in the DO loop will always be executed at least once. The comparison of A and B is done after the three statements have been executed.

The sequence of program development steps shown in figure H-6 applies when using pseudocode. The only difference is using pseudocode instead of flowcharts in the last step.

A pseudocode example is shown in figure H-9. This example portrays the same logic as the flowchart in figure H-5 and is relatively straightforward. One place where you might be confused concerns the end-of-data condition. The variable EOF-FLAG is initialized to zero, indicating that end of file (EOF) has not occurred. Then, the statements in PROCESS-PROCEDURE are repeated in a DO loop until EOF-FLAG becomes 1.

How does EOF-FLAG become 1? When END-OF-DATA is read in the NAME field, EOF-FLAG is set to 1. However, there is a problem. Once EOF is detected, we do not want to execute the remainder of the statements in the DO loop. To keep from doing this, we insert an IF statement. If end of data is reached, the statements under the ELSE will be skipped. Then, before another loop is made, the condition EOF-FLAG = 1 is checked. It will now be equal to 1, and the PROCESS-PROCEDURE will terminate.

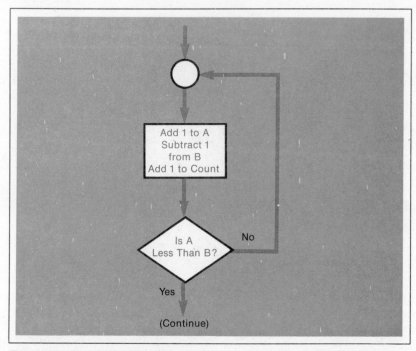

Figure H-8 Flowchart of DOUNTIL Logic

To see how this operation works, create some sample data and run through the logic. You might want to do this exercise with a friend to be sure you keep each other's logic straight.

Most data processing experts think this way of handling EOF is clumsy. They discovered that the logic can be simplified if the first record is read in the initialize paragraph. Then, when PROCESS-PROCEDURE is executed, a valid record will already be available. The record is processed, and the next read is then done at the bottom of the process loop.

This operation is shown in figure H-10. Note what happens if there is no data at all—if the first record is END-OF-DATA. In this case, EOF-FLAG will be set to 1 by the IF statement in the initialize paragraph. The DO loop in PROCESS-PROCEDURE will never be executed because EOF-FLAG will be 1 the first time through. This IF, by the way, is an example of an IF without an ELSE clause.

Do you think figure H-10 is simpler than figure H-9? Most professionals do. The logic may seem a little backwards to you the first few times you see it, however.

The first read can also be put in the initialize section of flowcharts. Figure H-11 shows this arrangement for the problem first illustrated in figure H-5. Note the read at the bottom of the figure. From now on, all

```
BEGIN EMPLOYEE-SUMMARY PROCEDURE
    DO INITIALIZE-PROCEDURE
    DO PROCESS-PROCEDURE
    DO WRAPUP-PROCEDURE
    STOP
END EMPLOYEE-SUMMARY PROCEDURE

BEGIN INITIALIZE-PROCEDURE
    SET NEMP TO 0
    SET TAGE TO 0
    SET TPR TO 0
    SET TPAY TO 0
    SET EOF-FLAG TO 0
END INITIALIZE-PROCEDURE

BEGIN PROCESS-PROCEDURE
    DOWHILE EOF-FLAG = 0
        READ NAME, AGE, PAY-RATE, EMP-PAY
        IF NAME EQUALS "END-OF-DATA"
            THEN SET EOF-FLAG TO 1
                 GO TO PROCESS-EXIT
            ELSE ADD 1 TO NEMP
                 ADD AGE TO TAGE
                 ADD PAY-RATE TO TPR
                 ADD EMP-PAY TO TPAY
                 PRINT NAME, EMP-PAY
        END-IF
    PROCESS-EXIT
    END-DO
END PROCESS-PROCEDURE

BEGIN WRAPUP-PROCEDURE
    SET AVG-PR TO TPR/NEMP
    SET AVG-AGE TO TAGE/NEMP
    PRINT NEMP, AVG-AGE, AVG-PR, TPAY
END WRAPUP-PROCEDURE
```

Figure H-9   Pseudocode Used to Express the Logic in Figure H-5

```
BEGIN EMPLOYEE-SUMMARY PROCEDURE
    DO INITIALIZE-PROCEDURE
    DO PROCESS-PROCEDURE
    DO WRAPUP-PROCEDURE
    STOP
END EMPLOYEE-SUMMARY PROCEDURE

BEGIN INITIALIZE-PROCEDURE
    SET NEMP TO 0
    SET TAGE TO 0
    SET TPR TO 0
    SET TPAY TO 0
    SET EOF-FLAG TO 0
    READ NAME, AGE, PAY-RATE, EMP-PAY
    IF NAME EQUALS "END-OF-DATA"
        THEN SET EOF-FLAG TO 1
END INITIALIZE-PROCEDURE

BEGIN PROCESS-PROCEDURE
   ┌ DOWHILE EOF-FLAG = 0
   │    PRINT NAME, EMP-PAY
   │    ADD 1 TO NEMP
   │    ADD AGE TO TAGE
   │    ADD PAY-RATE TO TPR
   │    ADD EMP-PAY TO TPAY
   │    READ NAME, AGE, PAY-RATE, EMP-PAY
   │    IF NAME EQUALS "END-OF-DATA"
   │        THEN SET EOF-FLAG TO 1
   └ END-DO
END PROCESS-PROCEDURE

BEGIN WRAPUP-PROCEDURE
    SET AVG-AGE TO TAGE/NEMP
    SET AVG-PR TO TPR/NEMP
    PRINT NEMP, AVG-AGE, AVG-PR, TPAY
END WRAPUP-PROCEDURE
```

Figure H-10 Alternative to Figure H-9 for Processing EOF

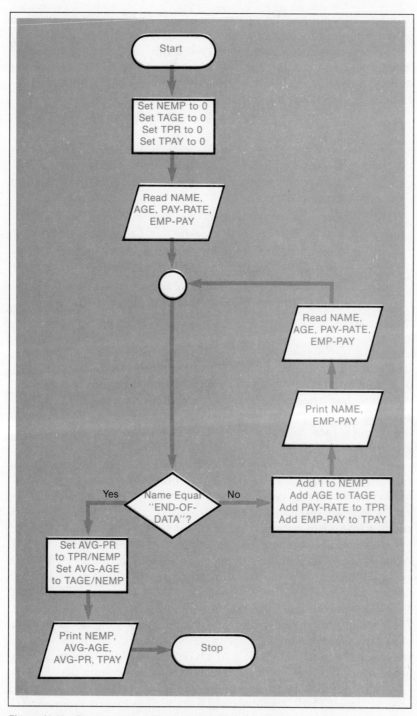

Figure H-11 Flowchart from Figure H-5 with Initial Read

of our pseudocode and flowcharts will have the first read in the initialize section. In almost every case, this action will result in better designs.

Again, the best way to understand this logic is to create some sample data and run through the logic. See what happens when the read is in the initialize paragraph and at the end of the process paragraph.

EXERCISES

H.7   Repeat exercise H.5, but use pseudocode instead of flowcharts to represent the logic. Process EOF as shown in figure H-9.

H.8   Repeat exercise H.5, but use pseudocode instead of flowcharts. Process EOF as shown in figure H-10.

H.9   Repeat exercise H.6, but use pseudocode instead of flowcharts. Process EOF as shown in figure H-9.

H.10   Repeat exercise H.6, but use pseudocode instead of flowcharts. Process EOF as shown in figure H-10.

SUMMARY

In this section we have discussed ways to design or develop the logic of simple programs. We began by describing the input/process/output cycle which is common to business computer programs. Next, we discussed a way to approach writing computer programs: First, specify the outputs, then specify the inputs, and third, develop the program logic.

One technique for showing logic is flowcharting. We use graphic symbols like rectangles and boxes to represent program logic. A few reminders for writing good flowcharts are shown in figure H-12.

After we discussed the input/process/output cycle, we added another feature to program logic. In some cases, there is a need for initializing activity before the input/process/output cycle is started. Also, in some cases, there is a need for termination activity after this cycle is finished. We showed how to represent this type of logic in flowcharts.

The last sections of this module were concerned with pseudocode. This is an English-like language for specifying program logic. We used procedures, simple imperative statements, IF-THEN-ELSE statements, and DOUNTIL and DOWHILE statements to specify program logic. Hints for using pseudocode are shown in figure H-13.

We have discussed only the essential techniques for designing program logic. These essentials will work well as long as programs are not complex. For more complex programs, more sophisticated techniques are required.

1. Every flowchart should have one and only one START and one and only one STOP.

2. Imperative statements should be enclosed in rectangles.

3. IF statements or decisions should be enclosed in diamonds. A question is always written inside a diamond. The question must be answered by Yes or No. Answers to the question are written on the arrows leading out of the diamond. Keep the direction of the arrows consistent. If the Yes is to the left in one place, keep it to the left in all places.

4. Input/output operations are shown in parallelograms.

5. DOWHILE and DOUNTIL structures should be presented as shown in figures H-7 and H-8.

6. Every line should have an arrowhead on it; otherwise, it may be hard to follow the flow of the program logic. When lines join, use the connector, or circle, symbol.

7. In general, the logic should flow from top to bottom, and left to right.

Figure H-12   Hints for Developing Program Flowcharts

Figure H-13   Hints for Writing Pseudocode

1. Break the program into small modules or procedures. For the programs you write, there will usually be initialize, process, and terminate procedures. For more complex programs, the process procedure itself may be broken into smaller modules.

2. Name all procedures. Use a name that describes what the procedure does. Start each procedure with a BEGIN statement and terminate it with an END statement.

3. Specify operations in the procedures by imperative (command-like) sentences.

4. Use IF-THEN-ELSE statements to show decisions. Indent statements under the THEN and the ELSE for clarity. Terminate the IF statement with an END-IF that is at the same margin as the IF statement.

5. Use DO statements for iteration. Remember DOUNTIL loop is executed once before the condition is checked. A DOWHILE loop will never be executed if the condition is untrue. Indent statements in the DO loop. Use an END-DO to terminate the DO loop.

6. Many times, pseudocode can be simplified if the first read statement is included in the initialize procedure. Then, A DOWHILE statement is used to control the input/process/output loop. The read statement is put at the end of the loop. Thus the pattern becomes:

   initialize (including the first read)
   process, output, input, repeat
   terminate

7. One of the chief advantages of pseudocode is its flexibility. You can do or write just about anything as long as it is logically correct and clear.

WORD LIST

(in order of
appearance in text)

Input/process/output cycle	*IF-THEN-ELSE*
Program variables	*DOWHILE*
Flowcharting	*DOUNTIL*
Pseudocode	*EOF*
Procedures or modules	

**QUESTIONS TO
CHALLENGE
YOUR THINKING**

A. You are given the task of designing an edit program. This program is to read new customer records containing customer numbers, names, credit limits, and account balances. Your program is to verify that the records conform to the following rules:

1. Customer number is all numeric.
2. Customer number is five digits.
3. Customer credit limit is one of the values 500, 1000, or 1500.
4. Customer balance is equal to zero.

Your program should list all of the records that do not conform to these rules. After all data has been processed, your program should print the number of records accepted and the number of those rejected.

Specify the outputs and inputs, and prepare a flowchart of this program's logic.

B. Same problem as A except specify the outputs, inputs, and pseudocode of the logic.

C. You are given the task of designing an inventory program. This program is to read inventory part records containing the following fields: part number, quantity on hand, item cost, item price, and reorder quantity. The program is to compute and print the following information for each part:

1. The inventory cost of the part (quantity times item cost)
2. The potential value of the parts on hand (quantity times item price)
3. The profit contribution of each part (price minus cost)
4. The difference between the number on hand and the re-order quantity

Furthermore, your program should produce a printed listing of all parts for which the quantity on hand is less than the reorder quantity. Additionally, your program should compute and print the total number of parts numbers, the total number of parts, the total inventory cost, and the total inventory value.

   Specify the outputs and inputs, and prepare a flowchart of the program logic.

D. Same problem as C except specify the outputs, inputs, and pseudocode of the program logic.

MODULE I

How to Write Simple BASIC Programs

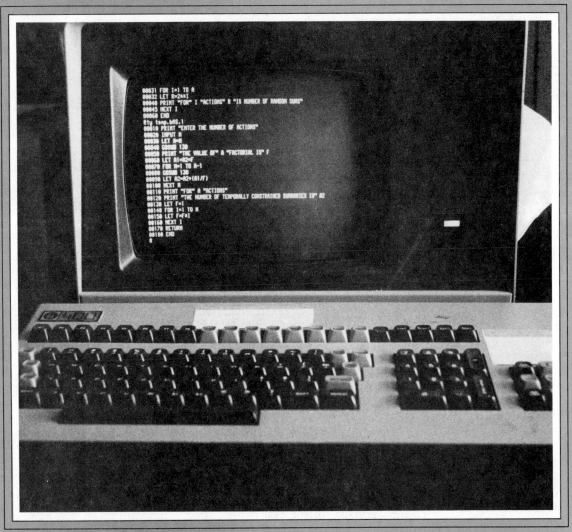

BASIC program on student terminal

SECTION 1—GETTING STARTED

Basic BASIC Statements
Running the Program
Program Testing

SECTION 2—ADDITIONAL BASIC STATEMENTS AND PSEUDOCODE IMPLEMENTATION

String Data and String Variables

The BASIC Assignment Statement

BASIC and Pseudocode

SECTION 3—PROGRAM LOOPS: THE FOR AND NEXT STATEMENTS

Population Problem

SECTION 4—TABLES OR ARRAYS

The Discount Program

This module is a continuation of Module H. If you have not read Module H, do so now before you read further.

In the last module, you learned there are two phases to developing simple programs: design, and programming and test. Module H considered design; you learned how to use flowcharts and pseudocode to specify program logic. In this module, you will learn how to program and test this logic using a language called BASIC. We will assume you have never programmed before.

The word BASIC is an acronym for the words *Beginners All-purpose Symbolic Instruction Code*. It is simple language that is easily learned and easy to use. There are many kinds of BASIC. Most computer manufacturers have a version of BASIC for their computer. Many of these versions have extensions or extra instructions that add more capability. Unfortunately, these extensions are not standardized; they vary from computer to computer. Therefore we will not discuss them here. Instead, we will stay with the commonly accepted version of BASIC.

When you finish this module, you will be able to write simple BASIC programs. If you decide you want to learn more about BASIC, you will have sufficient knowledge to understand any of the BASIC references listed at the end of this book. They will teach you more advanced concepts.

The purpose of this module is not to turn you into a programmer. Do not expect to be one when you finish. Rather, you should expect to learn what programming is like. You will experience some of the frustrations of professional programmers. Also, after this taste of programming, you may find you like it and want to learn more. Many professionals have started just this way.

You will do programming in one of three modes—depending on the hardware at your institution. First, you may use a CRT or other type of terminal. This terminal will be connected to a central computer. Alternatively, you may write programs on a microcomputer. In this case, you will type on a machine that has a computer inside it. Third, you may program in the batch mode. If so, you will punch your computer programs on cards that will be read by the computer. After you submit the cards, there will be a delay and then results will be printed. The first two modes are called *interactive* because you are directly connected to a computer. The third mode is called *batch*. Module I assumes you are programming in one of the interactive modes.

This module has four major sections. There are questions and programming exercises at the end of each. You should read a section, and then practice those concepts on the computer. Then read the next section and practice, and so forth.

To get started, you need to learn a few BASIC statements. Then you need to know how to use the computer to write the program. We will discuss these requirements in turn.

In the last module, we developed the logic for the following sales comparison problem:

> Read the names and sales amounts for pairs of salespeople. Compare the amounts sold, and print the name of the person who sold the larger amount. If the amounts are equal, print a message and both names. Repeat processing for several pairs of salespeople.

Since you are just getting started, let's simplify the problem. Instead of reading salesperson names, let's read salesperson numbers. Instead of printing salesperson names, we will print their numbers. Also, let's not worry about ties. If there is a tie, we will print salesperson number N2. The logic for this adjusted problem is shown in the flowchart in figure I-1.

Figure I-2 shows a BASIC program to solve this problem. It is a collection of BASIC statements. Each statement has a number fol-

**SECTION 1—
GETTING STARTED**

**Basic BASIC
Statements**

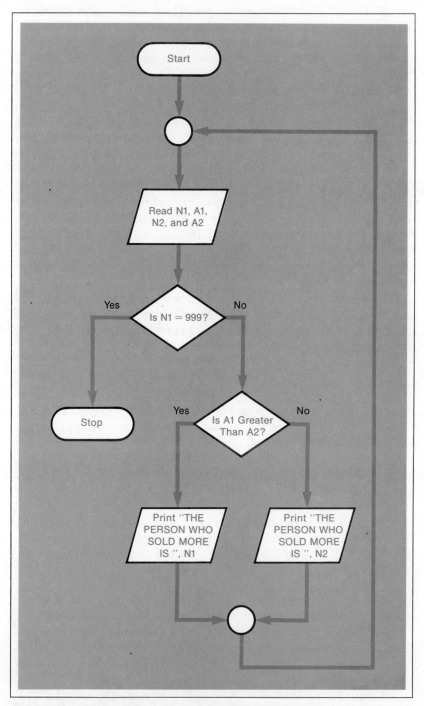

Figure I-1 Logic for Modified Sales Comparison Problem

```
 10  INPUT N1, A1, N2, A2
 30  IF N1 = 999 THEN 150
 50  IF A1 > A2 THEN 110
 70  PRINT "THE PERSON WHO SOLD MORE IS ", N2
 90  GOTO 10
110  PRINT "THE PERSON WHO SOLD MORE IS ", N1
130  GOTO 10
150  END
```

Figure I-2   BASIC Program for the Problem in Figure I-1

lowed by an instruction for the computer. The numbers are important because they determine the order of the statements. Thus, BASIC statement 10 comes before statement 30, which comes before 50, and so forth.

Note there are gaps between statement numbers. These gaps make it easy to insert new instructions if the program is changed. For example, if we want to insert an instruction between statements 30 and 50, we just give the new instruction one of the numbers from 31 to 49. The BASIC system will insert the new instruction in the correct location.

In Module H, we discussed *program variables*, or names of data items. The value of a variable can change as the program is run. Statement 10 in figure I-2 instructs the computer to obtain values for four variables: N1, A1, N2, and A2. We assume that N1 is the number of the first salesperson, A1 is the amount the salesperson sold, N2 is the number of the second salesperson, and A2 is the amount that person sold.

BASIC has very strict rules about variable names. They can be any of the 26 letters A to Z, or they can be a letter followed by a single digit. No other variable names are allowed. For example, the following are *valid* variable names:

         A3, J, K, I9, E0 (E-ZERO)

The following names are *invalid*:

         2J, JJ, I89, A#, EO (E-OH)

This rule is important to remember. *A variable name can be a single letter or a single letter followed by a single digit.* (As an aside, a zero is often written as $\emptyset$ and an oh is written as O to differentiate between the two.)

Now, how does this program work? What happens when the computer executes statement 10? The command INPUT means the computer is to obtain values for the four variables listed. It will ask for them from the person sitting at the terminal. When the computer executes statement 10, it will print a question mark (?) and then wait for the user to respond with four values.

On the terminal, it will look something like this:

```
? 100, 345, 400, 438
```

The computer types the ? and then the user types the first sales-person number (100), then a comma, then the first amount, a comma, and so forth. After the user has input all four values, he or she hits the RETURN key on the keyboard.

Using the above example values, after statement 10 is executed, N1 has the value 100, A1 has the value 345, N2 has the value 400, and A2 has the value 438.

Statements are normally executed in order in BASIC. Therefore, after statement 10 is executed, statement 30 will be processed. This statement is an IF statement. If N1 equals 999, then control will be transferred to statement 150. The statement can be read: "If N1 equals 999, then go to statement number 150." In this case the pro-gram will stop at statement 150.

If the condition is untrue (N1 is a value other than 999), then control will go to the statement following the IF. Thus in figure I-2, if N1 is 800 or 0 or 75 or any number other than 999, then statement 50 will be executed next.

Can you see what this program is doing? The value 999 is being used as a *signal* to indicate that all of the data has been read. When someone inputs a value 999 for N1, then the program will stop.

The value 999 is an example of a *program constant*. Program constants are numbers or groups of characters in quotation marks. (See statement 70.) Unlike variables, program constants do not change value during the run.

For the input values shown above, N1 will have the value 100. Since this is not equal to 999, statement 50 is executed. This is another IF statement. If A1 is greater than A2, then statement 110 is executed. Otherwise, statement 70 is executed. Compare these statements to figure I-1 to be sure the IFs are coded correctly.

For our data, A1 is 345 and A2 is 438. Therefore, since A1 is less than A2, statement 70 will be executed. Statement 70 is a PRINT statement. It causes words and numbers to be printed. When it is executed, the computer prints the words, "THE PERSON WHO SOLD MORE IS ", followed by the value of N2. It will look some-thing like this:

```
THE PERSON WHO SOLD MORE IS              400
```

The GOTO in statement 90 is executed next. It sends the com-puter back to statement 10 to obtain the next input values. Examine

```
? 100, 345, 400, 438
      THE PERSON WHO SOLD MORE IS          400
? 300, 417, 800, 345
      THE PERSON WHO SOLD MORE IS          300
? 50, 767, 28, 767
      THE PERSON WHO SOLD MORE IS          28
?999, 0, 0, 0
```

Figure I-3 Sample Run of the Program in Figure I-2

figure I-2 to see what happens when A1 is greater than A2. See the other PRINT statement in instruction 110? Do you agree the program is correct? Figure I-3 shows input values and results for several sets of data. Are the results correct for the data shown?

The program in figure I-2 is very easy to read and understand. More complex programs are harder to read and understand. BASIC provides a statement to improve program readability. It is called the Remark or REM statement.

REM statements contain comments about the program. They are intended to be read only by humans, and they are ignored by the computer. Figure I-4 shows the program from figure I-2 with REM statements included. Again, these statements are for people to read when learning what a program does. Also, note the PRINT in statement 05. This statement tells the person at the terminal what to do. From now on, all of our INPUT statements will be preceded by such a PRINT.

You really don't know if the program in figure I-4 works or not. The only way to find out is to key and run it. You should do this now.

Running the Program

Figure I-4 BASIC Program from Figure I-2 with Remarks

```
 05     PRINT "INPUT NUMBER 1, AMOUNT 1, NUMBER 2, AND AMOUNT 2"
 10     INPUT N1, A1, N2, A2
 30     IF N1 = 999 THEN 150
 50     IF A1 > A2 THEN 110
 60 REM      N2 SALES GREATER OR THERE IS A TIE
 70     PRINT "THE PERSON WHO SOLD MORE IS ", N2
 90     GOTO 10
100 REM      N1 SALES GREATER
110     PRINT "THE PERSON WHO SOLD MORE IS ", N1
130     GOTO 10
140 REM      STOP THE PROGRAM
150     END
```

The computer you will use is a general purpose machine. Before you can write BASIC statements, you must tell it what you want to do. It won't understand if you just start typing BASIC. You use *system commands* to tell the computer what you want to do, as well as who you are, who should get the bill for your computer time, and so forth.

Unfortunately, system commands are different for every computer. Therefore, you will have to ask your instructor what commands to use. When you find out, write them down. You can put them in figure I-5 if you want to.

Once you know the system commands, find a terminal or microcomputer, pull up a chair and sit down. You may have to turn the equipment on. Don't feel stupid if you can't find the switch. Ask. It may be in the back. Also, don't worry about breaking the computer. As long as you don't abuse it physically, you can't hurt it. The computer will take care of itself. It expects you to be a novice, and it won't let you do things that will hurt it. If you make mistakes, it will give you error messages, beeps, blank screens, or gibberish, but it won't let you hurt it.

Once the terminal or microcomputer is on, type in the system commands. Then, you can enter the BASIC program shown in figure

Figure I-5 Blank Space to Fill in Your Computer's System Commands

I-4. Type it exactly as shown. Put spaces where spaces are shown, and don't forget any commas.

Have you keyed the program in? Once you have, run it using the data in figure I-3. You will probably do this using the system command RUN. Do you get the same results? You should.

In Module H, we said the second phase of developing a simple program is programming and *test*. Testing is very important. Does the program really do what it is supposed to? Test the program you have just written. Try it when A1 equals A2, when A1 is less than A2, and when A2 is less than A1. Now, get nasty; try to trick it. What happens when A1 is zero? When both are zero? When A1 is negative but A2 is positive? What happens if you input a person's name instead of their number? Try all of these and any other conditions you can think of.

Program Testing

People are strange when it comes to testing. They like to skimp on it. As you will see, programming can be very creative. Often peoples' egos get involved in their programs. Looking for errors in a program can be like looking for defects in your personality. It's hard to do. However, testing is crucial. Even the simplest statements can have errors. A good assumption is, *Nothing works until you've shown that it does.*

Figure I-6 summarizes the BASIC statements introduced so far. The INPUT statement requests data from the user at the terminal. The IF statement branches based on variable values. The PRINT statement prints words and variable values. GOTO transfers the computer to the specified statement. The END statement stops the program, and the REM statement contains remarks for people using the program.

SECTION 1 SUMMARY

You have keyed in and run your first computer program. It wasn't so bad, was it? You might have found it was fun. Now practice what

Figure I-6 Summary of Statements Discussed in Section 1

Statement	Purpose	Example
INPUT	Obtain values from the user at a terminal.	`100 INPUT A,B,C`
IF	Conditionally transfer control.	`100 IF J = K THEN 200`
PRINT	Print words or variable values.	`100 PRINT "THE VALUES ARE ", A,B`
GOTO	Transfer unconditionally.	`100 GOTO 1000`
END	Stop the program.	`100 END`
REM	Insert a remark for a human (computer ignores it).	`100 REM     NOW OUT OF DATA`

you have learned. First, answer the following questions; then program either of the problems below.

I.1 Are you running programs in the batch or interactive mode?

I.2 What are program variables? What are the rules for BASIC variables?

I.3 Explain the difference between system commands and BASIC instructions.

I.4 Explain what happens when the following statements are executed:

a. `100     INPUT A, B, C`
b. `100     IF A = B THEN 200`
c. `100     END`
d. `100     PRINT "THIS IS THE ANSWER, ", A`
e. `100     PRINT "THIS IS THE ANSWER ", A`
f. `100 REM      THIS IS THE ANSWER`
g. `100     GOTO 10`

I.5 What is the good assumption about program testing?

P.1 Write a BASIC program that implements the logic in figure H-4. However, do not read the customer name, but read the customer number instead.

P.2 Write a BASIC program to implement the complete logic shown in figure H-3. Process ties as shown in the figure. However, read salesperson numbers instead of their names.

In this section you will learn about string variables and the assignment statement. You will learn more about IF statements. Also, you will learn how to implement the pseudocode statements IF-THEN-ELSE, DOWHILE, and DOUNTIL in BASIC.

In BASIC, a group of characters is called a *string*. The words "THE PERSON WHO SOLD MORE" are an example of *string data*. Variables that have string values are called *string variables*. These variables are named differently than variables having numeric values. Specifically, a dollar sign is added to the name of a variable that will have string values.

Figure I-7 shows the sales comparison program from figure I-4. However, instead of inputting and printing salesperson numbers, the

```
 05     PRINT "INPUT NAME 1, AMOUNT 1, NAME 2, AND AMOUNT 2"
 10     INPUT N1$, A1, N2$, A2
 30     IF N1$ = "EOF" THEN 150
 50     IF A1 > A2 THEN 110
 60 REM      N2 SALES GREATER OR THERE IS A TIE
 70     PRINT "THE PERSON WHO SOLD MORE IS ", N2$
 90     GOTO 10
100 REM      N1 SALES GREATER
110     PRINT "THE PERSON WHO SOLD MORE IS ", N1$
130     GOTO 10
140 REM      STOP THE PROGRAM
150     END
```

Figure I-7   BASIC Program from Figure I-4 with String Variables

program in figure I-7 processes salesperson names. N1$ and N2$ are string variables. They can have string values. In statement 10, the dollar signs signal to the BASIC system that the data to be input is *character* and not numeric.

The rules for naming string variables are similar to the rules for naming numeric variables. A single letter or a single letter with a single digit is allowed. Thus A$, J1$, W4$ are valid BASIC string variables. However, 1A$, 6$, or ABC$ are invalid string variables.

The difference between string data and numeric data is important. String or character data includes the 26 letters, the special symbols like #, %, &, and so forth, and the digits 0 through 9. Examples of valid string data are:

ABC

MAD+MONEY

RTS-40

MARY JONES

12345

The last example is all digits. However, even though it is all digits, it cannot be used as a number. Since it is to be read into a string variable, it will be string data. The program must not try to perform arithmetic on it. The number 12345 must be read into a numeric variable before it can be used for computation purposes.

Now, since salesperson numbers are not being input, the end-of-data check must be different. In statement 30, note the IF statement has been changed to check for the string EOF instead of the number

```
? MARY JONES, 10348, FRED SMITH, 9345
THE PERSON WHO SOLD MORE IS  MARY JONES
? JACK STALLONE, 8745, BILL NICHOLS, 11234
THE PERSON WHO SOLD MORE IS  BILL NICHOLS
? TIM BROWN, 23891, GWEN APPLE, 24647
THE PERSON WHO SOLD MORE IS  GWEN APPLE
?EOF, 0, 0, 0
```

Figure I-8 Sample Execution of the Program in Figure I-7

999. In BASIC, strings must be enclosed in quotation marks. Therefore, this statement compares N1 to "EOF" and not just EOF. This is the same way we specified character strings to be printed. We wrote PRINT "THE PERSON WHO . . .". Figure I-8 shows an example of one execution of the program in figure I-7. (Actually, 999 could still be used, but it would be the characters "999" and not the number nine hundred ninety-nine. For convenience we will use the characters "EOF" here.)

The BASIC Assignment Statement

Consider the problem of reading a sequence of 25 numbers and computing the total and average of them. Figure I-9 shows a flowchart of the logic to do this. It has an initiation section, a processing section, and a termination section.

At initiation, variables S and N are set to zero. Then values are read. Each time, the value is added to S. Also, 1 is added to N. When N equals 25, the process terminates. At this point, S has the sum of the numbers. In the termination section, S is divided by N to obtain the average.

Figure I-10 shows a BASIC program for this problem. Statements like $N = 0$ (statement 30) and $S = S + V$ (statement 90) are examples of assignment statements. They assign a new value to a variable.

BASIC assignment statements provide a broad capability. The fundamental form of the assignment statement is:

variable = arithmetic expression

Variable is the name of the variable to be given a new value, and the *arithmetic expression* is some combination of variables, constants, and the operators $+, -, *, /$. The operator $\uparrow$, which represents exponentiation, can also be used; but since it is not often used in business programming, we will ignore it.

Some examples of arithmetic expressions are:

$$A + B + C$$

$$A / Q1 - 75$$

$$1500.457 - B + (2 * B) / 2$$

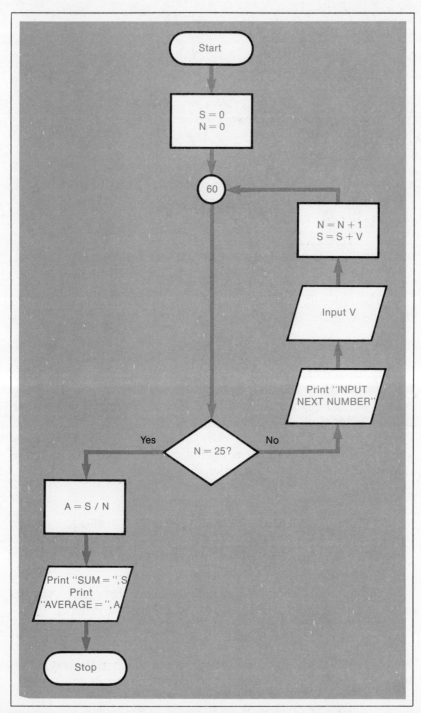

Figure I-9 Flowchart of Logic to Average 25 Numbers

```
10 REM        INITIALIZE N (THE COUNT OF NUMBERS READ) AND
20 REM        S (THE SUM OF THE NUMBERS)
30   N = 0
40   S = 0
50 REM        INPUT/PROCESS/OUTPUT SECTION
60   IF N = 25 THEN 120
65   PRINT "INPUT NEXT NUMBER"
70   INPUT V
80   N = N + 1
90   S = S + V
100  GOTO 60
110 REM        TERMINATION SECTION
120  A = S / N
130 REM        PRINT RESULTS
140  PRINT "SUM = ", S
150  PRINT "AVERAGE = ", A
160  END
```

Figure I-10   A BASIC Program to Compute the Sum and Average of 25 Numbers

The order in which operations are carried out is important. To illustrate, consider the expression:

$$2 + 4 * 3$$

Is the addition performed before the multiplication or the other way around? If we add first, the expression will be 6 * 3 or 18. However, if we multiply first, it will be $2 + 12$ or 14. From this you can see that the order of operations is important.

BASIC has very definite *rules* about the way that expressions are evaluated. The order of operation can be summarized by three rules. They are applied in the order shown:

1. Evaluate expressions inside parentheses first.

2. Evaluate multiplications and divisions before additions and subtractions.

3. Evaluate operations at the same level from left to right.

The following examples illustrate the use of these rules. Assume A has the value 5, B has the value 10, and C has the value 2.

$$J1 = (A + B) * C$$

Here, use rule 1. Evaluate inside the parentheses first. We add A to B to get 15 and multiply by C to get 30. Another example is:

$$L9 = A - B / C$$

Here, we use rule 2 since there are no parentheses. Division is performed before subtraction, so we divide B by C to get 5, and then subtract 5 from A to get 0. A third example is:

```
Z = A + B - 10 + C
```

Since there are no parentheses, and since only addition and subtraction are used, neither rule 1 nor 2 applies. In this case, we use rule 3 and evaluate from left to right. Z will be given the value 7.

This is a quick summary of assignment statements. If you want to know more, you can refer to one of the references at the back of this book. If you do refer to other books, you should be aware of one fact. In early versions of BASIC, the assignment statement had to be preceded by the word LET. Thus, instead of $N = A + B$, the programmer had to code:

```
LET N = A + B
```

This practice is no longer true for BASIC on most computers, but you may run into it if you read older books.

IF statements are broader than we have seen so far. The general format is:

More on the IF Statement

> IF condition THEN statement number

The condition can be quite complex. Its general format is:

> arithmetic expression-1   relation symbol   arithmetic expression-2

These arithmetic expressions are the same as those discussed for the assignment statement, and they are evaluated the same way. The six *relation symbols* in BASIC are:

Symbol	Meaning
=	equals
<	less than
>	greater than
<=	less than or equal to
>=	greater than or equal to
<>	not equal to

Examples of valid IF statements are:

```
IF A <= 100 THEN 800

IF Q1 + C = A + D + E THEN 800
```

```
IF A + B <= C THEN 800
IF A <> B THEN 800
IF (A + B) / C ⁎ E <= F / G THEN 800
```

It is possible to code very complex IF statements. As a general rule, however, it is better to keep them simple. Thus, the last IF statement would be better as three separate statements:

```
10 T1 = (A + B) / C ⁎ E
20 T2 = F / G
30 IF T1 <= T2 THEN 800
```

BASIC and Pseudocode

In Module H we discussed the three fundamental pseudocode structures: IF-THEN-ELSE, DOWHILE, and DOUNTIL. In this section you will learn how to represent each of these structures in BASIC.

An example IF-THEN-ELSE structure is shown in figure I-11*a*. The corresponding BASIC statements are shown in figure I-11*b*. Note that the condition is put into a BASIC IF statement. This statement transfers control to the THEN statements. The ELSE statements are inserted after the IF. They will be executed when the condition is not true.

A DOWHILE example is shown in figure I-12. Recall that a DOWHILE loop is performed only when the condition is true. In figure I-12*a*, the loop is to be performed only as long as A is less than B.

Figure I-11 Implementation of IF-THEN-ELSE in BASIC

```
IF A = B
    THEN SET A = A + 1
         SET B = B + 1
    ELSE SET A = A - 1
END-IF
PRINT A, B
```

a. Sample IF-THEN-ELSE Structure

```
100 IF A = B THEN 130        Condition
110 A = A - 1                ELSE statement
120 GOTO 150
130 A = A + 1
140 B = B + 1                THEN statements
150 PRINT "A AND B ARE ", A, B
```

b. BASIC Program Corresponding to IF-THEN-ELSE Above

```
DOWHILE A IS LESS THAN B
    ADD 1 TO A
    SUBTRACT 1 FROM B
END-DO
PRINT A
```

a. Sample DOWHILE Structure

```
100 IF A  = B THEN 140        Condition
110 A = A + 1
120 B = B - 1                 Loop statements
130 GOTO 100
140 PRINT "A = ", A
```

b. BASIC Program Corresponding to DOWHILE Above

Figure I-12   Correspondence of DOWHILE and BASIC Statements

Thus, if A is less than B, 1 will be added to A and 1 will be subtracted from B until A is greater than or equal to B.

Examine figure I-12*b*. The condition in the IF statement is backwards. The condition is: If A is greater than or equal to B. Why? If A is greater than or equal to B, then control will go to statement 150. It will skip over the loop. Otherwise, control will fall through to statement 110. The loop will be executed, and control will return to the IF in statement 100. In other words, the IF statement means, if the condition (A less than B) is not met, skip over the loop. Otherwise, execute the loop and return.

Figure I-13 shows the BASIC statements for a DOUNTIL structure. In figure I-13*a*, the loop is to be performed until A is less than B. The loop will be executed, and then the condition is checked. If the condition is true, the loop is not executed again. Otherwise, the loop is repeated.

Figure I-13*b* shows the corresponding BASIC statements. Note that the IF is at the bottom of the loop. 1 is added to B and 1 is subtracted from A. Then, if the condition is not true (A is greater than or equal to B), the loop is repeated. Otherwise, the PRINT is executed.

Figure I-14 is a copy of the pseudocode in figure H-10. A BASIC program that implements this logic is shown in figure I-15. Note how the IF statements and the DOWHILE structure are represented. The program starts at the INITIALIZE-PROCEDURE. The logic is simple enough that the DO statements need not be coded into BASIC. If we needed them, they could be coded into BASIC, but that is beyond the scope of this module.

```
DOUNTIL A IS LESS THAN B
    ADD 1 TO B
    SUBTRACT 1 FROM A
END-DO
PRINT A
```

a. Sample DOUNTIL Structure

```
100 B = B + 1
110 A = A - 1        Loop statements
120 IF A >= B THEN 100    Condition
130 PRINT "A = ", A
```

b. BASIC Program Corresponding to DOUNTIL Above

Figure I-13 Correspondence of DOUNTIL and BASIC Statements

SECTION 2 SUMMARY

Figure I-16 summarizes the BASIC concepts discussed in this section. These include string data and string variables, assignment statements, and more concepts of the IF statement. In addition to these statements, we showed how BASIC statements can implement pseudocode IF-THEN-ELSE, DOWHILE, and DOUNTIL structures.

The best way to reinforce these concepts is to write programs. The programming exercises and the programs below are especially recommended.

QUESTIONS

I.6 Which of the following are valid string variables:

a. N1$ d. A#
b. J7   e. P2$
c. JU$ f. A$

I.7 If J = 5, K = 3, and L = 4, what is the value of the following expressions:

a. J + (L / 2)   d. (J - K) / L
b. (J + L) / 2   e. J - K * L
c. J + L / 2

I.8 Explain the action of the following statements:

a. IF A * J = 20 THEN 457
b. IF (A + B) / C > M / 17 THEN 20
c. IF A / J <> D THEN 1800

```
BEGIN EMPLOYEE-SUMMARY PROCEDURE
    DO INITIALIZE-PROCEDURE
    DO PROCESS-PROCEDURE
    DO WRAPUP-PROCEDURE
    STOP
END EMPLOYEE-SUMMARY PROCEDURE

BEGIN INITIALIZE-PROCEDURE
    SET NEMP, TAGE, TPR, TPAY TO 0
    READ NAME, AGE, PAY-RATE, EMP-PAY
    IF NAME EQUALS "END-OF-DATA"
        THEN SET EOF-FLAG TO 1
        ELSE SET EOF-FLAG TO 0
END INITIALIZE-PROCEDURE

BEGIN PROCESS-PROCEDURE
    DOWHILE EOF-FLAG = 0
        PRINT NAME, EMP-PAY
        ADD 1 TO NEMP
        ADD AGE TO TAGE
        ADD PAY-RATE TO TPR
        ADD EMP-PAY TO TPAY
        READ NAME, AGE, PAY-RATE, EMP-PAY
        IF NAME EQUALS "END-OF-DATA"
            THEN SET EOF-FLAG TO 1
    END-DO
END PROCESS-PROCEDURE

BEGIN WRAPUP-PROCEDURE
    IF NEMP IS GREATER THAN 0
        THEN SET AVG-AGE TO TAGE/NEMP
             SET AVG-PR TO TPR/NEMP
             PRINT NEMP, AVG-AGE, AVG-PR, TPAY
        ELSE PRINT "ERROR--NO EMPLOYEES"
    END-IF
END WRAPUP-PROCEDURE
```

Figure I-14 Pseudocode for Employee Summary Problem (Based on Figure H-10)

```
10  REM        INITIALIZE
20     N = 0
30     T1 = 0
40     T2 = 0
50     T3 = 0
60     PRINT "INPUT FIRST RECORD--NAME, AGE, PAY-RATE, EMP-PAY"
70     INPUT N$, A, P1, P2
80  REM        SET EOF-FLAG AS APPROPRIATE
90     IF N$ = "EOF" THEN 120
100    E = 0
110    GOTO 140
120    E = 1
130 REM        START PROCESS-PROCEDURE--USING DOWHILE STRUCTURE
140    IF E <> 0 THEN 260
150    PRINT "EMPLOYEE ", N$, " HAD PAY OF ", P2
160    N = N + 1
170    T1 = T1 + A
180    T2 = T2 + P1
190    T3 = T3 + P2
195    PRINT "INPUT NAME, AGE, PAY-RATE, EMP-PAY"
200    INPUT N$, A, P1, P2
210    IF N$ = "EOF" THEN 230
220    GOTO 140
230    E = 1
240    GOTO 140
250 REM        WRAPUP PROCEDURE
260    IF N <> 0 THEN 290
270    PRINT "ERROR--NO EMPLOYEES"
280    GOTO 350
290    A1 = T1 / N
300    A2 = T2 / N
310    PRINT "NUMBER OF EMPLOYEES EQUALS ", N
320    PRINT "AVERAGE AGE EQUALS ", A1
330    PRINT "AVERAGE PAY RATE EQUALS ", A2
340    PRINT "TOTAL EMPLOYEE PAY EQUALS ", T3
350    END
```

Figure I-15 BASIC Program Corresponding to Pseudocode in Figure I-14

Figure I-16 BASIC Statements Discussed in Section 2

Concept or Statement	Purpose	Example
String Variable	To hold string or character data	N$, A1$
Assignment	To give new values to variables	A = A + 1
More IF	Conditional transfer	IF A + B > C - D THEN 100

Note: Questions I.9 through I.14 are programming exercises.

I.9   Input the following program to your computer:

```
10 INPUT A$, B
20 PRINT "A EQUALS ", A$, "B EQUALS ", B
30 GOTO 10
40 END
```

Experiment with data. What happens when you input numbers for A$? What happens when you try to input letters for B? How can you stop this program? Change this program to stop more conveniently.

I.10 Write a program to compute the expressions in question I.7. Print the results of the computations. Do the answers agree with this text?

I.11 Write a program that corresponds to the following pseudocode. Test the program to be sure it operates correctly.

```
READ A, B, C
IF A IS LESS THAN B
    THEN PRINT "A LESS THAN B ", A, B
    ELSE PRINT "A GREATER THAN OR
            EQUAL TO B ", A,B
END-IF
```

I.12 Write a program for the following pseudocode. Test it to be certain it works for all possible values of A and B.

```
INPUT A, B
SET N to 0
DOWHILE A IS GREATER THAN OR EQUAL TO B
    SUBTRACT 1 FROM A
    ADD 1 TO N
END-DO
PRINT "THE VALUES OF A, B, N ARE ", A, B, N
```

I.13 Write a program for the following pseudocode. Test it to be certain it works for all possible values of A and B.

```
INPUT A, B
SET N TO 0
DOUNTIL A IS GREATER THAN B
    ADD 1 TO A
    ADD 1 TO N
END-DO
PRINT "THE VALUES OF A, B, N ARE ", A, B, N
```

I.14   Write a program for the following pseudocode. Test it to
       be certain it works for all possible values of A and B.

```
INPUT A, B
SET N TO 0
IF A IS LESS THAN B
    THEN PRINT "A IS LESS THAN B"
         ┌DOWHILE A IS LESS THAN B
         │   ADD 1 TO A
         │   ADD 1 TO N
         └END-DO
    ELSE PRINT "A IS GREATER THAN OR EQUAL TO B "
         ┌DOUNTIL B IS GREATER THAN A
         │   ADD 1 TO B
         │   ADD 1 TO N
         └END-DO
END-IF
PRINT "THE FINAL VALUES OF A, B, N ARE ",
    A, B, N
```

PRACTICE PROGRAMS

The following problems are taken from Module H. You should have
designed the logic of these problems in that module. If not, design them
now, before you try to program them in BASIC.

P.3   Write a BASIC program for exercise H.1. Test your pro-
      gram to be sure it works for all possible data conditions.

P.4   Write a BASIC program for exercise H.2. Test your pro-
      gram to be sure it works for all possible data conditions.

P.5   Write a BASIC program for exercise H.3. Test your pro-
      gram as above.

P.6   Write a BASIC program for exercise H.4. Test your pro-
      gram as above.

P.7   Write a BASIC program for exercise H.5. Test your pro-
      gram. Do not try to write this program without a design;
      you're wasting your time if you do.

P.8   Write a BASIC program for exercise H.6. Test your pro-
      gram. Again, do not try to write this program without a
      design.

Loops, or instructions that are repeated over and over, are very common in programming. In the input/process/output cycle, all instructions in the cycle are repeated until some condition is reached. Because loops are so frequent, BASIC has special instructions to implement them.

Consider the program in figure I-10. The instructions in the input/process/output section are repeated 25 times. These instructions comprise the *processing loop*. The program in figure I-10 does not use any special statements for the loop.

Now, examine another version of this program in figure I-17. In this figure, two special BASIC statements (numbers 40 and 70) have been used to control the loop. These two statements work as a pair; they surround the statements to be repeated. The loop starts at statement 40 and it includes all of the statements through 70. Statement 40 has the following meaning:

> Start a loop using the variable N as a counter. Set N to 1 to begin with, and add 1 to N every time the loop is executed. When N is greater than 25, go to the next statement after the loop. (In our example, this will be statement 90.)

Statement 70 terminates the loop. It means:

> This is the end of the loop using the variable N. Add 1 to N and repeat the loop.

Thus, all the statements between 40 and 70 will be executed repeatedly. The first time they are executed, N will have the value 1.

SECTION 3— PROGRAM LOOPS: THE FOR AND NEXT STATEMENTS

Figure I-17 Sum and Average Program Using FOR and NEXT Statements

```
 10  REM       INITALIZE S (THE SUM OF THE NUMBERS)
 20    S = 0
 30  REM       INPUT/PROCESS/OUTPUT SECTION
 40    FOR N = 1 TO 25
 45    PRINT "INPUT NEXT VALUE"
 50    INPUT V
 60    S = S + V
 70    NEXT N
 80  REM       TERMINATION SECTION
 90    A = S / 25
100    PRINT "SUM = ", S
110    PRINT "AVERAGE = ", A
120    END
```

The second time, N will equal 2, the third time it will be 3, and so on. The last time through the loop, N will have the value 25.

The general form of the FOR statement is as follows:

FOR variable = initial value TO final value STEP increment

The variable is the name of a variable to be used as the index over the loop. The initial value is the first value the variable is to have, and the final value is the greatest value it is to have. The increment is the amount to be added to the variable each time the loop is repeated. In figure I-17, we did not specify an increment. If no increment is listed, BASIC assumes the increment is 1.

Figure I-18 shows a flowchart of FOR statement processing. If you compare this to figure I-12, you will see that BASIC FOR-NEXT structures are like DOWHILE structures. In figure I-18, the loop is performed while J is less than or equal to L. Figure I-18 shows how most BASIC compilers work; *however*, this varies from computer to computer. On your system, the FOR-NEXT may be implemented as a DOUNTIL. Write some FOR-NEXT statements on your computer and see.

Now, what if we do not know how many data items there will be? Suppose we know there will be no more than 25 values, and that end of data is signaled by a −9999. In this case, we will need to modify the program logic. Pseudocode for the modification is shown in figure I-19.

Figure I-20 shows a BASIC program to implement this pseudocode. Unfortunately, the FOR-NEXT structure is not capable of representing the full condition in the DOWHILE. It can limit the number of values to 25, but it cannot be coded to stop when no data remains. We would like to write:

```
50 FOR I = 1 TO 25 WHILE DATA REMAINS
```

But, unfortunately, this is not legal BASIC. Therefore, inside the loop, we check to see if the value is −9999. If so, we force the FOR statement to stop. We do this at statement 90, where N is set to 25, the maximum.

If you can understand the programs in figure I-18 and I-20, you are well on your way to understanding FOR and NEXT statements. We will discuss one more example so that you can check your understanding.

Suppose you want to estimate the United States population growth for different growth rates. You want to know the population in 2030 assuming it is 230 million in 1981. You will input a growth rate, and you want the estimate printed. Then you input another rate, and the next

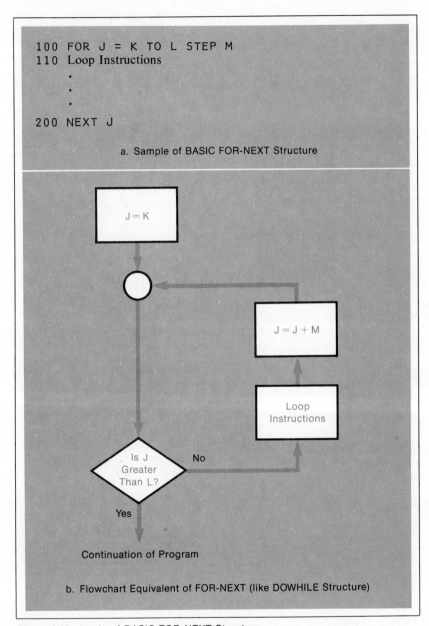

```
100  FOR  J  =  K  TO  L  STEP  M
110  Loop Instructions
        .
        .
        .
200  NEXT  J
```

a. Sample of BASIC FOR-NEXT Structure

b. Flowchart Equivalent of FOR-NEXT (like DOWHILE Structure)

Figure I-18 Logic of BASIC FOR-NEXT Structure

estimate is printed, and so forth. You will stop by inputting a growth rate of zero.

You know that the population at the end of each year equals the population at the start of the year plus the amount of growth. Thus, if

```
SET SUM TO 0, COUNT TO 0
DOWHILE COUNT IS LESS THAN 25 AND DATA REMAINS
    INPUT V
    ADD V TO SUM
    ADD 1 TO COUNT
END-DO
COMPUTE AVERAGE
PRINT RESULTS
```

Figure I-19   Logic for Average Program with a Variable Number of Values

```
 10 REM       INITIALIZE N1 (THE COUNT OF NUMBERS READ) AND
 20 REM       S (THE SUM OF THE NUMBERS)
 30    S = 0
 40    N1 = 0
 50 REM       INPUT/PROCESS/OUTPUT SECTION
 60    FOR N = 1 TO 25
 65    PRINT "INPUT NEXT VALUE"
 70    INPUT V
 80    IF V <> -9999 THEN 110
 90    N = 25
100    GOTO 130
110    S = S + V
120    N1 = N1 + 1
130    NEXT N
135 REM       TERMINATION SECTION
140    IF N1 > 0 THEN 150
145    PRINT "ERROR-NO DATA"
147    GOTO 190
150    A = S / N1
160    PRINT "TOTAL OF ", N1, " NUMBERS"
170    PRINT "SUM = ", S
180    PRINT "AVERAGE = ", A
190    END
```

Figure I-20   Sum and Average Program for a Variable Number of Values

the growth rate is 1 percent, then the population (P) at the end of the year is P + .01 * P. Knowing this, you develop the pseudocode in figure I-21.

Figure I-22 shows the corresponding BASIC. Note that figure I-22 strictly adheres to the pseudocode in figure I-21. Thus, there are two INPUT statements. The first one is needed to provide a value of

```
 INPUT I FROM TERMINAL
 DOWHILE I IS GREATER THAN ZERO
    PRINT THE VALUE OF I
    SET P TO 230, N TO 1981
    DOWHILE N IS LESS THAN OR EQUAL TO 2030
       SET P = P + I * P
       ADD 1 TO N
    END-DO
    PRINT P
    INPUT I FROM TERMINAL
 END-DO
```

Figure I-21   Logic for Population Estimation Problem

```
 05 PRINT "INPUT GROWTH RATE"
 10 INPUT I
 20 IF I <= 0 THEN 100
 30 PRINT "FOR GROWTH RATE ", I
 35 P = 230
 40 FOR N = 1981 TO 2030
 50 P = P + I * P             Inner            Outer
 60 NEXT N                    DOWHILE          DOWHILE
 70 PRINT "THE POPULATION IS ", P, " MILLION."
 80 INPUT I
 90 GOTO 20
100 END
```

Figure I-22   BASIC Program for the Population Pseudocode in Figure I-21

I to start the DOWHILE. The second one provides the next value of I in the outer loop. From an efficiency standpoint, the program could be improved by changing statement 80 to GOTO 10. Then, statement 90 could be eliminated. For simple programs, it is sometimes hard to see the beauty of the pseudocode. If you do more programming, you will find that your effort to understand the pseudocode structures will be worth it.

In this section we discussed the BASIC FOR-NEXT structure. We developed programs using this structure. Also, FOR-NEXT was related to the pseudocode DOWHILE structure.

**SECTION 3
SUMMARY**

QUESTIONS

I.15 Explain the operation of the following BASIC statements:

```
10 FOR I = J TO K STEP L
20 PRINT I
30 NEXT I
```

I.16 According to figure I-18, what will happen if J is greater than K in question I.15? What will happen if J is less than K, but L is greater than K?

The following BASIC program is needed to answer questions I.17 through I.21. Input it to your computer.

```
10 INPUT I, J, K, L
20 IF I = 0 THEN 80
30 FOR I = J TO K STEP L
40 PRINT I, J, K, L
50 NEXT I
60 PRINT "LOOP END ", I, J, K, L
70 GOTO 10
80 END
```

I.17 Run this program with $J = 2$, $K = 10$, and $L = 2$. Explain the results.

I.18 Run this program with $J = 2$, $K = 10$, and $L = 3$. Explain the results.

I.19 Run this program with $J = 10$, $K = 5$, and $L = 2$. Explain the results. Does your computer implement FOR-NEXT as a DOWHILE or DOUNTIL structure?

I.20 Run this program with $J = -5$, $K = 5$, and $L = 1$. What happens? If it works, explain the results. If it doesn't work, explain what happened.

I.21 Run this program with $J = 10$, $K = 1$, and $L = -2$. Does it work? If so, explain the results. If not, explain what happened.

PRACTICE PROGRAMS

P.9 Develop a BASIC program to compute the value of an investment. Suppose the amount invested, the interest rate, and the number of periods are input from a terminal. Your program should print the values read and the value of the investment that it computes. Use the same type of formula as was used to compute the population of the United States.

a. Design the program. Use either a flowchart or pseudocode to represent the logic.

b. Write a BASIC program that implements this logic.

c. Test the program. Make sure that it works for all relevant values. Print error messages for erroneous values.

P.10 According to history, the Indians were given $24 worth of trinkets for Manhattan Island. Suppose they had sold the trinkets for $24 and saved the money in a British bank at 6 percent, at 12 percent, or at 18 percent. Develop a BASIC program to determine what the $24 would be worth today.

a. Design the logic. Use either a flowchart or pseudocode to present it.

b. Write a BASIC program that implements this logic.

c. Test your program. Verify that the answers produced are correct.

SECTION 4—
TABLES OR
ARRAYS

This section presents the last of the major BASIC concepts that we will discuss. It concerns the definition and use of *arrays*. Do not let that term scare you; an array is simply a table.

To illustrate the need for arrays, consider the problem of a major wholesaler who provides discounts to customers based on the size of the order. The amount of the discount is as follows:

If the Order Is		
Greater Than ($)	*But Less Than or Equal to ($)*	*Then the Discount Is (%)*
0	500	0
500	1,000	3
1,000	5,000	5
5,000	10,000	7
10,000	Any amount	10

Now, how can the amount of the discount be determined in a BASIC program? First, consider how the discount is calculated without using arrays. Figure I-23 shows part of a BASIC program that does this.

This is an awkward program. It contains a long list of IF statements followed by a list of assignment statements. What happens if the company decides to have more breaks in their discount structure? If, for example, the company had 100 different discount breaks, there would be 100 IF statements and 100 assignment statements. There is a better way to develop this program.

(The program has already set A to the amount of the order.
D is to be set to the amount of the discount.)

```
210    IF A< = 500 THEN 300
220    IF A< = 1000 THEN 320
230    IF A< = 5000 THEN 340
240    IF A< = 10000 THEN 360
260 REM      A IS GREATER THAN 10000
280    D = .10
290    GOTO 400
300    D = 0
310    GOTO 400
320    D = .03
330    GOTO 400
340    D = .05
350    GOTO 400
360    D = .07
400    (The program continues from here.)
```

Figure I-23 Part of a BASIC Program to Determine Discounts without Arrays

Figure I-24 shows a table that holds this company's discount structure. The table has horizontal rows and columns. The first column has a maximum order amount, and the second has the discount.

This table can be used to determine the amount of the discount as follows. Compare the amount of the order to the items in the first column. Find the first row that has a value greater than the amount of the order. The discount in this row is the correct discount. Thus, if the amount of the order is 2,500, the first row having an amount greater than this quantity is row 3. The discount is therefore 5 percent. If the amount is 750, then row 2 has the discount. If the amount is 7,500, then row 4 has the correct discount.

Figure I-24 A Table Holding Discount Rates

	Columns	
	Amount	*Discount Rate*
Rows	500	0
	1,000	3
	5,000	5
	10,000	7
	100,000	10

The last row in the table must be an amount greater than any order can ever be. Here, it is set to 100,000. If the company ever has an order greater than this, an error will result.

Now, since we will be referring to these items in this table, we need to give each one of them a name. However, we must first give the table a name. Using our imagination, let's call it T for table.

Also, let's name the rows and columns. Again, using our imagination, we will call the first row, row 1; the second, row 2; and so forth. Also, we will name the columns, column 1, column 2, and so forth. Now, to identify a particular item, we simply state the table name, the row name, and the column name. Thus, T, row 1, column 2 refers to the value 0. T, row 3, column 1 refers to the value 5,000.

This naming technique is cumbersome; we need to shorten it. Let's put the row and column numbers in parentheses after the table name. If we do this, then $T(1,2)$ refers to the item in table T, row 1, column 2. $T(3,1)$ refers to table T, row 3, column 1. The names of the rows and columns are often called *subscripts*.

Tables can have different sizes. They can have from one to many rows, and they can have from one to many columns. The table in figure I-24 has five rows and two columns. The number of rows and columns is called the *dimension* of the table. The dimensions of the table in figure I-24 are five by two.

Before we can use a table in BASIC, we must define it; that is, name the table and give its dimensions. This procedure allows the system to reserve storage space for all of the values. A special statement, called the DIM or DIMension statement, is used to define a table.

To define the table in figure I-24, we would code the BASIC statement:

```
20 DIM T(5,2)
```

This code tells the system to reserve storage for a table with five rows and two columns. Note that the dimension statement is not referring to the last value in the table (the item whose value is 10). Rather it is informing the system of the maximum size of the table.

How can we get values into this table? We could do it with a long string of assignment statements like this:

```
30 T(1,1) = 500
40 T(1,2) = 0
50 T(2,1) = 1000
60 T(2,2) = 3
```
and so forth

This approach is tedious and would be even more so if the table dimensions were, say, 100,100. Also, what if we want to input the values in the table from a terminal? In this case we might code:

```
30  INPUT  T(1,1),  T(1,2)
40  INPUT  T(2,1),  T(2,2)
50  INPUT  T(3,1),  T(3,2)
and so forth
```

When statement 30 is executed, the user is expected to provide two values. The first will be put into position 1,1 of T, and the second will be put into position 1,2.

Examine the last three BASIC statements. Notice the pattern in the subscripts? The first subscript is 1 in statement 30, 2 in statement 40, and 3 in statement 50. We can use a variable to represent the first subscript.

For example, the table shown in figure I-24 could be filled by the following statements:

```
10  DIM  T(5,2)
20  FOR  I = 1 TO 5
30  INPUT  T(I,1),  T(I,2)
40  NEXT  I
```

Here we are using a FOR-NEXT loop to execute the INPUT instruction five times. The first time it is executed, I has the value 1, then it has the value 2, then 3, then 4, and finally 5.

This approach has even more appeal when you consider what would happen if the dimensions on T were 100,2. Without the FOR-NEXT loop, it would take 100 INPUT instructions to fill the table. However, with the FOR-NEXT instructions, it can be filled with just a few changes as follows:

```
10  DIM  T(100,2)
20  FOR  I = 1 TO 100
30  INPUT  T(I,1),  T(I,2)
40  NEXT  I
```

The Discount Program   Now, return to the original problem of computing discount rates. An algorithm for searching a table is shown in figure I-25. N is the number of rows in the table (5 for the table in I-24), and T is the table as defined above. The first operation checks if the order amount is too large (greater than 100,000 for I-24). If so, an error message is printed. Otherwise, the correct row is found, and the discount and amount due are calculated. Results are printed. Figure I-25a is a flowchart of this algorithm; part b shows the equivalent pseudocode.

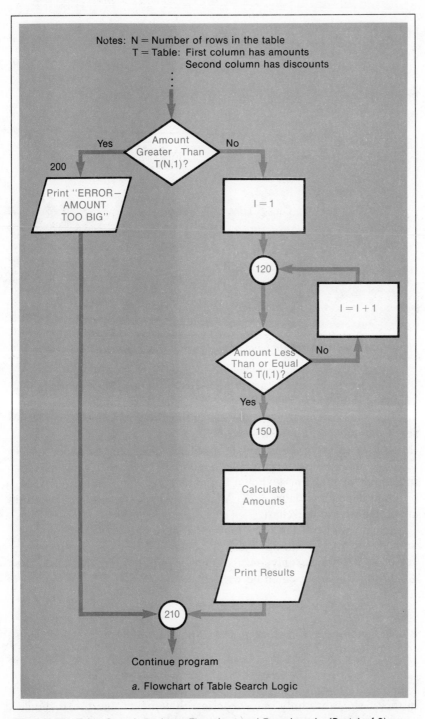

Figure I-25 Table Search Problem Flowchart and Pseudocode *(Part 1 of 2)*

```
                    Same variables as I-25a.
                              .
                              .
                              .

    IF AMOUNT GREATER THAN T(N,1)
        THEN PRINT ERROR MESSAGE
        ELSE SET I = 1
                DOWHILE AMOUNT GREATER THAN T(I,1)
                    I = I + 1
                END-DO
                CALCULATE AMOUNTS USING T(I,2)
                PRINT RESULTS
    END-IF

                    Continue program


              b. Pseudocode for Table Search Problem
```

Figure I-25   Table Search Problem Flowchart and Pseudocode *(Part 2 of 2)*

Figure I-26 shows part of a BASIC program. This program implements the logic in figure I-25. BASIC statement numbers are annotated on the flowchart. Thus, the 210 in the circle in figure I-25a represents statement 210 in figure I-26.

Now, to solve the complete problem, logic must be added to fill the table and to allow for multiple amounts to be input. A flowchart for the complete problem is shown in figure I-27. The complete BASIC program appears in figure I-28. Again, BASIC statement numbers are annotated on the flowchart.

So far we have described tables that have both rows and columns. Sometimes, a table will have just one column. For example, to store a list of stock prices, only one column is required. In this case, the dimension statement could be written:

```
10 DIM P(100,1)
```

P could then hold 100 stock prices. Another way that this dimension could be written is:

```
10 DIM P(100)
```

In this case, P has only one subscript. Statements that use P should specify only one subscript value. Statements to input values of P are:

Note: The following variables have already been given values in a previous
      part of the program:
      Al = the amount ordered
      N = the number of rows in the table
      T = the table in figure I-24
      .
      .
      .

```
100 IF A1 > T(N,1) THEN 200
110 I = 1
120 IF A <= T(I,1) THEN 150
130 I = I + 1
140 GOTO 120
150 D1 = T(I,2)
160 D2 = A1 * D1
170 A2 = A1 - D2
180 PRINT "AMOUNT ORDERED, DISCOUNT RATE, DISCOUNT AMOUNT, AMOUNT DUE"
185 PRINT A1, D1, D2, A2
190 GOTO 210
200 PRINT "ERROR AMOUNT EXCEEDS TABLE VALUES.  AMOUNT IS ", A1
210 Continue with program
```
      .
      .
      .

Figure I-26 Portion of BASIC Program to Implement Table Search from Figure I-25

```
10 FOR I = 1 TO 100
20 INPUT P(I)
30 NEXT I
```

Observe that only one subscript is specified in the INPUT statement.
Also, we used the variable name P instead of T. This is permitted; any
valid variable name can be a table name.

The array or table concept is a very useful and powerful one. We
have shown a way that tables are commonly used in business data
processing. However, there are many other applications. The practice
programs below show some of them.

**SECTION 4
SUMMARY**

Figure I-29 summarizes the BASIC statements discussed in this
module. This is only a subset of the BASIC language. If you are
interested, you can learn more from one of the references listed at the
end of this book. [78,81,87,99]

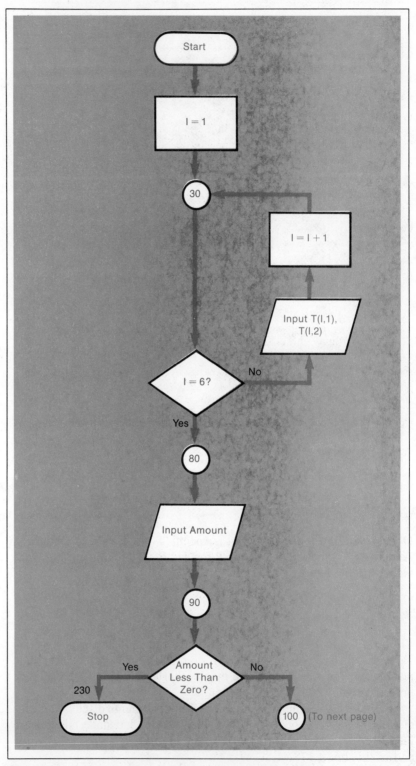

Figure I-27 Flowchart of Discount Problem Logic *(Part 1 of 2)*

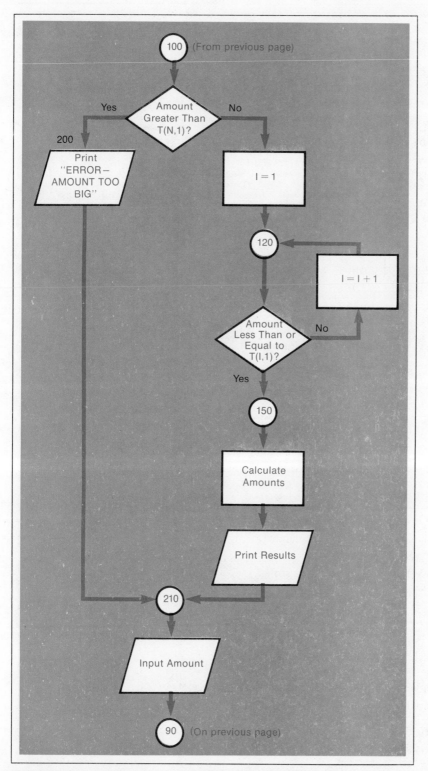

Figure I-27 Flowchart of Discount Problem Logic *(Part 2 of 2)*

```
10    DIM T(5,2)
20 REM     FILL TABLE
30    FOR I = 1 TO 5
40    PRINT "FILL IN NEXT AMOUNT AND DISCOUNT"
50    INPUT T(I,1), T(I,2)
60    NEXT I
70    PRINT "INPUT FIRST ORDER AMOUNT"
80    INPUT A1
90    IF A1 = 0 THEN 230
95 REM     FIND DISCOUNT RATE
100    IF A1 > T(5,1) THEN 200
110    I = 1
120    IF A1 <= T(I,1) THEN 150
130    I = I + 1
140    GOTO 120
145 REM     CALCULATE DISCOUNT AMOUNT AND AMOUNT DUE
150    D1 = T(I,2)
160    D2 = A1 * D1 / 100.0
170    A2 = A1 - D2
180    PRINT "AMOUNT, DISCOUNT RATE, DISCOUNT AMOUNT, AMOUNT DUE"
185    PRINT A1, D1, D2, A2
190    GOTO 210
195 REM     ERROR PRINT MESSAGE
200    PRINT "ERROR.  AMOUNT EXCEEDS TABLE VALUES.  AMOUNT IS ", A1
205 REM     GET NEXT ORDER AMOUNT
210    PRINT "INPUT NEXT ORDER AMOUNT"
215    INPUT A1
220    GOTO 90
230    END
```

Figure I-28 Complete BASIC Program for the Discount Problem

Figure I-29 Summary of BASIC Statements

Statement	General Format	Example
Assignment	variable = arithmetic expression	05 A = (B + C) / D
IF	IF condition THEN statement number	10 IF A = B THEN 100
Input	INPUT variable list	30 INPUT A, B, C
Output	PRINT variable list or character string (in quotes)	40 PRINT "AMOUNT DUE ", X
Stop	END	900 END
Repetition	FOR variable = initial value STEP increment Put instructions to be repeated here. NEXT variable	50 FOR I = 1 TO 99 STEP 2 100 NEXT I
Define tables or arrays	DIM variable (limit-1, limit-2) or DIM variable (limit-1)	05 DIM Q(20,5) 05 DIM Q(25)
Refer to tables or arrays	variable(subscript, subscript) or variable(subscript)	05 INPUT A(2,3) 05 INPUT A(J)

I.22   Explain what the following statements mean:

    a. `10 DIM R(50,50)`
    b. `10 DIM X1(1000)`

I.23   Which of the following are valid references for I.22*a* above:

    a. `INPUT R(23,4)`   c. `Z = R(23,4)`
    b. `T = R(-2,17)`   d. `Q = R(40,2)`

I.24   Which of the following are valid references for I.22*b* above:

    a. `INPUT X1(200)`   c. `T = X1(-5)`
    b. `X1 = 75`   d. `INPUT X1(0)`

P.11   An instructor has graded an examination and the scores range from 35 to 97. He or she has decided to assign grades as follows:

87 to 97	A
75 to 86	B
64 to 74	C
53 to 63	D
35 to 52	F

    Develop a computer program that the instructor can use to assign the letter grades. The input to the program is the student name and score. The output is the student name and the letter grade. Use a table to hold the grade scores.

    a. Design the program logic. Present it with a flowchart or pseudocode.

    b. Write a BASIC program to implement the logic.

    c. Test your program for correct results. Show that it works for all possible values.

P.12   For a major cross-country meet, runners are being assigned to starting groups based on their time at an earlier qualifying run. The group assignments are made as follows:

Previous Time	*Group Assignment*
35 minutes or less	1
36 to 40 minutes	2
41 to 50 minutes	3
51 to 60 minutes	4
Over 60 minutes	5

Develop a program to make the group assignments. Your program should input the runner's name and previous time. It should output the name and the group assignment.

a. Design the program. Present the design with a flowchart or pseudocode.

b. Write a BASIC program that implements the design.

c. Test your program for correct results. Show that it works for all possible values.

P.13 Develop a program to compute gross pay and taxes. Input the employee name, hourly pay rate, and number of hours worked. Give the employee time and a half for work in excess of 40 hours. Compute taxes on the following basis:

If Gross Pay Is Greater Than or Equal to	Less Than	Then Taxes Are
0	200	10%
200	600	$20 + 15% of the amount over $200
600	1000	$80 + 20% of the amount over $600
1000	1500	$160 + 40% of the amount over $1000
1500 or greater		$360 + 60% of the amount over $1500

Your program should output the employee name, gross pay, taxes, and net pay. Also, calculate and print the total payroll, total taxes, and total net pay.

a. Design the program. Present the design with a flowchart or pseudocode. *Hint:* Use a table with three columns.

b. Write a BASIC program to implement the design.

c. Test the program for correct results. Show that it works for all possible values.

WORD LIST		
WORD LIST	*BASIC*	*INPUT statement*
(in order of appearance in text)	*BASIC statement*	*IF statement*
	Statement number	*End-of-data signal*
	Program variable	*Program constant*

PRINT statement

REM statement

RUN command

Character data

String data

String variable

Assignment statement

Arithmetic expression

Relation symbol

Loop

FOR statement

NEXT statement

Loop increment

Array

Table

Subscript

Dimensions

DIM statement

MODULE J

Survey of Computer Programming Languages

A sample of programming languages

LANGUAGE SELECTION AT
DEMPCO ENTERPRISES

THE STATE OF
PROGRAMMING
LANGUAGES TODAY

PROGRAMMING
APPLICATIONS AND
LANGUAGES

  Business Applications

    BASIC
    COBOL
    PL/I
    RPG

Scientific Applications

  ADA
  ALGOL
  APL
  FORTRAN
  PASCAL
  Other Scientific Languages

Systems Applications

Special Purpose
Applications

LANGUAGE SELECTION AT
DEMPCO ENTERPRISES

LANGUAGE SELECTION AT DEMPCO ENTERPRISES

 Ben Katz shook his head in amazement and despair. What were these people talking about, and how important was it? Ben was the general manager of DEMPCO Enterprises, a position he had assumed two months ago. Just prior to that time, DEMPCO had been purchased by the company Ben worked for. He was the first manager after the realignment.

In front of Ben were two people from Data Processing. Jay had been a programmer at DEMPCO for 15 years. He was recognized as the person who kept the shop together. Susan was a young systems analyst who seemed to have a lot on the ball. She had worked at DEMPCO for only six months, but she had several years of experience before that.

The discussion concerned the future direction of programming at DEMPCO. Apparently, most of DEMPCO's programs were written in something called *assembler language*. This had Susan upset. She felt that these programs should be phased out and gradually replaced by programs written in another language. She seemed to vacillate about what other language should be used.

Jay thought the assembler language programs were fine. In fact, he thought they were excellent—very efficient, he said (although he never really indicated what he meant by efficient). Jay believed that programmers at DEMPCO should continue writing assembler language programs because they provided "efficiency" unavailable with other languages.

The issue had come to a head last Friday in a Data Processing staff meeting. Susan and Jay had had a confrontation about this issue. They had asked Ben for a decision on the company's future direction. Both Susan and Jay were threatening to quit if the wrong decision was made.

If you were Ben, what would you do?

In this module we will discuss computer languages. First, we will consider how languages have been developed and where they are today. Then, four types of computer programming problems will be defined. Languages commonly used for each type of problem will be briefly described. With that knowledge, we will return to DEMPCO Enterprises to see how the language selection issue was resolved.

You would probably be amazed to walk into a forest in the Pacific Northwest and find someone cutting down a 300 foot tree with an ax. Yet, in any midsized city, you will find some people writing computer programs with the equivalent of an ax. To understand why, consider how programming languages were developed.

THE STATE OF PROGRAMMING LANGUAGES TODAY

As stated in Module G, the first computers were programmed in binary using 0's and 1's. This process took a long time, and programs written in binary were very hard to change. Consequently, computer specialists looked for better ways to program. In the mid-1950s the first versions of *high level languages* were developed. These languages allowed programmers to write instructions which were closer to English than binary, but which could be translated into machine language.

The people who developed these early languages were truly pioneers. They had little theory to go by, and they developed languages by intuition. Some of the languages just grew. People considered the computers they had, and the problems they wanted to solve, and they developed the best language they could to solve the problems.

Unfortunately, pioneers are often shot down by arrows! Some of the languages were terrible! They never worked correctly; or they were very hard to use; or they directed the computer inefficiently; or the programs written in them were nearly impossible to read; and so on. Some never had enough time or money invested in their development to get a fair trial. All in all, over 1000 languages have been developed in the last 30 years. Of those, not more than 10 are in popular use today.

As languages were implemented, as they were used, and as one language was compared to another, principles of language design were developed. By 1970, many experts had a good idea of the best way to design languages.

A milestone in this process was the discovery in the late 1960s that all programming logic could be represented by three basic instruction patterns or *constructs: sequence, alternation,* and *iteration.* Sequence means that a group of instructions is to be performed in order.

Alternation means that the sequence of instructions to be performed is selected, depending on some condition. For example,

```
IF A IS LESS THAN B
    THEN
            /execute one or more statements/
    ELSE
            /execute one or more different
            statements/
END-IF
```

Iteration means that a sequence of instructions is to be performed repeatedly while (or until) some condition is true. For example, the following iteration might be used to calculate the year that some investment exceeds a million dollars:

```
DOWHILE PRINCIPAL IS LESS THAN 1000000
    ADD 1 TO YEAR
    COMPUTE NEW PRINCIPAL AT 10 PERCENT
END-DO
```

The iteration construct is discussed at length in Modules H and I.

This discovery meant that other instruction patterns were unneeded. It meant the logic of every program, no matter how complex, could be reduced to these simple building blocks. Some languages that had frills and extras beyond these patterns could be simplified.

Even more important, many languages represented one or more of these three patterns awkwardly. The alternation pattern, for example, is badly represented by several languages. (The BASIC language in Module I is one.) People began to see that programs written in these languages were hard to read, hard to understand, and hard to change.

Other principles were also discovered. These principles helped experts to understand the characteristics of a good programming language.

Unfortunately, by that time, several languages had become firmly entrenched in user organizations. These languages had some good characteristics, but they also had many bad ones. Thousands of programs had been written using them. Companies could not afford to completely rewrite the programs. They could not afford to retrain all of their programming personnel. Many programmers had spent years learning one or more languages. They did not want a new language to come along that would outdate their skills.

Therefore, there was, and is, tremendous economic, political, and personal resistance to new languages. Of the 10 most popular languages in use today, eight were developed before 1970. Seven were designed before 1965.

As you read this survey of languages, keep in mind that every one of them has major defects. However, every one of them also does something well. After all, they are the survivors of the 1000 or so languages that have been developed in the history of computing.

The story of computer languages is not finished. Today we have languages that were created in the pioneering stage. These languages will be improved or replaced. Sometime in the distant future, there will be languages that are easy to use, easy to read, and efficient. This development will occur in the course of your business career. You will deal with data processing personnel caught in the agony of this growth.

In the last 30 years, computer specialists have learned that there is no such thing as a typical computer program. Programs vary considerably; consequently there is no best computer language. Some languages are better for one type of processing and some are better for others. In this section we will investigate four categories of applications: business, scientific, systems, and special purpose. Each category requires a different type of programming language.

PROGRAMMING APPLICATIONS AND LANGUAGES

Business applications typically involve transferring large amounts of data, and business programs often execute many input/output instructions. However, once the data is in main memory, business programs usually perform few mathematical operations on it. Instead, data items are compared to one another, decisions are made, and changes are made to stored data. Structured reports are frequently produced.

Business Applications and Languages

Additionally, business applications are often on line. They may serve many users operating concurrently at many terminals. Users often want to access the same files of data, so program coordination is important. This is discussed further in Chapter 8.

Business is a dynamic activity, and business programs often change. Since the person who wrote a program is often not available to change it, business programs need to be easy to read and understand.

Order entry is a typical business application. To process an order, customer, inventory, and production records must be accessed. Data about customer credit, items on hand or in production, shipping addresses, etc., is processed to make order approval and shipping decisions.

Since hundreds of orders may be processed in a day, a tremendous volume of data may be transferred to and from the files. However, the processing of this data is simple arithmetic; no sophisticated mathematics is involved.

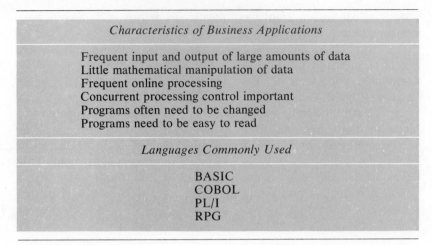

Characteristics of Business Applications
Frequent input and output of large amounts of data Little mathematical manipulation of data Frequent online processing Concurrent processing control important Programs often need to be changed Programs need to be easy to read
Languages Commonly Used
BASIC COBOL PL/I RPG

Figure J-1 Summary of Business Application Programming

Generally, several order entry clerks process the same files. If their access is not carefully controlled, they can interfere with one another.

These characteristics of business programs mean that a business programming language should have extensive input/output capability. It should be easy to do I/O, and data should be transferred efficiently. Also, the language should have a rich vocabulary for describing records, fields, data types, and so forth.

The logic of business processing is sometimes complex, so the alternation pattern (IF-THEN-ELSE) should be clear and easy to understand. Sophisticated mathematical vocabulary is unimportant.

Since online, concurrent processing is prevalent, the language should have commands for locking and unlocking records and for performing other types of program coordination.

The characteristics of business applications are summarized in figure J-1. This figure shows four languages commonly used for business programming. We will briefly describe each of these.

BASIC The acronym *BASIC* stands for Beginner's All-Purpose Symbolic Instruction Code. BASIC was designed in the late 1960s at Dartmouth College and was intended to introduce students to programming. As its name implies, it is an all-purpose language for beginners.

A simple BASIC program is shown in figure J-2. This program reads accounts receivable records and computes the number of accounts having a zero balance, the number having a positive balance, and the total of the balances. After all records are input, the results are printed. BASIC's primary virtue is that it is simple and therefore easy

```
010  REM       THIS PROGRAM PROCESSES ACCOUNTS RECEIVABLE DATA
020  REM       VARIABLE ASSIGNMENTS ARE:
030  REM       N1 = NUMBER OF ACCOUNTS WITH ZERO BALANCES
040  REM       N2 = NUMBER OF ACCOUNTS WITH POSITIVE BALANCES
050  REM       T  = TOTAL OF BALANCES
060  REM       N$ = NAME OF CUSTOMER
070  REM       B  = AMOUNT OF CUSTOMER BALANCE
100     N1 = 0
150     N2 = 0
200     T  = 0
225  REM       PROCESSING LOOP STARTS HERE
250     INPUT N$, B
300     IF N$ = "END" THEN 650
350     IF B = 0 THEN 550
400     N2 = N2 + 1
450     T = T + B
500     GOTO 250
550     N1 = N1 + 1
600     GOTO 250
625  REM       TERMINATION SECTION
650     PRINT "NUMBER OF ACCOUNTS WITH ZERO BALANCE IS ", N1
700     PRINT "NUMBER OF ACCOUNTS WITH POSITIVE BALANCE IS ", N2
750     PRINT "TOTAL OF BALANCES IS ", T
800     END
```

Figure J-2 Sample BASIC Program

to learn and use. BASIC has very primitive input/output capability, and its vocabulary for alteration is clumsy. As shown in Module I, iteration structures can be awkward to implement in BASIC.

BASIC is popular because it is simple, and it works well for small problems like computing the interest on a mortgage. However, because of its limitations, BASIC is not good for all business applications. When complex programs are written in BASIC, the code is usually hard to read and understand, and therefore hard to change.

Actually, BASIC's simplicity has turned out to be a disadvantage. BASIC has been applied to problems for which it is not suited. Beginners have learned BASIC, and then never graduated to one of the harder-to-learn but more powerful languages. As the beginner's programming skill improved, he or she took on more complex tasks, but carried BASIC along. After some period of time, a beginner's language is used to accomplish complex tasks. This paradox results in hard-to-read and otherwise undesirable code.

BASIC is offered with many small business computers and microcomputers. Often the computer vendor extends the capabilities of BASIC to allow for the sophisticated input/output needed for business data processing. This offer, however, is a trap. Once a company develops programs using the language extensions, they find it hard to switch to another vendor's computer. If they switched, all of the programs would have to be rewritten to remove the special commands. This modification would be very expensive.

To summarize, BASIC is an easy language for beginners to learn about programming. The standard language can result in hard-to-read and excessively complex programs. Vendors have augmented the language to give it more power. BASIC is often used with microcomputers.

COBOL   The acronym *COBOL* stands for COmmon Business Oriented Language. COBOL was designed by a committee of users and computer manufacturers in the late 1950s. The users wanted a language that would be suited to business problems and that would support sophisticated input and output processing.

COBOL is an old and established language. It is nationally standardized and supported by all major computer manufacturers. Between 60 and 80 percent of all business application programs are written in COBOL.

Figure J-3 shows the accounts receivable problem coded in COBOL. This is the same problem used to demonstrate BASIC in figure J-2.

Because COBOL was designed with business applications in mind, it has been very successful in the business environment. It has an extensive vocabulary for defining files, records, and fields. Its alternation and iteration constructs are much better than BASIC's.

Unfortunately, COBOL has disadvantages, too. It is a large language with many features. Like any committee project, everyone's good ideas were incorporated. Consequently, COBOL is easily misused, and it takes most people a year or so of programming to learn the language well.

Also, COBOL was designed to be *self-documenting*. Many lines of code must be written even for simple problems. A few years ago, someone said that when the weight of the cards containing the COBOL statements exceeds the weight of the computer, then the program is ready to run. Actually, COBOL was designed to solve medium and large business problems. It is time-consuming and frustrating to write small COBOL programs.

COBOL was designed before online processing existed. Therefore, the standardized language does not have any special commands to coordinate concurrent processing. Most manufacturers of computers with online capability have expanded their versions of COBOL to include such commands.

If there is *a* business programming language, COBOL is it. Over the years, COBOL has proven to be amazingly durable. It has the features necessary to handle most business processing problems. You

Note: A COBOL program has three parts, called *divisions*. The
IDENTIFICATION DIVISION names the program. The EN-
VIRONMENT DIVISION describes the files to be used; the
DATA DIVISION describes the format of the data. Finally,
the PROCEDURE DIVISION describes actions for the com-
puter to take. For simplicity, only the PROCEDURE DIVI-
SION is shown here.

```
PROCEDURE DIVISION.
    PERFORM A10-INITIALIZE.
    PERFORM A20-PROCESS UNTIL EOF-FLAG = 1.
    PERFORM A30-WRAPUP.
    STOP RUN.
A10-INITIALIZE.
    OPEN INPUT DATA-FILE
         OUTPUT PRINT-FILE.
    MOVE 0 TO EOF-FLAG.
    MOVE 0 TO NUM-ZERO-BAL.
    MOVE 0 TO NUM-POS-BAL.
    MOVE 0 TO TOTAL-BAL.
    READ DATA-FILE AT END MOVE 1 TO EOF-FLAG.
A20-PROCESS.
    IF BAL IS GREATER THAN 0
    ADD 1 TO NUM-POS-BAL
    ADD BAL TO TOTAL-BAL
    ELSE
         ADD 1 TO NUM-ZERO-BAL.
    READ DATA-FILE AT END MOVE 1 TO EOF-FLAG.
A30-WRAPUP.
    WRITE PRINT-REC FROM HEADER1.
    WRITE PRINT-REC FROM SUMMARY-DATA.
    CLOSE DATA-FILE PRINT-FILE.
```

Figure J-3 Procedure Division of a COBOL Program

probably do not go one day without handling a document or form that
was generated by a COBOL program.

PL/I PL/I stands for Programming Language I. It was developed
by IBM in the mid-1960s as a general purpose language that could be
used for all types of computer processing—business, scientific, and
systems.

Figure J-4 shows the accounts receivable problem coded in PL/I.
Compare this to the BASIC and COBOL programs in figures J-2
and J-3.

PL/I has many similarities to COBOL. The vocabulary for defining files, records, and data items is rich. A wide variety of input/
output techniques is available. The constructs for alternation and

```
ACCT_REC: PROCEDURE OPTIONS(MAIN);
```
Note: Definitions of variables go here. For simplicity, they are not
      shown in this example.

```
      ON ENDFILE (AR_FILE) EOF_FLAG = 1;
      EOF_FLAG = 0;
      NUM_ZERO_BAL = 0;
      NUM_POS_BAL  = 0;
      TOTAL_BAL    = 0;
      GET LIST (CUST_NAME, AMOUNT);
      DO WHILE EOF_FLAG = 0;
          IF AMOUNT GT 0
              THEN DO;
                   NUM_POS = NUM_POS + 1;
                   TOTAL_BAL = TOTAL_BAL + AMOUNT;
                   END;
              ELSE NUM_ZERO_BAL = NUM_ZERO_BAL +1;
          GET LIST (CUST_NAME, AMOUNT);
      END;

      PUT PAGE LIST ('NUMBER OF ZERO BALANCES IS ', NUM_ZERO_BAL);
      PUT SKIP(2) LIST ('NUMBER OF POSITIVE BALANCES IS ',
                       NUM_POS_BAL, 'TOTAL OF BALANCES IS ',
                       TOTAL_BAL);
      STOP;
      END;
```

Figure J-4   Portion of a PL/I Program

iteration are excellent. PL/I has all the features necessary for business application programming. Additionally, PL/I has features for scientific and systems programming that make it truly a general purpose language.

Unfortunately, all of these features mean that PL/I is complex. The PL/I learning period is lengthy. The designers of PL/I attempted to reduce the impact of this complexity by defining levels of the language. The idea was that beginners could easily use a subset of PL/I and never know that other features were available. The implementation of this idea has been only partially successful.

In spite of its excellent features, PL/I has not been readily accepted in the business community. There are several reasons for this rejection. First, for many years, PL/I was available only on IBM computers. Companies that developed programs in PL/I were in effect committing to use IBM equipment now and in the future. This commitment was more than most companies wanted to accept.

Second, the existing PL/I compilers do not generate efficient object code. Programs written in PL/I occupy more main storage than equivalent programs written in another language. They take more machine time to run.

Finally, although PL/I is an excellent language, it does not appear to have substantial advantages over COBOL for business applications. Therefore, it is not sufficiently better to justify switching languages and possibly becoming dependent on IBM. Consequently, most companies have stayed with COBOL.

RPG The acronym *RPG* stands for Report Program Generator. RPG is not a programming language like BASIC, COBOL, or PL/I, but sometimes it is called a programming language. Since many business reports are generated using RPG, you should know about it.

To use RPG, a programmer defines the format of input files by naming fields and specifying their lengths and types (numeric, character, etc.). Then, the programmer defines simple operations on fields, like "add all order amounts together." He or she then specifies that this total is to be printed on a report.

RPG is well named. It is useful for reading files and producing reports. However, when complex logic is involved, many experienced programmers will choose a programming language like COBOL or PL/I. An RPG example is shown in figure J-5.

Figure J-5 Sample RPG Program

```
010F* THIS PROGRAM CALCULATES THE NUMBER OF ACCOUNTS WITH ZERO
020F* BALANCES, THE NUMBER WITH POSITIVE BALANCES,
030F* AND THE SUM OF THE BALANCES
040FPAYROLL IP  F  80  80          READ40
050FREPORT   0  F 133 133      0F  PRINTER
010IPAYROLL AA   01
020I                                      1  20 NAME
030I                                     21  262AMT
010C     01      AMT       COMP 0                  10  20
020C     10      TPOS      ADD  1      TPOS     30
030C     10      TBAL      ADD  AMT    TBAL     82
040C     20      TNEG      ADD  1      TNEG     30
010OREPORT   H  201     0F
020O         OR         1P
030O                              56 'RECEIVABLE REPORT'
040O         H  2       0F
050O         OR         1P
060O                              26 'NUMBER OF ZERO BALANCES'
070O                              61 'NUMBER OF POSITIVE BALANCES'
080O                              90 'TOTAL OF BALANCES'
090O         T  1       LR
100O                       TNEG   15
110O                       TPOS   48
120O                       TBAL   86 '   , $0. '
```

Scientific Applications and Languages

A second category of languages includes those used for *scientific applications*. These applications differ from business applications in that they involve considerably less input/output. Although scientific applications do access stored data, this access is much less frequent and the volume of data transferred is much smaller than for business systems. However, the data that is transferred is heavily processed using complex mathematical and logical algorithms.

Scientific applications are usually batch-oriented. Sometimes online processing is used to input data to start a scientific program, but then the program executes autonomously. Few scientific programs are interactive, and few involve concurrent processing.

Statistical analysis is a typical scientific application. To estimate the impact of smoking on cancer, doctors may gather data about the health and smoking habits of 1000 people. This data will be input to programs that compute statistics such as the average rates of cancer among smokers and nonsmokers, the correlation of smoking with cancer, and other more sophisticated statistical estimators.

The amount of data read into the program will be small, at least in comparison to a business system like order entry. However, the data will be manipulated in mathematically sophisticated ways. The CPU will be very busy squaring and summing numbers, integrating probability functions, and so forth.

Also, there will be no need for several users to access the data concurrently. The researchers will be content to receive output reports one at a time.

Finally, scientific programs are not changed as frequently as business programs are. When changes do occur, they are usually additions to programs and not rewrites. For example, it is unlikely that a new method will be defined to compute the average or standard deviation of a sample of data. However, changes to order processing in business can and do occur frequently.

We have not defined scientific programs as programs used by scientists. Sometimes scientists use programs from the business category. For example, when scientists have applications involving lots of data, they use the computer as a business person would. In this case, the scientist is using business data processing techniques.

Figure J-6 summarizes the characteristics of scientific application programs and lists several languages commonly used. We will summarize these languages; but since this is a course in business data processing, this summary will be very brief.

ADA   *ADA* is the newest programming language in this book. It is being developed through contracts issued by the Department of Defense. The goal was to develop a scientific and systems language suitable for a national standard like COBOL.

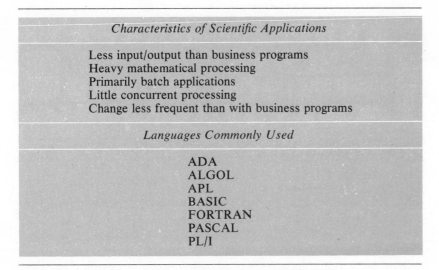

Characteristics of Scientific Applications
Less input/output than business programs Heavy mathematical processing Primarily batch applications Little concurrent processing Change less frequent than with business programs
Languages Commonly Used
ADA ALGOL APL BASIC FORTRAN PASCAL PL/I

Figure J-6 Summary of Scientific Application Programming

ADA is not an acronym. This language was named after Lady Ada Augusta Lovelace, who was a pioneer and important figure in computing in the 19th century. (See Module A for more information.)

ADA was announced in May of 1979 and became operational in early 1980. Although it is too soon to tell how the language will be accepted, early indications are that it is an excellent language and will receive widespread acceptance. ADA is a derivative of the PASCAL language.

ALGOL ALGOL stands for ALGOrithmic Language. It is one of the oldest programming languages. ALGOL was developed primarily for scientific programming. It has excellent alternation and iteration capability, and programs written in ALGOL tend to be easy to read and understand. ALGOL has limited input/output capability.

Although ALGOL never received much acceptance in North America, it has been widely used in Europe. It is the grandparent of several other programming languages including PL/I, ADA, and PASCAL (see below).

APL APL is an acronym for A Programmer's Language. This language is oriented toward problem solving at a terminal. It is especially useful for operating on arrays. APL has a host of language-unique commands for array processing.

Because there are many special characters in the APL language, an APL terminal or keyboard is required. (See figure J-7.) APL is known for its power. Very complex operations can be specified with

Figure J-7 Special Terminal Used for APL Programming

just a few variables and operators. Unfortunately, this also makes APL programs hard to read and understand.

Although APL has a large and loyal following, it is not as commonly used as languages like COBOL or BASIC. It is *primarily* available on IBM computers. This constraint, combined with the need for a special terminal and the large memory needed for the APL compiler, has limited its use. Even still, APL proponents claim there are few better languages.

FORTRAN *FORTRAN* is an acronym for FORmula TRANslator. It, like ALGOL, is an old language that was developed primarily for scientific programming.

FORTRAN is a prime example of a language that just grew. Originally, it was used to translate formulas, but people kept adding to its capability until it became a general purpose language. Unfortunately, FORTRAN is like an old miner's shack onto which rooms have been added year after year. It has little architectural integrity.

FORTRAN has limited input/output capability. Its alternation construct is awkward. Its iteration constructs are minimally acceptable. Programs written in FORTRAN tend to be hard to read and understand. Consequently, they are hard to change.

Amazingly, in spite of these disadvantages, more scientific programs have been written in FORTRAN than in any other language. There are many reasons for this strange situation. One is that many programmers (including your loyal and faithful author) didn't know how much better off they could be with other languages. Another is economic.

In the late 1950s and early 1960s a battle over which language to use was raging between FORTRAN and ALGOL. IBM supported FORTRAN, and other, smaller vendors supported ALGOL. Since IBM sold many more computers than other vendors, FORTRAN became the language most often used. FORTRAN's greater use occurred in spite of the fact that ALGOL is a much better language.

This awareness, however, is hindsight. In fairness to IBM, few people knew at the time that ALGOL was a better language. When the defects of FORTRAN became apparent, IBM developed PL/I, which had many features similar to ALGOL.

PASCAL The *PASCAL* language is named after Blaise Pascal, the French mathematician and philosopher. It was developed in the mid-1970s. PASCAL is an excellent language for scientific and systems applications, but has very limited input/output capability. The constructs for alternation and iteration are excellent, and complex data formats are easily represented.

PASCAL has received considerable acceptance in computer science and engineering departments at colleges and universities. It has had limited acceptance in industry. PASCAL and ADA are very similar, but ADA has more general input/output capability. Therefore, some experts think ADA will be used more often in industry than PASCAL.

Other Scientific Languages As figure J-6 indicates, both PL/I and BASIC are used for scientific applications. Recall that PL/I is a rich language that can result in excellent programs. Its chief drawbacks are that it is complex and the object code tends to be inefficient.

The same remarks can be made about BASIC for scientific applications as were made about BASIC for business applications. It is easily learned and can be effectively used for simple problems. Some professionals would say it is not suited for major programming efforts.

Systems Applications and Languages

The third category of applications are *systems programs*. These programs belong to the computer itself. The operating system, including compilers and utilities, is one example, and a database management system is another. Programs in this category can be very sophisticated. They contain complex logic; they are often executed concurrently; and they tend to be very large. Also, system programs run nearly continuously, so efficiency is very important.

The operating system is primarily involved with logic. Its logical operations include such tasks as selecting the next job; allocating files, main memory, and CPU time; and coordinating input/output operations.

Because relatively little I/O or mathematical processing is involved, these functions are not so important. The major requirement for a system programming language, therefore, is that it represent easily complex logic. The structures used to represent alternation and iteration should be clear and straightforward. Also, system programming languages need to be very efficient.

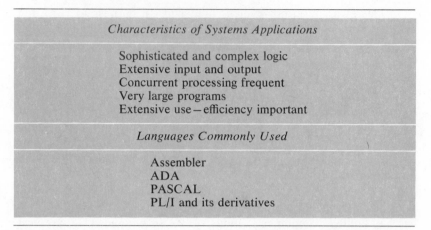

Figure J-8   Summary of Systems Applications Programming

Figure J-8 lists the characteristics of systems applications. Of the four languages listed, ADA, PASCAL, and PL/I have been discussed previously. Actually, PL/I has not been widely used for systems applications; however, its derivatives have. Also, it may be premature to put ADA in this list. ADA has not been available long enough to be used for major projects, although many people predict that it will be.

The first language listed for systems applications is called *Assembler Language*. Actually, this is not one language, but a class of languages. Each computer has its own assembler language.

Assembler language is midway between machine language and the higher level languages we have been discussing. It is more English-like than machine language, but not as English-like as COBOL or PASCAL.

The basic statement in assembler language is a machine instruction. However, instead of an instruction code like 01011010, the machine instructions are mnemonic (memory aiding) like ADD A, B or MOVE C, D. An assembler language program is a list of machine instructions written mnemonically. Figure J-9 shows an example of an assembler language program.

The major advantage of assembler language is its efficiency. Since assembler language is very close to machine language, the programmer can tailor the application to the machine in a way that is not possible in a higher level language. Also, some sophisticated operations can be performed only in assembler language. When these operations are required by the application (as they sometimes are for systems applications), the program must be written in assembler language.

Unfortunately, assembler language has major drawbacks. For one, it takes longer to program an application in assembler than it does in a higher level language. Also, assembler language programs are

```
ACCTREC   STM    14,12,12(13)    SAVE THE REGISTERS
          BALR   12,0            ESTABLISH ADDRESSABILITY
          USING  *,12
          ST     13,SAV+4        STORE SAVE AREA ADDRESS
          LA     13,SAV          GET NEW SAVE AREA ADDRESS
          OPEN   (ARDATA,INPUT,PRINTER,OUTPUT)
          SR     3,3             PUT ZERO IN R3
          SR     5,5             PUT ZERO IN NUMBER POSITIVE (R5)
          SR     6,6             PUT ZERO IN TOTAL BALANCES (R6)
          SR     7,7             PUT ZERO IN NUMBER NEGATIVE (R7)
*
*         NOW PROCESS
*
LOOP      GET    ARDATA,BUFFER     READ IN DATA: AMT IS IN BUFFER
          L      4,AMT
          CR     3,4             IS AMOUNT ZERO?
          BC     8,EQUAL         BRANCH IF IT IS.
          LA     5,1(5)          AMOUNT NOT ZERO. ADD 1 TO NUM POS VALUE
          AR     6,4             ADD AMOUNT TO SUM OF BALANCES
          B      LOOP
EQUAL     LA     7,1(7)          ADD 1 TO NUMBER OF ZERO ACCOUNTS
          B      LOOP
*
*         END OF DATA PROCESSING
*
ENDODATA  ST     5,NUMPOS
          ST     6,TBAL
          ST     7,NUMZERO
          PUT    PRINTER,MSG1       MSG1 HAS NUMZERO IN IT
          PUT    PRINTER,MSG2       MSG2 HAS NUMPOS AND TBAL IN IT
          CLOSE  (ARDATA,PRINTER)
          L      13,SAV+4        GET OLD SAVE AREA
          RETURN (14,12)         RESTORE REGISTERS
```

Figure J-9 Sample Assembler Language Program

hard to read and understand, and therefore hard to fix and change. Finally, assembler language is very system-dependent. Each computer has a different assembler language. If a business wants to change computers (especially to a different brand of computer), all of the assembler language programs must be rewritten.

Ten years ago, nearly all systems applications were written in assembler language. Today, this is changing. Although major portions of some operating systems are still written in assembler, other operating systems are written in PASCAL or a PL/I derivative. Other types of systems applications are also being written more and more in languages other than assembler.

As was mentioned in the DEMPCO case in the beginning of this module, at one time many business applications were written in assembler language. This fact is no longer true. The only assembler language routines around today are those left over from years ago. Assembler language is simply too hard to understand, and applications are too system-dependent.

**Special Purpose
Applications
and Languages**

The final category of program applications is the miscellaneous category. These are the *special purpose applications* like process control, operations research, computer simulation, and so forth. (See Chapter 3.) Because of the uniqueness of these applications, special languages have been developed for them. These applications account for a small percentage of programs, however, and we will not consider them further here.

Figure J-10 summarizes the languages surveyed in this module. Of these, the languages you are most likely to encounter are COBOL, BASIC, RPG, and PL/I. As you study figure J-10, pay particular attention to their features.

Figure J-10 Comparison of Programming Language Features

Language	Alternation Construct	Iteration Construct	Modularity	I/O Capability	Primary Uses
ADA	Excellent	Excellent	Excellent	Good	Systems, Scientific
ALGOL	Excellent	Excellent	Excellent	Good	Scientific
APL	Excellent	Excellent	Fair	Good	Scientific
Assembler	Poor	Poor	Excellent	Excellent	Systems
BASIC	Poor	Fair	Poor	Poor	Education, Simple Programs
COBOL	Excellent	Excellent	Fair	Excellent	Business
FORTRAN	Poor	Fair	Good	Fair	Scientific
PASCAL	Excellent	Excellent	Good	Poor	Education, Systems, Scientific
PL/I	Excellent	Excellent	Excellent	Excellent	General Purpose
RPG	None	None	None	Fair	Report Writing

Ben Katz didn't know what to think about the controversy regarding language selection. You know by now that assembler language probably was not the correct language for DEMPCO. Actually, Jay knew that too, but he was being defensive. He was good at coding assembler. He didn't want anyone to take his value away by eliminating his language. Also, he was afraid to try to learn a new language. Therefore, almost in spite of himself, Jay was arguing for assembler language.

Since Ben didn't know about programming languages, he asked one of the data processing supervisors at the parent company to advise him. The supervisor, Ruth Bennett, was known throughout the company to be an excellent manager as well as technically sharp.

It took Ruth about 30 minutes of talking with Jay to understand the situation. She knew assembler was the wrong language. She also knew why Jay was acting as he did. Without confronting him, she asked Jay and Susan to join her in a committee to determine the best language for DEMPCO in the long run.

Ruth never did confront Jay. She didn't want to because she thought he was sharp and she didn't want DEMPCO to lose his skills. Also, she felt Jay would make a good decision if language selection could be presented in a nonthreatening way.

Consequently, she asked Jay and Susan to consider the most important characteristics for programs at DEMPCO. Also, she asked them to develop a list of criteria for a programming language. After this, the committee met to weigh, or rank, the criteria.

Jay and Susan agreed that the most important characteristic of a program is *correctness*. Therefore, they wanted a language in which it would be easy to write and to correct the programs. On the second characteristic, they disagreed. Susan thought programs should be *adaptable*. She believed that many aspects of business at DEMPCO would change in the near future, and she wanted a language that resulted in easily changed programs. Jay thought programs should be *economical*. Susan asked him what he meant. He said that they should solve the problem with the minimum amount of CPU time and main memory space.

Since they disagreed, they decided to mention all three characteristics of programs at their meeting with Ruth. They also developed a list of language-selection criteria for the meeting.

Ruth was pleased with their work. She thought it was unimportant to decide which factor should be second and which should be third. She did point one fact out to Jay: programs can be economical by being efficient, but they can also be economical by being easy to write and test.

The committee used all three characteristics in developing the prioritized list of criteria in figure J-11. Although ease of learning was

Criteria	Level of Importance
Ease of learning	Low
Ease of use	High
Alternation construct	High
Iteration construct	High
Language documentation	High
Ease of maintenance	High
Program readability	High
Standardization	Medium
Portability	High
Program efficiency	Medium

Figure J-11 Ranking of Language Criteria for DEMPCO Enterprises

considered a criterion, it was not as important as other factors. The most important factors concerned ease of use, since the committee felt that a language that was easy to use would be most likely to result in correct programs.

Ease of maintenance (adaptability) and portability were also considered important. However, after some discussion the committee agreed that programming efficiency was only moderately important. Computers are simply becoming too cheap for that to be a major factor.

After the committee had developed this list of criteria, Ruth asked Susan and Jay to consider which language best fit the overall criteria. She told them to interview programmers who had experience in various languages and then to recommend the best language to the committee. Susan and Jay decided to consider assembler, BASIC, COBOL, and PL/I.

It was easy to eliminate one language. Both Jay and Susan believed it was important to maintain as much machine-independence as possible. They felt that using PL/I would tie them too much to IBM computers, so they eliminated it from further consideration.

As they investigated BASIC, it became apparent that the BASIC IF statement (see figure J-2) was inconvenient. They believed it would be difficult to develop complex programs in BASIC and that it would be easy to make errors with it. Consequently, they eliminated BASIC from consideration.

This left assembler and COBOL as choices. Ruth arranged for both Susan and Jay to take a one-week COBOL programming course. After this course, Jay changed his mind. He said he believed the advantages of a high-level language like COBOL would outweigh any programming inefficiencies. (Ruth guessed he also felt better about changing because he felt that he would be able to learn the new language.) Therefore, Jay and Susan recommended COBOL as the future language for DEMPCO, and Ruth concurred.

J.1 Name and describe the three fundamental programming constructs.

J.2 What significance do these three constructs have for programming languages?

J.3 Describe three reasons why some of the older, less desirable languages continue to be used.

J.4 Name five characteristics of business applications.

J.5 Give two advantages and two disadvantages of each of the following languages. Assume these languages will be used for business processing.
a. BASIC
b. COBOL
c. PL/I

J.6 Is BASIC a good business programming language? Explain why or why not.

J.7 Is COBOL a good business programming language? Explain why or why not.

J.8 What is the significance of COBOL being a standardized language?

J.9 What approximate percent of all business application programs are written in COBOL?

J.10 Describe four characteristics of scientific applications.

J.11 If FORTRAN is not considered a good language, why is it so widely used?

J.12 Describe four characteristics of systems applications.

J.13 What are the advantages and disadvantages of assembler language?

J.14 What measures of a good program did the staff at DEMPCO develop?

High level language

Sequence

Alternation

Iteration

Business applications

BASIC (or Beginner's All-Purpose Symbolic Instruction Code)

COBOL (or COmmon Business Oriented Language)

Self-documenting

PL/I (or Programming Language I)

RPG (or Report Program Generator)

Scientific applications

ADA

ALGOL (or ALGOrithmic Language)

FORTRAN (or FORmula TRANslator)

PASCAL

Systems applications

Operating system

Assembler language

Program efficiency

Program correctness

Program adaptability

Program economics

Program maintainability

Program portability

Machine independence

QUESTIONS TO CHALLENGE YOUR THINKING

A. What do you think about the way that DEMPCO selected a language? Do you believe they made a good decision? If you worked for DEMPCO, what would you have done differently?

B. Suppose a company is using a language that is inappropriate for its needs. What are the probable results of this situation? Is the company even likely to know that it is using the wrong language? How could a company find out if its application programming language is appropriate?

C. Some people claim that the language that we use limits or constrains the thoughts we have. For example, Sanskrit (an ancient human language) had more than 15 different words for love. Consequently, it is possible to describe nuances of love more specifically in Sanskrit than in English. How does this situation pertain to programming? How does the choice of language impact programmers? Can an inappropriate language constrain programmers? Can an appropriate language liberate them? What impact does this have on companies?

Bibliography

Part 1: Introduction

1. Ackoff, Russell L. "Management Misinformation Systems." *Management Science*, vol. 14, no. 4, December 1967, pp. 147–56.

2. Alter, S. L. "How Effective Managers Use Information Systems." *Harvard Business Review*, November–December 1976, pp. 97–104.

3. Colt, D. G. "Management Information Systems for Cash Management and Accounts Receivable Applications." *Management Accounting,* June 1969.

4. "Corporate War Rooms Plug into the Computer." *Business Week,* August 23, 1976, pp. 65–67.

5. Donelson, William S. "MRP — Who Needs It?" *Datamation*, vol. 25, no. 5, May 1979, pp. 185–94.

6. Drucker, Peter F. "What the Computer Will Be Telling You." *Nation's Business,* vol. 54, no. 8, August 1966, pp. 84–90.

7. Eliason, Alan, and Kent D. Kitts. *Business Computer Systems and Applications.* Chicago: Science Research Associates, 1979.

8. Freeman, Gaylord A. "The Role Top Management Must Play in MIS Planning and Implementation." *Proceedings,* Society for Management Information Systems, 1969.

9. Gorry, G. Anthony, and Michael S. Scott-Morton. "A Framework for Management Information Systems." *Sloan Management Review,* Fall 1971, pp. 55–70.

10. Leeson, Marjorie. *Computer Operations.* Chicago: Science Research Associates, 1978.

11. Lucas, H. J., Jr. *Why Information Systems Fail.* New York: Columbia University Press, 1975.

12. Mandell, Mell. "Computers: America's Chief Inflation Fighters." *Computer Decisions,* vol. 11, no. 2, February 1979, pp. 14ff.

13. Poppel, Harvey L. "The Information Revolution: Winners and Losers." *Harvard Business Review*, January–February 1978.

Part 2: Fundamental Business Computer Systems

14. Bohl, Marilyn. *Information Processing.* 3d ed. Chicago: Science Research Associates, 1980.

15. Brechtein, Rick. "Comparing Disk Technologies." *Datamation,* vol. 24, no. 1, January 1978, pp. 139–50.

16. Burch, John G., Felix R. Strater, and Gary Grudnitski. *Information Systems: Theory and Practice.* New York: John Wiley, 1979.

17. Carlson, Robert D., and James A. Lewis. *The Systems Analysis Workbook.* 2d ed. Englewood Cliffs, N.J.: Prentice-Hall, 1979.

18. Caswell, Stephen A. "The Changing World of Nonimpact Printing." *Datamation,* vol. 24, no. 11, November 1978, pp. 128–32.

19. *Data World.* Pennsauken, N.J.: Auerbach Publishers, 1980.

20. Gane, Chris, and Trish Sarson. *Structured Systems Analysis: Tools and Techniques.* Englewood Cliffs, N.J.: Prentice-Hall, 1979.

21. *Introduction to IBM Direct Access Storage Devices and Organization Methods—Student Text.* IBM Manual GC20-1649. White Plains, N.Y.

22. Kindred, Alton R. *Data Systems and Management.* Englewood Cliffs, N.J.: Prentice-Hall, 1973.

23. Moritz, Frederick G. "Conventional Magnetic Tape Equipment." *Modern Data,* vol. 8, no. 3, March 1975, pp. 51–55.

24. Orr, Kenneth T. *Structured Systems Development.* New York: Yourdon Press, 1977.

25. "Printers and Plotters." *Computer Decisions,* vol. 10, no. 8, August 1978, pp. 60–63.

26. Rubin, Martin, ed. *Documentation Standards and Procedures for On-line Systems.* New York: Van Nostrand Reinhold, 1979.

27. Stone, Harold, ed. *Introduction to Computer Architecture.* 2d ed. Chicago: Science Research Associates, 1980.

28. Weinberg, Victor. *Structured Analysis.* New York: Yourdon Press, 1978.

29. Yourdon, Edward, and Larry L. Constantine. *Structured Design.* New York: Yourdon Press, 1978.

Part 3: Advanced Business Computer Systems

30. Abrams, Marshall, Robert P. Blanc, and Ira W. Cotton, eds. *Computer Networks.* IEEE Tutorial JH3100-5, 1978.

31. Bingham, John E., and Garth W. P. Davies. *Planning for Data Communications.* New York: John Wiley, 1977.

32. Chu, Wesley, and Peter B. Chen, eds. *Centralized and Distributed Data Base Systems.* IEEE Tutorial EHO 154-5, 1979.

33. *Communications Solutions.* Delran, N.J.: Datapro Research Corporation, 1978.

34. *Data Communications Management.* Pennsauken, N.J.: Auerbach Publishers, 1979.

35. *Data Communications Primer—Student Text.* IBM Manual GC20-1668. White Plains, N.Y.

36. Date, Chris J. *An Introduction to Database Systems.* Reading, Mass.: Addison-Wesley, 1977.

37. *Executive Guide to Data Communications.* New York: McGraw-Hill, 1977.

38. Kroenke, David. *Database Processing.* Chicago: Science Research Associates, 1977.

39. Lefkovits, David. *File Structures for On-line Systems.* New York: Spartan Books, 1969.

40. Liebowitz, Burt H., and John H. Carson, eds. *Distributed Processing.* 2d ed. IEEE Tutorial EHO 127-1, 1978.

41. Martin, James. *Computer Data-Base Organization.* Englewood Cliffs, N.J.: Prentice-Hall, 1977.

42. Martin, James. *Telecommunications and the Computer.* Englewood Cliffs, N.J.: Prentice-Hall, 1976.

43. McQuillan, John M., and Vinton G. Cerf. *A Practical View of Data Communication Protocols.* IEEE Tutorial EHO 137-0, 1978.

44. McQuillan, John M., and David C. Walden. "The ARPA Network Design Decisions." *Computer Networks,* vol. 1, no. 5, August 1977.

45. Sanders, Ray. "Managing Data Communications." *Datamation,* vol. 24, no. 11, November 1978, pp. 43–47.

46. Thierauf, Robert J. *Distributed Processing Systems.* Englewood Cliffs, N.J.: Prentice-Hall, 1978.

47. White, Wade, and Morris Holmes. "The Future of Commercial Satellite Telecommunications." *Datamation,* vol. 24, no. 7, July 1978, pp. 94–102.

48. Bohl, Marilyn, *Information Processing.* 3d ed. Chicago: Science Research Associates, 1980.

49. Burch, John G., and Joseph L. Sardinas. *Computer Control and Audit.* New York: John Wiley, 1978.

50. "The Computer Bandits." *Newsweek,* August 9, 1976, pp. 58–61.

51. Dorf, Richard C. *Computers and Man.* San Francisco: Boyd and Fraser, 1977.

52. Goetz, Martin A. "Software Protection: You Bet Your Company." *Infosystems,* vol. 24, no. 7, July 1977, pp. 60–64.

53. Holoien, Martin O. *Computers and Their Societal Impact.* New York: John Wiley, 1977.

54. Kling, Rob. "EFTS: Social and Technical Issues." *Computers and Society,* Fall 1976, pp. 3–10.

55. Kling, Rob. *Passing the Digital Buck:Unresolved Social and Technical Issues in Electronic Funds Transfer Systems.* Public Policy Research Organization, University of California, Irvine. Report Number ICS-TR 87, 1976.

56. Krauss, Leonard I., and Aileen MacGahan. *Computer Fraud and Countermeasures.* Englewood Cliffs, N.J.: Prentice-Hall, 1979.

57. Mair, William C., Donald R. Wood, and Keagle W. Davis. *Computer Control and Audit.* Wellesley, Mass.: QED, 1978.

58. McCauley, Carole Sperrin. *Computers and Creativity.* New York: Praeger, 1974.

59. McCorduck, Pamela. *Machines Who Think.* San Francisco: W. H. Freeman, 1979.

60. McKnight, Gerald. *Computer Crime.* London: Michael Joseph, 1973.

Part 4: Special Computing Topics

61. Minsky, M. L. "Artificial Intelligence." *Scientific American,* September 1966, pp. 142–48.

62. Morrison, Philip, and Emily Morrison, eds. *Charles Babbage and His Calculating Engines*. New York: Dover Publications, 1961.

63. Morton, A. S., and M. L. Ernst. "The Social Impacts of Electronic Funds Transfer." *IEEE Transactions on Communications,* October 1975, pp. 1148–55.

64. Parker, Donn B. *Crime by Computer*. New York: Charles Scribner's Sons, 1976.

65. *Personal Privacy in an Information Society*. U.S. Government Printing Office, No. 052-003-00395, July 1977.

66. Rhodes, Wayne L. "Office of the Future, Fact or Fantasy?" *Infosystems,* March 1980, pp. 45–54.

67. Roberts, Jerome J. "Computer-Generated Evidence." *Data Management,* November 1974, pp. 20–21.

68. Rothman, Stanley, and Charles Mosmann. *Computers and Society*. 2d ed. Chicago: Science Research Associates, 1976.

69. Ryan, Frank B. "The Electronic Voting System for the United States House of Representatives." *Computer,* November–December 1972, pp. 32–37.

70. Sanders, Donald H. *Computers in Society*. 2d ed. New York: McGraw-Hill, 1977.

71. Turing, A. M. "Can a Machine Think?" *Mind,* 1950, pp. 2099–123.

72. Ware, Willis H. "Handling Personal Data." *Datamation,* vol. 23, no. 10, October 1977, pp. 83–87.

73. Weizenbaum, Joseph. *Computer Power and Human Reason: From Judgment to Calculation*. San Francisco: W. H. Freeman, 1976.

74. Wiener, Norbert. "Some Moral and Technical Consequences of Automation." *Science,* vol. 131, May 1960, pp. 1355–58.

75. Yasaki, E. K. "Bar Codes for Data Entry." *Datamation,* vol. 21, no. 5, May 1975, pp. 63–68.

Part 5: Structured Computer Programming

76. Arjani, K. A. *Structured Programming Flowcharts*. New York: Collegium, 1978.

77. Bernstein, M. K. "Hardware Is Easy—It's Software That's Hard." *Datamation,* vol. 24, no. 11, November 1978, pp. 32–36.

78. Bien, Darl, and Gregory A. Cook. *BASIC Programming with Quantitative Methods in Business*. New York: Petrocelli Charter, 1975,

79. Bohl, Marilyn. *A Guide for Programmers*. Englewood Cliffs, N.J.: Prentice-Hall, 1978.

80. Bohl, Marilyn. *Tools for Structured Design*. Chicago: Science Research Associates, 1978.

81. Bosworth, Bruce, and Harry L. Nagel. *Programming in BASIC for Business*. Chicago: Science Research Associates, 1977.

82. Brooks, Frederick P., Jr. *The Mythical Man-Month.* Reading, Mass.: Addison-Wesley, 1975.

83. Dijkstra, Edsger W. *A Discipline of Programming.* Englewood Cliffs, N. J.: Prentice-Hall, 1976.

84. Dijkstra, Edsger W. "The Humble Programmer." *Communications of the ACM,* vol. 15, no. 10, October 1972, pp. 859–66.

85. Gries, David, ed. *Programming Methodology.* New York: Springer-Verlag, 1978.

86. Hughes, Joan K. *PL/I Structured Programming.* 2d ed. New York: John Wiley, 1979.

87. Kemeny, John G., and Thomas E. Kurtz. *BASIC Programming.* 3d ed. New York: John Wiley, 1980.

88. McCracken, Daniel D. "The Changing Face of Applications Programming." *Datamation,* vol. 24, no. 11, November 1978, pp. 25–30.

89. McCracken, Daniel D. *A Simplified Guide to COBOL Programming.* New York: John Wiley, 1976.

90. Mills, Harlan D. "Top-Down Programming in Large Systems." In *Debugging Techniques in Large Systems,* edited by R. Rustin. Englewood Cliffs, N.J.: Prentice-Hall, 1971.

91. Myers, Glenford J. *The Art of Software Testing.* New York: John Wiley, 1979.

92. Noll, Paul. *The Structured Programming Cookbook.* Fresno, Calif.: Mike Murach and Associates, 1978.

93. Noll, Paul. *Structured Programming for the COBOL Programmer.* Fresno, Calif.: Mike Murach and Associates, 1978.

94. Orr, Kenneth T. *Structured Systems Development.* New York: Yourdon Press, 1977.

95. Sammet, Jean E. *Programming Languages: History and Fundamentals.* Englewood Cliffs, N.J.: Prentice-Hall, 1969.

96. Shelly, Gary B. *Introduction to Computer Programming: Structured COBOL.* Fullerton, Calif.: Anaheim Publishing Company, 1977.

97. Weinberg, Gerald M. *The Psychology of Computer Programming.* New York: Van Nostrand Reinhold, 1971.

98. Welburn, Tyler. "Toward Training the Compleat COBOL Programmer." *Interface,* vol. 1, no. 2, Spring 1979, pp. 40–42.

99. Wu, Nesa L'Abbe. *BASIC: The Time Sharing Language.* Dubuque, Iowa: William C. Brown, 1975.

100. Yourdon, Edward, and Larry L. Constantine. *Structured Design.* New York: Yourdon Press, 1978.

Glossary and Index

A

abacus, 356, 357

Access motion time The time required for a disk's access arm to move to a cylinder before reading or writing data. 165

access to computer room, 408

account numbers, 185, 399, 403, 464
  use in teleprocessing, 269

accounting computer systems, 64–72, 368, 420

Accounts payable system A business system concerned with recording, scheduling, and paying a company's debts. 70

Accounts receivable system A business computer system concerned with recording and reporting a company's receivables (debts owed to the company) and income. 70

ADA A new programming language intended for systems and scientific applications; named after Ada Augusta, the Countess of Lovelace. 360, 564–65, 570

Advanced Research Project Agency A governmental agency that sponsored the development of the first large-scale distributed processing system. 251–52, 373, 374

Aiken, Howard, 361, 364

ALGOL (ALGOrithmic Language) A systems and programming language developed in the 1950s; it has been used extensively in Europe. 368, 565, 570

Algorithm A set of specific actions to solve a problem in a finite number of steps. 43–47, 486
  for sequential file record-matching, 137–44

allocation of resources in business, 417–18

alphanumeric data, 380

Alpine Co-op A cooperative company that decided to acquire in-house computer systems to solve its member master, inventory, and other problems. This company is discussed throughout Part 2 of this book.
  acquisition of data processing personnel, 213–14
  alternative analysis, 210–12
  alternative decision, 212
  computer committee, 97–99
  dividend checks, 97
  feasibility study, 105–9
  hardware discussion, 136
  hardware for sequential member master file system, 125–36
  information needs, 94–99
  inventory accounting system, 201

job interview, 98–99
label and dividend check subsystem flowchart, 218
member maintenance subsystem flowchart, 216
member master file format, 131
member master file maintenance flowchart, 156
member master file system, 117, 214
  design, 215–22
  direct access update program, 176–81
  flowchart, 127
  hardware, 219
minicomputer alternatives, 200–201
order pricing system, 157–58
order pricing system flowchart, 158
organizational alternatives, 205–6
phases of systems development, 195
possible direct access systems, 156–58
procedures, 223, 224, 225–28
processing time for direct access member master file, 165–66
programs for sequential file processing, 137–44
project planning, 214
project team, 101
pseudocode for the dividend check program, 219–21
purchase update system, 137, 145–46
purchase update subsystem flowchart, 217
requirements study, 110–11
sequential file processing, 149
system alternatives, 207–8
as teleprocessing user, 238–39
training, 220, 227

Alternation programming construct One of the three essential programming patterns. Alternation is the IF-THEN-ELSE structure. The other constructs are sequence and iteration. 555–56

Alternative specification The third stage of the systems development cycle in which alternative solutions that will satisfy defined requirements are identified. 102, 104, 196–209

ALU. *See* arithmetic and logic unit

Amplitude modulation A technique of transforming binary data into analog signals. The size of the wave is different for 1's than it is for 0's. 247, 248

Analog transmission mode A technique for sending data that uses a continuous smooth wave instead of sharp peaks and valleys. Contrast with digital mode. 246–48

analysis of costs and benefits, 209–10

analyst/programmer. *See* programmer/analyst

APL (A Programmer's Language) A terminal-oriented language known for its power and brevity; used primarily for scientific applications. 565–66, 570

Application node In a distributed network, a computer that is used to process application programs. 320, 326

Application programs Programs employed directly by users to satisfy business needs. Contrast with operating system and system support programs, 29, 175–76
    in database processing, 300–303
    in distributed processing, 338–39
    in teleprocessing, 262–64

Arithmetic and logic unit The portion of the CPU that performs arithmetic and makes logical comparisons. 41, 480–81

ARPANET A government-sponsored, value-added communications carrier. 251–52

Artificial intelligence The application of computer technology to replicate or better the analytical capabilities of humans. 428–31

Assembler language A language mid-way between machine language (binary) and high-level languages like COBOL. Machine instructions are coded with mnemonic names. 554, 568–70

Atanasoff, John V., 365–66

audit needs for computer systems, 65

Automated office An office that makes extensive use of word processing, data processing, and electronic mail. A totally automated office would be paperless. 451–52

B

Babbage, Charles An English gentleman who pioneered the design of computers. Babbage designed the analytical engine, which had many of the characteristics of a modern computer, in the mid-1800s. 356–62

background processing, 369

Backup and recovery That portion of a business computer system concerned with saving data and restoring it in the event of a problem or disaster. 18 *See also* database processing; direct access file processing; distributed data processing; sequential file processing; teleprocessing
    role of DBA in, 308

BASIC (Beginner's All-purpose Symbolic Instruction Code) An easy-to-learn programming language; it is used primarily in educational institutions, and in businesses with microcomputers and smaller minicomputers. 17, 28, 511–51
    arithmetic expression, 522–25
    arrays, 539–45
    assignment statement, 522–25, 530
    business application, 558–60, 570
    character data, 521
    DIM statement, 541–45
    dimensions, 541
    DOUNTIL, 526–28, 534
    DOWHILE, 526–28, 534
    FOR statement, 533–37
    GOTO statement, 516–17, 519
    IF statement, 516, 519, 525–26, 530
    IF-THEN-ELSE, 526
    initializing BASIC variables, 522
    INPUT statement, 515–16, 519

    LET statement, 525
    NEXT statement, 533–37
    PRINT statement, 516–17, 519
    program constant, 516
    pseudocode, 526–28
    relation symbols, 525–26
    REM statement, 517, 519
    running a program, 517–19
    statement, 513–14
    statement number, 513–14
    statement summary, 548
    string data and string variables, 520–22, 530
    subscripts, 541
    tables, 539–45
    testing a program, 519
    variable name rules, 515, 521
    writing simple programs, 511–51

Batch The process by which data is collected and processed in groups. Used primarily for sequential file applications. 119
    data transmission, 244
    jobs, 239
    processing, 120, 243, 279
    programming, 513
    total, 145–47

Baud A term used to describe the speed of a communication line. It measures the number of times a line can change state in a second. A different and more informative term for business people is bits per second. Line speed in baud is less than or equal to line speed in bits per second. 246

benefits, analysis of, 209–10
    Alpine member master and inventory/pricing systems, 211
    word processing, 445

Binary A number system having two symbols, 0 and 1. Place values are based on powers of two. Binary is used by computers because 0's and 1's are easily represented electronically.
    arithmetic, 382–84
    digit, 120
    instruction codes, 476
    language programming, 555
    numbers, 124, 380–84

Bit A binary digit. Bits have the value of either 0 or 1. 120, 381, 456, 474–75

Bits per second A measure of the speed of a communication line that describes how many bits can be transmitted across the line in one second. 246

Block A group of records on a file that are read or written together as a unit. Records are grouped into blocks to reduce wasted space on tape or disk and to improve input/output processing speed. 132, 163

BPI. *See* bytes per inch

Buffer An area of main memory used as a temporary holding place for data during input and output. 132

business applications and programming languages, 557–63

Business computer system A collection of computer hardware, programs, data, procedures, and trained personnel that interact to satisfy a business need. 24

byte, 124, 474–75

Bytes per inch A term used to describe the recording density of magnetic tape. Common tape densities are 800, 1600, and 6250 bytes per inch. 131

capacity, disk, 164–65

Case statement A multi-branch structure in pseudocode. Useful when different actions are to be taken depending on the value of a variable. 177–78

cash machine, 155, 239
and microcomputer, 464

Cashless society A society in which all financial transactions take place electronically. Paychecks and other income would be deposited electronically, and all purchases would be made via check or electronic transaction. There would be no need for cash. 421.

CCP. *See* communication control program

Central processing unit The portion of the computer hardware that does the computing. It contains main memory, the arithmetic and logic unit, and other components. 26, 41, 256, 258

Centralized data Data that is stored in only one location in a distributed processing system. 340–43

centralized processing, 242

Channel Computer hardware that transfers data between main memory and input, storage, or output devices. 481

Character A single letter, digit, or special sign (like #, $). Characters are represented by bytes in storage. 36
representation in computer, 120–25

Character printer A printer that writes a full character. Contrast with dot matrix printer. 135

Check digit A digit that is added to a field to help verify correctness. 143

Checkless society A society in which all transactions take place electronically. All paychecks would be deposited electronically, and all purchases would be made by electronic means. There would be no need for checks. 420–22

Checks and balances A situation that exists when the authority and/or ability to perform an action is divided among two or more employees, 64, 66, 407–8

child, in record relationship, 289–91

Child-parent-grandparent processing A form of backup and recovery for sequential file systems. Three generations of master files and their transaction data are saved. When the fourth generation is created, the grandparent data is released. 147–48

class scheduling system, 34–55, 434

Clientele, system The people for whom a system exists. The consumers of the systems services. The clientele of the class scheduling system are students. Clientele for an airline reservation system are airline passengers. 31, 32

COBOL (COmmon Business Oriented Language) The most commonly used programming language for business applications. COBOL was developed by a committee of users and manufacturers in the late 1950s. 28
business applications, 560–61, 570
at DEMPCO Enterprises, 572–73

Code conversion The process of converting character codes used by one hardware component to those used by a different hardware component. Needed in teleprocessing and distributed systems in which hardware from different manufacturers is used.
in communications processing, 256–58, 262
in distributed processing, 338

coding conventions, data, 36–38

Common carrier A company that provides communication lines to the general public. For example, companies in the Bell System. 250

Communication The process of transmitting facsimile, data, or voice signals over distances.
control program, 262–64, 298–300, 337–39
front-end, 259–61, 270
specialists, 273
subnetwork, 332
terminals, 254–55

communication line, 17, 322. *See also* transmission line

Compiler A program that translates source program language statements into object code. Computer manufacturers provide a compiler for each language to be used on their computer. 477–79

Complement addition The process by which machines subtract in binary. 382–84

Complex network In a database, a many-to-many relationship among records in which the parents of a record can be of the same type. 291–93

components of a business computer system, 25–34 *See also* hardware; programs; data; procedures; personnel

computer
abuse, 432–35
applications for managers, 61–63
arithmetic, 379–94
auditing, 404–11
impact on business, 417–22
intimidation, 434–35
operators, 32
prompting, 54–55
service bureau, 96

computer crime, 64, 184, 269, 396–413

computer systems
in health professions, 422–24
in legal professions, 425–27
in politics, 427–28

computer-assisted design, 86

computers
and society, 415–38
history of, 364–71
today—the fourth generation, 371–75

Concentrator A computer used to process messages in a teleprocessing system. A concentrator combines/ distributes messages from/to terminals, it conducts polling, performs character conversion, and other communications functions. A concentrator does not do applications processing. It is physically remote from the applications processing computer. 256–58, 260–62

Conceptual view of database data The complete, organizational view of a database. 293–94

Concurrent processing The process by which the CPU executes several programs. For example, it may allocate a short amount of time (say 10 milliseconds) to each program in round-robin fashion. Portions of the programs are executed sequentially, but the process occurs so fast, it appears to humans the programs are executed simultaneously. 369, 481

Concurrent update problem Difficulties that occur when concurrently executing programs attempt to access and modify the same data. 270–72, 302–3
in distributed processing, 343
role of DBA in, 308

Conditioning of transmission line Special actions to increase the speed of a transmission line, 246, 250

Configurations of distributed hardware The pattern in which computers are connected in a distributed system. Three patterns are common: ring, star, and hybrid. 330–37

Consumer power and computers The way in which people can influence computer systems by selecting companies that provide high quality, responsible information service. 436

Contention line management A way of controlling traffic on a communication line. When a line is unused, terminals are allowed to broadcast at will. If two terminals initiate messages simultaneously, they must stop and transmit again, at different intervals. 252–253, 256–57

control
  of business resources, 419–20
  of computer resource, 404–11
  of computer systems, 396–413
  of direct access systems, 181–88
  of local data, 327
  of organizations, 417–18

control cycle, 82

Control field The key of a sequential file. Sequential master file records are normally kept in sequence of this field. 138

control totals, 409

controls, 219
  on business computer systems, 64–65
  for sequential systems, 145–47

conversions between number systems, 387–89

Core memory A type of main memory used by second- and third-generation computers. People sometimes incorrectly refer to today's main memory as core. 367

cost
  estimates of computer systems, 108
  feasibility, 100, 107, 109

Cost justification The process by which system costs are compared to benefits and the expenses of developing and operating a new system are determined (or not determined) to be worthwhile. 109, 461

cost/performance ratio. *See* price/performance ratio

costs, analysis of, 209

CPU. *See* central processing unit

Crash, system A failure or unexpected shutdown of the computer or teleprocessing hardware. 31 *See also* backup and recovery

cycle, input/process/output. *See* input/process/output cycle

Cylinder, disk The collection of tracks that can be read or written when a disk access arm is held in one position. There are as many tracks in a cylinder as there are recording surfaces on the disk pack. 161

D

Daisy wheel printer A character printer that produces high quality print. Often used with word processing systems. 447

Data One of the five components of a business computer system. 25, 29–31
  in alternative specification, 205
  bad, 142
  capture, 94

  encryption, 269
  integrity, 18, 269, 279–81
  preparation during systems development, 223

Data administrator A person responsible for the development, use, protection, and change of organizational data. 273, 410 *See also* database administrator

Data center resource controls Procedures to ensure the computer and related equipment is used only for authorized purposes by authorized people at authorized times. 408–9

Data communications The portion of a teleprocessing system concerned with transferring data. 238, 373

data compression, 256

data control, 18

data control personnel, 32

Data entry personnel People who convert source document data to computer-sensible form. Usually keypunch, key-to-disk, or key-to-tape operators. 32

Data management The portion of the operating system that provides data access services to application programs. Data management is concerned with creating, accessing, modifying, and deleting data. 175, 481

Data module A disk pack in a sealed cartridge. 162

Data movement time The time required to transfer data between main memory and an input/output device. 165

Data processing The process by which data is converted into information. 238 *See also* data vs information
  department, 6
  organizational placement, 406

data representation
  on direct access hardware, 159–69
  on magnetic tape, 122–23
  in main memory, 124
  on punched cards, 121–22

data set. *See* modem

data transfer time. *See* data movement time

Data utility A company envisioned to maintain large files and databases of data of interest to companies and individuals. Data utilities do not yet exist. 375

Data vs information Data is recorded facts or figures. Information is knowledge derived from data. 31

Database administrator The person or office concerned with managing database structure, activity, and the database management system. 307–11

Database dictionary A file or database describing database structure, related programs and systems, and other facts pertinent to the management of the database. 301–2

Database machines A computer devoted exclusively to providing database management services. 375

Database management system A large and complex program that serves as an intermediary between applications programs and the database. It is used to define and process a database. 282–83, 309, 375
  and distributed processing, 337–39, 342–43
  performance evaluation of, 309
  use of, 299–300

Database processing A style of data processing in which files and their relationships are integrated into a single resource. 375
  advantages, 283–85
  backup and recovery, 303–4
  cost, 286
  data, 288–97
  data activity management, 307–8

Database processing *(continued)*
definition, 281–87
disadvantages, 285–87
hardware, 286, 298
managing change to database structure, 308–9
overhead data, 294–97
personnel, 307–11
procedures, 303–6
programs, 298–303
training, 286
database sharing, procedures for, 304
DBMS. *See* database management system
Decimal A number system having ten symbols. Place values are based on powers of ten. Humans usually work in decimal. Computers can work in decimal, but they are not as efficient as when they work in binary.
and binary numbers, 380–84
computer representation, 391–92
Demodulation The process by which an analog signal is converted to a digital one. 247–48
DEMPCO Enterprises, 554–55, 571–73
Density The number of bytes or characters recorded per inch on magnetic tape. Common values are 800, 1600, and 6250. 131
Design The fifth stage of systems development in which specifications for hardware are developed, program logic is specified, data formats are constructed, procedures are defined, and personnel requirements are determined. 214–22
completion before coding, 221
detailed, 103, 219–21
flaw, 11
flowcharts, 45–47
of simple programs, 485–509
Design walkthrough A meeting of technical personnel in which design deficiencies are identified. 222
Development and testing The sixth stage of systems development in which hardware is installed, programs are coded and tested, data is converted to new formats, procedures are finalized and documented, and personnel are trained. 103–4, 222–28
difference engine, 358–60
Digit check An edit check to ensure that digits of a field conform to established conventions. 143
Digital transmission mode A technique for transmitting data in which messages are sent as digital (choppy) signals. Contrast with analog mode. 246–48, 260–61
Direct access A style of file processing in which records can be processed directly without regard for preceding or succeeding records. 154–91
data organization, 169–74
file and multiple keys, 295–96
file organization comparison, 174
flowchart symbol, 156
vs random terminology, 170
Direct access file processing, 92, 201, 482
backup and recovery, 186–88
data, 159–69
hardware, 159–69
nature of, 155–59
need for, 155–56
personnel, 189

procedures, 181–88
programs, 175–81
teleprocessing, 268
update program, 176–81
Disk A direct access device consisting of one or more surfaces mounted on a revolving spindle. Data is recorded in concentric circles called tracks. 159–66
cylinder, 161
data layout, 163–65
data transfer time, 165
pack, 159–60, 164
storage unit, 159–62
surface, 159–61
track, 159–61
Distributed data processing A style of processing in which more than one computer is used for applications processing. Generally, these computers are physically separate. 242–43, 255, 317, 375
advantages, 317, 320, 327–28
backup and recovery, 323, 326
characteristics, 326–29
cost, 334
data, 340–43
data directory, 341–43
disadvantages, 328–29
evolution, 326–27
examples, 317–26
hardware, 329–37
performance in, 334–35
personnel, 325, 326, 343–46
procedures, 346–47
program compatibility, 320, 322
programs, 325, 337–39
reliability in, 335–36
division/remainder for numeric conversion, 387–88
Documentation Written information, instructions, or procedures regarding the development, operation, use, or maintenance of a business computer system. 18, 47, 50–52, 223
of programs, 398
of requirements, 15, 102
Dot matrix printer A printer in which the characters are composed of small dots. 135
DOUNTIL A looping instruction in pseudocode. Since the test for condition is made at the bottom of the loop, the loop instructions are performed at least once. 44, 500–501, 507
DOWHILE A looping instruction in pseudocode. Since the test for condition is made at the top of the loop, the loop instructions may not be performed at all. 141, 177–78, 500–501, 507
Downline loading of programs In a distributed network, the process by which one computer loads programs in another. 339, 345
Drum A type of direct access device in which data is recorded in circles around the outside of a cylinder. 167–68, 367
Dump of main memory A printout of critical areas of main memory. Usually done when a program fails, and usually printed in octal or hexadecimal. 386
duplex transmission line. *See* full-duplex transmission line
Duplicated data The repetition of data on computer files. Usually occurs in file processing systems. 279–81, 284

EBCDIC. *See* Extended Binary Coded Decimal Interchange Code

Eckert, J. Presper, 364–66

Economies of scale Reductions in the cost of system operation because of an increase in system size. 242, 420

edit report, 66

Editing The process of examining input data to ensure that it is complete and conforms to established conventions. 66, 142–44, 216–18, 225
on intelligent terminal, 255

EDP (Electronic data processing), 404. *See also* data processing

EDP controls, categories of, 405

EDSAC. *See* Electric Delay Storage Automatic Calculator

EDVAC. *See* Electrical Discrete Variable Automatic Computer

EFTS. *See* electronic funds transfer

Electric Delay Storage Automatic Calculator, 365

Electrical Discrete Variable Automatic Computer, 365

Electronic funds transfer A computer system that truncates the flow of checks. Ultimately, electronic funds transfer may eliminate checks altogether. 420–22, 434

Electronic mail A computer-based document distribution system. Memos, letters, and other documents are created on CRTs and delivered electronically. 448–49, 452

Electronic Numerical Integrator and Calculator, 364–65, 456

Encryption The process of encoding computer data so that it cannot be understood by someone who intercepts it. Used particularly in teleprocessing systems. 269

end of file, 139, 491, 501–5
signal in BASIC, 516, 521–22

ENIAC. *See* Electronic Numerical Integrator and Calculator

EOF. *See* end of file

ERD Pharmaceutical Company, 14–20, 316–20

error, roundoff, 390–91

error correction, 50
in communication processing, 256
procedures for direct access systems, 183–84

error detection, in communication processing, 256

Evaluation and selection of an alternative The fourth stage in the systems development cycle. During this stage, alternatives are evaluated and one is selected. 103–4, 209–12

Even parity A convention in which the sum of the 1's in a column, row, byte, or other entity must be even. If odd, an error has been made. 123

Executable load module A program after compilation and processing by the linkage editor. 479

executive system. *See* operating system

Exponent The exponent portion of a number in scientific or floating-point form. 389–90

Extended Binary Coded Decimal Interchange Code One of the standard character codes. Each character is represented by an eight-bit byte. This code is used on all IBM computers, as well as computers by other major vendors. 122–23, 380, 391–92

External view of database data The user's or application program's view of a database. This view may be a subset or a reorganization of the conceptual view. 293–94

Fair Credit Reporting Act Federal legislation giving individuals the right to see and to challenge credit data that is kept about them. 435

Feasibility study The first stage of the systems development cycle. The possibility of satisfying a business need by a computer-based system is examined, and the cost, schedule, and technical feasibility are considered, 100–101

Field A group of characters that represents an item of data. Name and address are examples. 36

File A group of records. 37

File organization The structure and processing of a file. Sequential, random, and indexed sequential are the most common. 170, 174

file processing, disadvantages of, 279–81

financial computer systems, 72–75

First-generation computers Computers developed in the late 1940s and early 1950s. Circuits were constructed with vacuum tubes. 367

flag, 139

Floating-point numbers Numbers represented in scientific form. The value of the exponent determines the location of the point. Hence the term, floating-point. 124, 389–91

Floppy disk A flexible disk platter about the size of a 45 rpm record. Used mainly with small computers, intelligent terminals, and word processing systems. 167

Flowchart, program (or detailed) A diagram showing the flow of logic in a program. 45–47, 488
customer order problem, 493
employee pay problem (version 1), 497
employee pay problem (version 2), 505
hints for developing, 507
modified sales comparison problem, 514
salesperson comparison (version 1), 489
salesperson comparison (version 2), 492

Flowchart, system A diagram showing the relationship of files and programs. 35–36
class scheduling system, 36
order pricing system, 158
payroll system, 66–67

flowchart symbols, 35, 36, 46, 47, 66, 156

FORTRAN (FORmula TRANslator) A programming language used mainly for scientific programming; developed in the 1950s. 368, 566–67, 570

Fourth generation computers Computers today. The fourth generation is characterized by a tremendous decrease in the price/performance ratio of CPUs and other large-scale integrated circuitry. 371–75

fractions and roundoff error, 390–91

FRAMCO Distributing, 320–23

Freedom of Information Act Federal legislation giving individuals the right to obtain data about them gathered by governmental agencies. 435

Frequency modulation A technique for converting digital data to analog form. The frequency of the analog signal is changed depending on whether a 1 or a 0 is to be transmitted. 248

Front-end A computer that performs telecommunications tasks. It has the same functions as a concentrator, but resides physically close to the processing computer. 259–62, 270, 322

Full-duplex transmission line A transmission line that allows messages to be sent both ways, simultaneously. 248–49

G

general ledger system, 65, 70, 71
Global data In distributed systems, data that is used by application programs on more than one application node. 340–43, 346
Goldstine, Adele, 366
Goldstine, Hermann, 366

H

Half-duplex transmission line A type of transmission line in which messages can be sent in both directions, but not simultaneously, 248
Hard disk A disk pack or disk surface that is not a floppy. 167
Hardware Computing equipment—one of the five components of a business computer system. 25–27
   in alternative specification, 197–202
   negotiations for, 215
   specifications, 215
Hashing algorithm A method of transforming the value of a key into a physical address on a direct access device. 170–72, 295
Heads, fixed On a disk unit in which there is one read/write head per track. The heads need not move, therefore, access motion time is zero. 161
Heads, movable On a disk unit in which the read/write heads move back and forth across the cylinders of the disk pack. 161
Hewlett-Packard 7920 Disk, 164–66
Hexadecimal number system A number system having sixteen symbols. Place values are based on powers of 16. Used to abbreviate binary data. 384–87
Hierarchical configuration of computers A one-to-many relationship of computers in a distributed system. 330
Hierarchical record relationship A one-to-many relationship of records in a database. 288–91
High-level programming languages Programming languages that are closer to human language than either binary or assembler languages. 368, 477, 555
Hollerith, Herman, 121, 362–64
Hollerith code A method of representing characters on punched cards, 121
home computer, 458–59
Hopper, Captain Grace, USN, 327, 366
Hybrid computer configuration In a distributed network, a combination of ring and star computer configurations. 332–34

I

IBM, 164–69, 292, 364, 368
IDMS A database management system sold by Cullinane Corp. 292
IF-THEN-ELSE In pseudocode, a statement used to express conditional processing. 45, 499, 500, 507, 558 *See also* alternation programming construct.
Impact printer A printer that operates by causing characters to strike the paper. 133–35
Implementation The seventh stage of systems development during which a completed and tested business computer system is installed and business activity is converted to its use. 103–4, 228
IMS, 292
Indexed sequential file organization A file organization that allows both sequential and direct access processing. 172–74, 176, 179, 218
Information Knowledge derived from data. 31, 60, 63
Initial cost The cost of developing and installing a business computer system. 100, 108
initiation, designing for, 494–98
input data, 31, 42
input queue, 479
input/output equipment, specialized, 462–66
Input/process/output cycle The fundamental cycle of all business computer programs. Data is input, processed, and results are output. The process is repeated for all data. 42, 487
instructions, 27
Integrated circuit A large and complex electric circuit embedded on a small chip of silicon. 369
Integrated files Files, usually in a database, in which relationships among records are maintained. 288–93
Intel Corp., 372–73, 456
Intelligent copier A copy machine that can be connected to communications equipment. It can receive and transmit documents electronically. 448–52
Intelligent terminal A terminal containing a microprocessor or microcomputer. 254–55, 467
Interactive programming Programming in the online mode. The programmer interacts with the computer while developing program code. 513
Interblock gap The space between blocks of records on tape or disk. 131, 164–65
Internal view of database data The structure and appearance of a database to the machine on which it resides. Also called the physical view of the database. 294
Inverted file Database overhead that enables records to be processed by more than one key or by record relationship. 295–96
Iteration programming construct The concept of looping—one of the three basic programming patterns. The other two are sequence and alternation. 555–56

J

Jacquard, Joseph Marie, 362
Job management The portion of the operating system concerned with starting and stopping jobs, and the allocation of the computer's resources. 479

K

Kahn, Hermann, 431
Key A field of a record. For sequential systems, the master file records are normally kept in sequence of the key. For direct access and database systems, the key is used to locate a record directly—without processing records in sequence. 138, 169–70, 285, 294–96
key-to-tape hardware, 126–28
keypunch, 156

L

Labeled tape A magnetic tape that has identifying data recorded on the beginning and the end of the tape. 129
language translation, human, 428–29

Large-scale integrated circuits Large and complex circuits embedded in small pieces of silicon. 372

Leased communication line A communication line that is leased by a company for private use. Sometimes called private lines. 250–51

line, transmission. *See* transmission line

Line printer A printer that prints an entire line at a time. Contrast with character printer. 133–35

Link field Used mostly in database systems, a field in a record used to hold the address of another record. 296

Link/loader A system support program that transforms object code into an executable load module. 478–79

linkage editor. *See* link/loader

Linked list A data structure, used primarily in database processing, for maintaining the relationships of records. 296–97

Local data in distributed systems Data that is used by only one application node in a distributed system. 340–43

Lock commands Special instructions used by programmers to ensure only one user updates a record at a given time. This prevents the concurrent update problem. 302–3

locking of records, 271–72 *See also* lock commands
in distributed processing, 343

logic, developing, 43–47

Loop A sequence of instructions that are performed repeatedly until a condition is true. 44, 141–42 *See also* DOUNTIL and DOWHILE.

M

Machine language Sequences of computer instructions coded in binary. 368, 476–79

Magnetic ink character recognition Specialized input and output using magnetic ink. Used primarily in the financial industry. 464

Magnetic tape A device for recording data sequentially. Data is recorded as magnetized spots. Also, a reel of tape. 122–23, 129, 130, 132–33

Main memory A portion of the CPU that contains data and instructions. Programs must be brought into main memory before they can be run, and data must reside in main memory before it can be processed. 41
data representation, 124
in microcomputer, 456

Mainframe computer The largest and most expensive class of computers. 197, 199, 200, 458

Maintenance Activities to keep computer hardware in working order. Also, the repair of hardware. 17

management control, 63, 405–7

management functions, 60

Management information systems. Business systems to provide information to managers. Every company must have management information systems to exist, but these are not always computer-based. 60–63

Managing data activity In database processing, the function of the DBA to determine who can do what to which data, and to ensure that only authorized activity takes place. 307–8

Managing database structure The function of the DBA to ensure that only orderly, company-justifiable changes are made to the database structure. 308–9

Mantissa The fractional part of a number in scientific or floating-point form. 389–90

manufacturing computer systems, 81–87

Mark I computer, 364–65

market analysis, 14, 77

Mass storage device Storage hardware that combines direct access and magnetic tape technologies. 167–69

Master computer In distributed processing, a computer that controls another computer. 320
relationship with slave, 324–25

Master file A file of relatively permanent data usually kept in key order. Examples are employee master file, customer master file, and product master file. 65, 118

Materials requirements planning A manufacturing system that determines manufacturing materials requirements for specified levels of production. 85

Mauchly, John W., 364–66

Mean time between failures The average time between failures of hardware. 197–98

memory, with instruction and data, 474

message acknowledgment, 265–68

Message switcher In distributed processing, a computer that routes messages from one computer to another. 321–22, 334–35

MICR. *See* magnetic ink character recognition

Microcomputer The smallest and cheapest of the categories of computers. They contain microprocessors on a silicon chip. 197–98, 372, 455–67
applications, 458–66
and BASIC, 513
as component of a business computer system, 458
as component of a product, 458–62
and distributed processing, 323–26
and specialized input/output equipment, 462–66

microprocessor, 372, 446, 455

Minicomputer A medium-sized class of computers. Larger and more expensive than microcomputers, but smaller and less expensive than mainframes. 197–99, 371–72, 458

MIS. *See* management information system

Mode, transmission line Transmission lines can be analog or digital. 246–49

Modem (Modulator/demodulator) The hardware that converts a digital signal into an analog one, 248

MODREC, 396–98, 407–9, 411–12

Modulation/demodulation The process of converting (or de-converting) a digital signal into an analog one. 247–48

Module, program A group of program statements having a specified function. 223, 499

MRP. *See* materials requirements planning

MTBF. *See* mean time between failures

Multidrop line configuration A communication line to which several terminals are connected. 252, 256, 260–61

Multiple keys Primarily in database processing, allowing records to be accessed by more than one key. 294–96

Multiplexers Hardware that interleaves messages from many slow-speed terminals and transmits the composite signal on a single high-speed communication line. Multiplexers also perform the reverse process. 256–58

Multiplexing The process of interleaving messages from many slow-speed terminals into a single high-speed signal. 262

N

Narrowband transmission line A slow-speed transmission line, capable of 45 to 150 bps. 246

Network record relationships Records in a database having a many-to-many relationship. 291–93

Nine-track tape A type of magnetic tape in which characters are recorded across the tape in columns of nine bits. 122

Nonimpact printer A printer that produces characters through electrostatic, heat, or other means not involving striking the paper. 133–35

Nonunique key A key that allows more than one record to have a given value. Zip code is an example. 285

null-ELSE, 500

number representation, 379–94

number systems, conversions between, 387–89

numeric data, 380

numerical wheel calculator, 356, 357

O

Object code A source program that has been processed by a compiler but not the link/loader, 477–79

OCR. *See* optical character recognition

Octal number system A number system having eight characters and place positions based on powers of eight. Used to abbreviate binary numbers. 384–87

Odd parity A convention in which the sum of 1's in a row, column, byte, or other entity must be odd. If even, an error has been made. 123

Off-line input and output A style of processing popular with second-generation computers. 368, 370

Offline The characteristic of not being in direct communication with the computer.
application, 262
processing, 243
system, 159

offloading applications processing, 327

one-to-many relationship. *See* hierarchical record relationships

Online The characteristic of being in direct communication with the computer.
application, 262
processing, 243–44, 370
program development, 245
system, 158–59, 451
system and controls, 409–10

Operating system The set of computer programs that controls the computers resources. It performs job, task, and data management. 175, 368, 479–82
and database processing, 298–99
and direct access processing, 176, 179
and distributed processing, 337–39, 342–43
and programming, 491
and teleprocessing, 262–64

Operational costs The costs of running a system (as opposed to the costs of developing one). 100, 108

Operations personnel People who accept computer inputs, convert data to computer-sensible form, operate computer hardware, and distribute computer outputs. 31–32, 52–53, 273, 304, 344–45, 407

operator training, for direct access systems, 189

operators procedures, 49–50, 185–88

Optical character recognition A special type font is used for computer input of source documents. 464

Organizational controls Structuring organizations and locating personnel to achieve checks and balances in business activities. 407–8

output data, 31, 42

output equipment, 26

overflow area, indexed sequential file, 172–73

Overhead data In a database, data describing the database structure and relationships among records. 288, 294–97

P

packed decimal numbers, 124, 392

Paperless office An office of the future in which all correspondence is done electronically using communicating word processors, document distributions systems, and related equipment. 451–52

Parallel implementation A style of systems implementation in which the new system is run in parallel with the old one until the new system is shown to be correct and fully operational. 104, 228

parent, in record relationship, 289–91

Parity convention A rule stating that the number of 1's in a row, column, byte, or other entity must be either odd or even. If not, an error has been made. 123

Parity error A violation of the parity convention. 123

Parity track One of the tracks of a magnetic or paper tape that contains the parity bits. 122

Parker, Donn, 398, 401, 404

Partitioned data In distributed systems, data that is divided into subsets before it is distributed across the network of computers. 340–43, 346

PASCAL A programming language used primarily for scientific and systems applications; named for Blaise Pascal, a mathematician. 567, 570

Passwords Keywords, phrases, or numbers that must be specified before the system will allow an action to take place. 185, 269, 399, 403, 464

Payroll register A listing of payroll checks. 68

Personal computer A microcomputer that is inexpensive enough to be owned by individuals. 458–59

Personnel One of the five components of a business computer system. Categories of personnel are systems development, operations, users, and systems clientele. 25, 31–32, 205–6

Phased processing Dividing a system into portions to allow users to inspect intermediate results. For example, editing master file change data before modifying the master file. 66, 68, 145

physical view of database data. *See* internal view of database data

Piecemeal implementation A style of systems implementation in which the system is broken into subsystems, and are implemented one at a time. 104, 228

Pilot implementation A style of systems implementation in which the using organization is divided into groups, and the system is installed for one group at a time. 104, 228

PL/I (Programming Language I), 561–63, 570

place notation, 381

Plunge method of implementation A seldom justified style of systems implementation in which the old system is abruptly discontinued and the new system replaces it. This is a high-risk style of implementation. 103–4, 228

point-of-sale terminal, 462–64

Polling line management A style of line management in which the computer, front-end, or concentrator asks each terminal on its polling list if the terminal has a message to send. If so, the message is transmitted. 252–53, 256–57, 259–62

pre-edit report, 66, 68

Precompiler Primarily in database systems, a compiler that translates special commands into standardized language statements. It also records processing facts into the data dictionary. 301–2

price extension, 158

Price/performance ratio The cost of a computer system divided by a measure of its computing power. Recently of great interest because the price/performance ratio has fallen dramatically. 371–72, 458

printers, 133–35, 437

privacy, 422, 433–36

Privacy Act of 1974, 435–36

private communication line. *See* leased communication line

Procedures One of the five components of a business computer system. Written procedures are needed by operations, users, and systems development personnel, at the minimum, 25, 31, 205, 225–28, 399, 499

processing data, 31, 42

processing equipment, 26

processing standards, role of DBA in, 308

Program(s) One of the five components of a business computer system. There are three types of programs: operating system, system support, and application. 25, 27–29, 175

    in alternative specification, 202–4

    application, 29

    compatibility of, 8, 320, 322

    cost of, 375

    purchase of, 375

    purpose of, 472–76

    risk in buying, 203

    sources of, 202–4

    system support, 29, 175

    types of, 175

program

    algorithms, 43–47

    constant, 516

    editing, 142–44

    maintenance, 18

    translation, 476–79

    variable, 515

Program/data independence In database processing, a condition that permits some changes to be made to the database structure without changing all the application programs. 285

Programmable read only memory Main memory that is normally read only. Its contents can be changed only by unusual treatment like exposure to ultraviolet light. Used with microcomputers. 457

Programmer Systems development personnel who designs, writes, and tests programs, 31–32, 52, 345

Programmer/analyst Systems development personnel who analyzes business needs, designs systems, and writes and tests programs. 31–32, 52, 345

Programming language A vocabulary for instructing the computer. Programming languages vary from low-level binary machine code to high-level, English-like languages such as COBOL.

    for business application, 557–63

    comparison chart, 570

    constructs, 555–56

    criteria, 571–73

    machine language, 476–79

    purpose, 472–76

    for scientific application, 564–67

    for special purposes, 570

    state of today, 555–57

    for systems application, 567–70

    translation, 476–79

project team, 101, 109

PROM. *See* programmable read only memory

Prompting, computer A style of input in which the computer asks the user for data. 54–55

Protocol The packing and handling of messages between two communication programs. 264–68

Pseudocode A tool for expressing program and other logic. 44, 45, 488

    for Alpine's dividend check program, 219–21

    for class scheduling, 44

    designing logic of simple programs, 499–506

    for direct access processing, 178–80

    for employee pay problem 503–4

    hints for developing, 507

    for sequential file record matching, 139–42

punched card, 35

    for Alpine pricing, 157

    data representation, 121–22

    deck, 40

    early history, 359, 362–64

    hardware, 125

Q

query and response systems, 244

Query/update program A general purpose program for accessing and modifying database data. 285, 299–300

R

RAM. *See* random access memory

Random access file organization A style of direct access processing that enables rapid random access. Sequential processing is not possible. 170–72, 180

Random access memory Main memory that supports reading and writing to any location. 456

random vs direct terminology, 170

Range check An edit check to ensure input data is within established bounds. 143

Read check A condition that occurs when input equipment detects parity or other errors. 125

Read only memory Main memory that can only be read. The contents cannot be changed. 456

read/write tape unit, 129–30

Record A collection of fields about some entity. For example, the employee record, or the part record, or the customer record. 36

record blocking. *See* block

record code field, 126

record relationships, 283–85

    in database processing, 288–93

    physical representation of, 294–96

record-matching algorithm for sequential file processing, 137–44

recovery. *See* backup and recovery

Remote job entry The input and output of batch jobs from a remote terminal. 239, 254

Request for proposal A document asking vendors to bid prices on hardware, programs, supplies, or services. It normally includes a description of requirements and constraints. 201–2

requirements, change, 225

Requirements definition The second stage of systems development. During this stage, users are interviewed, their needs are determined, and a document of requirements is prepared. 102

Requirements document A document of system requirements. 15, 102

response time, 240

RFP. *See* request for proposal

rights and responsibilities for processing with databases, 304–6

Ring computer configuration In distributed processing, the connection of computers into a circle. 331–32
comparison with star, 334–37

RJE. *See* remote job entry

robotics, 431

ROM. *See* read only memory

Rotational delay For disk units, the time it takes data on a disk surface to revolve under the read/write head. 165

roundoff error, 390–91

RPG (Report Program Generator) A computer language for defining reports; used primarily in business applications. 563, 570

S

sales and marketing computer systems, 75–80

SAS-3 An auditing standard requiring auditors to examine the controls of data processing systems. 404

Satellite carrier A supplier of satellite-based communication lines. 250

schedule, of computer operations, 408

schedule feasibility, 101, 107, 109

Scheduling algorithm The logic in the operating system that determines the order of job processing. 479

Schema The complete organizational view of the database. Synonym for conceptual view. 286–87, 293–94, 301, 308
controlling changes to, 306

scientific applications and programming languages, 564–67

Screen formats The layout of data and input fields on a CRT or other video display device. 219–20, 225

scrolling on terminal, 255

Second-generation computers Computers developed during the late 1950s and early 1960s. Circuits were constructed of transistors. 367–68

Security A need in business computer systems to ensure that only authorized users can process authorized data at authorized times. 18, 185, 403, 464, 482
in teleprocessing, 269

self-checking fields, 143

self-documenting language, 560

self-instructional programs, 339

Sequence programming construct One of the three basic programming constructs. The others are alternation and iteration. 555–56

Sequential file processing A style of file processing in which records are processed in the sequence of their

control fields or keys. 92, 201, 482
backup and recovery, 147–48
characteristics, 118–20
data, 120–25
definition, 117–18
hardware, 120–25
personnel, 148–49
procedures, 144–48
programs, 137–44
record matching algorithm for, 137–44

Serial printer A printer that produces only one character at a time. Contrast with line printer. 133, 135

Service bureau A company that provides data processing services for other companies. 96

Seven-track tape Paper or magnetic tape that represents characters in columns of seven bits across the tape. 123

signed decimal numbers, 392

Simple network In database processing, a many-to-many relationship in which the parents of a record must be of different types. 291–93

Simplex transmission line A type of communication line in which messages can flow only one way. 248

single, double-arrowhead notation, 289

Slave computer In distributed processing, a computer that is controlled by another computer. 320

slide rule, 356, 358

society, impact of computers on, 415–38

software communications specialists, 273

Software house A company that markets standard program products and develops programs to specification. 203

sorting, 142, 218

Source code The form of an application program that is understandable to humans. It is processed by a compiler to become object code. 477–79

special commands for applications database programs, 301–2

Special purpose electronic machine A nonprogrammable computer developed for one and only one application. Since it is not programmable, it cannot perform a variety of jobs. 472–74

specialized input/output equipment, 462–66

Speed, transmission line The number of bits that can be sent across a communication line per second, 246, 249

standards
for Alpine documentation, 223
for database processing, 308–9
for distributed processing, 345

Star computer configuration In distributed processing, connecting computers to a central node. This node distributes messages to their destinations. 330
comparison with ring 334–37

Steering committee A group of senior management personnel who provide general direction to the data processing staff and who provide go/no-go decisions for the stages of systems development. 101, 109, 208, 212, 228, 407

Storage equipment Hardware, such as tapes and disks, used for data storage. 26

Storage medium A type of storage; e.g., cards, tape, or disk. 31

stored data, 31, 255

Structured programming A style of program development that produces easily maintained programs. Such programs generally have fewer errors than programs developed by other methods. Although it has not been emphasized, all the design and programming concepts in this text conform to the structured philosophy. 18, 485–551

Subschema A subset and reorganization of the schema. To the level discussed in this book, a synonym for external view. 293–94, 301, 309

Super-Burger Restaurants, 323–26

Supercomputers Computers composed of groups of microcomputers. 373

supervisor. *See* operating system

Surface, disk The magnetized part of a disk platter on which data is recorded. Also, the disk platter itself. 159–61

Switched communication line A dial-up communication line like a telephone line. 250–51

system, definition of, 24

system clientele. *See* clientele, system

system commands and BASIC, 518

system controls. *See* controls

system crash. *See* crash, system

System design The fifth stage in systems development. *See* design

system library, 477–78

system maintenance. *See* maintenance

System support programs A class of computer programs that includes compilers, utilities, and programs that provide system services. 29, 175

system testing, 18

system users. *See* users

System utility A program that provides a general, commonly needed service. Examples are sort programs, programs to move or copy files, programs to unload or reload data, and so forth. 142

Systems analysts People who design and develop all five components of a business computer system. They must be able to work closely with business users, managers, and technical data processing personnel. They need a broad background in both business and information systems. 31–32, 52, 345

systems applications and programming languages, 567–70

Systems development The process of building a business computer system.
  alternative evaluation and selection stage, 209–12
  alternative specification stage, 196–209
  controls, 411
  cycle, 92, 99–105, 194
  design stage, 214–22
  development and testing stage, 222–28
  feasibility analysis stage, 100–1, 105–9
  implementation stage, 228
  personnel, 31–32, 52–53
    in distributed systems, 344–46
    in teleprocessing systems, 273
  procedures, 49, 50
  requirements definition stage, 102, 110–11, 225
  staff, 202–3, 407
  steps, review of, 194–96
  summary of stages and activity, 230
  tasks during development and test stage, 224

Systems engineer A person who specializes in the application of a certain manufacturer's hardware. Usually employed by a computer vendor. 16

Tape, magnetic A medium for sequential data storage.
  for Alpine member master file system, 129–33
  data representation on, 122–23
  label, 129
  speed, 132–33
  unit, 129–30

Task management One of the major portions of the operating system. Task management controls executing programs; it allocates the CPU's resources. 479

technical feasibility, 100, 107, 109

telecommunications. *See* data communications

Teleprinter A terminal that can print hard copy. 254

Teleprocessing Data processing at a distance. Users are physically remote from the computer. Distinguished from distributed processing because only one computer processes application programs.
  application programs, 262–64
  applications, 243–45
  backup and recovery, 272
  at central computer site, 258–59
  and controls, 409, 410
  data, 268–70
  definition of, 237–46
  equipment, buyer of, 273
  hardware, 246–62
  personnel, 272–73
  procedures, 270–72
  programs, 262–64
  rationale, 240–42
  synchronizing processing in, 265–68
  users, examples of, 238–41

Tens complement A number which, when added to a specified number, equals ten. The tens complement of 6 is 4. 382

termination, designing for, 494–98

Testing The absolutely vital process of determining that systems do what they are supposed to do. Often inappropriately abbreviated. 18, 475–76

Text editor A program for manipulating text, data, or programs. Similar capability to word processing. 445

Third-generation computers Computers developed during the late 1960s and early 1970s. Integrated circuits replaced transistors. 369–71

Time slicing A process by which the CPU allocates small portions of time to programs. 480–81

Time-division multiplexing A multiplexing technique that allocates a small amount of time to each terminal. 256

Top-down design The structured design philosophy that specifies systems or programs should be developed from large general parts (top) to smaller, more specific parts (bottom). 214

Track, disk One of the concentric circles on the surface of a disk. 159–61

Track, tape One of the rows of bits on magnetic or paper tape. 122

training, 31, 52–55, 224–25

Transaction count A batch control to determine that all transactions have been processed. The number of transactions to be processed is calculated when input to the computer, recalculated by batch programs, and the two totals are compared on output. 145

Transaction file A batch of transactions used to update a master file. 118

Transaction processing Processing that conforms to the input/process/output cycle. 245

transistors, 367

transmission control, 265–68

Transmission line A medium for transmitting data. It may be wire, microwave, or satellite-based.
    conditioning, 246, 250, 398
    failure, 335–36
    management, 252–53
    mode, 246–48, 249
    protocols, 264–68
    sources, 250–52
    speed, 246, 249, 256
    type, 248–49

Transport speed, magnetic tape The time to move the tape through the read/write heads. 132–33

tree record relationship. *See* hierarchical record relationship

Truncated check flow In electronic funds transfer systems, the process of stopping the physical movement of a check. 421–22

Turnkey system A ready-to-use system of hardware and programs. Often announced as but seldom truly ready-to-use. 16–17, 204, 327

TYCON Construction Products, 6–14

Type, transmission line The direction and number of messages that can be carried on a transmission line. 248–49. *See also* simplex; half-duplex; duplex

U

UNIVAC I, 366

Universal product code A standardized technique for printing product identifiers using lines or bars. 464

unpacked decimal numbers, 391–92

UPC. *See* universal product code

updating a sequential file, 119

user training for direct access systems, 189

users procedures, 49, 50–52, 182–85, 187

Users The people who utilize a business computer system to accomplish their job. Examples are payroll clerks, order entry personnel, and financial analysts. Contrast with clientele, 31–32, 52, 102

V

vacuum tubes, 367

validation, 476

Value check An edit check to determine that input data conforms to an allowable value. 143

Value-added carrier A vendor of communication lines that leases undeveloped lines from other vendors and adds services like sophisticated error detection and correction. It then leases the improved capability to other companies. 251–52

variables
    initializing, 496
    in program, 488

VAX minicomputer, 371, 372

Views of database data The appearances of a database to different people or programs. The three views are external, conceptual, and internal. 288, 293–94

Voice grade transmission line A medium-speed transmission line capable of 1800 to 9600 bps. 246–47

von Neumann, John, 365

vulnerability, 422
    to computer crime, 403, 407
    in database processing, 286

W

Wagner Pleasure Boats, 236–37, 259–61, 263–64, 268

walkthrough. *See* design walkthrough

WATS line, 250, 260, 261, 290–310

Wideband transmission line A high-speed transmission line capable of 500,000 bps or more. 246–47, 260–61

Word processing Application of computer technology for the creation, editing, storage, printing, and transmission of documents. 87, 427, 439–53
    benefits, 445
    combined with data processing, 449–51
    definition, 440–45
    hardware, 446–48
    systems, 448–51

word processors
    backup of floppies, 446–47
    and CPU, 446
    delete command, 443
    and disk, 446–47
    insert command, 443
    network of, 450
    replace command, 441–43
    variable margins, 443
    workstation, 446

Write-protect ring A plastic ring that must be inserted in tape reels before the tape unit will write on them. 129, 130

Z

zoned decimal numbers, 391, 392